INDIA-PAKISTAN
IN
WAR & PEACE

Other Books by the Author

Self in Autumn

Anatomy of Flawed Inheritance

My South Block Years: A Memoir

Assignment Colombo
Indo-Sri Lanka Relations from 1985-1989

Across Borders
50 Years of India's Foreign Policy

Liberation and Beyond
Indo-Bangladesh Relations 1971-99

An Afghan Diary
Zahir Shah and Beyond

Indian Foreign Policy and its Neighbours

INDIA-PAKISTAN IN WAR & PEACE

J.N.Dixit

Routledge
Taylor & Francis Group

LONDON AND NEW YORK

First published 2002 in India by
Books Today, an imprint of The India Today Group

This edition published 2002
by Routledge
11 New Fetter Lane, London EC4P 4EE

Simultaneously published in the USA and Canada
by Routledge
29 West 35th Street, New York, NY 10001

Reprinted 2002

Routledge is an imprint of the Taylor & Francis Group

© 2002, J.N. Dixit
who asserts the moral right to be
identified as the author of this work

Typeset in Berling by Nikita Overseas (P) Ltd
Printed and bound by MPG Books Ltd, Bodmin

British Library Cataloguing in Publication Data
A catalogue record for this book is available
from the British Library

Library of Congress Cataloging in Publication Data
A catalog record for this book has been requested

ISBN 0–415–30472–5

Contents

Introduction

I originally wrote the introduction to this book as the Atal Behari Vajpayee–Pervez Musharraf summit concluded in Agra in July 2001. I thought my work was done, my assessment of a half-century and more of Indo-Pakistani relations complete. Three dates were to prove me wrong—11th of September, 13th of December and 12th of January. The attack on the World Trade Center in New York, the terrorist assault on the Parliament in New Delhi and Musharraf's "historic" speech to his people were only three signposts on the Indian subcontinent's roller-coaster journey in this period. The war in Afghanistan and the destruction of the Taliban regime changed many of the verities on which this book was based.

Yet, my purpose here is not to assess the consequences of the latest events, much less get carried away by them. There has to be a difference between quick journalism and reasoned analysis. It is appropriate to view even recent happenings through the prism of history. Such a larger view may indicate not a break from the past but perhaps continuity.

I was pondering the rationale for this book when the Musharraf-Vajpayee summit commenced in Delhi on the 14th of July. At a lunch hosted by the Indian prime minister, a brief conversation with a well-known Pakistani provided me with the initial arguments to articulate the relevance of this book. I came to know Cowasji Jehangir, an eminent Parsi citizen of Pakistan, during my tenure as India's high commissioner to his country between 1989 and 1991. I met him after a gap of ten years at Prime Minister Vajpayee's lunch. Jehangir belongs to a distinguished family of shipping magnates of Karachi. He has been fearless, highly intellectual and articulate in advocating human rights, civil liberties and liberal political values through the travails of Pakistani politics stretching over the past three or four decades. He did

9

not spend too much time on initial courtesies. "This summit," he said, "is a good thing but its relevance still lies in what the two heads of governments achieve." He was not terribly optimistic. He wondered why the establishment in either country didn't recognise the fact that: "*Nal main pani tak nahi hai our atom bomb bana liya hai. Kya Pakistani aur Hindustani bomb khayenge?*" He added: "*Popular nara hai Roti, Kapda aur Makan. In teenon cheezon kay liye pehle pani hona chahiyey, peace hona chahiyey. Aur dono taraf sey log bekar ki batain kartai hain*, Kashmir, Line of Control." (There is no water in the taps, water is drying up, and we have gone ahead to make a bomb. The populist aspiration trumpeted by politicians is food, clothing and shelter. But they forget for all these three things there must first be water as an elemental factor. This they do not realise. They waste their time talking of irrelevant issues, Kashmir, Line of Control. How foolish can we get.) What he said provided a post facto rationale for this book, which I had started early in 2000. It is 55 years since the Partition of India. The objective for which Partition was brought about has not been met. The objective was that once those Muslims who wanted a separate homeland got their homeland, the antagonism, apprehension and suspicion that underpinned the demand for Pakistan would disappear. The two countries would live in harmony and peace.

This was the aspiration of both Mohammed Ali Jinnah and Jawaharlal Nehru, first heads of government in the two countries. Exactly the reverse has happened.

So I felt that perhaps a panoramic survey of Indo-Pakistani relations covering the entire period since the inception of the idea of Pakistan might serve a purpose. Locked in adversity, burdened by inadequacies in terms of territorial and political identities, devilled by misunderstanding, suspicion and animosity—Indians and Pakistanis have much to think about. In a telling phrase, as Jehangir asked me at the prime minister's lunch, "Why are we in the subcontinent collectively so foolish?"

The idea of Pakistan predates Partition by 30 years. Chaudhary Rehmat Ali, a young student at Cambridge University wrote a monograph in January 1933 titled "Now or Never". In it he advocated a homeland for the Muslims of South Asia. He argued the future well-being of the Muslims in the region could not be ensured if they remained fragmented in different countries and particularly so in British India where the Hindus were in a majority. He talked of a Muslim homeland called "Pakistan" which would comprise Afghania (the North West Frontier Province), Punjab, Jammu and Kashmir, Sindh and Baluchistan. Significantly he did not talk of Muslim majority areas of Bengal and Assam as part of this "land of the pure and the faithful", though he hinted that other Muslim majority areas in the subcontinent could also unite as Muslim homelands and assume separate political identities.

The pre-Partition Muslim League of India rejected Ali's idea, describing it as chimerical and unpracticable. It was only towards the end of the decade of the 1930s, that the great Muslim philosopher and poet Alamma Iqbal recalled Ali's idea and speculated on his suggestion being a possible solution to the concerns and aspirations of Muslims in the British Indian Empire. It was only in 1940 at the Lahore session of the Muslim League, Jinnah formally proposed the idea and the "Pakistan Resolution" was passed. The territorial concept of Pakistan was expanded to Assam and Bengal. The rest is history.

Three specific events impelled me to undertake this longish analysis of how India and Pakistan have interacted in peace and war, influenced continuously by adversarial attitudes. The first was the Kargil war of summer 1999, waged by Pakistan within three months of Prime Minister Vajpayee's visit to Lahore, which on its part was a serious attempt by India to normalise relations. The Kargil experience was instructive as far as many people of India were concerned. The second event was the hijacking of the Indian aircraft from Kathmandu in December 1999 and the manner in which Pakistan reacted to the hijacking and then treated the hijackers and the criminals whose release they managed to achieve. The third event was General Pervez Musharraf ousting Nawaz Sharif, the elected prime minister of Pakistan, in a military coup (mercifully bloodless) and Musharraf's subsequent rejection of the Lahore process in November 1999.

One discerned that differences between India and Pakistan went beyond territorial disputes, political issues and attitudes of the establishments of the two countries to similar situations. I felt, therefore, that an attempt to take the journey backwards from the events of 1999 to 2000, to the beginnings of Partition and beyond might perhaps provide insights to the gridlock of Indo-Pakistani relations.

So the first two chapters deal with the hijacking of the Indian plane from Kathmandu to Kandahar via Dubai. The second chapter deals with Kargil. Indo-Pakistani relations in general are covered in reverse sequence of the chronological time-frame.

I was an observer of and participant in Indo-Pakistani relations from 1958 to 1994. As under-secretary (Pakistan) in 1964, I witnessed the events leading to the 1965 war. As director of the special division dealing with the East Pakistan crisis and subsequent liberation of Bangladesh I was a middle-level participant in Indian governmental action leading to the creation of Bangladesh. As ambassador and then high commissioner to Pakistan between

1989 and 1991, I saw the transition of Pakistan from long military rule to democracy under Benazir Bhutto, a transition that was approved by Chief of Army Staff General Mirza Aslam Beg on given pre-conditions. First, that Benazir would not do away with presidential powers to dismiss a prime minister, a power incorporated into Pakistan's constitution by military dictator General Zia-ul-Haq. Second, she would not interfere in any manner or exercise any executive authority in the affairs of the armed forces. Third, she would be guided by the armed forces in the conduct of her foreign and defence policies. Fourth, she would not stop Pakistan's nuclear weaponisation programme. Benazir agreed to these preconditions.

It was during my tenure as India's high commissioner that Pakistan vigorously reactivated the secessionist movement in Jammu and Kashmir in December 1989/January 1990. I could assert that I saw the beginnings of the proxy war against India.

As ambassador to Pakistan and as foreign secretary of India I participated in a series of discussions aimed at normalising Indo-Pakistani relations, putting in place mutual confidence-building measures and exploring the possibilities of multifaceted cooperation. This exercise achieved very limited and marginal results, which faded further between 1994 and the Kargil conflict.

So one felt that it would be worthwhile ruminating not only personally but also in writing in a systematic manner. The speculative hope in writing this book was that such a survey might throw up answers to a number of basic questions. It would go beyond normally articulated contradictions— two-nation theory versus the Indian commitment to a secular, pluralistic civil society; the Pakistani view that India is not reconciled to Partition and has a long-term agenda of re-absorbing Pakistan. The elemental questions needing an answer are: are the beliefs of India and Pakistan really antagonistic to each other at the profoundest psychological and emotional levels? Is there a difference of approach between citizens of the two countries towards each other and the attitude of the establishment? Or do the power structure truly reflect the attitudes of their respective people? If the latter is not the case, why is it that the positive attitudes of common people in the two countries have not influenced relations on constructive lines?

Why is it despite sharing so much in terms of ethnicity, culture, religion and language, India and Pakistan do not interact cooperatively—or is it that the very commonalities generate antagonisms. How has and how will the rise of religious extremism in both countries influence relations? How have the centrifugal, sub-national impulses in both India and Pakistan affected bilateral relations? Exactly how has the phenomenon called international terrorism changed the India-Pakistan equation? Has time eroded bitter memories of Partition in the younger generation of Indians and Pakistanis? How has the evolution of political institutions and processes of governance in the two countries affected the psyche and attitudes of the respective people?

In a manner this book is an attempt to think on these questions, if not answer them. Public memory is remarkably short and its attention span focuses on the immediate past and contemporary results. India's collective institutional memory is limited to perhaps the government—even in the government it is not very competent—and to a small section of analysts in civil society. Perhaps this book will jig the institutional memory. In no way can we fashion the future of Indo-Pakistani relations without understanding the past.

One discerned strange ironies of history, society and political evolution while researching and writing this book. Some are worth mentioning. The two-nation theory adopted by the Muslim League on the basis of which Pakistan was created did not really represent the broad aspirations and political convictions of the Muslims of pre-Partition India. Even the populace of those provinces of British India that became Pakistan did not provide full endorsement to the idea of "Pakistan". While East Pakistan broke away to become Bangladesh, the people of pre-Partition Punjab, the North West Frontier Province and Baluchistan were not enthusiastic about the creation of a separate Muslim homeland. Only a section of Muslims in Bengal, the United Provinces (now Uttar Pradesh), Bihar, Punjab and Sindh supported it.

The Muslim homeland was supposed to become the homeland of all the Muslims living in pre-Partition India. This did not happen. Nearly 50 per cent of the Muslim population remained in the Indian Republic, ultimately leading to an anticlimax where India today has a larger Muslim population than Pakistan and is the second most populous Muslim country in the world. The expectation and assessment of Pakistani and Indian leaders at Partition proved to be completely wrong. Jinnah announced in August 1947 that since Pakistan had been created, the reasons for Hindu-Muslim antagonism had come to an end and that India and Pakistan would live in harmony. His vision of Pakistan was that of a Muslim majority country, pluralistic, tolerant and democratic. Mahatma Gandhi was opposed to Partition. Nehru expressed sentiments similar to those of Jinnah about the future of Indo-Pakistani relations.

The only politician who anticipated the future was Maulana Abul Kalam Azad, the president of the Indian National Congress in 1947 and India's first minister for education. He predicted that the creation of Pakistan would harm the Muslims of India and create a crisis about their Islamic identity on both sides of the border. He had foreseen that ethno-linguistic and sectarian forces would affect both India and Pakistan, particularly Pakistan. He had a clear perception that India and Pakistan would drift into long-term adversarial relationship because Partition was a contrived political arrangement. It fragmented a civil society developed in the subcontinent over 1,100 years.

The separation of East Pakistan was the final nail in the coffin of the two-nation theory. Pakistan suffered from feelings of territorial inadequacy, religious identity and an ambition to play the role of protector of the Muslims of India. The anxiety for creating a certain credibility of Pakistan's Islamic identity resulted in the emergence of extremist Islam as a factor consciously cultivated by Islamabad's power structure.

At the cultural, intellectual and social levels, Pakistani decision-makers resorted to another policy orientation, that of identifying Pakistan more with countries of the Gulf and West Asia. Consequently, Pakistan cut itself adrift from its profound historical roots in subcontinental India, while at the same time it failed to find acceptance as an integral part of Islamic societies of the Gulf and West Asia. This was due to the simple fact that Islam in the subcontinent was different from Islam in West Asia and the Gulf region. Subcontinental Islam was a vibrant synthetic phenomenon resulting from hundreds of years of interaction between Arab, Turkie, Persian and Central Asian influences on the one hand and the equally rich and ancient Hindu influences. Pakistan diminished the content of its national identity by trying to narrow it down to West Asian and Gulf compartments. This has not been a very successful experiment at the social or emotional level.

In recent years the situation has been compounded by sectarian strife among Muslims in Pakistan. The Ahmedias have been excommunicated as non-Muslims. Shias and Sunnis are enmeshed in not just theological but violent conflict. Islam has not been able to transcend the deeper identities of Sindhis, Baluchis and Pathans, who resent the demographic and political domination of Punjabis. Even after half a century, Muslims who migrated from different parts of India to Pakistan are still called Mohajirs (migrants). In this context, speaking about the fate of non-Muslim minorities is irrelevant. At Partition, Hindus, Christians, Sikhs and so on constituted nearly 33 per cent of the population of West Pakistan. Information indicates today only five to seven per cent of the population of Pakistan consists of these minorities. The figure is perhaps even lower because the census is not conducted in Pakistan on a regular basis.

Tensions and fractiousness in Pakistani civil society keep simmering at a critical threshold. After the initial five years of attempts at establishing democracy, Pakistan has been continuously under military authoritarian rule even when democratic governments have been in power in the early 1970s and during the 1980s and 1990s. The consequence has been a disproportionately adversarial relationship with India. The deeper the faultlines in Pakistani society, the more adversarial became Pakistan's attitude and policies towards India.

Three arguments underpinned this negative continuity. One, India deprived Pakistan of territories that were rightfully its. So there are "unfinished tasks of partition". Two, at the deepest level India has not accepted Partition. Third, Hindu majority civil society in India wants to diminish and dominate the Muslims of India and Pakistan. None of these arguments is valid if tested on the criteria of the experience over the past 50 years.

There have been similar negative ingredients in Indian perceptions of Pakistan. The reason Britain partitioned India was to fragment Hindu areas into small political entities and ensure Pakistan's emergence as the largest and most cohesive political power in the subcontinent. Pakistan's ultimate aim is to fragment India. Pakistani invasion of Kashmir in 1948 and subsequent wars are a part of this continuous exercise. The Kargil war and the proxy war in Jammu and Kashmir are the latest examples of this pressure. India has not been decisive and surgical in resisting Pakistani subversion. India has voluntarily given concessions to Pakistan despite defeating it in all the major conflicts. Pakistan's long-term strategic objective is to ensure that India does not emerge as the most influential power in the South Asian region. The Pakistani power structure has a profound antagonism towards Hindu majority civil society in India. Pakistan has sought the support of a large number of Muslim countries and Asian and Western powers, (China and the US) to keep India on the defensive. Pakistan's continued questioning of Indian secularism, democracy and constitutional institutions is a deliberate attempt to generate friction within India. Pakistani support to secessionist and insurgent forces in Jammu and Kashmir, in Punjab and in the north-eastern states of India confirms this impression.

It is remarkable that despite mutually antagonistic perceptions, people-to-people contacts between India and Pakistan have survived. The process goes on however tentative it may be, and regardless of the difficulties it may face. More importantly, a conviction that it is only through mass contact between the people of India and Pakistan that political intransigence can be overcome is growing in both countries. Whether this is a correct perception or not is a different matter.

Some presumptions about Indo-Pakistani relations are often articulated. First, that common people in India and Pakistan want to come to terms with each other but it is governments that prevent this. Second, new generations of Indians and Pakistanis can break free of history. Third, normal economic and technological cooperation backed by cultural and intellectual exchanges will improve relations.

The concluding chapter of this book attempts to examine the validity of these presumptions. To give an initial reaction, however, the first two are not quite valid. This is the third generation of Indians and Pakistanis grappling with the challenges of normalising relations. One does not see memories of Partition fading away, neither disappearance of prejudices. The third assumption has potential. Pakistan has serious reservations about economic relations with India because it fears domination and possible exploitation by a larger neighbour. It will be rational to assume that the information revolution and economic globalisation will influence Pakistan and India to change their attitudes and policies.

One fervently hopes this happens.

The summit at Agra took place in mid-July 2001 and ended inconclusively. The presumption was that relations between India and Pakistan would be focused on retrieving the predicaments resulting from the Agra fiasco. This was the impression I received from my conversations with senior political figures in India even before the Agra summit took place. I had the privilege of meeting Prime Minister Vajpayee, Leader of the Opposition Sonia Gandhi and Foreign Minister Jaswant Singh before the summit took place. I also met the foreign minister of Pakistan, Abdul Sattar, and General Musharraf himself at the luncheon hosted by Prime Minister Vajpayee.

Whatever the public postures of these senior functionaries, they did not expect dramatic results at Agra. They were of the view that sustaining the dialogue would be a difficult process, on which the governments of the two countries would have to focus their attention.

These anticipations changed dramatically with the terrorist attack by Al-Qaida cadre on the 11th September, 2001. Two months later, Indo-Pakistani tensions reached critical levels after the attack on the Indian Parliament. General Musharraf is now in a dichotimous predicament. He cannot afford to offend the Islamic extremists in his country beyond a point if he has to survive. On the other hand, he has to be responsive to international pressure led by the United States, to disassociate himself from religious fanaticism and terrorism. As this book appears, Indo-Pakistani relations have gone into yet another almighty spin.

It is axiomatic and I accept that those who read this book may not agree with its assessments and conclusions. Every book reflects the processes of cognition and the impressions of an individual. Any shortcomings in this book are entirely my responsibility. I thank the publishers for their encouragement and support. I thank my colleague R.N. Sharma for his painstaking effort in preparing the manuscript of the book. I leave you with the hope that you will find this book worth your while.

J.N. Dixit

One

IC-814 to Kandahar

*T*here are few examples in the history of relations where two states have stagnated in a confrontationist mode, despite their civil societies having intense and wide-ranging commonalities. India and Pakistan, from their very inception as independent countries, have been stuck in an adversarial predicament owing to a number of reasons. The purpose in this book is not just to detail these reasons but to comprehend the undercurrents of perceptions, doubts, motivations and attitudes in the power structures and public opinion of both countries during wars and confrontations, interspersed with periods of tenuous peace, over the past 50 years.

A sequential survey should normally begin at Partition, in 1947, to be followed by a survey of the underpinnings of mutual antagonism, using the 1948-65, 1971 and 1999 military conflicts as points of reference. Such a gradual, logical and chronological approach would, however, diminish the sense of urgency with which India should assess and react to Pakistani antagonism towards India, which in some respects goes beyond territorial disputes like Kashmir or strategic worries about India's military capacities. It is to counter these prospects that one begins the process of description and analysis in reverse, beginning with the last (though not perhaps the latest) act of unprovoked violence against India, namely the hijacking of Indian Airlines flight 814 scheduled to fly from Kathmandu to Delhi on 24 December 1999.

The general details of this hijacking drama have been public knowledge since January 2000. Some of the more disturbing and politically critical details merit being brought to the reader's notice. Before proceeding to describe the dramatic event, it is relevant to understand the political machinations and policy orientations of Pakistan, in which such violent activities are rooted. It is equally important to know and understand how Pakistani public opinion reacted to the hijacking event. As a former member of the National Security Advisory Board, I can confirm that as Pakistan was compelled to pull back into its territory after the Kargil conflict of May-July 1999, the assessment of the Government of India and Indian strategic analysts was that the Government, the Armed Forces Headquarters and the Inter-Services Intelligence (ISI) agency of Pakistan would escalate terrorism and covert violence against Indian targets, not only in Jammu and Kashmir but wherever vulnerable targets were available. Even during the Kargil conflict, the assessment was that Pakistani authorities had infiltrated 1,500 to 2,000 well-equipped terrorist mercenaries into Jammu and Kashmir. This process of infiltration has continued. As a part of the plan to put India on the defensive, destabilise the Government and create higher levels of tension all over India, Pakistani subversive elements are being sent to other parts of India through Nepal, Bangladesh and some of the southeast Asian countries. Indications are that Kathmandu, Dhaka and Bangkok have become operational bases of the ISI to generate subversive activities against India, particularly in its northeastern states, where links between the Pakistani agency and violent secessionist movements are affecting the security environment. It is to be noted that there are direct international flights between Pakistan and Kathmandu, though passenger traffic on this route is not of a level where such direct flights would be commercially viable. The direct flights are a means of ferrying subversive personnel and their equipment to India's neighbours from where they fan out into different Indian states. There are confirmed reports about the ISI having training camps for violent separatist cadre of the northeast in Bangladesh and Bhutan since the middle of 1993. Apart from the direct air links between Pakistan and India's neighbours, the comparatively open borders between India and Nepal (without the requirements of formal travel documents) have been exploited by Pakistan.

Since Kargil, Pakistani terrorists have carried out terrorist attacks against civilians in Jammu and Kashmir, Himachal Pradesh and other parts of India. The covert supply of arms and explosives to its agents, disaffected individuals and organisations has steadily increased since July 1999. The objective is not just to get control over Jammu and Kashmir, but at the profoundest strategic level to weaken the Indian state and if possible to fragment India territorially. Nepal was chosen as a springboard for such operations in view of the Nepalese intelligence and administrative structures not being capable of effectively countering Pakistani operations, despite the good relations between Nepal and India, despite Nepal's desire to cooperate with India in nullifying Pakistani skulduggery.

The Facts and Chronology

It is against this background that the hijacking of the Indian Airlines flight took place on 24 December 1999. Indian Airlines flight IC-814, which was to fly from Kathmandu to Delhi, was hijacked within a few minutes of its takeoff at 1653 hrs. (IST). The Air Traffic Control at Palam airport, Delhi, received the first information of this hijacking at 1656 hrs. The initial information conveyed to the Air Traffic Control was that the hijackers were demanding the plane be taken to Lahore. No details about the number of hijackers or their demands were available. The plane was refused permission to land at Lahore. It was running short of fuel, so the hijackers agreed to the plane landing at Amritsar. It arrived at Amritsar at 1900 hrs. The hijackers demanded immediate refuelling. In the meantime, the Government of India activated institutional and operational arrangements to deal with the crisis. The Crisis Management Group, chaired by the cabinet secretary, was convened immediately. The National Security Guards (NSG) were placed on full alert. Procedures were commenced for the NSG's counter-hijacking unit to proceed to wherever the plane was supposed to land. A full Cabinet meeting was followed by a meeting of the Cabinet Committee on Security, which was to meet every evening till the hijacking ended seven days later, on 31 December 1999.

Instructions to authorities at Amritsar were to prevent the plane from taking off and to delay the refuelling till the counter-hijacking team arrived. The hijackers sensed that the plane was being deliberately delayed as they saw some heavy trucks and buses moving towards the runway to prevent takeoff. They abruptly decided not to refuel the plane and ordered the pilot at gunpoint to take off for Pakistan. The plane took off at 1949 hrs. without refuelling, and without permission from the Air Traffic Control at Amritsar. The hijackers again demanded that the plane be taken to Lahore. Pakistani authorities initially refused permission, but agreed when the pilot informed them that he would be forced to crash-land because of the critical lack of fuel. The plane was parked at Lahore airport from about 8.07 p.m. to 10.30 p.m. after being fuelled; the hijackers demanded the plane be taken to

Kabul. Kabul Air Traffic Control informed the pilot that there were no night-landing facilities there. At this, the hijackers ordered the plane to proceed to one of the Gulf countries; the choice fell on Dubai.

IC-814 landed at the Dubai airport at 1.32 a.m. on 25 December 1999.

At this, India's Ministry of External Affairs got in touch with the major world capitals, particularly Washington, those of the countries of the Gulf and of the permanent members of the UN Security Council. I happened to be in Washington and was calling on India's then ambassador, Naresh Chandra, when the information about the hijacking reached him with instructions to contact the concerned US authorities to generate pressure on Pakistan and the countries of the Gulf. Given the time difference between India and the US, the ambassador was aware that the plane had ultimately landed at Dubai. I was witness to the series of telephone calls and meetings Ambassador Chandra organised to activate the US Government. Both Deputy Secretary of State Strobe Talbott and the senior State Department official in charge of counter-terrorist activities, Ambassador Michael A. Sheehan, were prompt in conveying assurances that the US Government would fully cooperate with the Indian authorities. This included an assurance that, given the concurrence of the UAE Government, and the authorities at Dubai, the plane would not be allowed to take off from Dubai. The Indian ambassador to Abu Dhabi and the Indian consul-general at Dubai went into immediate consultations with the Dubai authorities.

While the hijackers were deciding on where to fly to from Dubai, they remained adamant about not releasing the hostages. They had already conveyed at Amritsar airport that they would start killing the hostages one by one if the plane was not refuelled and, if later, their demands were not accepted. They even announced that they had selected the initial hostages to be killed. One of them, a newly-married youth, Rupin Katyal, was stabbed to death by the hijackers because he did not strictly obey their orders and reacted with agitation and fright. The authorities at Dubai managed to persuade the hijackers to release 27 of the 180-odd passengers. The body of young Katyal was also offloaded at Dubai. IC-814 then took off from Dubai because the local authorities felt the lives of the hostages would be endangered if they delayed takeoff any further. The UAE government, perhaps, did not wish to get involved in the complicated discussions with the hijackers. The plane took off from Dubai at 8.20 a.m. and landed at Kandahar airport at 8.53 a.m. on 26 December, on receiving clearance from the Taliban authorities to bring the plane to Afghanistan. IC-814 remained parked at Kandahar airport till the hijacking ended on the evening of 31 December 1999.

As the hijacking drama progressed, the identity of the hijackers became known to the Government of India. They were: Ibrahim Athar, Sunny Ahmed Kazi, Shahid Akhtar Syed, Mistri Zahur Ibrahim and Shakir. Ibrahim Athar, the chief hijacker, was a resident of Bahawalpur in Pakistan and the brother of Maulana Masood Azhar, a leading figure of the Harkat-ul-Ansar and Harkat-ul-Mujahideen organisations. Shakir was a resident of Sukkur in Sindh, Pakistan. The remaining three hijackers were from Karachi. There was also Yusuf Nepali who later denied being involved in the hijacking but was cooperative with the hijackers and was a contact man. The Government of India considered the number of hijackers to be six, five of them Pakistani.

It would be worthwhile recounting the pattern of demands communicated to the Indian authorities, and Indian political and negotiating reactions to those demands. One can do no better than reproduce the extracts from the statements made by the Minister for External Affairs, Jaswant Singh, in both Houses of Parliament on 28 February 2000.

"In handling the situation arising from the hijacking, the Government set for itself clear priorities. These were (a) the earliest termination of the hijacking, (b) the safe return of the passengers, crew and aircraft, and (c) safeguarding national security. The manner in which the termination of the hijacking was secured met the priorities that the Government had set out."

"Soon after the aircraft reached Kandahar," the minister said, "a compaign to inform the international community about the incident began. Earlier, the foreign minister of Pakistan had been contacted to cooperate. Authorities in the UAE, as already informed, had also been asked for assistance. On 25 of December itself, I personally contacted several of my counterparts including those in the neighbouring countries, member countries of the UN Security Council and countries with nationals aboard the hijacked aircraft. The foreign secretary also spoke to some of his counterparts and heads of diplomatic missions in New Delhi. Pledges of support were received. After the arrival of the hijacked aircraft at Kandahar, upon our suggestion, the UN humanitarian coordinator for Afghanistan and representatives of countries whose nationals were aboard the aircraft sent special emissaries to Kandahar."

The Government of Nepal appointed a committee to investigate the Nepalese end of the hijacking. While the committee's report was not made public, action had already been initiated against some officials at Kathmandu's Tribhuvan Airport. The UAE authorities, after initial reluctance, responded positively to the request to permit IC-814 to land at Dubai. Their intercession with the hijackers led to the release of 27 passengers and the body of the murdered passenger.

The Pakistani authorities allowed the plane to land at Lahore airport after earlier refusing permission. To India's request for assistance, the Pakistani foreign minister said his government would act in accordance with law and "transparently". To facilitate the rapid move of India's high commissioner from Islamabad to Lahore, a helicopter was made available. Before, however, it could take off, the plane was allowed to leave Lahore at 2232 hrs. At Lahore, upon the suggestion of the captain, the hijackers offered to offload some women, children and injured persons. ATC Lahore declined. No death had occurred till then, though two of the passengers had been stabbed. Katyal succumbed to his injuries en route from Lahore to Dubai.

Flight IC-814 reached Kandahar at 8.33 hrs. on 25 December. The aircraft came within the control of the Taliban authorities, whom India did not recognise and with whom it had no official contact. Immediate contacts were established on the ATC channel between the Indian high commission in Islamabad and the Taliban mission in the city.

An official from India's high commission in Islamabad was sent to Kandahar on the morning of 27 December. Doctors and a relief crew reached Kandahar from Delhi on 27th evening itself. Officials accompanying this group met representatives of other countries present in Kandahar, UN officials, as also Taliban authorities, including Foreign Minister Wakil Ahmed Muttawakil. The team updated itself on the condition of the aircraft, the state of health of the passengers, and on what had transpired between the Taliban and the hijackers.

Direct discussions between the hijackers and Indian officials took place between the evening of 27 and 31 December. The hijackers initially demanded the release of Masood Azhar in return for ten Indians, five foreigners and some other passengers of their choice. This piecemeal approach was rejected outright by the Government. Both the Taliban and the hijackers were informed that until there was a formal, full and unambiguous detailing of demands, there could be no talks. It is significant that the Taliban then advised the hijackers to give their full demands. This was done. These were (a) release of 36 terrorists in Indian custody, including Masood Azhar; (b) the coffin of terrorist Sajad Afghani; and (c) payment of US$ 200 million. After these demands had been made public, the Taliban advised the hijackers that their clamour for money and Afghani coffin was un-Islamic.

Thereupon, the hijackers insisted that Masood Azhar be released in exchange for 15 hostages and such others as the hijackers may choose to release. This was again rejected by the Government. Finally, a full package was worked out for the release of all the hostages. The Government released three terrorists — Masood Azhar, Mushtaq Zargar and Omar Sheikh.

India had told the Taliban that the released terrorists would be brought to Kandahar Airport, whereafter they would be under Taliban control but not that of the hijackers. It was explicitly conveyed to the Taliban, the minister said, "that we expected that both the hijackers and the released terrorists would be treated as criminals in conformity with the law." The decision taken by the Taliban to allow the hijackers and released terrorists ten hours to leave Afghanistan "was their own."

Behind the Scenes

It is not the stark facts of the hijacking or the chronology of the flight that is of prime importance. What is relevant is to recount the information about Pakistan's full involvement in the hijacking, information which came out as a result of follow-up investigations. That the plan for the hijacking was the work of ISI agents located in Mumbai and Dhaka came to be known through intercepts of telephone calls between these operatives and London. The monitoring of these telephone calls was possible due to the technological assistance provided by the US. The ISI operatives arrested in Mumbai were Mohammed Rehan, Mohammed Iqbal, Yusuf Nepali, Abdul Latif Fasiullah and Salim Ahmed Quari. Preparations for the hijacking had commenced in the last week of September/first week of October. Abdul Latif, one of the Mumbai-based operatives, visited Kathmandu several times between October and end-November. He had discussions with the chief hijacker, Ibrahim Athar, both in Mumbai and in Kathmandu. Since reaching Kathmandu may have involved air routes through Bangladesh as well, ISI agents located in Bangladesh were also involved in the planning. They were Faizullah and Abdul Rahman from the Nurani Madrassa in Dhaka. The hijackers reached Kathmandu by various routes. The chief hijacker flew to Calcutta from Mumbai, took a train to New Jalpaiguri and proceeded to Kathmandu in the company of another hijacker, Akhtar Sayed. A third hijacker, Shakir, travelled by train from Mumbai to Gorakhpur and took a bus to Kathmandu. All the four hijackers were in position in Kathmandu by 15 December 1999. They had linkages with a Pakistan-based organisation, Harkat-ul-Ansar, which changed its name to Harkat-ul-Mujahideen after Harkat-ul-Ansar was declared a terrorist organisation by the US authorities.

It should be recalled that Masood Azhar, till the time of his arrest by Indian authorities in 1994, was one of the most violent and assertive leaders of the Harkat-ul-Ansar. The involvement of the Pakistani authorities in the hijacking is further proved by the fact that just before the departure of IC-814 from Kathmandu, Mohammed Arshad Cheema, first secretary consular of the Pakistani embassy in Kathmandu, accompanied by other officials arrived at the airport, went into the departure lounge and apparently had some last-minute discussions with the leader of the hijacking group. Cheema is known to be an ISI officer, and was responsible for supplying RDX to Sikh militants in 1998, a matter officially taken note of by the Indian mission in Kathmandu, as well as by the Government of India.

The destination to which the pilot of IC-814 was directed to proceed immediately after the hijacking was Lahore. ATC Lahore refusing the request initially was a farce. When the plane took off from Amritsar again without refuelling, the pilot warned the hijackers that because of extreme shortage of fuel, the plane might have to crash-land. The response of the hijackers to the pilot was "crash-land the plane, but in Pakistan". The plane was allowed to land at Lahore not at the request of the pilot but as a result of a direct conversation between the hijackers and ATC Lahore. The refuelling of the plane at Lahore too was done only after the hijackers spoke to ATC Lahore. Reports are that Pakistani military and intelligence officers were present in the ATC tower. The aircraft commander had persuaded the hijackers to agree to the offloading of injured women and children but ATC Lahore did not permit their release because Pakistan did not want to be seen as having had any agreements with the hijackers.

After takeoff from Dubai, ATC Kabul refused permission for the plane to land anywhere in Afghanistan but the plane was ultimately allowed to land in Kandahar, as ATC Lahore took the initiative to inform the pilot that Kandahar airport was ready to accept the hijacked aircraft. There is confirmed information that throughout the period of the hijacking from 24 to 31 December, the ISI controllers, the hijackers, and ISI operatives in Mumbai were in constant telephone contact with the amir of Harkat-ul-Ansar, Fazullur Rahman Khalil, who was in Pakistan. It is equally interesting to note that of the 36 terrorist prisoners whose release was demanded by the hijackers, only one was Kashmiri, one was from Afghanistan, one was a UK national of Pakistani origin. The remaining 33 were Pakistanis.

When the hijacking came to an end on 31 December, the hijackers as well as the terrorists released by the Government of India travelled straight from Kandahar to Quetta in Baluchistan (Pakistan). Maulana Masood Azhar, the main terrorist released, proceeded unhindered from there to Bahawalpur, his home in Pakistani Punjab. He later publicly announced that the hijackers as well as some of the terrorists released had gone back to

Jammu and Kashmir in India. Thus the hijackers and the terrorist mercenaries were allowed to go across the international frontier into Pakistan without any objections from the immigration authorities in the border control posts of Pakistan. They did not travel clandestinely but openly with attendant publicity, in the immediate aftermath of an internationally reported hijacking incident.

The hijackers as well as the terrorists released were members of the Harkat-ul-Mujahideen, previously known as Harkat-ul-Ansar. This organisation has the backing and patronage of the ISI. It is of particular significance that the Government of Pakistan had interceded with India's former high commissioner in Pakistan, Satish Chandra (now secretary to the National Security Council), for the release of Maulana Masood Azhar.

It is obvious that ISI contacts at Tribhuvan airport in Kathmandu allowed the hijackers to smuggle their arms into the aircraft and there must have been some collaboration by security, customs and immigration officials. Though the security arrangements were not as strict as they should have been, the smuggling of arms into an aircraft implies more than carelessness. Though the investigative report ordered by the Nepalese Government has not been publicised, that airport officials at Kathmandu have been suspended and put under investigation confirms this.

The attitude and role of the Taliban authorities in Afghanistan merits some analysis. The Taliban's anti-India stand on the Kashmir issue and its links with terrorist organisations operating in different parts of the world are well known. Their allowing an Indian aircraft to land at Kandahar must have been a difficult decision. It could be justified on humanitarian grounds, but any positive gestures towards the hijackers would have only worsened the image of the Taliban Government as a regime supporting terrorism. The Taliban's political sympathies, as expected, were with the hijackers, an attitude underpinned by the regime's political and military relationship with the Government of Pakistan, particularly with the ISI.

The Taliban fine-tuned its management of the hijacking crisis remarkably. Though the Taliban security forces surrounded the plane at Kandahar, they did not send any message to the hijackers to release the hostages and end the hijacking. To gain credibility as a government respecting humanitarian considerations, they assisted in the supply of medicines and food to the hostages in the plane. They also cautioned the hijackers that any killing of hostages on Afghan territory would result in the Taliban forces having to take countermeasures.

As mentioned in the statement of Foreign Minister Jaswant Singh, quoted earlier, the Taliban also asked the hijackers to withdraw the demand for $200 million, calling it un-Islamic. The Taliban gave facilities for representatives of the Government of India, UN representatives and other external non-governmental organisations to talk to the hijackers in the Indian plane. The Taliban offered safe conduct to the hijackers and the terrorists about to be released by the Government of India with an assurance that they would be given sufficient time to travel back to Pakistan safely. What should be a matter of concern, however, are reports that some additional arms might have been supplied by the Taliban authorities to the hijackers when the plane was stranded at Kandahar. The Taliban did not respond to the Indian request that the hijackers and the released terrorists be arrested and prosecuted under the internationally acknowledged legal requirements stipulated against hijacking.

In brief, the Taliban extended the minimum required cooperation to resolve the crisis, but there was no condemnation of the hijacking. The cooperation extended was to win over international public opinion. It was a hollow gesture.

The activities of Maulana Masood Azhar after his release confirmed the extent to which the Pakistani authorities were supportive of the hijack as well as Azhar's political and terrorist agenda. The Maulana was received with great fanfare at his home where local Pakistani authorities were present. He addressed a series of public meetings for six weeks after his arrival in Bahawalpur, claiming that the hijacking was not a crime but an act of *jehad* (holy war), that his organisation's basic political objective was to capture the Indian state of Jammu and Kashmir by force. He said he planned to recruit an armed cadre of half a million people to continue the *jehad* against India. This is the gist of the statement he made in Northern Sindh and parts of Pakistani Punjab. Audio cassettes of his speeches were prepared and distributed not only all over Pakistan, but in Jammu and Kashmir, Punjab, Haryana, Uttar Pradesh and northwestern Rajasthan in India. It was evidence of an extensive ISI network in different parts of India. To cap all this, Masood Azhar also got married with great fanfare.

In this context, it is difficult to swallow the denials issued by General Pervez Musharraf and other Pakistani authorities about their connections with the hijacking. It is impossible to believe that the Pakistani authorities did not have the means to apprehend the hijackers and the terrorists who should have been subject to prosecution under domestic and international law.

Apart from the patently unacceptable denials of involvement, Pakistan's claim was that the hijacking was carried out by indigenous Kashmiri militants. This again proved to be an inept exercise in mendacity. All the hijackers except Yusuf Nepali were Pakistani citizens. There were and are a large number of secessionist terrorists in the custody of the Indian Government. The demand of the hijackers was only for the release of terrorists who were Pakistani citizens. They did not demand the release of even one terrorist belonging to Pakistan-occupied Kashmir.

Other aspects of the Pakistani reaction to the hijacking need to be mentioned. The first reaction of the Government of Pakistan could be described as farcical but for its tragic implications. The Pakistani authorities decided that the hijacking was organised by the Indian intelligence agencies, particularly the Research and Analysis Wing (RAW), to put Pakistan in a bad light as a terrorist state, with the specific objective of sabotaging President Bill Clinton's visit to Pakistan. When this idea did not find any takers, Pakistani authorities claimed that they had no personal knowledge of the hijackers and that they were indigenous militants from Indian Jammu and Kashmir. They explained the interaction between Pakistani officials and the hijackers at Lahore as being motivated by humanitarian considerations. For nearly three weeks after the hijackers and terrorists had reached Pakistan, Government spokesmen, including General Musharraf, made the extraordinary claim that they were not aware of the whereabouts of the hijackers and released terrorists, while the latter were resorting to public pronouncements about their future anti-Indian projects.

The reaction of Pakistani public opinion during the hijacking was indicative of the collective mindset of Pakistani civil society. In the initial stages, the Pakistani media repeated the Pakistani Government's interpretation that the hijacking was organised by Indian intelligence agencies themselves to embarrass Pakistan before the international community. Once the plane landed in Kandahar and the demands of the hijackers became public, there was total silence about the contradictions between facts as they were emerging and the Musharraf Government's initial claims about India being the organiser of the hijacking. Even more disturbingly, the media and public opinion did not show any concern about civilian passengers being subjected to threats and trauma for a full week.

The reaction of the international community to the incident was equally bemusing. There was wide and daily coverage of the incident till the hijacking ended, but there was no condemnation of the organisation to which the hijackers belonged. There was no comment on Pakistan's resort to covert terrorist acts across international frontiers to capture the territory of a neighbouring state. Instead the Western media talked about Jammu and Kashmir being a flashpoint for a conflict in the context of India's and Pakistan's nuclear and missile weapon capacities.

Reviewing India's Decisions

After the hijacking ended there was no criticism of the Taliban or the Government of Pakistan for ensuring the safe escape of the hijackers and the terrorists released by India. The reaction was essentially an exercise in selective impartiality. Having said this, one must acknowledge that fairly strong messages went from the US and the Western democracies to the Government of Pakistan and indirectly to the Taliban to bring the hijacking to an end. There was much criticism about the manner in which India handled the hijacking incident. The validity of this criticism needs to be analysed and assessed. Views were expressed that India should not have succumbed to the demands of the hijackers, that it should not have allowed IC-814 to take off from Amritsar airport, that it should have ensured the plane remained stranded at Dubai airport, that the counter-hijacking action force should have neutralised the hijacking at Amritsar itself.

The facts should be described first. The decision to deal with the hijackers and to come to a compromise was taken after extremely tense discussions in the Cabinet Committee on Security by the minister for external affairs, and meetings with the prime minister were fraught with tense emotional protests by the relatives of the hostages. The Rashtriya Swayamsevak Sangh was firmly opposed to any dealings with the hijackers. Authoritative sources told me that in the cabinet discussions, one cabinet minister went to the extent of saying that he smelt an atmosphere of appeasement in the options being discussed. Home Minister L.K. Advani agreed to the decision of responding to the demands of the hijackers only reluctantly.

Could we have prevented the plane from taking off from Amritsar and Dubai? Judgements based on hindsight are irrelevant. However, some conclusions are inescapable. There was a lack of coordination in terms of speed and time between the authorities at Delhi and Amritsar. The runway was not blocked immediately after the landing of the plane at Amritsar. The NSG commandos did not scramble into their action/operational mode with sufficient speed. The hijackers had enough time to take off without facing any effective Indian resistance.

As far as the situation in Dubai was concerned, the authorities there had allowed the plane to land with reluctance and did not wish to get involved in a violent predicament. In any case, they did not wish to be participants in resolving the hijacking crisis at Dubai airport, which is a major civilian air traffic centre. Though they had initially given some assurances to the US authorities that they would prevent the plane from taking off, they could not fulfil this promise in the context of impinging on Dubai's international credibility as a safe place to travel for tourism and shopping purposes.

Once the plane landed at Kandahar, the question of any effective action by India became redundant. India was not even sure how the Taliban would deal with the hijacking, especially because it did not have any diplomatic mission in Kabul. The high commission established initial contacts with the Taliban mission in Islamabad. Ghanshyam, India's political consular at Islamabad, proceeded to Kandahar. He gave the assessment that the Taliban would be willing to receive an Indian negotiating team. Foreign Minister Jaswant Singh decided to send a negotiating team led by Vivek Katju, joint secretary incharge of Iran, Pakistan and Afghanistan in the Ministry of External Affairs. Katju was assisted by officers from the home ministry and other concerned agencies, Ajit Doval, Hooja and Razdan. It is to this team that the hijackers conveyed the series of demands, mentioned earlier in this chapter. The negotiations began with the first contact made by Ghanshyam with the Taliban on 27 December and ended with Jaswant Singh's visit to Kandahar with the terrorists whom the Government of India had decided to release. The other point of criticism has been about Jaswant Singh personally going to Kandahar, and thereby increasing the stature of the hijackers in psychological and public relations terms. He explained his rationale in the statement to Parliament: "I decided to go to Kandahar so as to ensure that the termination of the hijacking, the smooth release and safe return of the passengers and crew, took place without any last-minute hitch, also that should the need arise, prompt decisions could be taken on the spot.... My travel on the same aircraft as the three terrorists was entirely on account of logistical compulsions brought about by the limited infrastructural facilities at Kandahar airport."

Apart from briefing foreign governments and asking for their cooperation in countering Pakistan-sponsored cross-border terrorist acts, the Government of India sent direct communications to the Government of Pakistan. In its formal response, the Government of Pakistan said it would undertake to apprehend and prosecute any persons found on its territory, or the territory of Pakistan-occupied Kashmir, who may be suspected of the hijacking. Pakistan then proceeded to say that none of the hijackers was in any part of Pakistan, this after the ISI ensured the return of the hijackers, first to Pakistan-occupied Kashmir and then facilitating their re-entry into Jammu and Kashmir in India. That the hijackers were back in Jammu and Kashmir to carry on their violent activities was publicly announced by Maulana Masood Azhar in one of his speeches in Bahawalpur. Jaswant

Singh's assessment and response was: "As they (Pakistan) have rejected our dé marche, Pakistan's general commitment to act against the hijackers has to be assessed accordingly." In other words, there were and are no possibilities of Pakistan taking any action against these terrorists.

It is the public reaction after the hijacking was over that should impel India into introspection about how it handled the hijacking. Sections of public opinion and the media asserted India's image suffered thanks to giving into the hijackers. Some organisations like the RSS went to the extent of saying the Government of India acted in a cowardly manner. Others opined that India has reaffirmed the international assessment of it being a soft state. So were there other options that could have been exercised once the plane had landed in Kandahar?

In my assessment there certainly was one option. But it would have been a risky gamble. The option was to convey to the Taliban that as the hijacked plane was now in territory under its control, dealing with the hijackers for getting hostages released was entirely its responsibility. If it refused to persuade the hijackers to release the hostages and if it connived with them, the Taliban's links with cross-border terrorist groups would stand confirmed. Given the Taliban's inclination not to confront the international community, particularly Western democracies, it would have had to do something to end the hijacking. It would also have put Pakistan on the defensive, given its links with the Taliban. India could have refused to get involved in any direct negotiations with the hijackers. The risk was that the Taliban would have conveyed the demands of the hijackers to India and, if Delhi refused to meet those demands (which it would have, in the logic of the above policy stance), then the Taliban could have washed their hands of the whole matter, arguing that India was not cooperating. If consequently the hostages came to harm or if the plane was blown up, there would have been criticism of the Government of India, but at the same time, the Taliban would have been seen as being a party to the terrorist demands. The bottomline for examining the options that might have been exercised was whether India was willing to accept the loss of life of hostages to convey the critical message that it would not succumb to terrorist pressures. There are perhaps only two countries that have such a categorical policy approach on terrorism and hijacking cases: China and Israel. Since saving the lives of the hostages was the primary concern, the rest of the actions taken by the Government of India followed.

Though one wishes the Government of India had responded with effective action against the hijackers at Amritsar, and then taken an equally firm stand on putting responsibility on the Taliban, the matter was dealt with as effectively as feasible. If this experience heightens India's alertness and capacity for real-time response the trauma would have served a purpose.

What was lamentably contradictory was that the very people who pressurised the Government to compromise with the hijackers later joined the bandwagon of criticism. This shows the schizophrenia and dichotomies from which Indian media and public opinion suffer. This of course is endemic in democracies, where such opinions have to be respected, a problem not affecting authoritarian governments, or governments representing profoundly united public opinion like in Israel. It is equally worrying that the common people of Pakistan did not react to the hijacking in a manner influenced by humanitarian considerations. The attitude of the Pakistani Government was aggressive and hypocritical. Public sentiments in Pakistan remained prisoner to emotional and psychological antagonism towards India. This underlines the fact that while most of the world moves on to cooperative and rational interaction, India and Pakistan remain chained to irrational hostilities.

Two

Implications of the Kargil War

The India-Pakistan war in the Kargil sector on the Line of Control in Jammu and Kashmir lasted from 6 May to roughly the end of July 1999. It was the fifth large-scale conflict between the two countries. There seems to have been a subconscious reluctance on the part of both India and Pakistan to acknowledge the extensive nature of these conflicts, their territorial motivations and the violence inherent in them. Euphemisms are used. The military confrontations are described as "skirmishes", "intrusions", "warlike situations", or "limited military operations", whereas in fact, Indian and Pakistani armed forces were engaged in full-scale military operations against each other in 1947-48, twice in 1965 in Kutch and in Jammu and Kashmir (a war that expanded across the international frontiers between India and Pakistan), in 1971 during the East Pakistan crisis, and most recently in Kargil.

A significant and recurrent characteristic of these military confrontations has been that each time Pakistan initiated the confrontation covertly, whether it was in Kashmir, in Kutch or in former East Pakistan. When resistance to its moves was threatened with failure, Pakistan deployed its regular troops, which in turn invited full-scale military responses from India. Out of the four conflicts, it is only during the 1965 and 1971 conflicts that India formally declared that a state of war existed between India and Pakistan. Otherwise, there has been reluctance to accept the fact that all the major conflicts between India and Pakistan, were in fact regular wars in which the armed forces of the two countries engaged in operations against each other. The military conflict between India and Pakistan in Kargil in 1999 was not a skirmish, a border incident, or a marginal intrusion; it was a war. A war launched by Pakistan with definite and clear strategic, territorial and political motives, with premeditated planning and detailed preparation.

There is a political and emotional background to the Pakistani military initiative in Kargil, which has not been taken note of by public opinion on both sides of the border. Pakistan's Kargil effort was in some ways a culmination of various options exercised to acquire Jammu and Kashmir. It was also rooted in Pakistani calculations based on the experience of the failure of other efforts in Kashmir, particularly during the period 1989 to 1999. The arguments Pakistan put forward to realise its territorial claim were that Jammu and Kashmir becoming part of Pakistan was an unfinished task of Partition; since Partition was based on the two-nation theory and since Jammu and Kashmir was a Muslim-majority state (and contiguous with West Pakistan), it should be part of Pakistan. The second argument was that the people of Jammu and Kashmir have a right to self-determination. They were promised a plebiscite in order to exercise this right, from which India is reneging. Then there was the argument that the Government of India was violating human rights in Jammu and Kashmir. It was, therefore, the obligation of Pakistan as an Islamic country and an obligation of the international community to liberate Jammu and Kashmir from the Indian yoke.

When all these arguments failed to arouse the people of Jammu and Kashmir into a mass movement against India, and when the international community also failed to be convinced by these Pakistani arguments, Pakistan resorted to the final adventuristic reasoning that since both India and Pakistan have declared nuclear weapon capacities since 1998, if India is not asked by the international community to give up Jammu and Kashmir to Pakistan, the world must face the prospect of nuclear war between India and Pakistan on the Kashmir issue, the fallout of which would be dangerous not only for the Asian region, but for global stability and security.

This last argument did influence the international community. The consequence was pressure generated both on India and Pakistan from 1990 onwards to keep the bilateral dialogue going and to agree upon and implement as many confidence-building measures as possible to avoid the prospect of military confrontation. It is as a result of this pressure, as well as the Indian desire to avoid a military confrontation, that a number of discussions were held between the prime ministers of India and Pakistan and between the senior officials of the governments of India and Pakistan, including military officials, between 1989 and 1994. This exercise led to limited success, which found expression in the confidence-building measures agreed to between 1990 and 1993. These included the establishment of direct telephone hotlines between prime ministers, foreign secretaries and the directors-general, military operations. Agreement was reached on both sides to avoid holding military exercises at close proximity to the international frontier, and to give advance notice about land, air and naval exercises to each other. There was even an agreement on the treatment of diplomatic representatives. The implementation of these measures, however, clearly indicated that Pakistan conceived them to be limited tactical public relations exercises. Simultaneously, active support to subversive elements in Jammu and Kashmir and in other parts of India not only continued but has also increased. The commitment to make Jammu and Kashmir a part of Pakistan remained and remains an unalterable objective of the Pakistani power structure.

It is in this context that Pakistan launched "Operation Badr", the invasion of Jammu and Kashmir through the Kargil sector. It would be pertinent to mention the broad Pakistani political assessments and calculations on the basis of which Pakistan launched this campaign. The Pakistani assessment was that the credibility of Chief Minister Farooq Abdullah in Jammu and Kashmir was low. Pakistan believed that the Indian Army and security forces were involved in so many disparate activities that they would not be able to resist a coordinated large-scale military onslaught in an unexpected manner, in an unexpected area. The Vajpayee Government had lost a Motion of No-Confidence in the Lok Sabha in March 1999. Apart from being a coalition government, the Government of India was a "caretaker" Government, which would be busy in conducting general elections in the country. The anticipation was that the Vajpayee Government would not have sufficient credibility to take firm decisions against foreign aggression due to the volatile and uncertain political situation within India. Most important, the Pakistani assessment was that the Indian Army would not be able to resist and push back Pakistani forces once the latter entrenched themselves at strategic heights on the Himalayan ranges in the vital Kargil sector. This assessment was based on repeated reports in the Indian media about our army being short of officers and equipment and its morale being low throughout the 1990s. There was also the confidence that if Indian military resistance became unmanageable, Pakistan could resort to using nuclear weapons which would bring in international intervention, and at the same time temper Indian inclinations to expand the war and threaten Pakistan's general security as had happened in 1965 and 1971.

There was also the feeling in the Pakistani military high command that the Indian Army must be suffering from low morale because of its long-term deployment in counter-insurgency activities in Jammu and Kashmir and in other parts of India. In fact, the report of the Kargil Review Committee chaired by K. Subrahmanyam, quotes Lt. General Javed Nasir, former head of the ISI, as writing an assessment early in 1999, stating that "The Indian Army is incapable of undertaking any conventional operations at present, so how can one talk of their enlarging a conventional conflict."

Before proceeding to more specific political and strategic objectives of the Pakistani aggression in Kargil and before detailing the chronology of events, it is necessary to take note of the professional background and attitude of the key military figure who launched this aggression, General Pervez Musharraf, chief of army staff of Pakistan since 1998, who later, in October 1999, overthrew the democratically elected Nawaz Sharif Government and nominated himself as the chief executive of Pakistan. First, we must try to understand the policies he was inclined to follow in relation to India. Musharraf's public pronouncements provide some clear indications. As far as India is concerned, he was known to maintain a posture of political and military confrontation. He firmly believed that a sustained campaign of subversion and military intrusion would result in Pakistan achieving its objective of annexing Kashmir to Pakistan. His background and persona were factors affecting his initiating the Kargil misadventure. General Musharraf belongs to a Uttar Pradesh Muslim family. His grandparents and parents were residents of Delhi in the period immediately before Partition. Born in 1943, his family migrated to Pakistan when he was four. He grew up in Karachi and then in Gujranwala, ultimately being commissioned in the artillery branch of the Pakistani Army in 1964. He had a comparatively routine career till Pakistani President Zia-ul-Haq took notice of him because of his reputation as a devout Muslim officer and his links with a number of Islam-pasand politicians of Pakistan. Like Zia, General Musharraf has strong links with the Jamat-e-Islami of Pakistan. The first significant assignment given by Zia to Musharraf was to be in charge of training mercenaries recruited from various Muslim countries for fighting against Soviet troops in Afghanistan, in the concerned Directorate of Inter-Services Intelligence. There are reports that during this period he had contacts with Osama bin Laden, who was originally brought to Afghanistan by the US Central Intelligence Agency itself for constructing bunkers and tunnels for Afghan Mujahideen in different theatres of the conflict in Afghanistan. As part of his responsibility of training mercenaries, General Musharraf was also involved in financing their operations with the assistance of narcotic smugglers operating in the North West Frontier Province (NWFP) of Pakistan. An interesting sidelight to this phase of his career is that while intelligence establishments of the US and Pakistan valued his services, the Narcotics Control Establishment of the US Government was not enamoured of the general. This is given as one of the reasons why General Musharraf is a singularity in the Pakistani officers cadre in that he has never gone for any higher military training to US military institutions. He has done training only in the United Kingdom.

The year 1987 was a watershed in General Musharraf's career. He was made the brigade commander of the newly raised Special Services Group in the Siachen area, created to push back Indian forces from Siachen. He was responsible for a major attack on the Indian military post at Bilafond La, in the Siachen sector in September 1987. His forces were decisively defeated by Indian troops. He was given a special assignment in the summer of 1989 to suppress a revolt by the Shias in the Gilgit region against the Sunni-dominated local administration. General Musharraf supplemented his troops with Pathan tribesmen from the NWFP and Afghanistan for this operation in which hundreds of Shias were massacred and displaced. Pakistani newspaper and magazines like *Dawn* and *Herald* reported that Musharraf's troops invaded the Gilgit district along the Karakoram highway, destroyed crops and houses and killed a large number of the rural population. He followed this up with changing the demography of the Gilgit region by bringing in Punjabis and Pathans and settling them in Gilgit and Baltistan, in order to reduce the majority of Kashmiri Shias, who were the original inhabitants of the area. Musharraf has spent years with the Special Services Group in two separate assignments and claims to be the most knowledgeable expert on mountain warfare in the Pakistani armed forces. He values his identity as a commando more than as a gunner. The culmination of his field assignments was when he was appointed force commander, Northern Areas, which made him in charge of all military and subversive operations against Jammu and Kashmir. This assignment also brought him in close touch with senior officials of the ISI and extremist Islamic groups dealing with Afghanistan and subversion in Jammu and Kashmir. It was from the late 1980s and the mid-1990s that Pervez Musharraf established close links with groups like the Harkat-ul-Mujahideen and Lashkar-e-Toiba and Tabligi Jamaat. There are reports that Musharraf also has links with Osama bin Laden's international Islamic Front for Jehad against the US and Israel. Interestingly, Musharraf was also reported to be directly involved with an unsuccessful military coup against Benazir Bhutto in the autumn of 1995. The attempt was allegedly led by Major General

Zaheer-ul-Islam Abbasi, who succeeded Musharraf as force commander, Northern Areas.

The Pakistani media has reported that had the coup succeeded General Musharraf would have been the candidate for head of state. Both Abbasi and General Aziz (who was General Musharraf's chief of staff in 1999) were reported to be part of this coup. Throughout the 1990s, Musharraf and his senior associates were involved in the supply of finance and arms to various secessionist groups and mercenaries intruding into Jammu and Kashmir.

Coming to more recent developments, Pervez Musharraf was not enthusiastic about the Lahore meeting between Nawaz Sharif and Vajpayee. Even while the meeting was taking place, Musharraf had finalised plans for attacking India along the Line of Control in Jammu and Kashmir in the Kargil sector. He was the principal architect of the fourth major military conflict between India and Pakistan. Musharraf felt that he would succeed in his Kargil adventure because in his assessment conditions in India were politically uncertain, and the morale of the Indian armed forces was low owing to the poor leadership of Defence Minister George Fernandes and the soft leadership of Vajpayee. In fact a former chief of the ISI, Lt. General Assad Durrani, went to the extent of assessing during the initial stages of the Kargil conflict that Fernandes was perhaps the best Indian defence minister that Pakistan could hope for.

According to a study done by the Indian Institute for Topical Studies, Pervez Musharraf's approach towards India and the Kashmir question can be summarised as follows. The assessment is based on the pronouncements and interviews of Musharraf:

- The BJP is a party of "paper tigers", known more for verbosity than for action.

- Pakistan's nuclear and missile capability has ensured that India would not retaliate against Pakistan for occupying the ridges in the Kargil area.

- The fear of the possible use of nuclear weapons would bring in Western intervention, thereby internationalising the Kashmir issue.

- Pakistan should agree to a ceasefire only if it were allowed to remain in occupation of the Indian territory. There should be no question of the restoration of the status quo ante.

The interviews and speeches of General Musharraf since October 1998 show his thinking to be as follows:

• The acquisition of Kashmir by Pakistan can wait. What is more important is to keep the Indian Army bleeding in Kashmir just as the Afghan mujahideen kept the Soviet troops bleeding in Afghanistan.

• Even if the Kashmir issue is resolved, there cannot be normal relations between India and Pakistan because Pakistan, by frustrating India's ambition of emerging as a major Asian power on par with China and Japan, would continue to be the thorn in India's flesh. And so as long as it does so, Pakistan would continue to enjoy the backing of China and Japan.

This is Musharraf's professional background and it demonstrates the mindset of an assertive, theologically committed military figure. India's then high commissioner in Pakistan, Satish Chandra (now secretary of the National Security Council and chairman of the Joint Intelligence Committee), commenting on Musharraf's personality when he took over as chief of army staff of Pakistan in October 1998, indicated that Musharraf was hawkish, ambitious, and had long-standing links with several Islamic fundamentalist groups.

The question of why Pakistan decided to resort to massive territorial aggression against India in the Kargil sector, merits geopolitical, operational and psychological answers. As mentioned earlier, Pakistan had not succeeded in making any dent on the Indian political and territorial position in Jammu and Kashmir, despite the various political arguments and manoeuvrings it had engaged in since 1989. Pakistanis, therefore, felt something very drastic had to be done on the ground to disrupt the whole political and military hold of India in Jammu and Kashmir. All Pakistani military operations against India in Jammu and Kashmir had been launched on a southwest-northeast axis, through Jammu, from areas on the southwestern flank of Jammu and Kashmir. These had been successfully resisted by the Indian armed forces more than once during the past 50 years. So Pakistanis felt that the attempt to strategically dominate the Kashmir valley should be launched from a different location, west of the Indian-held areas up to the Line of Control. This approach was entertained by the Pakistani military command from the late 1970s onwards. The first attempt to get a foothold vis-à-vis the Kashmir valley was undertaken in the early 1980s in the Siachen glacier area because Pakistanis felt the demarcation of the Line of Control there could be ambiguously interpreted to justify their intrusion. It is relevant to recall that the Line of Control in Jammu and Kashmir has clearly been demarcated up to a grid reference point on the map, NJ 9842. It was agreed that it shall lie northwards from this grid reference towards the glaciers. Pakistan desired to take advantage of these cartographic formulations. Indian intelligence came to know about the Pakistani plans and Indian troops in pre-emptive operations moved forward and established posts at various points in the Siachen glacier region in 1984. Pakistani attempts to dislodge Indian troops from their positions in Siachen have repeatedly failed. Pakistan believed that a large-scale military operation across the LoC would draw away Indian troops from the Valley for border defence purposes, a situation that could then be utilised to heighten levels of terrorism within Jammu and Kashmir. The immediate assessment on the basis of which Pakistan launched the Kargil operations have been summed up in the Subrahmanyam Report:

(a) Pakistan's nuclear capability would forestall any major Indian move particularly across the international border. It was Pakistan's assessment that nuclear deterrence had worked in its favour from the mid-80s. Not an invalid assessment, objectively speaking.

(b) The international community would prevent the expansion of a conflict by intervening through bilateral mechanisms or through the UN. If Pakistan consolidated its gains across the LoC, the international community would accept the new situation, bettering Pakistan's negotiating position.

(c) China would be supportive of Pakistan's military operations.

(d) A weak and unstable government in India would be incapable of a firm response and would not expand the conflict into Pakistan across the international frontier.

(e) The Indian Army itself may not be able to respond effectively because of its counter-insurgency commitments in Jammu and Kashmir.

(f) Due to an inadequacy of resources east of Zoji La, India would not be able to react efficiently against intrusions before the Zoji La Pass opens for traffic by the end of May or early June.

(g) The Indian Army does not have troops sufficiently trained in high-altitude warfare, and would not be able to deploy adequate forces to counter a pre-emptive surprise Pakistani move. The Pakistani military intrusion if successful would disrupt the return of normalcy in the Valley.

The incursions across the Line of Control in the Kargil sector had been part of Pakistan's strategic options and war games since the mid-1980s. Senior journalist and adviser to Field Marshal Ayub Khan, Altaf Gohar, has confirmed that a plan to intrude in the Kargil sector by means of a major operation existed in the Pakistan Army Headquarters from 1987 onwards. But it was not operationalised by the successive governments of Pakistan till 1999. General Zia, during the last year and a half of his tenure, then Benazir Bhutto and Nawaz Sharif both pulled back from the Kargil plan, primarily because the chiefs of army staff, General Mirza Aslam Beg and General Jehangir Karamat, were not in favour of such a large-scale military operation to which an Indian response could have been unpredictable. General Pervez Musharraf however had a different mindset. He was deeply involved in various military operations in Pakistan-occupied Kashmir and the Northern Areas. He was frustrated about the debacle at Siachen for nearly a decade and a half. It was a region in which he had been militarily active. The comparatively uncertain political situation in India and the assessments about the state of preparedness and morale of the Indian forces made him feel that he could safely launch the Kargil operation in the preparation of which he had remained involved off and on from 1993 onwards as director general, military operations. Pervez Musharraf visited the Northern Areas of Pakistan-occupied Kashmir on 20 and 21 October 1998 accompanied by Lt. General Mehmood Ahmed, general officer commanding the 10th Corps of the Pakistani Army. The plan to launch an attack on Kargil was finalised during this visit and was given final shape in October and December 1998.

Prime Minister Sharif was briefed about the Kargil plan at the general headquarters of the Pakistani Army in Rawalpindi in January 1999; a month before he met Prime Minister Vajpayee at Lahore on 22 February 1999. Incursions by Pakistani armed forces commenced from the end of 1998, first for reconnaissance purposes and then to prepare the ground for a large-scale invasion across the Line of Control.

The process of incursions by regular Pakistani troops occurred during the period December 1998 to March 1999. By the last week of April and first week of May, Pakistani troops had crossed the Line of Control all along the Kargil region. They were positioned in the Batalik sector, in the Dras sector and Mushkoh sector, in the Kaksar sector, at Turtok and Chorbat La. The first clear perception that Pakistan was engaged in a large-scale invasion across the Line of Control occurred between the 2 and 5 May when forward units of the Indian Army got information about increased Pakistani presence from their local informants. The war (which commenced in May and came to an end in late July–early August) was fought along a 200 kilometre front on the Line of Control, stretching from Mushkoh valley to the Saltoro Ridge on the western flank of the Siachen

Glacier. Pakistan had not only crossed the Line of Control to a width of nearly 200 kilometres but had also moved into territory to a depth of 10 to 12 kilometres. The main battle was fought in excru-ciatingly difficult terrain, in extremely cold conditions, and at heights of between 10,000 to 18,000 feet.

The overall confrontationist phenomenon instigated by Pakistan resulted in regular war fighting (without it being openly declared) between Pakistani troops of the Northern Areas under force commander, Northern Areas Pakistan, and 10 Corps of the Pakistani Army, and nearly two and a half divisions of the Indian Army belonging to our Northern Command. While the Pakistani forces used light and heavy infantry weapons as well as heavy artillery and surface-to-air missiles, the Indian armed forces, apart from using similar weapons systems also operated with support from the Indian Air Force, involving both helicopters and fixed wing aircraft. The Indian Air Force lost two aircrafts and a helicopter in the initial phase of the operations but remained part of the collective coordinated military effort despite the losses. The Indian Navy went into a pre-emptive effective posture against Pakistan by deploying warships in the Arabian Sea, bottling up the Pakistani Navy and Pakistani shipping at Karachi, under what was called "Operation Talwar". Pakistan had labelled its invasion "Operation Badr". The Indian response of the army, air force and navy, was labelled "Operation Vijay", "Operation Safed Sagar" and "Operation Talwar". Another dimension of the Kargil conflict the Indian people should collectively acknowledge is that it was a costly war marked by high sacrifices and tragedy: 474 officers and other ranks of the Indian Army were killed and 1,109 were wounded. The largest number of casualties was among young officers who led their men from the front in the battle. The Kargil Review Committee Report gave the verdict that despite harsh battle conditions and heavy casualties, the morale of the Indian forces was extremely high. Young officers valiantly led soldiers who were deeply committed to the country.

The Geo-strategic Significance of Kargil

What was the motivation of Pakistan's military adventurism in Kargil? What was the extent of direct governmental participation in the aggression in the Kargil sector and the Line of Control? What are the lessons that India should learn from the Kargil experience? Should Pakistan be trusted to return to the negotiating table? Should the dialogue be continued? Given the apparent intention of Pakistan to continue its proxy war against India, to destabilise India, how should India deal with this threat? How should India assess the international reaction to the Kargil crisis? What are the lines on which Indo-Pakistan relations are likely to develop?

Before one proceeds to examine these points, it would be pertinent to describe the geo-strategic and demographic characteristics of Kargil and the factual and legal basis of the Line of Control that divides Pakistan-occupied Kashmir from the state of Jammu and Kashmir in India.

Geo-strategically, Kargil is a region of undoubted significance for the security of the Valley, Ladakh and our military positions on the Siachen Glacier. The area lying southwest from Ladakh straddles the approaches towards Siachen, towards Ladakh and to the Kashmir valley. The area lies within Indian territory east of the Line of Control and Siachen and the Saltoro Heights that are beyond the northernmost points up to which the Line of Control has been formally demarcated and delineated. (Grid refers to Point NJ-9842.) It should be remembered that Kargil is not a part of the Valley. It was originally a part of Ladakh, but was made a separate district because the majority of the people living in this district were Shia Muslims. If Pakistan could capture the Kargil area (stretching across 140 kilometres of mountain ranges) it could interdict the highway from the Valley to Ladakh and cut off India's approach to both Ladakh and Siachen. The Kargil sector of the Line of Control (covering the Mushkoh valley, Dras, Kaksar, Chhainikund, Shingo Batalik and Chorbat La), because of the terrain, was not manned in detail and around the year. There were gaps between brigades providing security to the Siachen region and brigades responsible for security at Kargil and Gurez. It was also felt that the composition of the Buddhist-Shia population of the area would be a natural preventive against any extensive Pakistani military intrusion. Regular Pakistani forces came across the Line of Control all along the 140-kilometre stretch, penetrating into Indian territory to a depth of 10 to 12 kilometres between March and May 1999. When challenged by India, Pakistan argued that it had not crossed into Indian territory, that the Line of Control in this sector was not clearly demarcated or delineated. It would be sufficient to keep the following facts in mind. The Line of Control is rooted in the ceasefire lines drawn up after the 1948 and 1965 wars with Pakistan. The present Line of Control was drawn up on the basis of the stipulations of the Simla Agreement of July 1972. The Line was drawn on the basis of mutual consent between the senior army commanders of India and Pakistan. The delineation of the Line has been shown on nine maps with detailed grid references in the appropriate scale. These have been countersigned by the military representatives of Pakistan. A matter of deliberate significance is that this Line was not a cease-fire line, but a Line of Control, not a Line of "Actual" Control, which might have implied the Line being a temporary arrangement. This was definitely not the intention. The agreement was on a permanent Line.

This Line of Control was respected by both sides for 27 years from 1972 to 1999. What then were the Pakistani motivations in violating it? The macro-level political motivations were manifold. First, the restoration of an elected government in Jammu and Kashmir and the gradual return of political stability and economic normality resulted in Jammu and Kashmir fading away as an area of crisis for the international community. Compounding this situation was an incremental success achieved by Indian security forces in countering and neutralising terrorist activities. The efforts of Pakistan in 1989 to destabilise and separate Jammu and Kashmir from India came to a naught. Some efforts had to be made to refocus international attention on the Kashmir issue within the framework of Pakistani objectives.

Second, strategic planners of Pakistan believed the international community was becoming supportive of a settlement of the Jammu and Kashmir issue on the basis of some kind of Line of Control. So it was decided to change the delineation of the Line of Control to a more advantageous position in favour of Pakistan. Shifting the Line of Control eastwards would enable Pakistan to continue its efforts to capture Jammu and Kashmir from a stronger position. Third, if this shift of the Line of Control could be consolidated in the Kargil sector, it would also have weakened India's strategic capacity to safeguard Ladakh and the Valley. The expectation was that the Chinese would not have minded Pakistan acquiring a more advantageous geo-strategic position on the southern and southeastern flanks of the Karakoram highway.

If this military conflict could be taken to the threshold of a tangible nuclear confrontation, the international community would intervene to pressurise India to compromise on Kashmir in a manner desired by Pakistan. To sum up, Pakistan's overall plans and detailed military objectives were assessed as follows by the Government of India:

(1) The plan was to have been kept top secret, which would involve the least number of people and avoid any activity opposite Kargil, which might indicate Pakistani intentions.

(2) Only an "in principle" concurrence without specifics was to be obtained from the Pakistani prime minister.

(3) A cover plan must exist to obfuscate the aggression and defuse any escalation in an early time-frame.

(4) The operation should help in internationalising the Kashmir issue, on which global attention had been flagging for some time.

With these terms of reference in mind, the Pakistani Army evolved a plan which was kept confined to the Pakistani chief of army staff (COAS), chief of general staff (CGS), director-general, military operations (DGMO), GOC 10 Corps and GOC force commander, Northern Areas (FCNA) who was made overall in charge of operations in the Kargil sector. Even the corps commanders were not kept in the picture. This has been completely substantiated by the taped telephonic conversation between the Pakistani COAS and CGS.

Pakistan's Aims

Pakistan's military aim in carrying out the intrusions was based on the following considerations:

(a) The intrusions would exploit large gaps, which exist in the defences in the sector on both the Indian and Pakistani sides of the Line of Control. The terrain is extremely rugged with very few tracks leading from the main roads towards the LoC. During winters the area gets heavy snowfall making movement almost impossible.

(b) The Zoji La Pass normally opens by end May/beginning June, so moving reinforcements by surface transport from Srinagar is not possible till then. Pakistan calculated that even if the intrusions were discovered in early May, as they were, the Indian Army reaction would be slow and limited, thereby allowing Pakistan to consolidate the intrusions more effectively. In the event, Zoji La was opened for troop induction in early May itself.

(c) The intrusions, if effective, would enable Pakistani troops to secure a number of domineering heights from where the Srinagar-Leh road could be interdicted.

(d) The intrusions would also draw in and tie down Indian reserves.

(e) The intrusions would give Pakistan control over substantial terrain across the LoC and enable it to negotiate from a position of strength.

(f) The intrusions would alter the status of the LoC.

Surprise and Deception

Apart from keeping the plan top secret, Pakistan decided on the following measures of surprise and deception:

(a) No fresh troops would be inducted into the Force Command, Northern Areas for the proposed operation. Any large-scale troop movement (two or three battalions) would have drawn India's attention.

(b) The artillery inducted into the Force Command, Northern Areas, during the heavy exchange of fire in July-September 1998, was not de-inducted. Since firing continued thereafter, though on a lower scale, this was not considered extraordinary.

(c) No reserve formations or units were moved into the FCNA till after the execution of the plan.

(d) The administrative bases for the intrusions were to be catered for from existing defences.

(e) Logistic lines of communication were to be along ridge lines and *nullahs*, well away from the tracks and positions of Indian troops.

Outline Plan

The plan, which was simple, was brought into effect by creating four independent groups from four infantry battalions and two companies of the Special Service Group (SSG), which were already located in the FCNA. These were:

(1) 4 Northern Light Infantry (NLI) Battalion, the FCNA reserve located in Gilgit.

(2) 6 Northern Light Infantry (NLI) Battalion (ex 62 Infantry Brigade) located at Skardu.

(3) 5 Northern Light Infantry (NLI) Battalion (ex 82 Infantry Brigade) located at Minimarg.

(4) 3 Northern Light Infantry (NLI) (ex 323 Infantry Brigade) located at Dansam.

SSG

The two companies of the SSG were to be allotted in smaller teams varying from 32 to 94 numbers among the four battalions.

Additional Resources

The groups were also allotted shoulder-fired Air Defence AD missiles of the Stinger variety. This coupled with 12.7mm AD machine guns integral to the NLI Battalions, gave them a modicum of air defence capability.

Use of Militants

Some militants from the Lashkar-e-Toiba, Harkat-ul-Ansar and Afghan war veterans were also grouped with each battalion to give it the facade of a *jehad*. After the intrusion, 800 or more militants were brought to the Skardu area for further reinforcements.

Artillery Support

Pakistani artillery numbering 20 batteries was to provide fire support to the intruding groups from the Pakistani side of the LoC. This ensured that each intrusion had the support of three to four batteries. Observation post officers from the Pakistani Army were also grouped along with line and radio communications.

Execution of Plan

The plan having been finalised, it was put into action towards the end of April. The main groups were broken into a number of smaller subgroups of 30 to 40 each for carrying out multiple intrusions along the ridge lines and to occupy the heights. The intrusions were in four main subsectors as under:

(1) Batalik	250	approximately
(2) Kaksar	100	approximately
(3) Dras	250	approximately
(4) Mushkoh Nullah	200-300	

Logistics

Logistic support was carried out by soldiers from within each battalion and the militants, with the route for supply along ridge lines and *nullahs*.

Reserves

After the plan had been implemented, Pakistan moved approximately a brigade of troops into the FCNA to recreate reserves.

Obfuscation Attempts

There has been a systematic and consistent effort by the Pakistani Government to obfuscate the issue. As directed by the Pakistani COAS, the foreign minister of Pakistan, Sartaj Aziz, spoke without consistency or substance. The shifting stand of Pakistan since then has been on the following lines:

(a) The LoC is delineated but not demarcated. This is the most brazen attempt at obfuscation. The line while not marked on the ground is clearly identified by both the armies and has remained so for the last 27 years.

(b) The Pakistani Army has been in occupation of these heights for a long time.

(c) The intrusion of the LoC is not by the Pakistani Army but by militants over which Pakistan has no control.

(d) The Pakistani Army is fighting in the Dras and Kargil sectors.

Much speculative analysis and obfuscatory prognosis has occurred about the Pakistani invasion of the Kargil sector. Questions are also being asked, motivated or otherwise, on whether there is any real evidence about direct Pakistani involvement in the conflict. It is time that we took note of the objective and incontrovertible realities about what Pakistan has been up to and, more importantly, have a clear perception of Pakistani ambitions on which India should predicate our future policies.

I personally visited Indian Army establishments where evidence of direct Pakistani military involvement in the conflict is available and is on display. There are arms and ammunition captured from regular Pakistani Army troops with markings and numbers of units to which the weapons belong. There are a large number of well-thumbed pay books with green covers and official emblems on them of Pakistani military officers and soldiers who were killed in battle in the eight weeks in question. India captured a sufficient number of operational and battle diaries kept by Pakistani military personnel. More important, it now has in its possession battle plans and battle directions given to Pakistani field commanders during this conflict which they had noted down in their diaries. There are also identity cards, uniforms and relevant military divisional and battalion shoulder patches of the Northern Light Infantry and other units of the Pakistani Army taken from dead Pakistani soldiers and officers. The most revealing and poignant material, evidence of Pakistan's direct involvement in the aggression, is the number of personal letters written to the soldiers by their family members. Some of them are of such an intimate nature that no civilised armed force or government would give publicity to them. The contents of these letters, mostly written in the Urdu script and in local dialects, have been methodically and precisely translated by Army Intelligence authorities. I have personally seen this material. It reveals interesting details of the methods and tactics adopted by the government and armed forces of Pakistan.

The plans for this violent ingress into India were drawn up some time in the autumn of 1998 and finalised by January 1999. The intrusion into the Kargil sector by Pakistani military personnel was not a regular, normal, large-scale military phenomenon. It was done gradually over a period of two months, perhaps in March and April. The operation was a carefully calculated exercise. Pakistan primarily relied on troops from the Northern Light Infantry to execute this aggression because soldiers of this regiment are mostly local young men from the mountainous regions of Skardu, Pakistan-occupied Kashmir, Baltistan, Gilgit and the North West Frontier Province. All of them are fully acclimatised to military activities at high altitudes. They were all ordered to shed their uniforms, put on *salwar kameez*, grow beards and wear skull caps. They were infiltrated in groups of three to four or five to take up positions all across the Kargil sector, which they did by the end of April. Their weapons, rations and other items of logistical support were taken across to the positions they had occupied in a parallel exercise by porters and yaks. The FCNA and the 10th Corps of the Pakistan Army provided command and control and full back-up support for the military operations. Heavy weapons like mortars, machine guns of various categories, and grenade launchers were supplied to the soldiers who were ordered to intrude into Indian territories in mufti. Roads and animal paths to carry military supplies were constructed to the maximum heights possible. Helipads were built to back up forward positions in Kargil taken over by the Pakistani forces in the absence of an Indian military presence in these areas at that point of time.

An interesting dimension of these Pakistani operations was that the irregulars, barring foreign mercenaries, were used as porters and logistical support personnel by the Pakistani Army. These cadre from Pakistan-occupied Kashmir and other parts of the northern areas, who were not in the regular Pakistani Army, were used as the logistical labour force. Most of the military operations were carried out by regular Pakistani Army officers and soldiers. Pakistan had also deployed squadrons of its helicopters and artillery to give cover to the military offensive. General Musharraf and chief of general staff of the Pakistan Army Headquarters, Lt. General Aziz, were direct planners and commanding officers of this operation at the highest level. This entire aggressive operation was conducted on the basis of full coordination and the consensus of the defence committee of the Pakistani cabinet which consists of the prime minister, the foreign minister, the defence minister, the information minister, the home minister and finance minister, plus the three service chiefs. There is sufficient evidence of this in Indian hands, while there is no evidence that the civilian segment of the Pakistani Government was averse to this operation. An interesting nuance, however, is that a fair number of corps commanders of the Pakistani Army were not informed of these plans almost till the Indian counter-offensive started. There are reports that General Musharraf and Lt. General Aziz have not been very popular with some of their senior colleagues because of this secrecy.

The Pakistani Army units were joined by mercenaries from the Afghanistan conflict and by members of the Taliban. The weapons available to the Pakistani aggressors and the logistical support system they enjoyed along with artillery cover and air support nails the lie that Pakistan had no direct involvement in the Kargil adventure. Indian forces undertook an extremely complex task in completing the counter-offensive. They did this without having the logical option of a total strategic and military offensive because of the political decision not to carry the battle into Pakistan-occupied Kashmir. That Indian forces succeeded despite this limitation is something that should not just be noted but acknowledged as a major feat of military and strategic success.

One must recall, for a complete understanding of what happened at Kargil, the manner in which the conflict was managed. Why was it that India was taken by surprise, and what was the public reaction to the conflict in India and Pakistan? The Kargil Review Committee's Report was placed before Parliament and it is now available to the public in book form. Details of the military operations, events leading up to the Kargil war, and other relevant issues have been amply covered in this report. So the objective is to touch upon those aspects of the conflict and the attendant issues that have not been described or assessed in detail in other writings.

Despite all the rationalisation resorted to by the Government and the Subrahmanyam Committee Report, the fact remains the Indian authorities failed to detect the military build-up by Pakistan in the Kargil area for a period of nearly eight months. The significant conclusions to be drawn from various commentaries and the Subrahmanyam Committee Report are first, that there was a general flow of information about the increased Pakistani activities across the Line of Control in the Kargil sector from various Indian intelligence sources, including the field officers of the Intelligence Bureau, IB, and RAW. Second, there were also clear indications that the theatre or field intelligence assessments of our army were inadequate and ambiguous. Third, the army command down to the echelons in Jammu and Kashmir did not assess the information available to them as indicative of any major operation or thrust by Pakistan till the beginning of May 1999. The assessment of the Northern Command was that Pakistani activities were of the usual kind for routine intrusion and skirmishes. Fourth, the information conveyed by the civil intelligence agencies, IB and RAW was not taken note of systematically or with any seriousness by the Army Command and Army Intelligence right up to the first week of May. And a matter of greater irony is that the reports of RAW and the IB were not sent to the chairman, Joint Intelligence Committee (JIC), in time.

Here it is necessary to refer to one conclusion of the Subrahmanyam Committee Report, stating that the director, Intelligence Bureau, did not send his report on incremental Pakistani activities in the Kargil sector to the officers and agencies directly involved in managing that sector or the Line of Control. This criticism merits some objective evaluation. There is confirmed information that the report of the director, Intelligence Bureau, Shyamal Dutta, was sent by him to the cabinet secretary, the principal secretary to the prime minister, and to the defence secretary. The criticism is that he did not send copies to the director general military operations, to the chief of army staff, to the secretary, RAW and to the chairman of the JIC.

Having some knowledge of the organisational structure of the government and the manner in which the reports were dealt with, the criticism of the Director, IB, appears to be excessive. The DIB's report to the cabinet secretary should have been taken note of by the Cabinet Secretary and he should have immediately sent copies to the secretary, RAW, and the chairman of the Joint Intelligence Committee, both of whom are part of the Cabinet Secretariat. The cabinet secretary should have suggested the national security adviser (principal secretary to the prime minister) convene a meeting of the Strategic Policy Group of the National Security Council, to discuss the DIB's report. The DIB's report to the cabinet secretary was routinely marked down without any action being taken. The response to the Subrahmanyam Committee's worries about the cabinet secretary's office, as to why this happened, was that the cabinet secretary's office receives so many reports from various agencies that the DIB's report was not taken note of in a focused manner. The principal secretary cum national security adviser was out of India when the DIB's report reached his office. And the drill in the Prime Minister's Office is that after being seen by concerned officers in that organisation, such reports are usually sent back to the DIB's office. The copies of the DIB's report which went to the Defence Ministry and the Armed Forces Headquarters were also treated in a routine manner and not brought to the notice of the chief of army staff, nor discussed in the chiefs of staff committee in time, according to the information which I have. The director, Intelligence Bureau's explanation as to why he did not send the report to everybody concerned was that he presumed the cabinet secretary and the DGMI, would share information with all concerned to take relevant action. It was not considered sufficiently satisfactory. Even more interesting is the fact that till the late spring and early summer of 1999, Secretary, RAW, Arvind Dave, was also holding charge of the post of chairman, JIC. It is legitimate to ask why he did not have RAW's information coming to him, to be examined by the JIC when he was in charge of that body also.

All this apart, due to reasons which are inexplicable, neither the divisional command in charge of the Kargil area, nor the north brigade command in charge of the Kargil sector, gave a focused assessment of the evolving situation between October 1998 and April 1999, though Brigadier General Surinder Singh later tried to claim he had sent relevant assessments in time. The Subrahmanyam Committee Report saw this as a post facto exercise in self-justification, which was a valid conclusion. Nor can the divisional commander or the corps commander be exonerated from the criticism of not having activated their own forward formations to be vigilant and send relevant information about the evolving ground situation, especially between February and May 1999. One cannot escape an overall conclusion that intelligence gathering was inadequate and sporadic due both to limitations in terms of equipment and resources and the human factor. Second, the information gathered was not systematically collated and assessed through the JIC, or through interdepartmental consultations that might have enabled the government and the Armed Forces Headquarters to anticipate possibilities with some accuracy. That the danger and threat of the Pakistani aggression was perceived only in the very last stages of the enemy's intensive intrusion and consolidation of its positions across the Line of Control confirms this assessment. The remedial recommendations made in the Subrahmanyam Committee Report on this particular aspect of the Kargil conflict generally endorse this conclusion.

Analysing the Situation

Detailed accounts of the military operations are available in journals and books written by mediapersons who covered the Kargil war and more comprehensively in the Kargil Review Committee Report. But some general curiosities about the conflict and how it was managed demand clarifications.

Once the fact of extensive Pakistani aggression across the Line of Control was realised, the Government of India's response was measured and decisive. Operation Vijay was launched in the middle of May with additional troops and the necessary weapons being deployed. The Cabinet Committee on Security met regularly and as often as necessary, including daily meetings. Service chiefs were in regular consultation with the prime minister, the defence minister and the national security adviser. The prime minister convened a special and combined meeting of all the component entities of the National Security Council — Cabinet members constituting the National Security Council and the members of the Strategic Policy Group of the Council, and all the members of the National Security Advisory Board. The long meetings on 7 June undertook a comprehensive review of events since the beginning of May, analysing the military and political implications of the evolving situation. Prime Minister Vajpayee instructed that a subgroup of the National Security Advisory Board should be immediately constituted to make an assessment and to convey suggestions to the national security adviser and the cabinet on the developments at Kargil. This group consisted of K. Subrahmanyam, Air Chief Marshal O.P. Mehra, Major General Afzal Karim, N.N. Vohra, former principal secretary to the prime minister and defence secretary, Sanjay Baru, economic writer, Raja Ramana, member, Rajya Sabha, and former chairman of the Atomic Energy Commission, and myself. Satish Chandra, chief of the JIC and secretary, National Security Council Secretariat, was the member secretary of this group. The group met twice a week from mid-June till the beginning of September on Mondays and Thursdays. Information about the Kargil war and internal and external developments related to it from various governmental, media and other sources were reviewed in this Advisory Group. Its assessments and suggestions were reduced to crisp memoranda or notes and forwarded to the national security adviser. These in turn, with the additional information available to the Cabinet, formed the basis of political and military action to resist and neutralise the Pakistani aggression.

There have been some rumours about the Indian Air Force being reluctant to join the military operations in the initial stages. This is not true. The chief of air staff, Air Chief Marshal Y. Tipnis, only made the rational point that the use of the air force would change the nature of the military conflict: that if India decided to deploy the air force in Kargil, India should be well prepared to anticipate the expansion of war beyond Jammu and Kashmir, and respond to expanded Pakistani offensives in other parts of India. Once the CCS and National Security Council affirmed their willingness to face the situation, the Indian Air Force joined the operations and played an effective and important role in the war.

The armed forces of the Government of India though taken by surprise functioned in a coordinated manner till the aggression was repulsed and the Pakistani forces pushed back across the Line of Control. The Indian forces had cleared the Pakistani invaders from all their major positions along the Line of Control by the first week of July and the decision taken was to mop up any remaining Pakistani positions whatever the cost. This was when the president of the United States provided a face-saving device to Prime Minister Sharif by suggesting that Pakistani forces withdraw into their own territory away from the Line of Control. The suggestion was reluctantly accepted by Sharif and by General Musharraf on 4 July, when an agreement to this effect was affirmed in the joint declaration issued at the end of Sharif's discussions with Clinton in Washington on 4 July.

The Subrahmanyam Report

Before one proceeds to discuss the political ramifications of the Kargil war, as they emerged, it would be pertinent to undertake a general assessment of the Kargil Review Committee Report prepared under the chairmanship of K. Subrahmanyam, one of India's most knowledgeable experts on strategic affairs. The committee consisted of K. Subrahmanyam as convener, the other members being Lt. General K.K. Hazari, former vice chief of army staff, and B.G. Verghese, an eminent journalist, scholar and professor at the Centre for Policy Research. Satish Chandra, secretary of the National Security Council Secretariat, was ex-member of this review committee. The terms of reference of the committee were the following:

1. To review the events leading up to the Pakistani aggression in the Kargil district of Ladakh in Jammu and Kashmir.

2. To recommend such measures as are considered necessary to safeguard national security against such armed intrusions.

The main report placed runs to 228 pages. In addition, it has 14 volumes of annexures, texts of testimonies given to the committee and extracts of reports and so on. The first point to be noted is that the committee completed its work in a remarkably short time — about four-and-a-half months. The next is that this is the first time that the Government has appointed a committee to review the causes and background of a major security crisis consisting of outsiders, instead of resorting to a purely in-house military inquiry. Third, this is the first time that the report of such a committee has been made public through Parliament. Previous internal reviews of military conflicts and crisis undertaken by the Government of India about the 1962 and 1965 wars were internal and have not been made public. Fourth, the report has not just confined itself to the immediate causation of the 50-day war but contains a comprehensive and wide-ranging analysis of the conflict-prone predicament of India and Pakistan in terms of the history, in terms of Pakistani motivations and India's reactions, in terms of the undercurrents of policies and mindsets, and in terms of the ramifications of how the Kashmir issue has been dealt with by India and Pakistan. It is also the first time perhaps that multidimensional recommendations have been made to fine-tune our intelligence, security and defence establishments.

One will deal with the criticism levelled at the Kargil Report, but before that it would be worthwhile summing up the answers to the question: could Kargil have been avoided? The Committee's sequential findings and recommendations (Chapters 12, 13 and 14 of the Report) address this subject. The conclusions briefly are: "Had the Indian Army sought to plug all conceivable loopholes, to frustrate every eventuality... and attempted to safeguard every inch of (unpopulated) territory, it would have meant the Siachenisation of Kargil along a wider front with correspondingly higher human and material costs. This would have been neither militarily nor politically cost-effective and... such a posture... would have enabled Pakistan to bleed India."

Indications are that the Kargil plan was originally formulated in the 1980s, but it was activated only after General Musharraf took over the command of the Pakistani army. Nawaz Sharif was fully aware of the Kargil implementation plan. While the Lahore summit between Vajpayee and Sharif did not lower the guard of the Indian decision-makers, there was a failure of intelligence inputs in terms of timely assessments which in turn resulted in our being surprised and our response delayed. The report says that while both RAW and the IB had communicated information about increased Pakistani activities in the Kargil sector, these reports were not channelled to all relevant authorities. It is also interesting to note the conclusions in the report that no specific indicators of a likely major attack in the Kargil sector, such as significant improvements in logistics and communications or a substantial forces build-up or forward deployment of forces, were reported by any of the agencies. The report goes on to say: "The critical failure of Intelligence was related to the absence of any information on the induction and de-induction of battalions and the lack of accurate data on the identity of battalions in the area of Kargil during 1998 and then onwards." The Kargil intrusion, according to the report, was essentially a limited Pakistani military exercise designed to internationalise the Kashmir issue which was tending to recede from the radar screen of the world community. The report refers to only one military officer, Brigadier Surinder Singh, as having failed in making correct assessments and not having initiated relevant anticipatory action.

Recommendations for remedial action in the report are wide ranging with suggestions for restructuring institutions, the improvement of procedures, reorganising arrangements for the flow of intelligence and so on. The volumes containing the annexures not only have texts of testimonies given and extracts of reports, etc., but also a wealth of information and data based on an extensive reading of books and documents dealing with security issues. The report itself contains footnotes with bibliographical references, emphasising the in-depth study with which the members of the committee desired to underpin their findings and recommendations. The historical context of the Kargil conflict has also been shown by the committee by detailing events leading to the previous conflicts with Pakistan.

Having touched upon the report's positive qualities, it is necessary to look at some of the inadequacies. These are not the result of oversight but of deliberate reticence. While there is a detailed description of the nature and content of the communications exchange from forward areas to Army Headquarters and back, there is no focused critical evaluation of the inadequacies or negligence that characterised the functioning of the army preceding the Kargil conflict. The report has focused mainly on the reasons for the complacency in the Northern Command in the pre-Kargil period, rather than on the critical shortcomings in observations, analyses and assessments at different levels in the command structure. There are some critical references of the divisional command level. But the report has been coy about critically evaluating the responses of the corps command and the Northern Army Command. There seems to have been no mechanism to ensure effective and real-time flow of information and assessments, from lower army echelons to Army Headquarters and the office of the chief of the army staff. There are only marginal references to the role that the Directorate General of Military Intelligence could have played. One understands that the internal assessment report prepared by the Armed Forces Headquarters itself was more forthright and critically introspective. This is the report prepared by General Reddy, which for obvious reasons would not be publicised. The rationale for not criticising the army might be that of not affecting the morale of the armed forces, which fought so bravely and sacrificed so much to regain Kargil. However, one wishes that the same amount of attention were given to the role of the armed forces as was given to the Intelligence Bureau (IB) and RAW.

This critical comment apart, one must unhesitatingly acknowledge that the report is a painstaking, methodical, scholarly and detailed analysis of a major military crisis. It is an important and substantial contribution in educating our Parliament and public opinion about several aspects of our national security concerns. The Government placing it before Parliament was a welcome initiative in introducing transparency on this sensitive subject, and one hopes that making the Kargil Review Committee Report available to the public will lead to reports on the previous conflicts with China and Pakistan, for example the Henderson Brooks Report of 1962 also being declassified. Involving the citizen in a national security debate is the strongest foundation for national defence.

Having ventured this general evaluation, one has to re-emphasise that there were a series of intelligence inputs with sufficient specificity between June 1998 and February 1999 about a qualitatively incremental intrusive posture on the part of Pakistan on the Line of Control in the Kargil sector. The IB reported increased activities on the borders and a continuing endeavour to infiltrate a large number of foreign mercenaries in the aftermath of the May 1998 nuclear tests. It also reported an increased movement of Pakistani armed forces in the Chore, Haldi, Saddle, Reshma, Masjid, Dhallan and Langer sectors along the Line of Control, and on the construction of a helipad at Khod on the banks of the Indus river. The Northern Command itself had reported on the continuous dumping of ammunition and rations, the movement of additional troops and the presence of an increased number of militants in civilian dress in the Skardu, Varcha and Matrol sectors, awaiting induction into Jammu and Kashmir. In December 1998, the Northern Command had given an assessment that there had been a three-fold increase in troop movements from November 1998 onwards, and a two-fold increase in vehicular and normal transport movement. In fact, normal transport movement itself was assessed to be about nine times what it had been earlier in 1998. Parallel to this, RAW and the IB conveyed the assessment (between September 1998 and November 1998) that the 7th Field Regiment of the 8th Medium Artillery Regiment of the Pakistani forces had been deployed in operational areas opposite the Line of Control in the Kargil sector. There was also the RAW assessment that the Pakistani Army had engaged contractors to ferry 100,000 kilograms of ammunition to posts in the Gultari, Hasan and Javed sectors. RAW had reported additional units of the Northern Light Infantry of Pakistan moving into the Gultari area in September 1998.

The Intelligence Bureau had conveyed the assessment to the Government of India that a limited swift offensive by Pakistan could not be ruled out. It also gave the information that Pakistan was training members of the Taliban, including training in the Balti and Ladakhi languages, and that these cadres were likely to be infiltrated through Kargil from April 1999 onwards. That specific information was available to the Government from different sources is clear. What became equally obvious at the beginning of the Kargil conflict was that these different strands of inputs were not collated and that an integrated assessment was not made.

Diplomatic Management

The initial official stance of the Government of Pakistan was that Pakistan was not involved in the invasion — that the crossing of the Line of Control was organised by indigenous mujahideen groups who took advantage of a comparative lack of attention of the Indian Army in the Kargil sector. It was said that India as usual was refusing to acknowledge the large-scale alienation of the youth of Jammu and Kashmir and their military prowess in challenging the Indian security forces. Both Sharif and Musharraf denied direct Pakistani involvement, almost till the end of May. It was only when Pakistani troops suffering casualties started becoming a matter of public knowledge that there was a reluctant acknowledgement of direct Pakistani participation. Once the Indian Army had come into possession of the diaries of Pakistani officers and soldiers, and once prisoners of war were taken by the Indian armed forces, India gave publicity to all of this and Pakistan could not maintain their mendacious obfuscation any more. So it changed track in its policy·statements on the conflict. The first point made was that the confrontation in Kargil occurred because the Indian Army was indulging in aggressive patrolling and the Pakistan assessment was that India would "do another Siachen" on Pakistan. The second was the Line of Control was not clearly demarcated in several sectors along the 700-odd kilometres. The third was skirmishes on the Line of Control were affecting Pakistani civilians across it in Pakistani territory to prevent which retaliatory action had to be taken. Fourth, the widespread military conflict in Kargil was the result of India's obduracy on the Kashmir issue.

This was the basic framework of the brief that was given to Pakistan diplomatic missions to convince the governments to which they were accredited. The additional point made by Pakistanis was that India had no right complaining about any alteration of the Line of Control especially in what they called undemarcated areas because India itself had violated the

Line of Control on different occasions over the past two decades. The Pakistani media was mobilised to project this governmental stance in contradiction of the original publicity posture of Pakistan disclaiming any involvement in the Kargil war.

The most significant politico-diplomatic initiative taken by Pakistan during the period was the visit of Sharif and Pakistani Foreign Minister Sartaj Aziz to Beijing as the Indian counter-offensive started succeeding. The Pakistani expectation was that there would be endorsement from China of the Pakistani interpretation of the critical situation. This in many ways was the logical expectation in the context of the close defence and strategic relationship between China and Pakistan. China's opposition to India's strategic visions and strong criticism of India's nuclear weapons programme may also be considered. But what Pakistan did not realise was that regardless of these considerations, China would not be in favour of internationalising the Kashmir issue, as China itself was sensitive to the possibilities of international intervention to deal with the Tibetan situation. China's reaction to the advocacy of Aziz and Sharif was that the Line of Control should be respected and that the conflict should be brought to an early end.

Indian Foreign Minister Jaswant Singh was to visit Beijing within two days of Aziz's visit there in June. Pakistan's hope was that Singh would be given a strong message by China supportive of Pakistan. In the event Beijing adopted a posture strictly within the framework of Chinese national interests. A significant aspect of these sensitive diplomatic activities was that the US and Chinese governments were engaged in close consultations with each other as the war progressed in Kargil. There was a convergence of US and Chinese interests in bringing the conflict to an early end and in ensuring that it did not escalate into a nuclear confrontation. The latter concern was of some immediacy because there were statements like those of the Pakistani Foreign Secretary Shamshad Ahmed Khan, towards the end of May, stating that if Pakistani security stood threatened to a point where it became a matter of serious concern, Pakistan would not hesitate to use any means or weapons at its disposal to counter the Indian threat. The matter was of sufficiently serious concern for President Clinton to have telephonic conversations with President Jiang Zemin just before Aziz's visit to Beijing. Clinton's advice to Jiang Zemin was that he should tell Aziz that Pakistan should pull back from its aggression and that friendly countries like China and the US should help Pakistan extricate itself from the mess in as honourable a way as possible.

A point to be noted is that Sharif and Aziz went to Washington after the disappointment they faced in Beijing fully aware that there was no support from Beijing and Washington for Pakistan having violated the Line of Control. It is equally interesting that while diplomatic representations were made on the part of Pakistan to all member countries of the UN and at the UN Secretariat, there was no move by Pakistan to activate the UN Security Council on this military conflict. The main reason was that Pakistan realised that it would not have the support of the US and the four other Permanent Members of the Security Council. India, in the context of its previous negative experience concerning the manner in which the UN dealt with the Kashmir issue and consistent with its policy of not accepting any international jurisdiction, had no interest in activating the UN Security Council.

That Pakistan failed in its diplomatic move, first to justify its aggression and then to achieve the end of the war without losing its credibility, was confirmed in the joint declaration Sharif was persuaded to sign by President Clinton on 4 July in Washington. The text of the joint statement recognised the critical situation created by the war, emphasised that the Line of Control in Jammu and Kashmir should be respected and stated that Pakistan had agreed to withdraw its troops into its own territory beyond the Line of Control. It was subject to this precondition that there were urgings of restraint and restoration of dialogue. The policy stances of other major powers on the Kargil war were in line with those of the US and China in every respect.

All foreign governments acknowledged that the war was initiated by Pakistan, that the Line of Control was violated by Pakistan as a unilateral provocative act, that Pakistan was directly involved in the aggression with its forces spearheading the attack on India, that respect for the Line of Control was an essential precondition to end the conflict and defuse tension. In official discussions and public pronouncements, practically all concerned governments articulated these views. There was also an acknowledgement that the Government of India and the Indian armed forces were justified in their counter-offensive, both from the political and military point of view.

Pakistan's political and military failure in this misadventure was primarily due to the Indian military successes in this difficult war. The international community perceived India's firm determination to end Pakistani aggression in the Kargil sector of Jammu and Kashmir, and it was clearly understood that India would not be agreeable to any interim political compromise which would allow Pakistan a foothold in Indian territory through political manoeuvrings. It was the ground reality of India's counter-offensive posture that generated the political impulses that eventually isolated Pakistan.

While the military stance of the Government of India was the critical factor in the process, the importance of parallel diplomatic moves to bring the origins and the implications of the conflict to the notice of foreign governments cannot be underestimated. Perhaps for the first time after the Bangladesh liberation war, India's foreign policy management and diplomatic moves were again characterised by purpose, a clear sense of priorities and coordinated efforts. It is worth recounting the Indian political and diplomatic effort also.

The Government had to ensure that the Kargil conflict would not result in an internal political upsurge in Jammu and Kashmir. The citizenry of Jammu and Kashmir had to be given a message that India was capable of resisting Pakistani aggression, of coping with any simultaneous subversive violence Pakistan could undertake. On a larger scale the Vajpayee Government had to convey the impression of being strong, determined and effective in resisting Pakistani aggression and defeating it, despite being a caretaker government. The Government also had the task of providing all the wherewithal necessary to the Indian armed forces at short notice, because the armed forces were not fully equipped to undertake largescale mountain warfare responsibilities. Creating an all-party consensus to back up India's military operations, and garnering similar support from Indian public opinion in general, were equally complex tasks. The positive anticipation about Indo-Pakistan relations generated by Prime Minister Vajpayee's visit to Lahore were still lingering. The Pakistani aggression first confused Indian public opinion and then made it critical of the Lahore initiative of Vajpayee. The consequence was doubt about the political judgement of the ruling coalition in dealing with Pakistan.

The general elections in India were four months away when war started in Kargil. Therefore, there was an undesirable amount of party politics in the reaction of various groups, particularly the main opposition, the Congress. The focus of the opposition parties was to question the Government's inability to anticipate the Pakistani aggression, rather than to give immediate unconditional support to the Government for launching the counter-offensive. Once India's armed forces swung into full action and the initial reports about hardships and bravery and the loss of life amongst our troops started coming in, the Government received general support. The liberal facilities provided to the media to visit the battlefront, the daily briefings given by a three-man team of an army officer, an air force officer and the spokesman of the Ministry of External Affairs helped in mobilising this support. Another important decision, which resulted in high levels of intellectual and emotional backing for the Government, was the decision to send back the bodies of the officers and jawans killed in Kargil to their homes in cities, towns and villages in different parts of India. It was the first time since Independence that the armed forces agreed to undertake this onerous responsibility. The physical and emotional impact of the bodies of the martyred soldiers in their hometowns and of the last rites being performed with military honours in public ceremonies aroused public feelings. Though no formal session of Parliament could take place because it stood dissolved, Prime Minister Vajpayee and his cabinet colleagues as well as senior members of the Ministries of Defence, External Affairs and Home and armed forces gave briefings to leaders of different political parties on a regular basis throughout the conflict.

The foreign challenges spawned by the Kargil war were equally complex. India had to counter the various arguments put forward by Pakistan in support of the war situation in Kargil, it had to successfully prove that Pakistani disclaimers about not being involved in the war were false. India had to convince the international community that the Kargil situation was the result of unprovoked aggression by Pakistan. It had to establish that the main body of the personnel who violated the Line of Control were regular Pakistani soldiers under the command of the Pakistan Armed Forces Headquarters.

With the benefit of hindsight, one can assert that India managed to meet all these objectives to a great extent. The Indian Foreign Office, led by Foreign Secretary K. Raghunath, undertook regular periodic briefings with the diplomatic corps located in Delhi. Communications went from the Foreign Minister Jaswant Singh and Prime Minister Vajpayee to their counterparts in all countries with which India has diplomatic relations.

While Vajpayee was in personal communication with President Clinton, Singh and National Security Adviser Brijesh Mishra, were in touch with their contacts, particularly in the governments of the five Permanent Members of the UN Security Council, with neighbouring countries and important countries like Japan and Germany and influential members of the Organisation of Islamic States. The message conveyed was that India would not stop its counteroffensive until Pakistani troops were pulled back from the Line of Control. No suggestions for an interim cease-fire and negotiations on the conflict situation would be accepted by India. India would not cross the Line of Control unless escalation of the levels and areas of conflict by Pakistan made it unavoidable. India remained committed to the policy of no first-use of nuclear weapons. If Pakistan used its nuclear arsenal there would be an appropriate Indian response. This was followed up by India providing specific evidence of the involvement of Pakistani troops in violating the Line of Control.

The firmness of purpose, the clarity of policy orientations, backed by India's actions in Kargil made an impact on the chancellories of a government in majority of countries. India's heads of missions in countries which were Permanent Members of the Security Council played a specially important role in garnering international support for India. Ambassador Naresh Chandra in Washington, High Commissioner Lalit Mansingh in London, Ambassador Kanwal Sibal in Paris, Ambassador S.K. Lamba in Moscow and Ambassador Vijay Nambiar in Beijing, under directions from the then Foreign Secretary K. Raghunath, carried out their political and diplomatic responsibilities with consummate tact. Permanent representative at the United Nations, Ambassador Kamlesh Sharma, played a similar role in New York.

The Telephone Tapes

India achieved an important and pre-emptive breakthrough in obtaining conclusive evidence of Pakistan's direct involvement in the Kargil aggression when our concerned agencies managed to intercept a telephone conversation between the chief of staff of the Pakistani Army, Lt. General Mohammed Aziz, and the chief of the army staff, General Musharraf, who was in Beijing with Nawaz Sharif. Indian agencies tape-recorded these conversations in which Aziz reported that operations in the Kargil sector were proceeding according to plan, and that Musharraf should ensure that the prime minister and his advisers did not succumb to any political pressure in their discussions. Some details of the movement of Pakistani troop units in the area also figured in this conversation. India gave enough publicity to this tape to expose the Pakistani claims of non-involvement in Kargil.

Pakistan's initial reaction was that the taped conversation was a concoction by Indian intelligence agencies, and that this was part of India's psychological warfare. It would be pertinent at this stage to highlight some of the undulation and contradictions in India's management of the conflict in its political and public dimensions. The foremost of these dichotomies was a statement made by Defence Minister George Fernandes in the early stages of the conflict stating that Pakistani armed forces had launched the aggression without the prior knowledge or endorsement of Prime Minister Sharif. Exonerating the prime minister of a government that had launched a large-scale offensive against India while the Indian forces were launching a counter-offensive could be considered bad for troop morale and could have given Nawaz Sharif a chance to exonerate himself before the leaders of important governments.

This is a valid criticism in the context of Sharif's proven awareness. But there is another rationale for Fernandes having made this statement at the initial stages of the conflict. He perhaps desired to provide a face-saving device and escape route for Sharif to pull back his troops, so that the conflict could be brought to an end as early as possible.

Fernandes's statement, however, resulted in speculation and seemingly justified criticism. Giving a good conduct certificate to Sharif could have been avoided. Then comes the episode of "the two initiatives", as the war was raging. The first was by a former foreign secretary of Pakistan, Niaz Naik, who visited Delhi in June, apparently with a message from Prime Minister Sharif. The second initiative was by the Indian Government, despatching and endorsing the journey of R.K. Mishra, former editor of the *Patriot* and now senior adviser to the Observer Group, to Pakistan, to convey India's message about the need for Pakistani withdrawals and India's willingness to end the conflict if that happened. Mishra was also entrusted with the responsibility of handing over the tape of intercepted conversation between Aziz and Musharraf to the prime minister and foreign minister of Pakistan. That Mishra's visit had the support and endorsement of the Government of India is clear from the fact that the joint secretary in charge of the Pakistan Division in the Ministry of External Affairs, Vivek Katju, went with him to Islamabad.

In the event the Government of Pakistan disowned the Naik mission because he was not given access to the higher levels of the Government. India said Mishra was sent only to hand over the Musharraf-Aziz tapes to prove Pakistani involvement in the Kargil war. Responding to the criticism about the joint secretary from the Ministry of External Affairs accompanying him, the Government of India's explanation was that Katju was sent to ensure the safe transportation of the tape to Pakistan because he travelled on a diplomatic passport.

There was also the questioning of the general advance assurance given by India that it would not cross the Line of Control. This was a legitimate query. Why had India given advance indications of its battle plans in the face of Pakistani aggression? Was there any need to announce in public our self-imposed restrictions in dealing with this aggression? A legitimate question on all counts. While referring to this point, one must mention in parentheses that there were sections of the armed forces, the Government and the National Security Council institutions who felt that India should have crossed the Line of Control and undertaken air strikes to hit the supply lines and staging posts of the Pakistani forces operating in Kargil. The Government of India as far as one knows did not impose any advance self-restraint on itself. All the options, including suggestions of the above type were examined and it was a measured and deliberate decision that there was no need to cross the Line of Control. This conviction gained ground as the battle on all fronts turned in favour of the Indian troops by the third week of June 1999.

One recalls that according to official estimates, the calculation was that the Indian armed forces would be able to push back the Pakistani troops across the Line of Control only by late August or early September 1999. The expectation was that given the terrain and the entrenched positions which the Pakistani troops were in occupation of, dislodging them would be a difficult exercise and would last for five months. One of the reasons for this was that compared to the Pakistani troops, who were mostly from the Northern Light Infantry and fully acclimatised to the weather and altitude where they were operating, Indian troops had to be mobilised from different parts of the country, apart of course from the units which went into immediate deployment from Jammu and Kashmir itself in the early stages of the conflict.

Troops from the northeastern states of India and central and south India were brought into the Kargil sector after brief acclimatisation exercises. It was felt that these troops would take time to adjust to the new battlefield conditions and then get into full action. The Indian armed forces' performance therefore was remarkably surprising, considering that they achieved all their major objectives by the first week of July, making the Pakistanis realise that the game was up.

International Reaction

What then was the general reaction of important countries to the conflict at Kargil? First, Pakistan itself. Foreign Minister Aziz arrived in New Delhi in mid-June, a public relations exercise aimed at the international community and not to solve the confrontation. The approach was that despite a raging military conflict, Pakistan was so reasonable that it had taken the initiative of sending its foreign minister to New Delhi to initiate a dialogue. India dealt with the visit in a manner responsive to this approach. Jaswant Singh received Aziz. The discussions were grim and to the point. The clear message given was that pretensions to dialogue were not going to succeed unless Pakistan pulled back completely beyond the Line of Control in Jammu and Kashmir.

Aziz went to China between 9 and 11 June and came to Delhi on 12 June. Despite the Chinese being less than supportive of Pakistan, Aziz stuck to the obfuscatory and aggressive Pakistani stance about Kargil having occurred because of India's intransigence and claimed that the role of Pakistan in relation to the infiltration was only supportive and not direct. A tragic and gruesome incident preceded Aziz's visit to Delhi. The Indian counteroffensive had gone into high gear on June. A unit from the Jat Regiment of the Indian Army was involved in operations in the initial stages. Ten soldiers of the regiment were killed and then their bodies were mutilated by Pakistani soldiers between 7 and 9 June. These bodies were handed over to Indian forward units in this terrible condition. The objective was obvious. It was a brutal and stupid exercise in psychological warfare to strike terror in the hearts of Indian soldiers. The consequence was counterproductive as far as Pakistan was concerned. The reaction of the Indian troops was disgust and intense anger. The handing over of the bodies was covered by the media, both Indian and foreign. The condition of the bodies angered the Government and the public in India, but it also evoked a highly critical response from the international community. A possible explanation is that, being confident of succeeding in their aggression, the Pakistani armed forces command decided to prevent any possibility of a cessation of hostilities due to Sartaj Aziz's visit to Delhi. In any case, Sartaj Aziz's mission was not going to succeed because a basic policy decision had already been taken by the Government of India to continue the military operations until the invader was beaten back.

But Aziz's mission to Delhi had one useful result. Both Pakistan and the international community got a clear signal from India that interim cease-fires and compromises would not be acceptable.

The first reaction of the US was a significant factor contributing to the denouement of the Kargil war. Diplomatic contacts relating to the evolving military situation were established both in New Delhi and Washington by the first week of May. Two incidents which crystallised US reaction to Kargil were, first, the shooting down of two fighter aircraft of the Indian Air Force by surface-to-air missiles on 27 May and the shooting of an MI-17 helicopter by a Stinger missile on 29 May. India had launched air strikes on 26 May. Brigadier Qureshi, the director-general of the Inter-Services Public Relations Office of the Pakistan Army, announced on 27 May, as the Indian aircraft were shot down, that Pakistan reserved the right to retaliate in whatever manner it considered appropriate. Simultaneously, Pakistan started justifying its military operations in Kargil, asserting that India had launched a full-scale war against Pakistan and that it had violated the Line of Control.

The first US reaction was to reject the Pakistani claims of violations of the Line of Control. The official spokesman of the US State Department said on 28 May, "To our knowledge, India has not struck over the Line of Control deliberately or accidentally." This was a response both to Brigadier Qureshi's statement and the assertion of Information Minister. Mushahid Hussain that "India has grossly violated Pakistan's territorial space and it is a threat to peace in the region".

Apart from being a factual assessment of the ground realities, the US stance was also rooted in concern that Stinger missiles and more sophisticated weaponry being used by Pakistani troops was from arms supplied to the mujahideen by the US at the height of the Afghanistan conflict in the 1980s. The US policy found more definite articulation when President Clinton publicly asked Nawaz Sharif to pull back from Kargil. He also announced that the commander-in-chief of the US Central Command, General Anthony Zinni, would be visiting Pakistan towards the end of June to encourage a defusion of tension. General Zinni arrived in Pakistan on 24 June and held extensive discussions not only with Prime Minister Nawaz Sharif, but also with General Musharraf and his senior colleagues at the joint chiefs of staff HQ. The central point of General Zinni's message was that President Clinton was emphasising the immediate need to de-escalate the conflict in Kargil so that new avenues for a dialogue on Kashmir could be explored. Zinni also stated that if Pakistan intensified the conflict and did not pull back it ran the risk of direct American support for India. The interaction between President Clinton and Jiang Zemin before Sharif's visit has been mentioned earlier in this chapter. The Chinese must have given some indication to Sharif of their discussions with the US and the evolving consensus among the major powers about the need for Pakistan to pull back. Sharif's meetings in Beijing were on 28 and 29 June. The 4 July meeting between Clinton and Nawaz Sharif took place in this context. The key paragraph in the statement issued at the end of Sharif's three-hour discussion with Clinton goes as follows: "President Clinton and Prime Minister Nawaz Sharif shared the view that the current fighting in the Kargil region of Kashmir is dangerous and contains the seeds of a wider conflict. They also agreed that it was vital for the peace of South Asia that the Line of Control in Kashmir be respected by both sides in accordance with the Simla Accord. It was agreed between the President and Prime Minister (of Pakistan) that concrete steps would be taken for the restoration of the Line of Control in accordance with the Simla Agreement."

While not pronouncing any value judgement on the substantive dispute of Jammu and Kashmir, the US accepted that Pakistan had violated the Line of Control and that the Simla Agreement was a relevant framework for dealing with Indo-Pakistani issues. Another reason leading to Nawaz Sharif's agreement to pull back Pakistani troops is attributed to indications given by India that if the withdrawals did not occur, India would expand the conflict and move across the Line of Control within 72 hours if the Clinton talks failed. Though there is no authentic confirmation of this possibility, this was the general impression, especially in the context of the statement by the chief of army staff, General V.P. Malik on 24 June, that, "If necessary we can cross the Line of Control in the supreme national interest. But the decision lies with the Cabinet." He added that there had to be a response to the well-conceived planned execution of military operations of the Pakistan Army which aimed at severing the road between Zojilla Pass and Ladakh. General Malik had chosen his audience well. He made these remarks to the military attaches of 28 foreign embassies in New Delhi. They were also shown weapons captured from Pakistani troops.

The reaction of the other major powers to the Kargil conflict evolved in the context of National Security Adviser Brajesh Mishra's meetings in Paris and Geneva during the Geneva Summit of the G-8 countries. Mishra handed over a detailed communication from Prime Minister Vajpayee to the National Security Adviser of the US, Sandy Berger, in which Vajpayee conveyed that India's capacity for restraint was reaching a threshold beyond which it could not be sustained. Mishra briefed the senior advisers of the heads of government of the G-8 countries in Geneva and separately briefed his counterparts in the French Government in Paris on 17 and 18 June. Translating its objections to the Pakistani military intrusion into India, into a concrete decision, France blocked and delayed the delivery of 32 Mirage fighter planes and three Augosta-class submarines. These were to be delivered to Pakistan under previously existing contracts. The US response to Mishra's advocacies was: "The US will initiate the necessary action in days and not weeks." As is evident from the Clinton-Sharif meetings, the US acted on its assurances. The G-8 had a paragraph on the Kargil conflict in the communiqué issued at the end of its summit meeting on 20 June 1999. The communiqué stated: "We are deeply concerned about the continuing confrontation in Kashmir following the intrusion of armed infiltrators who violated the Line of Control. We regard any military action to achieve the status quo ante as irresponsible. We, therefore, call for an immediate end to all these actions, the restoration of the Line of Control and for the parties to work for the immediate cessation of the fighting, for full respect in the future of the Line of Control and the resumption of dialogue between India and Pakistan, in the spirit of the Lahore Declaration."

Of all the members of the G-8, only Japan nuanced its policy in a curious manner. The Japanese Government stated that while it associated itself with the statement of the G-8 mentioned above, Japan's view was that, "As a result of the escalation of the fighting since last month, the militants have crossed the Line of Control. Japan, however, does not have sufficient means to verify whether the militants who have infiltrated are backed by Pakistani regular forces." Japan's stand aroused criticism and resentment in India. It was woodenly formalistic, sticking to an unrealistic neutral stance because the rest of the G-8 had acknowledged the direct involvement of Pakistani forces. The only explanation for the Japanese reaction which was obfuscatory and temporising is that Japan did not wish to endanger its economic interests and investments in Pakistan. Japan was also more critical of India's nuclear weapons programme than of Pakistan's. So there was a certain political and emotional background to the Japanese reaction.

Germany was more categorical in its approach. The German Foreign Office confirmed it had information that apart from Afghani militants, the Pakistani Army was involved in the intrusion in Kargil, violating the Line of Control. The German Foreign Office also mentioned the statements of US congressman Frank Pallone, the head of the Stimson Centre in Washington, Dr Michael Krepon, and of US congressman Gary Ackerman in support of the German stance.

The Chinese, while advising the Pakistanis to move back beyond the Line of Control, had a different assessment of events. The Chinese *Liberation Army Daily* in its issue of 12 June, just as Sartaj Aziz was departing from Beijing for New Delhi, indulged in the analysis that in the Kargil conflict the US stood to gain in any eventuality from a clash between India and Pakistan. The US aimed at weakening Pakistan and restraining India. As long as the conflict stayed within limits without escalating into a nuclear conflict, it was in the strategic interest of the US to play the role of arbiter. Aziz was of course told at the formal level that the Chinese considered it necessary to de-escalate the dangerous situation in Kargil. A clearer articulation of Chinese policies was made by Prime Minister Zhu Rongji on 28 June while talking to Sharif in Beijing. Zhu said it was the sincere hope of China that Pakistan and India would endeavour to maintain peace and stability in South Asia. He went on to say that the conflict in Kashmir had a historical background, with ethnic, territorial and religious ingredients. It could be resolved only through peaceful means. While reaffirming that China and Pakistan were permanent friends, who shared a profound and vigorous friendship, the Chinese view was that the conflict should be de-escalated and dialogue should be resorted to. Zhu then came up with a significant general statement on foreign policy, saying that the friendship of Pakistan and China was rooted in mutual understanding, trust, support, and non-interference in each other's internal affairs. The message was that while China valued Pakistan's friendship and the strategic partnership with Pakistan, China did not wish to get involved in India-Pakistan conflicts or controversies. China also implied that it shared the assessment of the important powers that the conflict could escalate into a nuclear confrontation to which China would be opposed. This last concern underpinned the reaction of the governments of France, Britain and Russia as conveyed to then foreign secretary K. Raghunath who held discussions on Kargil in London, Paris and Moscow.

The reaction of India's immediate neighbours in South Asia should remain part of the process of cognition about regional responses to Indo-Pakistani conflict. None of members of SAARC (Sri Lanka, the Maldives, Nepal, Bhutan and Bangladesh) articulated a clear value judgement about the origins of the Kargil war, though in discussions there was an acknowledgement of Pakistan having started the trouble. Second, there was genuine concern, even apprehension, about the conflict accidentally or deliberately escalating into a nuclear conflict. It was logical for these countries' immediate neighbours to urge both parties to stop the war by whatever means possible. India showed sensitivity towards the constraints as well as concerns of its immediate neighbours and did not press them to take India's side. As far as one recalls, only the then prime minister of Bangladesh, Sheikh Hasina Wajed, made a statement urging the cessation of hostilities and respect for the Line of Control and so on.

Pakistan had sought Iranian mediation with India in June, but Iran refused to get involved. Saudi Arabia was generally supportive of Pakistan during the Kargil conflict without expressing any definite views about responsibility for the crisis. It is understood that King Fahd and Prince Bander bin Sultan, the Saudi ambassador to Washington, played an important role in shoring up the sagging morale of the Sharif Government. Fahd told the Pakistani Minister for Religious Affairs Raja Zafrul Haq that Saudi Arabia would continue to extend its traditional support to Pakistan on the Kashmir issue. Prince Bander bin Sultan apparently played a behind-the-scenes role to convince the Pakistani military high command as well as Sharif that all would not be lost even if Pakistan pulled back to its side of the Line of Control.

The process of winding down the aggression commenced immediately after the 4 July agreement between Nawaz Sharif and Clinton. In consequence, the director generals of military operations of both India and Pakistan met at the Attari-Wagah border outpost near Amritsar on

11 July 1999. The Pakistani director general, military operations, informed his Indian counterpart that the withdrawal of Pakistani troops had already commenced from the morning of 10 July and would be completed by the morning of 16 July 1999. The Pakistani troops were not withdrawn as promised. Pakistani military high command requested an extension of the deadline by two or three days. Pakistani delay resulted in Defence Minister Fernandes warning the Pakistan authorities that if the deadlines were not met Indian forces would go into operation again. The Pakistani military authorities said they were requesting the extension so that they could withdraw in an orderly manner and also carry back whatever equipment they could. India agreed to extend the deadline by two days, but that did not result in Pakistan really withdrawing from all sectors. The Government of Pakistan tried to muddle the issue by saying that they had never agreed to any deadline. This was around 16 July. Pakistani troops in small groups remained entrenched in the Dras, Mushkoh valley, and Batalik subsectors. The Pakistan Government then came up with the sudden demand that India should vacate the Chorbat La, Siachen and Qamar sectors to restore the sanctity of the Simla Agreement on the Line of Control. This was a clear face-saving ploy. However, India rejected this demand and told Pakistan that the Indian armed forces were resuming their operations to mop up any Pakistani forces remaining on the side of the Line of Control in Dras, Mushkoh and Batalik. The Indian Army succeeded in clearing the entire area by 25 July. But the story does not end here. The time allowed to Pakistani troops to withdraw voluntarily beyond the Line of Control was utilised by them to mine and booby-trap the areas from which they were withdrawing. Indian forward patrols discovered this as they moved forward to occupy the positions vacated by Pakistani troops.

Foreign Minister Aziz, continued to push the claim that India had violated the Line of Control and occupied Chortbat La in 1972, Siachen in 1984 and Qamar in 1988. Conveniently, he refused to note that in each of these cases Indian troops did not cross the Line of Control as demarcated or implied in the 1959 and 1972 agreements. India only occupied positions on its side of the Line to pre-empt Pakistani moves to occupy Indian territory.

I have mentioned the Indian casualties earlier in this chapter. The figures for Pakistani casualties as assessed by Indian authorities towards the end of the conflict were — 745 Pakistani officers and soldiers had been killed and some 2,500 injured. While the war was costly in terms of human life for India, it was even more costly for Pakistan. That Pakistani troops mined areas being vacated was illustrative of a vengeful and frustrated mindset.

Future Prospects

How the Kargil war, which lasted nearly 50 days, influenced the future prospects of Indo-Pakistan relations is a matter worth examining. Its ramifications in terms of intergovernmental attitudes and interactions can be discerned in the events that followed. But what is also important to recall to complete our picture is the public perception and reaction to the war in India and Pakistan.

In the initial stages, say up to the beginning of June, the Pakistani media was successful in convincing the Pakistani public that the military confrontation in Kargil was between indigenous mujahideen and the Indian security forces. Pakistani public opinion swallowed the government propaganda hook, line and sinker. The media coverage and television discussions in Pakistan made the assessment that India was facing the logical "comeuppance" of its obstinate stand on Kashmir. Also expressed was the view that perhaps the Pakistani mujahideen campaign against India had entered its last and successful phase and would soon dislodge India from Jammu and Kashmir. There was also some sabre-rattling, taking off from the statement made by Foreign Secretary Shamshad Ahmed on 31 May when he said: "We will not hesitate to use any weapon in our arsenal to defend our territorial integrity." The general view expressed was that given Pakistan's nuclear capacity, India would not dare to launch any concerted operations against Pakistani forces and the mujahideen.

As the reports of Pakistani casualties started filtering back into Pakistan, there was a degree of concerned curiosity in public opinion about the military developments in Kargil. When the Indian Western Naval Command deployed itself south of Karachi, backed by additional ships from the India's Eastern Naval Command, apprehension emerged that the Kargil confrontation could become a full-scale war. But right until the first days of July, both the Government and the people of Pakistan remained convinced that the Indian armed forces would not succeed in pushing them back across the Line of Control and that international intervention, led by the US, would ensure Pakistan emerged unscathed from the Kargil war, with some territorial gains. Only when Indian troops captured all the vital posts along the Kargil front, including posts at great heights like Tiger Hill and Tololing, did Pakistani public opinion become aware of the debacle. It was not the Pakistani media who were instrumental in giving relevant information to the public. It was the Indian media, backed by information flows from third countries. Pakistan's diplomatic failures in Beijing and Washington could not be prevented from becoming a matter of public knowledge. It was only after Sharif was asked by Clinton to pull back Pakistan's troops that critical opinion about the Kargil operations started to be expressed in Pakistan. Many retired army officers — for example, General Mirza Aslam Beg, Air Marshal Noor Khan, Lt. General Kamal Matinuddin and Air Marshal Asgar Khan — expressed the view that the Kargil operation was ill-timed and ill-planned. However, an editorial in the *Friday Times* of 30 July 1999 said, "The Kargil operation was put on the drawing board by competent military minds many years ago." Kargil was presented as "a do-able" option when the time was ripe, partly as revenge for the loss of Siachen and partly as a political device to spur on the Kashmir mujahideen.

The basic belief among the Pakistani public was that the operations in Kargil were launched substantially by Kashmiri militants. It was not just right but inevitable that Pakistani armed forces supported these militants, when they came under pressure from Indian forces. There was a refusal to acknowledge that most of the mujahideen were foreign mercenaries diverted from Afghanistan because the Taliban had limited use for them. Nor was there any realisation that Pakistani armed forces and intelligence agencies were diverting these foreign mercenaries to Kashmir to prevent them becoming a volatile and disturbing factor in domestic politics. There was also a refusal to accept that Pakistani armed forces had launched an unprovoked aggressive operation against India. The general public in Pakistan continued to hold the view that Pakistan was drawn into the conflict within the framework of its declared diplomatic and political support of "the freedom struggle" of the Kashmiri people. Some sections of opinion felt the move on Kargil was politically and strategically aimed, with sharp motives. They realised that Pakistan's strategic assessment of international reaction was flawed, and that the tactical planning did not take into account the political and military response which would inevitably come from India.

There has subsequently been a reluctance to accept that Pakistan suffered heavy casualties compared to India and was dealt decisive military defeat in Kargil despite the element of surprise and having fought from entrenched positions. The interpretation of the debacle at Kargil in Pakistani public opinion, engineered by the Government, is that Pakistan had surprised and humiliated India and that Pakistan had achieved a tactical victory in Kargil. Pakistan only withdrew because of American pressure and nothing else. It is this broad facet of the Pakistani public perception that found expression in the criticism of Nawaz Sharif for having surrendered to American pressure when it was not necessary. This was one of the factors that contributed to the support for the military coup of Pervez Musharraf.

Sharif himself, before being overthrown, tried to rationalise the misadventure by saying that the objective of the Kargil operation was not military victory, but reactivating the Kashmir issue in the subcontinent and internationally. The operation was launched to signal to the Mujahideen and the people of India that Pakistani support was not just ideological but operational. Pakistani commentators also proceeded to express the view that if India did not agree to a compromise on Kashmir acceptable to Pakistan, "there would be many more Kargils". There was only a tiny minority of Pakistani analysts and thinkers who felt that Pakistan should not have jeopardised the tenuous peace at the subcontinent by undertaking this unprovoked military operation.

The public mood in India was in stark contrast to that in Pakistan. Factors influencing public opinion were, for example, the transparency concerning the progress of the war ensured by the free access given to the media. The sending back of the bodies of officers and soldiers killed in the war to their native towns and villages had an emotional impact on Indian public opinion. There was a general perception that India was caught off guard in terms of political assessment and military deployment. The feeling was generally shared that Pakistan had again lulled India into a mood of political complacency at the Lahore meeting between Sharif and Vajpayee in February 1999. The Government received dramatic support for launching the counter-offensive and pushing back the invading forces. There was general criticism of suggestions that Nawaz Sharif was not responsible for the operations and that India should stop military operations to give safe conduct to the invaders to go back to Pakistan. There was also criticism of using behind-the-scenes contacts to resolve the conflict, as was evidenced by the visits of former Niaz Naik to India and R.K. Mishra's and Vivek Katju's trip to Islamabad, as the war progressed. The feeling was that there should be no dialogue with Pakistan until the military operations against Pakistani troops were succesfully completed. As details of the war reached the public and as the last rites of soldiers killed in Kashmir were witnessed in different parts of India, emotive patriotism permeated the national psyche. There was a demand that individuals and entities responsible for the security of Jammu and Kashmir who failed to anticipate and detect Pakistani aggression should be identified.

A large number of seminars, workshops and discussions were organised on the Kargil war as it progressed. There was a general consensus in Indian public opinion, and even among the middle and younger ranks of the officers of the armed forces, that India should cross the Line of Control and hit Pakistani forces at their staging posts and supply depots. There were views expressed about expanding air operations and if necessary using the Indian Navy to neutralise the adventurist inclinations of the Pakistani power structure, particularly its military segment. I heard such views expressed not only in academic and civilian seminars but even in military think-tanks. There was an interesting and disturbing interface between the media and some military officers. The inclination of some officers to provide documents and give verbal briefings to the media, and to criticise the Government as well as the higher levels of the Indian military command, generated controversies in the public mind which could have affected the cohesion of the Government and the morale of the armed forces. Opposition political parties, while being complimentary towards the armed forces fighting at the front, did take advantage of these controversies to put the Government on the defensive.

The public's faith and trust in the armed forces stood profoundly restored during the war and at the end of it. There had been concern in the public mind about the state of the army based on analyses and commentaries in the media, which had averred that the armed forces were no more attractive to Indian youth: that the armed forces were not properly trained and equipped; that there was an incremental shortage of officers; that morale was low, especially among those deployed in Jammu and Kashmir; and political parties were playing politics with the armed forces and the defence establishments. Some of these critical evaluations were valid but the manner in which the armed forces rose to the occasion restored the public's faith.

The only aberration in opinion management during the war was India banning broadcast of Pakistani television networks. This was done of course to prevent Pakistani propaganda from reaching India. With hindsight one can say that this was an irrelevant misapprehension. The ground reality was that no amount of Pakistani propaganda could have affected the spirit and morale of the Indian public or the Indian armed forces.

The end result of the Kargil experience is that Indian public opinion is clear that Pakistan will continue its hostile activities against India and that India has to remain permanently alert. What then were the immediate prospects India had to anticipate?

First, there would be insistence from Pakistan and pressure from the international community, particularly the US, to enter into talks with Pakistan on Jammu and Kashmir. Second, to expect not a decrease but an increase in violent subversive activities by Pakistan, not only in Jammu and Kashmir, but also in other parts of India. This anticipation was not speculative. Sharif told the Pakistan National Assembly on 12 July 1999, "Though the volcanic eruption in Kargil has been brought under control, if

India does not discuss Kashmir in a meaningful manner, other volcanoes will erupt." This pronouncement had to be noted with his earlier statement that there could be many more Kargils if India did not come to terms with Pakistan on Kashmir. The spokesman of the ISI, Brigadier Qureshi, when asked whether the so-called Mujahideen were withdrawing gave the ambiguous response: "I do not know. We have appealed to them. Maybe they are dispersing towards Srinagar."

The following then are Kargil's lessons for India:

(a) Pakistan is not likely to agree to any practical solution of the Jammu and Kashmir issue on the basis of ground realities and reasonableness in the foreseeable future. It will continue its political campaign and overt military and terrorist operations against India, particularly in Jammu and Kashmir.

(b) Bilateral dialogue at the official and even at the highest political level with Pakistan should not be undertaken with any sense of excessive expectation, nor should these be predicated on the sincerity of Pakistan. Pakistan participates in these dialogues only as a stratagem to keep the Kashmir issue alive, to indulge in diplomacy and publicity.

(c) Pakistan's unalterable objective is to capture Jammu and Kashmir. The substance of its India policy is related to this objective.

(d) Pakistan will continue to foment military tension on the Line of Control and will indulge in intrusions to capture territory in Jammu and Kashmir. Pakistan will also engineer violence and terrorism in other parts of India in support of its proxy war in Kashmir. India should remain politically sensitive to these prospects at the policy level and should maintain continuous military alertness vis-á-vis Pakistan along the Line of Control as well as the international border. India will have to locate troops and security forces to the maximum extent possible on the Line of Control around the year.

(e) India should undertake a thorough overhauling of its intelligence-gathering and intelligence-assessment institutions and procedures both in functional and organisational terms. The interface between the intelligence agencies, the National Security Council and its adjuncts and the Cabinet Committee on Security Affairs has to be organised so that it does not face the surprise, as well as confusion in command control it faced during the initial period of the Kargil conflict.

(f) Firmness in dealing with Pakistan at the operational level, combined with restraint gets India international support.

(g) The support India got on the Kargil conflict from the international community was Kargil specific. There is no such support for India's overall stand on the Kashmir issue. The international community is keen that India and Pakistan quickly resolve this issue which, in their judgement, has the seeds of a nuclear confrontation.

(h) India must also acknowledge that a solution to the Kashmir dispute has the imperative requirement of being responsive to the desires of its citizens in Jammu and Kashmir.

(i) International support for India's general concerns about its territorial integrity, etc., will depend on our appearing to be reasonable and talking to Pakistan on Jammu and Kashmir. A static stance by India will result in Pakistan regaining international support.

(j) It is equally true that the international community does not support Pakistan's total claims on Jammu and Kashmir.

(k) Important powers are now inclined to a settlement of the Kashmir dispute on some kind of Line of Control plus a package deal for autonomy for the people of Jammu and Kashmir with the added proviso for normal and free interaction between people living in (Indian) Jammu and Kashmir and people living in Pakistan-held territories centred around Muzaffarabad. While India should be willing to resume dialogue with Pakistan, we must be clear in our mind that coming to a solution would be a gradual process spread over a decade or two. We must not let down our guard in any manner till then.

(l) A very important lesson to be kept in mind is the development of a US-China strategic consultation mechanism to deal with stability and security in a "nuclearly weaponised" South Asian region. President Bill Clinton and President Jiang Zemin were in more or less continuous contact during the period May to August 1999. The US and Chinese policy on the Kargil was coordinated at the highest level. India should be alert about the strategic implications of this development. Two superpowers having a converging approach on its security environment can impact India's freedom of options.

Three

Tunnel Visionaries

$\mathcal{T}$he abiding reaction among Indians and Pakistanis, when enmeshed in critical or conflict situations, is that of warped perception and selective interpretation. It is relevant to recount how this phenomenon impinged on the hijacking of the Indian Airlines plane in December 1999 and the Kargil war, and how it affects the prospects of any rational discussion between civil societies in the two countries.

Leaving aside the pronouncements of the Government and respective Army Headquarters of the two countries, it is interesting to note how non-governmental elements in the power structures of India and Pakistan reacted to events. Most interesting was the reaction of retired military officers in Pakistan to the Kargil conflict. In the initial stages of the conflict, they mouthed the official version of the military confrontation, stating that the Pakistani armed forces were not involved in Kargil, that the incursions into Indian territory were nothing but the capture of military posts on the Indian side of the Line of Control by indigenous mujahideen forces, that the mujahideen had proved again that they were more than a match for the Indian Army, that the Indian Government was levelling false accusations against Pakistan and Pakistani armed forces.

Once the Pakistani armed forces' direct involvement all along the Kargil front became undeniable, the interpretation underwent a dramatic change. The arguments that followed were that the Pakistani Army got involved in the conflict because India had carried the war across the Line of Control, both by land and by air. That the Pakistani armed forces had to give the minimum necessary support to the indigenous mujahideen, that in any case. Pakistani armed forces had only made defensive moves in the Kargil area where the Line of Control was not demarcated very clearly. This convoluted rationalisation was carried further with the claim that India has no rational or moral right to talk about the sanctity of the Line of Control because it was India that had violated the Line of Control by moving across and establishing offensive posts in the Siachen glacier area. The air operations carried out by India from the end of May onwards were described as violations of the Line of Control.

Once the Indian counteroffensive went into full swing, retired Pakistani military leaders endorsed the view expressed by their government authorities that if necessary Pakistan should not hesitate to use its missiles and nuclear weapons. Security experts asserted that the Pakistani military operations were fully justified in the context of their perception of the "oppression" to which Muslims in Jammu and Kashmir had been subjected from 1990 onwards.

Senior military figures, like General Mirza Aslam Beg, former chief of the Inter-Services Intelligence, Lt. General Asad Durrani, and Air Marshal Asgar Khan, former chief of air staff, attributed the failure of the Pakistani military initiative in Kargil to faulty strategic planning and inaccurate assessments about the morale and operational capacities of the Indian armed forces. Pakistani military leaders also criticised the civilian government and the Pakistani Foreign Office for making inaccurate and inadequate assessments about the strengths and weaknesses of the Indian Government, about the political situation in India and the political will of the Indian establishment. The view was also expressed that the Pakistani offensive in Kargil was not preceded by adequate and sufficiently extensive networking between the mujahideen and the Muslim population in the Valley. Their overall assessment was that had the military initiative been preceded by proper assessments and proper preparations, it was a brilliantly conceived plan that would have succeeded. There was also criticism of the Nawaz Sharif Government and the Pakistani Foreign Office for not having made effective diplomatic effort to back up the military move. There was the critical evaluation that Pakistan failed to inform and convince the major powers of the rationale of its military move and the legitimacy of its objectives within the framework of its Kashmir policy. The media and the public in general, took their cue from these informed assessments and evaluations, as they perceived them to be.

As during the previous conflicts with India in 1948, 1965 and 1971, the media and public were not given full information about the Government's role in the conflict. When it became clear that the Pakistani armed forces were being defeated and pushed back and that important powers and international public opinion were not supportive of Pakistan, the Pakistani media turned critical. The public fervour and support for the move diminished. But there was no regret about having initiated a military conflict or about the suffering which it caused. This was the case with Pakistani public opinion in general. The exception was, however, in public opinion in Pakistan-held Kashmir. There were civilian casualties on the Pakistani side because of long-range shelling by the Indian armed forces across the Line of Control. Non-combatants were killed and injured and normal life, to the extent that it existed, was disrupted. What was resented even more was the manner in which the Pakistani armed forces used the local male population to back up the military operations. They were mostly used for logistical purposes. Those among them who were on combat duty, were not provided with adequate equipment and rations when compared to their regular military colleagues. The Indian military establishment intercepted messages even from Pakistani armed forces personnel belonging to the northern areas, who were bitterly complaining against being abandoned on the Kargil heights without proper support and equipment. The crowning tragedy was Pakistani armed forces command refused to acknowledge their dead and to accept their bodies, all this to sustain the denial of the Pakistani involvement. The feeling of the people in Pakistan-held Kashmir and the Northern Areas was that they had been enmeshed in a highly violent military operation and then left to their own devices.

Reactions on the Indian side were equally complex and confusing. Though the large-scale intrusion by Pakistani troops was known by the Government from the beginning of May itself, the criticality of the situation was not made known to the public until almost the last week of May. During the first phase of the conflict, up to about the middle of June, there was apprehension in the media and in public opinion about the capability of the Indian armed forces to dislodge the Pakistani Army from the Kargil heights where they had consolidated their positions across a front of over 100 km. Even the most optimistic estimates were that India would barely manage to push back most of the Pakistani troops by September. Indian reaction was characterised by angry jingoism. There were advocacies for launching air strikes deep into Pakistani territory, and for launching offensives, if necessary, across the international frontier into Pakistani Punjab. As happens in unexpected critical situations, particularly so in a democracy where the media is free and there is a certain level of transparency about events as they develop, there was speculative criticism about the failure of the Indian intelligence agencies.

A New Transparency

Indian public opinion was critical of the Government for not allowing its forces to go across the Line of Control to take pre-emptive action against the Pakistani forces. The restraint shown by the Government of India and political justification given for the restraint were not accepted by the general public. An intense sense of patriotism permeated the Indian mindset. These feelings found expression in analyses, media reports, TV interviews and seminars and discussions throughout the country. There was considerable angst concerning our chief of army staff, General V.P. Malik, stating in the early stages of the conflict that though the Indian Army was facing a difficult situation, it would do its best with the wherewithal available to resist and neutralise Pakistani aggression. The fact that most of the counteroffensive operations were conducted by the infantry, that they counter-attacked an enemy entrenched at tactical heights in strategic positions across the entire battlefront, and that the fighting was done on steep gradients on foot, generated profound admiration for the courage and commitment of our soldiers and officers. The danger faced by our soldiers was graphically described to me by a member of the armed forces when he informed me that about 80 per cent of the initial battle casualties in the Indian Army were because of wounds received on the top of the head and above the shoulders with the enemy literally firing from the heights on advancing units. The high number of casualties is a proof of the difficult battle fought. A retired senior military colleague from Pune told me towards the end of the conflict: "This war was not won by the Government or the military high command. It was won by the young officers and jawans because of their grit and courage."

Two incidents during the war raised Indian public ire to vengeful heights. The first was the killing of an Indian Air Force officer, Ajay Ahuja, whose aircraft was shot down in Pakistani territory. There was clear evidence that he was alive after he crash-landed and that he was tortured before being killed. The second was Pakistani troops killing a number of Indian soldiers after their post was captured, and then mutilating their bodies, after which they were left on display at the post before the Pakistani troops were pushed back. Both the incidents happened in the first half of June. It was with difficulty that the Government restrained the forward units of our forces from undertaking a massive offensive across the Line of Control after these incidents occurred. Defence Minister George Fernandes and Foreign Minister Jaswant Singh had to make special efforts to calm public opinion after these harrowing incidents, manifesting the perverse and violent culture of the Pakistani armed forces. In some ways this war made a traumatic impact on the Indian psyche of the type which occurred at the end of the war with China in 1962. The conflicts with Pakistan in 1948, 1965 and in 1971 did not affect the collective Indian mindset as the Kargil war did.

Leaving aside the feelings of betrayal and patriotism and the desire to decisively push back the aggressor, there was also an accompanying feeling of inadequacy. There was criticism about India being timid, and on the defensive. A fair segment of the Indian strategic community, as it is called, felt that India's actions did not match its policy declarations. The points emphasised in this respect were that if Kashmir is an integral part of India and if the territory of Kashmir is violated by Pakistan, not once, but repeatedly, why is it that India does not strike back into Pakistani territory across the Line of Control?

The second question was whether international support for the political and diplomatic aspects of the Government of India's stand should be considered a decisive factor in safeguarding India's territorial integrity. The Indian restraint during the Kargil war seems to have been rooted in an anxiety to have international support. This may be important, but the ultimate responsibility of safeguarding one's territory depends on one's political will and physical ability to act decisively. Though India may have pushed back the aggressor, it was at very heavy human cost, resulting from the deliberate and unnecessary restraint practised by India.

The argument that India remained restrained to avoid a nuclear confrontation raises definitional questions. Why did India not call the bluff of Pakistan about using nuclear weapons? Given the Indian claim that India is superior to Pakistan in both conventional and nuclear weapons, and given the international community's capacity to prevent nuclear confrontation by direct military intervention, why was India inhibited? India should have subjected Pakistan to a test of its claims, according to this school of thought. The next question is, why did the BJP-led government not implement its announced policy of being operationally proactive against terrorist infiltration in Jammu and Kashmir? Why did India not exercise the right of hot pursuit from 1998 onwards across the Line of Control? Had the policy announced by Home Minister L.K. Advani been implemented India would have prevented infiltration into Kashmir early enough to preclude a full-scale war.

The Cost to the Nation

These questions remain under discussion even three years after the Kargil conflict. The synergy of these questions is aimed at generating profound collective introspection both in public opinion and in the Government. A former vice chief of army staff, Lt. General Moti Dhar, aptly sums this up in an article entitled "Blundering Through", which he contributed to the book, *Guns and Yellow Roses* (HarperCollins, 1999). He says: "The intrusion in Kargil was a national shame and hence accountability for such a blunder needs to be pinpointed if we are to ensure the security of the nation in future. Negligence has cost the nation approximately five thousand crores of rupees, heavy casualties to our troops and above all a shadow has fallen on the honour of the nation." He went on to recommend the appointment of a commission of inquiry of the type which the Government of Israel nominated to inquire into the failures of the Yom Kippur War in 1973 between Egypt and Israel. Two commissions have completed their work on the Kargil war since General Moti Dhar's recommendations. The Army Headquarters had set up internal inquiry committee and the Government nominated a committee under K. Subrahmanyam. Extracts of the Subrahmanyam Report are a public knowledge. But the internal report prepared for the Army Headquarters has not been published. The general impression, however, is that neither of these reports was imbued with the spirit of intense critical evaluation manifested in the Israeli Commission of Inquiry's report.

The intensity of thought and feeling about Kargil has diminished with time. The Government, however, has taken some action. India's defence budget has been augmented. An extensive review is being undertaken of all requirements, logistical support and weapon systems. That there is a move to diversify the sources of defence supplies for the Government of India is evidenced by discussions undertaken by the Defence Minister George Fernandes and the service chiefs during their interaction with foreign governments. But before one proceeds to any speculative prescriptions or future prospects, it is important to recall and analyse to the extent possible how the people of Jammu and Kashmir reacted to the Kargil conflict. They were the people most directly affected by the Pakistani aggression and attendant violence, which continues even now. Their feelings and reactions are, as they should be, a most decisive factor, and should influence India's Kashmir policies.

The glaring contrast between the public reaction in Jammu and Kashmir to the Kargil war when compared to the reactions of the people of the state in 1948 and 1965 is what one should take note of. In 1948, the public reaction was one of intense fear and apprehension against terror generated by the Pathan tribal infiltrators and the Pakistani troops backing them. Consequently, the Indian armed forces received public support throughout the 1947-48 operations against Pakistan. An undercurrent of alienation from

India emerged, particularly in the Kashmir valley, when Pandit Jawaharlal Nehru arrested Sheikh Mohammed Abdullah. Common people in the Valley felt that India was not fulfilling its promises and by arresting the most popular leader and sending him into exile and was embarking on some kind of authoritarian annexation of the state. Sheikh Abdullah's release from prison, just before Pandit Nehru's death, and his return to the mainstream of Kashmiri politics neutralised this feeling, resulting in positive and general support for India when Pakistan launched its second war in 1965. It was the population of the Valley that provided extensive advance information to the Indian armed forces when Pakistan launched its attack in September 1965, and the people were happy about India's defeating Pakistan. The period between 1965 and 1975 witnessed the revival of tensions and misunderstanding between the Government in Jammu and Kashmir and the Government of India. Sheikh Abdullah chafed at the progressive constitutional and political integration of the state into the Indian Union, but ultimately Indira Gandhi managed to arrive at compromises to assuage the Kashmiri leader's concerns.

The promises gave formal shape to the agreement reached between Mrs Gandhi's senior political adviser G. Parthasarathy and Kashmiri leader Afzal Beg. The Beg-Parthasarathy agreement brought some calm and stability to the Valley but it did not last long. The 1971 war with Pakistan occurred during this period. In the early stages of the war, the people and the leadership of Jammu and Kashmir held a detached view though they were critical of President Yahya Khan's rejection of the results of the Pakistani elections held late in 1970. Though Kashmir became a battleground in the 1971 war too, the political focus of the war was East Pakistan. The discriminatory and oppressive policies of Yahya Khan and Z.A. Bhutto and the violence perpetrated by the Pakistani armed forces on the people of the then East Pakistan resulted in a general feeling of relief and satisfaction among the people of Jammu and Kashmir who felt they were better off being part of India. Sheikh Mohammed Abdullah returned to power in 1975 and remained chief minister until he died in 1982. He was not at ease with the regime of Bhutto and was doubtful about the military regime of Zia-ul-Haq that succeeded. This contributed to his structuring a comparatively stable and cooperative relationship between the state of Jammu and Kashmir and the Central Government in Delhi.

Internal domestic concerns as well as an approach of caution towards India made Zia averse to any large-scale military adventurism against in his initial years, say between 1977 and 1981. It was only with the rise of Sikh militancy in early 1980-81 that Zia decided to support separatist terrorism in Punjab and also gradually revive secessionism in Jammu and Kashmir. Sheikh Abdullah's death coincided with Zia reviving Pakistani subversive activities against India in 1982. Mrs Gandhi and Rajiv Gandhi did not fully adhere to the compromises reached with Sheikh Abdullah and decided to integrate party politics in Kashmir with mainstream Congress politics. This affected the unity, credibility and sense of identity of the National Conference, the most important and popular political party in Jammu and Kashmir. The purpose here is not to describe or analyse the interaction between Mrs Gandhi and Rajiv Gandhi on the one hand, and National Conference leaders like Gul Shah, the son-in-law of Sheikh Mohammed Abdullah and Dr Farooq Abdullah, son of Sheikh Mohammed Abdullah on the other. The elections held in Kashmir between 1982 and 1989 lacked credibility in Kashmiri public opinion. Increasing maladministration and corruption in the governance of Jammu and Kashmir began a process of alienation which culminated in the violent terrorist/separatist movement of 1989-90. The decade between 1989 and 1999 was characterised by a fair segment of Kashmiri youth getting involved in the militant movement with the material and financial encouragement of Pakistan. This is apart from the direct involvement of Pakistani military personnel and Afghan mujahideen and mercenaries in violent subversive activities in Jammu and Kashmir. The Indian response was the extensive deployment of security forces in Jammu and Kashmir and a concerted effort to revive democratic political processes.

Opposition political movements got organised and operationally structured in the Valley with the apex body of the All Parties Huriyat Conference coming into existence. Pakistan-based militant outfits also got more directly involved in anti-Indian terrorist activities in Jammu and Kashmir. Despite these developments, Indian security forces managed to bring some level of normality to the state by 1996. This led to the holding of general elections, bringing Farooq Abdullah back to power. The situation gradually improved as evidenced in another election held in 1998 and Jammu and Kashmir sending elected representatives to Parliament. Developmental activities stood revived. Tourism restarted and there was a marginal sense of calm. It resulted in two developments unpalatable to Pakistan. First, the international community lost interest in the Kashmir issue. Second, the availability of cadres from the state for terrorist militant movements, sponsored by Pakistan, diminished, which compelled Pakistan to send more and more foreign mercenaries into the state to carry out cross-border terrorism and subversion. The common people in the Valley became exhausted and numb with the atmosphere of violence and tension. Their only interest was to somehow return to normal life and economic activities. They were equally disenchanted with India and Pakistan. It was in this situation that Pakistan launched its attack on Kargil. This is where the contrast between the public reaction to previous Indo-Pakistan wars became starkly clear. The average Kashmiri was indifferent and emotionally detached from the war between the armed forces of India and Pakistan. There was, of course, anxiety about personal welfare in the actual area of conflict. The people of Ladakh with its Buddhist majority and the people of Jammu with its Hindu majority were apprehensive about the Pakistani offensive and its consequences. In many ways they shared the reaction of the Indian public to the conflict, and were critical of India being taken by surprise.

The reaction in the Kashmir valley was quite different. In the initial stages there was support for the Pakistani military intrusion, the argument being that Pakistan directly challenging the Indian military forces and Indian jurisdiction over the state would change both the ground realities and the political terms of reference for negotiating a solution on the Jammu and Kashmir problem. Hopes were also expressed that if Pakistan succeeded in consolidating its position, and the Indian army failed in its efforts, new cease-fire arrangements would also be accompanied by mediation from third parties, particularly the US. Relief and happiness was also expressed by common people that the war in Kargil had reduced the presence of Indian armed forces and security personnel in the Valley and that as a result they would be free of surveillance and security-related activities. As the tide of the conflict turned against the Pakistani forces and as the news filtered in about Pakistan's decision to withdraw, bitterness and cynicism set in. Questions started being asked as to why the Pakistanis came in, if they could not take on the Indian armed forces, and why were they withdrawing in a hurry, thereby weakening the cause of self-determination of the people of Jammu and Kashmir. The bitterness manifested itself in the view that India and Pakistan were using the people of Kashmir as cannon fodder, that they were fighting over the possession of territory without commitment to the welfare of the people of Jammu and Kashmir. The international community's support for India's micro-level political stance that the sanctity of the Line of Control should be respected belied the initial hopes that the Pakistani military operation would result in direct mediation by the US and other foreign powers. The Pakistani Government not acknowledging direct involvement in the conflict at the beginning of the war and not accepting their casualties or giving any recognition to Kashmiri militants who died or were wounded in the Kargil heights led to disillusionment with Pakistan.

By July 1999 there was a general assessment that Pakistan and its supporters in the Valley would not be able to achieve their objectives by military or violent means, and also that the defeat at Kargil would prevent Pakistan from undertaking any major military or political initiative to ensure the separation of Jammu and Kashmir from the Indian Union. Both the media and public discourses in Jammu and Kashmir did not show any deep political or emotional involvement in Kargil. *Indian Express* correspondent Muzamil Zaleel, aptly summed up public reaction in the Valley when he wrote: "To most people of the Kashmir Valley, the Kargil war seemed a pale, distant and largely irrelevant echo of the terrible violence and suffering which they had experienced during the past decade. From May to July, the newspapers and television channels in India were filled with emotional accounts of brave jawans killed or wounded on the mountain tops, as bodies were brought home to grieving relatives amidst the massive outpouring of national patriotic fervour, but the Kashmiris felt so numb from the bloodshed that had taken thousands of lives in the Valley since 1989, were so alienated from the invisible power conflict only a hundred miles away, that they barely reacted at all even though the fighting was entirely in the name of Kashmir."

It was not their war.

The people of Kargil, who were most directly affected by the war, had a different reaction. They were generally angry. Pakistani shelling resulted in large-scale loss of life and property in the entire Kargil region. Nearly 25,000 people were displaced and a large number of villages in the area had to be evacuated totally, but there were no special arrangements for their re-settlement during the period of the war. They questioned Pakistan's involvement with the Muslims in Kashmir in the context of the havoc caused by Pakistani shelling in the area. The consequence was that the people of Kargil were supportive of the Indian military operation.

Despite the general indifference of the people of the Valley towards the war and their disappointment with the ineptitude of Pakistan, a phenomenon which worried them about the post-Kargil period was heightened terrorist activities in Jammu and Kashmir. Pakistan had managed to infiltrate nearly 1500 additional terrorists into the state, most of them belonging to the Lashkar-e-Toiba and Harkat-ul-Ansar. Both these groups, with their headquarters in Pakistan, consisted mainly of foreign mercenaries belonging to countries as distant as Somalia, Chechnya, Libya, Algeria and Sudan, leaving aside Afghans and Pathans from the North-West Frontier Province.

Reactions Within Pakistan

It would be pertinent to touch upon the post-Kargil reactions in Pakistan in the context of political developments there, before concluding this chapter. All the militant organisations created by Pakistan and supported by the Pakistani Government in their violent activities against India were totally opposed to the withdrawal of Pakistani troops. The Lashkar-e-Toiba, the Pakistani branches of the Harkat-ul-Ansar and later on Harkat-ul-Mujahideen and Al Badr Mujahideen, all held public meetings and mass rallies in Punjab, the North West Frontier Province and southeastern Baluchistan protesting against the withdrawal. Nawaz Sharif was blamed for succumbing to external pressure and not listening to the advice given to him by the Pakistan Army High Command that they could hold on to the positions across the Line of Control. Leaders like Ghulam Mohammed Shafi, secretary-general of the Pakistani Huriyat Conference, and Ali Hamza, leader of the Markaz-Dawa-ul-Irshad asserted that Pakistan was betrayed by the US at the moment of victory in Kargil, and that the prime minister of Pakistan was a victim of international conspiracies. Professor Hafiz Mohammed Sayed of the Harkat-ul-Ansar stated the withdrawal was not necessary and urged the jehad in Kashmir continue. All roads for the mujahideen should lead not only to Srinagar, but to Ladakh, to Doda and elsewhere. There were reports that once the Indian counteroffensive got into full swing some suggestions emerged in the Pakistani Armed Forces Headquarters that Pakistan should unilaterally withdraw from the Line of Control. The assessment in these quarters was that ultimately Pakistan would have to pull back to its side of the Line of Control due to international political pressures, even if it managed a temporary consolidation of its newly acquired positions on the Indian side. The suggestion in these quarters was that Pakistan should say that it had gone to the aid of the mujahideen operating in the Kargil area when Indians acting against these mujahideen had transgressed the Line of Control. The advocacy then would have been that Pakistan crossed the Line of Control in this process and taught the Indian forces a lesson, and that they were now unilaterally withdrawing in the interest of peace and stability.

Two factors resulted in this reported suggestion not getting implemented. First, the Indian Army's counteroffensive was determined, decisive and speedy in spite of the difficult terrain. Pakistani forces were not allowed sufficient time to regroup and declare a voluntary withdrawal. Indian military pressure was continuous and Pakistani withdrawals a cascading process of retreat. The second factor was that neither General

Pervez Musharraf nor Nawaz Sharif had the courage to face the criticism that would have been attached, personally, had they declared a unilateral and voluntary withdrawal, whatever their justification.

Political analysts and retired military and civil personnel of the Pakistani establishment felt there was nothing wrong in Pakistan undertaking the military operation in Kargil from any moral or political points of view. There was every justification for Pakistan, according to them, to feel that Jammu and Kashmir was unfairly integrated into India because of Maharaja Hari Singh's anti-Muslim prejudices and a conspiratorial nexus between the Government of India, Sheikh Abdullah and Hari Singh. Pakistan, therefore, feels itself to be an aggrieved party on the Kashmir issue. According to these circles neither India nor the international community has done anything to remedy the grievances of Pakistan. Therefore, Pakistan reserves the right to take desperate steps off and on, and tends to opt for policies of high risk. The most interesting rationalisation of the Kargil invasion came in a series of comments and statements by Mushahid Hussain, minister of information and broadcasting in the Nawaz Sharif Government, who became a friend when I was high commissioner in Pakistan. He was at that time a senior journalist. Mushahid has a profound sense of the danger relating to Pakistani identity. He is also deeply committed to the two-nation theory and the consequent ideological terms of reference governing the existence of the state of Pakistan. His views as articulated in the second half of 1999 give some idea of the manner in which the Nawaz Sharif Government and the Pakistani military high command perceived the public's attitudes on Kashmir, as a consequence of which Pakistan undertook the misadventure in Kashmir.

The argument ran on the following lines: Pakistan has a moral and political right to make Kashmir part of Pakistan; the experience of supporting militants in Indian Jammu and Kashmir has convinced Pakistani public opinion that a political solution of the Kashmir issue acceptable to Pakistan cannot be achieved unless the ground situation in Jammu and Kashmir is changed, weakening the jurisdiction of the Government of India in Jammu and Kashmir thus making the position of the Indian security forces untenable in Jammu and Kashmir; Pakistan was compelled to undertake the intrusion in the Kargil sector because of India's continued rejection of any dialogue with Pakistan on the status of Kashmir as an integral part of India. Situations like Kargil will continue to occur till India agrees to a compromise acceptable to Pakistan on the Kashmir issue.

Neither the Government nor the military high command expected the Kargil initiative to liberate Jammu and Kashmir from India. Pakistan had three objectives in undertaking the Kargil operation. First, to refocus international attention on Jammu and Kashmir, which was fading away due to Indian propaganda. Second, to convey a message to the people in the Kashmir valley that Pakistan would remain actively supportive of the movement of Kashmir separatists. Third, to diminish the confidence of the Indian armed forces, to underline their vulnerabilities, and to signal that Pakistan was capable of tactically and strategically posing effective threats to Indian-held Ladakh and Siachen.

The conclusion drawn by Mushahid Hussain and company is that Pakistan has succeeded in achieving all the three objectives, despite the embarrassment of the withdrawal. It was also felt that Pakistan's inclination to resort to military means was a result of an incremental feeling in Pakistani public opinion and in the Government of Pakistan, that there were no prospects of a negotiated settlement with India on Kashmir. Interestingly, a comment in parentheses about the results of the Lahore meeting between Vajpayee and Sharif is that it was a cosmetic initiative by India and a deliberate political move to weaken Pakistan's Kashmir policy and general security. The Kargil effort, therefore, was an act of desperation. There was, however, general agreement that the Kargil operation of Pakistan was an ad hoc and poorly planned exercise, which did not take into account the long-term consequences of this military move. There was also the view among the retired civil and military officers, like former foreign secretary Tanvir Ahmed Khan and Lt. General Talat Masood, a former chief of the Inter-Services Intelligence, that there was a lack of coordination and integrated planning between the political and military high commands during Kargil.

Pakistani perception was uniformly that troops had to withdraw not due to being defeated by the Indian armed forces, but due to American pressure. The discussions General Zinni, general officer commanding, the Central Command of the US Armed Forces, held with Nawaz Sharif and General Pervez Musharraf, were subjected to criticism in the Pakistani strategic community. It was felt that Zinni added the military and defence cooperation dimension to the political pressure being applied by the US to end the conflict and to withdraw across the Line of Control. There was quite an amount of speculation in India as to whether the military high command of Pakistan had really kept the political leadership of Pakistan informed about its Kargil plans. The general consensus was that the Sharif Government was taken into full confidence from the end of 1998 onwards about the Kargil military operation. Sharif denied this in his statements made at the Attock Jail early in June 2000. But more about this twist to the story later. Senior political and military figures of Pakistan are, however, agreed that a large-scale operation of the type undertaken in Kargil could not have taken place without Cabinet approval, whatever the circumstances in which the approval was obtained.

Another point of speculation in India and abroad was about the Kargil plans having been prepared from the mid-1990s onwards. Former Pakistan army chief General Mirza Aslam Beg stated that war gaming of the Kargil type may have been part of Pakistani strategic planning for Jammu and Kashmir but that there was no definite plan. Another former army chief, General Jahangir Karamat, categorically denied that there was any such plan during his tenure, when he succeeded General Arif Nawaz Janjua. The Islampasand parties of Pakistan and the various mujahideen groups were the most critical of the withdrawal of Pakistan's forces. They also felt that the Government of Pakistan need not have denied direct involvement in the Kargil conflict in the beginning, instead of acknowledging it only when proof of Pakistani troops fighting in the Kargil front was given publicity by the Indian armed forces. These extremist Islamic parties and mujahideen cadres have categorically declared their intention of continuing their violent operations in Jammu and Kashmir, as a jehad, which cannot be stopped till its objectives have been achieved. They have also stated that though the Pakistani Government had given certain commitments regarding the Line of Control, they expected not only continued but increased activities in Jammu and Kashmir. General Pervez Musharraf has given general indications that this expectation would be fulfilled. He has even justified jehad, stating openly in an interview given to an American newspaper on 24 June 2000, that jehad is not a terrorist and violent phenomenon. It is a "tolerant concept" embodying religious, political and social commitment to Islam for safeguarding the dignity and safety of Muslims.

One presumes Prime Minister Nawaz Sharif, till he was overthrown, shared most of these perceptions and orientations. His statements in June that he was not consulted, that he was not kept informed of the Kargil military operations in advance, merits an examination of the chemistry of politics and the interrelationships between the Pakistani armed forces and the political power structure of civil society in Pakistan. This is necessary to understand the more critical elements in Pakistan's Kashmir policy.

Defence Minister George Fernandes had remarked publicly towards the end of May 1999 that the attack on Kargil was a conspiratorial misadventure by the Pakistan armed forces and that perhaps Prime Minister Sharif was not informed in advance, that he was perhaps a victim of a *fait accompli*. The factual basis of this assessment was not clear, though one could speculate on the motives. Perhaps Fernandes had hoped that his remark would give Sharif a chance to distance himself from the military high command of Pakistan and enable him to overrule General Musharraf, leading to a quick withdrawal of Pakistani troops from the Line of Control. Fernandes was criticised for making this remark while the Indian Army was launching its counteroffensive against Pakistani forces. His trying to exonerate the prime minister of Pakistan was considered factually incorrect and detrimental to the morale of the Indian armed forces. Pakistani analysts rejected Defence Minister Fernandes's assessment as an attempt to create divisions in the Pakistani Government. There were indignant denials about the possibility of the Pakistani armed forces acting independently of the elected Government of Pakistan, especially when democracy was getting consolidated in Pakistan! In any case, Sharif remained involved in the Kargil conflict and its aftermath not only throughout June and July, but also up to October 1999, when he was ousted in a military coup by General Pervez Musharraf. It is ironic that nearly a year after the Kargil conflict, Sharif confirmed the speculation about the Pakistani military establishment having acted on its own in Kargil without taking Nawaz Sharif into confidence. In a number of statements early in June, Sharif asserted that the Pakistan armed forces had neither kept him informed nor had they consulted him before launching the invasion in Kargil. He made these statements at Attock and Lahore and in Karachi, when being taken for trials to these cities and from Attock where he was incarcerated. The points made by him can be summed up as follows:

(a) Plans were afoot in the Pakistani Army Headquarters for intruding into Kargil from the end of 1998 onwards. (b) Pakistani armed forces headquarters did not give him any information about these plans, nor did it consult him about the advisability of undertaking this military initiative. (c) Had he known about the plans regarding Kargil, drawn up by General Pervez Musharraf, he would either have nipped them in the bud as prime minister or, if he were not successful, he certainly would not have agreed to the meeting with Prime Minister Vajpayee in Lahore in February 1999. (d) He went to the Lahore meeting without any inkling of the Kargil plan and in general hoped to restore a substantive discussion with India to resolve the Kashmir issue and other pending problems affecting Indo-Pakistani relations. (e) He only came to know about the military operations in Kargil in the second half of April when military infiltrations across the Line of Control had already been initiated. Sharif's concluding accusation was that Musharraf was instrumental in getting Pakistan involved in a military misadventure that resulted in the defeat of the Pakistani armed forces and the erosion of Pakistan's credibility on the Kashmir issue. Sharif held

Musharraf responsible for a military debacle and for the political embarrassment of Pakistan. He accused Musharraf further of not having consulted the Pakistani military high command, the corps commanders of the Pakistani armed forces, or his principal staff officers in Pakistani army headquarters, the apex military body, for discussing and finalising this major military operation.

Sharif asserted that his government went along with Musharraf's plans in order to avoid divisiveness in the Government of Pakistan when it was engaged in a serious military operation. It was only when the Pakistani armed forces were facing military defeat that Sharif decided to arrange a compromise, in consultation with the US and China, which would extricate Pakistan from the quicksand of a military adventurist initiative. Sharif rationalised his discussions with President Bill Clinton and his decision to withdraw Pakistani troops from the Line of Control as a decision which was necessary to ensure national security and the territorial integrity of Pakistan, including Pakistan's jurisdiction over the Northern Areas and Pakistan-held Kashmir. He added an interesting footnote: that it was Musharraf himself who requested him to arrange for the extrication of the Pakistani armed forces from the Kargil crisis, with American help. Nawaz Sharif described the accusations against him about compromising Pakistan's interests and credibility in Kargil by the Islam-pasand parties and Musharraf as exercises in impracticable extremism and attempting to shift the responsibility for the fiasco from the Pakistani military command to the civilian government.

This self-justifying postmortem by Nawaz Sharif had some clear motivations. First and foremost, his aim was to restore his credibility with Pakistani public opinion as a person deeply committed to peace and stability. Second, he wished to convey to domestic political circles that despite the revival of democracy in Pakistan for nearly a decade, the Pakistani armed forces continued to follow their own separate agenda without any sensitivity towards constitutional requirements, institutional consultations or regard for the genuine interests of the common people of Pakistan. By implication he conveyed the message that Musharraf's military coup in October 1999 was a result of Sharif having opposed his aggressive policies on Kashmir. Fourth, he projected Musharraf as an army chief who did not even take his senior military colleagues, the corps commanders, into confidence before launching a major military operation. Another motive was to convey to the major powers of the world that the political parties and civil society in Pakistan were committed to a peaceful and practical dialogue with India on all pending issues, including Kashmir, but that it was the military establishment that always thwarted these efforts, to the extent of being capable of sweeping aside a democratically elected government.

The non-governmental political and strategic community in Pakistan did not accept Sharif's post facto revelations. They reserved judgement, expressing the general view that unless Sharif produced credible proof about his assertions, they were a self-serving exercise in the context of the critical legal and political predicament which he faces. Neither has Pakistani public opinion accepted his assessments, barring a faction of his own political party, the Pakistan Muslim League.

Public reaction to two other events in Indo-Pakistani relations are also worth noting, namely, the shooting down of a Pakistani reconnaissance plane on the Sir Creek Border between Sindh and Gujarat in August 1999 and the hijacking of the Indian Airlines plane from Kathmandu to Kandahar. There was natural indignation about the shooting down of the Pakistani plane and resulting loss of life of Pakistani military personnel, 22 of them who were in the plane. The Pakistani Government's accusations against India were not totally accepted by Pakistani public opinion. Questions were raised about the Pakistani Air Force undertaking such reconnaissance operations in the immediate aftermath of the Kargil conflict, especially when India was in a belligerent mood. The view expressed was that even if Pakistani interpretations of events were valid, was it necessary to undertake such activities when Pakistan's international credibility was low and when there was every likelihood of a decisive military response from India?

It was perhaps to neutralise this criticism that the Government of Pakistan took the case to the International Court of Justice (ICJ) at the Hague. India questioned the jurisdiction of the ICJ on the issue. The Indian advocacy was acknowledged and upheld by the ICJ in June 2000, which created further embarrassment for the Government of Pakistan. A Pakistani friend visiting Delhi reacted to the ICJ's decision and the denouement of the Kargil conflict by quoting the mid-19th century Urdu poet Zauk:

कम होंगे इस बिसात मे हम जैसे बदक़मार
जो चाल हम चले सो निहायत बुरी चले।

(There are few in this game of chess, as unlucky as we are.
We have gone wrong on every move we made.)

As far as the hijacking of the Indian Airlines plane in December 1999 went, Pakistani public reaction was both concerned and indifferent. The concern was that if the plane remained in Pakistan, Pakistan could again get embroiled in a controversy, and the international community would be supportive of India in the light of the increasing opposition to terrorism. The indifference was because in the middle of adjusting to the new military regime that had come into being in October 1999, the event was considered incidental and as part of the general support the ISI gave to terrorist cadre. Only the extremist Islamic parties and the militant groups in Pakistan endorsed the hijacking act. The general public was relieved when the hijacked plane left Lahore and ultimately landed in Kandahar: the buck had been passed on to the Taliban. There was of course some worry that the links between Pakistani authorities and the Taliban would result in Pakistan too being subjected to international criticism for the hijack. The hijackers' coming to Pakistan and Masood Azhar, one of the terrorists released by India to resolve the hijacking, staying in Pakistan for some time and getting married to boot did not help matters. In overall terms, Pakistani reactions to the critical events between May 1999 and June 2000 could be summed up as follows:

(1) The Kargil conflict and the other two events mentioned above could not be avoided by Pakistan because of the legitimacy of Pakistan's stand on Kashmir and in view of India's refusal to discuss a reasonable compromise (from Pakistan's point of view).

(2) The failure at Kargil is to be regretted, but it occurred because of military miscalculations, wrong political assessments and lack of coordination within the Pakistani Government.

(3) The failure also occurred because India had somehow managed to turn international public opinion against Pakistan and persuaded the US to bring pressure to bear on Pakistan.

(4) Support for the separatist activities in Jammu and Kashmir should continue, but should be planned more carefully.

(5) Sudden and extensive military operations should be avoided. The pressure on India should be gradual, continuous and incremental.

(5) There is no regret about the Kargil military operation itself. The regret, both in public opinion and in the Pakistani establishment, only about its failure.

(6) Pakistan should lobby major powers and international public opinion to generate pressure on India to meet Pakistani demands on Kashmir.

(7) There is no acceptance that despite the repeated failures of Pakistan's military operations in Kashmir since 1948, a solution lies in coming to

a practical compromise on the basis of ground realities without getting enmeshed in the ideological complexities of Partition.

One cannot escape the disappointing conclusion that both India and Pakistan are locked in inflexible mindsets. It must also be mentioned as a footnote that the sufferings of the civilian population during the Kargil war were no less on the Pakistani side of the Line of Control than on the Indian side. Media reports, particularly by foreign correspondents, highlighted the fact that in "Pakistan-held Kashmir" and in the Northern Areas there was much sorrow and resentment among the common people whose lives and families were affected by the unnecessary military operation.

Four

Wellsprings of Antagonism

*T*here is a school of thought which believes Indo-Pakistan hostilities originated in the long period of Muslim rule over India, which lasted nearly a thousand years before the advent of the European colonial powers. The implication is that the Muslims of India were willing to accept governance by other foreign powers like the French or British, but were not willing to face the prospect of being ruled by a Hindu majority in an India free from colonial domination. There is another school of thought that holds the view that the Hindu-Muslim synthesis achieved by Indian civil society (as the Muslim rulers settled down in India adopting India as a home) was fragmented by the extremist Islamic orthodoxy of Aurangzeb's rule from about 1658 to 1707. There have been speculative theories as to what would have happened had Shahjahan's eldest son Dara Shikoh succeeded to the Mughal throne rather than Aurangzeb, who killed his elder brother and usurped the throne. Historians have speculated that Dara Shikoh would have revived and continued the patterns of governance initiated by his great-grandfather Akbar the Great, policies which were followed to some extent by Dara's grandfather, Jahangir. Muslim assertiveness and Hindu resentment dating from the period of Aurangzeb bore the seeds of Hindu-Muslim antagonism, according to these theorists. A third theory about Hindu-Muslim tensions attributes them to the political forces at work during the British rule of India from the 18th century to Independence. This school of thought explains Hindu-Muslim antagonism as follows. The British to a large extent wrested political power from Muslim rulers in different parts of the country. Consequently, Muslims were neglected and deliberately subjected to discriminatory treatment in the initial period of British rule, whereas Hindus were favoured with opportunities to participate in the lower levels of administration and to become incrementally involved in economic and commercial activities. This enabled Hindus to become the more prosperous and progressive partners of the power structure of British India till the first decade of the 20th century. From being the rulers of India, the Muslim community became a comparatively backward and politically powerless segment.

Then there is the view that mainstream Indian politics, which in its initial phase was dominated by the urbanised English-educated middle class, was devoid of religious or communal overtones. But by the middle of the second decade of the 20th century, religious identities became resurgent, which ultimately led to the Hindu-Muslim divide, Partition and the creation of India and Pakistan. All these theories have elements of veracity, these crosscurrents spread over a period of nearly 250 years, have in some way or the other contributed to the origin of hostility between India and Pakistan. There are sufficient analyses available about the antagonisms between Hindus and Muslims from the 17th to the middle of the 19th century. One therefore concentrates on the more recent wellsprings of Hindu-Muslim tension and consequent Indo-Pakistan antagonism.

The political history of India after the 1857 Mutiny could be a proximate point of reference to understand the adversity between India and Pakistan. This analysis will be general in nature, whereas events and political attitudes from the beginning of the 20th century merit a more detailed assessment.

The first two decades or so after the British suppression of the Indian Mutiny found the Muslim community isolated and on the defensive. The trauma of the last Mughal emperor being imprisoned and sent into exile and of Muslim rulers in different parts of India being removed by political intrigues and military conquest — over a period of fifty years or so, from 1803 onwards — by the expanding British power left the community generally depressed and disoriented. The Hindus of northern India were equally victims of British disdain and arrogance but they did not carry the memory of having been part of the ruling community for a thousand years. Hindus eventually reconciled themselves to the ruling power politically, socially and culturally. They also became secondary partners to the British economic and technological endeavours in India. By the last quarter of the 19th century, however, interaction with the British power structure and intellectual circles raised the political and social consciousness of the Hindu community, resulting in an intellectual and social renaissance among Hindus, and the first stirrings of political assertiveness. The British Government of India perceived this as a subversive phenomenon, which needed counteraction. It came to the conclusion it should not allow this socio-cultural renaissance and political inclination towards the creation of a national identity to encompass the Indian Muslim community. The more perceptive members of the British power structure realised that with the introduction of telegraphs, posts and railway systems, people-to-people contact between different regions and communities would increase. This could result in a synergy of political and social impulses, gradually finding expression in an integrated national movement.

So a conscious decision was taken to exploit the existing divide between Hindus and Muslims. It was decided that the government should be more responsive to remedy the frustrations and angst of the Muslim community. The ingredients of this policy were to acknowledge and encourage a separate social, religious and cultural Muslim identity, neglecting the synthesis that had occurred from the 10th century AD onwards. It was also decided to respond to the political, economic, cultural and educational demands and aspirations of the Muslims in a compartmentalised way separate from the Hindus. The policy of divide and rule commenced.

However, one has also to acknowledge that the British approach was rooted in perceptions of the social, religious and cultural characteristics of Indian society. The caste- and taboo-ridden Hindu community, and the manner in which it interacted with Muslims in the religious and social spheres, resulted in perceptions about the separateness of the two communities. The perception of Indian history by the British — that they had replaced the Muslims who had dominated the Hindus — was simplistic, but nevertheless substantiated their view that Hindu-Muslim separateness could be exploited to play one community against the other. Whatever emotional criticism may be directed against this phenomenon, this approach helped Indian Muslims to break out of their despondent insularism and gradually join the Indian mainstream.

It is interesting to note that despite the British approach outlined above, there was no Hindu-Muslim divide for nearly the first three decades of the 20th century. Though separate political and social movements and leaders emerged in both communities, they generally cooperated with each other in the national movement for self-government. Leaders of Muslim organisations and the Indian National Congress participated in each other's meetings and movements till the mid-1930s, after which the drifting apart commenced, ultimately leading to Partition. This development in the mid-1930s was preceded by events and trends described below.

Separatist Trends

The leadership and membership of the Indian National Congress had started changing by 1910. The elite Anglicised leadership of the founding years changed with the emergence of leaders with more genuine roots in Indian religio-cultural values and a greater assertiveness against British authority. The likes of Dadabhai Naoroji, Surendra Nath Banerjee, R.C. Dutt, Badruddin Tyabji and Gopal Krishna Gokhale started getting replaced by individuals like Lokmanya Tilak, Bipin Chandra Pal and Lala Lajpat Rai and, a little later by Mahatma Gandhi. In my assessment both Lokmanya Tilak and Mahatma Gandhi contributed in some ways to the apprehensions and suspicions about the Hindu majority in the psyche of Indian Muslims. Indian nationalism was to be underpinned and strengthened by religious and cultural terms of reference and symbols. Tilak's reviving the Ganesh Chaturthi festival and references to Shivaji to invigorate Indian nationalism did not go down well with Indian Muslims, both in terms of religious beliefs and collective historical memory. Mahatma Gandhi's emergence as the foremost leader of the Indian National Congress in the 1920s generated further concern amongst Muslims. Though Gandhi was a firm believer in secularism and profoundly committed to rendering equal respect to all religions, his references to "Ram Rajya" and his including a recitation of texts from the Quran in his prayer meetings resulted in negative curiosities and concerns about his objectives. The average middle-class Muslim did not understand the profound sophistication of Mahatma Gandhi's approach to build an Indian national identity. "Ram Rajya" to the average Muslim was a prescription for Hindu domination. It was considered an attempt at diluting the unique qualities of Islam for political ends by a deeply religious Hindu leader. Even the brief emotional and intellectual collaboration between the Congress and the leaders of the Muslim community during the "Khilafat" movement did not last long. Maulana Mohammed Ali and Shaukat Ali parted ways with Gandhiji and became critical of him halfway through the Khilafat movement.

Despite all this a certain symbiosis continued between important Muslim leaders and those of the Indian National Congress. It is ironical that the creator of Pakistan, Mohammed Ali Jinnah, was hailed by Gokhale as the ambassador of Hindu-Muslim unity. Jinnah and Tilak were signatories to the 1916 Lucknow Pact. Perhaps both politics and personality clashes eroded the positive chemistry between the Muslim and Hindu leadership of the Indian National Movement. There is sufficient historical material available to indicate that Jinnah aspired to national leadership of both Hindus and Muslims but when he was (in his assessment) just at the threshold of acquiring this role, Mahatma Gandhi, Motilal Nehru, Jawaharlal Nehru, and Pandit Madan Mohan Malaviya, acquired importance in the Indian National Congress and emerged as mass leaders whereas Mohammed Ali Jinnah was averse to hobnobbing with common people except from a distance and from lofty heights. From the late 1920s onwards his attraction to the cadre of the Congress diminished. It resulted in his moving towards the leadership of the Muslim community, with which he was more at ease. He felt it was the Hindu communal approach that deprived him of the legitimate role of national leadership, usurped by others who were less able than him. One would do well to remember that Jinnah was a lawyer of the highest calibre and a successful barrister. Both Mahatma Gandhi and Jawaharlal Nehru were not of this eminence as lawyers. Motilal Nehru, though equally competent, was considered by Jinnah to be less distinguished because Motilal Nehru was not an England-returned barrister, but only a native lawyer who had made good. (It is well known that Jinnah never agreed to appear against Motilal Nehru in person in any case!)

A watershed in the break between the political leadership of Hindus and Muslims was the announcement of the "Communal Award" by British Prime Minister Ramsey McDonald in 1932. The Communal Award was based on the discussions held at the three Round Table Conferences on Indian political reforms held in London between 1930 and 1932. The Award provided for a representational and voting scheme for separate electorates, weighted representation and reserved seats for different communities in the provincial legislatures and the federal legislature of the Government of India that were to come into being under the Government of India Act of 1935. The Award provided for separate and reserved representation for Anglo-Indians, Christians, Europeans, Muslims and Sikhs. In 1934, the provisions of the Award were also extended to recruitment for government services, including quotas for Muslims and other minorities. All other Indians were categorised as general constituents. The Award initially provided for separate electorates and seat reservation for Untouchables amongst the Hindus. But Mahatma Gandhi went on a fast unto death and ultimately managed to persuade Dr Ambedkar to a compromise to have increased representation for untouchables under the general category.

What is important is the fact that Mahatma Gandhi and the Indian National Congress opposed separate representation for Muslims in the legislatures under this Communal Award as a "barrier to the development of Indian unity". What perturbed the Muslim leadership is that despite their claim to represent the Muslim masses, the Muslim League performed very poorly against the Indian National Congress in the elections to the provincial legislative assemblies held under the Government of India Act in 1937. The Congress swept the polls in most of India. Even in Muslim-majority provinces of British India like Bengal and Punjab, coalition governments with other political parties came into power in which the Muslim League had no role. Jinnah's suggestion, that keeping in mind the large Muslim community living in the United Provinces of Avadh and Agra (present-day Uttar Pradesh) it should have a coalition government, was rejected out of hand by the Indian National Congress which had won the majority of seats in that province. This was the last straw on the camel's back. The Muslim League felt that the Indian National Congress in the arrogance of its electoral victory was going to destroy the Muslim League and its claims to represent the Muslim community in India. The consequence was the Muslim League propounding the "two nation" theory under the leadership of Jinnah. The Muslim League accused the Congress of planning to deny Muslim rights in future schemes of Indian self-governance and insisted Hindus and Muslims constituted separate nations. Both must be equally accommodated in the subcontinent, with an autonomous homeland for Indian Muslims. This view found expression in the Pakistan Resolution passed by the Muslim League in 1940.

The Second World War fortuitously contributed to furthering the objective of the Pakistan Resolution. The British Government declaring war on behalf of India against the Axis Powers without consulting the leadership of the Indian National Congress resulted in the Congress resigning from the federal and provincial legislatures and dissociating itself from the British Government of India. Desirous of sustaining Muslim support for the war effort and for increasing recruitment of Muslims in the army, the British Government signalled its general support to the aspirations expressed in the Pakistan Resolution. The acceptability and clout of the Muslim League with the British Government qualitatively increased in the years just prior to India's independence. The Indian National Congress, however, did not show any foresight or sensitivity about these developments. The denouement was that the Muslim League emerged as a credible political force betwen 1942 and 1946 and succeeded in almost gaining parity with the Congress in the interim government formed in New Delhi.

Going back a little, the British Government sent a Cabinet Mission to discuss plans for political reforms and self-government in India. The mission (consisting of secretary of state for India, Lord Pethic Lawrence, president of the Board of Trade, Sir Stafford Cripps and first lord of the admiralty, Lord A.V. Alexander) discussed their proposals between March and June 1946 and suggested a composite plan on 16 May. The details of the plan are worth reproducing:

> The Cabinet Mission Plan proposed a Union of British provinces of India and the Indian princely states, with the central government dealing with external affairs, defence and communications. The new Central Government of the Indian Dominion was to have necessary financial powers to deal with these subjects. All other subjects and residual powers dealt with by the British Government of India were to be devolved to the Provincial Governments and the provinces of the princely states. The Central Government was to consist of an Executive and a Legislature, with the Executive being responsible to the Central Legislature. Any issue which affected the interests of either the Hindus or the Muslims was to be decided only by the majority of representatives of each community in each of the Legislatures voting separately. The British Indian Provinces were given the liberty to form sub-federal groups on the basis of the religious beliefs of people inhabiting each of the provinces. The Hindu majority provinces could join each other and create a Hindu sub-divisional group. The Muslim majority provinces of Punjab, the North West Frontier Provinces, Baluchistan, Sindh, Assam and Bengal could form a separate Muslim sub-federal territorial polity. The Central Constituent Assembly was to consist of 292 members elected on the basis of communal representation by provincial assemblies, 93 members were to be appointed by Maharajas, nawabs and princes of princely states. The interests of minorities and tribal groups were to be taken care of by a special advisory committee while drafting the constitution for the new dominion.

The plan was announced by the British Cabinet Mission despite not having received the consent of the Muslim League or the Indian National Congress. The plan conceded a number of demands of the Muslim League but rejected partition and separate Muslim state. The Mission also rejected the demand of the Congress for direct non-communal representation in the central legislature and the creation of a strong central government. The Congress was also against the federal subgroups suggestion mentioned above. The

Indian National Congress refused the plan and wanted more discussions for an alternative plan. The Muslim League's reaction was most militant. It called for direct action by Muslims in favour of Pakistan on 16 August 1946. Field Marshal Lord Wavell, the viceroy who presided over these developments, departed from India in March 1946 and Lord Mountbatten succeeded him with an overriding brief to arrange for the withdrawal of British rule by the summer of 1948. After his initial discussions with Indian leaders he came to the conclusion that partition was the solution. Barring Mahatma Gandhi, the Indian National Congress had become impatient to get independence and assume power. So this major national party agreed to the partition of India. Gandhi went to the extent of suggesting to the top leadership of the Congress that they should offer the prime ministership of India to Mohammed Ali Jinnah. But the groundswell of events made his suggestion irrelevant.

Subcontinental India suffered from extensive communal riots from Assam in the east to the North West Frontier Province in the west. Given the volatile situation Mountbatten hurried the process of partition, advancing the date for the British to leave India by one year, from June 1948 to 15 August 1947. The subcontinent stood partitioned with India and Pakistan emerging as independent dominions on 15 and 14 August respectively. Large-scale communal riots resulted in the displacement of nearly ten million people between India and Pakistan. A million people died. Partition and its attendant violence, instead of being a catharsis leading to normality, led to further controversies. The seeds of communal antagonism, sown over the previous 50 to 90 years, were sprouting through the ground as poisonous saplings.

The assumption shared by Pakistani and Indian leaders in 1946, that partition would be a clean and surgical break that would lay the foundations for a peaceful and stable relationship, proved to be wrong from the very beginning. Nor did ordinary people living in what was to become Pakistan or India anticipate that they would have to migrate. A large number of Hindus from Punjab, North West Frontier Province and Sindh, who had to flee as these provinces became part of Pakistan, initially did not think that they would have to go through the painful process of resettlement in India.

Similar was the mindset of the Hindus of East Bengal, which became East Pakistan. Again, Muslims living in the eastern portions of Punjab and West Bengal, as well as portions of UP, did not anticipate the violence which originated in Jinnah's call for Direct Action. The harsh realities of mass communal riots resulted in the migration of Muslims to West Pakistan and migration of Bengali Muslims from West Bengal to East Pakistan. Mutual anger and bitterness therefore characterised the mindset of the common people of both countries.

Leaving aside this immediate reason for hostility and suspicion, other developments provided the matrix for long-term antagonisms. The expectation of the Muslim leadership that Muslim-majority provinces and princely states would automatically become part of Pakistan in their full territorial extensions was not fulfilled. The British Indian provinces of Punjab and Bengal were divided in terms of narrow demographic specificity on the basis of the religious and communal affiliations of people inhabiting these provinces. Only half of Punjab and half of Bengal went to Pakistan. The Muslim League had expected Assam also to become part of Pakistan. But only some portions of Assam were made part of East Pakistan. But for the geographical isolation of the North West Frontier Province and Baluchistan, the people of those provinces were not terribly enthusiastic about becoming part of Pakistan. The Muslim-majority princely states of Junagadh, Hyderabad, Bhopal and Kashmir became integral parts of the new Indian Dominion by the end of 1948.

Muslim League leaders had also hoped for some portions of what is now northern Gujarat becoming part of Pakistan. This did not happen. Jinnah declared that he had got "a moth-eaten and truncated Pakistan". The manner in which the princely states of Hyderabad, Kashmir, Junagadh and Bhopal became part of India, and the logic of Pakistani frustrations relating to the accession of these states to India, will be discussed later. Suffice to say that the seeds of hostility about territorial identity germinated in these developments. The new Pakistani leadership attributed the territorial advantages accruing to India at the time of partition to Hindu perfidy and what they called "the pernicious anti-Pakistani collusion between Lord Mountbatten and the first Prime Minister of India Jawaharlal Nehru". The division of assets of the British Government of India between the two dominions of Pakistan and India also generated controversies. By some curious logic, Pakistan wanted a 50 per cent share of all the assets and not division of these assets proportionate to the territorial division of the subcontinent. This included the division of the foreign exchange assets, the assets of the British Indian armed forces and Government properties. Pakistan desired financial compensation for properties located in the new Dominion of India in order to utilise funds for building up infrastructural facilities in the newly created country. The Act passed by the British Parliament granting independence to India and the creation of the dominions and subsequent procedural arrangements were considered unfair by

Pakistan. There was some initial thinking that despite Partition, the new dominions would have common economic arrangements without customs and tariff barriers and that the transportation and communications infrastructure would remain integrated, serving both countries. These possibilities stood aborted with the Pakistani military operation in Kashmir, the intrigues between 1946 and 1948 to engineer an independent status for the large princely state of Hyderabad, and Jinnah's attempts to persuade the princes of Bikaner, Jodhpur and Jaisalmer to accede to Pakistan. By the end of 1948, India and Pakistan took decisions to treat each other as completely independent sovereign countries, separating the communications and transportation systems and putting in place customs and tariff barriers.

Mahatma Gandhi's suggestion to Nehru and Patel to be generous towards Pakistan in the division of assets, release of foreign exchange reserves, etc., was not accepted. His assassination in January 1948 removed the last moderating influence on interaction between India and Pakistan.

Historical Perspectives

It would be pertinent to take note of the origins of Indo-Pakistani antagonisms at a deeper political and strategic level before proceeding to an analysis of the events and attitudes in the two countries during the first two decades of their existence, from 1948 till 1959. Formal political accounts and personal archives of officials of the British Government and Muslim League leaders indicate that there was a certain pernicious geo-strategic plan that animated the exercise of Partition, particularly in British officialdom. The expectation was that the British Indian provinces would be divided and that they would constitute themselves into the dominions of India and Pakistan respectively. The British Government decided that all treaty arrangements between the British Crown and the princes of India would lapse at the time of Partition and that the maharajas, nizams and nawabs would resume their sovereign status over the territories they ruled and that it would be left entirely to their discretion to decide whether they wished to remain independent or to accede to India or Pakistan. This approach was rooted in the expectation that the major princely states (like Kashmir, Hyderabad, and the larger states of Rajasthan) would opt for independence rather than accede to one dominion or the other. The strategic scenario envisaged was that India would be a fragmented polity with British provinces constituting the new Dominion of India, but with the princely states making a patchwork of political entities retaining their linkages with the British Government, eroding the territorial and geo-strategic cohesion of India. In contrast, it was hoped that the Dominion of Pakistan would emerge as a united, cohesive territorial state rooted in Islamic unity, retaining a close relationship with the former imperial power in the context of the support which the British Government had given to the Muslim League for the creation of Pakistan. The policy anticipation was that Britain would still play a dominant role in the subcontinental political processes with a potentially weak India on the one hand and with the influence Britain would continue to exercise with Pakistan and the princely states of India. None of these expectations were fulfilled. British policy planners misjudged the capacity of the Indian princes to sustain their independence. They also underestimated the inclination and the strength of the people's movements in the princely states, which, though having been somewhat in isolation from the Indian National Congress, had become a part of the mainstream freedom movement from the third decade of the 20th century. They also failed to anticipate the dynamism, determination and political adroitness of Sardar Vallabhbhai Patel who ensured that the majority of the 500-odd princely states would accede to India. Kashmir, Hyderabad and Junagadh were the only exceptions, where political persuasion had to be backed by coercive means by the Government of India.

The process of integration of the princely states into India was characterised by high political drama in some respects. Jinnah is reported to have given the maharajas of Bikaner, Jaisalmer and Jodhpur the suggestion that they should accede to Pakistan because of their geographical contiguity with the western wing of the Dominion of Pakistan and in the context of their opposition to the Indian National Congress. The offer made by him was that he would accept any conditions stipulated by these princes for accession to Pakistan without any reservations or negotiations. These princes, however, were sensitive to public opinion in their kingdoms and did not accept Jinnah's offer. The maharaja of Indore decided briefly to declare his state independent and not to accede to India or Pakistan. The story goes that Sardar Patel invited him to come to Delhi to finalise the decision. His Highness Maharaja Malhar-Rao Holker got into his special train at Indore to travel to Delhi. The moment it entered the territory of the Indian Dominion, it was stopped at Ratlam, neither allowed to proceed to Delhi nor to go back to Indore. Then a message went to him that if he could not even move out of the limits of his state without the Government of India's cooperation, how was he going to manage a viable independent status? He came to his senses. Indore acceded to India.

Apart from Kashmir, the three other states which gave serious indications of wanting to remain independent were Hyderabad, Junagadh and Travancore. The maharaja of Travancore and the nawab of Junagadh decided to accede to India owing to the pressure of people's movements in their states. The nizam of Hyderabad held out till July 1948. The state of Hyderabad, the size of France, straddled south central India. Immediately after Partition, a militant Muslim group dominated Hyderabad's politics under an Islamic extremist, Qasim Rizvi. The nizam also opened up lines with Pakistan and with the UN Secretariat to ensure Hyderabad's emergence as an independent state. The people's movement in Hyderabad (a movement which included both Hindus and Muslims, barring the ruling elite advising the Nizam) was opposed to these moves. Hyderabad becoming an independent state covering a huge expanse of southern India would have been a political and strategic threat to the consolidation of the territorial identity of the Indian republic. It was after the failure of prolonged negotiations with the nizam that the Government of India decided to resort to the limited military operation which resulted in the integration of the state of Hyderabad into India. The entire military operation took less than a week. The swiftness with which the advisers of the nizam were overcome and were compelled to flee to Pakistan was proof enough of the inclinations of the people of Hyderabad as against the ambitions of the Nizam. The territories of the state of Hyderabad, with additional areas from the former British Province of Madras, today constitute Andhra Pradesh.

The Accession of Kashmir

Now we come to the question of the accession of Kashmir. Maharaja Hari Singh was inclined to declare Kashmir an independent state with himself as the monarch. He was not responsive to the inclinations of the National Conference or the Muslim League. While the Muslim League of Jammu and Kashmir desired Kashmir to become part of Pakistan, Sheikh Abdullah, the leader of the National Conference, was opposed to Kashmir becoming part of Pakistan. Nehru and Sardar Patel had conveyed to Jinnah and Liaqat Ali Khan that the accession of the princely states to one dominion or the other should not be decided upon by the maharajas and nawabs. They argued that it is the people of these princely states who should decide on their own future political status. Jinnah took a wooden constitutional stand (on the basis of his political anticipation) stating that on the lapse of paramountcy, sovereignty stood restored to the princes and that it was only they who had the political and legal legitimacy to decide on the future of the states over which they ruled. His anticipation was that the nizam of Hyderabad and maharaja of Kashmir would not accede to India. The point to remember is that it was

Jinnah and the top leadership of the Muslim League who refused to accept arguments about territorial arrangements on the basis of democratic dispensation or the people's will. The opportunistic wooden legality to which Pakistani leaders resorted did not succeed. The negative consequence has been a dispute over Kashmir which has bedevilled relations for 55 years.

Let us now recall the broad chronology of events leading to the first war between India and Pakistan on Kashmir. The last maharaja of Kashmir, Hari Singh, was a quintessential feudal autocrat whose reign was characterised by neglecting the aspirations of the people of Jammu and Kashmir. At Partition he perhaps suffered from the *follie de grandeur* of becoming a monarch to rule over a highly important strategic region. He resorted to the ploy of signing a Standstill Agreement with the Governments of India and Pakistan, stating that he would take some time before reaching a final decision on the status of Jammu and Kashmir. This deliberate dithering, and his having kept leaders of both the Muslim Conference and the National Conference in prison, generated internal disturbances in Jammu and Kashmir. The atmosphere was further vitiated by the communal violence of Partition. There were Hindu-Muslim riots in Jammu as well as violence against the rural Muslim peasantry in the Valley and the western portions of the princely state. The new Government of Pakistan took full advantage of the situation to violate the Standstill Agreement. Pakistan conveyed protests to Maharaja Hari Singh in September and early October 1947 stating that armed bands, which included the troops of the maharaja of Jammu and Kashmir, were attacking Muslim villages in the state and that Pakistan considered the situation fraught with danger. The response from Maharaja Hari Singh was that the disturbances referred to by Pakistan in its protest were created by Pakistan, which had elements of truth. Apart from the trouble created by the cadre of the Jammu and Kashmir Muslim Conference, who had links with the Muslim League, Pakistan-sponsored tribal infiltrators had commenced their violent operations in the western portions of the state by October. Retired Major General Akbar Khan of the Pakistan Army (who played the most significant role in engineering the tribal infiltration and then managing the full-scale Pakistani military operations in Jammu and Kashmir in 1947-48), has confirmed in his memoirs, (*Raiders in Kashmer*, 2nd edition, published by National Book Foundation, Islamabad in 1975) that as early as late August and September 1947 Pakistani political and military leaders meeting in Murree had discussed the measures and the time-frame for capturing Jammu and Kashmir and making it part of Pakistan. Akbar Khan asserts: "The accession of Kashmir to Pakistan was not simply a matter of desirability but an absolute necessity for Pakistan's separate existence." The leader of the Muslim Conference of Jammu and Kashmir, Sardar Ibrahim, who later became the first President of "Azad Kashmir", expressed the view by the autumn of 1947 that "the time for possible negotiations regarding Kashmir's accession to Pakistan was gone. The question therefore was whether the Government of Pakistan could move to take an active hand in the affair." Major General Akbar Khan acknowledges that he prepared a plan titled "Armed Revolt Inside Kashmir", which included measures by which a large Pakistani force could block Indian reinforcements or stop Maharaja Hari Singh or the anti-Muslim League National Conference leader Sheikh Abdullah, who was the most popular leader of the people's movement. What is even more important is that Akbar Khan confirms that he discussed this plan with the then prime minister of Pakistan, Liaqat Ali Khan, who endorsed it. Akbar Khan's impression of his meeting with Liaqat Ali Khan was that discussions were characterised by "an atmosphere of cheerfulness and confidence". It is well known that Akbar Khan, under the *nom de guerre* "General Tariq", personally led the tribal invasion of Kashmir.

Pakistan-inspired tribal attacks on Jammu and Kashmir reached full operational levels from 27 October 1947 onwards. The Muslim soldiers of the army of Maharaja Hari Singh deserted their posts. Pakistan-sponsored raiders captured Muzaffarabad and Poonch, and within five days had reached Baramulla, near Srinagar. This Muslim-majority town was subjected to massacres, arson and rape; later reports confirmed that of the population of 40,000 only 3000 people survived in this township. The raiders then moved towards Srinagar. It is at this stage that Maharaja Hari Singh in panic and under pressure decided to accede to India. It is on 27 October 1947 that the first airborne troops landed at Srinagar airport and went straight into the battle to push back the tribal invaders who had reached the outskirts of the airport.

It is true that people in areas which are now called Azad Kashmir were supporters of the pro-Muslim League pro-Pakistan Muslim Conference of Jammu and Kashmir, whereas people in all other regions of the princely state were supportive of Sheikh Abdullah's Jammu and Kashmir National Conference. It is also true that the cadres of the Muslim Conference had commenced disturbances against Maharaja Hari Singh's rule from 7 October onwards with support from Pakistan on the basis of advance information which they had that their agitation would be backed by tribal lashkars from the North West Frontier Province of Pakistan.

In fact, as the tribal infiltrators moved towards Baramulla, a Pakistan-sponsored Azad Kashmir Government was established on 24 October 1947.

This was a premature exercise because the Indian troops made steady progress in pushing back the tribal invaders. By December 1947, they were pushed out of the Valley and by the spring of 1948 the Indian Army had resumed its offensive to rid the remaining part of the state from Pakistani-sponsored invaders. It was late in 1947 and early in 1948 that the Pakistani Army decided to back up the tribal cadres.

The governor-general of Pakistan, Jinnah, personally ordered the deployment of Pakistani troops in support of the tribal invaders. This was initially objected to by the commander-in-chief of the Pakistani Army, who was a British General. But both Pakistani officers and British officers of the Pakistani Army functioning at lower levels favoured the introduction of Pakistani troops into Jammu and Kashmir. In the face of the increasingly successful counter-offensive by the Indian armed forces, Pakistani troops joined the tribals in military operations by the summer of 1948.

An interesting sideshow of this first war on Kashmir was that two high-level India-Pakistan joint committees, the Partition Committee and the Joint Defence Council, continued to meet to sort out the residual problems emerging from Partition. But by November-December, the deliberations of these bodies were overshadowed by the conflict in Kashmir. The last meeting of this series was held on 8 December 1947 with Liaqat Ali Khan and Jawaharlal Nehru as principal participants. The Pakistani prime minister had already destroyed the prospects of any constructive discussions by sending a telegram to Nehru in which he described Sheikh Abdullah as a "Quisling" of India and directly accused Nehru and the Government of India of launching a programme to eliminate the whole Muslim population of Jammu and Kashmir. The deadlock was final between India and Pakistan by mid-December 1947.

There is a general perception that Jawaharlal Nehru never seriously considered a comprehensive military initiative against Pakistan during the first Indo-Pakistan war in 1947-48. This is not true. Nehru in fact desired a general military campaign against Pakistan during the 1947-48 war, but did not succeed because the higher management of military and defence remained with the British during the first two years after India becoming independent. It is pertinent to recall how Nehru's inclinations were thwarted. The commanders-in-chief of the Indian Army and the Indian Air Force and Navy right till about the end of 1949 were British officers. Lord Mountbatten insisted on remaining the chairman of the Indian Cabinet Committee on Defence staking this claim on his background as supreme allied commander in South Asia during the Second World War. Field Marshal Lord Auchinlack was an influential figure in matters related to defence and division of the Indian armed forces between India and Pakistan in 1946-47. The first two commanders-in-chief of India were British, Generals Lockhart and Bucher.

The manner in which Lord Mountbatten, Lockhart and Bucher dealt with the Pakistani invasion of Jammu and Kashmir in 1947, scuttled the instinctive reactions of Nehru and Patel towards Pakistani aggression. These three British officers not just advised but bulldozed decisions against the wishes of Nehru and Sardar Patel, which resulted in India losing one-third of the territory of the state of Jammu and Kashmir. Recently revealed records show that Nehru and Patel had taken the view by December 1947– January 1948 that the Indian armed forces should launch military operations against Pakistan, exercising relevant strategic options to ensure Pakistan's withdrawal from Jammu and Kashmir. Mountbatten vetoed this advice as chairman of the defence council. It was he who gave the basic advice to Nehru to go to the United Nations, to offer a plebiscite with the general assurance that the British Government in combination with the United States would initiate effective action through the UN leading to Pakistan's complete withdrawal from Jammu and Kashmir. The inputs received from Major General Kulwant Singh commanding the forces in Jammu and Kashmir and from General Thimayya and Cariappa in the high military echelons of the Western Command nevertheless made Jawaharlal Nehru insist that while the political option of going to the UN was being exercised, India should simultaneously plan a military campaign against Pakistan to ensure a vacation of aggression in Jammu and Kashmir. Such orders were given to the commander-in-chief of the Indian Army, General Lockhart who insisted to Jawaharlal Nehru that it would not be possible to expel Pakistan-sponsored raiders from the Jhelum valley till the spring of 1948. Lockhart's successor Bucher soft-paddled the orders of Nehru to launch limited military operation against Pakistan. He confided to the US charge d'affaires in January 1948 that he had taken no steps to prepare the Indian Army for a cross-border operation. He pointed out that the Attlee Government on the advice of Mountbatten had cautioned Nehru against launching any military operation.

Meanwhile the UN Security Council was activated pro-forma, which was used as an excuse by Bucher to ignore Nehru's orders. It was only the clarity of purpose and innovation of General Thimayya and General Kulwant Singh which resulted in the successes of the limited operations they were allowed to undertake in Jammu and Kashmir.

It is pertinent to note that the field commanders Thimayya and Kulwant Singh not only operated effectively in military terms but their advice was against India going to the UN before recovering the whole territory of the state of Jammu and Kashmir. This advice was not heeded by Nehru though as in December, 1947, he had felt that going to the UN might not have been an exercise serving India's vital interests.

Referral to the United Nations

The Government of Pakistan suggested on 16 November 1947 that the situation in Kashmir should be referred to the United Nations with the objective of setting up an impartial administration in Kashmir, to be preceded by the withdrawal of all outside forces. This was the first of Pakistan's clever stratagems in international diplomacy. The cease-fire would have stemmed the military debacle Pakistan was facing. From Pakistan's point of view, the suggestion that outside forces should be withdrawn would have applied only to the Indian forces, because Pakistan was still disclaiming any direct involvement in the Kashmir conflict; the creation of impartial administration would have negated the accession of Jammu and Kashmir to India and foreclosed the possibilities of the National Conference and of Sheikh Abdullah assuming power. Neither Sheikh Abdullah nor the Government of India could accept this patently devious ploy. As Indian military operations continued, India decided to refer the issue to the United Nations within the framework of facts and Indian interests. India referred the case to the UN on 31 December 1947, under Article 35 of the United Nations Charter, which stipulates that any member of the UN may bring any dispute or situation which might lead to international friction or which is likely to endanger the maintenance of international peace and security to the attention of the UN Security Council or the General Assembly.

Pakistan's response to this reference, which was sent the very same day (31 December 1947), was uncompromisingly negative. India, therefore, followed up its reference of 31 December by formally appealing to the Security Council on 1 January 1948. The Indian reference to the Security Council stated: "There now exists a situation whose continuance was likely to endanger the maintenance of international peace and security owing to the aid which infiltrators, consisting of nationals of Pakistan and of tribesmen from the territory immediately adjoining Pakistan on the northwest, under directions from Pakistan for operations against Kashmir, a state which has acceded to the Dominion of India and is part of India. The Government of India requests the Security Council to call upon Pakistan to put an end immediately to the giving of such assistance which is an act of aggression against India. If Pakistan does not do so, the Government of India may be compelled in self-defence to enter Pakistani territory in order to take military action against infiltrators. The matter is therefore one of extreme urgency and calls for immediate action."

The manner in which the United Nations handled the Kashmir issue from 1948 onwards is a dismal story from India's point of view. Instead of taking action on the merits of the issue, on the basis of the constitutional and legal accession of Jammu and Kashmir to India, and instead of asking Pakistan to withdraw from its aggression, the United Nations over the years converted what should have been the issue of "invasion of Jammu and Kashmir, a part of India, by Pakistan" into "an Indo-Pakistan dispute".

Much has been analysed and written about this dispute over the last 55 years. It is pertinent to recount some of the relevant events. First and foremost, the point often forgotten in current discussions on Kashmir is it is Pakistan that resorted to the use of force to change a legal and constitutional decision to which it was a party, and it was India that referred the matter to the UN seeking a peaceful solution. Second, just before Pandit Nehru decided to refer the matter to the UN, there were strong suggestions from India's military commanders conducting the operations in Jammu and Kashmir in 1947 and in 1948 that they needed only a few weeks more to push back all Pakistani personnel and troops out of Jammu and Kashmir and that India need not go to the UN. Lt. General Kulwant Singh, senior commander of the Indian forces in Jammu and Kashmir at that time, according to reports, was categorical in giving this advice to the Government of India. But both Lord Mountbatten and Jawaharlal Nehru in their political wisdom refused to accept this advice. An even more interesting factor which is not widely known is that Sheikh Abdullah himself was not very keen that Indian forces retrieve the western areas of the state from Pakistani troops. The reason was that he was not sure of his popularity with and acceptance by the people who now inhabited Pakistan-occupied areas of Kashmir. His leadership and his political party, the National Conference of Jammu and Kashmir, did not have the same support in those areas which they had in the rest of Jammu and Kashmir. The people of the western regions of the state of Jammu and Kashmir were supportive of the Muslim Conference and the Muslim League. Sheikh Abdullah therefore endorsed India referring the case to the UN Security Council instead of having to cope with a portion of the state which would have opposed him after the completion of the military operations.

Another dimension of the faulty political strategy followed by India in 1947 and 1948 was India not referring the matter to the UN under Article 36 of the UN Charter, along with Article 35. Subclause 3 of this Article clearly provides that in taking action or making recommendations on any dispute under Articles 33, 34 and 35, the UN should take into consideration the legal dimensions of the issue brought to its notice and should as a general rule, refer the matter to the International Court of Justice (ICJ). Apart from this India should perhaps have referred the matter to the Security Council under Articles 6 and 7 of the Charter, focusing on Pakistani aggression against a province or state which had become an integral part of India. Even foreign experts like Joseph Corbel, chairman of the First UN Commission on India and Pakistan, have commented that India did not present its case to the Security Council forcefully enough in political as well as legal and constitutional terms.

The conclusion that one comes to is that India need not have gone to the UN at all because at that point of time it could have neutralised the Pakistani plans completely and permanently by military means. Second, even in our going to the UN, it was reticent and limited in its approach. Another physical and operational factor of historical interest is that while the Pakistani military commanders were full of fervour about the two-nation theory, and passionate about capturing Jammu and Kashmir, barring some exceptions, the Indian military commanders were not very happy about fighting their colleagues in the Pakistani Army who till a very short time ago, were their comrades in the British Indian Army. It should, therefore, be a relief in retrospect that despite these emotional misgivings, the Indian armed forces performed so efficiently in pushing back the invaders till they were stopped by higher political decisions.

In contrast to this, Pakistan was focused, aggressive and blatantly mendacious in its responses to the Indian reference of the issue to the UN. Pakistan responded to the Indian reference to the Security Council on 15 January 1948, entitling it: "Pakistan's Complaint Against India". Pakistan submerged the situation in Kashmir in a litany of accusations against India. The Pakistani response began by asserting that the Pakistani Government emphatically denied that it was giving assistance to the "so-called" infiltrators or that it has committed any aggression against India; on the contrary, solely with the objective of maintaining friendly relations between the two dominions, it had continued to do everything in its power to discourage the tribal movements by all means short of war. This assertion was followed by Pakistan accusing India of genocide of Muslims in Jammu and Kashmir, adding that India had taken over Junagadh and Hyderabad through unfair means. The Pakistani response described the Boundary Award of Sir Cyril Radcliffe as unfair and unjust. The response concluded by stating that Indian forces were "occupation forces" in the state of Jammu and Kashmir and that Indian policies reflected a general attitude of obstruction and hostility towards Pakistan with the objective of paralysing Pakistan at its very inception by depriving it of its rightful financial and other assets. This was followed by a macro-level political accusation that India had not accepted Partition, that the accession of Jammu and Kashmir to the Indian Dominion was brought about by "fraud and violence", and that India was now threatening Pakistan with direct military attack. By adopting this stratagem at the UN, Pakistan obfuscated its invasion of Jammu and Kashmir.

Another gap in India's initial presentation of its case was failure to inform the UN Security Council about the people's movement in Kashmir, i.e., Sheikh Abdullah and his party's role in opposing Maharaja Hari Singh's rule. It did not bring to the notice of the international community that the decision taken by Maharaja Hari Singh in fact had the general support of the most representative and popular party of the state of Jammu and Kashmir, the National Conference.

To cut a long story short, the UN and the major powers did not take note of the nature of the dispute as it was brought to the UN by India. Instead of questioning Pakistan's resort to force for territorial aggrandisement, the UN treated Pakistan on a par with India as a disputant on the issue. The resolutions passed by the UN Security Council between 1945 and 1949 created entirely unfair terms of reference to resolve the dispute, negating the constitutional and legal basis of the accession of Jammu and Kashmir to India as stipulated in the British parliamentary legislation partitioning India: creating the dominions of India and Pakistan, and laying down the procedures by which the princely states of the Indian subcontinent would determine their status. The UN also refused to acknowledge the political credibility and representative character of the Jammu and Kashmir National Conference and its leader Sheikh Abdullah. The focus was on organising a plebiscite. The only fair stipulation made by the UN was that Pakistani troops should withdraw from the territories of Jammu and Kashmir and that Pakistan should also try to ensure the withdrawal of the tribal invaders whom it had sponsored. No obligation was imposed on Pakistan to pull back its henchmen from Jammu and Kashmir. There was also arrogant indifference on the part of the major powers, both bilaterally and at the UN, about the Kashmir issue. The psychological implication was that newly independent states emerging from colonialism were not capable of managing their political affairs in a rational and practical manner and therefore the issue should be dealt with in a paternal and impartial fashion, which should include a certain sympathy for the weaker and newer state, Pakistan, and that allowances should be made for the mischief by Pakistan because of its frustrations about Partition, the Boundary Award and a majority of the princely states acceding to India.

A series of mediators then dealt with the Kashmir issue and made recommendations and suggestions to resolve it. The first United Nations Commission for India and Pakistan came into being in June 1948. Its chairman was Joseph Corbel from Czechoslovakia, father of the future US secretary of state Madeleine Albright. The other representatives on the Commission were from the US, Belgium, Columbia and Argentina. The efforts of this commission were followed by UN mediators General McNaughton in 1949, Sir Owen Dixon in 1950, Dr Frank Graham in 1951 and Gunnar Jarring in 1957. The suggestions and recommendations of all these gentlemen proved to be abortive because none of them was wholly acceptable to India and Pakistan.

Could the UN have dealt with the matter differently? Michael Brecher, the Canadian scholar, in *Struggle for Kashmir* (1953), gave some pointers that are still relevant. The questions the UN should have answered, according to Brecher, are: (1) Was Jammu and Kashmir's accession a legally valid act under the relevant British Parliamentary laws and acts granting independence to India and Pakistan? (2) Did Pakistan commit aggression in Kashmir? If so, an official condemnation and remedial action by the UN and its Security Council would have been in order. If not, the Security Council should have openly rejected India's case. (3) Is there a legitimate constitutional authority governing Jammu and Kashmir? (4) Is Azad Kashmir a legitimate entity? (5) Is the Azad Kashmir army a creation of Pakistan or an autonomous military force equipped and officered by a segment of Kashmiris, living in some portions of Jammu and Kashmir, opposed to the then maharaja?

Factual and objective answers to these questions will not be very palatable to Pakistan even now. Such answers would also hold up a mirror to the major powers of the world and the UN Security Council about the biased manner in which they dealt with the Kashmir issue. We now end the initial stage of the Kashmir story and move on to events and trends in Indo-Pakistan relations up to 1959, when Pakistan came under a military dictatorship.

The Human Dimension

Here we enter some of the emotional dimensions of Indo-Pakistani relations in the immediate aftermath of Partition. Mahatma Gandhi was assassinated as the first war on Kashmir progressed and India took the issue to the UN.

Despite his profound opposition to partition and his desire that India should play fair with Pakistan, once partition became inevitable, he found Pakistan's invasion of Jammu and Kashmir unacceptable and generally endorsed the Indian reaction to the Pakistani intrusion. His passing from the scene removed a deeply moral tempering and restraining influence on the interaction between the new power structures of India and Pakistan. On the other side of the border, Jinnah was facing terminal illness due to cancer. He also passed away towards the end of 1948. Thus the two foremost leaders of India and Pakistan had only a limited period of life to influence events after Partition. The second rung of leadership took over both countries within a year and a half of their emergence as independent nations. The consequence was Pakistan commencing its journey down the road to a more intensive Islamic identity, and to authoritarian and military rule, while anti-Pakistani sentiments entrenched themselves in the psyche of political circles in India rooted in the opposition to Partition and to Pakistani activities in Kashmir as well as on Hyderabad, Bhopal and Junagadh becoming part of India.

In terms of bland statistics, about ten million people migrated in both directions between 1946 and 1949. The geographical and demographic dimensions of this migration are of interest. Most Hindus and Sikhs from Punjab, Sindh and North West Frontier Province did not feel that their lives would be disrupted and that they would have to leave. The initial perception was that though Partition was regrettable, there would just be a change in administration. Life would go on as usual. Contrastingly, the Muslim League undertook a deliberate campaign amongst the Muslims in UP, Bihar, MP, Rajasthan, West Bengal, and princely Hyderabad urging that they migrate to Pakistan: a Muslim homeland in the subcontinent. Interestingly, the average Muslim living in these states was not very responsive to the Muslim League campaign except in Bengal, portions of Assam and East Punjab. It is the large-scale communal riots which followed after the direct action day organised by Mohammed Ali Jinnah in Calcutta, on 16 August 1946 that compelled Hindus and Muslims living on both sides of the border of areas that were to become Pakistan and India to think about forced migration. Most of Hindus and Sikhs in West Punjab, the North West Frontier Province and the northern portions of Sindh migrated to India. Most Muslims in East Punjab migrated to West Punjab and the North West Frontier Province. Most Muslims living in West Bengal migrated to East Bengal, which was going to become East Pakistan.

Hindus living in Sindh initially did not feel pressurised to migrate to India but violence against them increased from mid-1947 onwards, which resulted in their migration to Rajasthan and what was then the Bombay Presidency. Interestingly, most Muslims from UP, Bihar, Rajasthan, MP and the southern states of Hyderabad and Tamil Nadu who migrated to Pakistan were middle-class professionals. The majority of the Muslims in these states chose to remain in India, partially because they had neither the economic wherewithal nor a sense of economic security about going to Pakistan. Even more importantly, the ruling Congress Party undertook a special campaign to assure them of their safety and their citizenship rights in the Dominion of India, emphasising that the Constitution and governance in India would be rooted in the principles of religious and communal tolerance and secularism.

The final situation as it emerged was somewhat different from what the Muslim League had hoped for. Apart from not getting all the territories which it desired to become Pakistan, it did not succeed even in getting a major portion of the Muslim population to migrate to Pakistan. Rough statistics of the period indicate that out of the 100 to 130 million Muslims living in the Indian subcontinent, the population of Pakistan consisted mostly of Muslims who were already residents in regions which became Pakistan. Only a small percentage of Muslims living in the rest of India migrated to Pakistan. It is equally important to remember that the ruling Muslim political elite in Punjab and the North West Frontier Province were opposed to partition. The Muslim League carried the day because of the support it had amongst the people of these provinces. Between 35 and 42 million Muslims remained in India and did not move to the new Muslim homeland. While Muslims from the Indian portions of Punjab and Bengal went over and settled in Pakistani Punjab and East Bengal, the majority of Muslims who migrated from UP, Bihar, Rajasthan, MP, and the southern states of India settled in the province of Sindh in Pakistan because they were not easily accepted in Pakistani Punjab and the North West Frontier Province. About half a million Muslims from Bihar went to East Pakistan. These regional demographic characteristics of Muslim migration to Pakistan from India were to have far-reaching ramifications in the politics of Pakistan in the 1980s and 1990s.

I was a secondary school student in the princely state of Mewar (Udaipur) and then in Delhi from 1946 to 1949 and, like millions of my fellow countrymen, I too have personal memories of the emotional and physical dimensions of Partition. The princely states of Rajasthan had a sizeable population of Muslims belonging to different sects of Islam. Many of them had an important social and economic position dating back to Mughal times. Compared to the communal tension that affected

Hindu-Muslim relations in British India, in the first four decades of the 20th century there was no serious communal tension between Hindus and Muslims in the princely states of Rajasthan, almost till the beginning of 1948. There were Sunnis, Shias, Ismailis, Khojas and Bohras who were part of the civil society in the states of Rajasthan. It is only after Hindu migrants from southern Punjab and Sindh arrived in these states across the southern Punjab and Sindh border that tension emerged. I recall rich Sindhi migrants coming to Udaipur via Ajmer and the reverse flow of Muslims from Rajasthan into Sindh and southwest Punjab in Pakistan. The only difference between the travails affecting this mass of human beings across international borders was that the migration from Rajasthan to Pakistan and vice versa was not subjected to the kind of brutal violence migrants faced across East and West Punjab and across East and West Bengal.

I also recall the whole stretch of what was then an open maidan called the "Ramlila Ground" in Delhi, stretching from Ajmeri Gate to Delhi Gate and a little beyond, being hastily converted into a vast city of tents where the wave of migrants coming from Punjab and the North West Frontier Province were accommodated under difficult conditions. I also recall the sense of profound self-respect among these refugees who despite their difficult economic conditions did not resort to seeking alms. At that time I used to live in the walled city of Delhi in Sitaram Bazar and used to go for morning walks in this tented city. The incoming refugees were already engaged in setting up shop, putting up shacks for engineering and machine tool works; even the very young children were selling newspapers to earn a living. The spirit of enterprise and determination ultimately made these refugees from Punjab dominate the economic and social life of Delhi and its surrounding regions within two decades.

In contrast were the refugees who came from East Bengal to India. My late mother, Dr Ratnamayi Devi Dixit, was an ardent devotee of the Ramakrishna Mission, so she used to visit the headquarters of the Ramakrishna Mission at Belur near Dakshineshwar, which was then a suburb of Calcutta. I used to accompany her. I still remember the refugees from East Bengal crowding the railway platforms at Howrah and Sealdah. They were listless and showed a deeply defeatist spirit. Most of them were unwilling to move beyond the socially and culturally familiar surroundings of West Bengal. Somehow the spirit of enterprise and of defying circumstances was less visible amongst them. The proof of this contrast was that most of the refugee camps in northern India were disbanded and had disappeared by the late 1950s, whereas the refugee camps housing Bengali refugees continued for many many years in places like Salt Lake and Sealdah.

There were heartwarming incidents of human nobility and civilised behaviour in the middle of all this violence and bitterness. There was the incident of Jawaharlal Nehru discarding all concerns of personal security driving down to Connaught Place in the middle of anti-Muslim riots and angrily admonishing Hindu and Sikh rioters to desist from violence. There were a number of stories of Hindu neighbours all over northern India giving shelter to their Muslim friends and their families to save them from the fury of communal violence and then ensuring their safe passage to Pakistan. There were similar incidents of Muslims sheltering and giving advance warning to their Hindu and Sikh neighbours about impending violence in the Punjab and the North West Frontier Province in the cities of Multan, Lyallpur (now Faisalabad), Lahore, Rawalpindi and Peshawar. Then there were efforts undertaken on both sides of the border to recover abducted women and children and restore them to their families. The work done by women like Mridula Sarabhai and her counterparts in Pakistan during this period was a redeeming example of human civility.

Despite all the antagonism one has to acknowledge in retrospect that the period between 1947 and 1959 was still characterised by an attempt on the part of the political leadership of both countries to somehow resolve their controversies and lay foundations for a normal relationship. Jawaharlal Nehru interacted with successive prime ministers of Pakistan, beginning with Liaqat Ali Khan, then Nazimuddin, Mohammed Ali Bogra and Feroze Khan Noon. The controversies regarding Kashmir remained a high point of tension between the two countries and the violence against Hindus in East Pakistan in 1950 resulted in another wave of mass migration. Liaqat and Nehru decided to come to an agreement on some other issues: properties belonging to people who had migrated, technically labelled the "Evacuee Property" problem; treatment of minorities in both countries; the possibilities of restructuring economic and trade relations between two countries till recently part of an unified economy. In April 1950 Liaqat Ali Khan and Jawaharlal Nehru signed what was known as the Liaqat-Nehru Pact, also termed the Peace Agreement. They agreed on certain stipulations and codes of conduct for treatment of minorities in both countries, Nehru emphasising the seriousness of the problem because nearly half a million refugees had come to India from East Pakistan because of the renewed communal violence there in 1950. The two prime ministers also discussed the possibilities of cooperation in the spheres of transportation, irrigation, communications and evacuee property. Pakistan's major concern vis-à-vis India was ensuring the flow of canal waters from the river systems flowing to West Punjab, the head-waters of all of them being in India. A major Indian concern was regarding the evacuee property. Indian refugees had left behind property worth Rs 14,000 million in Pakistan, specially in West Pakistan, whereas Muslim refugees had left properties worth only Rs 2000 million in India (See Volume 1, *India-Pakistan: History of Unresolved Conflict* by Lars Blinkenberg, published by Odense University Press, 1998). Of these issues, those relating to evacuee property and canal waters were resolved by 1960. The agreement reached on the question of treatment of minorities, transportation, communication and trade remained unresolved. Liaqat Ali Khan's assassination in 1952 brought this initial chapter of Indo-Pakistan relations to an end. Nehru's relations with Mohammed Ali Bogra were particularly cordial. Their meetings in London and in Delhi in June and July 1953 marginally improved relations between India and Pakistan except on issues related to Jammu and Kashmir.

The Arrest of Sheikh Abdullah

Pakistan had created a separate territorial entity called "Azad Kashmir" in areas still under its occupation in early 1949 after the Indian military operations stopped. All mediatory efforts, concluding with the Jarring Mission in 1957, failed. The situation became more complicated with India dismissing Sheikh Abdullah from the post of prime minister of Kashmir and arresting him. The reason for this decision was the emergence of internal contradictions in Jammu and Kashmir. While Sheikh Abdullah desired an autonomous special status for Jammu and Kashmir within a general federal arrangement with India, the people of Jammu, a Hindu majority area, through their political party the Praja Parishad, started generating pressure for a complete and full integration of Jammu and Kashmir with the Indian Republic on a par with other states.

Sheikh Abdullah was profoundly opposed to this demand. The Jammu Praja Parishad also resented the progressively pro-Muslim policies of the Abdullah Government. Sheikh Abdullah's reaction resulted in the Jammu Praja Parishad resorting to violent demonstrations which exacerbated the crisis. Sheikh Abdullah in his anger described the advocacy of the Praja Parishad that the Indian Constitution should apply to Jammu and Kashmir in all respects as "unrealistic, childish and savouring of lunacy". He went on to describe the support for this advocacy in some sections of Indian public opinion as reflective of a "communal spirit which exists in India". Sheikh Abdullah's substantive inclination was that he should rule Kashmir fairly independently without Indian interference. It was his assessment that he would be able to achieve this objective with greater facility if Jammu and

Kashmir remained part of India. He was apprehensive about not having this freedom if Jammu and Kashmir were to be part of Pakistan; if the state became part of Pakistan he feared being swamped and neutralised by Muslim League politics. It was also his assessment that many senior members of his own party were inclined to sideline him, using the Indian connection. So he became more assertive and intemperate in articulating the view that he agreed to the accession of Jammu and Kashmir to India only for tactical purposes on the condition that it would have autonomous status.

Nehru tried to resolve this dilemma by signing an agreement with him in July 1952. But Sheikh Abdullah's personal ambitions and resulting policy pronouncements heightened the crisis. There were apprehensions in India that he may go back on his decision about the accession. He was therefore removed from the prime ministership on the basis of a move by the Jammu and Kashmir Legislative Assembly. His deputy, Bakshi Ghulam Mohammed, who was in close touch with the Government of India, succeeded him as chief minister, remaining in power till 1963.

The arrest of Sheikh Abdullah intensified tensions on Jammu and Kashmir with Pakistan. Pakistan raised the issue on an ascending scale at the Commonwealth Conferences and at the UN. India's position hardened proportionately, climaxing in the marathon debate in the Security Council in 1957. V.K. Krishna Menon pleaded India's case with vigour and in great detail at the Security Council, categorically defining the Indian position that Jammu and Kashmir was an integral part of the Indian Union, and that since Pakistan had not fulfilled any of the conditions contained in the UN resolutions for plebiscite, India would not agree to a plebiscite any more. Pakistan created the state of Azad Kashmir in the areas occupied by it. This made the demand for a plebiscite even more unacceptable.

Cold War Alignments

The hardened Indian position was also the result of two further factors. First, India perceived that the major Western powers were refusing to deal with the Kashmir problem on the merits of the issue in the context of legal and constitutional provisions under which Jammu and Kashmir acceded to India. Second, Pakistan had signed a series of defence agreements with the US between 1954 and 1955, agreeing to become a part of the American system of military alliances against the Soviet Union and its allies. Pakistan became a member of the Baghdad Pact and the South East Asia Treaty Organisation. The US and western democracies welcomed Pakistan joining them, in the exercise of containing communist expansionism. Pakistan's whole motive was to utilise the membership of these pacts to generate political and military pressure on India. India's refusal to join either of the blocs engaged in the Cold War and its commitment to non-alignment antagonised the US. The then US Secretary of State, John Foster Dulles, summed up the views when he said: "Those who are not with us are against us." The consequence was Pakistan getting general support from the major Western powers in its policy stances against India, particularly on Jammu and Kashmir. The deterioration of relations between India and China between 1956 and 1959 affected Indo-Pakistan relations. The Pakistani military establishment, led by then chief of the army staff, General Mohammed Ayub Khan, started taking note of the potentialities of developing an equation with China to put India on the defensive. Parallel to this, Pakistan's domestic politics was undergoing a qualitative transformation. Political leaders who had been part of the Pakistan movement and constituted the first generation of leadership of the Pakistan Government were fading away from the political scene. A combination of senior bureaucrats and military commanders had started dominating the power structure.

These critical political trends culminated in Governor-General Ghulam Mohammed stepping down and handing over power to General Iskander Mirza, who was backed by General Ayub Khan, in 1958. Power passed from the pre-Partition political class to a military-bureaucratic circle in 1959, with Ayub Khan taking over the presidency at the beginning of the 1960s. All the existing contradictions in Indo-Pakistan relations were now compounded by a major ideological chasm with India's commitment to democracy on the one hand and Pakistan's transformation into a military-bureaucratic authoritarian state on the other.

It would be relevant in parentheses to refer to the general feelings of the public about Partition and its aftermath. People belonging to the partitioned provinces of British India were first disoriented and then bitter because of the manner in which Partition affected their personal lives. Segments of public opinion in both India and Pakistan were permeated by communal extremism. The supreme manifestation of this was Mahatma Gandhi's assassination by a Hindu extremist with Hindu Mahasabha and RSS connections, Nathuram Vinayak Godse. Pakistani military intrusion into Jammu and Kashmir compounded these feelings of mutual antagonism, particularly in West Pakistan and in north and north central India. Similar adversarial feelings affected East Pakistan, portions of Assam and West Bengal. The mass migration of Bengali Hindus from East Pakistan was a major contributing factor to this bitterness in the eastern portions of India.

The pronouncements of senior political leaders in the immediate aftermath of Partition did not help matters. Senior leaders of Pakistan insisted the process of Partition was not complete and that India had retained Muslim-majority areas by political intrigue. Indian leaders on the other hand kept insisting that they had accepted Partition reluctantly and only because non-acceptance would have delayed independence. Maulana Abul Kalam Azad, the seniormost Muslim leader in the Indian National Congress, considered Partition an aberration and declared that it could not be a permanent phenomenon. He predicted presciently that Islam alone cannot be the basis for a national identity and that Pakistan would either reunite with India because of the profound historical and cultural commonalities of the people inhabiting the subcontinent or that Pakistan would break up because of ethno-linguistic diversities which cannot be overcome by a doctrine of national identity based on Islam.

Objectivity demands an acknowledgement of the fact that the rest of India, particularly the states of southern India, were not as traumatised by Partition as the northern states. They did not feel the direct political or economic impact of Partition. Once the Princely State of Hyderabad was integrated with the Indian Union, it was issues related to collective ethno-linguistic identities of people inhabiting the southern states that attracted the attention of the people in our southern regions, which ultimately led to the creation of the States Re-Organisation Commission and then the new states of Tamil Nadu, Andhra Pradesh, Karnataka, Gujarat and Maharashtra on the basis of ethno-linguistic demands. People and public opinion in Pakistan also went through a similar experience. Except for the public opinion in the Punjab and North West Frontier Province, there was no passionate feeling about Pakistani aspirations regarding Jammu and Kashmir. In fact, the people of the North West Frontier Province, Baluchistan, and Sindh were perturbed about the prospects of the domination by Punjab in the power structure of Pakistan, particularly after the demise of Jinnah and Liaqat. There was also a feeling of resentment about civil servants and bureaucrats, many of them from UP, Bihar and other former British Indian provinces, dominating the administration. There was further resentment in West Pakistan when three politicians from East Pakistan became prime ministers of Pakistan one after the other, H.S. Suhrawardy, Nazimuddin and Mohammed Ali Bogra.

The people of East Pakistan on the other hand had already started resenting the administration, the armed forces and police services being dominated by West Pakistanis. The declaration of Urdu as the only national language of Pakistan without any recognition being given to Bengali generated profound concern about identity. By 1952, the Language Movement in East Pakistan had become a critical political factor.

In overall terms, however, the processes of India's political consolidation contrasted with those in Pakistan. While India was getting consolidated on the basis of a democratic constitution and a cohesive institutional framework, Pakistan despite its efforts to develop along similar lines was unsuccessful in consolidating its democratic political structure and national identity. At the deeper intellectual level, this failure contributed to Pakistani apprehensions and suspicions about India.

Five

From Democracy
to Dictatorship and War

*P*akistan remained under military rule for nearly 14 years from 1958 to 1972. With the overthrow of the democratic government in 1958, power was assumed by General Iskander Mirza first, and then General Ayub Khan. In fact, the military-bureaucratic nexus had commenced dominating Pakistani political developments in the mid-1950s itself, after the assassination of Liaqat. The polity became disoriented from its ideological moorings. Its national identity was disrupted even before it could take the first faltering steps. The territorial inadequacies felt by the power structure of Pakistan in the beginning were compounded by incipient centrifugal pressures. The Pushtuns of the North West Frontier Province were not at ease at being part of the new country. Factors which resulted in this attitude were the domination of Khan Abdul Gaffar Khan and his elder brother Dr Khan Sahib in the politics of the North West Frontier Province. The Khudai Khidmatgar Movement had strong affiliations with the Indian National Congress. The Muslim League had not quite convinced the Pushtuns living in the North West Frontier Province and in the northeastern parts of Baluchistan about the virtues and advantages of the new Muslim homeland.

Similarly, the people of East Pakistan started having doubts about their proportionate share in the power structure of Pakistan. The insistence of

Jinnah and Liaqat that Urdu be the sole national language of Pakistan generated profound concern about cultural, linguistic and ethnic identity among Bengali Muslims. The Language Movement had become extremely purposive by1952. The coercive measures the Government took against the Language Movement only increased the centrifugal pressure in East Pakistan. The firing on Bengali students in Dacca, agitating for the recognition of Bengali as a national language in February 1952, sowed the seeds for the eventual separation of Bangladesh in 1971.

The insensitivity of the Government of Pakistan about manning of the senior administrative, political and military positions in East Pakistan without giving representation to East Pakistanis only heightened suspicions. The manner in which the three prime ministers of Pakistan who belonged to East Pakistan were treated by the bureaucracy and the military leadership in West Pakistan in the 1950s, seemed to confirm the validity of the anxieties. The perception was that Suhrawardy, Nazimuddin and Bogra being made prime ministers were acts of tokenism.

Pakistan's foreign and security policies also underwent a change from the mid-1950s onwards. The orientations of Jinnah and Liaqat, who envisaged Pakistan following an independent foreign policy, and the expectation of a normal relationship with India, changed barely a year after their assumption of power in 1948. The anxiety that India could still claim a large Muslim population as a part of its citizenry and the failure of the tribal-military misadventure in Jammu and Kashmir, made the Pakistani establishment come to two conclusions. First, that Pakistan's identity based on the two-nation theory could be strengthened only by a greater and more aggressively articulated Islamic identity that should claim closer geopolitical and cultural connections with Muslim countries of West Asia and the Gulf. Second, Pakistan, given its comparative military weakness vis-à-vis India, should seek military and defence equations with countries which may be antagonistic towards India in the context of their geo-strategic interests and ideological inclinations.

The US organised the North Atlantic Treaty Organisation (NATO), the Baghdad Pact (CENTO), the South East Asia Treaty Organisation (SEATO), and the Australia-New Zealand-US Security Pact (ANZUS). This exercise in encirclement was completed with separate security pacts signed by the US with Japan, and the Republic of China (Taiwan). Pakistan decided to become a part of this arrangement offering to be a link in these military pacts at the southern flank of Soviet Central Asia and at the northwestern edge of the Indian subcontinent. It took two steps to meet its geo-strategic and security objectives. It signed bilateral defence cooperation agreements with the US in 1954, and became a member of the CENTO and SEATO military alliances. It must be underlined that Pakistan's motivation in going down this path had only a limited convergence with the broad strategic objectives of the US. The US welcomed Pakistan as a minor link in its anti-communist strategic planning with the additional motivation that a Pakistan with security linkages with the US, could become a counter to the developing Indian links with the Soviet Union, and to a limited extent against the possible Sino-Indian equation, which seemed on the cards till the mid-1950s. Pakistan's joining of US-led military alliances was not rooted in any profound antagonism against communist states. Its expectation was that these military alliances would enable Pakistan to counter political or military threats from India.

By 1955, India had commenced its countermoves by expanding its economic, technological and military relationship with the Soviet Union. It is relevant to note at this point that General Iskander Mirza and General Ayub Khan had become members of the Pakistan Cabinet as minister for the interior and minister for defence respectively. Ayub was the main architect of the defence cooperation arrangements between the US and Pakistan. Therefore, when he assumed power as the military chief of Pakistan, he had to face two prejudices from India. First, he had replaced a democratic government and at least one prime minister, Bogra, with whom Nehru had established a certain rapport. The second disadvantage was the knowledge in India that Ayub was the person who had fashioned the close US-Pakistan defence relationship between 1954 and 1959. Having said this, objectivity demands that one analyse Ayub Khan's India policies at least until the year 1964 with detachment. During this period, he desired to restore political stability, good governance and a clean and efficient administration within Pakistan. He wished to assuage the feelings of his East Pakistani compatriots. He also wished to remedy the setbacks that Pakistan had received in Jammu and Kashmir between 1947 and 1950. More important, he wanted to see if he could break the political impasse which India and Pakistan had reached on Kashmir.

By 1957, India had come to the conclusion that the United Nations and the Western powers were not going to accept the Indian stand on Kashmir. Consequently, it had pulled back from its original offer of holding a plebiscite in Kashmir. Krishna Menon had stated all this in the United Nations Security Council session debates in 1957. India's Kashmir policy had undergone a qualitative change compared to what it was between 1947 and 1952. General Ayub wished to defreeze the stalemate.

The Water Problem

General Ayub Khan was equally concerned about the major economic threat which India could pose for Pakistan. The headwaters of all the rivers flowing into Punjab and then joining as tributaries of the Indus were in those portions of Jammu and Kashmir and Punjab that were in India. Pakistan's agriculture and food security depended on some durable agreement with India ensuring uninterrupted flow of waters through the river basins of Jhelum, Ravi, Chenab and the Satluj. He was keen to come to an agreement with India to meet this objective. China's acquisition of Tibet and the rapport between China and India and the Soviet Union and India in the mid-1950s concerned Ayub. One remedial measure he put in place was the defence linkage with the US, which was both multilateral and bilateral. He was strategically adroit enough to feel that, if possible, he should also come to some understanding with India about avoiding a confrontation.

He did initiate policies to meet these objectives during the first five years of his tenure, until about 1964. He inducted more Bengali civil servants into the administration of East Pakistan. He also increased the recruitment of Bengali officers into the Pakistani armed forces and he certainly brought about more efficiency in the domestic administration of Pakistan. Realising that the province of Punjab and its people were the dominant political factor in the Pakistani polity, he decided to shift the capital from Karachi to Islamabad, near Rawalpindi. The other factor influencing this decision was his valid judgement that he should remain proximate to headquarters of the Pakistani Army and the main military cantonments of Pakistan at Rawalpindi and in other parts of Punjab.

As far as the sharing of river and canal waters was concerned, given the economic importance of the issue, it roused emotions and widespread bitterness between India and Pakistan, even threatening a possible war. Pakistan was of the view that as a lower riparian state, it should be given full access to the river and canal waters, particularly of the Ravi and Satluj which formed part of the boundary between India and Pakistan. Short-term arrangements were somehow put in place between 1947 and 1951. Two eminent Americans made suggestions which ultimately resolved this problem. David Lilienthal, former chairman of the Tennessee Valley Authority, after discussions with the then US secretary of state, Dean Acheson, visited Pakistan in February 1951, after which he made the suggestion that "India and Pakistan work out a programme jointly to develop and jointly operate the Indus Basin River System, upon which both nations are dependent for irrigation waters. With more dams and irrigation canals the Indus and its tributaries could be made to yield additional water which each country needs for increased food production." He went on to suggest that the World Bank, with the support of the United States, might function as a facilitator to bring India and Pakistan together to negotiate an agreement for this purpose and then possibly finance the implementation of the agreement they reached. The then president of the World Bank, Eugene R. Black, supported Lilienthal's proposals. By the spring of 1954, World Bank experts had put forward proposals. The waters of the three eastern rivers — Ravi, Beas and Satluj — should be utilised exclusively by India. The waters of the three western rivers — Indus, Jhelum and Chenab — would be used exclusively by Pakistan. A new set of canals would be constructed to convey waters from the western rivers to those areas of Pakistan which until Partition had depended for their irrigation on water from the Ravi, Beas and Satluj. Lastly, in the transition period when these canals were being constructed, India would ensure the minimum necessary water supplies to Pakistan. India accepted these proposals in their entirety, but Pakistan had some objections, which from their point of view were logical. During the above-mentioned interim period, Pakistan could suffer from canal water shortages.

The World Bank in the meantime promised large-scale financial and technical assistance if an agreement based on its proposals could be finalised. After a series of meetings in Rome, London and Washington, an agreement was finalised just when Ayub took over as supreme authority in Pakistan. It would be pertinent to mention that the three individuals who deserve unqualified credit for the finalisation of this agreement were W.A.B. Illif, then vice-president of the World Bank, and senior technocrats G. Mueen-ud-Din from Pakistan and N.D. Ghulati from India. The agreement was made possible because Ayub, untrammelled by political considerations and with his military background, gave the necessary political impetus, which already had the endorsement of Nehru. The Indus Waters Treaty between India and Pakistan was signed on 19 September 1960 at Karachi by Nehru, Ayub and Illif and was ratified in January 1961. It had, however, come into force retroactively before the monsoon season of 1960, i.e., from April onwards. Welcoming the resolution of this problem, considered almost intractable since 1947, General Ayub Khan made a public statement, the text of which speaks for itself:

> The signing of the Indus Water Treaty is an event of historic importance to the two countries concerned. And if I may say so, in all humility before the whole world, the solution of a problem

of this magnitude on the peaceful settlement of which depended the lives and livelihood of millions of people, has been achieved after very difficult negotiations which have dragged on for over a decade.

I had mentioned the Pakistani apprehensions about China's intentions after the latter's takeover of Tibet. They were rooted in speculation about the Chinese attitude towards Pakistan in the context of Pakistan being a partner in the US-led military alliances. But by 1959, these apprehensions were no longer a factor in Pakistani policies. Sino-Indian relations had started running into difficulties, with Chinese maps claiming large segments of Indian territory in Ladakh, in the border areas between UP and Tibet and in the northeast, especially areas in Nagaland and Arunachal Pradesh. India had discovered the Chinese building a road in Aksai Chin in Ladakh and protested. Border skirmishes between Indian and Chinese border patrols gradually increased and had reached a repetitive confrontation pattern by 1959.

A Joint Defence Agreement

Though Pakistan was watching the deterioration in Sino-Indian relations, and was in the process of determining new options in its China policy, it felt some kind of a No War or Defence Agreement with India would reduce the possibilities of China impinging on the security environment of Pakistan and India. Though Pakistan had rejected a suggestion from Nehru in 1949 for a No War Pact, Ayub revived the proposal in another form on 24 April 1959. Pakistan had rejected India's No War Pact offer in the immediate aftermath of its troops and lashkars being defeated in Jammu and Kashmir, considering Nehru's suggestion as an attempt to prevent it from taking any military initiative to capture Kashmir.

Ayub's offer was for a joint defence agreement. The year 1959 is significant because it was in the spring and summer of this year that the break-up between the Dalai Lama and the Chinese leadership became final. The Dalai Lama escaped into India and was given political asylum. The Government of Pakistan was concerned about the direct Chinese intervention in Tibet. This was given expression to by the Pakistani ambassador in Tokyo, Mohammed Ali, who said on 20 April 1959 : "The Tibetan issue has jolted Asian people out of their complacency. The Tibetan revolt should have more impact on Asia than the invasion of Hungary by Russia. The Chinese have followed the same pattern, which should open the eyes of Asia to the danger of red imperialism."

Nehru's response to Ayub's proposal for a joint defence agreement was acerbically short. He inquired: "Who is the joint defence aimed at?" Speaking in the Lok Sabha on 4 May 1959, Jawaharlal Nehru said: "I am all for settling our problems with Pakistan and living normal, friendly and neighbourly lives. But we do not want to have a common defence policy which is almost some kind of military alliance. I do not understand against whom people talk about common defence policies." Nehru was still immersed in the idea that India's positive relations with China could be sustained and that they were an essential factor for Asian peace and stability. He considered any agreement with Pakistan as hobnobbing with a junior partner in the Cold War. So he rejected Ayub's offer.

Another reason for this rejection was Nehru's assessment that such a defence agreement with Pakistan would be utilised by Pakistan as a springboard to force a compromise on Jammu and Kashmir which would suit Pakistan. Nehru's position on Jammu and Kashmir had hardened considerably over the previous decade, first because of the 1947-48 war with Pakistan; second, because of the unsatisfactory manner (from India's point of view) in which the UN dealt with the issue; and third, the political uncertainties about Kashmir's status which Sheikh Abdullah tried to create in the early 1950s, compelling Nehru to have him dismissed from the premiership of Jammu and Kashmir and imprison him. Nehru also perceived the joint defence agreement as a measure against an external threat. He preferred a bilateral No War Pact with Pakistan.

Ayub was disappointed with Nehru's response. In his autobiography *Friends not Masters* he states: "There was nothing sinister in the proposal. Nor was I the first one to have made it. The Qaid-e-Azam thought that it was of vital importance to Pakistan and India as independent sovereign states, to collaborate in a friendly way, and jointly to defend their frontiers both on land and sea against any aggression." Ayub was quoting an interview given by Jinnah to a Swiss newspaper *Neue Zurcher Zeitung*, Zurich, on 11 March 1948. To correspondent Eric Streiff, he said: "Our own paramount interests demand that the Dominion of Pakistan and the Dominion of India should coordinate for the purpose of playing their part in international affairs and in the developments that may take place." Analysts of both countries have been critical of Nehru's rejection of Ayub's offer and then they proceed to the conclusion that it was in consequence of Nehru's rejectionist approach that Ayub turned Pakistani policies to befriend China. But Ayub's motivations for offering a joint defence pact found a clearer expression after he met Nehru briefly at Palam airport on 1 September 1959, when he said: "What I had in mind was a general understanding for peace between the two countries. I emphasised that the prerequisite for such understanding was the solution of big problems like Kashmir and the canal waters. Once these are solved, the armies of the two countries could disengage and move to their respective vulnerable frontiers. This would give us the substance of joint defence. That is, freedom to protect our respective frontiers." India's former high commissioner to Pakistan, Kewal Singh, commented on this statement, saying: "Ayub thus confirmed the views of our officials who believed that his joint defence proposal was not sincere but was aimed at forcing India to give up her position on Kashmir and the Canal Waters dispute." Whatever the points of debate may be, Pakistan commenced its overtures to China late in 1959.

If one looks back on the ups and downs characterising Indo-Pakistani relations during the Ayub era, the signing of the Indus Waters Treaty and his offer of a defence pact were the last positive elements in them. Once President Ayub Khan consolidated himself in power, Jawaharlal Nehru rightly came to the conclusion that sending eminent political figures to interact with the Pakistani leadership as in the pre-Partition days, as India's high commissioners to Karachi would not be useful. The Indian representative had to be a person knowledgeable about the socio-cultural background and mindset of the new military power structure. Nehru, therefore, chose Rajeshwar Dayal, a former member of the British Indian Civil Service (ICS) who had served the pre-Partition British Government of India for nearly fourteen years. Dayal had joined the ICS in 1933 and had served mostly in UP before Partition. During this period he had served a stint as the district officer in Agra at a point of time when General Ayub Khan was also posted in the Agra Cantonment as a young officer of the British Indian Army in the late 1930s. Ayub and Dayal had struck up an acquaintance during this period which resulted in some kind of personal contact being maintained. Dayal was appointed India's high commissioner to Karachi early in 1961, in the expectation that his personal rapport with Ayub Khan might help in restoring some normality to Indo-Pakistan relations. The brief period that he served in Karachi, about a year from 1961 to 1962, was influenced by the personal friendship between Ayub Khan and Dayal to the extent it could be. But it could not transcend the adversarial chemistry of relations rooted in the Kashmir issue and in Pakistan's growing defence relationship with the Western camp.

One also has to add that Rajeshwar Dayal could not give focused attention to Indo-Pakistan relations during his tenure in Karachi. He was simultaneously involved with the United Nations peace-keeping initiatives in the Congo and its aftermath, following Patrice Lumumba's and Dag

Hammerskjold's assassinations. In any case, Dayal's heart and intellect were more involved with the UN rather than with what was considered by many ICS officers in the Foreign Service as the diplomatic backwaters — South Asia. This attempt at utilising personal equations for larger political purposes did not succeed, as is usual in most cases.

The period between 1959 and 1961 witnessed a deterioration in Sino-Indian relations, which was to culminate in the war of October-November 1962. The deep differences on the boundary between India and China came out into the open from 1959 onwards, when border clashes between Indian and Chinese border patrols started taking place with painful regularity. Discussions between Chou En-Lai and Nehru on the boundary question were abortive. The official-level boundary talks between 1959 and 1961 became progressively acrimonious and polemical. The last round held in Rangoon in 1961 signalled their complete breakdown. The Chinese also began to establish additional forward border posts and to strengthen their patterns of border patrolling.

Zulfiqar Ali Bhutto

The relevance of making a general reference to deteriorating Sino-Indian relations lies in the fact that President Ayub Khan's government watched these developments with interest. One individual in Ayub's government who was an assiduous observer of Sino-Indian relations during this period, and who sought to exploit the situation to Pakistan's advantage, was Zulfiqar Ali Bhutto. He had joined Ayub's government as its youngest cabinet minister, dealing with the portfolios of information, petroleum and energy resources, commerce and ultimately foreign affairs. While Ayub was reticent about improving relations with China, given his understanding of the Cold War equations between the US on the one hand and China and the Soviet Union on the other, Bhutto was a more perceptive observer of the nuances and undercurrents of interstate relationships. He had taken note of a series of confrontations between the Soviet Union and the US during the late 1950s and early 1960s, which began with Russia's shooting down of the U-2 spy plane and culminated in the Cuban missile crisis in 1962. His conclusion was the USSR's strategic and foreign policy concerns would be focused on the US and Western Europe, it might not be inclined to support India fully, despite the evolving closeness between Moscow and New Delhi since 1955.

Bhutto was also equally quick in taking note of the ideological and political differences emerging between China and the Soviet Union. He correctly assessed the negative chemistry between Nikita Khrushchev and Mao Zedong and also discerned some anxiety on the part of the Soviet Union to project communist unity against the challenges posed by the US and the Western democracies. He therefore started advocating Pakistan's foreign and security policies should work on improving relations with China as an important and immediate objective. He gave the valid assessment that if such a Sino-Pakistan equation could be established it could counter India's capacity to threaten Pakistan. He also argued that it would enhance the security of East Pakistan in case there was an Indian threat there. Ayub was initially reluctant to accept Bhutto's advice, but his views changed when the Sino-Indian conflict occurred. India suffered a decisive military defeat. In the initial stages of the conflict the Soviet Union did not give even political support to India, and no military assistance came to India during the conflict. In contrast, the Americans were quick to respond to India's request for political support and military assistance. The positive response of the US, despite India's non-aligned foreign policy proved that Bhutto's analysis regarding China was valid. Bhutto was authorised to open up contacts with China, which he did effectively and successfully.

The first tangible manoeuvre he undertook was the boundary agreement he signed with China relating to those portions of Jammu and Kashmir under Pakistani occupation and bordering western Tibet and Xinjiang. Bhutto correctly discerned Chinese anxieties and interests in consolidating their position in Tibet, and organising a secure communication network between Tibet and Xinjiang. The construction of a road in the Aksai Chin area belonging to Ladakh was a part of this exercise. It sparked off the Sino-Indian boundary controversy. Bhutto, with Ayub's approval, offered geo-strategic security to the Chinese communication links between western Tibet and Xinjiang and also for the land route for trade with Pakistan from Tibet by offering to cede the entire stretch of territory at the northern edge of Jammu and Kashmir to China, and to draw a new Sino-Pakistan international boundary. This agreement was signed in the aftermath of India's military defeat by China in 1962. Bhutto achieved three objectives in one go. He gave concrete proof of Pakistan's interest in having a long-term relationship with China and created a vested interest for China in sustaining such a relationship. By ceding territory belonging to the old state of Jammu and Kashmir, which was (and is) technically claimed by India, he destroyed India's jurisdictional stand on the area by creating a ground reality whereby India would have to contend not only with Pakistan but with China in establishing its claim on the area and regaining it. Third, by signing the boundary agreement with

China, he endorsed the Chinese stand on border issues: that borders drawn up during the colonial period have no permanent or legal validity.

Pakistan had made a suggestion to China for the demarcation of the boundary between Xinjiang on the one hand and Gilgit on the other on 3 May 1962, even before the Sino-Indian war. The Sino-Pakistan boundary agreement was signed on 2 March 1963. It resulted in China recognising and supporting Pakistan's stand on the Kashmir issue at that point of time. It is also interesting to note that during the Sino-Indian war in October-November 1962 there were suggestions from President John F. Kennedy to Ayub asking him to assure Nehru that Pakistan would not take any action on the Indo-Pakistani border. Kennedy's view was that if this assurance could be given to India, it could shift more forces from its western borders to counter the Chinese military threat. Ayub's response to Kennedy's message, sent on 28 October 1962 was categorically negative. He wrote: "I am surprised that such a request is being made to us. After all what we have been doing is nothing but to contain the threat that is constantly posed to us by India. Is it in conformity with human nature that we should cease to take such steps as are necessary for our self-preservation?" One speculates whether the Pakistani response would have been different had India accepted Ayub's proposal for a joint defence agreement. In fact, an additional negative development was Pakistan being strongly critical of the support given to India during the Sino-Indian conflict by Western democracies led by the US. An example was the then Pakistani foreign minister, Mohammed Ali, speaking in the Pakistan National Assembly saying: "Some of our allies and friends in their wisdom have decided to rush arms and equipment and military aid to India, which is posing a threat to our [Pakistan's] safety and security." Ayub added in his speech on the occasion: "The large expansion of the Indian Army is aimed at subjugating its small neighbouring countries, particularly Pakistan."

A critical consequence of the Sino-Indian conflict and Western military assistance flowing into India was the pressure generated on India to resolve the Kashmir issue on terms acceptable to Pakistan. The US and the UK were concerned about the Pakistani reactions to the support they had given to India against China, a support which was extended in the context of Cold War considerations. While their expectation was that the support extended to India might make it more amenable to their strategic orientations, they were realistic enough to know that there was no certainty India would fulfil these expectations. The long-term interests of the Western democracies necessitated their being responsive to Pakistan's declared apprehensions about India.

The result was the arrival of two special envoys, one from the US and another from the UK, to persuade India to reopen discussions on the Kashmir issue — on the backburner since the Security Council debates of 1957. Ambassador Averell Harriman came with suggestions from President Kennedy and Duncan Sandys from the UK came to back up Harriman's efforts. Their recommendations were detrimental to Indian interests. They implied that India should accept substantial territorial readjustments and should withdraw most of its troops and security forces from Kashmir. A generous assessment of Western motives given by some analysts was that in their desire to resist the Chinese threat to South Asia, the Western powers were attempting to create a better understanding between India and Pakistan. This was a patently blinkered assessment of Pakistani policies because by the time Harriman and Sandys were making their advocacies to India, the Pakistanis were already engaged in opening up lines with China and negotiating the boundary agreement, an agreement that more than settling the boundary between Pakistan and China was aimed at putting India on the defensive.

Nehru had to respond to the pressure from the US and the UK in the context of the support they had extended to India against China. Nehru and Ayub agreed to start a dialogue at the political level. Indo-Pakistan discussions on Kashmir commenced in Rawalpindi on 27 December 1962. The Indian delegation was led by then minister for railways, Sardar Swaran Singh, the Pakistani delegation by newly appointed foreign minister Zulfiqar Ali Bhutto. The atmosphere at the discussion was spoilt ab initio by the Pakistani government announcing just a couple of days before the talks started that Pakistan and China had reached an agreement to delineate the boundary between Pakistan-occupied Kashmir and China. Bhutto demanded a solution based on the UN Resolutions from 1948 to 1953 while Swaran Singh stressed that Jammu and Kashmir had become an integral part of India. The same arguments were repeated in five more rounds of discussions in Delhi and Rawalpindi, which followed till May 1963. It must also be mentioned that Sandys was openly pro-Pakistan in his advocacies to India on Kashmir, while Harriman assiduously emphasised that the US wanted a fair and objective solution and that it was not demanding any quid pro quo for the military assistance it gave India.

There were interesting facets to the 1962-63 negotiations between Swaran Singh and Bhutto. My colleagues from the Ministry of External Affairs who participated in these discussions have told me that there was a stark difference between the negotiating styles. Bhutto, many years younger than Swaran Singh, was assertive, polemical and focused on specific points of interest to Pakistan. He also indulged in his penchant for political and strategic analysis about Pakistan's geopolitical interests and its ethnic and geopolitical claims on Jammu and Kashmir. Bhutto was also tense and somewhat acerbic in his presentations. Swaran Singh in contrast was laid back, and soporifically self-confident. Throughout the negotiations he insisted that Pakistan could not lay claim to Jammu and Kashmir on the basis of a unilateral assertion based on the two-nation theory or speculative claims on parts of Indian territory. He emphasised the resolution of the Jammu and Kashmir issue had to be based on the legal and constitutional stipulations that governed the partition of India. Swaran Singh's approach was deliberately descriptive and ambulatory. The story goes that after the first two rounds of negotiations, Bhutto told members of his delegation that "the objective of the Sardarji was not to negotiate but to exhaust him [Bhutto]". Bhutto is reported to have said that it was impossible to have a logical and meaningful discussion with Swaran Singh. One speculates that being the seasoned politician that Swaran Singh was, he decided to confound Bhutto and the Pakistani delegation by adopting negotiating tactics which would firmly safeguard India's interests, and at the same time convey a clear message to Pakistan that unilateral demands for a Pakistan-oriented compromise on Kashmir would not wash. That this message was absorbed by Pakistan became clear when it launched military operations in Jammu and Kashmir within two years of the breakdown of negotiations on 16 May 1963.

Lal Bahadur Shastri

Jawaharlal Nehru passed away in May 1964 and Lal Bahadur Shastri replaced him as prime minister. Though one of the most respected leaders of the Congress Party with a reputation for moderation, efficiency and integrity, Shastri had little experience of international relations. Compared to Nehru he was practically an unknown figure, even to the Pakistan power structure. There was also his reputation of being non-assertive and accommodating with an aversion for confrontations, in direct contrast to the Pakistan leadership, with a military figure like Ayub as head of state and an aggressive foreign minister like Bhutto. Bhutto was also imbued with the ambition of making Pakistan a major power in South Asia. The failure of the 1962-63 discussions resulted in Pakistan coming to the conclusion that the US and the Western powers would not be critical of Pakistan if it resorted to force again to acquire Jammu and Kashmir. The assessment was Western powers would be inclined to assuage Pakistani feelings and be responsive to their concerns resulting from the short-term political and defence cooperation undertaken with India during the Sino-Indian war. The two-year period between 1962 and 1964 witnessed critical developments in Indo-Pakistani relations with high levels of violence against the Hindu minority in East Pakistan. After the breakdown of talks on Jammu and Kashmir, Pakistan also mounted a sustained publicity and diplomatic campaign against India. Pakistan had a handle to do this because there was retaliatory communal violence against Muslims in West Bengal and Bihar. Eventually, these developments culminated in two military conflicts with Pakistan — one in the Rann of Kutch in the summer of 1965 and a second large-scale conflict in Jammu and Kashmir in August-September 1965.

Pakistan felt India was demoralised after being defeated by China and that the army was weak, psychologically vulnerable and dispirited. Second, the assessment was that after Nehru's death, the Indian political system was subject to great uncertainties and that the government had a weak leader in Shastri. Third, it somehow came to the conclusion that the people of Jammu and Kashmir had been alienated from India, particularly after India's defeat by the Chinese. The Pakistani expectation was that the people, particularly in the Valley, would rise to secede from India as soon as Pakistani armed forces actively intruded into Jammu and Kashmir. Fourth, Pakistan felt that the international community would not oppose their military intervention in the context of India having shown a total unwillingness to change its stand on Kashmir during the 1962-63 talks. The assessment was that even if the Western powers did not support the Pakistani military operations, they would not oppose them. Fifth, the exploratory military operations which Pakistan launched in the Rann of Kutch had resulted in some marginal successes for the Pakistani forces, which confirmed assessment of the Indian Army's vulnerability.

So the Pakistanis concluded that they could safely take on the Indian Army in a limited theatre operation of their choice, namely, in Jammu and Kashmir. The expectation was that India would respond militarily only in areas where Pakistan launched military operations.

The conflict in Kutch, characterised by off-again on-again short battles was brought to an end by a cease-fire signed on 30 June 1965, with both governments agreeing to settle the boundary conflict in Kutch either by ministerial discussions through an international tribunal. Shastri simultaneously offered a No War Pact to Pakistan again, which was rejected. The dispute on the border in Kutch went up for consideration to the International Tribunal under the chairmanship of a Swedish judge, Gunnar Lagergen. Other members of the Tribunal were Dr Nasorullah Intzam of Iran, nominated by Pakistan, and Dr L.S. Bebler of Yugoslavia, nominated by India. The Tribunal had 170 sittings between 1965 and 1967 and gave its final award on 21 February 1968, demarcating a boundary which was accepted by both governments. The only segment of this boundary not demarcated at that point of time was the boundary at Sir Creek, which is still hanging fire. But as mentioned before, the Pakistani military initiatives in Kutch were to make an assessment of India's military capacities and somehow convinced it that Indian armed forces could be overcome in Jammu and Kashmir. The plans for invading Kashmir and organising its separation from India were well under way from early spring 1965. Bhutto was the primary political architect of this military misadventure.

The plan was first to infiltrate thousands of tribals and organised lashkars from the NWFP and from Pakistani-occupied Kashmir into the Indian side of Jammu and Kashmir. Their task was to disrupt all the communication networks, to attack military installations and centres of command and control, and to capture airports and strategic points on important road links between the Indian parts of Jammu and Kashmir. Once these operations were launched these intruding cadre were to seek help from the people of Jammu and Kashmir to dislodge the Indian security forces and the elected government of G.M. Sadiq. The establishment of a Revolutionary Governing Council of Jammu and Kashmir, would then be announced. It would declare the separation of Jammu and Kashmir from India and its intention of joining Pakistan. If this initial push did not succeed in meeting all these objectives, the Pakistani armed forces were to participate directly. A decision was also taken to project these critical developments as an indigenous uprising with which Pakistan had nothing to do. The plans were to be put in operation by the Pakistani authorities on the night of 5 August 1965, with large numbers of Pakistan-based infiltrators moving into Jammu and Kashmir across the ceasefire line. Interestingly, Pakistan chose to indulge in a farcical gesture of courtesy to uphold the myth of its non-involvement in the conflict about to begin.

The new Indian high commissioner to Pakistan, Kewal Singh, reached Karachi on the afternoon of 5 August 1965. Though the ceremony for the presentation of credentials was fixed for 10 August, he got a message from Rawalpindi that as a special gesture of courtesy, Ayub would receive him the very next morning, that is, 6 August. Overcoming various logistical difficulties, including obtaining his Letters of Credence by a special courier from Delhi, Kewal Singh reached Rawalpindi and presented his credentials to President Ayub Khan. Ayub, in his speech, emphasised that he was reciprocating every move from India for a better understanding and cooperation between the two countries. Ayub expressed regret that both

India and Pakistan were spending vast sums of money on defence due to their unfortunate relationship, money that should have been diverted to economic development. Ayub was spouting these positive sentiments while being fully aware that thousands of Pakistan-trained and well-armed guerrillas had started crossing the cease-fire line about 12 hours earlier.

It was during the first five days, between 5 August and 10 August 1965 that one of the basic Pakistani assessments was proved wrong. Instead of people in the Valley rising in support of the guerrillas, and acting against their government and security forces, the local population gave continuous and detailed information about the movement of infiltrators to India's security forces. The population actively participated in resisting the infiltrators, in tracing them and in having them either neutralised or arrested. It is obvious that Ayub desired to get the formal accreditation of the Indian high commissioner over before news about Pakistani infiltration into Kashmir reached the world at large. He also wanted to prevent an Indian diplomatic withdrawal as the infiltration was supposed to be a spontaneous internal movement in Jammu and Kashmir. The Indian high commissioner not presenting his credentials because of the conflict might have let the cat out of the bag. Kewal Singh was instructed on 9 August to convey a firm message to Ayub about India's determination to resist the infiltrators and to push them back. Kewal Singh did not get the appointment for nearly 24 hours, as the security situation in Jammu and Kashmir deteriorated. Foreign Minister Bhutto received Kewal Singh at about 7 p.m. on 10 August and promptly disclaimed any Pakistani links with the evolving violent situation in Kashmir. Bhutto in his public pronouncements stated: "No stretch of the imagination can put the blame for whatever is happening in Kashmir on Pakistan. It is a spontaneous uprising of the people of Kashmir." He also indulged in clever anticipatory tactics, saying that India was preparing for an attack on Pakistan to retaliate against the genuine people's movement against India in Jammu and Kashmir.

The whole plan of infiltration aimed at separating Jammu and Kashmir from India and absorbing it into Pakistan was carefully prepared. It was called "Operation Gibraltar", and there is confirmed information on record that preparations for the 1965 conflict had been under way since April/May 1965. Emergency ordinances were promulgated by Ayub, raising the strength of Pakistani reservists and the strength of the paramilitary mujahideen force to more than 100,000. These cadres were given intensive military training at Murree and adjacent areas under the supervision of Major General Akhtar Hussain Malik, GOC of the 12th Division of the Pakistan Army. Foreign Minister Bhutto actively participated in discussions leading to the finalisation of the Gibraltar Plan. Operational techniques were based on the tactics of the People's Liberation Army of China and Algerian guerrillas. The plan envisaged the destruction of the logistical command and control systems of the Indian security forces and the administration of the elected government of Jammu and Kashmir. Once the initial operations succeeded, a revolutionary council would set up a provisional government of free Jammu and Kashmir. This government was ultimately to be backed by two divisions of the Pakistani armed forces masquerading as Kashmiri freedom fighters and guerrillas.

Though the Pakistani government and media reported successes by the so-called freedom fighters, the picture became clear by the end of August. Some of the prisoners taken by the Indian security forces revealed themselves to be regular officers of the Pakistani armed forces. They confessed to having prepared for the attack for nearly six months, to three months' intensive training before they launched themselves into Indian territory. American and British correspondents located in Delhi, Rawalpindi and Karachi confirmed in their despatches by the middle of August that the infiltration was undertaken by Pakistan-officered commandos and that they had proceeded in pre-planned missions to bomb bridges, army depots and several other government installations. The chief military observer of the UN in Jammu and Kashmir, General Nimmo, confirmed to Secretary General U. Thant, that the infiltrators were from Pakistan and had been trained and supported there.

Later information indicated that before India and Pakistan were formally engaged in the war, mujahideen infiltrators numbered about 150,000. These infiltrators were organised into eight forces. Each of these forces consisted of six groups of mujahideen infiltrators, numbering 110 men in each company. Approximately 5,000 infiltrators moved into India's Jammu and Kashmir between 5 August and 10 August. They failed in their mission because of local resistance from the people and by the locally supported Indian security forces. It became clear to the Pakistani authorities that the use of force in a clandestine form was failing. Pakistan therefore decided to take, direct, pre-emptive military action against India. It launched an open attack with heavy armour on 1 September in the Chhamb district, where the ceasefire line ran into the international border, and was aimed at disrupting the main communication line between Jammu and Poonch, and Jammu and Srinagar. The attack was on the Chhamb Jaurian salient. The political and strategic objective was to isolate the Indian security forces in Jammu and Kashmir, and stop them from getting any support from the main military bases in India; and to encircle and cut off communications between

Indian and the Kashmir valley and then proceed to internationalise the Kashmir issue to the disadvantage of India.

An Unexpected Decision

The attack in the Chhamb sector came as a surprise. If India were to be defeated there, the Pakistani armed forces would have proceeded into Jammu and Kashmir from the southwestern flank while the infiltrators expanded their operations from the west and northwest. Pakistan made this strategic move on the basis of the assessment that India would not expand the scope of the conflict beyond the territories of Jammu and Kashmir. This is the second assessment that went wrong. The first Pakistani attack changed the whole nature of the conflict. India had to take remedial action to disrupt Pakistani plans. First, it expanded the operational dimensions of the conflict by calling on the Indian armed forces, including the Indian Air Force, to counter the Pakistani armoured thrust in Chhamb and Jaurian. Prime Minister Shastri then took a totally unexpected decision, as far as Pakistan was concerned. He authorised the Indian armed forces to expand the scope of the war beyond Jammu and Kashmir, across the international border with Pakistan. They were authorised to launch offensives into Pakistani Punjab aiming at Lahore and Sialkot. It was now Pakistan's turn to be surprised. They had not anticipated India expanding the area of conflict to cover the most important province of Pakistan — Punjab, threatening its capital, Lahore. The primary Indian military objective was to relieve the Pakistani military pressure in the Chhamb-Akhnoor sector. Pakistan had to withdraw its forces from Chhamb and Akhnoor to resist the Indian offensives aimed at Lahore and Sialkot. India reduced both the inclination and ability of the Pakistani Army to directly invade Jammu and Kashmir, instead putting Pakistan on the defensive.

The systematic resistance against the Pakistani operations in the Punjab sector disproved two other predications on which Pakistan had based its operations. First, that the macro-level political power structure of India under the leadership of Lal Bahadur Shastri would not be capable of responding in a cohesive and decisive manner; second, that the Indian armed forces were demoralised due to their defeat by the Chinese.

As a consequence of the 1965 war which ended on 22 September, India controlled 720 square miles of Pakistani territory in Punjab, and Pakistan was in control of 220 square miles of Indian territory in Rajasthan. There were 12,500 Indian casualties; 2,700 killed, 1,500 either prisoners of war or were missing, 8,400 wounded. On the Pakistani side 3,000 were killed,

2,000 taken prisoner or missing, and roughly 9,000 were wounded. Pakistan lost 200 tanks with another 150 tanks put out of action. India lost 175 and 190 tanks with 200 tanks being put out of commission temporarily. Pakistan is reported to have lost 32 per cent of its armour, while India lost 27 per cent. Neither the Indian nor Pakistani navy played any significant role in the 1965 war. There are no definite figures concerning the loss of aircraft but on all counts both sides fought each other to a stalemate in the air. Pakistan lost 43 aircraft, India 59. The point to remember is that the Indian Air Force matched the performance of the Pakistani Air Force despite Pakistan having better aircraft like the F-104s and F-86s and Sabres when compared to India's World War II-vintage Gnats, Hunters, Mysteres, Vampires, Canberras, Packets, Dakotas and Austers. The most advanced aircraft the Indian Air Force had in 1965 was the MIG-21.

Though India claimed victory in the 1965 war, in purely operational and military terms it was a draw with no decisive military victory for either side. It was in politico-strategic terms and policy objectives that Pakistan was defeated. It was an incontrovertible fact that Pakistan initiated the conflict by organising first the massive tribal infiltration into Jammu and Kashmir under the covert invasion titled "Operation Gibraltar", and when it failed, deployed its regular army not only in Jammu and Kashmir but at the southern edge of the cease-fire line in the Chhamb-Jaurian sector, as part of "Operation Grand Slam".

The nomenclature tells its own story. The Arab general Abdur Rahman Tariq-ibn-Ziyad, whose forces captured Gibraltar in AD 711, ordered his men to burn their boats. (The older name of Gibraltar was Jibal-ul-Tariq.) When his soldiers asked how they would return to the Maghreb, General Abdur Rahman told them that the plan was to capture not only Gibraltar, but all of Spain (which the Muslims did between the 8th and 9th centuries) and that it was going to be a Muslim homeland. There was no question of returning to their places of origin. The psychological and emotional motivation for the Pakistan-sponsored infiltration into Jammu and Kashmir was obviously to make it part of Pakistan and a homeland for the Muslims. Pakistan was appealing to the collective historical and assertive Islamic memory of a conquest of nearly a thousand years earlier.

India was without doubt taken by surprise. But once retaliatory action commenced, the objectives were very clear: first to completely thwart any kind of Pakistani territorial acquisition, the second to resort to multiple options to make the military resistance to Pakistan successful. Prime Minister Shastri and his senior advisers took the conscious decision not to limit the area of conflict, but to expand it, to qualitatively reduce Pakistan's capacity to concentrate its forces. The third decision was to carry on military operations only up to the point where Pakistan was compelled to pull back from its military misadventure in Jammu and Kashmir. At no point of time was there any motivation to capture a major Pakistani city or to remain in military domination in any part of Pakistan. When India launched its offensive across the international frontier, Pakistan accused India of hegemonistic designs. The Pakistani public and diplomatic analysis of Indian objectives was that it wanted a comprehensive defeat of the Pakistani Army, that India desired to capture and integrate large portions of Pakistan back into India and that the aim was to undo Partition. There was also a more cautious school of Pakistani analysts who assessed that the Indian objective was to capture the major cities of Lahore and Sialkot, to hold them under occupation, and then to dictate peace terms.

Military analysts and scholars, however, later came to the conclusion that India had a limited objective. First, the retaliation against the onslaught in the Chhamb-Jaurian sector was to relieve Pakistani military pressure there. India's objective was only to relieve Akhnoor, and then to reduce the across-the-border pressure being engineered by Pakistan in Jammu and Kashmir. In fact, India was somewhat surprised at the speed with which its forces moved into the vicinity of Lahore during the 1965 war. Objectivity however, demands the acknowledgement that Lahore was well defended. Capturing the city itself would have been a very difficult task, and keeping and holding it even more so.

One must mention in parentheses that there were no land operations between East Pakistan and the eastern states of India of any significance. There was a very short air battle in the eastern sector, with Indian aircraft bombing Chittagong and Pakistani aircraft bombing selected air bases and air defence centres in West Bengal and Assam. This was a marginal phenomenon.

By the third week of September, international efforts got into full swing to bring an end to the conflict. The US took the first initiatives. Once General Nimmo, the United Nations military observer confirmed Pakistani infiltration and the Pakistan armed forces' direct involvement in Jammu and Kashmir, the US, instead of cutting all flows of military supplies and equipment to Pakistan urged that India and Pakistan should allow the UN secretary-general to resolve the issue. The Pakistani armed forces had used US-built armour, aircraft and a variety of radar and communication, and surveillance equipment supplied to it by the US against the Indian Army. The US again assumed an impartial stance in this conflict between India and Pakistan. The US, conscious of its defence and strategic links with Pakistan and its somewhat disappointing experience in security and political cooperation with India after the Sino-Indian war of 1962, decided to be even-handed. This was despite repeated requests from the US Ambassador in New Delhi at that time, Chester Bowles, urging direct pressure at the earliest possible moment on both sides, particularly on Pakistan to accept the cease-fire. Even Bowles did not show any elementary sensitivity about the situation or about Indian concerns. When the Pakistanis escalated the conflict on 1 September 1965, by launching their regular forces in the Chhamb-Jaurian sector, Ambassador Bowles asked Indian Foreign Minister Swaran Singh to be cautious, warning that a military thrust by India at some more favourable point against the Pakistani move would almost certainly touch off a war.

Swaran Singh, of course, told Bowles that he should concentrate on persuading Pakistan not to use US-supplied Patton tanks against India's armed forces, an action that was contrary to assurances given by the US to India. The attitude of the US seemed to be that if Pakistan succeeded in its efforts, there would be no harm. Reacting to Bowles' suggestion that military supplies be cut off to Pakistan, the then secretary of state, Dean Rusk, informed the ambassador: "The highest-level decision taken here is not to engage in direct pressure on either Pakistan or India for the time being but to place primary reliance on the UN. Given existing strains in relations with both parties, we do not believe such further actions as threats to suspend military aid along the lines you suggested is likely to halt the fighting at this time." The US only indicated its willingness to generally support UN Secretary-General U. Thant's efforts. It was only as the UN pressure for a cease-fire mounted that the Americans even-handedly stopped military assistance to both India and Pakistan.

Encouraging the Russians

Objectively speaking, US policies in 1965 disappointed both India and Pakistan. India was logically upset about US-supplied Pakistani military equipment being used against it. Pakistan was equally, if not more, upset at the US not giving open support and pulling back from certain aspects of military and economic assistance. In any case, the US was not interested in undertaking a genuine mediatory effort because that might have involved a dilution of its strategic and defence relationship with Pakistan. The Cold War was at its height. The US, therefore, indicated to the Soviet Union that it would have no objection to a Russian mediatory effort. The discussions leading to the Tashkent Conference in January 1966 will be touched upon later but the American endorsement of the Soviet role in this South Asian crisis is worth understanding. Rusk explained the US rationale as follows: "We encouraged the Russians to go ahead with the Tashkent idea because we felt that we had nothing to lose. If they succeeded in bringing about a détente at Tashkent, then there would be peace on the subcontinent between India and Pakistan and we [the US] would gain from the fact. If the Russians failed at Tashkent, at least the Russians would have the experience of some of the frustration that we had faced for 20 years in trying to sort out things between India and Pakistan."

The point not articulated by Rusk was that if the Russians failed, Pakistani links with the US would become closer and India would be disillusioned with the Russians and may move towards the US. Rusk summed up the US attitude when recording for the Oral History section of the Lyndon B. Johnson Library: "India and Pakistan allowed the matter to escalate very fast on both sides, contrary to the advice that was being given to them by the US. So we in effect shrugged our shoulders and said well, if you are going to fight, go ahead and fight, but we are not going to pay for it." Another factor that influenced Washington policy-makers was that with the US becoming more involved with the Vietnam War, South Asia's importance in US political and security priorities declined. Washington, given its interests and involvement in Southeast Asia and the Far East, seemed willing to let Moscow be a major player in South Asian security affairs.

UN Initiatives

UN Secretary-General U. Thant and members of the Security Council were fully aware of the factual origins of the 1965 conflict in terms of Pakistan's massive covert and violent invasion of Jammu and Kashmir in the first week of August. General Nimmo, and his assistants in their reports to their headquarters clearly confirmed that Pakistani intrusions had taken place on a massive scale. Despite the factual position being observed by their own observers, the UN Security Council and the UN Secretary-General did not call for the withdrawal of the Pakistan-sponsored invaders from Jammu and Kashmir throughout August. The violent situation was only taken note of and general appeals were made for the restoration of peace.

The UN became more active only when the proxy war launched by Pakistan transformed itself into an open conflict and war was declared on 1 September 1965, when the Indian armed forces launched their counteroffensive against the military thrust on the Chhamb-Jaurian-Akhnoor salient. The reaction of the UN was again pusillanimous and woodenly formalistic. U.Thant issued appeals for a ceasefire, for the cessation of hostilities by both sides, the restoration of the ceasefire line, etc. He appealed to Ayub to observe the ceasefire instead of demanding that Pakistan pull back its tribals and its army to its side of the ceasefire line. India was asked to be restrained in its retaliatory action! The Pakistani response to U.Thant's appeal was of disdainful silence, while India said it would act with restraint if the UN persuaded Pakistan to withdraw its infiltrators and regular forces. But what was important was the tone of the letters of the secretary-general to both India and Pakistan. It confirmed the assessment of the UN not being inclined to take a stand on the cause of the conflict. U.Thant, in his letter to both governments dated 1 September (given the time difference between the subcontinent and New York of nearly nine and a half hours, the letter must have been issued after the war expanded across the international frontier between India and Pakistan), wrote: "Without any attempt to apportion blame it may be said that such actions now come from both sides of the line, involving an increasingly large number of armed men on each side and take place in the air as well as on the ground. Most serious of all, it is my understanding that regular army troops from both countries are now engaged in military actions along and across the Line."

There was a deliberate disinclination to take note of Pakistan's initiating the conflict without any provocation. The UN Security Council met on 4 September. It passed a resolution calling on both governments to forthwith take all steps for an immediate cease-fire and to equally respect the cease-fire line and withdraw the armed forces, of both sides, that had transgressed the Line. An interesting point is that this resolution was moved by the non-permanent members of the UN Security Council with none of the five permanent members taking any active part. They were busy managing affairs behind the scenes within the framework of their own respective strategic and political interests. There was no criticism of Pakistan trying to alter by force the territorial arrangements of Partition, underpinned by law and constitutional arrangements.

Secretary-General U.Thant visited Islamabad and New Delhi in the second week of September 1965. In his discussions with the prime minister of India and the president of Pakistan he called for an immediate and unconditional stoppage of hostilities by 14 September 1965. The Government of India responded immediately, accepting U.Thant's proposal provided Pakistan also accepted his suggestion. India also demanded that once hostilities ceased, Pakistan should withdraw its infiltrators and troops from Jammu and Kashmir and other parts of India. Pakistan indicated that it was agreeable to a ceasefire with its troops and infiltrating cadres remaining where they were while India should withdraw its troops from the Punjab. There was a clear contrast between the responses of India and Pakistan to the UN initiatives. Whereas India only made demands regarding troop withdrawals and so on, related to the actual conflict, Pakistan wanted the ceasefire to be conditional with all the old issues being revived. They wanted a UN military presence in Kashmir. They demanded that India agree to a plebiscite and they also showed an inclination to stay on inside the Indian territories where they had managed to gain some kind of foothold.

The secretary-general in his reports to the Security Council between 1 September and 16 September 1965 did not refer to the calculated disinclination of the five permanent members of the Security Council to act in unison to defuse the crisis. His reports did not take note of one of the big powers giving active political support to Pakistan and generating indirect military pressure on India. There was a reluctant acknowledgement of Pakistan's obduracy and its direct involvement in initiating the conflict. U.Thant in his report of 16 September, acknowledged that while India had accepted his suggestions, Pakistan had not. He also acknowledged in the report that a large number of tribesmen from the North West Frontier Province of Pakistan were participating in the conflict inside Jammu and Kashmir and on the border with India.

While all this was happening, the Soviet Union issued an appeal to the governments of India and Pakistan, expressing concern about the conflict and offering its good offices to organise a dialogue. This information was reported to the Security Council meetings on 17 September and 20 September 1965. By the 20th, there were general indications from both India and Pakistan that they might respond to the Soviet Union's offer. The Security Council passed a resolution on the 20 September demanding a cease-fire between India and Pakistan on the 22nd, the subsequent withdrawal of the forces of both parties to the positions held by them before 5 August 1965. The resolution asked the secretary-general to provide the necessary assistance to ensure the supervision of the ceasefire and to call on all states to refrain from any action that may aggravate the situation in the area. The resolution concluded by stating that the UN would consider steps that should be taken to help in the settlement of the Jammu and Kashmir issue.

In any case, neither Pakistan nor India had the capacity to remain involved in a prolonged conflict unless it became totally unavoidable. The suspension of military and economic assistance by the US and Britain to Pakistan in the later stages of the 1965 war had reduced its capacity to stay engaged in a military confrontation. While India was better placed in terms of conventional military capacities, in comparative terms, defence supplies from the Soviet Union had been reduced. Both India and Pakistan had lost 27 to 30 per cent of their armour and aircraft and Pakistan had to acknowledge that it was not going to achieve the objectives for which it had launched the offensive in Jammu and Kashmir. India had achieved the specific but limited objectives it had in mind in responding to the Pakistani offensive. The political and military realities and the ground situation persuaded both countries to respond to the suggestions for a ceasefire and a bilateral conference.

The general military conflict came to an end on 22 September and a ceasefire gradually came into being by December 1965. The Soviet Union had offered its good offices in the third week of September. On November 21, 1965 Prime Minister Alexei Kosygin renewed his invitation to India and Pakistan to come for a bilateral conference at a location in the Soviet Union acceptable to both sides. India and Pakistan accepted this renewed invitation in the first half of December 1965. It was agreed that the meeting would be held in Tashkent (in the Uzbek Soviet Republic) in the first week of January 1966.

The Chinese Role

The Tashkent Conference and its results had an impact not only on Indo-Pakistan relations but also on Pakistan's domestic politics. Analysis of the Tashkent deliberations should be preceded by a reference to the Chinese role during this conflict and the Soviet motivation in getting involved to bring this conflict to an end. There was a qualitative improvement in relations between China and Pakistan in the immediate aftermath of the Sino-Indian war of 1962. Pakistan had garnered additional goodwill from China by ceding territories belonging to Jammu and Kashmir to China, as mentioned earlier. China was also concerned about the incremental proximity between India and the Soviet Union and the American willingness to give military assistance to India after the border war. Bhutto had clearly initiated new orientations in Pakistan's foreign policy: developing close relations with China to counter "threats" from India. China was still not a member of the UN or its Security Council. So having a substantive cooperative relationship with Pakistan would not only serve the purpose of keeping India on the defensive but would also provide it with a foothold in Pakistan, a member of the Western system of military alliances aimed at, among other things, containing China. Pakistan could be a valuable source of information. A relationship with Pakistan would weaken a link in the Western chain of alliances stretching from Turkey to the Philippines. China, therefore, decided to back Pakistan by generating indirect political and military pressure on India during the conflict. Chinese Foreign Minister Marshall Chen Yi visited Karachi on 4 September 1965, within four days of open war between the two countries commencing. He had discussions with Zulfiqar Ali Bhutto. At a press conference at the end of his discussions, Chen Yi declared, "China fully supported the just action taken by Pakistan to repel the Indian armed provocation in Kashmir."

When the Indo-Pakistan war expanded, China decided to add a critical dimension to the tense situation. The Chinese Foreign Office lodged a strong protest with the Indian embassy in Beijing on 7 September accusing the Government of India of successive violations of Chinese territory and sovereignty by Indian troops and warned that China would take the necessary remedial action. The Chinese Government went on to repeat that it gave full support to Pakistan in its just struggle against Indian aggression. The Chinese resorted sanctimonious threats that "responsibility for any consequences arising out of its [India's] criminal aggression, will rest entirely with India". As Pakistani troops were repelled from the Chhamb-Jaurian sector, and as their armoured thrust in the Kasur-Khemkaran sector was neutralised by the Indian armed forces, the Chinese sought to compel India to divert some of its forces to the eastern parts of India on the Sino-Indian boundary.

The director-general for south Asia of the Chinese Foreign Office summoned the Indian chargé d'affaires in Beijing at midnight on 16 September and handed over a protest note, extracts of which are worth quoting. Accusing India of aggressive activities against China through the territory of Sikkim, the note alleged that "Indian troops had built a large number of military works with the objective of aggression against Chinese territories in Tibet". It went on to say: "There are now 56 such military works wantonly encroaching upon Chinese territory and violating her sovereignty. The Chinese Government now demands that the Indian Government dismantle all its military works within three days of the delivery of the present note and immediately stop all its intrusions along the Sino-Indian boundary and China-Sikkim boundary. India should return the kidnapped border inhabitants and seized livestock and pledge to refrain from any harassing raids across the boundary, otherwise the Indian Government must bear full responsibility for all the grave consequences arising therefrom." The note then proceeded to gratuitously refer to the Kashmir question and the ongoing Indo-Pakistani military conflict: "The

Chinese Government has consistently held that the Kashmir question should be settled on the basis of respect for the Kashmiri people's right of self-determination as pledged to them by India and Pakistan. This is what is meant by Chinese non-involvement in the dispute between India and Pakistan. But non-involvement absolutely does not mean failure to distinguish between right and wrong. It absolutely does not mean that China can approve of depriving the Kashmiri people of their right of self-determination or that she can approve of Indian aggression against Pakistan under the pretext of the Kashmir issue. So long as the Indian Government oppresses the Kashmiri people, China will not cease to support the Kashmiri people in their struggle for self-determination. So long as the Government of India persists in its unbridled aggression against Pakistan, China will not cease supporting Pakistan in her just struggle against aggression. This stand of ours will never change, however many helpers you may have such as the US, the Modern Revisionists and the US-controlled United Nations."

Not only did China threaten India openly, it went on to give expression to its strategic concerns by being critical of the US, the Soviet Union (Modern Revisionists was the code name for the Soviet Union) and the UN. India's response to these Chinese fulminations was non-polemic and firm. It simultaneously alerted its forces in the eastern sector, particularly on the Sino-Indian boundary from UP to Arunachal Pradesh.

The involvement of the Soviet Union in the 1965 war and the Tashkent meeting marked a noteworthy shift in the Soviet Union's South Asia policy which lasted for about seven years, from 1964 to 1971. It must be remembered that the two Soviet leaders who were the architects of the initial phase of close relations between India and the Soviet Union, Brezhnev and Khruschev, were out of power by the end of 1964. Brezhnev and Kosygin, with Communist Party of Soviet Union (CPSU) ideologue Suslov, constituted the centre of the power structure. Brezhnev desired changes in foreign policy in the context of the troubles the Soviet Union had had with the US and China from 1955 to 1964.

The Soviet Union was also interested in creating a geo-strategic atmosphere on the southern and southeastern flanks of Soviet Central Asia. This would ensure the security of the Soviet Central Asian republics and prevent the emergence of centrifugal impulses in this region. There was also a desire to have access to the warm waters of the Gulf and its energy resources. Soviet policy planners therefore felt that an excessive and one-sided involvement with India should be replaced by an attempt to open up lines with Afghanistan and Pakistan and if possible with Iran. The Indo-Pakistan conflict of 1965 provided an important opportunity to the Soviet

Union to take such an initiative. The US, enmeshed in Vietnam, and worried about a nuclear weapon–equipped and antagonistic China — China had conducted its nuclear weapons tests in September 1964, changing the strategic balance in Asia as far as the US was concerned — was becoming interested in some sort of an understanding with the Soviet Union, as confirmed by the Soviet ambassador to the US, Anatoly Dobrynin, in his memoirs *In Confidence*. Not desiring to be seen as moving away from its ally, Pakistan, during the 1965 conflict, the US was willing to let the Soviet Union play an enhanced political role in South Asia. The US also felt the USSR's undoubted influence on India would be more effective in persuading Delhi to bring the conflict to an end. The Soviet Union had also indicated to Pakistan a willingness to expand bilateral economic and technological ties between 1964 and 1965. These were the factors that underpinned the Soviet initiative to host the Indo-Pakistani meeting.

Good Offices

Soviet Prime Minister Alexei Kosygin sent communications on 20 August, 4, 7, and 8 September and then on 21 November to President Ayub Khan and Prime Minister Lal Bahadur Shastri, offering good offices for settling the differences between India and Pakistan. Shastri and Ayub Khan agreed to a bilateral meeting in Kosygin's presence, to be held at Tashkent in the Uzbekistan Republic of the Soviet Union. The Tashkent Conference lasted from 4 to 10 January and was held in a tense atmosphere. Shastri was accompanied by Foreign Minister Sardar Swaran Singh and Defence Minister Y.B. Chavan. Ayub was accompanied by Ghulam Farooq, minister for commerce, Khwaja Shahabuddin, minister for information, and Zulfiqar Ali Bhutto, foreign minister. Prime Minister Kosygin was accompanied by Foreign Minister Andrei Gromkyo and Defence Chief Marshal Malinovsky. All the delegations were accompanied by senior officials.

In assessing the significance of the Tashkent meeting two points must be kept in mind. First, both sides came to the meeting because of international diplomatic pressure. Second, both India and Pakistan had clearly divergent objectives. India desired the restoration of the cease-fire line, plus an agreement that it should be allowed to retain control over the strategic passes Indian troops had captured at Hajipur and in the Poonch-Uri and Kargil sectors. Control over these strategic positions was important to India because these were the routes through which Pakistani infiltrations had taken place since 1947. India also desired a commitment that Pakistan would abjure the use of force to settle the Kashmir dispute. India was clear that it would not allow the status of Kashmir as an integral part of the Indian republic to be a subject of discussion at the conference. Pakistan's objectives were exactly the opposite, the most important being to re-open the question of Jammu and Kashmir's accession to the Republic of India. Pakistan desired India to vacate all the strategic passes its troops had captured. Pakistan was not willing to give any assurance about not using force to change the status of Jammu and Kashmir. If possible, Pakistan desired the revival of Kashmir as an international issue to be discussed at the UN which would lead to the implementation of the UN resolutions of 1948 selectively, in sum ensuring that Kashmir become part of Pakistan. The aim was to achieve politically what it had failed to do militarily.

Kosygin had separate meetings with Ayub and Shastri, soon after their arrival in Tashkent on 3 January 1966. The tripartite conference started with Kosygin addressing it on the afternoon of 4 January at the Tashkent Municipal Hall in the glare of international publicity. Nearly 300 representatives from the world media had arrived in Tashkent. The inaugural statements made by Shastri and Ayub were anodyne, stressing the importance of peace, the settling of disputes by negotiations, etc. Kosygin's statement was formal and politically correct, particularly emphasising the fact that the Soviet Union had no desire to play an interventionist role. Kosygin said: "The future of Indo-Pakistan relations rests with India and Pakistan, with their readiness to demonstrate goodwill and mutual understanding and persistence in achieving positive results. On its part, the Government of the Soviet Union will in every way promote the realisation of these noble aims. We are ready to render our good offices for the successful work of this meeting. All those for whom peace is dear, are following this meeting between the president of Pakistan and the prime minister of India with great attention and hope. They believe in the wise statesmanship of the leaders of Pakistan and India, they wish success to the Tashkent meeting and peace and well-being for the Indian and Pakistani peoples."

The discussions on 5 January between Shastri and Ayub and their accompanying cabinet ministers (the latter met separately) indicated the deep differences of approach. Discussions between Sardar Swaran Singh and his counterpart, Bhutto were particularly acrimonious, with Bhutto insisting that India must renounce the legal and constitutional status of Jammu and Kashmir as part of India, and agree on a settlement according to Pakistani demands. A draft agreement or treaty, presented by the Indian side, had provided for the mutual withdrawal of forces, peace on the frontiers, good neighbourly relations, the settlement of disputes by peaceful measures and abjuring the use of force. The Indian draft was rejected in toto by the Pakistani side while India remained adamant about not discussing the status of Jammu and Kashmir. Prime Minister Kosygin did not participate in the discussions on 5 January but he met Ayub and Shastri separately trying to find a compromise. It became clear by the forenoon of 6 January that the talks had been deadlocked.

Kosygin then decided to take an active role. He spent up to eight to ten hours each day on 6 and 7 January talking separately to Ayub and Shastri. A further attempt was made on 7 January to reconcile the differences when Shastri and Ayub met separately for two hours without anybody else present. Even this meeting confirmed that the Indian and Pakistani positions were irreconcilable.

It was Kosygin who ultimately managed to break the logjam. He had long private discussions with Ayub and Shastri on 8 and 9 January 1966, while Gromkyo spoke to Swaran Singh and Bhutto. The differences of opinion were profound but all the three participants had a shared concern that the conference should not fail. The Soviet Union's political and diplomatic credibility would suffer a setback if that happened. Ayub and Bhutto could not return to Pakistan without showing some results after the dismal failure of their military initiative. This was the first major international conference to which Shastri had gone where Indian interests were directly involved. Hence he too had an interest in its success. The two crucial points of difference were the manner in which the Kashmir issue should be referred to in the final document summarising the results of the conference, and the question of India vacating crucial border passes. Kosygin's persuasion succeeded with both Shastri and Ayub on the first point; a mutually acceptable draft emerged constituting the first part of the Tashkent Declaration. It said: "Both sides will exert all efforts to create good neighbourly relations between India and Pakistan in accordance with the UN Charter. They reaffirmed their obligations under the Charter not to have recourse to force and to settle their disputes through peaceful means. They conceded that the interest of peace in their region and particularly in the Indo-Pakistan subcontinent, and indeed the interests of the people of India and Pakistan, were not served by the continuance of tension between the two countries. It was against this background that Jammu and Kashmir was discussed and each of the sides set forth its respective position."

The second point of difference, about the vacation of the passes at Hajipir, Kargil and the Uri-Poonch Bulge, was a serious point. Shastri was ultimately persuaded by Kosygin to withdraw Indian troops from these positions on the basis of two arguments. First, that the UN Resolutions of August and

September 1965 had clearly recommended the withdrawal of forces by both sides, to positions which they had occupied before 5 August 1965. The second argument was that India vacating these posts would serve the larger interest of stability in Indo-Pakistani relations. Shastri reluctantly agreed, while Bhutto was not at all happy about the formulation in the Tashkent Agreement stipulating that both sides should abjure the use of force.

The Tashkent Declaration was signed at 4.30 p.m. on 10 January at the Tashkent Municipal Hall. In retrospect, the Declaration and the agreements therein were a tenuous patchwork exercise to defuse tensions for a short period, not the basis for a normal, cooperative relationship. As if foreshadowing the ephemeral contribution that the Tashkent Declaration was to make to Indo-Pakistan relations, Prime Minister Shastri had a heart attack around midnight on 10 January and died. Instead of coming back to explain the significance of the agreement to the Indian people, it became a funerary journey for the Indian delegation. Kosygin and a grim-looking Ayub served as pall-bearers as the coffin was loaded onto the Indian aircraft. It was on a sombre and tragic note that the Tashkent Conference ended.

That the results of the conference generated discontent in both countries, was evident within days of its conclusion. While politically knowledgeable circles and strategists outside the government generally accepted the unavoidability of the Tashkent Conference and its results, public opinion did not quite accept the government's assessment that the Tashkent Declaration signified the beginning of an era of normality and reasonableness between India and Pakistan. There was a feeling in India that the government should not have gone to the Tashkent Conference without demonstrating military superiority in clear and categorical terms by capturing a couple of major Pakistani cities. While it had succeeded in thwarting Pakistani plans, the fact that the war in overall terms was a stand-off, had not seeped into public knowledge. The view was that a victorious India, due to some lack of political will, had rushed to Tashkent due to international pressure. There was particular resentment about Shastri's decision to vacate the strategic passes at Hajipur, Kargil and Poonch-Uri. The armed forces were resentful of the decision and are still so, four decades after the event. The view of the army and the assertive segments of India's strategic establishment has been that the vacation of these posts is the reason for all the subsequent Pakistani infiltration and shenanigans in Jammu and Kashmir. The overall public reaction was that while the Tashkent Conference might have brought the war to an end, India did not take political advantage of the military successes it had achieved because of a desire to get good-conduct certificates from the major powers and the UN.

Ironically, Pakistani public reaction was similar but due to different considerations. First and foremost, President Ayub Khan's political decline, leading to his ultimate exit from office, commenced. Bhutto was the trigger in this process. Though a participant at the Conference, Bhutto disowned its results immediately after returning from Tashkent, calling it a "surrender and a betrayal" of Pakistani interests. He also attributed the military failures of Pakistan to Ayub's mismanagement of the military operations. Within a week of the conclusion of the conference, by 18 January there were hostile demonstrations by students, and riots in Lahore. The opposition groups, antagonistic to military rule, the intelligentsia and the bar associations, mounted a campaign against Ayub. An emotional dimension was added with the processions of Pakistani war widows on the streets of Lahore and Peshawar, shrilling that their husbands had sacrificed themselves in vain because of the betrayal at Tashkent.

Ayub was accused of selling Kashmir to India. He was sufficiently concerned about this accusation to make a radio broadcast on 14 January 1966, saying that nothing in the Tashkent Declaration deflected Pakistan from its firm stand on Kashmir, and that the Kashmiris must exercise their right of self-determination. He also promised that once the withdrawal of forces was completed, he would urge the UN to implement its resolutions on Kashmir within the framework of Pakistani interests. The two reasons for the widespread criticism and disappointment about the Tashkent Declaration in Pakistan were: first, the military offensive was presented to the Pakistanis as a determined exercise to liberate Jammu and Kashmir from Indian domination, which was going to be successful without any doubt; second, the resentment against the military rule of Ayub had crystallised by 1965. The military setback inflicted on Pakistan and Pakistan's failure to get any commitment on Jammu and Kashmir from India in Tashkent, provided an opportune handle to opposition politicians to discredit Ayub. Bhutto was a prime mover in this enterprise and in disowning the Tashkent Agreement. He had strongly opposed the signing of the Declaration and Ayub Khan had overruled him. Now he fully utilised the groundswell of public criticism to question the motivation and performance of Ayub. He began an anti-Ayub political campaign, which led to his founding the People's Party of Pakistan and ultimately emerged as a leader in his own right. While Ayub had the support of some senior politicians and governors, and though he attempted to explain the rationale of the Tashkent Declaration to the Pakistani public through them, the aura of efficiency and decisiveness which he had had until the beginning of 1965 vanished. His command and authority over the officer cadres of the armed forces had also diminished, because of the failure of the military effort.

By the end of 1966, the operational relevance of the Tashkent Declaration to bilateral equation had disappeared. The Pakistani establishment, including Ayub, refused to refer to the stipulations in the Tashkent Declaration as a basis for structuring future Indo-Pakistan relations. The Government of India continued to refer to it off and on, on a pro-forma basis whenever Indo-Pakistan relations went through any critical phase between 1966 and 1972. The Declaration was chanted more like a mantra than used as a functional framework for fashioning India's Pakistan policy.

Indira Gandhi Enters the Scene

The Tashkent Agreement, signed in January, started becoming defunct by March 1966. In the interim period Indira Gandhi had taken over as prime minister. She conveyed to President Ayub Khan that there would be a continuity in India's policy decisions incorporated in the Tashkent Agreement. She also indicated that an Indian delegation led by Sardar Swaran Singh would visit Islamabad in March, and she invited Foreign Minister Bhutto to come to India at his convenience thereafter.

By 25 February 1966, the armed forces of India and Pakistan had withdrawn to their pre-August 5, 1965 positions. The Indian delegation consisting of Foreign Minister Sardar Swaran Singh, Minister for Shipping and Civil Aviation N. Sanjeeva Reddy, Minister for Commerce Manubhai Shah and Foreign Secretary C.S. Jha reached Islamabad early in March. The purpose of the discussions as envisaged by the Indian side was to take follow-up action on the Tashkent Declaration, especially those segments relating to the normalisation of relations and the commencing of bilateral cooperation beginning with the creation of institutions like the Joint Commission, and its subcommissions for economic communication and cultural cooperation.

Pakistan's Foreign Secretary Aziz Ahmed, in the opening session of the official-level discussions, said that unless the Kashmir issue was discussed, and unless there was an agreement with India for the creation of permanent institutional arrangements to discuss and find a solution concerning the status of Kashmir, the other stipulations for the normalisation of Indo-Pakistan relations could not be discussed. Foreign Minister Bhutto, opening the ministerial-level discussions the next morning categorically asserted that unless India agreed to discuss and then change the status of Jammu and Kashmir, Pakistan would not be in a position to discuss other follow-up action as per the Tashkent Agreement. Bhutto refused to discuss urgent issues that were the consequence of the 1965 war, relating to communications, the restoration of properties and ships captured, and the movement of people and goods between the two countries. He categorically refused discussions on long-term commercial, civil aviation and economic cooperation. Thus, this high-level bilateral discussion stood aborted. It became clear that the Pakistani power structure, starting to be dominated by Bhutto, had no interest in implementing the Tashkent Agreement. The only limited objective which Pakistan had in participating in the Tashkent Conference seemed to be not to antagonise the US and the Soviet Union, and to extricate itself from a conflict situation in which it was on the defensive.

The benefit of hindsight brings to notice another factor that resulted in Pakistan pulling back from its commitments at Tashkent. The Language Movement against the imposition of Urdu, which had commenced in East Pakistan early in 1950, had evolved into a full-fledged movement for autonomy led by Sheikh Mujibur Rahman. In a collective meeting of opposition parties held in Lahore on 5 and 6 February 1966, Mujibur Rahman announced his famous six-point demand for autonomy.

India looked upon these demands with sympathy because it was deeply sensitive to the linguistic and ethnic marginalisation of East Pakistan by West Pakistan. Public opinion in West Bengal had taken note of the economic discrimination and exploitation from which East Pakistan suffered. Another factor underpinning this general sympathy for East Pakistan and its leaders, was that East Pakistan was not supportive of the hostility and antagonism entertained by the power structure of West Pakistan against India.

Bhutto resigned from the government and went into open opposition against Ayub by the middle of 1966. The brief exercise to bring some rationality into Indo-Pakistan relations disappeared by the beginning of 1967. In an editorial on 4 April 1967, the newspaper *Dawn* recommended that: "Pakistan should soon get rid of whatever remains of the post-Tashkent euphoria, brush up on its realism once again, and continue to prepare internally and through the strengthening of outside and dependable foreign relations for whatever the future holds." The period between 1960 and 1971 saw relations drifting into somnolent hostility. Ayub had to grapple with the political and agitational impulses generated against him by Bhutto, which were utilised by other political parties both in West Pakistan and East Pakistan to question the legitimacy and efficiency of the military government.

The 1967 elections gave Mrs Indira Gandhi a thin majority. She was also threatened by widespread internal factionalism in the Congress Party, so her focus was on political survival and related domestic concerns. The seriousness of the crisis which she faced could be gauged by the fact that the ruling Congress Party split in 1969, with the Old Guard, which had engineered Mrs Gandhi becoming prime minister (defeating Morarji Desai), standing marginalised in national politics. A development of long-term political and strategic significance was the notable enhancement in the defence expenditure of both India and Pakistan.

One notes an almost geometrical progression in the defence expenditure in both countries between the years 1966 and 1971. In 1966-67, Pakistan's budget was US$ 473 million or about 19 per cent of government revenue. India's defence expenditure was US$ 1171 million or 17 per cent of its budget. By 1970-71, Pakistan's military budget had grown to 32 per cent of its revenue, that is US$ 625 million. India's defence budget had increased by 25 per cent to US$ 1466 million, while the size of the Indian armed forces remained static at one million men and Pakistan's at around 350,000. Pakistan had increased its armoured strength, not only replenishing the losses it suffered in 1965, but increasing its number of tanks to 1439, compared to India's 1320. India took countermeasures. It acquired 745 aircraft, compared to Pakistan having only 447 planes. Most of the military supplies to Pakistan came from China, but what bothered India was that in keeping with its logic of organising the Tashkent Agreement, the Soviet Union also gave some defence supplies to Pakistan.

Domestic unrest in Pakistan took a dramatic turn when an attempt was made on Ayub's life in 1967. Bhutto and other opposition leaders were arrested. The consequence was widespread agitation and disturbances all over Pakistan. Ayub's position became untenable and he relinquished the presidency in 1969. He was replaced by the then chief of the army staff, General Yahya Khan. Yahya did not have the sophistication and urbanity of Ayub. His mindset was more anti-Indian than that of most of the senior figures in his government. He was convinced that all the trouble and agitation in East Pakistan was the result of Indian conspiracies and direct Indian involvement. The East Pakistan leader Sheikh Mujibur Rahman was arrested more than once between 1956 and 1970, culminating in his being accused of high treason in the Agartala conspiracy case. Yahya was essentially an individual with a narrow authoritarian military vision. He faced twin challenges. The first was consolidating his position in the face of increasing public agitation for the restoration of democracy, the most important challenge being posed by Bhutto, emerging as a leader of political consequence with mass support in West Pakistan. The second challenge was posed by Mujibur Rahman and his Awami League, was becoming more strident about demands for autonomy, a new constitution for Pakistan, and general elections.

Yahya's personality and inclinations were also a factor affecting the internal politics of Pakistan and relations with India. His make-up was that of an officer of the British Indian Army, aloof, somewhat feudal, not interested in, in fact averse to, the processes of mass politics. He had neither the patience nor the political sensitivity to manage the politics of the disturbed situation within Pakistan in the aftermath of the 1965 war and the Tashkent Conference, now compounded by the groundswell of opposition to military rule. His approach to India therefore was essentially distant and hostile, both because of his angst about Pakistani military failures in the 1965 war, and his having to be responsive to the anti-Indian strands in the mass movement coming into being under Bhutto.

Mrs Gandhi, who came to power in the spring of 1966, was facing an equally difficult political predicament. She was to go in for general elections in April 1967, within a year of coming to power. The Indian economy was suffering from food shortages, inflation and increasing disparities between the urban rich and the rural poor. Agricultural and industrial production was falling, India's foreign debt obligations were increasing. In the general economic survey of 1966-67, the Reserve Bank of India assessed that 35 per cent of the Indian population was undernourished. Mrs Gandhi sought advice not only internally but from foreign experts; on the latter's advice she devalued the rupee, but she did not undertake the matching economic reforms and restructuring to take full advantage of the devaluation. She nationalised banks and, instead of modernising and liberalising, proceeded to increase government control over the economy. The consequence was the Congress Party suffering major losses, but not losing power in the 1967 elections. The Congress Party's strength in the Lok Sabha decreased from 361 to 284. As against nearly 45 per cent of the votes cast in favour of the Congress Party in 1962, it got 40.9 per cent of the votes in 1967. It also lost power in some of the provincial legislatures. The two important parties that gained from the Congress's electoral losses were the right-wing Swatantra Party and what in foreign circles was called a Hindu Nationalist Party, the Jan Sangh. The Swatantra Party increased its strength from 18 to 42 seats in the Lok Sabha, and the Jan Sangh more than double, from 14 to 35 seats.

To compound all this Mrs Gandhi faced intensive factionalism in her own party. Morarji Desai and elder leaders of the Congress, S. Nijalingappa, Sanjeeva Reddy and K. Kamaraj, blamed the electoral setback on her. This critical personal predicament monopolised Mrs Gandhi's attention. A side-effect was the drift in India's policies towards Pakistan, which became mostly reactive to Pakistani policy towards India.

In overall terms, the period between 1958 and 1970, barring the signing of the Indus Waters Treaty between India and Pakistan in 1960, was characterised by a downward curve in relations. Three factors influenced India's perceptions and attitudes towards Pakistan during this period. Pakistan's foreign and defence links with the US and China contrasted with India's commitment to the non-aligned movement, the leadership of which was considered an important factor in India's foreign policy. Political and emotional distances increased between India and Pakistan, especially in the context of Pakistan going under military rule. The third factor was Pakistan resorting to force to settle scores with India in 1965 and to gain Kashmir on the basis of mistaken perceptions of India's vulnerabilities.

One cannot help mentioning three anecdotes manifesting the flavour of Indo-Pakistan relations during this period. The first incident occurred in February 1966, when India's then high commissioner to Pakistan, Kewal Singh, went to meet Ayub after the Tashkent Agreement. Ayub was on a hunting trip in the estates of Bhutto in Larkana, Sindh, and Kewal Singh was asked to come to Larkana for the meeting. The exchanges between Kewal Singh and Ayub proceeded on expected lines, with mutual assurances about the necessity to build normal relations on the basis of the Tashkent Agreement. The discussions were followed by a dinner at the end of which ghazals were sung and dances were performed by some young artists from Karachi who were brought in by Bhutto for the entertainment of the guests. Kewal Singh told me years later that the last ghazal sung at this function was Faiz Ahmad Faiz's ghazal (poem) which was:

गुलों मे रंग भरे, बादे नौबहार चले।
चले भी आओ कि गुलशन का कारोबार चले।।

(Let the breezes of the spring blow and
fill the flowers with deep colours.
Come on beloved, do come, so that the romantic
business of the garden may pick up momentum.)

Kewal Singh recalled that at the end of the dinner one of the senior Pakistani officials told him in a bantering tone that the Indian high commissioner should not think that this ghazal in any way signified the political mood of the Pakistan Foreign Office with Bhutto being foreign minister. The high commissioner should understand that it was just a quicksilver expression of traditional Pakistani entertainment and hospitality.

The second anecdote is about the son of the first Indian commander in chief, K.M. Cariappa, who was a fighter pilot in the Indian Air Force, being shot down in Pakistan in the 1965 war when he was on a sortie. The younger Cariappa, who later rose to become an air marshal in the Indian Air Force, was taken as a prisoner of war. Ayub reportedly sent a personal message to Cariappa, by then retired from the Indian Army, that he (Ayub) would like to release his son as a special gesture because of Ayub's old connections with Cariappa in the British Indian Army. General Carriapa's response has passed into the folklore and tradition of the Indian armed forces. His message to Ayub Khan was: "I have thousands of my sons fighting in this war. Every Indian prisoner of war is my son. There is no need for any special gesture regarding my son. No exception need be made."

The third anecdote was conveyed to me by India's former foreign secretary, my senior colleague K.P.S. Menon (Jr.) who served as consular in Islamabad from 1966 to 1968. Soon after the ceasefire of 1965 was declared, one of the Pakistani brigade commanders deployed in the forward areas of Pakistani Punjab sent a general message to the forward formations of the Indian Army asking whether there were any former students of the Doon School on the Indian side. If so, he would like to meet them and talk to them despite the recent conflict. Menon told me he did not know whether there was an Indian response or not, but it is my assessment that there must have been some army officers with a Doon School background on the Indian side too, who must have responded if the opportunity were there.

Whatever nuances concerning the chemistry of Indo-Pakistan relations these anecdotes may convey, the substantive predicament was a downward drift in relations. It set the stage for the momentous events in the subcontinent which began at the end of 1970 and culminated in the break-up of Pakistan with the creation of Bangladesh.

Six

The Break-up of Pakistan:
Mujibnagar to Simla — The Advent of Zia-ul-Haq

*Y*ahya Khan and the Pakistani Army agreed to the stepping down of Field Marshal Ayub Khan because he was the focus of public animosity. Yahya's expectation was once Ayub departed from the scene, Zulfiqar Ali Bhutto would fall in line and the armed forces could continue in power. This was an illusion. By the end of 1969 and the beginning of 1970, the opposition parties both in West and East Pakistan were clamouring for a return to democracy.

Ayub's experiment in what he called "basic democracies", that is the creation of district-level and provincial councils through an electoral college consisting of people with minimum levels of educational qualifications and property ownership, could not replace the logic of universal adult franchise as the basis for genuine democracy. Yahya had come to realise that he would have to hold elections sooner rather than later. By the spring of 1970 he had given indications he would hold general elections in Pakistan by the end of the year. But the atmosphere, particularly in East Pakistan, was volatile. It ultimately affected Indo-Pakistani relations for most of the 1970s. It is relevant therefore to describe in some detail the events leading to the break-up of Pakistan after the war of 1971.

As if to presage the violence and trauma that the people of East Pakistan (later Bangladesh) were to face throughout 1971, the province was struck by a fearsome cyclone in the second week of November 1970, just a few weeks before the general elections scheduled by Yahya for December that year after eleven years of military rule. The elections were originally scheduled for October but were held in mid-December. The results of the National Assembly elections as well as the East Pakistan Provincial Assembly Poll produced a landslide victory for Sheikh Mujibur Rahman's Awami League. The party won 162 out of the total of 313 seats in the National Assembly, securing a clear majority. Similarly, his party won 288 out of 300 seats in the Provincial Assembly.

But I am getting ahead of the story. Between 150,000 and 200,000 people were reported killed by the cyclone and the tidal wave that hit coastal East Pakistan in November 1970. Perhaps two million people were affected by the floods that devastated the region. The sympathy and assistance from the international community was immense. The military regime's paranoia concerning India however showed itself even in such tragic circumstances. India offered prompt relief in terms of medicines, foodgrains, tents and medical personnel, and even planes and helicopters for relief operations. While Pakistan accepted assistance from all over the world, Yahya Khan turned down Indian aid saying that what came from other sources was enough and that Pakistan did not need India's assistance. This despite the fact that it would have been the speediest source of relief. The cyclone was used by certain West Pakistani politicians and military rulers to postpone the scheduled general elections; Bhutto, president of the People's Party, advocated postponement by a few months. He had support from certain segments of the military, its intelligence having accurately assessed that the election would bring Mujibur Rahman to power on the basis of a genuine mandate from the people. Apart from using the cyclone as an excuse, riots and disturbances were instigated by the Government in Khulna, Dacca and other district headquarters. The restoration and maintenance of law and order were to provide compelling additional reasons for postponing the election.

Aware of these machinations, the Awami League had warned the Central Government of the prospect of a poll postponement and emphasised that such a move would result in widespread protests. The Awami League in West Pakistan as well as other political parties in the West conveyed similar messages in their public pronouncements and in their exchanges with the military regime. The PPP and Islam-pasand parties of West Pakistan were the only ones which adopted an ambivalent attitude.

In the event, elections were held and the results confirmed the apprehensions of the military regime. On all counts Sheikh Mujibur

Rahman would have become prime minister of Pakistan, and a senior leader of his party the chief minister of East Pakistan. One of the main resolves in his election manifesto was that were his party to come to power it would draft a new constitution providing for the decentralisation of power and autonomy for the constituent units of Pakistan. An elaboration of this election promise indicated that the proposed constitution would use the six-point programme of autonomy as its terms of reference. Neither the Yahya regime nor the People's Party which had emerged second in the National Assembly, was ready to accept the electoral verdict. Bhutto was more categorical in his opposition to the Awami League coming to power than even the generals who ruled Pakistan at that time. In a statement in Lahore on 20 December 1970, Bhutto asserted that no new constitution could be framed nor any government established at the centre without the cooperation of his party. He went on to make the extraordinarily illogical assertion that the People's Party of Pakistan was not prepared to sit in the opposition benches of the National Assembly. While acknowledging that Mujibur Rahman had a clear majority in the National Assembly, he voiced the view that a majority alone does not count in national politics. Explaining his position he said that while the Awami League may have a majority of seats in the National Assembly, the People's Party of Pakistan had won clear majorities in the provincial assemblies of Sindh and Punjab. As the real power of the central government originated in these provinces, no central Government in Pakistan could be constituted without the PPP's participation. The Awami League leaders from East Pakistan, like Mujibur Rahman and Tajuddin Ahmed, secretary of the party, responded that the people of Pakistan, particularly East Pakistan, were not ready to accept Sindh and Punjab as the bastions of power. They emphasised the importance of respecting the electoral verdict.

Bhutto's Preconditions

It was clear by the end of December 1970 that the Yahya regime and Bhutto were not going to allow Mujibur Rahman to form the national government or to commence drafting a new constitution responsive to the aspirations of the people of East Pakistan. Public and polemical exchanges between the leaders of East Pakistan and Bhutto characterised events during December 1970 and January 1971. Bhutto's non-cooperative attitude prevented Yahya from setting in motion even the procedure to convene the National Assembly and create a democratic government in Pakistan. The political debate deteriorated to a level where the Awami League's electoral victory was questioned by Bhutto saying that it was the result of subversive activity by India. He proceeded to accuse the Awami League leadership of being a pro-Hindu organisation that was going to affect the Islamic identity of Pakistan through the thinly disguised stratagem of incorporating the six-point autonomy provisions into the proposed constitution.

While these political pyrotechnics proceeded, the military regime faced the problem of maintaining its domestic and international credibility. Yahya, during his detour to Dacca in the middle of a state visit to China in January 1971, reiterated that he was keen to transfer power to the elected representatives, that he would convene the National Assembly as early as possible, and that Sheikh Mujibur Rahman would be the prime minister of Pakistan. Bhutto responded with convoluted political and legal arguments, the main burden of which was that while the Awami League could form the government in East Pakistan, the government at the centre would have to be a coalition between the People's Party of Pakistan and the Awami League. Also that the position of prime minister should not go automatically to Mujibur Rahman and the issue should be resolved through compromise on the basis of power-sharing arrangements. Yahya had announced by late January or early February 1971 that the National Assembly would be convened at Dacca on 3 March 1971. Bhutto meanwhile put forward the additional demand that the new constitution of Pakistan should be drafted not on the basis of the six-point programme but after fresh discussions on all those six points. He wanted the Awami League to accept modifications he had in mind to preserve the authority of the Central Government and the unity of Pakistan. He declared in a statement in Peshawar on 15 February that members of the National Assembly from his party would not attend the session in Dacca on 3 March unless Mujibur Rahman accepted his preconditions.

It should be noted that the majority of political parties in West Pakistan did not support Bhutto's obstructionist stand against the Awami League and his deliberate attempt to sabotage the restoration of democracy. By the last week of February Bhutto went on record to say that there was no room left for negotiations with the Awami League and that he was adopting the path of non-cooperation. Mujibur Rahman was ready for practical political compromises despite Bhutto's shenanigans. He held meetings with Yahya and with Bhutto in the last week of February in Dacca. Though the discussions were abortive, Mujibur Rahman confirmed in a lengthy press statement issued on 24 February that he was willing to have detailed and constructive discussions with the leaders of West Pakistan and with Yahya to resolve the problems which were in debate. He also confirmed that Yahya had assured him in the last week of February that there would be no postponement of the date for convening the National Assembly. Yahya had either become a pawn in the hands of Bhutto or a partner in the perfidious plans the politician had in mind. After having assured Mujibur Rahman that the National Assembly would be convened as scheduled on 3 March he announced on 1 March that due to a lack of consensus between the political leaders of West and East Pakistan, he had decided to postpone the convening. He gave the additional justification that he was compelled to take this decision because of the generally tense situation created by India in East Pakistan.

There is some background to this artificial and unwarranted accusation. India had wholeheartedly welcomed the holding of a general election in Pakistan in December 1970 and had taken note of the completion of the electoral process on 17 January 1971, expressing the hope that a genuinely representative government under the leadership of Mujibur Rahman would be established. Pakistan's behaviour towards India during the Sino-Indian conflict, the growing collusion between Pakistan and China (of which Bhutto was the main architect under Ayub), and the 1965 war with Pakistan made India view Pakistani military dictatorship with reservation. Therefore when India supported the democratic processes in Pakistan, it was natural for Yahya, from his narrow point of view, to transfer some blame for the contradictions in Pakistani politics to the Government of India.

There was widespread resentment against Yahya's decision to postpone calling the National Assembly into session. When the Pakistani authorities fired on Awami Youth League members holding demonstrations against this decision on 2 March 1971, Mujibur Rahman reacted with legitimate anger. In a press statement issued in Dacca on 2 March he announced a massive programme of civil disobedience. He said a province-wide hartal would be observed each day from 3 to 7 March. All work would be brought to a standstill in East Pakistan, both in government and non-governmental spheres, including public utility services, transport and communications. He announced that 3 March, the day when the National Assembly was expected to come into session, would be observed as a day of national mourning and that he would address a public meeting that evening at Paltan Maidan in Dacca. He also announced that he would declare further programmes of protest. These protests were completely successful, although they were accompanied by disturbances against which the military regime used coercive force, the army and police being deployed in all major cities. Mujib's demand that these forces should be withdrawn and the democratic process brought back on track was ignored.

A noteworthy parallel development was that except for the Muslim League and the PPP, the other political parties in West Pakistan supported Mujib's demand that the election results be respected and power be handed over to the Awami League. Even a regional political party like the Punjab Pakistan Front passed a resolution on 3 March in which it opposed Bhutto's stand on the formation of the new government. Malik Ghulam Jilani, convenor of the Front, released the text of the resolution. It declared: "In the opinion of the Punjab Pakistan Front Organising Committee, a decision is being forced on the country by the reckless and unsupportable ambition of one single person who claims to speak in the name of Pakistan although he has a clear majority in barely one of the four provinces of West Pakistan." Maulana Ghulam Ghaus Hazarvi, general secretary of the West Pakistan unit of the Jamait-ul-Ulema-e-Pakistan, criticised Bhutto for talking in the language of ultimatums and creating a crisis.

All governmental activities in East Pakistan came to a standstill with protests against postponing the convening of the National Assembly and the delay in installing Mujibur Rahman as prime minister. There were violent incidents with army and police firing in Dacca, Tongi, and Rajshahi. Some 50 people were killed and 600 injured because of governmental repression between 3 and 6 March. The violent law and order measures taken by the military regime were under the declaration of martial law. Mujibur Rahman made a four-point demand on 7 March to restore normality. He asked for the immediate annulment of martial law, for troops to be sent back to their barracks, for an inquiry into the killings that had occurred between mid-February and 7 March and for the transfer of power to the elected representatives of the people. Meanwhile, he indicated the non-cooperation movement and protests would continue till power was transferred to the Awami League. The massive support for Mujib in East Pakistan and the support given to him by all the major political parties and leaders of West Pakistan — except Bhutto and the Muslim League — persuaded Yahya that he must recommence negotiations. He therefore arrived in Dacca in mid-March 1971. Bhutto also joined the talks, not with a problem-solving approach but with his own motives. The first was to score a possible publicity point because he had agreed to talk to Mujibur Rahman despite his fundamental differences with the East Pakistani leader. His second motive was more important (which one discerns with the benefit of hindsight): that of ensuring that Yahya did not succumb to Mujibur Rahman's advocacies, which would have thwarted Bhutto's ambitions. Details of the discussions between Yahya, Bhutto and Mujibur Rahman between 17 and 25 March 1971 have been public knowledge for 26 years now — they need no recapitulation. The main feature of these negotiations was that Yahya and Bhutto tried to persuade Mujibur Rahman to agree to power-sharing in the Central Government. Mujib was also pressurised to tone down his demand for autonomy and his determination to draw up a new constitution for Pakistan. Mujibur Rahman's response was negative. He made the valid point that any discussions on a future constitution of Pakistan should be discussed in the National Assembly. No a priori assurance could be given to the military regime or to Bhutto.

As the talks were moving towards an anticipated failure, Mujibur Rahman made his famous speech at the Rama Maidan on 7 March in which he said (in my rendering from Bengali), "The struggle now is for liberation and self-rule; the struggle this time is for independence." There have been reports that Mujib was reluctant to take this categorical public position on independence as negotiations were to continue till 25 March. He wanted to wait for the final outcome without adopting any decisive position on breaking away from Pakistan. It was the student leaders of the Awami League sharing the dais with him who virtually compelled him to make a declaration of independence on 7 March 1971. Tofail Ahmed, Abdul Razak, Abdul Kuddus Makhon and Abdur Rab were among them.

As Bhutto remained obstinate and Yahya Khan was not ready to offend him, hoping that a stalemate would enable military rule to continue, the talks failed. Bhutto's personal ambition and scepticism were evident even while he participated in the talks. Senior Bangladeshi friends told me later, when I was assigned to be India's first diplomatic representative in Dacca, that Bhutto would make fun of Mujib and other East Pakistani leaders almost every evening after the talks were over. He was satirical, derisive and completely confident of getting his way after the crisis, which he had created. In the meanwhile, public unrest was growing and Yahya decided to crack down on the people. He ordered the imposition of martial law and a military operation against the Awami League and particularly its youth wing from the afternoon of 25 March. These were confidential orders — he gave no warning to Mujib about his intentions.

The Military Crackdown

Bhutto left for Karachi on 25 March the day on which Yahya had promised to convene the postponed session of the National Assembly. The orders for military operations were directed not only against the Awami League and its youth wing but pre-emptive military measures were ordered against the East Bengal Regiment of the Pakistani Army and the East Pakistan Rifles.

Similarly, East Pakistani police barracks in all the major cities were to be surrounded by West Pakistani forces and neutralised. The military crackdown commenced a little before midnight on 25-26 March. This was not a sudden and ad hoc decision — the plan to scuttle the election results through military means was already in hand from the beginning of March. Pakistani troops in plain clothes were being flown into Dacca on the commercial flights of Pakistan International Airlines. The Pakistani Navy had also begun transporting troops and supplies to East Pakistan from the beginning of March, and by the third week the military regime had deployed a division plus a brigade in East Pakistan. Additional subversive activities were undertaken by specially trained commandos of the Pakistani Army who infiltrated the protest marches and demonstrations to make them violent so that the consequent military crackdown could acquire legitimacy. Indian intelligence agencies monitoring the developing crisis had given advance information about these goings-on. Bhutto and Yahya had planned a parallel political stratagem to lull Mujib into complacency and isolate him from like-minded leaders of West Pakistan. This stratagem worked because, despite the disturbances and turmoil, the Mujib-Yahya negotiations made apparent progress during the ten days preceding the military crackdown. Yahya agreed to Mujib's demands to end martial law and for the transfer of power. As a quid pro quo, Mujib agreed to Yahya remaining the interim president of Pakistan until a new constitution had been drafted and finalised. He also agreed to Yahya's suggestion that in the constitution formulation exercise, the National Assembly and the provincial assemblies should meet separately and not jointly as was originally planned. Mujib agreed to separate meetings in response to Bhutto's apprehension that a joint meeting of the provincial assemblies and the National Assembly on drafting the constitution might have severely isolated the Pakistan People's Party with Mujib joining up with the leaders of Baluchistan, the North West Frontier Province and Sindh. The loose points were tied up and Yahya told Mujib that a proclamation embodying the agreement followed by a notice for the convening of the National Assembly would be issued on 25 March. It was this apparently rational pattern of discussion that made Mujib pull back from the non-cooperation protests from 15 to 25 March.

The build-up was completed by the afternoon. Lt. General Tikka Khan was given instructions to launch a district-wise military operation against the Awami League and the people of East Pakistan on the evening of 25 March. Yahya flew out of Dacca within a couple of hours of giving these orders. Tikka Khan now had 70,000 troops under his command in East Pakistan. West Pakistani troops outnumbered the troops of the East Bengal

Regiment, the East Pakistan Rifles and the East Pakistan Police Force. He launched genocidal operations with brutal precision. His troops attacked and killed all the personnel at the regimental headquarters of the East Pakistan Rifles at Peel Khana in Dacca. West Pakistani troops also attacked the headquarters of the Dacca police at Rajbagh. There was military resistance from the Bengali personnel of these military and paramilitary organisations but they were facing an overwhelming force that included armour and artillery.

Pakistani troops also attacked the campus of Dacca University and Bengali troops in all the major metropolitan centres. The worst carnage was at Jagannath Hall in Dacca University and in the girls' hostel there. Hundreds of students were killed and the university building was seriously damaged. Mujib went underground sometime around midnight. A pre-recorded broadcast by him declaring East Pakistan a newly independent country called Bangladesh went on the air from clandestine radio stations established by the Awami League in Rangpur and Rajshahi districts in the northwestern part of the country. Simultaneously, the battalion commander of the East Pakistan Regiment at Chittagong, Major Ziaur Rahman (who became president of Bangladesh in 1976-77), briefly captured the Chittagong Radio Station and broadcast a declaration announcing the establishment of free Bangladesh and appealed to all Bengali military and paramilitary personnel to resist the Pakistani Army. In fact, Ziaur Rahman's broadcast came a little earlier than Mujib's broadcast and he was the first Bengali officer of the Pakistani Army to declare his loyalty to the new country.

General Tikka Khan captured all the radio stations and communication centres in East Pakistan by the forenoon of 26 March. A systematic programme of killing and arrest commenced. Meanwhile, Mujib stayed at his residence in Dhan Mandi in Dacca to remove uncertainty about his whereabouts and to sustain the confidence of the liberation movement. Pakistan military personnel arrested him on the night of the crackdown and flew him out to Rawalpindi.

India was closely monitoring the situation. Prime Minister Indira Gandhi, in a series of statements in both Houses of Parliament between March and May 1971, expressed growing concern about developments in East Pakistan and India's support for the restoration of democratic processes. She also strongly criticised the military action of the Government. Her views had the support of all political parties and the unqualified support of Indian public opinion. Parliament unanimously advised that the Government of India support the fulfilment of the aspirations of the people of East Pakistan.

Part of the conspiracy against the people of East Pakistan was to prepare the ground for a military conflict between India and Pakistan as the military regime was scuttling the election results. The ploy used was the hijacking of an Indian Airlines plane to Lahore by Pakistani agents claiming to be Kashmiri secessionists, early in March 1971. Pakistan's expectation was that India would launch some sort of limited intelligence and military action to revenge the hijacking of the Indian plane in response to which Pakistan could engineer another military conflict with India and use it as an excuse to justify the massive military operations against the people of East Pakistan. But India's response was sober. It suspended overflights of all Pakistani aircraft over Indian airspace by mid-March, and moved the International Civil Aviation Organisation (ICAO) to take corrective action against the Pakistan-sponsored hijacking of the Indian plane. India's case was strengthened by the Pakistani military regime's failure to take any effective measures against the hijackers, and Bhutto himself meeting them. India sent two diplomatic representatives to lobby countries represented on the executive council of the ICAO to seek their support for remedial action against Pakistan on the hijacking case. Dr S.P. Jagota, the then director of the Legal and Treaties Division of the External Affairs Ministry, went to countries in Western Europe, North America and South America represented on the ICAO Council to argue India's case. I went to Eastern Europe, Scandinavia and the Arab countries in the same capacity. The ICAO took some procedural measures but it did not have any visible impact. The most notable memory that I have of this special mission was that most of the Arab countries temporised and did not express full support for the Indian case. The deputy foreign minister of Libya was the most frank among my interlocutors. He told me that whatever the pros and cons of the issue, Libya had to take a sympathetic view of any action taken by another Muslim country like Pakistan.

India not reacting violently to this provocation left Pakistan in limbo. The hope of the military regime and of Bhutto that their conspiracy in East Pakistan could be covered under an emerging conflict situation with India was not fulfilled.

India Goes Slow

To get back to the developments in East Pakistan from 27 March, Mujib was arrested, so the second rung of the Awami League leadership took charge of the emerging liberation struggle. Most of them escaped from Dacca and reached the eastern districts of the Indian state of West Bengal. An independent Government of Bangladesh was established on the Indian border and the location of the Government was named Mujibnagar. The new Government, headed by its designated vice-president, Syed Nazrul Islam, issued a proclamation on 10 April in which the following points were affirmed: that Bangladesh was an independent sovereign republic; that Sheikh Mujibur Rahman would be the president of the new state; that Syed Nazrul Islam was designated vice-president and supreme commander of the armed forces of the republic; and that the government under him would exercise all executive and legislative powers of the state. Tajuddin Ahmed was designated prime minister while Kamaruzuman would be the home minister. The Government ordered a full-scale liberation war against the Pakistani regime. It appealed to all Bengali military and paramilitary personnel and youth to join the Bangladesh freedom forces.

A delegation from this new government visited Delhi to request India's recognition and military assistance. India assured support for the fulfilment of the aspirations of the people of East Bengal and urged the Government of Pakistan to release Sheikh Mujibur Rahman and to negotiate a peaceful political settlement.

The prime minister of Bangladesh, Tajuddin Ahmed, simultaneously appealed for international support and arms aid for the liberation struggle. Significantly, all the important powers expressed sympathy for the people of East Pakistan but did not show any inclination to support them actively. The only positive element was a shared view that Pakistan should respect the results of the elections, restore democracy and release Sheikh Mujibur Rahman. While this surrealistic political theatre was in progress, the Pakistani military crackdown intensified. In the initial stages of this process, civilised members of the Pakistani power structure started dissociating themselves from the policies of Yahya and Bhutto. The most prominent amongst them was Lt. General Sahebzada Yakub Khan, who was the then Governor of East Pakistan. He resigned his post and returned to West Pakistan as his sage advice was overruled by the politically blind military regime and Bhutto. Bengali military personnel and Bengali youth combined to form several groups of freedom fighters and commenced military resistance to the Pakistani forces.

The second phenomenon was the massive exodus of refugees from East Pakistan into the Indian states of West Bengal, Assam and Tripura. By the middle of April, the liberation struggle in Bangladesh had become an operational fact. However, it took nearly seven months for the world to acknowledge this struggle as a political reality. Even India was cautious in publicly proclaiming its support for the break-up of a neighbouring country through military means till August-September 1971, though by the end of

May, the inner deliberations of the Government of India considered supporting the liberation struggle as unavoidable. The Mujibnagar Government operating from the Indian border was provided with headquarters at 18, Camac Street in Calcutta. The Ministry of External Affairs opened a full-fledged secretariat in Calcutta to liaise with the Mujibnagar Government under Nazrul Islam and Tajuddin Ahmed. It was headed by a senior officer of the Foreign Service, A.K. Ray, who had been deputy high commissioner in East Pakistan, and was joint secretary in charge of the Pakistan Division in New Delhi when the crisis blew up.

Political and psychological factors characterising the crisis made India's involvement in the liberation struggle inescapable. The point to be underlined is that India's support was not a preplanned, conspiratorial strategic response to the continuous threats Pakistan had been posing against the unity and territorial integrity of India right since Partition. The first step that India took was to indicate its clear sympathy for the triumph of democracy in East Pakistan and the fulfilment of the legitimate aspirations of the people of Pakistan (as a whole) as manifested in the December 1970-January 1971 elections. In the immediate aftermath of the crackdown and the arrest of Sheikh Mujibur Rahman, senior leaders of the Awami League had escaped to India and sought support for the establishment of a government in exile. India's first formal step was to allow the establishment of such a government. The second move was to give refuge to the military and paramilitary personnel who had escaped as they were particular targets of the extensive military crackdown.

The ferocity and indiscriminate military violence caused intense and widespread resentment among the people of East Pakistan against West Pakistanis in general and the military regime in particular. By about the end of May, several Bangladeshi resistance groups had come into existence. Former local members of the army who had defected to the cause commenced resistance under the leadership of Major Ziaur Rahman and the then seniormost former East Pakistan army officer present in Bangladesh, Col. M.A.G. Osmani. Other senior Bangladeshi officers like Lt. General Wasiuddin happened to be in West Pakistan and were put under house arrest. Members of the youth wing of the Awami League constituted themselves into Mukti Bahinis under the leadership of bold and charismatic persons like Sheikh Fazlul Haq Moni (a nephew of Mujibur Rahman), "Tiger" Kader Siddiqui, Tofail Ahmed, Abdul Razak, Abdul Kuddus Makhon and so on. These groups, despite lack of formal training and political experience, showed a clear sense of priorities. They knew that finance and arms were most important to make the resistance movement effective.

Instead of attempting to stabilise the administration of East Pakistan, the military regime resorted to extremely violent military repression. The Bengali personnel manning the lower echelons of the administration fully supported the call for a break with West Pakistan and for the establishment of Bangladesh. Taking advantage of the situation the resistance groups captured armouries and arsenals in most places except Dacca. They also captured the treasuries at various district and some subdistrict headquarters. Having acquired this money they sought Indian assistance, which was given, to convert a portion of these resources into foreign exchange for purchasing essential communications equipment and other items needed to carry on their struggle.

By the middle of May the flow of refugees had reached alarming proportions. By the third week of May there were between five and a half and seven million East Pakistani refugees causing demographic pressures on Assam, Tripura and West Bengal and straining the resources of these Indian states. Although it extended general support to the cause of the East Pakistanis, India was cautious not to take macro-level diplomatic or political steps in support of the liberation struggle. While providing facilities for the establishment of an interim government and giving general support to the resistance movement, India had not given formal recognition to what came to be known as the Mujibnagar Government.

Ambassadors to the UN

Responding to the large-scale influx, Mrs Gandhi established a separate department to deal with the East Pakistan refugees under the charge of the Secretary, Rehabilitation, Government of India. India first took up the East Pakistan issue in the United Nations as a refugee problem. Ambassadors to the UN in New York and Geneva were instructed to give detailed factual briefings to the Economic and Social Council of the UN (ECOSOC) the United Nations High Commission for Refugees (UNHCR) and other related agencies about the violent events in East Pakistan and their negative fallout on India. Similar instructions went out to all diplomatic missions. While this was the initial approach, the internal views at the highest levels in the Government were characterised by nuances and differences of opinion. Mrs Gandhi had appointed a core group of senior advisers to deal with the crisis. The persons constituting this group were D.P. Dhar, who was chairman of the Policy Planning Committee of the Government of India, P.N. Haksar, principal secretary to the prime minister, T.N. Kaul, foreign secretary, R.N. Kaw, director of the Research and Analysis Wing of the Cabinet Secretariat, and P.N. Dhar, secretary in the Prime Minister's Office. At the Cabinet level, the principal advisers were Swaran Singh, Y.B. Chavan and Jagjivan Ram.

The results of the internal cogitation, which I describe below are based on my memory of secondary briefings I received on these discussions from D.P. Dhar and T.N. Kaul. I became involved because at the time I was in charge of work related to the specialised agencies of the United Nations as deputy secretary in the UN Division of the Ministry of External Affairs. As India chose to use the handle of refugee influx to highlight the East Pakistan issue at the various fora of the United Nations, I was designated as coordinating officer for this work at the middle level. By end-June 1971 I was detached from the UN Division and a special unit or bureau was created to deal with the crisis, of which I was nominated director. As I was dealing with the preparation of papers, basic policy notes and briefing points, I was given guidance and instructions by both D.P. Dhar and T.N. Kaul on the basis of the discussions in which they were participating. This is how I came to know about some aspects of the differing views on Indian policy.

Mrs Gandhi's initial and instinctive reaction was to give immediate recognition to a free Bangladesh and to back the liberation struggle and the resistance movement with full military support. However, Foreign Minister Swaran Singh held the view that while ultimately this was what India might have to do, it must ensure that its credibility and political correctness was not questioned. Swaran Singh felt that India should not face collective international opposition from the greater powers as well as from the United Nations on the basis of a possible accusation that India was interfering in the affairs of a neighbouring country with the aim of fragmenting it. P.N. Haksar, as far as I recall, shared this view, whereas D.P. Dhar was more inclined towards immediate drastic action against Pakistan. When Mrs Gandhi consulted Defence Minister Jagjivan Ram and the then army chief, General (now Field Marshal) Sam Manekshaw, both of them reportedly told her that while India could exercise her military option, a precipitate military campaign in the summer and monsoon months might create problems and delay the successful completion of the campaign. General Manekshaw expressed the view that he should be allowed sufficient time to prepare the Indian armed forces for deployment against Pakistan as he correctly anticipated that he would have to fight the war on two fronts. Mrs Gandhi's advisers also pointed out that apart from ensuring international credibility regarding the Indian initiative in responding to this crisis, India should take into account the possibility of Chinese political and military support to the Pakistani regime. This would be apart from the support the US under President R.M. Nixon would extend to Pakistan. Consequently, an evolutionary policy stance was adopted aimed at freedom to exercise the military option if interim measures taken did not resolve the East Pakistan crisis. India, therefore, decided on a policy approach having the following elements:

- The East Pakistan crisis could be resolved only if Pakistan respected the results of the general elections and assured the fulfilment of the legitimate political and constitutional aspirations of the people of Pakistan, especially East Pakistan.

- To achieve this objective the military regime should immediately release Sheikh Mujibur Rahman from custody enabling him to return to Dacca, and should recommence political negotiations with him.

- Pakistan should ensure the return of all East Pakistan refugees to their homes, undertaking to guarantee their safety, honour and economic well-being.

- Pakistan should immediately stop the military crackdown on the people of East Pakistan, and Pakistani troops should return to their barracks.

- The international community should pressurise Pakistan to resolve the East Pakistan crisis by peaceful means; this advice and pressure should be generated through bilateral diplomatic channels and the United Nations.

- The United Nations and its specialised agencies should initiate immediate steps to give relief and rehabilitation assistance to millions of East Pakistani refugees in India and those who had become shelterless within East Pakistan due to the military crackdown.

The Pakistan response to this policy stance was to level the familiar accusations about Indian conspiracies to break up Pakistan. There was no response to the suggestion of releasing Sheikh Mujibur Rahman unconditionally, or about reopening political negotiations with him. Pakistan also engaged in propaganda, saying that the refugees who had come into India were really rebels and "secessionist miscreants" and that the majority of them were Hindus. It also accused India of giving support to the Government in exile and to the East Pakistani resistance groups — an accusation that was factually correct. The number of refugees had reached eight million by July, and there was no indication of Pakistan pulling back from its confrontationist stance. There was also an increasing feeling in the Government of India that exercising the military option in support of the freedom struggle of Bangladesh was inevitable.

The Indo-Soviet Pact

The most significant strategic step that India took in preparation for this possibility was to sign an agreement on peace, friendship and cooperation with the Soviet Union. It had been under negotiation for nearly six years, since the mid-1960s. The contents of the agreement, its finalisation and the date of its signing were kept completely confidential. The Soviet Foreign Minister, Andrei Gromyko, flew into Delhi on 5 August and the Indo-Soviet agreement was signed in the Cabinet Room of South Block on the morning of 7 August 1971. The agreement had significant clauses guaranteeing mutual cooperation for ensuring each other's security. Without going into clause-by-clause details, the most important political and strategic clauses were those that stipulated both countries guaranteed each other's security; that if there was any perceived threat by either party to the agreement they would enter into immediate consultations to fashion remedial countermeasures; that they would not enter into any arrangement or agreement with other countries which would be detrimental to each other's security interests; and that they would cooperate with each other to strengthen security.

The agreement was received with much criticism from Pakistan as well as the US and other Western democracies. As far as India was concerned the general objective of the agreement was to provide a legal and political basis to seek Soviet assistance in case India's security was threatened by any country. The specific objective was to provide a basis for future support from the Soviet Union in case the US and Pakistan, or Pakistan and China acted in concert to thwart any military operations India might undertake in support of Bangladesh's liberation struggle. India was prompt in emphasising that the Indo-Soviet agreement was not based on any aggressive or assertive intentions. Nor did it preclude India's willingness to enter into similar agreements with any other country responsive to such arrangements. The substantive political perception generated by the agreement, however, was that India had moved significantly forward in giving operational assistance to the liberation struggle of Bangladesh. Apart from coping with the refugees and sustaining the liberation struggle indirectly, India also had to take note of the fact that the US had increased its military supplies to the Pakistani regime. India also noted that Sri Lanka was being used as a transit point for the airlifting of military supplies and troops to East Pakistan.

General Yahya Khan announced that he was going to order Mujibur Rahman's court martial for waging war against Pakistan within three days of India signing the agreement with the Soviet Union, that is by 10 August 1971. The trial was to be in camera without providing Mujibur Rahman any legal defence and without allowing any impartial observers to be present. Both Mrs Gandhi and Sardar Swaran Singh sent messages to the UN secretary-general and to the heads of diplomatic missions in New Delhi objecting to the Pakistani decision, and pointing out this would exacerbate the political crisis.

Henry Kissinger visited Delhi in July 1971 to caution India against supporting the liberation struggle and pointed out that the US remained fully supportive of Yahya. He stated early that India should expect the US to oppose any Indian initiative in support of the liberation of Bangladesh. His meetings with Mrs Gandhi, P.N. Haksar and other Indian officials were tense and unproductive. Kissinger was assertive and somewhat supercilious. He received a firm and equally disdainful response from his Indian interlocutors, details of which are available in Kissinger's memoirs and the memoirs of the then foreign secretary, T.N. Kaul.

Kissinger proceeded from New Delhi to Islamabad from where he was to undertake his secret mission to Beijing to reopen diplomatic and political relations between the US and China. Yahya and Bhutto had been the intermediaries who had organised the political exchanges as well as the logistics that culminated in this momentous visit. Pakistan was an extremely important strategic instrument assisting the US in creating this new equation with China. It was natural, therefore, for the US to be fully supportive of the military regime of Pakistan.

To revert to Colombo being used as the air transit point for transporting Pakistani forces to East Pakistan, and to how India reacted to it, Mrs Gandhi deputed Sardar Swaran Singh to Colombo late in August to persuade Mrs S. Bandaranaike to withdraw this facility. She was also to be reminded that India had come to her assistance in overcoming the violent Janata Vimukti Perumana (JVP) agitation against her. Mrs Bandaranaike was not very responsive initially, till Swaran Singh politely told her that if Sri Lanka did not agree to the Indian request, India might be compelled to take interceptive action to prevent Pakistani defence supply flights from landing at Kathunaike airport in Colombo. In the event India did not have to take any drastic action; Mrs Bandaranaike agreed to the Indian request.

The extent of US support to the military regime in Pakistan can be gauged by the fact that Kissinger and the Nixon administration ignored, and indeed rejected, factual reports about atrocities and the violation of human rights which were sent to Washington by the then US consul-general in Dacca, Archer Blood. Blood was ostracised, isolated and recalled and a diplomat called Spivak replaced him in Dacca. The only measure that the US was willing to take was to offer some monetary assistance for the East Pakistani refugees in India. The US refused to ask Pakistan to release Mujibur Rahman or to undertake political negotiations with him.

There were both fundamental strategic considerations and immediate political compulsions for India to support the liberation struggle in Bangladesh. In the years following the partition of India, Pakistan had used its eastern wing for subversive activities and secessionist movements against India. Apart from sending the Hindu population of East Pakistan as refugees to India, East Pakistan was also utilised as a base for financing and supplying arms to separatist groups operating in the northeastern states of India, whether they were Naga or Mizo. As the China-Pakistan equation came into being and progressed into a defence and political partnership from 1962 onwards, India's defence planning had to take into account the possibility of fighting a war on two if not three fronts if there was to be a conflict situation with Pakistan. Such a war might also lead to Chinese support of Pakistan in its eastern wing and a conflict situation on the Sino-Indian borders.

This perception was not just speculative. When the Tashkent Agreement was signed after the Indo-Pakistan conflict of 1965, Zulfiqar Ali Bhutto had described it as a national humiliation and diplomatic betrayal. Bhutto's remedy and revenge was to advocate not just the acquisition of Jammu and Kashmir by force but the dismemberment of India in its eastern extremities. Stanley Wolpert in his biography of Bhutto, *Zulfi Bhutto of Pakistan: His Life and Times*, states that Bhutto sent a top secret memorandum to Field Marshal Ayub Khan in the aftermath of the 1965 war that stated: "The defence of East Pakistan would need to be closely coordinated with Chinese actions both in NEFA and also possibly in the regions of Nepal and Sikkim. It would be necessary to provide the Chinese with a link-up with our forces in that sector. I envisage a lightning thrust across the narrow strip of Indian territory that separates {Pakistan} from Nepal. He is referring to the Jalpaiguri-Siliguri-Bagdogra salient on Indian territory. From our point of view, this would be highly desirable. It would be to the advantage of Nepal to secure its freedom from isolation by India. It would solve the problem of Sikkim and Tibet and for us Pakistan a stranglehold over Assam whose disposition we can then determine" (page 93).

The erosion of India's territorial integrity and the dismemberment of India through the instrumentality of an anti-Indian nexus not only between Pakistan and China but between Pakistan and other smaller neighbours of India was the basic motivation of Pakistan's India policy. It should be remembered that though Ayub ruled till 1969, and Yahya from 1969 to 1972, Bhutto was the most influential political voice of Pakistan, both domestically and internationally from the winter of 1965 onwards. Bhutto's orientation regarding India heightened Indian strategic threat perceptions. The ramifications of Bhutto's political views on Indo-Pakistan relations were multifaceted. East Pakistanis felt that their defence and security did not matter much to the central authorities in Islamabad. They noted that Pakistan was more inclined to delegate the responsibility of defending East Pakistan to China than strengthen East Pakistan's defences by locating sufficiently well-equipped military forces.

As the movement for autonomy gained strength in East Pakistan from 1954 to 1956, public opinion in India, particularly in West Bengal, became supportive of the movement. Whatever the formal stance of the Government of India, the realities could not be ignored by policy-makers. Though India did not want a reversal of history after Partition and the reintegration of Pakistani territories with India, it nevertheless remained deeply convinced that religion alone did not make a nation. Two wings of Pakistan with an intervening stretch of over a thousand miles of Indian territory was a geographical and political incongruity. The possibility of a strategic nexus between China and Pakistan centred on East Pakistan was an additional factor that contributed to Indian support for the movement for autonomy in East Pakistan. If the people of East Pakistan, driven by socio-ethnic and linguistic factors and in the face of an irrational and obstinate negation of their basic rights and aspirations, wished to secede from Pakistan, India could have no objection. If Indian endorsement and support could result in the emergence of a friendly entity, it would be beneficial. A non-hostile Bangladesh in place of a hostile East Pakistan was considered desirable.

These were the strategic considerations. The immediate provocation was, of course, the humanitarian disaster that followed the brutal military crackdown on the civilian population. Additionally, the economic and demographic burden imposed on West Bengal, Assam, Tripura and Manipur due to the large-scale influx of refugees called for decisive steps. In any case, in no circumstances could the Government of India ignore the emotional and ethnic sympathy of the people of West Bengal for East Pakistanis.

Opposite Aims and Effects

Pakistani propaganda against the movement led by Mujibur Rahman only served to enhance Indian support for the freedom movement. Pakistan argued that India had fraudulently engineered Mujibur Rahman's electoral victory to break up Pakistan. Second, that the freedom fighters of Bangladesh were a minority group of secessionists. Third, that Mujib's political programme was foisted on him by India, and therefore the international community should prevent India from working against the territorial integrity of Pakistan. India was encouraging the flow of refugees into its territory for financial gain and to contrive a situation for politically separating East Pakistan from West Pakistan.

India's decision to support the East Pakistan freedom movement was fraught with the danger of backfiring. By 1971, India had faced centrifugal tendencies in its northeastern states and in Tamil Nadu caused by ethno-linguistic and cultural motivations. Supporting the freedom movement of Bangladesh could present India with a similar dilemma. It was however felt that a positive response to the Bangladeshi movement would reduce the chances of states like West Bengal agitating for separate identities. In operational terms any support or military intervention in East Pakistan would lay India open to the accusation of interfering in the internal affairs of a country that was also a recognised member of the United Nations. If India eventually got involved in a military operation, it would have to face charges attracting international law and critical international public opinion. By the end of April, Mrs Gandhi and her advisers had come to the conclusion that India should prepare domestic public opinion for the likelihood of extending formal and active support to the liberation struggle of East Pakistan. It was also considered necessary to undertake a comprehensive and detailed diplomatic initiative to make the chancelleries of the world aware of India's concerns.

Apart from setting up a special unit in the External Affairs Ministry to deal with the crisis, Mrs Indira Gandhi established a separate branch secretariat of the ministry in Calcutta to liaise with the Bangladesh Government in exile. A.K. Ray, who led it, had extensive contacts with the leadership of Pakistan across the board. He was known for his high intellectual calibre and courage of conviction. He was assisted by another Foreign Service officer, Ms Arundhati Ghose, then the deputy secretary who was later to become India's permanent representative to the UN at Geneva and ambassador to the Conference on Disarmament. The branch secretariat at Calcutta was entrusted with the task of liaising with the

Mujibnagar Government, coordinating the Central Government's views and policies with the state government of West Bengal, and facilitating logistical support for the Mukti Bahini, the freedom fighters of Bangladesh. The then director of External Publicity, S.K. Singh, who was also spokesman of the Foreign Office, was given the focused responsibility of coordinating the publicity campaign for the Government's East Pakistan/Bangladesh policies.

Mrs Indira Gandhi decided to involve a number of senior politicians and ministers in fine-tuning India's policy and in briefing foreign governments. Swaran Singh, K.C. Pant, Y.B. Chavan and Jagjivan Ram were assigned different responsibilities to mobilise domestic and international support for India's policies. Swaran Singh undertook a tour of the important capitals of Europe and North America between May and September 1971. K.C. Pant visited a number of Asian and South and central American countries. Mrs Indira Gandhi's close confidant and friend Mohammed Yunus was deputed to argue India's case with the Muslim and Arab countries. The diplomatic missions to the UN in Geneva and New York were strengthened. The Economic Division in the Ministry of External Affairs was reorganised and R. D. Sathe, the joint secretary in charge of it, was given special responsibility to deal with the assistance that may be required by the Bangladeshi Government in exile.

These basic organisational and political arrangements were in place by the end of May 1971. There were three special matters which India had to cope with. The first issue was to assist the Bangladesh Government in exile to establish linkages with the East Bengali diaspora in different parts of the world to enable them to obtain funds and support. The second issue was related to the large number of Pakistani government employees of Bengali origin who had resigned from their jobs and had commenced championing the cause of Bangladesh's liberation. Many of them wanted to come and stay in India, eventually to move to Bangladesh when the liberation struggle would be brought to a successful end. The third issue was to ensure that Pakistan did not succeed in moving the United Nations General Assembly and the Security Council to act against India, especially utilising the special relationship that existed between Nixon and Kissinger and Yahya.

The defection of East Pakistani government officials proved to be an incremental phenomenon between May and December 1971. The very first defection was by a young East Pakistani second secretary in the Pakistan High Commission in New Delhi, Shabuddin, in March 1971. He was the first Pakistani civilian officer to formally resign from the Pakistan

Government. It was a spontaneous and emotional reaction to the military crackdown. He resigned and sought political asylum in India which was promptly given. He was followed by the entire Bengali component of the Pakistani consulate general in Calcutta. Because the consulate was in West Bengal and this Pakistani mission was dealing with problems affecting East Pakistan's relations with West Bengal and Assam, the majority of the personnel at this mission, including the consul-general, were East Bengalis. Since India had not formally recognised Bangladesh, these officers were requested to assist the Bangladesh Government in exile, and form the nucleus of the emerging foreign office. Khondakar Mushtaq Ahmed, the foreign minister of the Government in exile, and his foreign secretary, Mehbubul Alam Chashi, started dealing with the defection of East Pakistani diplomatic personnel with the assistance of the branch secretariat of the Ministry of External Affairs in Calcutta and other concerned agencies. Indian diplomatic missions abroad were directed to respond positively to requests for political asylum from East Pakistani employees of the Government of Pakistan.

By the middle of June nine million refugees had migrated to India. Large refugee camps had to be opened in West Bengal, Tripura and Assam as the military repression continued unabated. Martial law remained the basis of governance of East Pakistan. After the initial indiscriminate violence, the Pakistani military concentrated on eliminating political activists, intellectuals, academics, artistes and former government employees. Bengali youth were a special target of Tikka Khan. The atrocities against women became a part of his pogrom. The Pakistani Army created paramilitary vigilante forces, called Razakars and Al-Badrs, who took over the dubious task of pursuing their fellow citizens after each military operation. A significant number of these paramilitary forces were recruited from amongst migrants from UP and Bihar who felt that their future interests would be safeguarded only if they supported West Pakistani terror. The ethnic dimension of this repression structured by the military regime created a deep divide between the Bengalis and non-Bengalis of East Pakistan.

International reaction to the developing crisis was characterised by a curious contradiction. Despite the censorship imposed by the Pakistan Government, stories of military repression, violence and the horrendous violations of human rights reached international public opinion through the media. There was growing support and sympathy for the cause of Bangladesh's liberation. In stark contrast to this the majority of governments, not only of the Western democracies but also the countries of the Non-

Aligned group and the socialist bloc, were opposed to the liberation of Bangladesh or the fragmentation of Pakistan. Most of them advised India not to get involved while expressing the hope that the Pakistani Government would resume a political dialogue with the leaders of East Pakistan. This type of governmental reaction was both logical and expected. No government could countenance the territorial disintegration of a state nor could it endorse any external support or intervention which would accelerate the process. The majority of Western democracies had close strategic relations with Pakistan because it had been a member of the Western system of military alliances. A large number of non-aligned countries were ruled by military dictators or authoritarian regimes, so there was sympathy amongst them for Yahya. China supported Pakistan as it had had a decade-long political and strategic equation with that country. The Soviet Union and East European countries, while they strategically and politically supported India, would still not openly back Bangladesh's liberation till it had become inevitable. Signals from the United Nations and its specialised agencies were that they would be willing to mobilise resources for helping the refugees and would try and persuade the Yahya regime to release Sheikh Mujibur Rahman for a political dialogue. None of the multilateral fora ventured a value judgement on the military repression of East Pakistanis or the disregard by the military regime of the fair and acknowledged electoral verdict of the people of Pakistan.

President Yahya Khan remained defiant. He had commenced the court martial of Sheikh Mujibur Rahman in Rawalpindi jail. All the indications were that the charge of high treason would be upheld and that he would be sentenced to death. The other senior politician in jail with him was Kamal Hossein, who was to become foreign minister of Bangladesh later. He was in danger of being sentenced to life imprisonment. It was clear by the beginning of September that neither the Pakistani government nor the international community was willing to end the oppression of the East Pakistanis or to explore the possibilities of a solution through political dialogue. The inevitability of a confrontation with Pakistan because of Indian support for the liberation struggle was clear. It was with this background that the Indian delegation prepared to go to New York for the United Nations General Assembly session in mid-September 1971. It was also decided to send a special delegation of the Bangladesh Government in exile to the UN to try to draw the international community's attention to the critical situation and to seek support for the liberation movement. It was towards the end of September that India changed gear to give operational support to the freedom fighters of Bangladesh.

By the end of August 1971 it was clear to India that the military regime of Pakistan was not in a mood to seek a practical political compromise on the East Pakistan crisis. Pakistan's policies as they crystallised between April and August, pointed towards the following broad trends:

- Sheikh Mujibur Rahman was to be tried and awarded the death sentence and, after the verdict was amended, be given a long prison term so that he could not re-emerge as a factor in East Pakistani politics.

- Pakistan should garner external support again t the liberation struggle, using the argument that the Government of l akistan would not allow the fragmentation of the country under the disguise of decentralisation.

- Pakistan would take back all the Muslim refugees but not the Hindu refugees who had "escaped" to India.

- Even the return of the refugees would be subject to the condition that the United Nations and the Western democracies would provide all the resources for their settlement.

- The Awami League would be abolished and would not be allowed to participate in politics in East Pakistan.

- The Government of Pakistan, without any reference to the election results of January 1971 would draft a new constitution. (This vide the declaration by General Yahya Khan of 28 June 1971.) The proposed constitution would provide for partial autonomy for East Pakistan and would allow participation in the government by all East Pakistani politicians except those who along with Mujibur Rahman had secession. This would include the entire leadership of the Awami League, which had won the general election in 1971.

- East Pakistan would remain under martial law and military operations would continue till the situation stabilised fully. A civilian government could take over in East Pakistan towards the end of 1971, were stability to return.

- India's support to the liberation struggle was to be projected as subversive intervention aimed against the unity of Pakistan. This issue would be brought up before the UN General Assembly and the Security Council as a threat to peace and regional stability.

- India's support was to be first contained and then neutralised by obtaining defence supplies from the US and by making specific defence cooperation arrangements with China focused on the East Pakistan crisis, as also by generating international opposition to India's role. The expectation was that if Pakistan succeeded in forging these equations and continued its military operations, the East Pakistani struggle would falter without direct Indian military intervention.

India's major foreign policy concern at this point was to persuade the US not to oppose the Bangladesh liberation struggle; to ensure Sino-Pakistani collusion did not sustain the discriminatory military regime in East Pakistan; to ensure to the maximum extent possible that the United Nations and its Security Council did not make any move supporting the policies of the military regime, and to forge an understanding with the Soviet Union to function in tandem with India to ensure the success of the liberation struggle.

Nixon's Chemistry

Western democracies led by the US were concerned about the violation of human rights and the military repression in East Pakistan but would not support the liberation struggle. China was far ahead of them, fully supporting the Yahya regime. The Soviet Union had a comparatively ambiguous approach till August 1971. It sympathised with the liberation struggle, supported India but did not openly declare itself in favour of the independence of Bangladesh. The beginning of the US-China détente and Kissinger's visit to Beijing in July 1971 brought about a qualitative change in Soviet policies. Their strategic interests were transformed in view of this evolving US-Pakistan-China nexus. The Soviet Union signed the Treaty of Peace, Friendship and Cooperation with India in the first week of August 1971, conveying it would stand by India against any Chinese military threat caused by the East Pakistan crisis.

The attitude of the Nixon administration was anti-Indian on the entire gamut of issues relating to developments in East Pakistan. Nixon's antipathy towards India was neither rooted in ideology nor coloured by political factors. It was entirely a matter of Nixon's flawed personal chemistry with Mrs Gandhi, going back to the time when he was vice-president under President Eisenhower. Nixon had visited India in the early 1960s at a point of time when his reputation was very high as a "Cold Warrior" and the winner of "the kitchen debate" with Khruschev in Moscow. He was treated rather perfunctorily by Mrs Gandhi and the Indian leadership because both Jawaharlal Nehru and Indira Gandhi had a better personal equation with Kennedy and Lyndon Johnson as well as the leadership of the Democratic Party. Nixon had proceeded to Pakistan from India. In contrast to the treatment in New Delhi, he was lionised by Field Marshal Ayub Khan and the Pakistan Government. He never forgave Mrs Gandhi and the Government of India for the lack of attention and high courtesy he thought he deserved. Mrs Gandhi on her part has been described in her interaction with President Nixon as aloof and indifferent. The US nevertheless was an object of primary attention in India's foreign policy at that point of time. While Nixon and Kissinger were temporising and obfuscating, depending upon their perceptions of US strategic interests, the US public opinion and US Congress were becoming increasingly concerned about Pakistani military violence against its own citizens. They were generally sympathetic towards the people of East Pakistan. The Indian ambassador in Washington, L.K. Jha, and the Indian deputy chief of mission, M.K. Rasgotra, were entrusted with the difficult and complex task of lobbying US public opinion and the US Congress to bring pressure on the Nixon government to desist from following an active anti-Bangladesh and anti-India policy. On all counts, they served India's interests with great determination and diplomatic adroitness. Their efforts marginally inhibited Nixon from giving full operational military support to the Yahya regime during the India-Pakistan war of 1971.

Foreign Minister Swaran Singh visited Washington in June 1971 to brief US authorities about the developing tragedy in East Pakistan. He urged the US Government to stop military assistance and to apply economic sanctions against the Yahya regime to extract from it a positive response for the people of East Pakistan. The effort proved futile. Nixon and Kissinger owed too much to Yahya for his help in establishing contact with the Chinese leadership. It was during late August and early September 1971 that the US decided to adopt the policy that came to be known as "the tilt in favour of Pakistan". Though a general policy statement was made about the US discontinuing military support to Pakistan, supplies continued. From late August onwards messages started coming suggesting that the US would discontinue economic assistance to India if it persisted in supporting the East Pakistan movement. An interesting example of political theatrics took place when the US ambassador to New Delhi, Kenneth Keating, told Mrs Gandhi at a meeting in her South Block office that the US wished to avoid taking the embarrassing decision to stop economic assistance to and cooperation with India and hoped that India would reconsider its policies on the East Pakistan issue. Mrs Gandhi's response was prompt and decisive. She told Keating that there was no need for the US to feel embarrassed and suggested the immediate closure of the US Aid Mission Office in New Delhi. She stuck to her decision. The office, located in a well-appointed complex of buildings on what was then known as Mehrauli Road (now Aurobindo Marg), was closed down. The building was converted into a hotel (Qutub Hotel) by the India Tourism Development Corporation.

India decided to undertake a vigorous and comprehensive advocacy of the East Pakistan cause at the UN General Assembly session in September 1971. It was also decided in consultation with the prime minister of the Bangladesh Government in exile, Tajuddin Ahmed, that his government would send a separate delegation to New York in the company of the Indian delegation to lobby the General Assembly. Information about the Bangladesh delegation coming to New York was conveyed to Ambassador L.K. Jha, who in a discussion with Kissinger late in August suggested that this delegation would be able to convey an objective and informed assessment of the attitude of the people of East Pakistan. This might help the US Government in giving constructive advice to President Yahya Khan to be reasonable.

The US, however, used this advice to serve its own purposes. Qayyoom, a member of the East Pakistan Awami League who was in touch with the Bangladesh Government in exile, approached an officer of the US consulate-general in Calcutta, George Griffin, claiming he had been designated to establish contacts with the US. The US consul-general was authorised to interact with Qayyoom. Qayyoom apparently told Griffin that if Mujibur Rahman was released and invited for political negotiations, a faction of the Awami League might settle for less than full independence and agree to the decentralisation of power within the framework of Mujib's six-point agenda. This message was conveyed to Yahya through the US ambassador in Islamabad, Joseph Farland. Yahya's response was that the Americans should continue contacts with that section of the Awami League inclined towards such a compromise. However, he did not make any firm commitments about releasing Mujib.

What was happening behind the scenes was that a faction of the Bangladesh Government in exile, led by its foreign minister, Khondakar Mushtaq Ahmed, desired negotiations with the Yahya Government through the mediation of the US. Tajuddin Ahmed learnt about the contacts between Khondakar's representative Qayyoom and Griffin and alerted D.P. Dhar. Indian agencies consequently began to monitor contacts between Qayyoom and Khondakar Mushtaq Ahmed with the US consular office. By September end, the Government of India had definitive information about Khondakar Mushtaq's disaffection with the Government in exile. Khondakar was to lead the Bangladesh delegation to the UN. His plan was to negotiate with the newly appointed civilian governor of East Pakistan and members of the Pakistan delegation to the UN, and with the commencement of these negotiations, disown the policies and declarations of Sheikh Mujibur Rahman. He had resolved to do this without informing the Mujibnagar Cabinet or the Government of India. Kissinger partially confirms these developments in the first volume of his autobiography, *White House Years* (pp. 869-873). But he gives quite a different version of the conversation between Qayyoom, Khondakar and the officials of the US Consulate.

D.P. Dhar felt that decisive remedial measures needed to be taken to prevent possible compromises that might affect the personal safety of Mujibur Rahman and harm the larger cause of Bangladesh freedom. He advised Tajuddin Ahmed that he should remove Khondakar from the foreign ministership and also relieve his foreign secretary, Mahbubul Alam Chashi. Dhar advised that Khondakar be given another portfolio in order to maintain the unity of the Mujibnagar Government. Tajuddin Ahmed was in favour of his complete removal from the government. Ultimately, President Nazrul Islam persuaded Tajuddin away from such drastic action. Khondakar was removed from the foreign ministership and was stopped from leading the Bangladesh delegation going to New York. Tajuddin then appointed a trusted grassroots Awami League member, Abdus Samad Azad, as foreign minister.

There were some differences between A.K. Ray, in charge of the Ministry of External Affairs' branch secretariat in Calcutta, and D.P. Dhar and T.N. Kaul, the foreign secretary, over the manner in which this critical development was dealt with. Ray felt the ministry was "over-interpreting" the implications of the contacts between Khondakar and Griffin. He also felt India's advice to Tajuddin Ahmed to remove Khondakar could be perceived by the Mujibnagar Government and a section of the Awami League as domineering and interfering. It could lead to factionalism in both the Mujibnagar Government and the Awami League. It was also Ray's assessment that India should not view the contacts in question with paranoia. Perhaps he felt these could contribute to the US modifying its attitude towards the East Pakistanis. However, the liberation struggle and India's support for it had proceeded too far to permit a reversal of the process, for that would certainly not have the approval of the freedom fighters and the people of East Pakistan. This, combined with the calculated equivocation of the Yahya regime and the steadfast obstinacy of Bhutto, convinced India and the Mujibnagar Government that the US initiative was more a tactical move to save Yahya than a genuine effort at finding a fair settlement.

The UN Debates

It is against this background that the Indian delegation led by Sardar Swaran Singh participated in the UN General Assembly debates on the Bangladesh crisis. Thirty-five of the 117 countries represented at the UN referred to Bangladesh in their policy statements in September-October 1971. Sardar Swaran Singh made his main policy statement on 27 September. He informed the assembly: "The Pakistan authorities have torn up the solemn declarations and conventions to which Pakistan had subscribed. Pakistan has desperately tried to divert attention from its outrageous actions. Its actions have made so many serious inroads into much that the UN Charter stands for that it would indeed be a travesty of international law and a mockery of international justice to suggest that what is involved is an internal issue. It is even less an internal issue when one keeps in mind that other nations are having to support the enormous cost of the massive exodus of Pakistani citizens into India."

Swaran Singh went on: "In our view the flow of refugees will not stop nor will the refugees already in India begin to go back until a political solution acceptable to the elected representatives of the people has been found. Secretary-General U. Thant and many other distinguished statesmen, politicians and leaders of public opinion have consistently maintained that as a first step towards a political solution, Sheikh Mujibur Rahman, the leader of the Awami League, should be set at liberty without delay and negotiations should be started with him. It has been proved beyond doubt that he alone can speak on behalf of the people of East Bengal. He and he alone symbolises and represents the aspirations and will of the people of East Pakistan. Apart from these actions, which the Pakistanis themselves can take, what can the international community do in these circumstances? First and foremost, action which the Assembly and all other international organs within or without the UN system can take is to impress upon the military regime of Islamabad the fact that force will not succeed and that therefore a political settlement between the military regime and the already elected leaders is essential. We consider it wholly short-sighted to wait until the worst crisis has arisen. Bilaterally, all governments can do their utmost to ensure with whatever means available to them, that the military regime stops its repression, enters into negotiations with the elected leaders to achieve a political settlement with their consent and send the army back to barracks. Only by these measures will the flow of refugees be stopped and the refugees already in India be able to return home. Only by the measures I have suggested will the threat of famine be alleviated and normal conditions restored. If these measures are not taken, if attempts are made to divert attention by various analyses and wrong accusations, then the prospects are indeed gloomy. We, here in this Assembly, may argue in a sophisticated manner as long as we like but those who have been the victims of aggression and who are fleeing from terror and massacres will not have such a tolerant outlook. They will not forgive us or those who do not stand by them in their hour of trial."

I recall that Aga Shahi, the permanent representative of Pakistan to the United Nations, interrupted Sardar Swaran Singh's speech twice by raising points of order. Both points of order basically accused India of interfering in the internal affairs of Pakistan. But a more interesting point of order was raised by Jameel Baroody, ambassador of Saudi Arabia at the United Nations for a very long period of time. He was prompted to interrupt Sardar Swaran Singh by the Pakistani delegation. Baroody proceeded to the podium and suggested that the United Nations was already seized of the problem of the refugees in India, so there was no need for India to raise the issue in the general debate. He then went on to make the extraordinary suggestion that Sardar Swaran Singh need not deliver his whole speech; the text of the speech had already been distributed to the members of the General Assembly and could be taken as read. This would save the time of the General Assembly and would also help avoid controversies.

Sardar Swaran Singh gave appropriate answers to the points of order raised by Baroody and Aga Shahi, and he insisted on delivering his whole speech. What was particularly notable was his sense of humour and its display as he came down from the podium after delivering the speech. All of us in the delegation asked him whether he was not upset about the interruptions, particularly the one by the Saudi ambassador. Sardar Swaran Singh's response was: "You young people should understand that before I became the foreign minister or joined the cabinet, for many years I was a lawyer practising in the courts of Jalandhar and other parts of Punjab. I am used to calculated and frequent interruptions by lawyers and their harassment. But Baroody underestimated me if he thought that I would give up making the speech to gain cosmetic approval from these delegations in the General Assembly."

The upshot of the debate was the stark revelation that members of the UN do not react to critical political developments in member states on the basis of the merits of the issues or moral considerations of democracy and the rule of law, which the UN upholds. When the agenda item on the East Pakistan crisis was put to vote, a resolution in which India demanded the fulfilment of the aspirations of the people of East Pakistan, an overwhelming majority of the UN membership, as far as I recall 111 out of 114 countries, voted against India. There were two votes cast in favour of the resolution, those of India and Bhutan. One or two abstained. This voting pattern in turn was used by the Pakistani delegation and the US as the basis to argue that India should be pressurised to withdraw its support to the East Pakistan freedom movement.

In the General Assembly, 117 members participated in the general debate of whom 55, excluding India and Pakistan, referred to Bangladesh in their statements. These references can be classified under the following categories:

1. Twenty-four countries stated that the problem should be tackled from a humanitarian point of view, but made no reference to the political aspect of the problem. These were: Argentina, Australia, Chile, China (Taiwan), Egypt, Ghana, Jamaica, Japan, Laos, Liberia, Libya, Mexico, Madagascar, the Netherlands, Nicaragua, Syria, Tanzania, Thailand, Turkey, Uganda, Uruguay, Yemen (Aden), Yemen (Sanaa) and Zambia.

2. Eight countries stated that the primary concern should be humanitarian, and called for the restoration of normality in East Bengal as a prerequisite for the return of refugees, etc. These were: Afghanistan, Ceylon ("accelerated democratic and constitutional procedures"), Equador, Finland, Italy, Nepal, the UK ("a return to civil government") and Yugoslavia.

3. Fourteen countries, apart from expressing humanitarian concern, specifically stated that a political solution should be evolved to meet the situation in East Bengal. These were: Austria, Belgium (also counted in category 4), Cyprus ("the humanitarian problem has its roots in a political situation and the secretary-general has put the proper emphasis on this issue"), France, Guyana, Ireland, Malta (referred to a solution based essentially on "political accommodation"), Mongolia ("means in accordance with the interests of its population"), New Zealand ("durable, political settlement"), Norway, Poland (called upon Pakistan "to adopt measures to reach an appropriate political settlement of the crisis situation in East Pakistan"), Sweden, the US, and the USSR.

4. Five countries acknowledging the humanitarian aspects of the problem, stated that it should be settled between India and Pakistan with or without the assistance of the UN. These were Algeria, Indonesia, Iran, Lebanon, Sierra Leone and Belgium (primarily included in category 3).

5. Saudi Arabia by taking a pro-Pakistan stand constituted a category by itself.

6. Three countries, Ethiopia, Iceland and Israel, made only passing reference to the problem.

Twelve countries "specifically" stated that the situation in East Bengal involved human rights, or took the line that a political solution in East Bengal should be reached in consultation with the elected representatives of the people. Such statements can be classified in the following categories:

(a) Eight countries specifically stated that the East Bengal situation involved human rights: Belgium, Ecuador, ("protests against massacres in East Pakistan which are a violation of the sacred nature of human life"), Ireland, Malta (the refugee camps are "the direct result of political and military action" and the refugees "have their inalienable human rights"), Madagascar (called for "humaneness in the conduct of repressive operations"), New Zealand, Sweden and Uruguay.

(b) Four countries "specifically" stated that a political solution should be reached in consultation with the elected representatives of the people: France ("a political solution based on the consent of the Pakistani people"), Mongolia ("a settlement by political means in accordance with the interests of its people"), New Zealand, and Sweden ("a political solution based on the will of the people as expressed through the ballot").

It is interesting that only India and four other countries in the entire UN advocated a political settlement of the East Pakistan crisis in consultation with the people of East Pakistan. The reaction of all the other countries was both ambiguous and pusillanimous.

Plus Ça Change...

It was clear to India by the third week of October that the international community was not likely to support the liberation struggle or the fragmentation of Pakistan. This was an attitude both logical and in conformity with the general principles of international law. The international community was willing only to provide some marginal economic assistance for the relief and rehabilitation of East Pakistani refugees who had come into India. The continuing military repression was eroding the operational effectiveness of the various groups of freedom fighters. The majority of Islamic countries and the Western democracies led by the US were supporting the Yahya regime.

A worrisome aspect of the situation was Pakistan's success in persuading some segments of the international community and some of the multilateral fora to question the veracity of India's claims about the number of refugees who had crossed over from East Pakistan. The special secretary in charge of the East Pakistan refugee problem, G.S. Kahlon, advised Sardar Swaran Singh that India should allow visits by eminent and credible foreign observers to these refugee camps and then get these visitors to address press conferences attended by both Indian and foreign journalists. Since international support for Pakistan was likely to increase, bringing upon India additional pressure, it became necessary to make a careful assessment of whether a liberation struggle with only general support from India would succeed or whether it would require Indian military support. This carried the risk of an open military confrontation with Pakistan. An evaluation had to be made about the countries likely to support India, the way the UN might react.

India extended a general invitation to journalists and observers from within the country and from abroad to visit the refugee camps themselves. Three eminent persons who visited the camps between October and early November in 1971 were Senator Edward Kennedy, chairman of the sub-committee on human rights and refugee problems of the US Senate, André Malraux, former culture minister in Charles de Gaulle's Government in France, and Prince Sadruddin Aga Khan, the United Nations high commissioner for refugees. Senator Kennedy and Malraux went back convinced about the Indian claims and the critical predicament of the refugees. They also endorsed the validity of the Bangladesh cause. Prince Sadruddin Aga Khan acted with the utmost political correctness, and consciously moderated the political sensitivities which he no doubt possessed. I accompanied him to West Bengal, Assam and Tripura and on his tour of the refugee camps at Salt Lake City in Calcutta and near Guwahati and Agartala. He also had meetings with the chief minister of West Bengal, Siddhartha Shankar Ray, and the governor of Assam, B.K. Nehru. Since Prince Sadruddin wanted to be seen as making an assessment of the situation without the interfering presence of the Government of India, he was allowed free access to the registration process, and individually to the refugees without any governmental monitoring or presence. Because of his family's intimate links with Pakistan and his own inclination to be impartial as a senior UN official, Prince Sadruddin Aga Khan was a deeply disturbed man, having been greatly moved by the tragic predicament of the refugees. In his discussions in Delhi with the senior advisers of Mrs Indira Gandhi, he conceded that he came to India with some scepticism but was going back convinced of the enormous and tragic complexity of the East Pakistan problem.

Senator Edward Kennedy sought separate meetings with representatives of the Mujibnagar Government, which were organised both in Calcutta and Delhi. He returned to the US and spoke understandingly in the Senate, in American political circles and before the American media about the plight of the Bangladeshis. Malraux was so moved he wrote about his desire to mount an Indian Army tank and wage war against the military oppressors of East Pakistan. Being transparent about the ground situation and allowing foreign observers access to the refugees made an impact on world public opinion. By the middle of October, Pakistan started receiving serious appeals and suggestions from distinguished persons and even from some governments to release Mujibur Rahman and to resume negotiations.

Meanwhile D.P. Dhar asked me to prepare a position paper for consideration by the cabinet committee dealing with East Pakistan. I was asked to analyse and assess the likely reaction from major world powers and from the United Nations members to India providing open military support to the liberation groups of Bangladesh, an action that had the potential of an open war with Pakistan. He also asked S.K. Singh, then director in charge of external publicity, and me to visit Calcutta. He wanted us to speak to representatives of the Mujibnagar Government and the West Bengal Government to evaluate whether the Government in exile and the various freedom fighters' groups could sustain their military operations, considering the size and operational capacities of the Pakistani Army.

S.K. Singh and I visited Calcutta in late September and in the first half of October. We jointly submitted a report to D.P. Dhar providing a categorical assessment that the Pakistani Army was becoming progressively successful in neutralising the freedom fighters, including the groups consisting of former members of the Bengal Regiments and East Pakistan's paramilitary forces and police personnel ably led by former officers of the Pakistani Army including Major Ziaur Rahman. As far as I recall, our assessment was that the Pakistani Army would overcome the resistance movement at the latest by January or early February 1972, unless India improved its qualitative support to the liberation cadres, even at the risk of another Indo-Pakistan war.

The position paper I prepared about the likely international reaction to an Indo-Pakistan war contained the following assessments:

1. The international community was ambivalent about the prospects of an independent Bangladesh coming into existence.

2. There would be no disappointment or concern about the resulting predicament of the people of East Pakistan.

3. If the Pakistan military regime succeeded in stabilising the situation, the world would accept the fait accompli and support the Pakistani Government.

4. If India moved in the direction of a military conflict with Pakistan, the US, the Western democracies and China would not only oppose India but provide full political and indirect military support to Pakistan. But the military support would stop short of direct involvement in the war by Pakistan's supporters and allies.

5. The Muslim countries would give general political support to Pakistan's military regime but it was unlikely that they would give any meaningful material assistance to Pakistan. The members of the Non-Aligned Movement would not have a united approach to the East Pakistan crisis. The movement was fragmented. It would indulge only in impartial admonitions while the majority of its members would support Pakistan's advocacy of the importance of its territorial integrity.

6. Except for Bhutan, India's neighbours would have reservations about direct Indian involvement in the context of their own real or imagined threat perceptions. Russia would be generally supportive because of its strategic calculations vis-à-vis the US-China and the China-Pakistan-US nexus.

I also gave the general assessment that even though Russia would be sympathetic towards India, the United Nations and the Security Council would intervene successfully if the prospective war or conflict were prolonged. I concluded with the general opinion that the timing, the nature and the content of future support to the liberation struggle of Bangladesh should be decided primarily on the basis of consultations with our intelligence agencies and the armed forces headquarters. If their advice was that open support would result in a surgical and short successful operation, then India should consider this option. If their assessment was that the conflict was likely to be a long one, the Government should be cautious.

Mrs Gandhi's Initiative

Another overarching political factor that impacted on Indian policies at this particular point of time was the tremendous groundswell of public opinion not only in Bengal and Assam but all over India in support of the Bangladesh liberation struggle. There was growing impatience in Parliament and in the media about India not providing open military support. Leaders like Siddhartha Shankar Ray and Triguna Sen stressed the emotive support for the struggle from the people of West Bengal.

By the third week of October when the UN General Assembly debates were coming to an end, Mrs Gandhi decided she would undertake a direct and personal diplomatic initiative, visiting the capitals of important powers to explain to them India's predicament and persuade them to make a last attempt at influencing Pakistan to release Mujibur Rahman and restart political negotiations. In contrast, the Yahya regime's attitude was becoming progressively truculent. An example was Yahya's behaviour at a press conference at the United Nations headquarters when he visited the General Assembly in September-October 1971. Halfway through this conference one of the foreign correspondents asked him to confirm or deny the results of the general elections in which Mujibur Rahman had got a majority. The correspondent went on to quote the statistics of the election results and asked Yahya Khan for some additional factual information about the proportion of Bengali citizens in Pakistan compared to the citizens from other provinces constituting his country. Yahya's response was startlingly rude and inept. After emphasising the legitimacy of Pakistan's military operations in the post-election period in East Pakistan, he said something to the effect that he was the president of Pakistan and could not be bothered about giving statistics and factual information. Then he pointed his finger at one of the senior officials sitting with him at the conference, probably Aga Shahi, his ambassador to the UN, and told the correspondent that he must ask such questions from "one of my stooges". "They would be able to give you this kind of routine information," he said.

Meanwhile, the Mujibur Rahman trial continued. All indications were that a ruthless sentence would be awarded to him. Mrs Gandhi commenced her world tour in November, visiting Moscow, Washington and West European capitals. In the days preceding this, from mid-October onwards, India had stepped up its support to the Bangladeshi freedom fighters. Indian Army and naval units were put on alert to give support to the freedom fighters were the Pakistani forces to take any decisive military action affecting Indian territories. Nixon was naturally aware of these developments. He had already created what has come to be known as "Washington's Special Action Group" in his National Security Council to deal with East Pakistan crisis. Nixon also initiated a series of exchanges with the Soviet Foreign Minister Gromyko and asked Kissinger to interact with the Soviet ambassador in Washington, Dobrynin, to pressurise the Russians to function in tandem with the US to prevent India from providing support to the liberation struggle. The Soviet response was tactical but firm. Gromyko had told Nixon on 29 September that though avoiding war in the subcontinent was desirable, it was the Soviet Union's judgement that the risk of war would entirely be rooted in "Pakistani provocations and intransigence". By early October, Nixon had asked Alexander Haig, the deputy national security adviser to Kissinger, "to hit the Indians again on their refusing to agree to the proposals of withdrawal of troops from the East Pakistan border, in reciprocation of which Pakistan would also pull back its forces". The US Senate and House of Representatives were progressively critical of the administration's pro-Pakistan tilt, which only provoked Nixon to be more aggressively pro-Pakistani. His entire approach was to continue support to Yahya and Bhutto, and to somehow sustain the basic position of the West Pakistan power elite on the political future of East Pakistan. Bhutto and Yahya were encouraged to articulate a number of vague and shifty proposals for a political settlement.

Mrs Gandhi received a sympathetic and supportive hearing in the Soviet Union and a non-committal response from other European countries. She had two meetings in Washington with President Nixon on 4 and 5 November 1971. There is no better description (though from the American point of view) of these crucial meetings between Mrs Gandhi and Nixon than the one given by Kissinger in *White House Years*. He says:

> Nixon had no time for Mrs Gandhi's condescending manner. Privately, he scoffed at her moral pretensions, which he found all the more irritating because he suspected that in pursuit of her purposes she had in fact fewer scruples than he. He considered her indeed a cold-blooded practitioner of power politics. On August 11th, Nixon had admitted to the Senior Review Group that in Mrs Gandhi's position he might pursue a similar course. But he was not in her position — and therefore he was playing for time. He, as did I, wanted to avoid a showdown, because he knew that war would threaten our geopolitical design, and we both judged that East Pakistan's autonomy was inevitable, if over a slightly longer period than India suggested. In fact, India never put forward a specific timetable, implying throughout that yesterday had already been too late.

Mrs Gandhi, who was as formidable as she was condescending, had no illusions about what Nixon was up to. She faced her own conflicting pressures. Her Parliament would be meeting in two weeks, thirsting for blood. Though she had contributed no little to the crisis atmosphere, by now it had its own momentum, which, if she did not master it, might overwhelm her. Her dislike of Nixon, expressed in the icy formality of her manner, was perhaps compounded by the uneasy recognition that this man whom her whole upbringing caused her to disdain perceived international relations in a manner uncomfortably close to her own. It was not that she was a hypocrite, as Nixon thought; this assumed that she was aware of a gap between her action and her values. It was rather that for her, her interests and her values were inseparable.

The conversation between Nixon and Mrs Gandhi the next day confirmed the never-never land of US-Indian relations. Mrs Gandhi made no reference to Pakistan at all. The entire meeting was confined to world view matters in which Mrs Gandhi asked penetrating questions about our foreign policy elsewhere, as if the subcontinent were the one corner of peace and stability on the globe. She gave us honour grades everywhere, except there. Nixon on his part was willing enough to ignore the subject of the previous day, partly because he dreaded unpleasant scenes, partly because he correctly judged that this was Mrs Gandhi's way of rejecting the various schemes we had put forward. It was a classic demonstration of why heads of government should not negotiate contentious matters. Because their deadlocks seem unbearable, their tendency to avoid precision is compounded. Thus, Mrs Gandhi's visit ended without progress on any outstanding issue or even on a procedure by which progress could be made.

As mentioned earlier, in October, the director in charge of external publicity in the Ministry of External Affairs and myself, as director in charge of the special unit dealing with the East Pakistan crisis, were sent to Calcutta. We were told by the officials in Prime Minister Tajuddin Ahmed's office that while guerrilla warfare could continue for many years, the various groups of freedom fighters would not be able to overcome the Pakistani military without direct Indian military support. Col. (retd.) M.A.G. Osmani, who was the titular head of all the freedom fighters, gave the clear assessment that if there was no direct military support from India, the youthful groups fighting the West Pakistan Army would ultimately fade away. The following specific suggestions were made by the Mujibnagar Government to the Government of India:

1. The Bangladesh Government should be given formal recognition and Bangladesh's existence as an independent country should be legally acknowledged by the Government of India.

2. A joint command should be formed by the Indian armed forces and the Mukti Bahini to draw up immediate plans for full-scale military operations against the Pakistani armed forces in Bangladesh.

3. India should indicate to the United Nations that given the dilatory attitude of the majority of members, India and Bangladesh would not countenance any intervention by the United Nations that may be aimed at compromising or scaling down the demand for complete independence.

Mrs Gandhi had decided to respond positively to all of these demands by the time she returned from her trip to Washington. Intelligence sources had conveyed to her that the Special Action Group of the National Security Council of the US, under instructions from President Nixon, had commenced orchestrating strategies at the United Nations and in the important capitals of the world to resist the liberation struggle of Bangladesh and to sustain the approach of Yahya and Bhutto towards the political crisis in East Pakistan. India therefore came to the conclusion that before the US took any pre-emptive action to back Pakistan, the Bangladeshi freedom fighters' efforts should be given more operational support. By mid-November, Mukti Bahini groups had intensified operations sufficiently all over Bangladesh to make the Pakistani military command a trifle desperate. Bangladeshi freedom fighters, after each of their operations, were receiving sanctuary in Indian territory. The military high command in Pakistan therefore decided on a policy of hot pursuit into Indian territory, including some air strikes, despite East Pakistan having only 12 or 14 planes.

Matters came to a head between 15 and 31 November when Indian troops started retaliating against this Pakistani move. The incident that has come to be known as the Battle of Boyra, on 22 November was in fact the beginning of the military conflict between India and Pakistan. Yahya Khan warned from Islamabad that if India did not desist from supporting the liberation struggle, Pakistan would not limit the conflict to the eastern sector, that India should be ready to face the consequences on its western borders also.

Anticipating the prospect of an open conflict and preparing to give more support to the liberation struggle, Indian troops were put on the alert and requests were sent to the Soviet Union for defence supplies. The Soviet

Union readily responded and by mid-October Soviet military supplies had started reaching India. Following the Battle of Boyra, the Government of India decided to put in place all the procedural and legal arrangements necessary for India's direct military support to the liberation struggle. An advance team of Indian civil and military officials from Delhi went to Calcutta, as far as I recall, between 28 and 30 November to finalise a draft agreement between the Government of India and the Mujibnagar Government on the creation of a joint military command. It was also decided that once the command was formed and operations launched, Mrs Gandhi would announce the formal recognition of Bangladesh. She was visiting Calcutta between 1 and 3 December for some Congress Party engagements and functions organised by the West Bengal Government. She was to meet the president and prime minister of the Mujibnagar Government and formalise India's participation in the liberation struggle.

The creation of a joint command became a thorny issue for a brief period in the last week of November. The Indian military command's stand was that it was imperative to have a unified centralised chain of command. They were not happy about the creation of a joint command with general (the rank was given to him for the assignment) Osmani being designated as joint supreme commander of the forces that would operate in East Pakistan. Prime Minister Tajuddin Ahmed felt that his Government's political credibility as well as the discipline and loyalty of the freedom fighters could only be assured if a joint command were formed in which the commanders of the Bangladeshi freedom fighters, with General Osmani as the head, had a role to play. Ultimately D.P. Dhar, under direction from Mrs Gandhi, was able to persuade the Indian High Command to accept a joint command structure, with General Osmani as the counterpart of General Officer Commanding-in-Chief of the Eastern Command, Lt. General Jagjit Singh Aurora. The agreement on a joint command was negotiated and signed between 1 and 3 December 1971. The decision was to get directly and operationally involved in the liberation struggle some time towards the end of the first week of December. India was aware that once its armed forces got directly involved, they would be carrying out the major portion of the operation, while the Mukti Bahini units would shoulder the important responsibility of disrupting the administration, communications and military coordination of the East Pakistani forces inside East Pakistan. It was also clearly understood that once the operations started, the command and control would rest with the Indian military headquarters in Delhi and in Calcutta. The creation of a joint command was essentially a political arrangement respecting Bangladesh's political status and sensitivities.

In a manner, Indian military involvement had already commenced from October onwards. Indian commandos and marines had already started infiltrating East Pakistan with groups of Bangladeshi freedom fighters. The presence of trained Indian military personnel had increased the efficacy of the guerrilla war being conducted by the freedom fighters. Indian military liaison officers also helped in resolving controversies and soothing tempers between the different groups of freedom fighters which were generally operating autonomously. There was a group led by Tiger Kader Siddiqui, and another led by Sheikh Fazlul Haq Moni, a nephew of Sheikh Mujibur Rahman. Then there were the ex-military, paramilitary and police personnel of East Pakistan who functioned under the guidance of military officials like General Osmani and Major Ziaur Rahman, later to become president of Bangladesh.

"Exactly What One Had Expected"

Mrs Gandhi completed her engagements in Calcutta late in the evening of 3 December. She and her party, which included D.P. Dhar, some West Bengal politicians, and middle-level officials dealing with Bangladesh like Peter Sinai and me boarded a special plane around 7 p.m. for Delhi. As the plane reached the airspace a little east of Lucknow, the pilot asked D.P. Dhar to come to the cockpit and speak on the communication system as there was an urgent message from New Delhi. Mr Dhar spent three or four minutes in the cockpit, came out and spoke to Mrs Gandhi, walked back to his seat and turned to us who were sitting behind him and said: "The fool has done exactly what one had expected." General Yahya Khan had carried out pre-emptive air strikes on Indian air bases in northwestern India in Jammu, Punjab and in Rajasthan and had also launched ground attacks on Indian territory. General Manekshaw, chief of army staff, had already commenced retaliatory action. Most of northern and northcentral India was under a blackout in anticipation of further strikes.

Instead of flying to New Delhi, Mrs Gandhi's plane was diverted to Lucknow airport. We remained at the airport for nearly two hours and took off again around 10 p.m., landing at Palam around 10.45 p.m. Defence Minister Jagjivan Ram was at the airport to receive Mrs Gandhi. All of us drove directly to the Army Headquarters in South Block. Mrs Gandhi, Jagjivan Ram, Swaran Singh and senior officials went straight into the Operations Room. We were asked to wait outside. General Manekshaw proceeded to brief Mrs Gandhi and her cabinet colleagues about the counteroffensive which India had launched in the western sector. He also asked Mrs Gandhi's permission to commence operations in the eastern sector, which was immediately given. Mrs Gandhi proceeded to the Cabinet Room in the western wing of South Block to preside over an emergency meeting she had summoned while flying into Delhi. The cabinet took the decision to declare a state of war with Pakistan, to recognise Bangladesh and to allow the opening of a Bangladesh diplomatic mission in New Delhi immediately.

By the early hours of 4 December army groups belonging to the Eastern and Western Commands had launched full-scale operations against Pakistani forces. The army and navy were ordered to commence offensive operations, blockades and interceptions of Pakistani aircraft and ships forthwith. Mrs Gandhi announced the formal recognition of Bangladesh in Parliament on 5 December. Parliament unanimously endorsed the decision and declared its unqualified support for the military operations. Humayun Rashid Chowdhury, the seniormost Bangladeshi diplomat formerly belonging to the Pakistan High Commission, was designated as Bangladesh's first chargé d'affaires in India and was accorded the unusual honour of being received by both Houses of Parliament in a joint session.

One incident reflects the spirit of quiet confidence and humour that characterised the Indian military high command at the beginning of the conflict. I have mentioned Mrs Gandhi going to the Operations Room for a military briefing at midnight on 3 December. I was told by some colleagues who were in attendance that as she entered the Operations Room, she noticed a bottle of Scotch and a couple of glasses on the table. Fastidious as always, there was a frown on her face and she directed an enquiring look at General Manekshaw. The story went that General Manekshaw said to Mrs Gandhi: "Madam, the brand name of that whisky is Black Dog. It's the whisky that Yahya Khan drinks. I am quite sure that I shall overdrink him and outfight him, so please do not be angry." Years later, I inquired of Field Marshal Manekshaw, in the summer of 1998, whether the story was true. His laconic response was: "Yes, the story is generally true, but I do not quite remember what I told her. I must have been my usual irreverent self."

India simultaneously launched a diplomatic campaign in support of its military initiative. Communications from Mrs Gandhi and Foreign Minister Swaran Singh were sent to all heads of state and governments giving the background of the crisis in the region, explaining why India was compelled to give open support to the liberation war. The UN Security Council met in a continuous emergency session from 4 December to deal with the evolving crisis. The Pakistani ambassador to the United Nations, Aga Shahi, backed by US Ambassador George Bush and Chinese Ambassador Huang Hua, demanded immediate Security Council intervention against India. The Soviet ambassador, Jacob Malik, made a speech supporting India and the rationale of its actions. While the Security Council began to deal with the third war between India and Pakistan, India's ambassador to the UN, Samar Sen, summed up the situation in the words: "None can remove us from our path by mere resolutions and mere exhortations. The question of a cease-fire, as I have already mentioned, is one not between India and Pakistan, but between the Pakistani Army and the Bangladeshi people. Therefore, let us hear them before we go further into this debate."

The Attendant Political Events

A number of descriptive and analytical books have been written about the 1971 war, which lasted just about a fortnight. These have ranged from political analyses to military descriptions. While the commander of the Pakistani forces in East Pakistan, General A.K. Niazi, has come out with his account after a gap of nearly 27 years, his Indian counterpart, Lt. General J.S. Aurora, has yet to give his version of the campaign. It would not be appropriate for me to comment on the military operations because I had no direct involvement in them. I was only an indirect witness to the political processes and decisions. I will therefore focus on the attendant political events, and then describe the dramatic events leading to the formal establishment of Bangladesh as an independent country.

First, a summary of the broad objectives and characteristics of the military campaign as I recall them. The primary objective was to give full operational support to the freedom fighters for a decisive defeat of the Pakistan Army, ensuring the transformation of East Pakistan into the free republic of Bangladesh.

A consequent objective was to make sure that Pakistan did not take advantage of the conflict situation to intrude into Jammu and Kashmir and capture it. Another goal was to counter as decisively as possible any invasion from Sindh and Punjab, leading Pakistan to acquire Indian territory in the western sector. India also proposed to take tactical and procedural political initiatives at various important world capitals and at the United Nations. This was necessary to prevent any bilateral or broad political move by the international community aimed at rendering the Indian response to Pakistan abortive, and delaying the creation of Bangladesh. The higher political direction for military operations to meet these objectives was given by Prime Minister Indira Gandhi with the assistance of her principal secretary, P.N.

Haksar, and chairman of the policy planning committee, D.P. Dhar. Operational and detailed guidance was given by General Manekshaw, Air Chief Marshal P.C. Lal and Admiral S.M. Nanda. The theatre commander in the eastern sector was Lt. General Aurora and in the western sector Lt. General K.P. Candeth.

The broad strategy worked and all the objectives set by India were fully achieved. The Pakistani forces in East Pakistan were decisively defeated, with India taking 93,000 prisoners of war, the largest number of soldiers taken prisoner in world history and comparable only with the Russian army capturing the entire corps of Field Marshal Von Paoli in the battle of Stalingrad. The prisoners included all the generals serving in East Pakistan. On the western front, India pushed back the Pakistani forces from the Rann of Kutch. India had captured strategic locations in Jammu and Kashmir and about 5000 square kilometres of Pakistani territory in southern Punjab and Sindh, when it declared a unilateral cease-fire in the western sector on 16 December 1971. This is a compressed summary of the military campaign.

It is the political and diplomatic dimension of the campaign that is of more abiding interest. While the prime minister and defence minister Jagjivan Ram dealt with the situation in Delhi, the foreign policy aspects and manoeuvres at the UN were handled by India's practical and phlegmatic foreign minister, Sardar Swaran Singh, and the foreign secretary, T.N. Kaul, with the assistance of the Indian ambassador at the UN, Samar Sen. As war broke out, there were insistent messages from all the major powers asking India to stop military operations and agree to a ceasefire. The Soviet Union was the only exception. While urging a cessation of the military conflict, the Soviet Union emphasised that this could be possible only after Yahya had released Sheikh Mujibur Rahman and showed meaningful responsiveness to the aspirations of the people of East Pakistan. As mentioned earlier, consideration of the developments in East Pakistan/ Bangladesh shifted from the UN General Assembly to the Security Council as soon as war broke out. Neither India nor Pakistan was a member of the Security Council in December 1971. A meeting was summoned procedurally by the president of the Security Council and the secretary-general of the UN, but basically at the initiative of the US. The main purpose of the Security Council coming into session was to pass some sort of a collective resolution mandating India and Pakistan to stop the war and begin a political discussion. In all, 35 statements were made by permanent representatives of the member countries and by India and Pakistan between 4 and 21 December.

Interestingly, except for statements by the Polish representative, most of the statements were made by the American, British, French, Chinese and Soviet representatives. Of course, statements were also made by Ambassador Samar Sen and his Pakistani counterpart, Aga Shahi. The five permanent members of the Council were represented by very distinguished individuals. For the US it was George Bush, who later became the US president; France was represented by Kosciusko Mortzei, later to become secretary-general of the French Foreign Ministry; China's spokesman was Huang Hua, a future foreign minister; while Russia and Britain were represented by Jacob Malik and Sir Colin Crow. Aga Shahi eventually took over as foreign minister of Pakistan, and Samar Sen, bringing history full circle, became India's second and long-serving high commissioner in Bangladesh. The main trends in the Security Council discussions were as follows:

Pakistan accused India of deliberately creating a separatist movement in East Pakistan and of giving it open military support. India's statements concentrated on the unavoidability of its support to the liberation struggle of Bangladesh because of political and socio-economic reasons relating to the influx of refugees into India. The Americans, the French and the British, supported by most of the non-permanent members of the Security Council temporised or took an impartial stance. They urged an immediate cease-fire and resumption of a political dialogue. None of these members addressed the basic cause of the crisis, namely, the non-fulfilment of the legitimate political verdict given by the people of Bangladesh. The Soviet Union and to some extent Poland touched upon the crux of the problem.

Seventeen resolutions were introduced in the UN on the Bangladesh crisis — four in the General Assembly and thirteen in the Security Council — between 4 and 7 December. Thirteen more resolutions were introduced in the Security Council between 12 and 21 December. The resolutions moved by the US, the USSR and Poland were the most significant. The US consistently demanded an immediate end to all Indo-Pakistan hostilities, called for an immediate withdrawal of Indian and Pakistani forces from each other's territories, and appealed to both countries to create an atmosphere conducive to the return of Bangladeshi refugees to their country, and to use the secretary-general's good offices for this purpose. There was not a single reference to the political aspirations of Bangladesh or the manner in which these should be fulfilled.

The Russian resolutions in contrast were brief and to the point. These called for a political settlement in East Pakistan, which the USSR believed would automatically end the military hostilities, and urged Pakistan to direct its armed forces to stop all violence towards the people of East Pakistan. The draft resolution introduced by China was condemnatory of India, and to withdraw its forces from Pakistani territory. It suggested that all states should support Pakistan in its just struggle to resist Indian aggression. The other resolutions moved by France, the UK and the non-permanent members of the Security Council conformed to the US resolutions.

The most significant resolution moved in the Security Council was the one proposed by Poland (draft resolution No. S-10453) on 14 December 1971. It sought the stipulation on behalf of the Security Council that power would be peacefully transferred to the lawfully elected representatives of the people of East Pakistan led by Sheikh Mujibur Rahman, who should be released immediately. The resolution conditioned a ceasefire on this. As a follow-up Poland wanted the withdrawal of Pakistani armed forces to pre-set locations in East Pakistan from where they should be sent back to West Pakistan. The repatriation of Pakistani forces and West Pakistani civilians and the return of refugees was to be managed under the supervision of the United Nations. The resolution suggested that once these conditions were fulfilled, the Indian forces should immediately withdraw from Pakistani territory. It also suggested that neither country should retain any territory captured by it during the military conflict.

The Soviet Union as far as I recall, cast vetoes in favour of India about seven times between 4 and 16 December against US and Western-sponsored resolutions. The Polish and Soviet resolutions, which generally supported Bangladesh's cause and the Indian stance, received similar veto treatment from the Western permanent members of the Security Council. It was only when the war reached the concluding stage, between 12 and 14 December, that some resolutions in the Council, such as those moved by France, began to refer to the need for a political settlement and a response to the Bangladeshis' aspirations. The broad outcome was that because of India's close relations and strategic equations with the Soviet Union, the Security Council was prevented from taking any mandatory punitive action against India. Had there not been a Soviet veto, President Nixon's pro-Pakistan tilt would have found expression in a Security Council initiative that would have aborted the Bangladesh freedom struggle and resulted in a monumental strategic setback for India.

This assessment is partially based on my experience as secretary to the Indian delegation at Security Council meetings throughout December 1971. It was the polemics of the Security Council debates and the tactical political moves made by India and Pakistan that lent a sense of drama to the discussions on the East Pakistan crisis. Half way through the debate, some time between 9 and 12 December, the Chinese permanent representative Huang Hua, while reacting to the Soviet veto on one of Beijing's resolutions, resorted to ideological polemics and criticised the Soviet Union. He questioned the Soviet Union's socialist credentials, its inability to sustain socialist solidarity in the world and its motivations. Jacob Malik's response was witty. After he had answered all the points of criticism, he told Huang Hua that the Soviet Union had no complexes about its socialist identity. It was China that should do some introspection about its socialist integrity. Malik said China had once sent an emperor to Russia — the reference was to the last Ming emperor, Pu Yi, who went to Manchuria when it had come under Soviet control. The Russians had transformed him into a librarian and sent him back home where he did useful work as a Chinese citizen. The point was that the Russians had sent another Chinese home after training him in library science — a reference to Mao Zedong — and China made him an emperor, full of whims and fancies. Which country then was genuinely socialistic, Malik asked.

Sardar Swaran Singh and the Surrender

Swaran Singh arrived in New York on 10 December for the Security Council debate. The task of preparing the first draft of his speech was entrusted to me and C.V. Ranganathan, then first secretary in our permanent mission at the UN, and later ambassador to China and France. We prepared a compressed and pointed peroration. Swaran Singh took one look at the draft and declared it would not do. He said we must prepare a long speech covering the entire history of the alienation of the people of East Pakistan from their parent country. He added that he proposed to speak for at least two days. We accordingly prepared a long speech that ran into 20 printed pages. The statement had an amplificatory second section that ran into another nine printed pages. Swaran Singh delivered this on 12 and 13 December. Once in a while he insisted on consecutive rather than simultaneous translation. The Security Council is the only forum where a delegate can demand his speech is sequentially translated into four official UN languages and may disallow a simultaneous translation, because of the seriousness of the issue he is speaking on. The obvious result is that the speaker gains time.

By the morning of 14 December, local time in New York, it was clear that the military conflict would end in another 12 to 24 hours. We asked Sardar Swaran Singh why he was insisting on a long speech that might distract the Security Council members' attention from the issue. He replied that he had to gain sufficient time for India to bring the conflict to a decisive end without being thwarted by any Security Council decision. His political assessment was accurate, as it was obvious by 11 December that patience was wearing thin at the United Nations. Even the Russians had started urging India to end the conflict quickly as they felt they could not continue their opposition to the West's moves at the UN for very long.

As events progressed towards the defeat and surrender of the Pakistani Army in Dacca, the Security Council met on 16 December. Zulfiqar Ali Bhutto, who was leading the Pakisan delegation at the Council, was vitriolic in his denunciation of India. In view of the time difference between New York and the subcontinent, Sardar Swaran Singh received information about the surrender at Dacca some time during the morning of 16 December, local time in New York. He addressed the Security Council, giving information about the surrender and India's decision to declare a unilateral ceasefire on the western front from 8 p.m. Indian Standard Time on Friday. He urged the Security Council to ensure that India's unilateral ceasefire declaration was respected and implemented. Bhutto, sitting three or four yards from Sardar Swaran Singh at the circular conference table, tore up all the Council documents in front of him, fulminated and accused India of violence and aggression, and declared that Sardar Swaran Singh had bloodstained hands. He asserted that the Security Council could not play any useful role when the vital interests of member countries were affected. Bhutto then walked out of the Council meeting. The permanent representative of Pakistan, Aga Shahi, had the presence of mind to remain because he realised that this was the moment when Pakistan needed international support and sympathy. He continued to hold his seat till the Council was adjourned.

Sardar Swaran Singh's Foresight

The surrender at Dacca took place at 4.30 p.m. on 16 December 1971 at the Race Course Maidan. Lt. General Niazi signed the Instruments of Surrender while Lt. General Aurora signed the documents accepting the surrender. There was some drama preceding the surrender ceremony to which I will come later, but to return to the UN. As the Security Council meeting was coming to an end on 16 December, Sardar Swaran Singh passed a note to Foreign Secretary T.N. Kaul saying he wished all the Indian delegates to meet him in the lounge outside the Council Chamber immediately after the meeting was adjourned. We were all curious about the purpose. Sardar Swaran Singh came out and conveyed two or three very precise instructions we were to follow strictly. He said that no Indian delegate should be seen at the bar in the delegates' lounge in the coming 48 hours. He also cautioned us not to be boastful or jingoistic in our conversation with other delegates about the victory of the Indian Army and the liberation of Bangladesh. He said we must limit ourselves to responding to inquiries. He stressed that in our response we should underline that the break-up of Pakistan was a tragedy, that the cause of the tragedy was entirely due to the unreasonableness of the Pakistani military regime, that India's support to the liberation struggle was unavoidable and that India's declaration of a unilateral ceasefire in the western theatre of war was proof it had no aggressive designs. We were all impressed by his political sensitivity and foresight. The prescription which he gave could still apply to similar events and moments in history.

One incident in the military operations preceding the surrender of the Pakistani forces at Dacca is worth mentioning. The cabinet of the government of East Pakistan was summoned for a meeting by the governor of East Pakistan around 13 or 14 December to decide on measures to counter the increasing and imminent pressure of the Indian military advance. Indian military intelligence received advance information about this meeting and its timing. It was to be held in the large conference room in the left wing of the building (as one faces it from the main gate) of what later came to be known as "Banga Bhawan". Indian Air Force jets carried out a precision rocket attack on this room a few minutes before the meeting was due to begin. No other part of the building was damaged. (I saw this room soon after the surrender, on 16 December.) The rockets had hit and extensively damaged only this room and its conference table. My Bangladeshi friends told me later that this air operation specially unnerved the East Pakistani rulers and perhaps hastened the unconditional surrender.

To get back to the UN again, it would be pertinent to mention that there was a direct message from General Niazi to the UN secretary-general on 11 and 12 December that a ceasefire be immediately demanded under the aegis of the UN and that Pakistani armed forces be evacuated by ships and planes arranged by the UN. The message was signed by Major General Rao Farman Ali, Niazi's political adviser and chief of staff. His message did not have any formal endorsement from President Yahya Khan. In any case, the conflict was in its last stages during the week, 10 to 17 December 1971.

The last act of the play at the Security Council meeting was the adoption of a resolution (No.307 of 1971) on 21 December 1971. Taking note of the cessation of hostilities, the Indian declaration of a unilateral ceasefire and Pakistan's acceptance of it, the Security Council demanded that the ceasefire be made durable. It recommended the withdrawal of

Indian and Pakistani forces. It called upon member states to refrain from any action that might aggravate the situation in the subcontinent. This particular clause was perhaps a signal to Pakistan and China that they should not join together to revive the conflict.

I use the word "play" because throughout the East Pakistan crisis, the UN, virtually subject to superpower politics, failed to comprehend its seriousness and took no initiative to address the substantive issue, that is the fulfilment of the political aspirations of the people of East Pakistan. Nor did the UN or the Security Council take any step to stop the genocidal military operations of the Pakistani Army against the people of Bangladesh. Even as the Council dealt with the issue, the division of opinion was purely along strategic and Cold War lines. In a way, this helped India carry through the policy of supporting the freedom struggle with the Soviet Union's backing. But the most significant lesson India learnt once again — a lesson previously discerned from the manner in which the UN dealt with the Pakistani aggression in Kashmir — was that the UN cannot play an effective role in resolving political crises on merit alone, unless there is consensus among the Permanent Council members. The lesson is still valid, in terms of the UN's post–Cold War response to crisis situations.

It is time to move to events in India and Bangladesh between 3 December 1971 and 9 January 1972. The second date is a watershed in the history of Bangladesh because it was on the afternoon of that day that Sheikh Mujibur Rahman returned to Dacca after an interval of nearly nine months. During of his long imprisonment in West Pakistan he was on the brink of execution more than once.

I have mentioned the broad strategic approach adopted by the Indian military high command in conducting the war. Once open war was declared, after Pakistan's pre-emptive air strikes, the Indian Army took upon itself the main burden of regular combat with the Pakistani forces. The different groups of freedom fighters played a most crucial role in carrying out strikes behind Pakistani military lines and at the forces' concentrations. They also guided the movement of the Indian forces throughout the campaign in territory with which the Indian Army was not very familiar. They provided highly valuable psychological, logistical and operational intelligence about the Pakistani forces in East Pakistan. The Mukti Bahini cadre under the guidance of their leaders, General Osmani, Maj. Ziaur Rahman, Sheikh Moni, Tiger Siddiqui, Abdul Rab, Tofail Ahmed, Abdul Razak, also functioned as a valuable link between the people of East Pakistan and the Indian armed forces. Though the war finished in a fortnight, it was fraught with many tensions and contradictions. Intelligence sources had indicated the possibility of China coming to the assistance of Pakistan — information India had factored into its strategic planning. General Niazi's memoirs and other accounts of the conflict written by Pakistani authors confirm Islamabad's misplaced expectation that China would back its general political support with military intervention. India had to have contingency plans to deal with this possibility. Relations between General Osmani and senior military officials of the Eastern Command were somewhat tense. Although in terms of the Joint Command operational responsibilities were vested in the GOC-in-C, Eastern Command, General Osmani rightly wanted to be seen in an operational role in planning the war strategy, and Prime Minister Tajuddin Ahmed's efforts to persuade him to function in tandem with the Indian commanders irritated him at times.

Indian forces were short of missiles, ammunition, artillery shells and various categories of essential equipment that they had to obtain urgently and on an uninterrupted basis from the Soviet Union. The close contacts D.P. Dhar and T.N. Kaul had with the Soviet Union, both having been ambassadors to Moscow in the 1960s, helped. This was of course backed up by the mutually responsive and good equation between Mrs Gandhi and Brezhnev. The Indo-Soviet Treaty of Peace, Friendship and Cooperation signed in August 1971, proved to be the most significant political and diplomatic leverage during the 1971 war. Two Soviet deputy foreign ministers, Firyubin and Kuznetsov, were of particular help to India. It should be underlined that the pro-Pakistani tilt of President Nixon and his Washington Special Action Group on the East Pakistan crisis was apparent in the interaction between the US and the Soviet Union. Washington sent several proposals to Moscow between October and December 1971 to persuade India to stop supporting Bangladesh's freedom struggle. The main elements of these proposals were that the Soviet Union should persuade India to end its support of and break off relations with the Mujibnagar Government, and pull back its troops deployed on Pakistan's borders. The quid pro quo offered were vague assurances about the release of Mujibur Rahman, commencement of a dialogue with him, and general assistance for taking back East Pakistani refugees from India. The Soviet Union did not succumb.

The Soviet airlifting of military equipment to India commenced from the last days of October. As the assessment in New Delhi pointed towards the possibility of an Indo-Pakistan armed conflict, Marshal Pavel S. Kutakhov, deputy defence minister and chief of staff of the Soviet armed forces, visited India in November. The US on its part tried to persuade General Yahya Khan to step down. He was asked to agree to a unilateral withdrawal of Pakistani troops from East Pakistan and to the commencement of a political dialogue with Mujibur Rahman.Yahya agreed on 2 November to a unilateral withdrawal but equivocated over reviving a political dialogue. His stand was that he would talk only to East Pakistani politicians who were not involved with the liberation movement. This ruled out dialogue with the Awami League. Yahya was still playing games without realising the gravity of the situation.

Another significant development was the US cutting off economic and military aid as well as military sales to India in November. It has not been public knowledge that throughout November and the first half of December, Nixon held a series of secret meetings with the Chinese ambassador to the UN, Huang Hua, to consider what kind of Chinese pressure could be exerted on India to prevent it from supporting the liberation struggle. When war actually broke out, the Chinese reaction to Kissinger's proposals for a compromise on the East Pakistan crisis was negative. China wanted the matter to be decided in the Security Council and suggested that firm action be taken against India and the East Pakistan separatists, instead of seeking a compromise. Interestingly, there was no Chinese signal about extending any operational military support to Pakistan.

Seven Days and the Seventh Fleet

By 10 December seven days after war was raging both in East and West Pakistan, the US began to show concern about the threat to the territorial integrity of West Pakistan as a result of the Indian onslaught. A significant aspect of this anxiety was that India might eject Pakistani troops and officials from "Azad Kashmir", as Pakistan-occupied Kashmir is known. The Indian ambassador to the US, L.K. Jha, was called to the State Department more than once and asked for assurances that India would not liberate Pakistani-occupied Kashmir and would not attempt any territorial annexation in West Pakistan. Jha assured the Americans that India had no territorial ambitions in West Pakistan, but as far as Pakistan-occupied Kashmir was concerned, India would take a decision dependent on the military situation. He said he would seek instructions from Delhi. It was this anxiety about the disintegration of West Pakistan, coupled with the hope that a telling strategic signal from America might prevent the separation of East Pakistan, that led the US to order the Seventh Fleet, led by the aircraft carrier *Enterprise*, into the Bay of Bengal. The Seventh Fleet crossed the straits of Malacca on 13 December 1971, and sailed into the Bay of Bengal. The ostensible justification offered for the arrival of the Seventh Fleet, armed with lethal weapons, tactical nuclear warheads and strike aircraft, was that it was moving towards Chittagong port to safeguard foreigners in East Pakistan, and to evacuate them from an area where war had reached critical dimensions, threatening the civilian population. The operational implication of this move, however, was the possibility of American marines and soldiers landing in East Pakistan and intervening in the military operations, backed by the air and firepower of the Seventh Fleet.

India was naturally concerned at this development. At cabinet meetings held on 13 and 14 December in New Delhi, apprehension was expressed by several of Mrs Gandhi's ministerial colleagues to the effect that India must slow down the military campaign and establish diplomatic contacts at the highest level with the US and Western powers as well as with the Soviet Union. Mrs Gandhi consulted military leaders who, while recognising the seriousness of the threat posed by the Seventh Fleet's intervention, advised against a slowdown in the campaign, whatever the consequences. The Ministry of External Affairs also advised that succumbing to US pressure would affect India's credibility and international status in a profoundly negative way.

It was in the context of the Seventh Fleet's presence in the Bay of Bengal that the two Soviet deputy foreign ministers, Firyubin and Kuznetsov, arrived in New Delhi. In discussions with them, D.P. Dhar and Mrs Gandhi conveyed India's determination not to succumb to US military pressure. They also indicated that India expected the Soviet Union would stand by it at that moment of crisis. It was also pointed out to them that Yahya had formally requested military support under the defence arrangements Pakistan had signed with the US in 1954 and 1959, and under the terms of Pakistan's membership of CENTO and SEATO. Firyubin and Kuznetsov had come to New Delhi carrying briefs from President Brezhnev formulated on the basis of his interaction with President Nixon. At the superpower level a stage had been reached where the Soviet Union was not ready to jeopardise its gradually growing détente with the US. It desired a practical strategic equation with Washington in the context of the US new and expanding relations with China. The message the Soviet ministers brought with them was in substance the following. The Soviet Union would convey an appropriate message to the US to ensure the withdrawal of the Seventh Fleet from the Bay of Bengal, and that India should complete the operations in East Pakistan by December end. Once the operations in East Pakistan were successfully completed, Moscow wished that India should declare a ceasefire, stopping military operations in the western sector. The Soviet ministers pointed out that the USSR had steadfastly supported India in the Security Council by casting its veto. However, this was an exercise which could not be continued.

The Soviet Union sent a cautionary message to the US, late on 13 December or on the 14th morning, that the Soviet fleet in the Western Pacific had been alerted about the presence of the *Enterprise* in the Bay of Bengal and that it would be sent to stabilise the situation in East Pakistan. The message apparently also contained an assurance to the US that India would declare a unilateral ceasefire in the western sector after the operations in East Pakistan were over. India agreed to the suggestions that came from the combined pressure of the US and the Soviet Union. The only stipulation that India made was that it would not disengage itself from the conflict in East Pakistan till the liberation of Bangladesh was achieved. India indicated simultaneously to the Soviet Union that operations in East Pakistan would be over by 15 or 16 December. The Seventh Fleet started to withdraw from the Bay of Bengal by 15 December.

India's armed forces did a paradrop around Dacca on 13-14 December. By then Indian troops had taken control of most of the East Pakistan territory and bottled up the Pakistani troops at their divisional and brigade headquarters. Manekshaw had leaflets airdropped demanding immediate and unconditional surrender, giving assurances that the Pakistani troops would be treated under the Geneva Convention and other provisions of international law. General Niazi agreed to an immediate ceasefire and surrender. The surrender ceremony was fixed for 4.30 p.m. on 16 December 1971. The ceremony took place as scheduled at the Race Course Maidan at Dacca. The signatures of the two generals, one surrendering and the other victorious, were affixed at 4.31 p.m. and the ceasefire came into immediate effect in the eastern theatre. I was told by military colleagues that after signing the instruments of surrender and handing over his personal weapon (a pistol), Lt. General Niazi told Lt. General Aurora that whatever the outcome of the conflict, he hoped Aurora would tell the world that Niazi had given him a good fight, that he had fought well. Simultaneous with the surrender, India announced that it would implement the unilateral ceasefire on the western sector from 8 p.m., Indian Standard Time, on 17 December 1971. India informed the UN Security Council and all the world capitals about this decision.

A major political mistake at the surrender ceremony was the Indian military high command's failure to ensure the presence of General M.A.G. Osmani at the ceremony, and of not making him a signatory. The formal excuse explaining his absence was that his helicopter did take off but could not reach Dacca as per schedule. But there was widespread suspicion that his helicopter had been sent astray so that he could not reach Dacca in time, and the focus of attention at the ceremony would be on the Indian military commanders. This was an unfortunate aberration. It generated much resentment in Bangladeshi political circles. Osmani's presence at the surrender ceremony could have helped avoid many of the political misunderstandings that affected Indo-Bangladesh relations in the early days of Bangladesh's independence.

The end of the conflict in the eastern theatre was fraught with problems. Keeping 93,000 prisoners of war in safe custody, while managing a post-war situation, was both logistically and in terms of law and order a nightmare. There were no guarantees that some sections of the Pakistani prisoners of war would not mutiny and create a violent situation. There was the real danger of the people of Bangladesh resorting to retaliatory violence against the prisoners of war and the civilian officials who had supported Pakistan. Several groups of the Mukti Bahini were in an emotionally volatile mood. They had to be prevented from going on a rampage against the paramilitary cadre created by the Pakistani Government to maintain law and order in East Pakistan. Compounding the critical situation was the presence of nearly 200,000 Mohajirs, migrants mostly from Bihar and UP, who were concentrated in the Mirpur suburb of Dacca. These people had actively collaborated with the Yahya regime and were a particular target of the wrath of Bangladeshis. They had to be protected.

The political debacle and military defeat of 1971 destroyed the myths and deterministic predications on which Pakistan's India policy was fashioned. The myths destroyed were:

1. That India could never be united and politically cohesive enough to fight a decisive war with Pakistan.

2. That India as a pacifist and soft state dominated by the Hindu ethos could not match Pakistan's martial traditions.

3. That India's democracy was tentative and floundering with so many internal problems that it could not have any impact on Pakistan's subcontinental policies and moves.

4. That East Pakistan would not stand firm on its demand for liberation, under Pakistani military pressure.

5. That East Pakistanis, being Bengalis (though Muslims), were generally permeated by the Hindu ethos. In the face of sufficient coercive authority, they would stop their military operation.

6. That Indian encouragement to the freedom movement could be contained by a combination of Pakistani military strength and US support.

7. That the aversion of the international community to the breaking up of states and respect for the concept of territorial integrity would prevent the leaders of Bangladesh from achieving their objectives.

8. That the permanent members of the Security Council would act in time to prevent Pakistani military adventurism from becoming a Pakistani military debacle.

9. That the close friendly relations between Pakistan and China would result in China's active military intervention in favour of Pakistan.

10. And last, but most important, that the Pakistani decision-making elite would be able to successfully practise its own brand of politics, disregarding the democratic impulses of Pakistani society.

Pakistan emerged from the 1971 conflict disoriented and diminished. But whatever one's critical evaluation of Bhutto during the five years of his stewardship of Pakistan, he restored the national spirit, some sense of self and a purposive capacity for national restoration to his people and his country. Retrieving Pakistan from the political predicament of the defeat was the first priority in Pakistan's India policy in December 1971. By February-March 1972, communication between India and Pakistan commenced. Pakistan's priorities were to get the 93,000 prisoners of war released to prevent Bangladesh from holding war crime trials against Pakistani army officers and other ranks, to retrieve nearly 5000 square miles of captured territory and to ensure to whatever extent possible that Pakistan's stand on Kashmir did not get diluted or neutralised for good.

Though the Pakistani Army stood discredited and was in general disarray, it still remained the most organised segment of the establishment. Bhutto had to keep it on his side to achieve the above objectives. He also had to re-establish Pakistan's political credibility with the international community. He opted for a measured purging and reorganisation of the Pakistani military high command and began to cultivate Islamic countries.

India on its part had signalled the substance of its politico-military intentions by declaring a unilateral ceasefire on the western sector with the surrender of the Pakistani forces in the eastern sector. Any approach of a military nature or territorial acquisitiveness in West Pakistan would not have been a practical proposition. Nor would this have been acceptable to the international community, particularly to countries that were supportive of India's attitude and activities during the East Pakistan crisis. The experiences of the 1948 and 1965 wars with Pakistan were well learnt by India. It did not wish again to be part of a third party mediation process in which Pakistan would assume an artificial air of injured innocence and claim compensatory post-conflict compromises. It was in this context that India commenced negotiations for post-war normalisation of the situation with Bangladesh on the one hand and Pakistan on the other. Details of discussions held in Islamabad, Delhi and Murree between February and July 1972 have been discussed and analysed over the past three decades as have the negotiations between India and Bangladesh. These exchanges ultimately led to the signing of the Simla Agreement — and there begins the current stalemate in Indo-Pakistani relations.

The Simla Agreement

For a retrospective view of Pakistani motivations and statements from November 1971 to July 1972, it is necessary to understand the contents of the Simla Agreement and the negotiations that preceded it. Yahya Khan's pre-emptive air strikes on air bases in northern India had resulted from his growing frustration at not being able to effectively counter the increasing vigour of the freedom movement in Bangladesh and from a strategic perception that if he escalated the internal conflict in East Pakistan into an interstate war, it would ensure him greater power as well as UN intervention to prevent the break-up of Pakistan. While the operational decisions on the air strikes were military decisions by the Pakistani armed forces establishment, the strategic plan underpinning the air strikes was the result of Bhutto's fertile but flawed imagination. His argument was that expanding the conflict into a state of war with India would not only help in aborting the freedom struggle, but might also revive the question of Jammu and Kashmir at the UN.

Bhutto's influence on events during the conflict should not be under-estimated. In the last stages of the two-week conflict there was much confusion and contradiction in Pakistani moves. There were suggestions from the Pakistani Army command in East Pakistan that Mujib should be released and sent back — to pull the rug, as it were, from under the arguments of the freedom fighters. The central authorities in Rawalpindi did not accept this recommendation because of Bhutto's continuing apprehension that Mujib's triumphant return to East Pakistan would again endanger his own political ambitions and future. It was the same logic that resulted in Bhutto refusing to accept the Soviet and Polish resolutions in the Security Council in December 1971, advocating an immediate cease-fire, the return of Mujib, the restoration of democratic government in Pakistan on the basis of the electoral results, the withdrawal of Indian troops and the removal of Pakistani troops to West Pakistan. When Major General Rao Firman Ali, the second seniormost officer in Lt. General Niazi's headquarters in Dacca, sent a direct message to the Security Council indicating the willingness to accept an immediate ceasefire, the central authorities in Islamabad and Rawalpindi dissociated themselves from the initiative. They sent a message to Niazi that "Chinese activities" were likely to commence.

What is to be noted is that Bhutto was leading the Pakistani delegation to the Security Council meetings on the East Pakistan crisis. Despite his negative experiences concerning China and the US during the 1965 war, he still held on to the hope of Chinese and US intervention. The Chinese did not undertake any activities except to support Pakistan in deliberations at the UN, while the US naval task force steamed into the Bay of Bengal and steamed out again without making any impact. After berating Sardar Swaran Singh in vituperative language, Bhutto tore up the agenda papers and resolutions in the Security Council on 16 December 1971, threw them on the table and walked out. His expectation being that the conflict would continue in the western sector, he had hoped for a continuation of the Security Council meetings in which India could be put in the dock for aggressive intentions against Pakistan. India's declaration of a unilateral ceasefire in the Western Sector only increased his frustration and bitterness. This was the second time that he had failed in his anti-Indian adventurism. It was a bitter and vengeful Bhutto who became the president and chief martial law administrator of Pakistan in early 1972.

The Bhutto era in Indo-Pakistani relations had two phases. The first period, from 1972 to 1975, was that of Pakistan trying to salvage the political and military damage it had suffered in 1971, without altering the basic orientation of its adversarial attitude towards India. During the second period, from the end of 1974 to 1977, Bhutto felt that he had achieved his interim objectives and that he could now take strategic steps to achieve parity with India in all subcontinental equations.

For a start, he initiated establishing internal political and constitutional processes to consolidate his power, a pan-Islamic international credibility, and generating political and economic pressures on India for the return of prisoners of war and captured territory. He encouraged an anti-Indian stance in Pakistan's India policies to neutralise the impact of the military defeat and to create the impression that Pakistan was bloodied but not bowed. He refused to recognise Bangladesh. He orchestrated anti-Indian propaganda in the Pakistani media, about Jammu and Kashmir and self-determination for its people and about India maltreating its minorities — not only Muslims but also Sikhs. Support to Sikh separatists found political expression with his advent to power as early as 1972. He emphasised the importance of China in countering Indian hegemonism in the South Asian region and cautioned India's other neighbours against its expansionist motives.

Bhutto undertook a tour of Iran, Turkey, Morocco, Algeria, Tunisia, Libya, Egypt and Syria in the very first month of taking over power in January 1972. Though he announced that the objective of his visit was to convey his thanks to these Muslim countries for their support and assistance in rebuilding Pakistan's military strength and economy, the larger political objective was to see if an Islamic alliance could be forged to counter India's influence and stature in Asian, West Asian and Gulf politics. He succeeded in this effort, as later events showed. Pakistan was accepted as host for the summit of the Organisation of Islamic Countries (OIC) to be held in 1974. The flow of resources for Pakistan's military and economic revival also commenced. Though he took Pakistan out of the Commonwealth in retaliation for the grouping's temporising role during the East Pakistan crisis, Bhutto continued to cultivate Britain. Though disappointed with the US and China, he reopened talks with them to get support for the post-war damage-control exercises he was undertaking. He even conveyed messages to the Soviet Union not to precipitate any one-sided action in favour of India.

Though Bhutto was the architect of Pakistani policies seeking proximity with China and creating distances from the US-sponsored military alliances in the 1960s, he now asserted that the US-sponsored military alliances, of which Pakistan was a member, had reacquired their relevance for Pakistan in the context of the Indo-Soviet treaty of 1971. He put all these processes into motion between January and April 1972 with a view to strengthening Pakistan's negotiating position with India. Talks ultimately commenced at Murree in February and April 1972. Bhutto agreed to participate in the summit at Simla in July 1972 in an atmosphere of dichotomy. He had to ensure that domestic public opinion did not visualise him as a supplicant. At the same time, he had to get back Pakistani prisoners of war and territory and re-establish the case on Jammu and Kashmir. He also had to ensure that Bangladesh did not put Pakistani military officers on trial for war crimes. This was a daunting brief. He carried it through in great measure.

During the initial days of my assignment in the Indian embassy in Bangladesh in 1972, the Prime Minister Tajuddin told me that when Bhutto decided to release Mujib between 4 and 7 January 1972, he took the first step towards safeguarding the interests of the Pakistani military. Before his release and departure via London and Turkey, Bhutto is reported to have told Mujib that as a quid pro quo for his release he should help in freeing the prisoners of war and in not holding war crime trials. Bhutto is reported to have used the argument of solidarity among Muslims in support of his advocacy. He also reportedly reminded Mujib of his own contribution to the Muslim League's struggle for Pakistan before Partition, whatever the later differences and controversies might have been. Mujib's policies and attitudes on the issues between 1972 and 1974 lend credence to these reports.

Two competing approaches were advocated by Mrs Gandhi's advisers for the Simla discussions. One group sought to take full advantage of the military victory and make the release of prisoners of war and the vacation of captured territory conditional on Pakistan relinquishing all claims to Jammu and Kashmir and agreeing to a final settlement of the issue. If Bhutto rejected these demands, the advocacy was to continue a state of armed hostility short of war. The second group of advisers, perhaps with a more realistic and larger vision of working for subcontinental peace and stability, advocated the vacation of territory and the release of prisoners of war, but subject to the condition of Bhutto agreeing to a reasonable compromise on Jammu and Kashmir, and to structuring the provisions of the agreement in a manner that would encourage him to have peaceful relations with India and maintain his political credibility at home.

The negotiations at Simla were painful and tortuous. They almost broke down, but were retrieved after a long personal discussion between Mrs Gandhi and Bhutto. The provisions of the agreement and its implications have been studied, analysed, criticised and evaluated threadbare. It is not the formal clauses of the agreement that have to be taken into account, but the reported indications given by Bhutto to Mrs Gandhi in resolving the Kashmir issue that are of relevance in dealing with current Indo-Pakistani controversies.

There have been repeated reports from Pakistani and Indian official participants in the Simla discussions, as well as from media representatives present there in July 1972, that Bhutto had agreed to settle the Jammu and Kashmir issue on the basis of evolving ground realities. The Line of Control was to replace the ceasefire line between Pakistan-Occupied Kashmir (PoK) and Jammu and Kashmir. These reports now stand confirmed by P.N. Dhar, the then secretary and later principal secretary to the prime minister, in an article in *The Times of India* 4 April 1995. Mrs Gandhi and her advisers were clear that the basis for a durable solution to the Kashmir issue should be firmed up at Simla. But there were differences of opinion among her senior advisers, both in the Cabinet and at the official level about methods. The general information I have is that D.P. Dhar, who was an important adviser, desired a categorical and formal agreement by Pakistan to recognise the Line of Control as a de jure border, and that the release of Pakistani prisoners of war and the vacation of Pakistani territory should be conditional on Bhutto agreeing to this. The Indian side negotiated for this approach and its inclusion in the Simla Agreement right till the last minute. The Pakistanis could not agree.

Every indication was that the talks would fail, at which point Bhutto requested a private one-to-one meeting with Mrs Indira Gandhi late in the evening of 2 July. The private meeting began at 6 p.m. and lasted an hour and a half. According to information made available later, Bhutto agreed to the following points:

- He acknowledged the Kashmir issue should be finally resolved and removed as a hurdle in Indo-Pakistan relations.

- He agreed that the Line of Control could gradually be converted into a de jure border between PoK and Jammu and Kashmir. However, he requested that these commitments of his should not be included in the formal agreement or in the form of a written commitment. He said if this were done, it would endanger his survival and the emerging democratic setup in Pakistan. He was in the process of establishing civilian control over the armed forces. That process would be jeopardised.

- He was of the view that after the trauma of the separation of Bangladesh and military defeat, giving up Kashmir immediately and formally would deepen hostility against India in Pakistani public opinion. It would bring forces representing such hostility into the power structure. He conveyed that he would take steps after his return to Islamabad to first integrate PoK and other related territories of the old princely state of Jammu and Kashmir on the Pakistani side with the federal territories of Pakistan. Over a period of three to five years he would be agreeable to convert the Line of Control into a de jure border.

The Line of Control

Mrs Gandhi and Bhutto apparently agreed that once the Line of Control was stabilised as a border, all normal cross-border people-to-people contact would be restored. There was speculation on whether Bhutto's offers and commitments should be incorporated into some sort of secret memorandum or clause in the agreement. Both Bhutto and Mrs Gandhi agreed it would be inconsistent with the spirit in which the Simla discussions were held that nothing should be hidden from the public of India and Pakistan. According to P.N. Dhar, Mrs Gandhi asked Bhutto: "Is this the understanding on which we proceed?" He replied: "Absolutely, *Aap mujh par bharosa keejiye* (trust me)." As far as one knows, there is no written record of these agreements between Bhutto and Indira Gandhi due to his specific request. But Mrs Gandhi was sufficiently convinced, not so much of Bhutto's sincerity but of his compulsions and limitations, to go ahead with the Simla Agreement. It was signed late at night on 2 July 1972.

To some extent Bhutto did follow up on his offers. When the commanders drew the new line dividing the positions of Indian and Pakistani troops, it was called the Line of Control and significantly not the Line of Actual Control. The signal was that a Line of Control is permanent and will evolve into a boundary. Second, Bhutto detached the Northern Areas, originally part of the state of Jammu and Kashmir, and integrated them into the federal territories of Pakistan. He also structured greater political, administrative and constitutional control over Pakistan-occupied Kashmir. But by the second half of 1976 he was enmeshed in domestic political controversies. While he took the above steps to signal his following up on the assurances given to Mrs Gandhi, he also started resiling from his stand on Jammu and Kashmir by the beginning of 1973.

India agreed to release the prisoners of war in consultation with the Government of Bangladesh and vacate territory. It sought in return Pakistan's recognition of Bangladesh. As for the war crimes trials, India took the stand that this was a matter that had to be finally decided by the Government of Bangladesh, though India would assist in finding a reasonable compromise. This was the substance of the negotiations that led to the Simla Agreement.

Bhutto's detachment of the Northern Areas from PoK and then assuming more constitutional, political and administrative control over PoK itself in the aftermath of the Simla Agreement gives credence to the reported inclination for a compromise on Jammu and Kashmir. Later events and Pakistan's policies during the late 1970s and 1980s may cast doubt on Bhutto's sincerity. But at Simla, his compulsions must have lent a measure of reasonableness to his negotiating stance. He could not go back empty-handed from Simla. He did not. As far as Pakistan was concerned, despite coming to the negotiating table as a defeated party it returned a political gainer. There was agreement for the return of the prisoners of war and for the vacation of territory. At the formal level, the Jammu and Kashmir issue remained an acknowledged issue. Bhutto could claim he had retrieved Pakistan's interests, despite military defeat, on issues that really mattered to Pakistan. The Simla Agreement also led to the reopening of embassies. India chose to send somebody specially appropriate as ambassador to Pakistan. K.S. Bajpai, a senior contemporary of Bhutto's at Oxford, was posted to Islamabad. For about two years Indo-Pakistan relations drifted through an apparent and tentative normality.

Having achieved his immediate objectives, Bhutto concentrated on the two remaining aims: preventing the war crime trials and re-establishing Islamic links with Bangladesh. Though a bitter rival, Bhutto was accurate in his perception about Mujib's subconscious Islamic inclinations and his innate reservations about India, which Mujib viewed through the prism of his complexes about West Bengal. From 1973 onwards Bhutto sounded Mujib about Bangladesh joining the OIC, with the attractive proposition of Bangladesh emerging as a major South Asian Islamic country. When Mujib responded positively to this courtship by other Islamic countries, it was conveyed Bangladesh would get recognition from Pakistan and admission to the OIC if war crime trials were not held. The deal was struck some time between November 1973 and January 1974.

Mujib participated in the Islamic summit in Lahore in February 1974, despite a fair amount of opposition and doubts from his old comrades in the Awami League. Mujib returned, Pakistan recognised Bangladesh, and Bhutto was invited to visit Dacca. Bhutto's interaction with Bangladesh during the period had a single motive: to erode the political and strategic objectives achieved by India in the 1971 war. In the process he sought to revive the Islamic consciousness in Bangladesh. In private conversations, he is reported to have told his senior party advisers that India might have created Bangladesh, but he would see that India would have to deal with not one, but two Pakistans, one in the west and another in the east.

A digression here would reveal the accuracy of his assessment of the Bangladeshi psyche and also his capacity to achieve maximum domestic impact. During his visit to Dacca in July 1974, the roads from Tejgaon airport to his guest house were chock-a-block with the citizenry. It was not a hostile crowd, given that this very people had bayed for his blood in 1971. Being the acting high commissioner for India, I was in the reception line. When I was introduced, he shook hands with me and turned to Mujib and then producing something between a statement and a query said: "Now that we are rearranging subcontinental geography according to the wishes of the people, Mr Dixit, I suppose you and I could talk about settling the Kashmir issue accordingly." The subject he raised was indicative of his thinking. The occasion he chose and the person to whom he spoke were inappropriate except as an attempt to satirise Mujib and his attitude towards India. What followed was profoundly significant and an indication of the shape of things to come. As the motorcade moved out, Mujib's car was decorated with garlands of chappals and anti-Awami League slogans were shouted together with slogans such as: "Bhutto Zindabad", and "Bangladesh-Pakistan Friendship Zindabad". The diplomatic motorcade followed the main motorcade and as my car reached the junction where the road turns left to the Intercontinental Hotel and the government guest house, the crowd, recognising the Indian flag, shook and jostled my car and shouted anti-India slogans. I returned to my office chastened and ruminating about the twists of history and politics.

Earlier, in the United Nations General Assembly session in 1972 — on Pakistan's instigation and of course on the basis of its own calculations — China had vetoed Bangladesh's admission to the UN. Bangladesh was admitted after its contacts with Pakistan were established. But the story does not end there. Apropos of Bhutto's machinations, Bangladeshis were keen he pay homage at the Martyrs' memorial at Sawar with formal military ceremony. Bhutto was most reluctant. The ceremony was to be held on Friday afternoon, so he first delayed going there, saying that being a devout Muslim he had to offer Friday prayers and therefore he could not go at the scheduled time. However, he could not withstand Bangladesh's insistence and proceeded there late in the afternoon, not in the formal attire appropriate for the occasion but in casual clothes with a golfing cap, to place a wreath. He said that his going was conditional on no military ceremony being held. According to reports no military ceremony was held.

Mujib's Assassination

There were three results of Bhutto's visit to Bangladesh that had an impact on Indo-Pakistan and Indo-Bangladesh relations. He persuaded Mujib to reabsorb into the Bangladeshi military and civil services those Bangladeshi officers who had not endorsed the freedom movement, some of whom were still returning from Pakistan and other places. Second, he sowed the seeds for the revival of the Islamic character of the Bangladeshi polity by advising Mujib that now that he was free, he should gradually reclaim his country's Islamic identity to consolidate his domestic political position as well as counter excessive influence by India. Third, he told Mujib that to balance

India's influence and to retain Bangladesh's freedom of options, a good equation with Pakistan would be both relevant and necessary. Mujib's actions and policies from 1974 and till his assassination in 1975 indicate that his words were not ignored.

Two events that made a negative impact on Indo-Pakistan relations in 1974 and 1975 were India's successful underground nuclear test at Pokhran on 18 May 1974, and the assassination of Mujib on 15 August 1975. The Pokhran test gave Bhutto the necessary handle to arouse adverse Pakistani public opinion against India. It enabled him to augment the military strength of Pakistan not only with the help of Islamic countries but also with the assistance of the US and China, based on their apprehension of a nuclear-armed India. He vowed that Pakistanis would acquire a nuclear weapon even if they had to eat grass. The military coups and counter-coups that followed, ending in the assassination of practically the entire political leadership of the Bangladesh freedom struggle and enabled Pakistan to establish a nexus with Bangladesh. Within six years of Mujib's assassination, the Bangladeshi power structure was permeated by people with pro-Pakistani and extremist Islamic inclinations. This is not being said as criticism, but as a description of the changes in politico-strategic terms that took place in Bangladesh.

The period between 1974 and 1977, when Bhutto was on the way to being ousted from power, was essentially a period of drift in Indo-Pakistan relations with strong undercurrents of antagonism and tension. Having achieved his objective of the release of prisoners of war and the vacation of territory under the Simla Agreement, Bhutto had commenced retracting from some of the commitments inherent in it. Education Minister Pirzada, speaking in the National Assembly on 7 September 1972, barely two months after the agreement was signed, stated: "The president had categorically stated that Pakistan was not bound to the withdrawal of UN observers under the Simla Accord. The Government had no intention of asking the UN to withdraw its observers." (*The New Pakistan* by Satish Kumar, 1978, p. 243.)

The Pakistani media and ministers, from the second half of 1972, voiced the view that by agreeing to bilateralism in dealing with the Jammu and Kashmir issue Pakistan had not closed the option of using other instrumentalities, including the UN, to resolve the issue. There was delay in the withdrawal of Indian troops from captured territories; there was a delay in the release of prisoners of war because of Bhutto backing out of his commitment to recognise Bangladesh; there were skirmishes in the Rajouri sector between Indian and Pakistani forces; and even after the drawing of the Line of Control, military tensions continued.

From 1975 onwards, Bhutto became more and more enmeshed in domestic political controversies. His attempts at restructuring the polity were flawed because of his authoritarianism and ambition. The more he faced domestic opposition and crises, the more was his inclination to underline the dangers from India to consolidate his own position. By 1975, he started asserting Pakistan's need to have a firm and adversarial position against India in the context of the Indo-Soviet treaty of 1971, the Indo-Bangladeshi Treaty of Peace, Friendship and Cooperation of March 1972, India's nuclear test of May 1974 and Pakistan's commitment to keep the Jammu and Kashmir issue alive.

Foreign secretary–level talks took place as a follow-up of the Simla Agreement between 1974 and 1977. They ensured the maintenance of contracts and superficial calm. But by the end of 1975, Bhutto had lost interest in building Indo-Pakistani relations. Though embassies were retained and rail and civil air links were restored, political and economic interaction remained minimal. A trade protocol signed in 1974 did seek to stimulate the restoration of commercial relations. The only silver lining during this period were the trilateral and bilateral agreements signed between India, Pakistan and Bangladesh in April 1974, dealing with the repatriation of prisoners of war, the return of non-Bengalis from Bangladesh to Pakistan, and the not holding of war crime trials. In the event, only a small number of non-Bengalis were allowed to enter Pakistan. The issue remains a festering problem between Bangladesh and Pakistan. It was the bilateral agreements that restored the travel facilities between India and Pakistan in principle. But this did not result in the restoration of normal people-to-people contacts, because of Pakistan continuing with restrictive passport and visa procedures.

If one were to draw a balance sheet of improved trends in Indo-Pakistan relations, from India's point of view the foundations for the current controversies and antagonism were laid during this period. Despite the general commitment given by him at the Simla negotiations, Bhutto revived the issue of Jammu and Kashmir as the main hurdle to normalising relations, reasserting Pakistan's claims on Jammu and Kashmir. He launched Pakistan's nuclear weapons programme — commencing with Dr Abdul Qadir Khan's clandestine journey to Larkana — to make Pakistan a nuclear weapons state. The beginnings of the OIC being used as an instrument for Pakistan's policies towards India were made with the Lahore summit in 1974. Though people generally blame Zia-ul-Haq for the extremist Islamisation of the Pakistani polity, the process was begun by Bhutto because of his personal populist motives, which had their negative ramifications on relations with India. It was Bhutto who assiduously and purposefully rebuilt the strength of the Pakistani armed forces with the admonition that the humiliation of 1971 had to be avenged.

Within two-and-a-half years of his assuming power in Pakistan, by the end of 1974, the moderation and rationalism in Bhutto's approach towards India had disappeared. Despite his irritation with the US because of Kissinger acknowledging India's pre-eminent role in South Asia, he found encouragement from the US to build up Pakistan as a politico-military counter to India with the restoration of economic relations and military supplies by 1975-76. He could revert to his adversarial mindset primarily because he had politically retrieved what had been lost by Pakistan's defeat in 1971.

Zia's Coup

By 1975, the tenuous momentum to normalise Indo-Pakistan relations went into a sluggish drift. Bhutto had reverted to his strategic vision of reviving Pakistan as a most important power in south Asia. Though full-fledged ambassadorial relations were restored and some limited steps were taken to revive trade and cultural cooperation, Bhutto was not interested in these processes. Neither was Mrs Indira Gandhi for that matter. By 1975 both Bhutto and Indira Gandhi were enmeshed in domestic political turmoil. Mrs Gandhi had to declare an internal emergency and Bhutto had to go in for elections, in 1977, which he unnecessarily rigged, aiming at an overwhelming electoral victory. The rigging was a combination of voting irregularities and violence. It was the violence he engineered that led to his terminal debacle.

There was a curious parallelism in the political destinies of Mrs Gandhi and Zulfiqar Ali Bhutto in 1977. Mrs Gandhi lost the general elections in March 1977 and was out of power for nearly three years. Bhutto's authoritarianism and intrigues led to a military coup by Zia-ul-Haq. Soon after being ousted from power, Bhutto was arrested and imprisoned on charges of conspiracy to murder and abetment to murder a political rival. He was sentenced to death and despite appeals and requests from various heads of state and government, the sentence was carried out on 1 April 1979. His execution in many ways had the inevitability of a Greek tragedy — a flamboyant life violently cut short, perhaps because of his self-destructive ambition and nonchalance. It must be mentioned that Mrs Gandhi appealed to General Zia not to carry out the death sentence. Morarji Desai who had become prime minister of India, refused to make such an appeal, despite suggestions to do so.

It took nearly a year and a half from 1977 for Indo-Pakistani relations to emerge in any discernible pattern. Pakistan's new ruler, Zia-ul-Haq, remained in power for eleven years. In this time he dealt with three prime ministers — Morarji Desai, Indira Gandhi and Rajiv Gandhi. This phase of Indo-Pakistani relations will be dealt with in the next chapter but a postscript on how the Government of Pakistan itself dealt with the trauma of the military defeat by India in December 1971 will be pertinent.

The general public reactions to the conflict as it evolved have been mentioned in the earlier portion of this chapter. But more detailed information about the critical introspection carried out by Pakistan became a matter of public knowledge with the commission report prepared by Justice Anwarul Haq Hamoodur Rahman, submitted to the Bhutto Government on 23 October 1974. The report was kept secret for 28 years until it was leaked to the Pakistani paper *Jung*. The commission was established by Z.A. Bhutto soon after he took over in December 1971, and was headed by the chief justice of Pakistan, Hamoodur Rahman (a Bengali who had remained loyal to Pakistan during the 1971 war). It consisted of Justice S. Anwarul Haq of the Supreme Court of Pakistan, Justice Tofail Ali Abdur Rahman, chief justice of Sindh and Baluchistan, and Lt. General (retd.) Altaf Qadir, who was entrusted with the task of enquiring into the circumstances in which the commander of the Eastern Command of Pakistan surrendered, and the members of the armed forces of Pakistan under his command laid down their arms.

The report rejected the claim of the Pakistani Government and army headquarters that Pakistan was not really defeated, that the army in the East was just betrayed. The commission charged both the Pakistani armed forces high command in Islamabad and all the senior officers of the Eastern Command of the Pakistani Army with subverting democracy, violating constitutional processes, precipitating civil disobedience and armed revolt, violence against civilians and encouraging murder, rape and looting. The commission categorically affirmed that the Pakistani armed forces were defeated and the defeat was due to a lack of professionalism, a lack of character in the officer cadre — and a collective and deliberate decision not to respect the democratic verdict of the people of Pakistan. The leaders of a number of political parties of West Pakistan were blamed as co-conspirators with the armed forces. The report confirmed the civilian population not only in East Pakistan, but in West Pakistan too, was completely opposed to Bhutto's political intrigues, which prevented Mujibur Rahman from becoming prime minister. It also opposed the military crackdown on the civilian population of Bangladesh by General Tikka Khan and Lt. General Rao Ferman Ali.

What is interesting is that Bhutto and the heads of government who succeeded him refused to publicise this report for nearly three decades, the main reason being the concern of the Pakistani armed forces high command that its credibility and reputation would be damaged. Equally interesting is the fact that while Bhutto sent Yahya and General Gul Hasan, the then operational chief, into obscurity, he condoned General Tikka Khan becoming chief of army staff and Lt. General Rao Ferman Ali, the key figure in the violence against civilians in East Pakistan, becoming chairman of the powerful Fauji Foundation. Both these military officers remained part of the power structure of Pakistan even during Zia-ul-Haq's time. Even at the time of writing, the Hamoodur Rahman Report has not been officially given to the public. The text has become public knowledge covertly, through an exercise in investigative journalism.

In conclusion, one wonders if India's deep-seated anxiety to restore peace and stability in the subcontinent, reflected in Indira Gandhi agreeing to sign the Simla Agreement, was misplaced. Should India have been slower in releasing the prisoners of war, and in vacating Pakistani territory and the areas in Jammu and Kashmir? Should it have agreed to the ambiguous formulations on the Jammu and Kashmir issue in the agreement, instead of insisting that Pakistan accept the ground realities. In sum, should India have been slower in waging peace, which is always more difficult and complex than waging war?

A portentous footnote to this period is that it was in March 1972 that Bhutto initiated Pakistan's nuclear weapons programme which culminated in the tests in the Chagai Hills in the last week of May 1998. But more about this in the chapter on India and Pakistan's nuclear weapons programmes.

Seven

Coup to Coup:
Pakistan, 1972–1999

*C*ompressing the complex pattern of relations between India and Pakistan during a 22-year time-span is not easy. Pakistan during this period (1977-99) had the governments of Zia-ul-Haq, Benazir Bhutto, Ghulam Mustafa Jatoi, Nawaz Sharif and Moinuddin Qureshi, with Benazir Bhutto and Nawaz Sharif coming back to power twice through elections. The government in India also went through parallel changes in leadership. Morarji Desai came to power in March 1977, a few months before Zia overthrew Bhutto in a military coup. Desai was succeeded by Charan Singh, Indira Gandhi, Rajiv Gandhi, V.P. Singh, Chandra Shekhar, P.V. Narasimha Rao, H.D. Deve Gowda, I.K. Gujral and Atal Behari Vajpayee. The point to remember is that Indo-Pakistan relations at one level were subject to political uncertainties and changes of governmental leadership, and at another level the general adversarity was punctuated by brief periods of thaw and normalisation, especially after democracy was revived in September 1988 with Benazir becoming prime minister.

Zia ruled Pakistan for 11 years continually dealing with three Indian prime ministers, Morarji Desai, Indira Gandhi and Rajiv Gandhi. (I am not counting Charan Singh's brief six-month tenure towards the end of 1979.) Zia's long tenure lent a certain continuity to his India policies. Despite his fomenting trouble in Punjab and generating tensions in Jammu and Kashmir, his period in office was characterised by a certain stability in Indo-Pakistani relations, which was in contrast to the volatility and tensions which characterised the period between 1969, when Ayub was ousted, and 1977, when Bhutto was overthrown.

One should begin with the persona of Zia and the political concerns and motives that animated him. Though a Punjabi, he was not from the heartland of west Punjab, which dominated the military power structure of Pakistan. So he had to prove himself to be more of a west Punjabi Muslim in his attitudes towards domestic politics in Pakistan as well as towards India. Belonging to the elite armoured corps and not having a high military reputation, he had a continuous anxiety about consolidating his image in the officers' cadre and other arms of the Pakistani armed forces. Though not an admirer of Ayub Khan's Sandhurst-based military culture, he was of the view that ultimate political power should vest with the army, as this safeguarded the interests of the armed forces. The armed forces, as he saw it, were the only cohesive entity in Pakistani society capable of nurturing national integrity and stabilising its foreign relations. His training abroad and his foreign assignments made him politically ambitious. The close connections he developed in the course of these assignments with the power structures of the US and Saudi Arabia, which played the most important role in Pakistani politics, fashioned his world-view, his conceptions about relations with Islamic countries and his attitude towards India and South Asian politics.

Apart from the armed forces, Zia had the additional support or connivance of liberals and democrats, the opposition parties and the orthodox Islamic elements in overthrowing Bhutto. This was proved by the lack of opposition to the actions Zia took against Bhutto after dismissing him, between July and November 1977 — Bhutto was accused of conspiracy to murder, was arrested and ultimately the Supreme Court rejected a writ petition filed by Nusrat Bhutto against the imposition of martial law and endorsed the decision of the chief of the army staff in this respect. Domestically, Zia consolidated his position within the army power structure and lulled public opinion by a greater Islamisation of society through laws and edicts on the one hand and the promise of elections on the other. He considered Bhutto's elimination from politics imperative for his survival. He also knew that political parties, particularly those with comparatively modern and rational terms of reference like the PPP or the Awami Party, posed a danger. He therefore initiated action for the activation of Islamic political parties like the Jamait-e-Islami. In the sphere of foreign policy, during the first half of his regime he decided on having a calibrated adversarial relationship with India. As an important supportive element to this last segment of foreign policy, he decided to cultivate all of India's south Asian neighbours.

In 1977, the new leadership both of India and Pakistan wanted to change the nature of relations between the two countries to prove that each one of them had different terms of reference and a different orientation compared to the governments they had replaced. The new governments in both countries came to power following political turmoil and general disaffection amongst the people. But that is where the similarities stopped. While Morarji Desai with his genuine, almost theocratic commitment to Gandhian idealism, was determined to see if a normal equation could be established with Pakistan, Zia wanted to refashion relations in a manner whereby compromises made by Pakistan due to the compulsions of the defeat in 1971 could be removed. He wished to revive and restrengthen the Pakistani Army to redress the imbalances created by the East Pakistan crisis. The Pakistani military and religious establishment was also of the view that the Janata government, with its natural desire to prove it was different from the Indira Gandhi government, would be more vulnerable to Pakistani stratagems. Pakistan, of course, did not expect the Desai government to dilute India's stand on Jammu and Kashmir or on other issues. But Zia certainly expected it would not be overcommitted to the operational clauses of the Simla Agreement. He therefore commenced eroding the Agreement's governing relevance to bilateral relations.

The period 1978 to July 1979 was characterised by a surrealistic thaw in relations — surrealistic because both Zia and the Janata government went through a "minuet" of manifesting good intentions and giving some content to it at the public level, while in terms of realpolitik neither the concerns nor the attitudes underwent any change in India or Pakistan. In the 1980s and 1990s it was claimed that despite the (future) Bharatiya Janata Party (BJP) being a major partner of the Morarji Desai government and its leader Atal Behari Vajpayee being the foreign minister, Indo-Pakistani relations acquired a positive ambience, which disappeared with the return of Mrs Gandhi. This is a superficial view. An elaboration of this assessment is made in the next chapter.

Let us first consider the facts. Vajpayee initiated the process by going to Pakistan on 6 February 1978. Amir Mohammad, adviser to Chief Martial Law Administrator Zia, visited India in late February and stayed on till March, having discussions with Agriculture Minister Surjit Singh Barnala. L.K. Advani, then information and broadcasting minister, visited Pakistan in November. The high-water-mark was Prime Minister Desai's meeting with General Zia in Nairobi on 31 August 1978. Both were attending the funeral of President Jomo Kenyatta. Apart from these high-level contacts, India and Pakistan signed the bilateral agreement on the building of the Salal dam and Aga Shahi, then adviser on foreign affairs, came to India for this purpose. There were official-level discussions for reviving cooperation in the fields of commerce, railway transport and agriculture. After a decade, direct sporting contact also commenced, with hockey and cricket matches. Pakistan also agreed to the reopening of the Indian consulate-general in Karachi. In September 1978 India reciprocated by agreeing to the opening of a Pakistani consulate in Mumbai. There were also gestures at the human level. India provided wheat seeds to Pakistan and Pakistan sent tents, milk powder, medicines and cotton sheets as relief material for flood-affected areas in India.

These developments could be called confidence-building measures of a non-military nature. But what is interesting is that the Pakistani side assiduously avoided any direct bilateral discussions on the main controversial issues. While the visits of the delegations were more frequent and covered a wider spectrum of subjects during their discussions, they did not result in any concrete steps except for the agreement on the Salal dam. On the substantive side, statements by Pakistani leaders, and various incidents and events, showed a pattern of creating the basis for sustaining bilateral controversies.

It was during the period 1978-80 that Pakistan established connections with extremist Sikhs in Punjab and elsewhere with a view to fomenting Sikh separatism. The number of Sikh pilgrims allowed to visit Pakistan was deliberately increased by Zia. He also directed that apart from the relevant Wakf authorities and the ministries dealing with religious affairs, Sikh pilgrims should be contacted and attended to by officials from the Pakistani intelligence agencies and armed forces. The objective was to influence our Sikh citizens and to recruit operatives for long-term subversive purposes, India realised this only in the first half of the 1980s, with tragic consequences.

In May 1978, the Karakoram Highway straddling the Khunjerab Pass was opened to general traffic. In October Zia visited the highway, which runs through territories India claims as part of Jammu and Kashmir. He did not miss the opportunity of trying to get indirect acknowledgement of Pakistani jurisdiction over the area by inviting the Indian ambassador along with 15 other important ambassadors, to accompany him. The Indian ambassador however declined the invitation.

By the end of 1978, traditional attitudes regarding India began to be rearticulated. Aga Shahi, Zia's de facto foreign minister, demanded a just and honourable solution of the Jammu and Kashmir issue in the UN General Assembly session on 4 October 1978. Later in the month, when Zia was asked whether the visa system between India and Pakistan could be abolished as a further step towards improving bilateral relations, he said that there was no question of abolishing the visa system. During Advani's visit to Pakistan, his Pakistani counterpart expressed concern about disturbances at Aligarh. The year 1978 ended on a note of déjà vu. The Pakistani Foreign Office issued a trenchant press release questioning Vajpayee's statement in the Indian Parliament on 6 December in which he had rejected the jurisdiction, in India, of the UN Commission on the Protection of Minorities. A study conducted by this Commission had listed Jammu and Kashmir among the problems affecting minorities still awaiting settlement. Vajpayee had naturally questioned this motivated intrusiveness. Not satisfied with just issuing a statement criticising Vajpayee, the Indian ambassador was summoned for a tutorial by the Pakistani Foreign Secretary on 7 December. While reasserting the Pakistani stand on Jammu and Kashmir and Pakistan's right to speak about Muslim minorities in India, Zia allowed progress on those aspects of Indo-Pakistani interaction that would benefit Pakistan or meet its covert motives. In January, Pakistan agreed to the constitution of the Permanent Indus Commission under the Indus Waters Treaty of 1960. Zia allowed a four-member public sector delegation representing the Heavy Mechanical Complex at Taxila to visit India. The point should not be missed that this complex is a supportive estate to Pakistan's military industrial units at Wah.

The Janata India Foreign Office, was perhaps under the impression that its transparency would neutralise the adversarial motivations of Pakistan. In late 1978 and the first half of 1979, Pakistan received informal signals from India and direct signals from other channels that India would not stand in the way of Pakistan's desire to join the Non-Aligned Movement. To avoid procedural objections, Pakistan announced its withdrawal from CENTO on 12 March 1979. SEATO was already defunct. Foreign Secretary Shah Nawaz visited India towards the end of May and went back with a general assurance from his counterpart, Jagat Mehta, that India would not oppose Pakistan's entry into the Non-Aligned Movement. India's logic was that showing a positive attitude would defang Pakistan. This proved to be wrong, and Zia, speaking at the Non-aligned conference in Havana on 6 September 1979, stated that Pakistan was determined to seek a resolution of the Jammu and Kashmir problem in accordance with the relevant UN resolutions and "the spirit of the Simla Agreement".

Lest one carry away the impression that it was only Zia who was gradually reversing the embryonic positive trends of 1978, Benazir Bhutto, then in opposition, made her own contribution. In a press conference in Karachi on 25 June 1979, she raised the question as to why the Government of Pakistan had not protested against the anti-Muslim riots in several parts of India. She accused Zia of being silent when Muslims were being "slaughtered" in India. During the UN General Assembly and in the meetings of the UN Committee for Elimination of Racial Discrimination, Aga Shahi, apart from insisting on the Pakistani stand on Jammu and Kashmir, went further and asked the UN to urge the Indian Government to take steps for the preservation of the autonomy of educational institutions of the minority communities, particularly the Muslims. Obviously, Pakistan wanted to take full advantage of this autonomy to foment disaffection among India's Muslim citizens. These policies towards India proceeded apace with the increasing theocratisation and Islamisation of Pakistani society. Zia, apart from introducing Islamic studies and subjects like the ideology of Pakistan and the two-nation theory in the educational syllabi, also established a separate set of Shariat courts, right up to the high court level, by February 1979.

By this time, Morarji Desai's government had collapsed and Charan Singh's government had taken charge. The new government was confused and inept. Pakistan with its repetitive trait of negative optimism about Indian politics expected a vulnerable India in 1980. So 1979 ended with Pakistan raising the ante on Kashmir. While visiting POK on 15 November, Zia said Pakistan would continue to support the Kashmiri people's right to self-determination.

In retrospect, therefore, the question of whether there really was a thaw in relations during the Morarji Desai-Charan Singh period deserves an answer. Without any intention of assuming a friendlier-than-thou posture, it cannot be denied that India made a genuine attempt to normalise relations with Pakistan. The initiatives taken for high-level visits, for bringing about normality in economic and commercial relations, for improving people-to-people contacts, all came from India. India endorsing Pakistan's willingness to join the Non-Aligned Movement was not the only positive gesture. Some indications were given late in 1978 and 1979 that if Pakistan wished to return to the Commonwealth, India would not stand in the way.

The Sikh Mindset

Pakistan's response to these endeavours was not totally negative, but it was selective. On certain economic and infrastructural projects like the Salal project, Pakistan's response was positive. It encouraged people-to-people contacts, but with a negative motivation. While Muslim citizens of India were given freer access to Pakistan for familial or religious purposes, access to Hindu visitors remained limited. But the more sinister aspect was to infiltrate the Sikh people and the Sikh mindset.

It was during the period 1978-80 that larger numbers of Sikh pilgrims were welcomed to Pakistan. Leaders of these groups were entertained at the highest levels of the military and religious leadership. It is a matter of both pride and a proof of India's national sense of self that the vast majority of Sikh pilgrims who went to Pakistan did not get subverted by Pakistani intrigues and activities. Some did, but what is significant is that Pakistan succeeded more in this respect with non-resident Indian Sikhs in the US and Canada than with Sikhs in India. The proof is Punjab as it is today, despite the travails it went through in the 1980s. Pakistan took advantage of India's goodwill. To some extent I would call it our naïveté.

The basic lesson of this period is that there was a consistency in Pakistan's policies towards India. Both Bhutto and Zia, in 1977 and 1978-79 respectively, reasserted that the Kashmir issue had to be resolved by reversing the processes of history with the revival of UN jurisdiction. Both said that a no-war pact with India, or any bilateral stabilisation or defence agreement, could be signed only after the Kashmir dispute was resolved on lines Pakistan desired. It was Bhutto who added a geometrical dimension to the arms race in the subcontinent by openly declaring Pakistan's intention to initiate a nuclear research programme aimed at "weaponisation". Zia, long before Benazir or Nawaz Sharif, had initiated the proposal for a south Asian regional non-proliferation arrangement that would stifle India's nuclear research, nuclear technology and nuclear weapons programmes.

Pakistan's attitude to all suggestions for expanding commercial, economic and technological cooperation continued to be negative. Anti-Indian propaganda remained an abiding phenomenon in the Pakistani media, despite commitments given to mutually abjure from doing this in the Simla Agreement. The so-called thaw, in the historical sense, was an illusion. It was a tactical exercise on the part of Pakistan. It was an exercise in misplaced optimism by India.

Having come to this overall conclusion, it would be relevant to jog public memory in India about the role of Atal Behari Vajpayee, minister for external affairs, under Desai. Even years later, Vajpayee was still considered the most reasonable Indian foreign minister by the Pakistani Government and politically aware sections. In retrospect it should be remembered that it was Vajpayee who reopened high-level talks with Pakistan, and, more important, with China after a gap of time. That these endeavours did not lead to any concrete results is a different matter.

Between March 1980 and August 1988, Zia-ul-Haq dealt with two Indian prime ministers, Indira Gandhi and Rajiv Gandhi. I have asserted in the earlier parts of this chapter that the eleven-year tenure of Zia was a period of comparative stability in relations. I use the adjective "comparative" advisedly, because even this period of general normality Indo-Pak relations was punctuated by controversy. Zia's support to Sikh separatism in India came into full bloom in this time and had to be suppressed by a military operation. Zia's regime heightened tensions between Indian and Pakistani military forces in Siachen. India and Pakistan came to the brink of another war due to what is popularly known as Operation Brasstacks. The assassination of Mrs Gandhi in 1984 and Zia-ul-Haq in 1988 climaxed the phase of Indo-Pakistan relations in a sense, because in the following decade India dealt with a democratic Pakistan with hope and positive anticipation. Let us move on then to a chronological description and assessment of this period.

Mrs Gandhi returned to power within about a fortnight of Zia getting onto a winning strategic track at the end of 1979, with the Soviet Union directly and militarily intervening in Afghanistan between 27 and 29 December 1979. The chemistry of the relations between Indira Gandhi and Zia was bound to be unusual, given Zia's memories of 1971. India's "measured and balanced" reaction to developments in Afghanistan gave the Zia regime a handle to be critical of India. India's reaction to Afghan developments was based on India's acknowledging some of the positive orientations of the "SAUR" Revolution and the subversion which it faced continuously from Pakistan and others following Daud's overthrow. The second important factor was, of course, India's close relationship with the Soviet Union.

Mrs Gandhi's message to Zia to spare Bhutto's life, early in 1979, when she was out of power, must also have influenced Zia's mindset about India under her leadership. Zia had, in fact, commenced his two-track policy of continuing an adversarial relationship with India on the one hand, while projecting an image of desiring peace and normality with India on the other. When Ambassador K.S. Bajpai called on the Pakistani Foreign Office to express concern over the US decision to lift the embargo on the supply of arms to Pakistan on 1 January 1980, the Pakistani response was that it had made a long-standing offer to enter into negotiations with India for a mutually balanced reduction of forces. This response was widely publicised by Pakistan. During the same month, Zia, while inaugurating the foreign ministers' conference of the OIC, made a deliberate and provocative reference to Kashmir.

Taking note of the upward curve in tensions between India and Pakistan on the Afghan issue, on India and Pakistan buying arms from the Soviet Union and the US respectively, Mrs Gandhi deputed Foreign Secretary R.D. Sathe to Islamabad. Sathe met Zia, Aga Shahi, General Arif and the finance minister. He also took a personal communication from Mrs Gandhi to Zia. The Indian objective was to remove Islamabad's misunderstandings about the Indian view on Afghan developments and to explain that the military supplies being obtained from the Soviet Union were not so much for a qualitative upgrading of the weapons systems of the Indian armed forces, but only to replenish and maintain them at appropriate levels. Sathe also took this opportunity to convey India's serious concern about the large-scale subsidised military assistance that Pakistan was going to receive from the US spread over a period of three years, amounting to about $ 4 billion. In these exchanges, Pakistan raised the philosophical question about each country having a right to determine what its security requirements were. Sathe agreed that conceptually this would be logical, but each country's defence policies should be based on legitimate and objective requirements and that the political limitation and norm should be that any country's arms expenditure and procurement policy should not generate tension in the region. Pakistan chose to give selective publicity to Sathe's response, saying that "India accepts that Pakistan's arms acquisition policies are legitimate". This had to be promptly contradicted. These discussions were, as usual, resultless.

The Games Begin

Two important high-level political meetings followed Sathe's visit. Mrs Gandhi sent Sardar Swaran Singh as a Special Envoy to Pakistan from 10 to 14 April and he met Zia and Aga Shahi. Mrs Gandhi met Zia in Salisbury on 18 April. Mrs Gandhi had two motivations. First, to make an initial assessment of Zia's foreign policy and strategic intentions and, second, to counter Zia's public relations exercises in which he was projecting himself as a man of peace. There were marginal positive developments on the economic side. Pakistan decided to purchase 300,000 tonnes of iron ore from India in March; the deal was finalised on 21 May. In June, the civil aviation authorities of both countries began talks.

Zia felt he had to keep up the momentum of pretence apropos of normal bilateral contacts. He therefore sent Aga Shahi to India during the period 15-17 July. The discussions were again on Afghanistan and on normalising bilateral relations. While they were held in a functional and practical manner, Aga Shahi could not restrain himself from giving expression to his own anti-Indian mindset and to Pakistan's basic negative orientations while meeting intellectuals, the press and the public. He was critical of India's stand on Kashmir and Afghanistan and of India's defence postures. This received wide publicity both in India and Pakistan and in the international media.

India had to respond to put the record straight even if it resulted in Aga Shahi's visit ending on a negative note. I was the official spokesman of the Government of India on foreign policy and was duly instructed to give an official briefing to the press. My briefing appeared in all the Indian newspapers, with critical comments on Aga Shahi on the morning of 17 July, the day he was to leave for Islamabad. While Indo-Pakistan relations were slated to continue on a dreary course, I acquired minor celebrity status by being publicly snubbed by Aga Shahi at the departure ceremony. Before going into his special aircraft, he shook hands with everybody. Coming down the line, he looked through me but did not extend his hand to me for the farewell handshake. The incident could have resulted in a scene, had it not been for the standard training in etiquette that civil servants like me were given during our probation, namely, that you do not extend your hand for a handshake to any senior person unless he first extends his hand towards you. Protocol is not just ceremony but common sense, and also a shield against embarrassment and controversy. The then ambassador of Pakistan, Abdul Sattar, being sharp as ever, had noticed what happened at the airport. He underlined the importance of the gesture to me at a party a few days later at Bhai Mohan Singh's residence. Bhai Mohan Singh was (and still is) the consul-general of Monaco. Sattar said that it would have been prudent if I had refrained from briefing the Indian press. My response was somewhat in the vein, "The fault, dear Brutus, does not lie in our stars, ... we are underlings."

By 1981, two years had gone by since the execution of Bhutto. Zia was consolidating his hold over the power structure of Pakistan through four instrumentalities. First, nurturing his relations with the armed forces and retaining the position of supreme commander; second, cultivating religious leaders and Islam-pasand parties; third, augmenting Islamisation through political, juridical and academic means; and fourth, exploiting to the full the apprehensions of Islamic countries about the Soviet presence in Afghanistan. Zia structured his foreign and defence policies on these elements, bringing rich dividends to Pakistan. From 1981 onwards, his two-track policy towards India — that of an apparent peace offensive, while encouraging covert moves to erode India's unity, influence and strength — crystallised.

The peace offensive was multidimensional. Between 1981 and 1982, responding to India's suggestion, Zia agreed to the exchange of sailors from fishing craft that had strayed into each other's waters during fishing activities and been captured. He agreed, for the first time, to the Indian ambassador addressing the Pakistani public on PTV on India's Republic Day in 1981. He removed objections to Indian artistes and dancers visiting Pakistan. Ustad Amjad Ali Khan, Ustad Asad Ali Khan and danseuse Bharati Shivaji gave performances in Pakistan. He agreed to the revival of sports meets between India and Pakistan in cricket and hockey. On the initiative of Ambassador K. Natwar Singh he received a group of students from his almandite in New Delhi, St Stephen's College, in October 1981. He endorsed the recommendation of Indian and Pakistani officials that both countries participate in trade fairs in each other's territory. Most important of all, the spokesman of the Pakistan Foreign Office announced on 15 September Pakistan's readiness to enter into immediate consultations with India "for the purposes of exchanging mutual guarantees of non-aggression and non-use of force in the spirit of the Simla Agreement".

There was some background to all this. It was not Zia making unilateral moves on these fronts. On 10 January 1981, Natwar Singh had delivered a letter from Indira Gandhi to Zia in which she had strongly urged the normalisation of relations between the two countries and building an atmosphere of peace and stability, especially in the context of the disturbed situation in Afghanistan and the development aspirations of the people of the subcontinent.

The most significant event in the first half of 1981 was P.V. Narasimha Rao's visit to Pakistan between 8 and 11 June. He was then minister for external affairs. Rao met Zia, Aga Shahi and a number of ministers and senior officials. He also went to Lahore and Karachi and addressed civic receptions and the Pakistan Institute of International Affairs. Despite the undercurrents of animosity, Rao's visit was assessed in positive terms. It restored high-level political contact. It defused tensions. Both sides managed to have a detailed exchange of views on contentious issues like Afghanistan and Kashmir. They also agreed in principle to encourage people-to-people contacts. In fact, both sides agreed to make their respective visas for each other's nationals valid for visiting four cities in each other's country, instead of three. Pakistan's decision to participate in trade fairs in India was also a result of Rao's discussions. Rao's address to the Pakistan Institute of International Affairs in Karachi was significant not only for its content, but also because an Indian cabinet minister had addressed a public forum in Pakistan after a gap of a decade and a half. Rao's advocacy for transcending all animosities and establishing a durable and practical relationship for mutual benefit made a particularly positive impression on his audience.

On the political front, Pakistan increased its propaganda and rhetoric on the Kashmir issue. There was continued criticism of India's defence capacities and views on the Afghanistan situation. In his speech to the UN General Assembly on 2 October 1981, Aga Shahi referred to Kashmir as the only outstanding dispute, which should be resolved in the spirit of the Simla Agreement and in the light of UN resolutions. The formal erosion of the stipulation of bilateralism in the Simla Agreement had commenced.

Pakistani intelligence had infiltrated some sections of the Sikh community in the Indian state of Punjab through the Sikh pilgrims, who were being encouraged to visit Pakistan in large numbers. On 14 September 1981, Pakistan formalised its proposal for a non-aggression pact and transmitted it to the Government of India through Natwar Singh. India responded to this draft by giving a seven-point aide-memoire detailing additional elements. This was done on 24 December 1981. The Pakistan Government's suspicions and apprehensions were not only shown in macro-level political activities, but also at significant levels of human relationships. On 6 December 1981, Natwar Singh requested the Pakistan Foreign Office for permission to visit Wali Khan, son of Abdul Gaffar Khan, for lunch at Charsadda near Peshawar. Wali Khan had invited Natwar Singh and the deputy chief of mission, Lambah, along with their wives, to his village home. The Pakistani Government refused permission. So much for the peace offensive.

The year 1982 began on a note of cautious optimism between the two countries, with Ambassador Abdul Sattar handing over on 12 January an eight-point response to Indian suggestions regarding the agreement on non-aggression and non-use of force. Aga Shahi visited Delhi from 29 January to 1 February to discuss this agreement and also to exchange views on the establishment of a joint commission for multifaceted cooperation. Mrs Gandhi suggested India and Pakistan sign a treaty of friendship and cooperation halfway through Aga Shahi's visit. The joint press statement issued at the conclusion of Aga Shahi's visit announced that delegations of the two countries would meet in Islamabad by the end of February 1982 to continue discussion on agreements for non-aggression, friendship, non-use of force, etc.

The abiding jinx on attempts at mutual normality manifested itself again. Within two weeks of Aga Shahi's visit to Delhi, Aga Hilali, the leader of the Pakistani delegation to the UN Human Rights Commission in Geneva, made a vitriolic attack on India on the issues of Kashmir, treatment of minorities, etc. It resulted in an equally acrimonious response from B.R. Bhagat, MP, of the Indian delegation. By 24 February responding to parliamentary and public pressure, the Government of India called off the proposed Foreign Secretary–level talks to be held in Islamabad from 1 to 4 March.

Continuing the process of integrating areas which were formerly part of the princely state of Jammu and Kashmir, Zia confirmed direct Pakistani jurisdiction over Gilgit, Hunza and Skardu. He appointed three observers from these Northern Areas to the Pakistan Federal Council on 3 April 1982. Our chargé d'affaires, Lambah, promptly protested against this. Two days earlier, Zia, in an interview given to senior Indian political columnist Kuldip Nayar, had said that as far as Pakistan was concerned, Gilgit, Hunza and Skardu were not part of the disputed territory of Jammu and Kashmir. Pakistan's involvement with Sikh militancy became more active from the end of 1981. On 29 September 1981, the Amritsar-Srinagar flight was hijacked. On 4 August 1982, an Indian Airlines plane flying on the same route was hijacked by Dal Khalsa activists, but apprehensive of its direct contact with militants coming into the open, Pakistan compelled the plane to return from Lahore to Amritsar.

On 1 June 1982 Pakistan handed over a revised draft agreement on non-aggression, renunciation of force and promotion of good neighbourly relations to Natwar Singh, who by then had returned to Delhi to work as special secretary in the Ministry of External Affairs, in charge of Pakistan and West Asia, as well as of the forthcoming Non-Aligned summit. India handed over a draft agreement for the establishment of a joint commission on 26 June. On 11 August, M.K. Rasgotra, then Indian foreign secretary, handed over an Indian counter-draft of a treaty of peace, friendship and cooperation. Zia met Mrs Gandhi in Delhi on 1 November during a transit visit while returning from a tour of the Far East and Southeast Asia. This was the first regular, formal, bilateral meeting between Mrs Gandhi and Zia. The meeting resulted in two decisions: the establishment of a joint commission and the continuation of discussions on the two draft agreements on peace, friendship, non-aggression, etc. On 2 November India and Pakistan signed a protocol agreeing to exchange information on each other's nationals imprisoned or detained in the other country and providing for consular access to such persons. There was some progress in people-to-people contact through delegations of chambers of commerce and of academics.

Two further significant developments took place in 1982. Pakistan and China signed a protocol on the opening of the Khunjerab Pass border between POK and the Xinjiang province of China, an adverse strategic development as far as India was concerned. The second was the emergence of basic differences between India and Pakistan during foreign secretary–level talks from 22 to 24 December in New Delhi between Niaz Naik and Rasgotra on the no-war pact and friendship treaty proposals. There were many political nuances and security considerations underlying the differences. Pakistan was not ready to extend the stipulations and provisions of these proposed agreements. It was a definitional divergence of views on what constituted India's territorial integrity. Pakistan was also averse to abjuring foreign military bases in its territory.

Compared to the period 1977 to 1982, the year 1983 could be called a period of comparative quietude. Zia visited Delhi for the seventh Non-Aligned summit in March. This was perhaps the only event where there was manifest tension. Zia could not, for domestic-political as well as external-diplomatic reasons, avoid mentioning Kashmir in his general statement to the Non-Aligned summit. Though my assignment at this time was that of India's ambassador to Afghanistan, halfway through the conference I was entrusted with the responsibility of briefing the Indian press on certain specific issues, because of my previous incarnation as Foreign Office spokesman. Mrs Gandhi, after taking note of Zia's references to Kashmir, specifically instructed me to counter them appropriately and firmly. Zia had mentioned Kashmir as a pending problem needing resolution for regional peace, stability and so on. In my briefing, I said that we agreed with Zia that Kashmir was a pending problem. But, I explained, it could be resolved if Pakistan vacated all territories occupied by it in the old princely state of Jammu and Kashmir, which had acceded to India under relevant parliamentary acts and regulations. I had commenced the briefing just prior to Zia's statement coming to an end in the plenary session. The publicity the Pakistani delegation expected to get from his statement was neutralised by Mrs Gandhi's prompt instructions on the matter.

Despite these contretemps, the Indo-Pakistan agreement on the establishment of a joint commission was signed on 10 March 1983, in the presence of Zia and Mrs Gandhi. Delegates from the chambers of commerce and industry from both countries exchanged visits between February and April and agreed to augment trade and industrial cooperation. External Affairs Minister Narasimha Rao visited Pakistan on 4 June to co-chair the first meeting of the Indo-Pakistan Joint Commission. The subject of non-aggression, non-use of force and the friendship treaty again came up during the discussions between Rao and his counterpart, and the only decision taken was that further discussions would be held.

The second half of 1983 was characterised by mutual accusations. Both blamed each other for fomenting centrifugal forces. Pakistani authorities accused India of encouraging Sindhi separatism. India accused Pakistan of encouraging Sikh separatism and fomenting disaffection in Jammu and Kashmir. Speaking about this matter in the Pakistani Majlis-e-Shoora on 5 November, Foreign Minister Yakub Khan made highly critical references to India, which were dismissed out of hand by the Government of India. The more the pretensions towards change, the more things remained the same.

The year 1984, the last year of Mrs Gandhi's leadership, was suffused with ambiguities and tensions. The joint commission and its sub-commissions on economic relations, information, education, travel, tourism, etc., commenced tentative activities. Despite the continuing differences on Kashmir and Pakistan's increasing involvement with Sikh terrorists, delegations of political leaders, particularly Muslim political leaders and jurists, including judges of the Supreme Court, were exchanged. The foreign secretaries of India and Pakistan, Niaz Naik and Rasgotra, met in Delhi and Udaipur in the first week of March. They met again in Islamabad between 19 and 25 May 1984. Agriculture Minister Rao Birendra Singh and Information Minister H.K.L. Bhagat visited Pakistan in April and July respectively. But the point to note is that none of these exchanges had any lasting impact.

In contrast, the political temperature went up. India's decision to carry out the death sentence on Maqbool Butt, the Kashmiri militant leader, after the murder of Indian diplomat R.H. Mhatre by the Jammu and Kashmir Liberation Front in Birmingham, India's becoming aware of the weapons' orientation of Pakistan's nuclear programme and Pakistan's cooperation in this field with China, the increasing evidence of Pakistan's financial and material support to Sikh militants, and the hijacking of Indian Airlines planes to Pakistan on 5 July and 24 August 1984 by Sikh militants inflamed passions. On 19 June 1984, speaking at an Iftar party in Islamabad, Zia said that India's accusations were without foundation and highly irresponsible. He compounded his mendacity by unwarranted and pernicious pronouncements regarding Indian Muslims. He said: "Even when Muslims were victimised in India, I kept quiet. My heart bled for them, though it may be India's internal affair." Pakistan's labour minister, Ghulam Dastgir Khan, made the same accusation at a reception in London: "Mrs Gandhi has massacred thousands of Sikhs in Punjab and thousands of Muslims in Maharashtra."

Pakistan took full propaganda advantage following Operation Bluestar. There is reliable information that Zia had authorised the Inter-Services Intelligence (ISI) Agency from 1981 onwards to give training, weapons and logistical facilities to Sikh militants. This was reflected in the increasing terrorist violence in Punjab, Delhi, Haryana and parts of Rajasthan. It culminated in the tragedy of Operation Bluestar in June 1984, and the assassination of Mrs Gandhi on 31 October 1984. An example of Pakistani reaction to Operation Bluestar was the statement by Defence Minister Mir Ali Ahmed Alpur on 26 June in which he said: "What has happened in the Indian Punjab is more than what happened in the Jallianwala Bagh massacre. By praying in the Golden Temple, Mrs Gandhi cannot wash away the bloodstains of these killings on her clothes. It is against civilised behaviour to destroy a shrine." The question arises whether this criterion should be suitably applied to Muslim rulers, beginning from Mahmud Ghaznavi to Aurangzeb and even to latter-day rulers of Pakistan.

Zia was, however, prompt in conveying condolences on Mrs Gandhi's assassination. He also attended the funeral, where he had his first meeting with the new prime minister, Rajiv Gandhi. Later in December, when Rajiv returned to power after the elections, he sent the customary congratulatory message. Mrs Gandhi's assassination closed an uncertain chapter in Indo-Pakistan relations.

Islam's General

After suffering initial ostracism for engineering a military coup, for replacing a democratic government and for hanging its prime minister, Zia gained acceptability. His regime got legitimised primarily because of the Soviet intervention in Afghanistan and his willingness to be part of the US-led Western coalition. The US and Saudi Arabia also played an important role in consolidating his regional and international position. He first faced a dilemma in reacting to the Iranian revolution in 1979, and then in fashioning a balanced attitude in terms of Pakistan's interests in Iran and Iraq. He performed the tightrope act well enough, generally functioning within the foreign policy and strategic parameters designed by the West.

In contrast India's Afghanistan policy safeguarded its interests, but generated problems vis-à-vis the Western world. These were, however, managed fairly well despite pressures. Reaction to the Iranian revolution was more positive and practical than that of Pakistan. But India negated its possible benefits by taking a neutral and equidistant stand on the Iran-Iraq war. For India it was a Hobson's choice, because India had good relations with both countries and substantive economic interests in sustaining friendly equations, particularly so with Iraq. India's reaction to West Asian developments during this period increased Pakistan's capability to mobilise the OIC to further its policy objectives, especially its negative contents.

From 1969 practically up to 1992, India suffered withdrawal symptoms in relation to multilateral Islamic fora and discussions, despite claiming to be the second largest Muslim country in the world. I do not think India was unaware of the importance of interacting with the Islamic fora, but the bilateral aspect of Indo-Pakistani relations influenced the attitude to the OIC deliberations. This could be described as a flaw.

It was an assertive Pakistan poised for military and diplomatic success that Rajiv Gandhi had to deal with. The political atmosphere was tense and qualitatively at a higher pitch when compared to the previous decade. There were suspicions about Pakistan's hand in Mrs Gandhi's assassination, which was plausible in the context of the increasing political and material support Khalistan extremists were receiving from Pakistan. Zia was claiming the high moral ground on the Afghanistan situation. He had authorised military operations to capture the Siachen Heights earlier in 1984. They were neutralised effectively and in time by Mrs Gandhi and the then defence minister, R. Venkataraman. The Pakistani move towards Siachen had the dual objective of capturing strategic heights, which would expand Pakistani control over the land salients stretching northeast towards the Karakoram ranges, and of creating a base for a politico-strategic revival of the Kashmir issue. Pakistan was taking full diplomatic advantage, through its propaganda, after Operation Bluestar.

Rajiv's stance towards Pakistan during the early years of his prime ministership has to be viewed in the context of an overall approach on foreign policy issues. His public pronouncements and statements in Parliament between December 1984 and May 1985 provide some indications: ensuring the continuity of a foreign policy geared to safeguarding India's vital interests while structuring new and original initiatives to meet problems on hand. He asserted: "A new government has taken over the country." He reminded the people: "60 per cent of the Indian electorate is below 40 years of age." He emphasised: "For nation-building the first important requisite is peace; peace with one's neighbours, peace in the world." And to meet this imperative, "one cannot remain mired in the past, one must remain flexible".

Zia first met Rajiv Gandhi on 4 November 1984 at Mrs Gandhi's funeral. He told the Pakistani press that he had received a positive response to his desire to improve relations between the two countries. While there was no change in the substantive aspects of Pakistani policies relating to Punjab and Kashmir between January and May 1985, there was a general thaw in Indo-Pakistani interaction. Zia attended India's Republic Day celebrations. The Indian ambassador, K.D. Sharma, was invited by the

Pakistan army headquarters to speak at the National Defence College. India's new foreign secretary, Romesh Bhandari, had a bilateral meeting with his Pakistani counterpart in Male on 1 February. On 5 March Zia authorised the trial of those Sikhs who had hijacked the Indian Airlines aircraft in 1981. He followed it up by authorising the trial of those who had hijacked another Indian Airlines plane to Lahore on 4 July 1984.

Adversarial and Assertive

The first substantive discussions between Rajiv and Zia took place in Moscow on 13 March 1985, where both had gone to attend Chernenko's funeral. This resulted in Foreign Secretary Romesh Bhandari's visit to Pakistan between 4 and 6 April. But from June onwards, the abiding adversarial psyche of Pakistan surfaced again. Foreign Minister Yakub Khan, in an official statement in Islamabad, categorically rejected Indian claims to the Siachen glacier, which, he said, "was part of the Northern Areas of Pakistan". Minister of State for Foreign Affairs Zain Noorani, speaking in the National Assembly, asserted, "Rajiv Gandhi is repeating baseless statements about Pakistan's peaceful nuclear programme." He also reasserted Pakistan's presumed role of being the protector of India's Muslims.

Rajiv's response as far as Siachen was concerned was to strengthen our military control over the area. To Pakistani presumptions about protecting minorities in India, and to the nuclear programme, he was firm and measured. His overall approach was to encourage interaction where possible. Zia was not averse to this. Yakub Khan led a 14-member Pakistani delegation to India for the second meeting of the Indo-Pakistan Joint Ministerial Commission established during Mrs Gandhi's time. Instead of the usual controversies, not only were agreements for mutual cooperation signed but also separate agreements on agricultural cooperation were brought into force.

In 1965, Rajiv and Zia had three more meetings, apart from the one in Moscow. They met in New York in October at the 40th session of the UN General Assembly. They met in Dhaka for the first SAARC summit on 7 December and in Delhi after Zia's tour of Bangladesh and Sri Lanka. At these meetings they agreed that foreign secretaries should carry forward the discussions, specifically on finalising a bilateral agreement for mutual friendship. Drafts for the agreement had already been exchanged. While these generally positive orientations were being followed in a tenuous manner, Pakistani paranoia kept finding expression. Speaking in the Pakistani Senate on 29 October Yakub Khan stated that in the event of any attack on the Kahuta nuclear facilities, Pakistan would have no option but to retaliate. What was curious was that the provocation for the statement remained — and remains — indiscernible. Despite the abrasiveness reflected in Yakub Khan's and Zain Noorani's statements there seemed to be a general sense of ease in Indo-Pakistan relations. This was reflected when the Pakistan's minister for finance and planning, Mahbubul Haq, led a high-powered delegation to India between 14 and 16 November. He was accompanied by Secretary-General for Economic Affairs Aijaz Naik, and Commerce Secretary Mukhtar Masood.

At a more human level, recalling a personal encounter with Zia in Colombo in December 1985 would be relevant. The Pakistani ambassador in Colombo hosted a large reception in Zia's honour during his official visit to Sri Lanka after the SAARC summit. When I was introduced to him as India's high commissioner, he gave proof of his sharp memory. He remembered that I had been with the Indian delegations that had visited Pakistan with Sathe and Narasimha Rao in 1980 and 1981 respectively. With a touch of humour he said, "Mr Dixit, I am intrigued by the Indian ambassadors in neighbouring countries. Your new ambassador to Islamabad is Mr S.K. Singh. I have just come from Dhaka where I met your high commissioner, Mr Chadha, and now I meet you again. Why is it that all of you are short-statured? Is there some structured policy about the size of Indian ambassadors?" I replied: "Sir, you know there is this general complaint about India being a big country. Therefore, I think Mr Rajiv Gandhi has decided to send people of short stature like me to project a 'low profile' despite India's capacities and powers." Zia's response was: "Well, well, this is a reasonable explanation." I could not have imagined a Pakistani president having this kind of bantering conversation with an Indian diplomat in the 1970s.

There was also a piquant situation arising out of the Sri Lankans insisting on taking Zia to Anuradhapura to pay obeisance to the Mahabodhi tree. He was subjected to the ritual of carrying a *thali* (tray) full of flowers and incense towards the tree. The Sri Lankan TV, Roopvahini, showed him walking towards the tree with the tray but did not actually show him placing it in an act of worship, which I am sure he did not do. But there was mischievous amusement among local Indians as well as Sri Lankans, because he had to almost indulge in *butparasti* (idol-worship) in contradiction of the Nizam-e-Mustafa.

The year 1985 ended with Rajiv Gandhi's invitation to Khan Abdul Gaffar Khan to participate in the centenary celebrations of the Indian National Congress. Zia did not stand in the way. Earlier, he had resented the conferment of the Bharat Ratna on the "Frontier Gandhi" in the early 1980s.

The second half of 1986 was characterised by more manifest support to Khalistani separatists. Pakistan encouraged visits by a large number of Sikh pilgrims from the US and the UK. These were timed to coincide with Guru Nanak's birthday. Pakistani intelligence authorities also orchestrated contacts between non-resident Indian Sikhs coming to Pakistan and Sikh *jathas* from India. One pernicious result of this interaction was that some Indian diplomatic liaison officers attached to Indian Sikh *jathas* were physically attacked, mostly by Sikhs from abroad, at places of pilgrimage in Pakistan. Despite Rajiv Gandhi's idealistic and visionary desire to normalise relations, these factors introduced caution and realism into his Pakistani policies.

The even tempo of relations with occasional ups and downs was maintained throughout 1986. The year began with the visit of the then finance minister, V.P. Singh, to Pakistan. The trap ended in the Agreed Minutes of his discussions being signed, focusing attention on the normalising of bilateral trade. The signal for a rational approach was manifest in the agreement between Rajiv and Zia to resolve the problems related to the military confrontation between India and Pakistan on the Siachen glacier. The first round of talks on Siachen between Indian Defence Secretary S.K. Bhatnagar and Pakistani Defence Secretary Ijalal Haider Zaidi, was held in Rawalpindi from 10 to 12 January 1986. It was inconclusive. Meanwhile, Pakistan continued to harp on the Kashmir issue. Mohammed Khan Junejo had been appointed prime minister by Zia on 23 March 1985. He was later elected president of the Muslim League. It was in this context that India took official note of the Pakistan Muslim League Council passing a resolution to the effect that Indo-Pakistan relations could be normalised only after the Kashmir issue was settled on the basis of UN resolutions. The council's resolution was passed and publicised soon after Romesh Bhandari's second five-day visit to Islamabad on 16 January.

The process of chipping away at the foundations of the Simla Agreement continued in more subtle ways when compared with the latter part of the Bhutto era. The contradictory duality in Indo-Pakistan relations continued, with meetings of the subcommissions on education, culture and sports, expert-level exchanges in the sphere of agricultural research, and the signing of agreements on the avoidance of double taxation and the marginal liberalisation of visa regimes. Rajiv met Junejo on 18 March at Stockholm at Prime Minister Olaf Palme's funeral. They agreed to continue bilateral contacts on various issues and to interact with each other for the second SAARC summit, to be held in Bangalore in November 1986.

In the autumn of 1986 the seeds of suspicion were sown. They sprouted into a forest with the potentiality of a conflagration by the beginning of 1987. The reference is to Operation Brass Tacks, the annual military exercise of the Indian Army with some special dimensions structured by the then chief of army staff, General Krishnaswamy Sundarji. General Sundarji had undertaken a structural rationalisation, modernisation and qualitatively improved mechanisation of the Indian land forces. He wanted to test the operational efficiency of his reforms, including inter-service coordination between the Army, Navy and Air Force. Operation Brass Tacks was the result. It had the clear stamp of his assertive and confident mindset.

Zia had been under domestic political pressure since July–August 1986. Ghulam Mustafa Jatoi had launched the National People's Party. The Movement for the Restoration of Democracy was launched on 14 August by Nusrat and Benazir Bhutto in collaboration with practically all the major parties except the Muslim League. The inconclusive second round of defence secretary–level talks on Siachen in June, with the Indian Army remaining dominant in the glacier affected Zia's reactions. Though some marginal progress was made in the middle of this tense atmosphere in reviving contact in the fields of telecommunications, agriculture and rail links relations were receding again into the traditional grooves of tension and mutual suspicion. The SAARC summit at Bangalore was used by Rajiv and Junejo to have an overall review of relations. They agreed that foreign secretaries and home secretaries of the two countries should continue the dialogue on pending political agreements and on border-monitoring arrangements. The meetings duly took place in December but without results. The Rajiv-Junejo meeting in Bangalore was overshadowed by India concentrating more on trying to evolve a political solution to the ethnic problem of Sri Lanka in consultation with President Junius Jayawardene and the Tamil military leadership. Curiously, Junejo did not raise the question of Operation Brass Tacks in any significant manner. Perhaps, he was not even fully informed of the evolving threat perceptions by Zia and the Pakistani Army.

Junejo's dismissal was a watershed in Pakistani politics. The mutual disenchantment between Junejo and Zia could be traced to first Junejo's growing confidence as a political leader who could have become a challenge to Zia's authority and second, Junejo's fundamental differences on foreign and defence policy matters with Zia, specially relating to the Afghan situation, and with West Asian countries like Iran and Iraq. After becoming president of the Muslim League, Junejo started taking a more active and assertive stance on foreign policy issues, intruding into what Zia considered, his domain. There were reports that Junejo was initiating equations with Mohajir as well as Sindhi politicians, ultimately with a view to abrogating the Eighth Amendment of the Pakistani Constitution, which gave Zia the right to override the elected prime minister. His dismissal was a categorical assertion by Zia of his intention to hold on to supreme power in Pakistan regardless of his protestations about gradually restoring democracy.

The homily of Henry Brooke Adams, US diplomat and historian, that "power when wielded by abnormal energy is the most serious of facts" got transmuted to the situation on the ground in Indo-Pakistan relations during the winter of 1986 and the beginning of 1987. While Operation Brass Tacks was peaking towards the end of the year, based on the energetic mindset of General Sundarji, Pakistan, apprehending an attack, took equally rigorous steps to move to forward positions on the border during its winter exercises under orders from Zia and on the advice of Lt. General Hamid Gul of the ISI. When the Pakistani armed forces did not withdraw from their forward positions after the winter exercises in January, Indian armed forces were placed on an operational alert, from 23 January onwards. The general perception was that the confrontation could degenerate into a conflict. India undertook a number of moves, through countries like the US and even directly with Pakistan, to defuse the tension. Things did not move towards de-escalation. Junejo telephoned Rajiv on 27 January. Rajiv was prompt in extending an invitation to Junejo to send high-level representatives to resolve the problem. Pakistan's foreign secretary, Abdul Sattar, arrived in New Delhi on 30 January 1987 for five days of detailed discussions to de-escalate the border crisis. His delegation comprised three senior officials from the Pakistani armed forces and Defence Ministry. It was agreed in principle that a gradual withdrawal of troops from both sides should commence as early as possible and a further round of talks should be held. Patience and wisdom prevailed over the advocates of military adventurism on both sides. The first phase of the mutual withdrawal of troops in the Ravi-Chenab sector was completed between 11 and 19 February 1987.

Zia decided to project a reasonable and peace-seeking image for Pakistan despite the military tensions. Rajiv was equally desirous of normalising relations whatever the duality of Zia's motives. An invitation was extended to Zia by the Board of Control of Cricket in India to come and witness the Indo-Pakistani cricket series. Zia visited India between 21 and 23 February accompanied by 68 government officials and public personalities. Though his discussions with the Indian leadership did not have any concrete results, his visit was projected as a major diplomatic initiative. The second round of discussions to de-escalate border tensions was held in Islamabad within four days of Zia's return, from 27 February to 7 March. The secretary in the Ministry of External Affairs, Alfred Gonsalves, along with the additional secretary (Defence), N.N. Vohra, and senior officials from the Directorate General of Military Operations went to Islamabad and met their counterparts, who were led by Abdul Sattar. In contrast to the comparative reasonableness in approach during the 30 January–4 February discussions, this second round was characterised by acrimony and truculence on the part of Pakistan. Perhaps the withdrawal of Indian troops earlier in February led to this stance. Gonsalves cautioned the Pakistani side about the implications of stemming the momentum of de-escalation. In the event the talks concluded more or less successfully. Tensions mounting since September-October 1986 got defused.

The perennial roller-coaster nature of Indo-Pakistan relations, however, could not be avoided. Senior Indian journalist Kuldip Nayar was on a visit to Pakistan towards the end of February and the beginning of March. His Pakistani friend Mushahid Hussain, then editor of *The Muslim*, offered to organise a meeting between Nayar and the architect of Pakistan's clandestine nuclear projects, Dr Abdul Qadir Khan. Dr Khan confirmed to Kuldip Nayar that the US Central Intelligence Agency's assessment that Pakistan possessed nuclear weapons capability was correct. This has been known to the Government of India since 1983-84. But the publication of Nayar's interview in Indian and foreign media, including the Pakistani media, made it appear a sensational revelation.

A phenomenon to be kept in mind when analysing the motivations of Abdul Qadir Khan speaking to Kuldip Nayar is the calculated and continuous public relations exercise of the Pakistani Government to use Indian journalists and political commentators to generate dissension in Indian policies and where possible to scare or frighten India. It is a different matter that Indian journalists, even those who are passionate about peace between Pakistan and India despite challenging realities, have not completely fulfilled Pakistani expectations. At the risk of provoking objections and criticism, I must mention Pakistan has made this attempt with senior and thoughtful journalists like George Verghese, Pran Chopra, the late Dilip Mukherjee, Ajit Bhattacharya, Bhabani Sen Gupta, and the late Rajinder Sareen. But in overall terms this Pakistani effort has not succeeded.

Rajiv, reacting to the revelation about Pakistan's nuclear capacities in the Lok Sabha on 3 March said: "We have been trying to improve relations with Pakistan, but some serious problems remain. There is a clandestine effort for a nuclear weapons programme. It has been gathering momentum for the past several years. Those who had the responsibility and means to halt this programme have failed to do so. Instead they have helped Pakistan to launch an ambitious armaments programme. The present situation is that notwithstanding legal safeguards against proliferation, Pakistan continues to get assistance. It is quite extraordinary. Let there be no mistake about the determination and capacity of the people of India to defend their sovereignty and integrity." It was obvious from this statement that India had been monitoring Pakistani nuclear developments since 1974-75 when Bhutto, reacting to India's Pokhran nuclear experiment, had announced his intention to make Pakistan a nuclear weapons power even if "Pakistanis had to eat grass". It was also obvious that India knew which countries provided expertise and material for Pakistan's nuclear weaponisation programme.

There has been some debate about why Dr Khan confirmed Pakistan's nuclear military capacities to an Indian journalist. It could not have been an impulsive declaration or an act of accidental indiscretion. It is also a curious coincidence that Mushahid Hussain, who had been and is close to the Pakistani armed forces establishment, organised the interview. It is now generally acknowledged that the interview was an orchestrated attempt at coercive diplomacy by Zia. He was riding high due to the Afghan situation. US interest in backing him for its strategic purposes made him feel safe enough against any negative fallout in American public opinion about his evolving nuclear weapons capacity.

About a month or two after Dr Khan's interview with Kuldip Nayar there were reports in the Western media that Pakistan may be in possession of four to seven nuclear devices. On seeing these reports in Colombo, where I was high commissioner, I made enquiries with the ambassador of Pakistan in Colombo, Brigadier Tariq. Tariq's reaction was coy and ambiguous. He remarked, "Mr Dixit, you will agree that all of us do take care to meet the requirements of our security environment." Holland, Germany, the US and France contributed to Khan's nuclear efforts. It is to be noted that it was only on the initiative of Senator Larry Pressler that the executive branch of the US government was persuaded to take any substantive action against Pakistan in conformity with its non-proliferation and arms control objectives. The Indian response was not panicky. India conveyed to Pakistan and the world that the revelation did not surprise it, that it was aware and observant of the phenomenon, that while continuing its efforts for non-discriminatory non-proliferation and disarmament, it was aware that the vocal advocates of the Nuclear Proliferation Treaty (NPT) had contributed to Pakistan's covert nuclear weapons policies and that India was capable of meeting this threat both at the political and technological levels.

Pakistan's reaction to the Indian involvement in Sri Lanka was also negative and critical. Apart from breaking up Sri Lanka's links with the US and even Israel — in assistance to fight the Tamils — Pakistan was vocal in its objections to India espousing the cause of the Tamils. The standard accusations against India voiced by the Sri Lankan Government were endorsed and publicised by Pakistan. There was the usual bilateral contact between Rajiv and Junejo at Kathmandu on 7 November 1987 during the SAARC meeting. There was a bland exchange of views and the pious hope of continuing efforts for normalising relations. An important but admittedly unrelated event that gave additional legitimacy to Benazir Bhutto's claim to the leadership of Pakistan in terms of the Islamic ethos was her marriage to Asif Zardari on 18 December.

Khan Abdul Ghaffar Khan passed away in the third week of January 1988. Rajiv nonplussed Zia by informing him that he would visit Peshawar to pay his last respects to the great leader of the Indian freedom movement. That Rajiv chose to bypass Islamabad did not please Zia. The Indian prime minister visited Peshawar on 20 January with a high-level delegation, spent about an hour and a half in Peshawar before the funeral and flew back. There were reasons for this unusual behaviour. He wanted to convey a sense of disdain and disillusionment about Zia's policies towards India. He also wanted to convey to the people of Pakistan that the visit was to pay respects to Ghaffar Khan and to acknowledge his identity as a secular, nationalist leader of the subcontinent.

In any case, Zia was deeply engaged in the final stages of the negotiations with the Russians and Americans about the Afghan situation while coping with the support that the Movement for the Restoration of Democracy was garnering inside Pakistan. The increasing clout of Pakistan in Afghan developments due to the US-Soviet rapprochement during the Mikhail Gorbachev regime was a matter of concern to India. While India had reservations about the Soviet military presence in Afghanistan, it was supportive of the modernisation and secularisation of Afghan society. The rapidly changing scenario had the seeds of marginalising India.

After informal exchanges with the Russian and Pakistani missions in New Delhi, Rajiv Gandhi spoke to Zia over the phone on 25 February 1988 and invited him for a bilateral visit with a special focus on Afghan developments. Zia countered by reminding Rajiv Gandhi that he had visited India twice. Therefore, he requestd Rajiv to come or send a personal envoy. Both leaders then decided that the foreign secretaries of the two countries should meet. Zia was not enthusiastic about acknowledging any Indian interest or role in Afghanistan. He therefore postponed the foreign secretaries' meeting scheduled for 1 March. After much procrastination, this meeting took place on 3 May. Pakistan refused to touch upon any substantive aspects of the Afghan issue during the talks. The Indian foreign secretary, K.P.S. Menon, came back with a clear impression that Pakistan would prevent Indian participation in the solution of the Afghan crisis. In contrast to the Brezhnev-Andropov regimes of the Soviet Union, which considered India as an important balancing factor in stabilising the Afghan situation, Gorbachev in his anxiety to move his troops out of Afghanistan agreed with the Pakistani-Saudi argument that Indian involvement would offend Islamic sentiments in Afghanistan.

A massive explosion at the ammunition depot at Ojhari near Rawalpindi on 10 April 1988, killed nearly a hundred people and injured over a thousand. It interrupted the normal political processes in Pakistan. There have been strong and recurrent suspicions that the explosion was not accidental and that it was triggered by the ISI itself to avoid detailed accounting of arms, ammunition and other military supplies that were to be returned to the US with the withdrawal of Soviet forces from Afghanistan. Another theory is that the explosion also provided the cover to distribute arms to cadre employed by ISI in different covert operations, including those against India in Jammu and Kashmir and in Punjab.

India had awarded the Bharat Ratna to Badshah Khan. Zia retaliated by conferring the highest civilian award of Pakistan, "Nishan-e-Pakistan", on former Indian prime minister Morarji Desai for his promotion of better ties between Pakistan and India. Zia did this four days before his demise in an air crash near Bahawalpur on 17 August. His death resulted in a sudden and qualitative metamorphosis of the power structure of Pakistan. For the first time a Mohajir officer (originally from Azamgarh, UP), General Mirza Aslam Beg, became chief of army staff. Ghulam Ishaq Khan became the president.

The conspiracy leading to Zia's assassination remains shrouded in mystery. Pakistani authorities conducted an investigation through their Federal Intelligence Bureau, through the ISI and through technologists from the company that manufactured the plane. Representatives of the American Federal Bureau of Investigation were also participants. The general conclusion was that some boxes of mangoes were loaded into the plane just before it took off and that there was some kind of a time fuse that released a gas, disabling the pilot, the co-pilot and the flight engineer. The perpetrators of the conspiracy have not been clearly identified as yet. There has been speculation that the air crash was engineered by Pakistani Shiite Muslims critical of Zia's Sunni Wahabi-oriented Islamisation policies. Another school of thought believes that members of the air force or the intelligence services having links with the Pakistan People Party organised this assassination. There is a third school of thought that some segments of the Pakistani ISI itself, apprehensive of Zia's drastic action against them for the Ojhari camp disaster, might have eliminated him. There was even far-fetched partisan speculation that the US, desirous of a change of leadership in Pakistan with some semblance of democracy, might have encouraged anti-Zia elements towards this violence. But the mystery remains.

In retrospect, the Zia era was marked by a comparative stability and absence of any large-scale military conflict between the two countries. It was also less turbulent in terms of personal interaction between the leaders of India and Pakistan, primarily because their domestic political concerns were more dominant. Zia had to legitimise his status in the post-Bhutto period. He had to deal with domestic dissent and had to manage relations with the US and Islamic countries to serve his interests in Afghanistan. India, under four prime ministers, had to face the post-emergency trauma, uncertainties generated by the Janata and Charan Singh governments, and separatist violence. How does one summarise the main points of Zia's policies? He encouraged cooperation in surface transport, civil aviation and postal services. He also encouraged cooperation to a limited extent in agriculture and financial and taxation matters. He supported people-to-people contacts, particularly with the Muslim and Sikh citizens of India, for subversive purposes. That he did not succeed goes to the credit of the Indians whom he targeted. He diverted arms received for the Afghan crisis to anti-India elements. By augmenting the weapons stockpile of the Pakistani Army, he contributed to the arms race in the subcontinent. He accentuated the process by galvanising Pakistan's nuclear weapons. Several SAARC leaders have personally confirmed to me that during his exchanges with them Zia constantly underlined the dangers of Indian hegemony and even told them that Pakistan's nuclear weapons capacity served the purpose not only of its own security but also of the smaller neighbours of India. Therefore, he pleaded, they should support the weapons orientation of Pakistan's nuclear policies.

The Benazir Bhutto Years

In opening up the lines of communication with Benazir, and being aware of the hurdles that the entrenched military and Zia elements in the power structure would place, Rajiv Gandhi decided to use an unorthodox approach. He first sent Aftab Seth, former consul-general of India in Karachi and who like Benazir had been to Oxford University to meet her, once it became clear that she would be the next prime minister. Seth's brief was to assure Benazir of the positive attitude that India would have towards the newly elected democratic Government of Pakistan. This was followed by Rajiv sending a joint secretary in his own office, a Foreign Service officer called, Ronen Sen, to meet Benazir and her advisers before the SAARC summit took place in Islamabad in December 1988. Sen's brief was to underline that while Rajiv Gandhi would be coming for the SAARC summit, he was willing to utilise the opportunity to focus attention on structuring Indo-Pakistan relations in a new and constructive framework. Benazir reciprocated the gesture and designated Iqbal Akhund, her foreign affairs adviser, and a Pakistani Parsi confidant, Happy Minwalla, as points of contact between Rajiv's office and her office. Though she had to retain Yaqub Khan as the foreign minister on the advice of Ghulam Ishaq Khan and the armed forces, he was not part of this process of back channel contacts. One must underline that these contacts were not secret. They were open.

Rajiv returned from his visit to Islamabad after participating in the SAARC meeting immediately after Benazir had become the prime minister. They interacted with each other for a year between December 1988 and December 1989. Rajiv Gandhi's mindset about Pakistan was that of creating a positive atmosphere for bilateral relations, shedding the heritage of suspicion and hostility of the past. But this approach was not romantic, it was tempered with realism. His own pronouncements at the end of 1988 constitutes the best manifestation of his policies. Speaking at the inaugural session of the fourth SAARC summit in Islamabad on 29 December he said, "I am particularly happy to be here when the people of Pakistan have elected you, Madam Prime Minister, to lead your great country to progress and prosperity, rooted in democracy. I bring greetings to the people of Pakistan from their sisters and brothers in India. We rejoice in the prospect of friendship and cooperation between India and Pakistan ... here in Pakistan, democratic elections have led to the installation of a new government under your distinguished leadership, giving rise to hope everywhere in the subcontinent of a new dawn of friendship and cooperation between us." This was the normative aspect of his approach, his vision about Indo-Pakistan relations.

Speaking at the impromptu press conference at Delhi airport on his return from Pakistan on 31 December 1988, he was asked: "Were you able to convince the prime minister of Pakistan that policies of military nuclear programmes and support to terrorists are to be given up?" His response was: "I had very useful talks with Prime Minister Benazir Bhutto.... We high-lighted the major problems, the difficult areas, and also the less difficult areas where it could be easier to work. I felt that there is definitely a mood on both sides to try and get things back on the track to normalising the situation between our two countries. I can also say with confidence that we believe that the People's Party's policies will be much better than the earlier policies, essentially in the more difficult areas." Another questioner asked: "You have said that you are confident that the policy of the PPP in future will not be as it has been before. However, you are already aware of the PPP's and her father's policies. What new change have you now found in her that you have the confidence that her future policy will considerably improve relations between Pakistan and India?" The prime minister responded: "These are your words, not mine."

It is one of the abiding paradoxes of Indo-Pakistan relations that despite a general awareness of political realities, any change of government in either country always generates some optimism and positive expectations. Public perceptions about Rajiv and Benazir overseeing Indo-Pakistan relations were even more optimistic. There were assessments on both sides of the border that being young, not having been subject to the psychological, emotional and political trauma of Partition, they would be more willing to shed the burdens of the past. Neither of them had any direct part to play in the previous Indo-Pakistan conflicts. So the hope was that the attendant complexes and prejudices would not affect them. There was also the involuted analysis that Benazir being the daughter of the man, who signed the Simla Agreement might have a greater commitment to fulfil its objectives. Mrs Gandhi's request to Zia not to carry out the death sentence against Zulfiqar and India's general support to the Movement for the Restoration of Democracy also resulted in expectations. India's consul-general in Karachi, Mani Shankar Aiyer (now a distinguished and articulate Member of Parliament), and Aftab Seth had kept in touch with Benazir, despite frowns from the Zia regime, when she was in the opposition. Her own pronouncements after her electoral victory reflected a rational and practical attitude towards India.

The Geneva Agreements on Afghanistan having been signed and the time-frame for the withdrawal of Soviet troops having been finalised, the US was also keen on stabilising the situation in South Asia, particularly in the context of its concern regarding nuclear weapons and nuclear technology proliferation. It was the American view that the gradual establishment of a peaceful working relationship between India and Pakistan would reduce the propensity of both countries towards nuclear "weaponisation". On India's part, Rajiv had kept the general momentum of interaction with Pakistan open, even during the interregnum between Zia's demise and Benazir's coming to power.

Rajiv had three meetings with Benazir during his stay in Islamabad. Three bilateral agreements were signed. First, on the prohibition of attack on each other's nuclear installations and facilities; second, on cultural cooperation. Third, on avoidance of double taxation on incomes derived from international civil aviation transactions. They agreed to set in motion meetings for cooperation in trade, civil aviation, railways, tourism, and border monitoring and management. They also agreed that discussions on Siachen on delineating land borders in the Sir Creek area and on the Tulbul project would be continued. It was also agreed that the Ministerial Commission on Bilateral Cooperation would be revived.

When I called on Rajiv late in February and then again early in March, he asked me to take assiduous follow-up action on the agenda that he had set for Indo-Pakistani relations during his visit to Islamabad. He also informed me that the situation in Kashmir and Punjab was generally discussed by him with Benazir. She told him that there was no Pakistani involvement in Punjab and that if there was any, she would rectify the situation. As far as Kashmir was concerned, she affirmed to him that she would be willing to resolve the issue within the framework of the Simla Agreement. But no details were discussed. Rajiv Gandhi was particularly keen on preventing a nuclear arms race in south Asia.

Even before I assumed charge as ambassador to Pakistan on 16 April, there was almost unprecedented interaction between the two countries. Between January and April 1989, high-level delegations from India visited Pakistan to strengthen commercial contacts. Between May and June, delegations were exchanged to resume substantive cooperation in civil aviation, railways, transport and tourism. Indian delegations visited Islamabad and Karachi to discuss civil aviation and rail traffic matters during May. Pakistan's minister for tourism, Yusuf Raza Gilani, led a delegation to India to participate in a bilateral conference of Indian and Pakistani tour operators. All three visits resulted in agreements on enhancing civil air traffic between the two countries and restoring travel for nationals of both countries by train, all seven days of the week.

The third round of home secretary-level talks was held in Islamabad between 21 and 24 May 1989 and the fifth round of talks on Siachen between the defence secretaries was held on 14-17 June. The home secretaries, J.A. Kalyana Krishnan and S.K. Mehmood, discussed the possibility of cooperation between the border security forces of the two countries in monitoring cross-border illegal activity and patrolling the border to counter infiltration. An interesting nuance in the Pakistani stand was that they were willing to have only "parallel patrolling" of the borders by the border security forces and not "joint patrolling" which we suggested. They also agreed to liberalise the visa regime. It was agreed that the number of places which Indians and Pakistanis could visit in each other's country would be increased, that prior police verification requirements before granting visas would be liberalised to some extent, that the periodicity of visas would be increased and that the requirement of reporting to police stations on arrival in each other's country would be made easier.

Discussions on Siachen between Defence Secretaries Naresh Chandra and Izlal Haider Zaidi, though inconclusive, showed some forward movement. For the first time, armed forces commanders on both sides commenced an exercise to determine the points to which both Indian and Pakistani troops should withdraw. These discussions also concentrated on the manner in which the area could be kept free of conflict or future military activity. Discussions on delineating the boundary in the Sir Creek area were characterised by detailed exchange of information and cartographic data on the basis. Both the Indian and Pakistani sides acknowledged that delineating the boundary on the land was not complex in itself, but that the manner in which the delineation would take place might have implications in determining the maritime boundary stretching out to the Arabian Sea. This posed problems because of Pakistani ambitions and claims in this regard. The discussions therefore did not lead to any substantive agreement. As a follow-up of the fifth round of defence secretary–level talks on Siachen, the army commanders of India and Pakistan met in Delhi for two days, on 10 and 11 July. The director-general of Pakistan Joint Staff Headquarters, Lt. General Imtiaz Wahrraich, came to India. The Indian delegation was led by Lt. General V.K. Singh, director-general, military operations. There was tentative agreement on points to which Pakistani and Indian troops should move back from their existing positions on the Siachen glacier. The two governments agreed at the end of the discussion that army commanders should meet again in August at Islamabad.

The bilateral visit of an Indian prime minister to Pakistan took place on 16 and 17 July after a gap of 30 years. Rajiv Gandhi accompanied by Sonia Gandhi, External Affairs Minister Narasimha Rao, Natwar Singh, minister of state, and a number of senior officials arrived for a tightly scheduled visit. Discussions, primarily one-to-one between the two prime ministers, were supposed to be the beginning of frequent, direct, personal contacts, as was agreed during Rajiv's SAARC-connected visit in December 1988. The conclusion of the visit, however, was an anti-climax. Benazir concentrated more on the Kashmir issue and wanted Rajiv Gandhi to signal some shift in India's firm stand on Kashmir so as to increase her credibility with the military and Islamic constituencies in Pakistan that were accusing her of being soft on India. He reminded her of the discussions that had led to the signing of the Simla Agreement and told her that a practical and realistic approach was required rather than demands for unilateral concessions by India. Her misplaced expectation was that Rajiv, with his lack of involvement with the events leading to Partition and with his genuine desire to improve relations with Pakistan might be willing to compromise on the Kashmir issue. She had considered this expectation a sine qua non to neutralising the pressure on her by the extreme Islamic elements and the hawks in the Pakistan armed forces establishment. Rajiv was to hold a joint press conference with her on the morning of 17 July, before his departure for Delhi. Both leaders delayed the press conference as Benazir insisted on one more one-to-one bilateral discussion to bring Rajiiv round to her views on Kashmir. This meeting was held in a room adjacent to the press conference hall. It was inconclusive. But Rajiv remained firm about India's interests. He articulated this view clearly in the press conference that followed.

Benazir was on the defensive after Rajiv's visit. She commenced reverting to old Pakistani policy stances. Foreign Minister Yakub Khan visited Delhi towards the end of July and offered to mediate between India and Sri Lanka as Sri Lanka refused to host the SAARC Summit in 1989 unless the Indian Peace Keeping Force (IPKF) withdrew. He offered Islamabad as a venue for Indo-Sri Lankan bilateral discussions, a suggestion pregnant with political motivations and implications. India politely told Yakub Khan that while his offer might be laudable, it did not suit India.

The meeting between the military commanders of India and Pakistan on Siachen took place as scheduled in Islamabad in August. While the mechanical and operational aspects of the arrangements for mutual withdrawal or redeployment of troops were more or less finalised, the Pakistani delegation introduced two new points they had been generally hinting at during the previous discussions. First, while agreeing that troops would be redeployed at mutually agreed upon points, they refused to confirm cartographically the point from which their troops would withdraw. They also refused to put on record details of the posts from which they would withdraw. Second, withdrawal would be subject to India generally agreeing that the Line of Control, or notional line determining the jurisdiction of each country, should be drawn tangentially northeastwards to the Karakoram ranges from the northernmost grid reference point clearly identified in the maps about the Line of Control, namely, grid reference point NJ-9842. The objective was clear. They not only wanted India to vacate its strategically secure position on Siachen, making the area a no-man's land, but also wished to lay claim to several thousand square miles of Indian territory south and southwestwards from the Karakoram range to establish future legal claims on the area. One had come to an impasse.

In the meantime, some of the old allies of Benazir in the Movement for the Restoration of Democracy had joined the opposition. She was under domestic political pressure which found manifestation in the no-confidence motion moved against her on 31 October 1989. She survived the motion by a narrow margin of 12 votes and had to induct into her cabinet three members of the Islami Jamhori Ittehad (IJI) who had voted in her favour. By late autumn, Rajiv was deeply involved in preparing for general elections in India. Opposition politics in Pakistan and electoral policies in India impinged on bilateral relations. By the beginning of 1990, Rajiv was out of power. A new incarnation of the Janata Government led by V.P. Singh with I.K. Gujral as foreign minister took over. Indo-Pakistan relations were to go into a spin from the end of 1989 onwards because of the violent and volatile developments in Kashmir. The tenuous hopes of a new beginning came to a somewhat abrupt end in December 1989.

How did this denouement take place? The brief answer could be the contradiction between the expectations on the part of Benazir and the predications on which Rajiv structured his policies. Benazir's expectations arose from her memories of her father's discussions with Indian leaders. She felt that India would deal with her in a more accommodating manner since her father had been a signatory to the Simla Agreement, which had formed the basis for a conflict-free relationship between the two countries for nearly two decades. She, however, overlooked the fact that within months of signing the Agreement her father had started resiling from the imperative bilateral tenets. She also concluded India might be willing to compromise on vital issues like Kashmir and Siachen.

The predications on which Rajiv fashioned his policy were quite different. His basic anticipation was that if he engineered positive and substantive cooperation, it would create the necessary atmosphere of mutual trust and confidence that could ultimately lead to practical solutions to intractable problems. He was willing to sign a treaty of peace, friendship and cooperation, to meet Pakistani concerns. His suggestion about not attacking each other's nuclear facilities was transformed into a bilateral agreement. It was a step towards stabilising the nuclear non-proliferation atmosphere in the subcontinent. He was willing to review and rationalise ground rules for monitoring and stabilising the security environment on the Indo-Pakistan border.

Long before US officials like Robert Gates and J. Bartholomew visited India in 1990-91, Rajiv had offered to sign a memorandum of understanding with Pakistan to prevent mutual airspace violations. He had desired substantive expansion of bilateral trade and the mutual granting of Most Favoured Nation (MFN) status. India in any case was doing this under its obligations to the General Agreement an Tariffs and Trade (GATT). He was a strong advocate of both countries adopting non-discriminatory and free trade regimes. This initiative had some impact as Pakistan expanded the list of permissible imports from India to Pakistan from a little over 400 items to a little over 700 items in 1988-89. Rajiv offered to support joint economic and technological ventures. He desired cooperation in tourism, culture, science and technology and was keen on increasing people-to-people contacts with liberalised travel arrangements.

When I called on Rajiv before assuming charge in Islamabad, he articulated the macro-level policy approach. He said all the suggestions he had made to Zia and to some extent to Benazir were confidence-building and risk-reducing methods. Five months before he went to Pakistan for his bilateral visit, he told me that Pakistani responses to his suggestions had been sceptical and unsatisfactory. He was also clear in his mind that there was no question of India compromising on its interests, Kashmir and Siachen, non-proliferation and arms control, and structuring the military balances on the subcontinent.

Mutual disappointment between Benazir and Rajiv was therefore inevitable. If Rajiv had continued in power and if Benazir had not faced pernicious domestic challenges, they could perhaps have made small beginnings in resolving the contradictions.

The above optimistic assessment is not rooted in facts or in reason, but in the impression I had about the attitude of both Rajiv and Benazir on the basis of my conversations with them between August 1989 and December 1989. Rajiv Gandhi lost power in the winter of 1989. V.P. Singh replaced him with Gujral as the foreign minister. The so-called kidnapping of Rubiya Sayeed, daughter of Mufti Mohammad Sayeed, by militants and the V.P. Singh Government succumbing to the demands of the terrorists to get her released, was a watershed. The Government of India and the Government of Jammu and Kashmir surrendering to the terrorists convinced them that they could relaunch their violent secessionist movement on a full scale against India. The Government of Pakistan, specially its military establishment and the Inter-Services Intelligence, came to the conclusion that the Government of India, being a weakly cobbled-together coalition, would not be able to put up any effective resistance to heightened terrorist activities or covert interference. By December 1989, Pakistani violence increased. Consequent tensions between India and Pakistan put the bilateral dialogue and the implementation of various agreements reached during Rajiv tenure, into a spin.

The period between November 1989 and June 1991 was overshadowed by incremental terrorist violence in Jammu and Kashmir and on occasions heightened tensions on the international border between India and Pakistan. Benazir remained in power till October 1990, when she was dismissed on charges of corruption and maladministration. Nawaz Sharif assumed charge after an electoral victory in the winter of 1990. The two Indian prime ministers who dealt with them in this period were V.P. Singh and Chandra Shekhar.

Despite accentuated terrorism in Jammu and Kashmir, India's minister for external affairs, Gujral, felt that efforts should continue to get Indo-Pakistani relations back on track. Benazir had a different motive in continuing contacts with India. So though the motivations were different, there was a convergence of views about restoring contacts on hold since August-September 1989. Benazir sent Abdul Sattar as her special envoy to Delhi early in January. Sattar (now foreign minister of Pakistan) had served in Delhi as high commissioner between 1978 and 1982. His mission was primarily to make an assessment of the vulnerabilities of the new government under V.P. Singh, while the declared objective was to establish contact with the new power structure of India. Sattar went back to Islamabad and briefed the Benazir Government about the weakness of the Indian coalition and the contradiction between V.P. Singh's cautious and tense approach towards Pakistan and Gujral's desire to open up lines of communication. Benazir decided to give a formal expression to Pakistan's public posture of reasonableness towards India by deputing her foreign minister, Lt. General Sahibzada Yaqub Khan, to Delhi from 21 to 23 January 1990. Another motivation of the Yaqub Khan mission seemed to be to pressurise, perhaps even intimidate, India on the Jammu and Kashmir issue. He was stern and admonitory in his pronouncements. He emphasised that Benazir was deeply disappointed by Rajiv not being responsive to her suggestions regarding discussion on the status of Jammu and Kashmir. He cautioned Gujral that war clouds would hover over the subcontinent if timely action was not taken.

Gujral was quite upset with Yaqub Khan's message. After a lengthy discussion with Prime Minister V.P. Singh, he decided to give a strong message to Yaqub Khan. The high commissioner of Pakistan, Babar, was holding an official dinner in honour of Yaqub Khan, to which Gujral went.

He asked me to convey to the Pakistan high commissioner that he would like to have a private meeting with Yaqub Khan after the dinner, at the high commissioner's residence itself. This meeting took place, at which I was present. Gujral told Yaqub Khan that the warnings and accusatory remarks made by him (Yaqub Khan) during the course of the day were unacceptable and they had caused concern and resentment in the Government of India. Gujral said that such an attitude of Pakistan would only evoke a firm and decisive response from India.

Brinkmanship

The Yaqub mission was an exercise in futility. What compounded the situation was Benazir's moving on to take a highly militant and aggressive posture on Jammu and Kashmir vis-à-vis India. Solidarity weeks, rallies and strikes were sponsored and organised with the support of the Pakistan Government. Various Islam-pasand parties and groups announced that there would be mass crossings by Pakistani civilians into the territory of Jammu and Kashmir as also into portions of northern Punjab. I was given instructions by the Government of India to caution the Government of Pakistan against such adventurist activities. I told Pakistani Foreign Secretary Tanvir Ahmed Khan as well as US Ambassador Robert Oakley that civilian crossings and mass hysteria across the Line of Control and across the international frontier would be met with decisive responses by the Indian armed forces. The message apparently did not make an impact. A mob of about two or three thousand people crossed into the Indian side of the Line of Control from Chakothi in Pakistan-occupied Kashmir. A similar crossing was attempted by seven hundred to a thousand civilians from a point northeast of Sialkot. Initially, the Indian security forces asked the civilians to go back, using public address systems. But the Pakistani mob was so full of militant confidence that they started burning the crops on the border and the wooden stakes and pillars on which the Indian observation posts were built. It was only when matters reached this stage that the Indian security forces fired on the mob, resulting in the death of six or seven Pakistani civilians. Once this happened, no further attempts at civilian crossings and agitations were made. Pakistan went back to infiltrating militants and mercenaries. Pakistani propaganda and international diplomatic efforts took advantage of these tense incidents to argue the traditional case on Kashmir. Direct attacks on government installations and security forces in Kashmir were parallelly organised.

By April 1990, Prime Minister V.P. Singh came to the conclusion that a public message should be conveyed to Pakistan about India's intention of taking decisive countermeasures. In a speech in the Indian Parliament on 10 April, he announced that India would respond extensively and decisively against Pakistani violence and interference. He followed this up by a speech to the Indian security forces on the Ganganagar border in Rajasthan saying that India was in the process of initiating military measures against Pakistan. Singh's statement generated some concern in the Government of Pakistan. I was summoned to the Pakistani Foreign Office to explain matters. I conveyed that if Pakistani pyrotechnics and aggressive intervention continued, Pakistan should be prepared to face a military response from India. I conveyed a similar message to US Ambassador Oakley. Some time during the first half of May 1990, Oakley called me to his office for an urgent meeting. He produced some photographs taken through US satellite imagery and told me that the photographs were of the build-up of Indian armour on the Rajasthan-Sindh border and on the northern edge of Rajasthan, which could be perceived as a threat to the southern portions of Pakistani Punjab. He wanted to know whether India was in the process of launching an operation against Pakistan to reduce Pakistani violence and pressure in Jammu and Kashmir. I told him that I had no such information and I would check with the Government of India and get back to him. But there was a sufficient sense of alarm in Islamabad. I was informed by my concerned officers in the high commission that there was a movement of large trucks loaded with containers out of the Kahuta nuclear facilities near Islamabad. The guess of my informant was that this was nuclear equipment and also the components of missiles Pakistan was importing from China. Oakley told me that Pakistan apprehended some kind of military operation by India across the international frontier. I received information and instructions within 36 hours of my conversation with Oakley from Cabinet Secretary Naresh Chandra that India had no plans or intention to launch any military operation against Pakistan, particularly across the international border into Sindh or Pakistani Punjab. I was also told to convey that India would certainly retaliate militarily against violence inside Jammu and Kashmir. I made a specific request to Ambassador Oakley to tell the Pakistani military high command and the Inter-Services Intelligence directorate to cease and desist from their adventurist inclinations. Oakley not only conveyed the message to all the seniormost levels in the Pakistani government, but his messages also resulted in what is known as the Gates diplomatic mission to Pakistan and India in the summer of 1990.

These are the events that resulted in later inaccurate speculation about the imminence of an Indo-Pakistan war in 1990, with possibilities of some kind of nuclear confrontation. There was none of the danger or brinkmanship later sensationalised in the book *Critical Mass* by two American authors. Robert Gates, US deputy national security adviser, visited Pakistan and India and took the trouble to meet Benazir in Europe. He represented the US policy orientation of ensuring that things did not get out of hand in view of the heightened tensions in Jammu and Kashmir. Gates also had a brief to convey categorical cautionary admonitions to India and Pakistan about their nuclear weapons programmes. The Gates mission did not result in any abatement of Pakistan-sponsored separatism in Jammu and Kashmir. He, however, achieved one concrete result. He told the Pakistanis to resume a dialogue with India on putting in place the confidence-building measures Rajiv had proposed in 1989. He made this suggestion on the basis of the Government of India indicating its willingness to engage in such a dialogue. The consequence was a new round of foreign secretary–level talks commencing on 17 July 1990 with Foreign Secretary Muchkund Dubey visiting Islamabad. Dubey and his Pakistani counterparts, Tanvir Ahmed Khan and Shahryar Khan, had four rounds of talks between July 1990 and October 1991. These discussions did not result in any forward movement towards a practical solution to the Kashmir issue, but they proved useful in putting in place a number of political and confidence-building measures. These involved both sides giving advance notice of military exercises, being restrained in flights of air force planes and patrolling by their respective navies, completing procedural formalities for bringing into force the Indo-Pakistan agreement on not attacking each other's nuclear installations, and so on.

The year 1990 presented a paradoxical situation in Indo-Pakistan relations. Governments in both countries were vulnerable, as they were essentially coalition governments. Tensions in Jammu and Kashmir were kept at a high level by Pakistan. The Janata Government was more anxious to prove Rajiv's foreign and defence policies wrong than to assess them objectively. This could have been neutralised by Pakistan structuring practical equations with India. Had Pakistan acknowledged the necessity to distance itself from violence in Kashmir and agreed to concentrate on larger and more important aspects of bilateral relations, it could have been beneficial to both countries. But there is an inevitability about Pakistan's inability to extricate itself from its almost atavistic religio-communal compulsions regarding Kashmir. While this was so, the general positive push given to Indo-Pakistani relations by Rajiv Gandhi went into slow motion during the Janata period.

By November 1990, Nawaz Sharif came to power in Pakistan and Chandra Shekhar became Indian prime minister owing to the disintegration of the Janata Government. During Chandra Shekhar's brief tenure between November 1990 and May 1991, Indo-Pakistan relations continued in their negative drift except for two events. Chandra Shekhar met Nawaz Sharif during the SAARC summit in Male between 21 and 23 November 1990, during which they decided to establish a direct hotline. They also took a decision to activate the hotline between the offices of the foreign secretaries and the directors of military operations. It is a different matter that hot-line conversations between the directors-general of military operations remain routine and the prime ministerial hotline has seldom been used, as has the hotline between the two foreign secretaries except towards the end of 1992 and in the second half of 1993. The second event was a consequence of the tragic assassination of Rajiv Gandhi on 21 May 1991. I was informed of it around midnight on 21 May. I conveyed this information immediately to the president of Pakistan, Ghulam Ishaq Khan, and Nawaz Sharif. Ishaq Khan came to the high commission of India to sign the condolence book. Nawaz Sharif decided to lead the Pakistan delegation to the funeral of Rajiv Gandhi.

On 24 May 1991 Nawaz Sharif called me for a meeting and made the request that he would like to have a separate meeting with Prime Minister Chandra Shekhar, apart from the courtesy call. Chandra Shekhar readily agreed. He hosted a lunch for Nawaz Sharif and his delegation on 25 May as most of them were departing from Delhi. The lunch was held at 7 Race Course Road, with only members of the Pakistani delegation and senior officials of the Ministry of External Affairs present. After the initial courtesies, Nawaz Sharif suggested that Chandra Shekhar and he should have a separate and private discussion.

The lunch proceeded normally. Nawaz Sharif and the delegation left for the airport. He was seen off around 3 p.m. from the Palam Technical Area. Chandra Shekhar called me back for a meeting after the departure of the Pakistani delegation and I met him later in the evening. He called a meeting of senior officials of the Ministries of External Affairs, Defence and Home to review Indo-Pakistani relations at 11.15 a.m. on 27 May. The conclusion arrived at at this meeting was that Pakistan's anti-Indian activities in Kashmir would continue, even if Nawaz Sharif may not be supportive of these activities. The prime minister asked me to see him again at 7 Race Course Road on 28 May. He informed me of the main purpose of Nawaz Sharif wanting to see him alone at the lunch two days earlier. Nawaz Sharif after emphasising the imperative need to improve Indo-Pakistan relations told Chandra Shekhar that the only problem standing in the way of normalisation was the Kashmir issue and that the only practical solution would be that both India and Pakistan should move back from claiming total jurisdiction over the entire territory of the old princely state of Jammu and Kashmir. He then told Prime Minister Chandra Shekhar that his government should seriously consider allowing either plebiscite in the Valley, that ultimately India could keep Ladakh and Jammu while Pakistan would retain areas of POK and that the Valley would accede to Pakistan. Chandra Shekhar told me he told Nawaz Sharif not to make impractical, utopian proposals.

Two events proved that this reaction of Chandra Shekhar made Nawaz Sharif move back to an adversarial stance. First, addressing the National Defence College of Pakistan in Rawalpindi on 6 June he put forward a proposal for subcontinental non-proliferation with some new dimensions. He suggested that India and Pakistan should sign a formal agreement to eliminate all weapons of mass destruction and that this agreement should be guaranteed by the US, China and the Soviet Union. He also proposed that a five-power conference of representatives of India, Pakistan, the US, the Soviet Union and China should be held to negotiate such an agreement and to create a system of guarantees or a security umbrella by the three superpowers. He recommended this as a practical step towards achieving nuclear non-proliferation in South Asia.

Second, he proposed that an international conference should be held in Islamabad with the backing of the Pakistan Government to discuss the systematic violations of human rights in "Indian-held Kashmir". His proposals were generally endorsed by the US, while the Soviet Union and China kept their own counsel. The latter two only made enquiries about India's reaction to the proposals. India rejected them on the grounds that South Asian nuclear non-proliferation could not be achieved in a foolproof manner by a compartmentalised approach concentrating only on the Indian subcontinent.

Rumours and Rhetoric

P.V. Narasimha Rao became the prime minister of India in June 1991. As foreign minister he had met Benazir in December 1988 and in July 1989. Rao had frequent interaction with Nawaz Sharif between October 1991 and May 1993. He met him at Harare (during the Commonwealth summit) in October 1991, again in Colombo in November 1991 during the SAARC summit, and then in Rio de Janeiro, Davos, Jakarta and Dhaka in 1992 and 1993 during the summit, the economic summit, Non-aligned summit and then again at the SAARC summit in April 1993.

I do not recall the exact date (in October 1991) on which I happened to meet Benazir, then in the opposition, at a reception in one of the embassies in Islamabad. When I greeted her, she remarked: "Mr Dixit, I am hearing good rumours, I believe you are going to be the next foreign secretary of India. I am glad that somebody who has lived in Pakistan and who knows Pakistan is going back to the Foreign Office. Despite the current difficulties I hope that during your tenure in office, we will be able to improve our relations." I replied the rumours she had heard about my going back to Delhi were not entirely baseless but that the decision had not been formalised or announced.

A brief reference to the prevailing trends and happenings in Pakistan, just preceding my assuming charge in Delhi, is relevant. Benazir had lost the elections in October 1990 and Nawaz Sharif had become the prime minister. While there was no change in the substance of Pakistani policies, Sharif had considerably toned down the anti-India rhetoric on Kashmir and other issues during the later part of 1990 and most of 1991. By the time I prepared to return to Delhi, Nawaz Sharif had already met Prime Minister. Chandra Shekhar at the Maldives SAARC Summit in November 1990. He had also met Prime Minister Rao at the Harare summit in October 1991. Talks at the Foreign Secretary level were continuing as scheduled. The fifth round was held in Islamabad on 30 September and 1 October 1991. During these talks, Foreign Secretary Muchkund Dubey, and his Pakistani counterpart, Shahryar Khan, had agreed to expert-level meetings on the Tulbul navigation project, on the demarcation of the boundary in Sir Creek and on the finalisation of an advance declaration on Pakistan and India's decision to abjure chemical and biological weapons. It was agreed that the sixth round of talks would be held in Delhi in early 1992.

Shahryar Khan had visited Delhi between 18 and 20 August 1991 as a special envoy of the prime minister of Pakistan. He brought a communication from Nawaz Sharif addressed to Rao in which the former assured the latter of Pakistan's desire to move towards the normalisation of relations in a purposeful manner. When Shahryar Khan called on the prime minister, he requested a meeting with the defence minister. It was agreed to. He also called on Foreign Secretary Dubey. Shahryar Khan's visit was, in a manner, a repetition of that of his predecessor, Abdul Sattar, to New Delhi between 7 and 11 January 1990, when the V.P. Singh Government was in power. Like Sattar, Shahryar Khan's objective was to assess the mood in India and the likely policies of Rao's new government in relation to Pakistan. The most important aspect of Khan's visit was the verbal assurance he gave to Prime Minister Rao and Defence Minister Sharad Pawar that Pakistan would take definite steps to prevent subversive activities in Jammu and Kashmir originating from Pakistani territory. The words he used were: "India will see a qualitative change in the situation on the ground." He declared that in this context both countries should undertake a discussion on the Kashmir issue as well as on all other issues in an attempt to normalise Indo-Pakistan relations.

It was with this background that the fifth round of talks at the foreign secretary level took place on 1 October 1991. Decisions taken by Dubey and Khan about expert-level meetings were implemented in the stipulated time-frame. The seventh round of talks on the Tulbul navigation project took place between 12 and 15 October 1991. Further discussions on the delineation of the boundary in the Sir Creek area and on clearly demarcating the maritime boundaries between the two countries were held between 25 and 28 October 1991. The foregoing discussions were affected by tension in Ayodhya and attempts by certain Indian political parties to damage the Babri Masjid structure. A Pakistan Foreign Office spokesman issued a statement on 2 November: "The Government and the people of Pakistan are outraged and anguished over the desecration and damage to the Babri mosque." During my farewell call on President Ghulam Ishaq Khan on 12 November he reiterated Pakistan's desire to establish peaceful relations with India on the basis of justice and sovereign equality. When I met Prime Minister Nawaz Sharif the next day, he introduced a nuance of regionalising bilateral disputes: "SAARC should be made more effective in order to promote peace and development of the region."

It was, therefore, in a contradictory atmosphere engendered by negative ground realities clashing with positive trends in domestic political discussions regarding Pakistan that I assumed charge as foreign secretary on 1 December 1991. On 12 December the Jammu and Kashmir Liberation Front chief, Amanullah Khan, put a spanner in the works by announcing that his cadre would cross the Line of Control in Kashmir from Pakistan occupied Kashmir on 11 February 1992. The Government of India issued instructions to the chargé d'affaires in Pakistan, Bhadra Kumar, to convey a message to the Pakistani authorities that India would hold them entirely responsible for any tension arising out of this decision and that Pakistan should prevent this intended crossing of the Line of Control. Late in December, as a sort of follow-up to his meeting with Prime Minister Narasimha Rao in Harare, Nawaz Sharif gave an interview to the editor of the *Hindustan Times*, H.K. Dua, in which he stated that India and Pakistan should raise the level of discussions on Kashmir. Sharif suggested that both countries should commence a dialogue at the political level to resolve the Kashmir issue and other bilateral issues.

The first official act related to Pakistan in which I was involved after becoming foreign secretary was to ensure that India and Pakistan exchanged lists of nuclear installations and facilities as stipulated in the Indo-Pakistan agreement on non-attack (on each other's nuclear installations). There were reservations among experts on both sides of the border regarding the propriety of such a step. Prime Minister Rao, however, decided that we must honour our commitment which, in my judgement, was the right decision. We exchanged the lists on 1 January 1992. The next decision in which I was involved was related to deciding who would be my successor at the mission in Pakistan. The prime minister asked me to give him a list of three or four names. He had decided, in principle, that the person had to be from the career Foreign Service, since he felt that a person appointed from political or media circles might attempt to utilise the assignment to further his image or political aspirations back home. A career officer would not be subject to this temptation and would thus be more detached and professional.

I listed four officers who had previously dealt with Pakistan, at the senior level, either in our mission in Islamabad or from Delhi. On our flight back from the Caracas G-15 summit, the prime minister told me that he had chosen S.K. Lambah, former joint secretary in charge of Pakistan, Iran and Afghanistan and former deputy chief of mission in Islamabad. Lambah had the additional advantage of having a large number of contacts across the entire spectrum of the Pakistani establishment. His family originated from Peshawar, and he spoke fluent Punjabi. Further, Lambah had worked with me as first secretary (political) during my assignment in Bangladesh between 1972 and 1974. Both of us were among the first to arrive in Dhaka after the liberation of Bangladesh to open the Indian mission in its new incarnation as India's embassy. When I informed him of the prime minister's decision to send him to Islamabad, he promptly agreed and left his post as consul-general in San Francisco without even completing his tenure there. He assumed charge on 23 January 1992. Lambah then served as our ambassador in Bonn and Moscow, retiring from service in 2001.

Despite all the supposedly positive signals sent by the Nawaz Sharif Government to India, the assurances conveyed by Shahryar Khan in August 1991 that the situation on the ground would change were not adhered to. The Pakistan Government orchestrated a nationwide protest against India on 5 January 1992. A number of rallies were organised and the day was dubbed the "Right of Self-Determination Day for Kashmir". Sometime later we received a message that Nawaz Sharif would be in Davos, Switzerland, for the International Economic Conference between 30 January and 3 February, a conference which Prime Minister Rao was also scheduled to attend. There was a suggestion from Pakistan that the two should meet at Davos. The meeting eventually took place on 2 February. When Nawaz

Sharif repeated his desire for normality and peace, Rao pointed out that despite their previous meetings at Harare and the earlier message conveyed through Shahryar Khan, there was no change in Pakistani policies towards India on the issue of Jammu and Kashmir. Rao inquired how Nawaz Sharif could sustain the credibility of his political assurances when they contrasted so sharply with realities on the ground. Sharif responded with the standard Pakistani line that his government was trying to do its best to pull back from confrontationist activities but that Pakistani public opinion and its reflection in certain agencies of the Pakistani Government could not be brought under control so quickly. He reiterated that attempts towards the normalisation of relations should continue at the highest political and official levels. Rao indicated that though he had no objection to contacts being maintained, prospects of good relations would remain uncertain, if Pakistan did not change its attitude.

That the Pakistani leaders, regardless of their political affiliations, remain prisoners of an all-embracing anti-Indian stance was proved when, within three days of meeting Prime Minister Rao, Nawaz Sharif gave a call for a strike all over Pakistan "to express solidarity with Kashmir". The strike was observed on 5 February with the total support of the Pakistani Government. The very next day, the National Assembly of Pakistan adopted a resolution critical of India on the issue of Kashmir, and reiterated support to the separatists. Anti-Indian activities did not stop here. JKLF cadre attempted to cross the Line of Control on 11 and 12 February. Fourteen people were killed and nearly 115 people injured in this attempt. Nawaz Sharif sent six ministers of his cabinet to mobilise international opinion against India on the Kashmir issue. The important countries lobbied by Pakistan were Saudi Arabia, Oman, Morocco, Senegal, Cape Verde, Nigeria, Brazil, Ecuador, Venezuela, Malaysia, Indonesia, Egypt and China. One of my preoccupations through December 1991 and January and February 1992, was to counter these Pakistani moves.

Since the late President Zia's visit to Jaipur in 1987 in exercise of "cricket diplomacy", this game had become a catalyst for encouraging positive trends in bilateral relations. President K.R. Venkataraman sent a message of congratulations to his counterpart Ghulam Ishaq Khan on the victory of the Pakistani cricket team in the World Cup tournament on 25 March 1992. Thinking back, I wonder whether such exchanges between heads of state serve any useful purpose. In my opinion they only serve to increase the scepticism of public opinion in both countries about the incongruity of it all.

The period between March and August 1992 was a specially tense one in Indo-Pakistan relations because of a number of violent incidents that affected even the diplomats of both countries. JKLF cadre tried to cross the Line of Control again on 30 March 1992 but this time Pakistani authorities themselves prevented their attempt. India was also witness to another provocative phenomenon engineered by Pakistan. The Imam of the Jama Masjid, Delhi, Abdullah Bukhari was invited to visit Pakistan. He spent a fortnight there, lionised as a "sensible leader and protector of minorities" in India. Prime Minister Nawaz Sharif received him twice during his visit, which lasted from 5 to 20 May.

On 1 April 1992, Indian authorities apprehended an official of the Pakistan high commission, Arshad Ali, for his involvement in espionage activities. He was caught while meeting an Indian official whom he had subverted. Earlier in March, the Border Security Force (BSF) had apprehended four Pakistani military personnel who had crossed over into Indian territory. India kept them in custody for nearly two months and ultimately returned them on 13 May. I had felt that after checking the antecedents of these military personnel and debriefing them, India should have sent them back promptly but it was decided otherwise by the Home Ministry and Defence Ministry. The consequence of deporting Arshad Ali and holding the Pakistani military personnel was that one of the senior officers in the Indian mission in Islamabad, Consular Rajesh Mittal, was abducted by Pakistani intelligence agencies just outside his house on 24 May. He was taken to an interrogation centre and was subjected to violent interrogation techniques, including beatings and electrical shocks, for nearly seven hours. He was released after vigorous protests by High Commissioner S.K. Lambah. Though he was declared persona non grata and asked to leave Pakistan within 48 hours with his family, the Pakistani authorities did not guarantee him safe passage from Islamabad to Lahore or the assurance that he and his family would be allowed to take the normal Indian Airlines commercial flight from Lahore to Delhi with the necessary medical personnel in attendance. Lambah's requests in this context to the Pakistani authorities in Islamabad and an approach to the Pakistan High Commission in New Delhi received a negative response. After his release, Mittal was in a physically debilitated condition. In fact, he was a stretcher case. I conveyed that India would like to send an air force plane to bring him and his family back. The Pakistani authorities refused even this request, stating that they could not allow an air force plane to land in their country. Ultimately, after discussions with Foreign Secretary Shahryar Khan, a BSF plane was sent.

I personally went to receive Mittal in the technical area of Palam airport, New Delhi. I was aghast at what I saw. An officer in his late 30s or early

40s, of medium height and healthy build, had become a human wreck. His face, hands and feet were swollen and black and blue with beatings; his eyes could open only halfway. His wife could barely speak except to declare emotionally that she was grateful that her husband was alive and that she and her children had arrived back safely. I learnt later that apart from subjecting the officer to violence during the interrogation, Pakistani intelligence had hurled filthy abuses and anti-Hindu remarks at Mittal.

Mittal had to undergo a long process of medical treatment and rehabilitation. Our reaction was to expel two Pakistani Consulors , S.F.M. Endrabi and Zafrul Hasan, from Delhi. There was a comic denouement apropos of these gentlemen being expelled. When they were escorted to the Pakistani aircraft at Delhi airport, they walked into the aircraft in normal physical condition. The next day, the Pakistani media reported seeing them descend from the aircraft in Pakistan bandaged at various places and claiming that they had been subjected to physical abuse and violence. There must have been some midair arrangements on the flight between Delhi and Lahore/Islamabad, to counter Indian indignation at the diplomatic "courtesies" extended to Mittal by Pakistani intelligence agencies.

Apart from lodging a formal protest with the Pakistan High Commission and Foreign Office, India suggested to the Pakistani side that whenever the next round of foreign secretary–level talks were held, there must be an additional item on the agenda — agreement on a code of conduct governing treatment of each other's diplomats. Shahryar Khan readily agreed. Rao had his fourth meeting with Nawaz Sharif on 14 June 1992 at Rio de Janeiro, at the Earth Summit. Rao was not keen on this meeting, in the context of the ground realities of Indo-Pakistan relations. We, however, persuaded him to meet Nawaz Sharif, basically to ensure that Pakistan did not exploit a refusal for publicity and propaganda purposes. It was during this Rio meeting that it was decided to hold the sixth round of talks at the foreign secretary level in mid-August in New Delhi.

Shahryar Khan arrived on 16 August. We held three days of discussions, extending up to the afternoon of 19 August. In my personal meeting with Shahryar Khan before the formal discussions commenced he pointed out he would have to first state the Pakistani view on the Kashmir issue. I replied that while each one of us had to stick to his respective briefs, instead of responding to him point by point, as it would be a waste of time, I would rather concentrate on positive aspects on which we could achieve something. Having common sense and a professional approach Shahryar Khan agreed that after we had made our respective statements on Kashmir, we could move on to more substantive issues on which some useful work could be done. Shahryar Khan made a firm but non-polemical statement on the Kashmir issue. The flights of abuse and peroration that one of his predecessors, Tanvir Ahmed Khan, used to routinely indulge in were completely absent. After listening to him I observed that there were obviously fundamental differences in Indian and Pakistani thinking on how to deal with the Kashmir issue. I mentioned to him that the question of India in any way compromising its unity and territorial integrity did not arise. I then suggested that instead of continuing with purposeless debate on the issue, we should move on to the other items on the agenda. That is what happened. In comparative terms, this sixth round of talks yielded more concrete results related largely to mutual confidence-building measures. As a result, India and Pakistan exchanged instruments of ratification of the agreement on prevention of airspace violations by military aircraft and the agreement on advance notice on military exercises, manoeuvres and troop movements. A joint declaration on the complete prohibition of chemical weapons and another agreement on the code of conduct for the treatment of diplomatic and consular personnel by India and Pakistan were also signed. Preparatory work for these agreements was done during the fifth round of talks between Dubey and Shahryar Khan held in Islamabad on 1 October 1991. Another important decision taken during the sixth round of talks was to resume discussions at the Defence Ministry and armed forces level to defuse the confrontation at Siachen.

Shahryar Khan also called on Rao and handed over a letter from Nawaz Sharif in which the latter proposed bilateral negotiations on Kashmir under Article 6 of the 1972 Simla Agreement. This article, which was the last clause, stipulated that the heads of government would meet again at a mutually convenient time in the future to evolve a final settlement of Jammu and Kashmir, apart from discussing other issues. As part of the confidence-building measures, I handed over a formal invitation from India's chief of army staff to his Pakistani counterpart to visit India. The Pakistani authorities accepted the invitation only in principle, though some tentative dates had been suggested. The visit never took place.

Rao replied to Nawaz Sharif's letter on 29 August. The main points were that India was willing to have discussions on issues related to Kashmir under the Simla Agreement but that such discussion could not be held in a compartmentalised framework of just one article of the agreement. Rao pointed out that the discussion could be held only if Pakistan fulfilled its obligation to improve bilateral relations and bring about normality in interaction between India and Pakistan. Nawaz Sharif's communication was obviously an exercise that had ulterior publicity motives. India's response had necessarily to be clear and firm, even at the risk of Pakistan using it to slander India by saying it had rejected suggestions to discuss Kashmir.

The Jakarta summit of the Non-Aligned Movement was to be held in September 1992. Once again we received a message that this opportunity should be used for arranging a meeting between Rao and Sharif. This fifth meeting between the two prime ministers took place on 3 September. For appearances' sake, both told the assembled Indian and Pakistani mediapersons that such contacts in themselves were contributory to tempering the situation and defusing tension. Prime Minister Rao later admitted he considered these meetings with Nawaz Sharif as merely cosmetic.

A Downward Slide

The last quarter of 1992 and the first quarter of 1993 witnessed events that impelled a downward slide in Indo-Pakistan relations. While the manner in which the Kashmir issue impinged on foreign relations during my assignment in South Block will be discussed separately, it is worthwhile at this point to mention the shifts in Pakistani stances and policies regarding Kashmir. By the middle of 1992, Pakistan shifted away from its argument advocating the separation of Kashmir from India on the basis of the so-called "doctrine of self-determination". The world at large, taking note of the negative aspects of the disintegration of the Soviet Union and Yugoslavia, was not terribly keen to support arguments regarding "self-determination" which would affect the integrity of plural societies or multilingual, multiethnic and multireligious states. Seeing that its assertion about Kashmir was not evoking a positive response, Pakistan changed tracks to new political arguments to justify its views on Kashmir. It started highlighting "violations of human rights" and alleged "excesses by Indian security forces against a genuine anti-Indian mass movement in Jammu and Kashmir".

Human rights, in any case, had become a fashionable theme and one that various countries harped upon as a part of the new world order envisaged by former US president George Bush. Pakistan too found this subject a conveniently effective diplomatic and propagandist ploy. The second argument used by Pakistan was based on Western apprehensions about nuclear weapons proliferation. Pakistan started telling other countries that if India did not allow Kashmir to become part of Pakistan, there was likelihood of an open war between India and Pakistan which could lead to a nuclear holocaust. Thus, the Pakistanis insisted, in the interests of the settlement of a long-standing issue and in the larger interests of human rights and preventing nuclear conflict, Pakistan should get Kashmir.

India countered this Pakistani move, which was supported to some extent by the US and its Western allies, by simply assuring important powers that India had no desire to go to war with Pakistan and even if a military conflict occurred, it would not be the first to use nuclear weapons. India also pointed out that while Pakistan had covertly and overtly confirmed that it had nuclear weapons from 1985-86 onwards, India made no such claims. As far as the human rights argument of the Pakistanis was concerned, the response was to adopt an approach of greater transparency, by inviting genuinely impartial foreign observers to come to Jammu and Kashmir. At the same time, India conveyed to the UN in New York, to the Human Rights Commission in Geneva, and to the OIC Secretariat in Saudi Arabia that the passing of resolutions against India on Kashmir-related issues would be a futile international exercise. India would not succumb to any pressure where its territorial integrity and unity were involved. It also briefed practically every member of the UN about its perceptions of the stratagems being adopted by Pakistan, to somehow internationalise the Kashmir issue. The result was that despite several attempts throughout 1992 and 1993, and despite the passing of some resolutions by the OIC, India's position on Kashmir remained uneroded in international fora. In fact countries such as China, Japan, Germany, the UK and even Iran to some extent understood India's political position and tempered Pakistani activities.

The destruction of the old Babri Masjid structure at Ayodhya on 6 December 1992, however, put the fat in the fire. Pakistan took full advantage of this socio-political tragedy. Nawaz Sharif expressed a deep sense of shock and sorrow. The Pakistani Government handed over a formal aide memoire protesting against the demolition. There were strikes and processions all over Pakistan. The Indian Airlines office in Lahore was set on fire by a mob on 7 December. The residences of Indian officers and staff at Islamabad and Karachi were subject to stone-throwing. On 7 and 8 December a number of temples, churches and gurdwaras were destroyed by Pakistani mobs on the rampage. The culmination was the ransacking and burning of the residence of Indian Consul-General Rajiv Dogra in Karachi, with government connivance. As I was away in Dhaka preparing for the SAARC summit, to be held later in the month, I asked my senior colleague, Secretary K. Srinivasan, to summon the Pakistani high commissioner, Riaz Khokhar, and convey strong objection to Pakistan's anarchic reactions to an internal incident in India.

Srinivasan and Joint Secretary Bhadra Kumar had more than one meeting with Khokhar and his subordinates in Delhi. India demanded an appropriate expression of regret and compensation for the damage done to the Indian mission in Pakistan and for the violence diplomatic staff was subjected to. The situation put Nawaz Sharif in a dilemma. On the one hand, he had to be responsive to the religious hysteria in Pakistan. At the same time, he had to ensure that Pakistan's international image was not tarnished, a highly likely eventuality in the context of the attack on Indian missions and the destruction of non-Muslim places of worship in Pakistan. His government resorted to the ploy of continuing to issue critical statements about India, passing condemnatory resolutions in the Pakistan National Assembly, organising strikes and protests, and accusing India of mistreating its minorities. In addition, Sharif announced that non-Muslim religious structures destroyed in his country would be repaired at government cost and that the Government of India would be paid appropriate compensation for the damage to its properties in Pakistan. As far as I know, neither of these assurances was fulfilled till I retired on 31 January 1994. Two casualties of the Babri Masjid incident were the SAARC summit, not held as scheduled in December 1992, and foreign secretary–level talks in February 1993, to which Shahryar Khan and I had agreed, which were postponed indefinitely.

Earlier, the sixth round of talks between the defence secretaries of India and Pakistan regarding Siachen had been held from 2 to 5 November 1992. Defence Secretary N.N. Vohra and his Pakistani counterpart Syed Salim Abbas Jallani almost finalised the agreement for the redeployment of Indian and Pakistani troops. I expected that this would put an end to a strategically futile and economically costly confrontation. Three factors prevented the agreement from getting governmental approval in India and Pakistan. First, Pakistan continued to harp on the precondition that India should agree to the Line of Control being notionally accepted as running northeastwards from the grid reference point known as NJ-9842. Second, Pakistan continued to express reservations about finalising a joint cartographic document that would pinpoint positions from which troops of both countries should pull back. Third, the Indian government had reservations at the political level about approving the agreement reached at that point of time because of increased levels of Pakistan-sponsored violence in Jammu and Kashmir and also because of the intensity of the hostile diplomatic and publicity activities against India that Pakistan was engaged in. It was felt that Indian public opinion and Parliament would not be supportive of any move forward on Siachen at that point.

At the official level, we felt if this was the case, we need not have got into the very detailed discussions we had with Pakistan in November 1992. Even though the exercise turned out to be futile, I feel in retrospect that these talks between the defence secretaries of the two countries did work out in fair detail the mechanics and geopolitical conditions for the disengagement of troops. The agreement could still form the basis for a future solution of the Siachen problem.

There were faint silver linings in these dark clouds of hostility. Ministers of state for foreign affairs of both countries (M.H. Kanju from Pakistan and Eduardo Faleiro from India) met each other in Dhaka and then New York during the SAARC and UN conferences. India sent relief supplies to victims of the devastating floods that hit Pakistan in September 1992. Pakistan accepted these supplies. The year 1992, however, ended on a negative note with the Government of Pakistan asking India to drastically reduce its staff strength at its consulate-general in Karachi, from 64 to 20, creating immense hardships for the common citizens of both India and Pakistan who were dependent on consular services to facilitate visiting each other's countries.

India was still recovering from the initial aftershocks of the destruction of the Babri Masjid (on 6 December 1992), when a series of bomb blasts rocked Bombay on 12 March 1993. Nawaz Sharif indulged in the formality of sending a message of sympathy to our Prime Minister Rao on the Bombay blasts. Preliminary investigations, however, established by 17 March that the blasts were orchestrated by the ISI of Pakistan, which utilised Dawood Ibrahim, the Memon family, and their criminal associates to heighten the already tense communal atmosphere in India born of events in Ayodhya. There was another sinister motive behind the bomb explosions. They were perpetrated in Bombay, the most important centre for economic activities in India. The bombs were exploded to coincide with the general timing of the announcement of the Indian Budget for the year 1993-94. The objective was to create an impression in the international community that India was prone to violence and instability. Pakistan hoped that the consequence of this strategy would be to reduce investment and technology transfers.

As far as I recall, I spoke to Foreign Secretary Shahryar Khan over the hotline on 17 or 18 March and gave him advance information that preliminary evidence indicated the involvement of Pakistan in these bombing incidents. As expected, he responded by saying that this accusation would not be acceptable to Pakistan and that if there was any genuine evidence, it should be conveyed to Pakistan. After obtaining evidence from the Maharashtra state government and from our own concerned agencies, we passed on the information, with documentary proof, to High Commissioner Riaz Khokhar, on 23 March. The most substantive element in this evidence was proof that six members of the Memon family had reached Karachi on 17 March via Delhi. The Government of India asked for these people to be traced and for their extradition to India. Pakistan's response was formalistic. It first said that it would try to trace them, then asked for more information. Finally it declared they were not traceable.

Despite increasing levels of tension, Prime Minister Rao agreed that, wherever possible, routine contacts should be maintained with Pakistan, short of formal bilateral interaction, till the atmosphere improved. In keeping with this approach, Vice-President K.R. Narayanan had a brief exchange of views with Pakistani's caretaker prime minister, Mazari, in Colombo, where both had gone for Premadasa's funeral in May 1993. The Permanent Joint Indus Water Commission met in Delhi. A culmination of sorts was the sixth meeting between Nawaz Sharif and Narasimha Rao in Dhaka during the delayed SAARC summit in April 1993. Rao was not at all inclined to go through the cosmetic exercise again. My counterpart, Shahryar Khan, faced the same reaction from his prime minister, though for different reasons. Nawaz Sharif was anxious about domestic public opinion in Pakistan castigating him for having meetings with the Indian prime minister. Both of us, however, felt that howsoever resultless such a meeting may turn out to be, it might at least serve the purpose of reviving serious dialogue non-existent since August 1992. As it happened, the two prime ministers met for about 20 minutes at the end of the concluding session of the SAARC summit. It was a one-to- one meeting. While flying back from Dhaka, Prime Minister Rao told me that Nawaz Sharif had indicated a willingness to revive the foreign secretary–level dialogue and that I should follow it up. Later, in a review meeting in Delhi, the prime minister articulated his basic assessment of Indo-Pakistan relations. Rao did not expect any concrete positive developments in the foreseeable future, but he felt that there was no harm in India keeping the dialogue open while remaining fully aware of the prospects of subversion and hostility from Pakistan. He told me that whenever the next round of foreign secretary–level talks took place, I should keep in mind a basic perception, that while India had the resilience to face Pakistani hostility, it was for Pakistan to decide whether or not it wished to continue this drift in bilateral relations based on hostile attitudes and subversive policies. It was also for Pakistan to assess whether this approach would ensure its future unity and stability. It was with this background that Shahryar Khan and I exchanged messages about the possibilities of a bilateral meeting to be held in Cyprus in October 1992. We also agreed that perhaps we could fix new dates for the next round of talks at the foreign secretary level. On my reporting the details of these exchanges to the prime minister, he expressed his approval of both developments.

The internal situation in Pakistan had changed since April 1993. President Ghulam Ishaq Khan dissolved the National Assembly and dismissed Nawaz Sharif on 18 April soon after the latter's return from the SAARC meeting in Dhaka. Nawaz Sharif filed a petition in the Pakistani Supreme Court against the decision, on constitutional grounds. The court admitted Sharif's petition and restored him to power on 26 May. Sharif also received a vote of confidence in the Pakistan National Assembly the very next day. Soon afterwards, however, he was ousted from power again. Elections were held in September–October 1993 and Benazir Bhutto emerged victorious. The period between Nawaz Sharif's final ouster in 1993 and Benazir's return was comparatively calm, with Pakistan having an acting Prime Minister, Moin Qureshi, former high commissioner to India, and former foreign secretary, Abdul Sattar, was foreign minister in this interim arrangement.

Shahryar Khan and I held three meetings between 18 and 21 October 1993 in Cyprus, during the Commonwealth summit. These talks were held against the backdrop of the infiltration of terrorists into the Hazratbal shrine on the outskirts of Srinagar, the capital of Jammu and Kashmir. Shahryar Khan and I, however, agreed tentatively to resume foreign secretary–level talks in January 1994, with dates to be fixed later. Benazir, meanwhile, decided to attend the Commonwealth summit in Cyprus, though she had regained power just about a week earlier. She made her inevitable references to Kashmir and India in critical terms in her policy statement though she was less jingoistic than usual, perhaps bearing in mind that she was addressing a gathering of heads of state and government. Prime Minister Rao had decided to send Manmohan Singh, the Indian finance minister, to the summit because state-level elections were being held in India. This was also because of the indisposition of Minister for External Affairs Dinesh Singh.

A Personal Touch

Two incidents that occurred at the summit stand out in memory. Benazir had come for the summit only for a day and a half. After finishing her policy statement at the summit meeting, as she was walking past the Indian delegation, I stood up and greeted her. She remarked that now that she was back as prime minister she hoped to reverse the negative slide in Indo-Pakistan relations. She told me that Shahryar Khan and I should finalise dates for the next foreign secretary–level talks soon. The second incident occurred at the retreat at Paphos where the heads of government had gathered. As they were meeting in camera, Shahryar Khan and I were sitting at a restaurant just outside the conference room and chatting. We had known each other for nearly four years and I had always known him to be an elegant and courteous person. Whatever may have been our formal negotiating stands on bilateral issues, our interaction at the personal level had never been subject to the irrelevant negative dramatics that normally characterised the attitudes and conversation of Indian and Pakistani diplomats. As we bantered in a friendly manner, Sri Lankan Prime Minister Ranil Wickramsinghe walked out of the conference room. He paused at our table and remarked: "Looking at you two talking to each other who would believe that India and Pakistan are at each other's throats most of the time!" He walked on, leaving both of us to ponder the dichotomy he had observed. On my return to Delhi, Shahryar Khan and I had discussions over the telephone and through diplomatic channels about the next foreign secretary–level talks. Even as a joint announcement was being made that these talks would be held in Islamabad between 1 and 3 January 1994, the Hazratbal shrine crisis reached critical levels. Even after the announcement of the dates of the talks, Shahryar Khan and I had doubts about their being held because of the contretemps at Hazratbal. A group of militants had taken shelter in the Hazratbal mosque, and the Indian Army was forced to lay siege there. This lasted from 17 October to 16 November 1993, after which the militants surrendered; not a single shot was fired.

Good sense, however, prevailed. I went to Islamabad for the talks on New Year's Day 1994. Benazir Bhutto was in Karachi. The Pakistani media hastened to interpret her not being in Islamabad during the talks as a firm signal to India about Pakistan's unwillingness to compromise on any basic issue. They were, however, proved wrong. Prime Minister Bhutto invited me to call on her in Karachi and made a special aircraft available.

Discussions between the two delegations on 1 January were formal; I recalled the contents of Prime Minister Rao's message of congratulations to Benazir on her assumption of power in 1993, in which he had indicated that India would be willing to discuss all issues relating to Jammu and Kashmir within the framework of the Simla Agreement. Shahryar Khan, welcoming this approach, pointed out that Pakistan was firmly supportive of the right of Kashmiris to self-determination and that any discussion on Kashmir had to take this factor into account. I replied that this was a complex matter that would need patient negotiations. We then moved on to other subjects such as Siachen, Sir Creek, determining the maritime boundary, and reviving meetings of the Indo-Pakistan Joint Commission for Economic Cooperation. Shahryar Khan kept stressing that progress on these matters could be made only after some move forward on Kashmir. I told Shahryar Khan after the meeting that evening, in a one-to-one conversation, that I had brought six working papers containing proposals to normalise relations between India and Pakistan and that I had orders to hand them over to the Pakistani authorities. He told me that he would respond to these proposals after I met Benazir.

I called on Benazir at her official residence in Karachi at 2.30 p.m. on 2 January. We spent an hour in discussions; Shahryar Khan was also present. Benazir stressed the importance she attached to normalising Indo-Pakistan relations. She welcomed the information conveyed to her by Prime Minister Rao, that India was willing to discuss issues related to Kashmir. She went on to make a strikingly emotional and reasonable point. She declared: "Mr Dixit, two generations of Indians and Pakistanis have been held hostage by the Kashmir issue. We should not allow this tragic predicament to continue. We must solve the problem and move towards fruitful cooperation and normalcy in relations." She asked Shahryar Khan and me to continue our efforts sincerely. At that stage, I left the meeting. Shahryar Khan stayed back for further instructions from the prime minister. He told me on the two-and-a-half-hour flight back from Karachi to Islamabad that he would like to know about the confidence-building measures and other proposals I had brought. He also told me that despite what Benazir Bhutto had conveyed to me, she was on the defensive as far as domestic politics in Pakistan were concerned, as she was being accused of being soft towards India by allowing foreign secretary–level talks to take place, especially when Indian security forces had surrounded the Hazratbal shrine and were engaged in intensive operations against Kashmiri militants.

I responded that it would not be a practical approach to stipulate preconditions in terms of internal developments in India for continuing foreign secretary–level talks. I then agreed to give him general details of the proposals I had brought. There was a formal dinner on the evening of 2 January 1994 after which I told Shahryar Khan that I would outline Indian proposals to him in a one-to-one meeting. Given the certainty that my hotel room would be bugged, I told Shahryar Khan that I did not want our conversation to be recorded by the Pakistani intelligence agencies. I therefore told him that I would rather meet him for breakfast at the poolside garden of the hotel where I was staying. Shahryar Khan agreed, and we met at this location early on the morning of 3 January. I outlined the confidence-building measures I had in mind. Khan's response appeared curious and out of character. He admitted that while he would normally have asked me to formally hand over the proposals, he had instructions not to receive any proposal from the Government of India at that time. He added that India had to agree to three preconditions before the proposals could be considered. First, it should remove the security forces surrounding the Hazratbal shrine where the terrorists were ensconced; second, it should reduce the overall size of its security forces in Kashmir; and third, it should be willing to discuss the modalities for a compromise on the future status of Kashmir, taking into account Pakistani concerns and the views of Kashmiri Muslims. I replied that I felt all the three preconditions were impracticable, but agreed to convey them to the Government of India. I also stressed that a dialogue aimed at peace should not be subject to preconditions. The matter ended there, with Khan stating that he was following the instructions given to him.

The morning meeting with Shahryar Khan was followed by my call on the foreign minister of Pakistan, Sardar Asif Ali. This turned out to be an abrasive experience. Instead of having a conversation, Ali spoke as if he were addressing a Pakistani public meeting. He repeated the familiar criticisms and accusations against India. I had to reply in kind. At the end of the day, I came away with the distinct impression that there were no possibilities of any change in Pakistani policies towards India. Shahryar Khan and I addressed a joint press conference late in the afternoon of 3 January at Islamabad airport. Neither of us wished to convey to the media the stalemate which we had reached, so both of us tried to talk of positive trends in response to the various questions we were asked. The Pakistani press corps was aggressive and critical. One of its members asked me towards the end of the conference what India's reaction would be to a Pakistani resolution on human rights violations by India, which had every likelihood of being passed at the next Human Rights Commission meeting in Geneva in February 1994. I did not mince my words: "Even if several resolutions are passed in various fora of the United Nations," I replied, "they will still not succeed in subverting India's territorial integrity or separating Jammu and Kashmir from India."

Soon after this, I boarded the special aircraft to fly back to Delhi. When I landed, the deputy secretary in charge of my office, Atul Khare, showed me a wire service news item datelined Islamabad. From this report I learnt that Shahryar Khan had continued the press conference after my plane had taken off from Islamabad airport. He had mentioned that the question of any further talks at the foreign secretary–level did not arise unless India discussed the status of Kashmir and removed its security forces from the Hazratbal shrine. I had received some indications of this attitude during my one-to-one meeting with Shahryar Khan, just before my departure from the hotel. I had enquired from Khan when the next talks at the foreign secretary level would be held. I needed to know so that we could mention the dates in the joint statement we were to issue at the end of the visit. As per instructions given to him to put off further rounds of discussions, we finally had to resort to a non-commital sentence in the last paragraph of the press statement: "The two sides will consult each other on the question of further talks at the foreign secretary or other levels."

Pakistan then resorted to a clever diplomatic and publicity act. Its government sent two proposals for confidence-building measures on 18 January. The first proposal suggested detailed modalities for the holding of a plebiscite in Jammu and Kashmir within the framework of the UN resolutions, which India had repeatedly stressed had become irrelevant. The second proposal detailed measures required to create an "appropriate climate for the peaceful resolution of the Jammu and Kashmir dispute and other issues". The second proposal, apart from repeating accusations against India, outlined the preconditions that Shahryar Khan had mentioned to me on the morning of 3 January. Both were patently impracticable proposals without any relevance to political realities.

My last act relating to Pakistan as foreign secretary was to send on 24 January the six working papers containing India's proposals for normalisation of relations to Islamabad. The first proposal was the signing of an agreement on the maintenance of peace and tranquillity along the Line of Control in Jammu and Kashmir. The second was to sign an agreement to pull back troops from the Siachen area. The third was to reach an accord demarcating the boundary at Sir Creek and determining the maritime boundary between the two countries. The fourth was to finalise the agreement on the Tulbul navigation project. The fifth suggested reviving activities of the Indo-Pakistan Joint Commission for Mutual Cooperation covering a wide field of activities. The final proposal was to put in place mutual confidence-building measures related to security and disarmament.

There was an important element in the sixth proposal. India suggested that the Indo-Pakistani Agreement on the Prohibition of Attack on each other's nuclear installations should be extended to include population centres and economic targets. India also suggested an agreement by which both sides would undertake not to be the first to use or threaten to use their nuclear capabilities against each other.

India and Pakistan rejected each other's proposals. It was back to square one.

In Conclusion

Highlighting the general trends in Pakistan's policies towards India, which I discerned during my foreign secretaryship, would be an appropriate conclusion to this section. First, Benazir's failure to persuade Rajiv to give up India's stance on Kashmir made her revert to old, hostile approaches. She could not help taking such a stand, due to her own tenuous position in the power structure of Pakistan. Second, both she and Nawaz Sharif correctly perceived that the US would continue its sophistical tilt in favour of Pakistan on the Kashmir issue. Third, the revival of the agitation in Jammu and Kashmir provided Pakistan an opportunity to reintroduce Kashmir as an issue in its foreign policy. Fourth, Pakistan had adopted a three-track approach to explain the Kashmir issue. Through this approach, the Pakistanis had hoped to:

(1) conduct a proxy war on the ground, aimed at the fragmentation of India. If Pakistan achieved success in this regard, it would weaken India, and serve the purpose of conveying to the Pakistani people that Bangladesh's separation and Pakistan's military defeat in 1971 had been avenged;

(2) mobilise Islamic countries against India on the Kashmir issue on the basis of the tenet that "Islam was in danger" and that "Muslims were being persecuted by India"; and

(3) mobilise international public opinion in support of Pakistani political and territorial objectives, using the arguments of self-determination, the violation of human rights, and the possibility of nuclear war.

Pakistan's policies of fragmenting India were not concentrated in Kashmir alone. Pakistan's intelligence agencies had been actively engaged in encouraging ethno-religious and linguistic fissiparous tendencies in India, stretching from Punjab, through central south India, right up to the north-eastern states. That Pakistan has not really succeeded in its efforts so far is a measure of the resilience of the Indian polity, Indian public opinion, and Indian institutions. However, Pakistan is not likely to give up these efforts in the foreseeable future. The only semantic difference I noticed between Benazir Bhutto and Nawaz Sharif, was that Benazir had shades of her father's impulsiveness and aggressiveness. She was also more sensitive and vulnerable to international and domestic political pressures and to public opinion. Nawaz Sharif, in contrast, was quite practical, more circumspect and comparatively patient.

Another impression I carried away from my spell in the Foreign Office, was that despite all claims to the contrary, the Pakistani armed forces and the Islamic parties in Pakistan remained the centre of the power structure. The operational manifestation of this phenomenon was the influence of the Islamic clergy on Pakistani domestic and foreign policy, and the autonomous power of the Inter-Services Intelligence agency.

Pakistan is a negative factor that adversely affects Indian regional policies and South Asian regional cooperation. This is the reality that cannot, and should not, be wished away. It is in this context that, towards the end of my tenure, I was getting more and more convinced that India should shed its ambiguity about acquiring nuclear weapons status. However, I was conscious that I was not fully capable of assessing the technological and economic implications of this stand. Towards the end of my assignment in Pakistan, a senior Pakistani well-wisher the late Mazhar Ali Khan — who was also a friend of Jawaharlal Nehru — told me in mid-1991 that the suspicion and misunderstandings born of Partition could only be removed when the people of India and Pakistan could be able to meet each other without the restrictions imposed on them by the power structures in both countries. He added that these power structures sustained these restrictions only to safeguard their own vested interests. He was right in objective terms. The limitations of my professional experience prevent me from reaching the high moral ground from which he spoke.

I would like to add two "footnotes" that I think are relevant.

As already mentioned, the Hazratbal shrine was infiltrated in October 1993 by militants. Consequently, Indian security forces had cordoned off the area around the shrine. A day after this event, the chief of army staff, General Bipin Joshi, rang me up over the scrambler to ask what the reaction of the international community would be if troops made a forced entry into the shrine. He also stated: "My commanders at the operational level around Hazratbal are telling me that they can clear the shrine in about two hours flat." General Joshi, however, held the view that larger political considerations, both in domestic and international terms, would be involved in taking a decision regarding the operation to flush out the terrorists. He was right, as well as thoughtful, in taking into account the larger picture. I suggested that subject to the home minister's and the prime minister's orders, my view was that there should be no repetition of the June 1984 Operation Bluestar, which resulted in damage to the holy Sikh shrines at the Golden Temple, Amritsar, quite apart from human casualties. I maintained that although I was not knowledgeable about the precise ground situation nor did I fully comprehend the technical and logistical aspects of the military operations required, my advice would be to lay siege to the Hazratbal shrine and gradually flush out the terrorists. General Joshi agreed with me entirely. Eventually, he decided to adopt this very approach while tackling the situation.

However, both General Joshi and I were overruled by the Jammu and Kashmir authorities and by some politicians belonging to the Congress and the National Conference with regard to certain aspects of the proposed operation. For instance, we had suggested that all food supplies should be cut off and only water should be allowed into the shrine. Both these suggestions were rejected. On the contrary, the terrorists were provided vast amounts of food, including biryani. Such a move demoralised Indian security forces, whose basic strategy was defeated. This move also generated criticism among the public in the rest of India. Home Secretary Naren Vohra also shared the views held by General Joshi and me.

The second aspect of Indo-Pakistan relations that I had to consistently monitor and report to the Defence Ministry and the Apex Committee of Secretaries on National Security pertained to Pakistan's aggressive diversification of the sources of its defence supplies. The Pressler Amendment had resulted in the US withholding the $3.2 billion military assistance package to Pakistan. This amendment had stipulated that military assistance to Pakistan should be continued only if the US president could unambiguously certify that the country was not arming itself with a nuclear arsenal. Neither President Bill Clinton (during the first two years in office) nor his predecessor, George Bush, was able to give such a certificate to Pakistan after 1990. Consequently, supply of a wide range of sophisticated military equipment, as also advanced combat aircraft (such as F16s) and long-range artillery, was held up. Moreover, the US had also decided to withdraw several warships it had leased to the Pakistan Navy. Such developments impelled Pakistan to go on a "shopping exploration". Islamabad showed an inclination to make full use of the disintegration of the Soviet Union in December 1991 to acquire nuclear weapons. Pakistani defence and military delegations undertook a series of visits from late 1991 till the end of 1994 to various East European countries, particularly Poland, the Czech Republic, Ukraine and Romania as also to the Russian Federation, to negotiate the purchase of items such as aircraft, tanks, armoured personnel carriers, and artillery and other lethal weapons.

Given the pressing need for foreign exchange and economic resources in East European countries, the entire region became a buyer's market as far as military equipment was concerned. Pakistan also concluded discussions with West European countries such as France and Germany, and the US, as well as with Scandinavian countries, for obtaining submarines, howitzers, various categories of short-range missiles and so on. In view of these disquieting developments, Indian embassies were asked to closely monitor Pakistani operations and keep New Delhi regularly informed in the event Pakistan became, a steady, if not a massive, importer of arms from these countries.

Pakistan's arms import policies were facilitated further by President Clinton and Senator Hank Brown functioning in tandem to restore military supplies to Pakistan by modifying the stipulations of the Pressler Amendment. During my tenure in office, I held the view (which I still do) that it was pointless for India to indulge in emotional fulminations against the US for supplying arms, or against Pakistan for procuring them. India must clearly perceive that these are matters decided upon by both countries concerned in terms of their national and strategic interests. India's reaction should be practical and measured towards the US and should avoid confrontationist criticism as well as whining. Instead, India must do what it has to, namely, upgrade and enhance its defence capacities in terms of weapons and military technology to counter Pakistani moves.

This was the stand adopted by Prime Minister Rao, though politicians pointed out that the dry, rational approach adopted here was not enough. Some degree of emoting could not be avoided. Because the ruling party did not emote or complain or make public statements, the opposition would criticise as well as embarrass the Government. I did not buy this argument. I felt that the government and the ruling party should educate public opinion and keep the people informed of the rationale of their policies. The opposition would then have only a limited capacity to condemn or find fault with the policies.

Indo-Pakistan relations between 1996 and 2000 do not lend themselves to any cogent or structural narrative. India was subject to political transitions with three prime ministers, if not four, assuming power during this period, while Pakistan saw the removal of its democratically elected government by a military coup. After Narasimha Rao's departure, Vajpayee, Deve Gowda, Gujral and again Atal Behari Vajpayee, assumed power. India went through three general elections during this period. Nawaz Sharif returned to power, replacing Benazir Bhutto and the Moin Qureshi Government in the general elections in 1996. He lasted for about three years, till 12 October 1999, when General Pervez Musharraf ousted him, assuming the curious title of "Chief Executive of the Government of Pakistan".

Indo-Pakistani relations and people-to-people interaction have been replete with contradictory characteristics during this period. The stalemate reached when the Benazir Government in 1994 was overcome primarily due to two reasons. Nawaz Sharif made restoration of normal relations with India and the solution of the Kashmir issue by negotiations a major element in his 1996 election manifesto. He was elected with a substantive majority despite the declared opposition to his intended policies towards India by the Islam-pasand parties. Coincidentally, I.K. Gujral became foreign minister in the Deve Gowda Government and then became prime minister in 1997. Nawaz Sharif's practical approach of having a working relationship with India and Gujral's deep conviction about normalising relations with Pakistan as being imperative for regional peace and stability, augured well for Indo-Pakistan relations for a brief period. Gujral met Nawaz Sharif at the UN, at the SAARC summit in Colombo and at the Commonwealth summit in Edinburgh.

Bilateral dialogue was restored from the end of 1996 onwards, though not without irrelevant controversies and inhibitions from both India and Pakistan. India wanted a comprehensive discussion suggesting the Government of Pakistan agree to a decision to hold meetings of the working groups on all outstanding subjects. The subjects were: Kashmir, Siachen, the settlement of Sir Creek boundary, issues related to the Wullar Barrage (or Tulbul hydel project), liberalisation of travel facilities, revival of cultural cooperation, restoration of economic cooperation and trade relations, and the demarcation of the maritime boundary. Much was made of the fact by the Indian media that these nine issues "were defined and a definite agenda was worked out for the first time". This assertion was totally inaccurate. These nine issues had been on the Indo-Pakistani agenda since 1983. They were specifically catalogued when Rajiv met Benazir Bhutto late in 1988. Then there was much hype about the suggestion that separate working groups would be dealing with each of these individual subjects for the first time. This again was proof of a very short public memory because separate official-level working groups dealing with each of these subjects had met alternately in Islamabad and New Delhi between 1988 and 1994.

Leaving aside this deliberate negation of institutional and political memory, it was the manner in which the substance of this restored dialogue was dealt with, that left the impression of irrelevancies being the governing factor. Pakistan insisted that Kashmir should form the subject matter of a separate working group which would be led by the foreign secretaries of the two countries. It suggested political and security issues be discussed separately. The Pakistanis went on to demand that the issue of Kashmir be discussed first and the other issues later, depending on the progress made on Kashmir. India opposed the idea of discussing Kashmir separately.

The result was that all the bilateral discussions in the restored dialogue between foreign secretaries got enmeshed in controversies concerning the agenda for the talks for nearly two-and-a-half years from 1996 to the end of 1998. The Indian foreign secretaries who carried the burden of these talks, Salman Haider and K.V. Raghunath, were victims of the politics of the Indian political leadership in not wanting to discuss Kashmir separately, and of the obstinacy of Shamshad Ahmed Khan, the Pakistani foreign secretary, who seemed to be an expert in orchestrating a dialogue of the deaf. The virtues claimed by the "Gujral Doctrine", of having restored dialogue after a gap of two years, disintegrated in the meaningless discussions between 1996 and 1998. Even so, it is to be acknowledged that Gujral and Nawaz Sharif had a personal rapport and a genuine desire to bring relations back on track. Gujral had the limitation of being part of a coalition government while Nawaz Sharif had the limitation of the attitudes of Islam-pasand parties and the armed forces and, curiously, even the Foreign Office establishment.

It is worthwhile mentioning an incident to prove this point. A major Indian industrial house, the Ambanis, had shown an interest in the production of natural gas in Pakistan and of constructing a pipeline to bring this gas to India and, if possible, to ultimately link this pipeline with their Gujarat project and with gas coming from Turkmenistan. They had preliminary discussions with their Pakistani business counterparts and with the Government of Pakistan on this matter. The Government of India was willing to buy natural gas from Pakistan, and Nawaz Sharif was supportive of the project. During the bilateral discussions between Gujral and Sharif on the margins of the Commonwealth Heads of Government Conference in Edinburgh in 1997, Gujral raised the question of cooperation on this project. Nawaz Sharif was in the process of making some preliminary remarks and giving a positive response, when Foreign Secretary Shamshad Ahmed Khan intervened, interrupting his own prime minister, stating that such a project of Indo-Pakistan cooperation could not be undertaken unless the Kashmir problem was resolved in a satisfactory manner and that there would be opposition from Pakistani public opinion to such cooperation unless this precondition was fulfilled. Curiously, the discussion came to an abrupt end. Nawaz Sharif did not question the propriety of his foreign secretary butting in on a prime ministerial exchange.

Prime Minister Deve Gowda did not take any interest or play an active role in these proceedings. Gujral was very much the initiator and implementor of foreign policy both as foreign minister and later as prime minister. While this political networking was going on, violence in Kashmir continued unabated. Pakistan continued to agitate the Kashmir issue at the United Nations as well as at the United Nations Human Rights Commission deliberations. Despite WTO stipulations, Pakistan refused to have normal trading arrangements with India, and continued to be obstructive about projects under the SAARC umbrella. Relations remained in the doldrums despite the positive motivations inherent in the Gujral Doctrine. The problem was that the doctrine was not rooted in reality.

The Recent Past

The Vajpayee Government assumed power in March 1998. Within eight weeks of the BJP-led coalition assuming charge, India conducted its Shakti series of nuclear weapons tests on 11 and 13 May 1998. Pakistan followed suit by conducting nuclear weapons tests at the Chagai Hills a fortnight later on 27 May. International reaction to these developments were highly critical, despite Vajpayee making a statement in Parliament that India would not conduct further tests in the foreseeable future and that India would adhere to the principle of No-First-Use. The Government of India landed itself in an embarrassing position because of some highly assertive statements made by Home Minister L.K. Advani and the then minister for parliamentary affairs, Madan Lal Khurana, in the immediate aftermath of India's nuclear tests. Advani warned Pakistan that given India's enhanced military capacities, India may undertake pre-emptive action against Pakistani terrorist interference in Jammu and Kashmir. Khurana challenged Pakistan to choose any time, any place to confront India where "Pakistan will now be taught a lesson". The Pakistani response was equally aggressive and uncompromising, based on the confidence acquired by the Pakistani establishment because of nuclear tests and missile capacities.

The most significant consequence of the possession of nuclear weapons was the direct and multidimensional pressure on the governments of India and Pakistan to resume a bilateral dialogue quickly, not only on the Kashmir issue but also to prevent a nuclear confrontation. The US took the lead in this process, with full support from the remaining four nuclear weapons powers, France, Russia, the UK and China. Equally important was a general groundswell of public opinion in India and Pakistan supporting the resumption of high-level political dialogue. This particular trend found expression in Prime Minister Vajpayee's pronouncements that he was willing to meet Nawaz Sharif and in Nawaz Sharif responding to these signals in a lengthy interview given to Shekhar Gupta, editor-in-chief of the *Indian Express*. In the course of the interview he made two points: first, that he was still committed to the election promises he had made to restore normal relations between India and Pakistan; second, that he invited Vajpayee to come to Pakistan for discussions. To cut a long story short, there was a flurry of official-level bilateral discussion between August 1998 and January 1999. Vajpayee accepted Nawaz Sharif's invitation and agreed to go to Lahore on 22 February 1999. This was going to be a visit by an Indian prime minister to Pakistan after a gap of nearly ten years, after Rajiv Gandhi's visit to Islamabad in July 1989. Vajpayee decided to dramatise the occasion by travelling by bus from Amritsar to the Wagah-Attari border. This was also to be the inauguration of the bus service between Lahore and New Delhi.

Public opinion in India and Pakistan was a study in contrasts. The Indian media waxed eloquent about a "new dawn in Indo-Pakistan relations", "a new chapter in goodwill and cooperation being opened", etc. Pakistani public opinion was less enthusiastic; the gesture was welcomed in a subdued manner. This contrast was reflected in the physical atmosphere surrounding Vajpayee's trip as it took place. Apart from the print and audio-visual media hype, Vajpayee decided to lead a delegation consisting of prominent individuals representing all the important spheres of the civil society of India. There were politicians, former civil servants, media representatives, prominent artistes, cinema actors, litterateurs and so on. The entire route between Amritsar and the Indo-Pakistan border was decorated and a large number of people lined the route, with much music, much dancing and an infectious atmosphere of festivity. All this enthusiasm was dampened because on the very morning of the visit, 22 February, Pakistan-sponsored terrorists had massacred a number of civilians at Rajouri, Jammu and Kashmir. Despite this Vajpayee proceeded to Lahore. The atmosphere on the other side of the border was quite different. Nawaz Sharif accompanied by his foreign minister was there to receive Vajpayee, but there was no public attendance of any significance and none of the armed forces chiefs were present when Vajpayee inspected the guard of honour. The welcome was correct but subdued with a somewhat distracted looking Nawaz Sharif doing the honours.

The two prime ministers boarded a helicopter and proceeded to Lahore. Their talks resulted in two documents: the Lahore Declaration and a Memorandum of Understanding, to ensure strategic nuclear restraint. The declaration was generic in content, confirming the commitment of the two prime ministers to meaningful discussions to normalise relations. It was the Memorandum of Understanding on strategic restraint that was more substantive and important. It supported the creation of an expert working group to discuss measures to ensure restraint, to prevent accidental nuclear confrontation and to put in place confidence-building measures focused on preventing a nuclear war between the two countries. This group was to commence its work by March/April 1999.

The welcome given in Lahore to Vajpayee was better than the one accorded to him at the Wagah-Attari border. The service chiefs were present, but there was no public reception. Later there was a well-attended official reception at the Governor's House. Vajpayee was at his best in Lahore. In a speech at the reception, he underlined India's sincere and deep desire to have friendly and cooperative relations with Pakistan to ensure peace, stability and the economic well-being of the subcontinent and so on. Nawaz Sharif's response was equally positive. The pièce de résistance of the visit was Vajpayee's decision to visit the Minar-e-Pakistan, a monument commemorating the creation of Pakistan. No Indian leader had visited the monument, and he made a very important political gesture there, describing his visit as a categorical affirmation of India's commitment to the sovereignty, unity and stability of Pakistan. He implied that his visit should remove all doubts as to India not having accepted Partition or wanting to reabsorb Pakistan.

Vajpayee returned on 23 February hoping he had broken the logjam in Indo-Pakistan relations. But he was conscious that the prospects were dicey. As he got into the bus at Amritsar, he had information about the massacre at Rajouri, and a journalist asked him about the journey he was beginning. Vajpayee's response was that he was going to Lahore with "mixed feelings" and "uncertain anticipations". Later weeks were to prove how valid he was in his cautious approach. Even otherwise, incidents during his visit and its immediate aftermath in Lahore indicated the shape of events to come. There were public demonstrations against his visit to Lahore. These had to be quelled by police action. A group of religious leaders and representatives of the Islam-pasand parties washed the entire platform surrounding the Minar-e-Pakistan after Vajpayee's departure "to purify it from the malign impact of the visit of an infidel prime minister of the enemy country". No immediate follow-up action could be taken on the decisions reached at the summit because the Vajpayee Government came under challenge from opposition parties, losing a no-confidence motion in March 1999. Likewise Nawaz Sharif got enmeshed in controversies about corruption and his relations with the armed forces. So this important visit remained a question-mark.

The relevance of the visit was further drowned in the quagmire of the Kargil conflict within two-and-a-half months of Vajpayee's Lahore initiative. The conflict, lasting for 50 days, left the fabric of Indo-Pakistan relations in complete tatters, as detailed at the beginning of this book. The political, military and strategic failure of Pakistan at Kargil generated internal divisive pressures in the country that culminated in the rift between the elected government and the high command of the Pakistan armed forces. This led to Nawaz Sharif trying to dismiss the army chief, General Pervez Musharraf, when the latter was on a visit to Colombo. Sharif had earlier compelled the resignation of Army Chief Jahangir Karamat as army chief and the removal of the navy chief. But he acted on the basis of misplaced and excessive confidence while dismissing Musharraf. The drama characterising Musharraf's landing in Karachi, and the military coup carried out in Islamabad as he was landing are a matter of public knowledge and need no repetition. Musharraf assumed charge as Chief Executive of Pakistan on 12 October 1999. Within days he disowned all the decisions taken at the Sharif-Vajpayee meeting in Lahore in February. India was totally opposed to the revival of military dictatorship in Pakistan. The two years that Pervez Musharraf has been in power in Pakistan have seen a downward curve in relations. Except during 1971 and the East Pakistan crisis, Indo-Pakistani relations have never been as bad as they are as this book is being written. The details of what has happened in the past half-year and the prospects for Indo-Pakistani relations will constitute the contents of the last chapter, a sort of epilogue to this book.

The decade of the 1990s began with promising prospects. The first year of the new millennium has witnessed their fading away in a mist of violence and heightened antagonism. But one would be remiss if one did not point out some positive details on this broad canvas. During the period 1977 to May 1999, people-to-people contacts were sustained in tenuous and tense circumstances. India and Pakistan played cricket matches, during some of which Indian spectators applauded the Pakistani performance with enthusiasm. Artistes like Ghulam Ali, Nusrat Fateh Ali, Iqbal Bano and Reshma from Pakistan were repeatedly received in Indian cities with appreciation and admiration. Zeba Bakhtiar, the daughter of a Pakistani attorney-general, acted in the film *Henna* produced by Randhir Kapoor. Dilip Kumar and Saira Banu were warmly received in Pakistan, Dilip Kumar being decorated with a high civilian decoration.

I recall Randhir Kapoor and Rishi Kapoor visiting Islamabad in connection with their film *Henna*, in 1990, when I was high commissioner there. They expressed a desire to visit their ancestral home in Peshawar, and the Pakistani authorities gave prompt permission. They were subjected to showers of rose petals when they entered the lane where their ancestral house was situated, and they were accorded an equally warm welcome in Lahore. Shatrughan Sinha was another such welcome visitor. Dancers like Bharati Shivaji and Kiran Sehgal visited Pakistan in the late 1970s and early 1980s, and were received by enthusiastic audiences. Indian and Pakistani authors and poets exchanged visits. I recall welcoming Faiz Ahmad Faiz, as the secretary in the Indian Council for Cultural Relations in 1979, and Vajpayee presiding over a function at which he was honoured. Another poet who has won the heart of Indians is Ahmad Faraz, who keeps coming to Delhi, though of late Pakistani authorities do not let him come. Human rights activists like Asma Jahangir and journalists like Mariana Babar are visitors to India and are held in high esteem by their Indian counterparts. In this same strain I must also mention the Islamabad International Women's Club sending a delegation to India in 1989. They not only visited Delhi and Jaipur but also went to Srinagar, where they were personally received by the then governor, general (Retd.) K.V. Krishna Rao, who hosted a reception for them in Gulmarg. These are instances that have precedents going back to the time of Partition.

The point one is making is that despite the intractabilities and tragedies of Indo-Pakistani relations, there is an undercurrent of reasonableness and common sense in segments of civil society on both sides of the border that gives one some hope about the future.

Eight

Kashmir:
The Intractable Bone of Contention

*T*he second chapter of this book dealt with the 50-day Indo-Pakistan Kargil war in the summer of 1999. The conflict was essentially a result of the long-standing dispute between India and Pakistan on the Kashmir issue. Issues related to this dispute have been touched upon in the earlier chapters of this book, particularly the period up to 1965, and then again while discussing the aftermath of the Indo-Pakistan war of 1971. The objective here is to analyse the problems related to Kashmir in a somewhat autonomous context, and to speculate on the prospects of some solution over a period of time. The fact of the matter is that India will still have to resolve the current crisis in Kashmir, by structuring a solution responsive to the aspirations of the country's citizens resident in Jammu and Kashmir. In the second stage, India and Pakistan will have to structure a compromise on the crisis, which is rooted in Pakistan's views and claims regarding Jammu and Kashmir. Some elemental historical realities and facts have to be kept in mind in analysing the problems.

1. It should be remembered that the princely state of Jammu and Kashmir, now bifurcated between India and Pakistan, was an artificial creation of the Dogra imperium supported by the British authorities in the middle of the 19th century.

2. Jammu and Kashmir has a multi-ethnic, multi-lingual, multi-religious civil society. It is not a homogeneous area with an Islamic identity, as claimed by Pakistan.

3. If one looks at history, Jammu and Kashmir was an integral part of Indian kingdoms and empires during the early Hindu and Buddhist periods. In the more recent Mughal period, the western areas of Jammu and Kashmir, now under Pakistani jurisdiction, were mostly controlled by the Afghan kings and indirectly by representatives of the Persian empire. The eastern portions of Jammu and Kashmir, now with India, were under the jurisdiction of the Mughals.

4. At Partition, the Hindu Dogra king of Jammu and Kashmir, Hari Singh, had the initial ambition of making Kashmir an independent state. There was opposition from the people of Jammu and Kashmir to this. Both Sheikh Abdullah of the National Conference and the leaders of the Muslim League of his princely state opposed the idea.

5. Hari Singh acceded to India under the provisions of the Independence Act passed by British Parliament in 1947. He was under pressure due to the tribal and military invasion of this princely state by Pakistan. He needed Indian military protection.

6. The point that the accession of Jammu and Kashmir to India was a desperate decision stood neutralised because the most representative political organisation of the people of Jammu and Kashmir, the National Conference, endorsed the accession of Jammu and Kashmir to India under the leadership of Sheikh Abdullah.

7. Indian leaders had suggested both to the British Government and to Jinnah, the founding father of Pakistan, that the princely states of India should decide their future status on the basis of the aspirations of the people of each of these princely states and not on the needs and inclinations of their princely and feudal rulers. Neither the British authorities nor Jinnah accepted this suggestion. They insisted that it was the princes and not the people who should decide the future status of these states. Jinnah's fond hope was that the rulers of states such as Bhopal, Hyderabad and Junagadh would accede their territories to Pakistan.

    Jinnah also hoped that the state of Kashmir, especially with the Muslim majority in the Valley, would rise against Maharaja Hari Singh and Kashmir would emerge as an independent entity or accede to

Pakistan. When Jinnah's hopes did not materialise, Pakistan engineered a tribal invasion in October 1947.

8. It was India that went to the UN in 1948 hoping that the international body would make Pakistan vacate the territory occupied by it and make it desist from disrupting the constitutionally valid decision taken by the maharaja of Kashmir to accede to India. India agreed to a plebiscite subject to certain very specific conditions, the most important of which was that Pakistan should withdraw all its troops and vacate the entire territory of the former princely state of Jammu and Kashmir. This Pakistan refused to do and still refuses to do. It was against this background that India initiated democratic processes in Jammu and Kashmir and, at the same time, rejected any further role for the UN or any external party in resolving the dispute. India had time and again objected to Pakistan agitating the Kashmir issue as an "unfinished task of the partition".

Failing to acquire Kashmir by subversion and international pressure, Pakistan has fought three wars with India to meet this objective by military means. Pakistan has been unsuccessful and continues to be unsuccessful in this adventurist endeavour. Pakistan insists that Kashmir is the core issue preventing the normalisation of relations with India. For India too, it is a core issue because India cannot allow any part of its territory and any of its peoples to be alienated from the Indian republic on the basis of religious affiliation. Such an eventuality would destroy the basic terms of reference on which independent India came into existence, the terms of reference of a pluralistic, multi-religious, multi-lingual, national territorial identity.

The qualitative heightening of terrorism and secessionism, with the accompanying violence supported by Pakistan since the end of 1989, was peaking towards the end of 1991. The Ministry of External Affairs basically had three tasks to perform in relation to problems resulting from Jammu and Kashmir. The first was to prevent the operational or institutional internationalisation of the issue. This could have led to Kashmir's separation from India. The second task was to present Indian perceptions and the Indian case on Kashmir to the international community at the bilateral level as well as in international fora, such as the UN. The third task was to interact with the Home Ministry and the Government of Jammu and Kashmir in order to keep them informed of international attitudes and reactions developing and to get authentic information so as to reinforce the Indian case internationally.

The overall attitude of the international community towards the issue during the period 1991 to 1999 can be summed up as follows:

1. Regardless of the historical and legal validity of India's geographical claims on Jammu and Kashmir, the world at large perceived the state as a disputed area between India and Pakistan.

2. The international community was not interested in the merits of India's case or even in the plight of the people of Jammu and Kashmir. Its main concern was that the confrontation between India and Pakistan on Jammu and Kashmir should not degenerate into a general military conflict and, even more important, into a nuclear holocaust.

3. While most countries (barring some Islamic countries such as Saudi Arabia and Turkey) acknowledged Pakistan's interference in and support to secessionist forces in Jammu and Kashmir, they did not (and do not) accept the Indian view that the entire problem had arisen only because of Pakistan's political and material support to such forces and to foreign mercenaries. In their perception the agitation in Kashmir was also sparked off due to the social and economic frustration and alienation of substantive segments of the population in the Valley. The rest of the world held the view that any violation of human rights by Indian security forces had become inevitable and unavoidable in a situation where armed political agitation was sought to be suppressed by coercive methods.

4. The US and other Western countries were keen that India and Pakistan engage purposively in a dialogue to resolve the Kashmir problem. They were willing to assist in, mediate and engineer a dialogue by whatever means possible, depending on the willingness of India and Pakistan to accept any practical suggestions. This policy attitude has undergone a qualitative change since the Indian and Pakistani nuclear tests of May 1998. These countries are now more assertive and coercive in their desire to expedite a solution to the Kashmir issue. Their inclination is to persuade India to be more compromising, which India cannot do.

Muslim countries, while temporising on the Kashmir issue, and taking an impartial stand at the bilateral level with India, were collectively supportive of the Pakistani position on Jammu and Kashmir. Such support found expression in the Organisation of Islamic Conference resolutions, in deliberations at the UN in New York and Geneva, and in the meetings of the UN Human Rights Commission. By the end of 1992, India also faced the predicament of having mercenaries from Afghanistan, from the Gulf countries and from Africa joining terrorist and secessionist elements in Jammu and Kashmir.

An interesting shift took place in Pakistani policies on the Kashmir issue from 1991 onwards. Realising that the strategy of detaching Kashmir from India on the basis of the ethno-religious argument would not find acceptance in the international community, Pakistan advocated the separation of J&K from India on the grounds of upholding the principles of self-determination. Such separation was offered as a remedy to the violations of human rights in the state. Pakistan claimed that the accession of the state to India had been organised by spurious means, which contradicted the provisions of the political and legislative decisions meant to govern the determination of the people's will at the time of India's partition.

Alistair Lamb's book, *Kashmir: A Disputed Legacy* (Oxford University Press, Karachi, 1993) and the then US assistant secretary of state, Robin Raphael's statements questioning the legal basis of J&K's accession to India in October 1947 supported Pakistan's standpoint. In addition to the foregoing argument, Pakistan started generating international apprehension that if India did not compromise on Kashmir, the prospect of a nuclear war between the two countries was strong. The unfortunate aspect was that the US not only backed Pakistan's viewpoint but also picked up this issue to pressurise India to fall in line with Washington's agenda on nuclear non-proliferation and missile development.

There was reluctance on the part of Indian political leadership to accept that the disturbances in Kashmir were not entirely due to Pakistani activities but were also due to the alienation of some segments of the J&K population. There was no consensus in Indian public opinion or in the Indian Parliament on how to deal with the dilemmas. There was (and there is) consensus that Jammu and Kashmir should not be allowed to break away from India under any circumstances, but there was no integrated or cohesive view on how to meet the aspirations of the people of the state, how to assuage their feelings of alienation. During Narasimha Rao's tenure as prime minister, the home minister, S.B. Chavan, and the minister of state for internal security, Rajesh Pilot, kept working at cross-purposes. The Government of Jammu and Kashmir and the state administration were not functioning in coordination with either the security forces command or with the Home Ministry/External Affairs Ministry. While everybody paid lip service to the need for restoring the political process and acknowledged that the critical situation in Jammu and Kashmir could not be resolved by coercive force alone, no structured policy resulted. Both Parliament and public opinion remained divided on tackling the problem at the national level. One school of thought advocated the abrogation of Article 370 of the Indian Constitution, which granted certain special privileges to Kashmir and changing the demographic composition of the population of the Valley. Another school of thought wanted still greater autonomy for Jammu and Kashmir.

A Bizarre Situation

Apart from Pakistan, other countries took full advantage of the ambiguities and limitations of New Delhi's approach to the Kashmir problem and exerted pressures regarding human rights, mainly to accept external assistance and mediation. There were also differing views on how to neutralise Pakistani support to secessionist and terrorist elements in Jammu and Kashmir. Some politicians, civil servants and intellectuals advocated a preventive and reactive role. However, some hawkish elements wanted to carry the conflict into Pakistan-occupied Kashmir and, if necessary, into Pakistani territory itself to destroy terrorist bases. The Ministry of External Affairs was interested in the cosmetic rather than the substantive responsibilities related to India's Kashmir policy. As mentioned earlier, one of New Delhi's main objectives was to prevent any resolution critical of India or providing for third party intervention in the dispute from being passed in international fora. Another objective of the MEA was to counter Pakistani publicity. It had to persuade various governments about the legitimacy of India's stand and inform them about the dangers of ethno-religious fragmentation that would affect the nations of South Asia if Kashmir were allowed to secede. One aspect of handling of the Kashmir issue was the lack of any structured institutional mechanism to deal with the entire crisis on a continuous basis at the highest levels. There were periodic meetings held by the prime minister and the home minister. Meetings were also held between the Government of Jammu and Kashmir and its advisers and officials of the central Government. These only be described as event specific and episodic. The cabinet secretary used to conduct weekly meetings of an apex committee of secretaries, of which the home secretary, the foreign secretary and the chiefs of intelligence organisations were members. These meetings also dealt with specific events or incidents and the corresponding remedial action. There was no strategic planning or policy to resolve the internal situation in Kashmir, or to face the Pakistani challenge. There were some attempts at long-term planning and some calibrated policy formulation during the period when Naresh Chandra was the cabinet secretary (between 1989 and 1992), but his two successors, S.

Rajgopal and Zafar Saifullah, just could not cope. The situation was compounded further by Governor Krishna Rao refusing to interact with the home secretary or the cabinet secretary, and at times with the army and intelligence chiefs, on procedural and protocol grounds. It was bizarre. Nevertheless, the Ministry of External Affairs took the following steps within the narrow field of its jurisdiction.

Apart from increasing the frequency, content and range of briefings to diplomatic missions abroad, it strengthened India's permanent missions to the UN in Geneva and New York to cope with the spurt in debates on Jammu and Kashmir. The Intelligence Bureau and the Home Ministry prepared special briefing material, including audio-visual presentations for publicity purposes. The combined recommendations of the Ministries of External Affairs, Home and Defence led to the prime minister allowing greater access to foreign political figures and agencies to Jammu and Kashmir so that they could get a first-hand impression of what was happening there. Access was allowed to resident ambassadors in New Delhi, to parliamentary delegations from different countries and to the International Commission of Jurists. The Home Ministry furnished detailed data and evidence on Pakistan-sponsored terrorist activities as well as reports on action taken by the Government of India to monitor and uphold human rights. Such data and evidence were transmitted to Pakistan as well as to the governments of important countries. This move neutralised Pakistani diplomatic and propaganda efforts against us to a great extent. A conscious decision was taken to reopen contacts with the Secretariat of the Organisation of Islamic Conference in Saudi Arabia in order to keep its officials briefed about developments in Jammu and Kashmir. Also organised was a pattern of continuous discussions and briefings with heads of missions of Muslim countries in New Delhi.

The Ministry of External Affairs' initiatives for publicity and transparency were resisted by the Government of Jammu and Kashmir, by the operational levels of the Home Ministry and by the security forces. All of them felt that such exercises in liberalism would not only be exploited by the separatist forces but also create an image of India being on the defensive. In overall terms, however, our openness paid dividends. Nevertheless, there were contretemps the MEA encountered as a result of its initiatives. There was a strong likelihood that Pakistan would sponsor a resolution reviving the UN jurisdiction over Jammu and Kashmir and that this resolution would be passed during the UN General Assembly's session in 1993. The External Affairs Minister Dinesh Singh, despite his infirmities, made a special effort to canvass the support of other foreign ministers against the Pakistani move.

I had also gone to participate in the General Assembly session during the course of which I held individual and collective meetings with permanent representatives of the Islamic countries, the European Community and all the five permanent members of the Security Council. I also held separate discussions with permanent representatives of China and Iran; these two countries were themselves being threatened with critical resolutions related to human rights. I assured them that if they could influence Pakistan to pull away from moving its resolution against India, we would give them reciprocal support. All this lobbying eventually resulted in the Pakistan resolution being aborted. The UN, however, managed to retain its toehold on the Kashmir issue due to two factors. First, the UN Secretary-General, Boutros Boutros Ghali, made a special reference to the situation in Jammu and Kashmir in his report to the General Assembly, despite our objections. Second, US President Bill Clinton contributed to the process by pinpointing the situation in Kashmir as a flashpoint in South Asia that merited international monitoring. Clinton's reference to Kashmir in the same breath as Bosnia and Somalia did not exactly help matters. This reference led to speculation in the Ministry of External Affairs and in the Indian press that Robin Raphael was up to her usual tricks, and had slipped in the reference to Jammu and Kashmir in Clinton's speech. The other temporary problem we faced resulted from a call made by the External Affairs Minister Dinesh Singh on Boutros Boutros Ghali in the third week of October 1993. Ghali, during the course of this conversation, said that he was quite willing to be of assistance to India and Pakistan in resolving the Kashmir issue. He went on to say that his assistance need not be construed as an intrusion by the Security Council or the UN. Dinesh Singh, always polite and courteous, made some general remarks thanking the secretary-general, and welcoming his good intentions. These remarks were interpreted by the secretary-general's staff as an indication from the Government of India that Ghali could play a mediatory role in tackling the Kashmir issue.

When my senior colleagues pointed out this interpretation to Dinesh Singh, he wanted the situation to be rectified immediately. Therefore, that very afternoon a communication was sent to the secretary-general which clarified that Dinesh Singh's remarks should not be misinterpreted or misconstrued. This communication generated some confusion, which we ultimately resolved by (as far as I recall) a telephone conversation between Prime Minister Rao and the UN secretary-general in which Rao clearly told Ghali that while the latter's goodwill and desire for the normalisation of relations between India and Pakistan was appreciated, India did not envisage any mediatory or jurisdictional role for him or the UN in Kashmir.

Simultaneously, some important steps were taken for the establishment of the Indian Human Rights Commission and for structuring an effective brief on questions of human rights for the UN Conference on Human Rights in Vienna in June 1993. We also established a special publicity cell to project India's policies and views on Jammu and Kashmir. This cell functioned under the jurisdiction of the Home Ministry.

In some respects a disproportionate amount of attention was given, and energy spent, by the Ministry of External Affairs to deal with the external dimensions of the Jammu and Kashmir issue. There were moments when I felt that India should concentrate on internal crisis management in Jammu and Kashmir and then proceed towards a political solution of the problem. I also felt that no harm would have come to India had it clearly told Pakistan and other countries that it did not propose to react to their publicity, diplomatic pressures or political blandishments on this issue.

Based on my experience of dealing with revived tension in Kashmir since 1989-91, I feel that India has to take three steps urgently to tackle the problem. First, India has to maintain its jurisdiction over Jammu and Kashmir and ensure necessary levels of law and order so that the people there can feel a sense of security against the depredations of terrorists and secessionists. Second, India has to undertake innovative political initiatives to restore genuine democracy and set up autonomous political arrangements responsive to the aspirations of the people. Third, India should nip in the bud Pakistan-sponsored violence and terrorism by all means possible, hopefully without getting enmeshed in an open military conflict with that country. But if Pakistan crosses the thresholds of tolerance with respect to Indian security concerns, it should not be inhibited in taking decisive action.

Ever since the situation in Kashmir became volatile, in 1989-90, a number of proposals have been put forward for resolving the problem. Detailing some of them here would be relevant:

1. Acknowledging the current Line of Control in Jammu and Kashmir as the international border between India and Pakistan, thereby stabilising the situation and then allowing normal interaction between Kashmiris staying in what is now called Pakistan-occupied Kashmir and those on the Indian side of Jammu and Kashmir. This was the proposal which the late Zulfiqar Ali Bhutto reportedly gave general assurances to fulfil during the Simla talks in 1972.

2. UN resolutions should be revived, leading to a plebiscite.

3. Working out a new standstill arrangement on Kashmir between India and Pakistan and placing the territory of the state under some UN

trusteeship mechanism to be followed a few years later by a plebiscite or referendum for ascertaining the views of the people there. A segment of the Jammu and Kashmir Liberation Front leadership made this proposal in 1992. Two plebiscites could be held, one on the Indian side and other in PoK. The results of both plebiscites should form the basis of a solution.

4. Both India and Pakistan should renounce their claim and jurisdiction over Jammu and Kashmir and make it an independent state.

5. The Kashmir valley may be ceded to Pakistan, while India retains Ladakh, Jammu and other areas.

Except for the first proposal, which matches ground realities and safeguards the territorial integrity of both India and Pakistan, all the other proposals are bound to generate opposition on one count or another.

The strategic environment specific to the state of Jammu and Kashmir and also to its neighbourhood has undergone profound changes over the past three decades, particularly after the overt nuclear weapons programmes of India and Pakistan. An uncertain situation prevails in Afghanistan, while China continues to hold large tracts of Jammu and Kashmir territory in its possession under its boundary agreements with Pakistan in 1963. Both Pakistan and China are well placed in the northern and northwestern flanks of Jammu and Kashmir as far as territorial control is concerned. Apart from these factors impinging on India's policies, some other highly relevant questions arise about the aforementioned proposals, barring the first one. Can Pakistan and India accept Jammu and Kashmir becoming an independent state? Can India maintain effective jurisdiction and control over Ladakh, Jammu and Punjab, if it were to accept the Valley and Muslim-majority areas acceding to Pakistan or becoming independent? Can India ensure its own internal unity in demographic, ethnic and religious terms if any of the proposals, except the first one, were given serious consideration?

It would be rash to suggest instant solutions because there are just so many imponderables. But some aspects are clear. First, the issue related to Jammu and Kashmir cannot be resolved by coercive force or military means alone. Second, India has to look at itself in the mirror and acknowledge the frustration and alienation of a section of its citizens who live in an area of paramount strategic and security interest to it. These frustrations have to be overcome by political means and positive responses on the basis of democratic principles. This can be done only by reviving the basis of democratic principles and political dialogue by all available means.

Arguments and Solutions

Having underlined the fact that a negotiated settlement is unavoidable if one is to find a durable solution to the Kashmir problem, it would be pertinent to take note of the rationale of the Pakistani stand on Jammu and Kashmir. The historical argument given by Pakistan is Jammu and Kashmir has not been an integral part of the Indian polity under different empires and kingdoms for the past one thousand years or so. This is not a historically correct claim, because Jammu and Kashmir was part of the Gupta and Maurya empires and also of the Mughal empire. Second, the territories of Jammu and Kashmir in more recent times were part of the Afghan empire and the kingdom of Punjab which is now Pakistan. Third, Jammu and Kashmir has a Muslim population and, therefore, under the two-nation theory it should become part of Pakistan. The next argument is that since this did not happen at the time of Partition, making Jammu and Kashmir a part of Pakistan is the unfinished task of Partition. An additional argument which is not formally expressed but which forms part of the Pakistani rationale is that the alienation of East Pakistan on its becoming the independent country of Bangladesh with Indian military support has to be avenged and this redressal can only be achieved by ensuring that Kashmir breaks away from the Indian republic and becomes part of Pakistan.

There is also the geo-economic concern of Pakistan that the headwaters of practically all the rivers flowing into Pakistan are in Jammu and Kashmir. The Pakistani worry, therefore, is that if Jammu and Kashmir remains under the control of India, Pakistan can be held hostage by India cutting off the water supply. The fact of the matter is that despite there having been four wars with Pakistan, India never thought of taking such action. The treaty signed on the sharing of the waters of the Indus has remained operational, despite these wars. Regardless of this reality, Pakistan has this apprehension and Pakistani politicians articulate this concern with frequency.

The basic approach of India for finding a solution to the Kashmir issue is based on three terms of reference. First, that there should be no alienation of the territory of the former princely state of Jammu and Kashmir which is now part of the Indian Union and that the solution has to be within the framework of the Indian constitution. Second, a solution has to be responsive to the basic anxieties and aspirations of the people of Jammu and Kashmir. Third, that a solution should be based on the existing ground realities and the jurisdiction exercised by Pakistan and India in Jammu and Kashmir on both sides of the Line of Control.

I have referred to the Agreement reached between Zulfiqar Ali Bhutto and Mrs Indira Gandhi at Simla in July 1972 that once the Ceasefire Line was converted into the Line of Control, the Line of Control should be converted into an international boundary, Pakistan keeping territories it had and India retaining jurisdiction over areas under its control since 1947.

Participants at the Simla Summit have in later years confirmed that such an agreement was reached and that Bhutto pleaded with Mrs Gandhi not to make his commitment a part of the formal Simla Agreement for his own political survival and the survival of democracy in Pakistan. Mrs Gandhi and her advisers made the mistake of accepting this request. What is interesting, however, is the fact that Zia-ul-Haq tacitly accepted this arrangement and never questioned the legitimacy of the Line of Control in political terms, though he occasionally tried to alter it through military means. The most prominent example of this was his trying to take control of the Siachen Glacier area. He did not succeed because of India having advance information about this effort and taking pre-emptive military action in the area in 1984.

More noteworthy are the unpublicised diplomatic initiatives taken by the Government of India to find a solution to the Kashmir issue on the basis of the Indira Gandhi-Zulfiqar Ali Bhutto agreement to convert the Line of Control into the international border, after the revival of democracy in Pakistan in 1988 September. The then foreign secretary of India, Muchkund Dubey, was authorised to revive this proposal in discussions with Prime Minister Benazir Bhutto by the V.P. Singh Government. Dubey made this suggestion to Benazir Bhutto, recalling her father's commitment to Indira Gandhi during her call on the Pakistan prime minister in the summer of 1990 in Islamabad. Benazir's response was that though she was at Simla with her father, he had not mentioned anything about any commitment on the Line of Control. She added for good measure that even if there was such a commitment much water had flown down the Jhelum and Ganges since 1972. The circumstances had changed. India and Pakistan should discuss a solution to the Kashmir problem afresh in the context of the critical situation there. She was referring to the armed secessionist movement that had affected Jammu and Kashmir since the end of 1989.

I was authorised to repeat this offer to Prime Minister Nawaz Sharif in November 1991 soon after the announcement of my appointment as foreign secretary. I raised the possibilities of a solution to the Kashmir problem on the basis of the Line of Control with Sharif during my meeting with him just before I left for New Delhi to assume my new post. Sharif's candid response was that as the leader of the Pakistan Muslim League he could not go by speculative reports regarding a commitment given by Zulfiqar Ali Bhutto more than two decades earlier. He emphatically told me that neither the Government nor public opinion in Pakistan could accept a solution on the basis of Line of Control.

The fundamental reason for this intransigent pull back from the position taken by Bhutto in 1972 in Simla was the assessment by the Pakistani power structure that Kashmir was ripe for separation from the Indian Republic from 1989 onwards and that the Indian state did not have the political will or the stamina to sustain Jammu and Kashmir as an integral part of India. The large-scale military aggression launched by Pakistan across the Line of Control in Kargil in the summer of 1999 was an operational expression of this. It would be pertinent to recall that Pakistan questioned the legality and sanctity of the Line of Control during the Kargil conflict. Nawaz Sharif and his foreign minister, Sartaj Aziz, and General Pervez Musharraf claimed Pakistan had not violated the Line of Control because, according to them, it was never clearly demarcated. They went further to argue that the small-scale military skirmishes that had occurred on the Line of Control, and Indian forces occupying the Siachen Heights, had altered the Line of Control and that it had no legitimacy. Pakistan went even further in laying the basis for territorial extension into India by saying that while there was an international frontier between India and Pakistan, it too was not clearly defined. Pakistani spokesmen claimed between 1999 and 2001 that there was a "working border" between the two countries which is different from the formal cartographic delineation of the international frontier. The objective was to justify intrusions into India south of the Line of Control to gain strategic territorial advantage in the region for launching operations into Jammu and Kashmir.

Pakistan had opted for a parallel policy of undertaking military operations against India in Jammu and Kashmir, while at the same time making policy statements aimed at eroding the sanctity of the Line of Control and the northern segment of the international border between India and Pakistan.

India in contrast remained committed to territorial arrangements finalised at the Simla Agreement and at the consequent negotiations between senior military commanders. India remained steadfast despite the grave provocation of the Kargil war. It must be mentioned that till about the third week of June 1999, sections of the policy-making entities of the Government of India seriously considered the option of crossing the Line of Control to stem the Pakistani invasion of the Kargil region in Jammu and Kashmir. The then chief of army staff, General Ved Malik, publicly confirmed in January 2002 that operational planners at the Indian Army Headquarters had prepared contingency plans to cross the Line of Control to destroy the supply depots and supply routes of the Pakistani armed forces engaged in the invasion of Kargil.

A subgroup of the National Security Advisory Board, of which I was a member in 1999, had recommended that India consider carrying out air strikes and launching a military operation across the Line of Control. This small subgroup of the NSAB was created on the instructions of Prime Minister Vajpayee on 7 June 1999. It consisted of seven members, including Air Chief Marshal (retd.) S.K. Mehra and K. Subrahmanyam. We collectively felt that a quick end to the war could be achieved by strikes across the Line of Control. The recommendation was forwarded to the National Security Council. It was, however, kept as an option "in reserve" and was not implemented because it became unnecessary by the first week of July. As far as I recall we forwarded this recommendation to the Government in the third week of June 1999.

General Musharraf's statements as late as 12 January 2002, emphasised that Government of Pakistan would not accept any solution of Kashmir based on the Line of Control. Political reality, suggests Pakistan is not inclined towards any practical solution to the Kashmir problem based on ground realities that have evolved over 50 years. It is in this context that the Indian Government's initiatives with various political groups within Kashmir need to be recalled and assessed.

In the recent past there has been a flurry of activity on the part of the Government of India and various militant groups in Jammu and Kashmir about resuming a dialogue. Segments of the media, in their wisdom, have described these as initiatives to achieve long-sought-after peace in Jammu and Kashmir. One would agree that peace is much desired and imperative. But I would not call the steps for interaction between governmental representatives of India and the militant groups a peace initiative. Factually speaking, these are only initiatives to resume a dialogue hoping for arrangements that may eventually bring about peace. The evolving situation related to Jammu and Kashmir has to be examined and assessed in three dimensions: first, the factual background and ingredients leading to the recent agreement to have talks; second, the motivations and circumstances underpinning this initiative for a dialogue; third, the prospects of this impending dialogue in the context of the objectives that all the parties concerned have in mind normatively and in terms of practical possibilities. The events and measures that led to the declaration of a ceasefire by the Hizbul Mujahideen merit recounting. The Government of India decided to resume a meaningful dialogue with all parties and segments of public opinion in Jammu and Kashmir early in 2000. By late spring and summer, senior leaders of the Hurriyat Conference were released from jails and sent back to Kashmir. Meanwhile, the prospects of the Central Government's offer to the Hurriyat generated concern in the mind of Chief Minister Farooq Abdullah and his party. This led to the state legislative assembly passing a resolution endorsing the report of the Autonomy Committee.

In parallel, the Central Government orchestrated back-channel contacts with the leaders of the All Parties Hurriyat Conference. R.K. Mishra of the *Observer* group, former foreign secretary M.K. Rasgotra, even the chief of the Research and Analysis Wing, A.S. Dullat, were deployed for these contacts. Track II contacts with Pakistan were also activated. Two delegations of journalists and women visited New Delhi and Islamabad respectively in July 2000 and January/February 2001. There was some participation by Kashmiri activists based in the US. Individuals like Farooq Kathwari, Ghulam Nabi Fai of the Kashmir American Council, Mohammad Ayub Thakur of the World Kashmir Freedom Movement, Mushtaq Jeelani of the Kashmiri Canadian Council, and Mansoor Ejaz, a New York banker, were conduits for contacts with Kashmiri militants. Their efforts had the backing of the State Department and American think-tanks specialising in South Asian affairs. The most recent announcement by principal secretary to the prime minister, Brajesh Mishra, told of Rasgotra being authorised to initiate contacts with the Pakistani establishment using non-official channels. Rasgotra, accompanied by four Foreign Service officers, proceeded to Islamabad in the first week of August 2000. Other members of the delegation were former foreign secretary Salman Haider and former ambassadors Manorama Bhalla, Alan Nazareth and C.V. Ranganathan. They were received by Pakistani Foreign Minister, Abdul Sattar. These strands of discussions first resulted in the Hizbul Mujahideen declaring a three-month ceasefire, indicating a willingness to talk to the Government of India without any preconditions. While the local leader of the Hizbul Mujahideen, Abdul Majid Dar, made this offer, the Supreme Council of his organisation, based in Pakistan initially opposed it. It then reluctantly agreed to exploratory discussions. The other Pakistan-based militant groups like the Lashkar-e-Toiba and Harkat-ul-Ansar have labelled the Hizbul's initiative as a betrayal.

The head of the Lashkar-e-Toiba, Mohammad Saeed, stated on 31 July 2000 that the jehad would continue against India till Kashmir becomes part of Pakistan. The policy was transmuted into action soon enough with the Lashkar attacking and killing six soldiers at the Bandipora military base. Violence continued in Srinagar despite the Indian Army suspending operations against Hizbul Mujahideen. The Hizbul nominated a four-member delegation to discuss the modalities for the dialogue with the Government of India. It comprised Ghulam Ali (leader of the Kashmiri American Council), Mushtaq Geelani (World Kashmir Freedom Movement) and Mohammad Ali Saqib (member of the Overseas Kashmiri Citizens' Committee). The Hizbul indicated that it would nominate additional members from its senior cadre to the negotiating team. The Government of India responded by inviting the Hizbul to talk to an Indian team led by Home Secretary Kamal Pande.

Meanwhile, various informal contacts continue to portend a dialogue. Public pronouncements by both sides were confusing and contradictory.

But more than anything else, one should take note of the motivations and impulses underpinning these recent initiatives. There is definitely behind-the-scenes American pressure on Pakistan and on India to resume discussions to bring about normality in Kashmir, both with the militants and between India and Pakistan. The US establishment wanted some tangible progress to occur by the time Prime Minister Vajpayee visited in mid-September 2000 for bilateral talks with President Bill Clinton. Clinton's commitment to take personal interest in issues related to Kashmir had to be translated into some concrete developments for the credibility of America's South Asia policies. Pakistan agreed to support the dialogue without giving any commitment about discontinuing cross-border terrorism. Pakistan felt supporting the dialogue would enable it to tell the US that it has persuaded the militants to declare a ceasefire. Pakistan wanted to make the same claim at the UN General Assembly and the UN Security Council in September 2000, when Vajpayee was in New York. If India refused to resume the dialogue, it could be projected as unreasonable, and if India resumes the dialogue and it ended in a stalemate, India can continue to be accused of obduracy.

There has been much oscillation in the thinking about various categories of political dialogue. Ceasefires have been declared and withdrawn and conditions stipulated, denied and then restated by both sides. Indian delegations have met the Hizbul and the Hurriyat and covert talks have been held by R.K. Mishra and M.K. Rasgotra. Hurriyat leaders came to Delhi in the third week of August 2000 and had meetings with the Pakistani high commissioner and officials of the US embassy. Abdul Majid Dar asserted that the talks had "only been delayed and not derailed" and that they could resume in two or three months, while his chief, Salahuddin, asserted that the talks had broken down. Leaders of the Lashkar-e-Toiba and other outfits announced that the betrayal of the jehad by declaring a ceasefire and having discussions with the infidel Government of India would not be allowed.

All the protagonists involved in the Kashmir tragedy seem to be on a roller-coaster from which they wish to get off, but cannot; the Indian objectives in order of priorities are (a) the cessation of all violence and terrorist acts; (b) to ensure that those portions of Jammu and Kashmir that are part of India do not get separated from the territories of the Republic of India; (c) to ensure that any compromise arrived at on the basis of discussions with various opposition groups representing the people of Jammu and Kashmir does not dilute the strategic position of India in the state; (d) to ensure that it does not result in any ceding of territory to Pakistan; and (e) that the compromises reached should be such that they contribute to neutralising the centrifugal forces in other parts of India.

The objectives of the opposition and secessionist forces are not crystal clear. There are differing objectives entertained by them, but first and foremost, these groups wish the withdrawal of the extensive and large-scale presence of the Indian military and security forces in Kashmir. Some of them want the complete withdrawal of these forces. A segment of the people of Jammu and Kashmir want autonomy of the type which the state had between 1948 and 1953. Another segment of people want Jammu and Kashmir to become an independent political entity with security guarantees from the international community and from India and Pakistan in particular. A third group wish the state to become a part of Pakistan, and then there is a fourth segment of people, belonging to Ladakh and Jammu, who wish the state to remain an integral part of the Indian republic.

Pakistan's objectives are clear: (1) it considers the acquisition of Jammu and Kashmir the unfinished part of Partition; (2) its claim to Kashmir is firmly rooted in the two-nation theory; (3) it desires to invalidate the provisions of the Indian Independence Act and the Instruments of Accession which the maharaja of Jammu and Kashmir signed acceding the state to India; (4) it also questions the decision taken by Sheikh Abdullah to make Jammu and Kashmir a part of India; (5) it is of the view that continuing cross-border terrorism and violent intervention, including sending mercenaries and non-Kashmiri cadres to create a conflict situation in Jammu and Kashmir, will achieve the above objectives.

A contradiction permeating the approach of the parties to these discussions should also be noted. While India and a section of the people of Jammu and Kashmir are convinced that the final solution of the Kashmir dispute can only be through political means and negotiations, the opposition militant groups particularly those based in Pakistan, are convinced that their jehad, has to be continued. It will defeat India through either a process of attrition or by a direct military defeat inflicted by Pakistan on India; that will solve the problem. Successive governments of Pakistan have been and are of the view that Pakistani objectives would be met by a combination of covert military operations and organising international pressure, intervention or mediation, the latter to be generated by raising the levels of violence in Jammu and Kashmir to the threshold of regional tension. This would compel international intervention in the context of the nuclear weapons capabilities of India and Pakistan.

These are the fundamental realities, in the context of which India has to fashion its policies on Jammu and Kashmir and towards Pakistan. Analysing what has happened recently, one must keep in mind the lessons for future action. The Hizbul Mujahideen announced the decision for a unilateral ceasefire and a willingness to negotiate with India on the basis of clearance given by the ISI and the military government of Pakistan. The reasons for this initiative were: first, the apprehension that India's discussions with certain Hurriyat leaders and India's moves to devolve further powers to the state of Jammu and Kashmir would have marginalised the Pakistan-supported political and military elements in Jammu and Kashmir. Second, perhaps, the Hizbul wanted a recess in military operations to regroup and re-equip itself to meet the sustained pressure by Indian security forces and the political developments in Jammu and Kashmir. Once talks started, the Hizbul headquarters in Pakistan and the ISI feared that negotiations may take off and Pakistani long-term plans would be thwarted. Hence, the demand for Pakistan's presence at the talks, after the negotiations commenced, and the very short period given to India — almost like an ultimatum — to respond within two-and-a-half days, by 8 August 2000.

Though this attempt at commencing negotiations with secessionists failed, there have been suggestions both from the Hurriyat and the Hizbul that the talks could and should be revived. There was even an offer that in the initial stages Pakistan need not be a party to the discussions.

At the most fundamental level, the issue of Jammu and Kashmir is no longer a legal or territorial dispute for both India and Pakistan. The issue is now a question of the ideological basis of their respective national identities. For Pakistan, acquiring Kashmir will be a revived confirmation of the two-nation theory. For India, alienation of any portion of Jammu and

Kashmir because of its being a Muslim-majority area will be a denial of the secular, pluralistic terms of reference of India's national identity. So India agreeing to cede any part of Jammu and Kashmir, that is now an integral part of India is and would be out of the question.

Structuring meaningful political discussions on the complex issues related to Kashmir is going to be an extremely difficult and intractable exercise. The Farooq Abdullah government is not happy about the Government of India's willingness to talk to representatives of secessionist groups. The constituent groups of the All Parties Hurriyat Conference have internal differences about a possible solution. The JKLF, led by Yasin Malik, desires an independent sovereign state for Kashmir. The other groups want Kashmir to be part of Pakistan. All the groups of the Hurriyat want Pakistan to be a party to negotiations with the Government of India and they reject greater autonomy or any solution within the framework of the Indian Constitution. The principal leaders of the All-Party Hurriyat Conference remain totally opposed at present to any consolidation of Jammu and Kashmir's integration with the Republic of India under any new arrangement. The National Conference led by Dr Farooq Abdullah wants restoration of the pre-1953 status of Kashmir accepting India's sovereignty only in matters related to finance, external affairs and communications. Both the major political parties of India, the Congress and the BJP, are opposed to the restoration of the pre-1953 status. They consider it the first step towards Kashmir breaking away from India. They are also opposed to tripartite discussions, with Pakistan as a participant.

Compounding these contradictory approaches are the profound reservations the people of Jammu and Ladakh have about any new arrangement based on the demands of the extremist Islamic secessionist groups of the Kashmir valley. It must also be remembered that apart from being responsive to the aspirations of the peoples with different ethnic, religious and linguistic affinities constituting the population of Kashmir, any political solution would also involve an amendment to the Indian Constitution. This can be managed only with the general national consensus. Collective opinion in India is not likely to condone the whole or partial alienation of any part of India on the basis of language, religion or the sort of definition of nationhood that led to the partition of India. After the Pakistani invasion of Kargil and the hijacking of the Indian Airlines aircraft in December 1999, there is a profound antagonism in India towards making Pakistan a party to any discussions on Kashmir. There is also a perception that Kashmir is no longer a territorial dispute rooted in the communal demography of the Valley. Any political, social or territorial alienation of

Kashmir from India would have a negative impact on the political and territorial unity of India. International reactions are also important. While the world at large is opposed to Pakistani participation in and support of secessionism, the view is that Kashmir is a dispute between India and Pakistan with serious implications for regional stability and security and also that the aspirations of the people of Kashmir should be met.

India's approach should be to work towards meaningful autonomy for Jammu and Kashmir, bringing the people of the state into the mainstream of the Indian democratic process, with the Line of Control gradually converting itself into a permanent border between India and Pakistan. Efforts to achieve this objective through political discussions should be initiated, however long drawn the effort may be.

Nine

India and Pakistan — Nuclear Weapons States

$\mathcal{T}$here is much literature available on the history of India's and Pakistan's nuclear weapons programmes. India's overall policy on non-proliferation issues, specially during the 1990s, could be summed up as follows:

1. Willing to join any genuine effort at bringing about arrangements for non-discriminatory non-proliferation, arms control and disarmament.

2. Not willing to join any interim discriminatory regimes, including the Comprehensive Test Ban Treaty, regardless of assurances and security guarantees the US and others were willing to offer.

3. Opposed to a South Asian nuclear weapons-free zone and to any conference aimed at meeting this limited objective.

4. Willing to participate in a broader Asian conference with a large number of participants to discuss the possibilities of creating a nuclear-free zone in the whole Asian landmass and its adjacent seas, provided that all the countries of the region, plus all the countries that have the nuclear weapons capacity to affect the security environment of the region, undertake mutual and equal obligations.

5. Indicated that details pertaining to the terms of reference, the objectives and the participants in the conference (if held at all) should be worked

out carefully and that it should be comprehensive. India would participate in such a conference only if there was a formal a priori assurance that the proposed enlarged Asian conference would be an interim step towards holding a global conference on nuclear non-proliferation and disarmament within a definite time limit.

6. Clearly indicated to all interlocutors that India would develop and deploy missiles of various categories depending upon its security requirements and that it would not accept unilateral or admonitory stipulations and "disciplinary measures" from any quarter.

7. When the US changed its position on nuclear testing, thus enabling the beginning of negotiations, we agreed to work together to finalise the Comprehensive Test Ban Treaty provided it was universal, really comprehensive and non-discriminatory. Regarding the US proposal on observing fissile material production restraint unilaterally or bilaterally, with Pakistan, India was successful in moving the issue to the UN General Assembly and then to the Conference on Disarmament, where it has remained stalemated since 1994.

India conveyed to the US and to the other nations during bilateral discussions that the extension of the Non-Proliferation Treaty should be subject to changed realities in nuclear developments all over the world and that the treaty should be reviewed and extended only on the basis of genuine international consensus.

The purpose here is to summarise the immediate background of India becoming an overt nuclear weapons state and to examine the ramifications of Pakistan following suit. The reasons for India undertaking the nuclear weapons tests and declaring itself an official nuclear weapon state are the following. First and foremost, the progressively deteriorating security environment India has faced since the late 1980s activated successive Indian governments to go nuclear. Second, the incremental restrictive and discriminatory international regimes being put in place would have not just stifled but put a complete stop to India realising its potential in the field of space and nuclear technologies. This spurred India to exercise the nuclear option. Third, India was averse to adjusting to a new international strategic and technological order in which the existing five nuclear weapons states would remain a dominating factor for a prolonged period of time. Fourth, India required a long-term and sophisticated defence capacity in the context of its own post-Independence experience of its territorial integrity being threatened more than once. Fifth, India took note of the fact that when other states with nuclear weapons capabilities were subjected to restrictive pressures, these states either overcame the pressures by becoming nuclear weapons powers themselves (such as France and China), or succumbed to international pressure and had their nuclear capacities capped, rolled back or eliminated (Argentina, South Africa and Brazil). India chose the first option.

The first criticism levelled against India is that by conducting these tests it has abandoned its unqualified commitment not to acquire nuclear weapons and missile capacities. This is not true. New Delhi had noted the discriminatory orientations of the nuclear weapons powers at the time of the very inception of India's own nuclear programmes. Political and technological elements of the statute on the establishment of the International Atomic Energy Agency (IAEA), discussed at the conference to finalise this statute in 1957, gave clear indication of its prospective discriminatory orientations. India articulated its reservations. While abjuring the acquisition of nuclear weapons, despite suggestions to the contrary by the US in 1963, it took note of the Chinese nuclear weapons programme in 1964, and decided to build up infrastructure capacities for a nuclear deterrent of its own. India's building a plutonium-processing plant in 1964 was an affirmation of this intention. India's refusal to sign the nuclear Non-Proliferation Treaty in 1967-68 and conducting the peaceful nuclear explosion test at Pokhran on 18 May 1974 were clear signals that it was aiming at acquiring basic nuclear weapons capacities and would keep this option open.

The post-Pokhran I reaction of nuclear weapons powers led by the US heightened India's misgivings about a restrictive non-proliferation policy. Multilateral technical discussions on safeguards procedures, and transfer of technology policies of nuclear weapons states changed the very definition of non-proliferation. It initially aimed at only preventing the acquisition and proliferation of nuclear weapons. The definition was extended to cover all related technologies. Similarly, the objective of safeguards was changed to monitor and supervise nuclear and space technologies being used for peaceful purposes. This approach was embodied in the concept of the full-scope safeguards of the IAEA, which India consistently opposed. Full-scope safeguards were also going to be discriminatory, as these were not applicable to the facilities and laboratories of the nuclear weapons states.

If one recalls the provisions of the 1978 Nuclear Regulatory Act of the US, its primary target was to control and diminish India's nuclear, technological and defence capacities. The deleterious impact that agreements on regional and subregional nuclear weapons-free zones had on the nuclear self-reliance capacities of countries like Brazil and Argentina — the Treaty of Tlatlalco — was also taken note of by Indian defence planners. India was convinced that regional and subregional nuclear-free zones were irrelevant in terms of non-proliferation. Nuclear weapons have global reach and most of the regions anyway had at least one nuclear weapons power already. India also noted that the discriminatory terms of reference governing the NPT remained the guiding principle of all international regimes being put in place, whether it was the missile control technology regime, the Comprehensive Test Ban Treaty, or the proposed Fissile Material Cut-off Treaty.

Since the beginning of the 1990s, there was a clear political message for India vis-à-vis the pressure exerted on South Africa to totally give up its nuclear weapons options the moment a black African-majority government came to power, and the enormous pressure exerted on (and financial incentives running into over a billion dollars given to) Ukraine to do likewise. The end of the Cold War and the end of the US-Soviet confrontation did not change the discriminatory and self-aggrandising attitude of the nuclear weapons powers on non-proliferation issues. Their static and self-serving approach was manifested in all the discussions related to non-proliferation of every category held after the Cold War. India, consequently, had to fashion a practical though disciplined deterrent-oriented response. This was the objective it sought to fulfil in May 1998.

The purpose of recalling these trends is to underline the fact that India's nuclear policies have not developed in a vacuum. They were essentially a graduated and measured response to international non-proliferation trends India perceived as a threat to its long-term security interests. It is the same motivation that made India commence its missile development programme, given a pronounced impetus by Rajiv Gandhi from 1984 to 1989, a process that has continued to date.

The conventional wisdom that Pakistan commenced its clandestine nuclear and missile weapons programme only after the Indian nuclear tests of 1974 is factually incorrect. In their book *Islamic Bomb* (Vision Books, Delhi, 1981), Steve Wiessman and Herbert Krosney assert that right from the mid-1950s, Zulfiqar Ali Bhutto (when he became a minister in Ayub Khan's cabinet) was an advocate of Pakistan developing nuclear weapons. Pakistan's defeat in 1971 strengthened Bhutto's conviction. He took the decision that Pakistan should have a nuclear weapons capacity two years before India's 1974 tests in Pokhran. His articulated logic was that Pakistan should have such an overwhelming superiority in non-conventional weapons that India would never be able to defeat Pakistan in conventional warfare.

Pakistan consistently increased its nuclear weapons and missile capacities from 1972 onwards and by 1987, Pakistan was in possession of a limited number of nuclear devices. During 1987 and 1988, Pakistan improved its military missile arsenal, with Chinese help, culminating in a situation where, between 1996 and 1997, senior Pakistani political and military figures asserted that they were capable of adopting a nuclear and missile posture against India. The firing of the potential IRBM missile, Ghauri in April 1998 — and the claims of the creator of the Pakistani nuclear weapons programme Dr. Abdul Qadir Khan that Pakistan had an effective military arsenal — could not be ignored by India. Regardless of marginal scepticism and doubts expressed by experts in India and abroad about Pakistan's capacities, the following facts have to be taken note of.

Pakistan today has 14 laboratories and nuclear facilities in the Chagai Hills, Kundian, Chashma, Lakki, Isakhel, Wah, Golra Sharief, Rawalpindi, Sihala, Kahuta, Khushab, Lahore, Multan and Dehra Ghazi Khan. These facilities include tritium and uranium enrichment plants, mining facilities, a laboratory for uranium hexafluoride conversion, weapon-manufacturing centres, fuel fabrication centres, nuclear testing facilities, heavy water manufacturing facilities, plutonium-reprocessing facilities, milling facilities, nuclear reactors and a well-equipped research and development capacity.

One does not have to go into such detail about Chinese nuclear and missile capacities, which have evolved since 1964 and made China a member of the nuclear weapons powers club. Over the years, the US has conducted 1032 nuclear tests, Russia 715, France 210, the UK 45 and China 45. France and China conducted these nuclear tests as late as 1996, just as the Comprehensive Test Ban Treaty was being finalised. As of May 1998, the US possessed 12,070 nuclear warheads, Russia 22,500, France 500, the UK 380 and China 450. Even if the Strategic Arms Limitation Treaty (SALT) and Strategic Arms Reduction Treaty (START) get finalised and implemented, the US would retain about 10,000 nuclear weapons, 3500 strategic, 1000 tactical and 5500 warheads in reserve till the year 2007. The Russians will retain 11,000 nuclear weapons, 3500 strategic, 2500 tactical and 5000 warheads in reserve. There would be no significant qualitative change in the nuclear arsenals of France, the UK and China. Indian threat perception in the context of this international weapons environment, stretching well into the first decade of the 21st century, is realistic.

India becoming a nuclear weapons state is logical in terms of national interests, as well as international precedents. The UK and France need not have become nuclear weapons powers. They did despite having a guaranteed nuclear security umbrella provided by the US and also by NATO. Israel's non-declared nuclear weapons status has occurred despite security guarantees from the US. The UK, France and Israel became nuclear weapons powers with encouragement from the US. For China it was the logic of the Cold War that led to the imperative for self-reliance. South Korea and North Korea acquiring nuclear weapons capacities have more or less the same logic, based on the Chinese presence. South Africa's nuclear weapons status was sustained and supported till Nelson Mandela came to power. A black-majority democratic regime could not be trusted with capacities as the white racist Pretoria regime had been. One cannot forget the ethno-racial logic of South Africa being persuaded to give up its nuclear weapons status not only because black South Africa may not have been a reliable strategic ally but also because of an unarticulated feeling that such sophisticated technology could not be handed over to a majority of Africans in South Africa.

I would like to indulge in a diversion about this concept of "rogue states" and "irresponsible states". It has become part of the lexicon of non-proliferation disarmament and arms control discussions. This concept was introduced by the industrially advanced countries led by the US. Countries like Libya, Iraq, Iran, North Korea and to some extent Syria have qualified for it. Now India and Pakistan are potential candidates.

The objective criteria for the irresponsible use of weapons of mass destruction are the following: (1) if such a weapon is used by one country against another that does not have similar weapons of mass destruction (WMD); (2) if the WMD-processing country uses such a weapon without provocation or genuine military requirement; and (3) if an WMD-equipped country uses such weapons against a defenceless civilian population. If a country meets these three criteria, it merits the description of being irresponsible. It should be clarified that one does not hold a brief for the adventurist and impulsively violent policies of President Saddam Hussain or Colonel Muammar Gaddafi. But if the criteria are objectively applied, there has been only one case when they were fulfilled without any inhibition or compunctions. The US bombing of Hiroshima and Nagasaki August 1945. Perhaps the nuclear weapons states should occasionally look into the mirror before applying such adjectives to other states.

India's Nuclear Weapons Status

Let me return to the main story. The new Bharatiya Janata Party Government in New Delhi took the politically radical and dramatic step of conducting five nuclear tests, three on 11 May and two more on 13 May

1998. These tests included one 45 kiloton thermonuclear test and two subcritical subkiloton tests. India asserted its nuclear weapons capacities overtly and declared itself a nuclear weapons state. It can now be mentioned that Prime Minister Narasimha Rao was quite close to conducting a nuclear test towards the end of 1995. But various external and domestic pressures inhibited him.

The period between the summer of 1994 and the end of 1997 saw the finalisation of the Comprehensive Test Ban Treaty despite India's reservations about its discriminatory nature. India's conducting thermonuclear and nuclear tests had the following implications: First, it affirmed its status as a full-fledged nuclear weapons state. Second, these tests confirmed the sophisticated level of Indian technological capacities in high-energy physics and nuclear engineering with facilities for computer simulation and subcritical tests in future. Third, India acquired a strategic position as a balancing factor both in regional and international power equations. Fourth, regardless of the intransigence of the five nuclear weapons powers, objective terms of reference for future arms control and disarmament processes stood changed with the principle of discriminatory restrictions facing a question mark.

International reactions to the radical politico-strategic initiative taken by India were varied. Most were overwhelmingly negative. The first and foremost concern of New Delhi was to convince the international community that India's only purpose in overtly declaring its nuclear weapons capacity, and confirming it by operational experiments, was to meet India's security requirements and, this capacity would be managed with restraint and responsibility, posing no threat to peace and stability.

A number of questions were raised about the Government of India's decision to go nuclear in terms of its defence capacities. They need answers. The first question asked was: Why did India end its ambiguity and carry out the test? The answer lies simply in the security environment around India stretching from Diego Garcia in the west in an encircling arc right up to Pakistan, the Gulf and the Straits of Hormuz. There are a number of countries with a nuclear weapons presence in this entire region, one of which Pakistan has threatened to use nuclear weapons missile capacities against India more than once. Pakistan's relations with other nuclear weapons powers such as China and the US cannot be ignored by India. Second, the conducting of tests was necessary for India to ascertain for itself what its capacities were, to make the Indian public generally aware of these capacities, and to impart a sense of confidence. The second question asked is about the timing of these tests. Why did India go in for these tests in

1998? The reasons were twofold. First, the tests were necessary for technological and operational reasons, the objective being to lay the foundation for India to develop a deployable deterrent capacity against potential threats. India had already delayed this process; a delay that had affected its security. Second, any further delay would have entailed a straitjacket of punitive and discriminatory stipulations, which would have become operational under the CTBT by the end of 1999, further compounded by the Fissile Material Cut-off treaty coming up for discussion in the Conference on Disarmament. The third question asked is about the legitimacy of a minority and coalition government taking such a vital decision. In terms of seats in Parliament and related statistics, the Vajpayee Government may have been a minority government, but in terms of voting patterns in the 1996 and 1998 elections there can be little doubt that the BJP's foreign policy and security policy orientations had the general support of the Indian public and that, unlike the preceding Deve Gowda and Gujral governments, the Vajpayee Government was led by the largest single party in the Lower House of Parliament (Lok Sabha). In terms of public opinion, conducting the tests had the general endorsement of the people of India. The fourth criticism levelled is that the government did not consult various parties before taking the decision. Such sensitive decisions are not preceded by public debate and political consultations. Mrs Gandhi did not consult political parties before the 1974 nuclear test. As far as I recall, such decisions by the five nuclear weapons powers in the aftermath of the Second World War were not preceded by consultations and transparency. The requirements of political secrecy and technological confidentiality preclude such consultations. More important, India has been engaged in prolonged detailed and multifaceted discussions on the nuclear weapons issues over the last 26 years. At each stage of the evolution of the Indian attitude, there was a general national consensus on what was done. This criticism had more to do with party politics than with genuine principles.

An additional question needing an answer is whether India's economic modernisation and development would be affected irretrievably because of the sanctions that would inevitably be imposed in the aftermath of the nuclear tests. The assessment in informed government circles as well as by strategic and economic experts was that the sanctions would create problems for India in the short run. But India's basic natural and human resources and the inherent strength of the Indian economy would be able to withstand the pressure of these sanctions provided India fulfilled three requirements: that of remaining politically stable and united, that of engaging in constructive discussions with all the important world powers to reassure them, and that of continuing with economic liberalisation and reform purposefully. One speculation was that Defence Minister George Fernandes's critical remarks about China were in preparation for the nuclear tests. There was no such link as far as one could ascertain.

What were Indian reactions to external criticism about its tests? New Zealand and Australia withdrawing their high commissioners from India was an exercise in blatant hypocrisy, given that these countries continue to have relations with nuclear weapons states that have conducted nuclear tests nearer to their territories and whose nuclear capacities provide a security umbrella for them. Japan's criticism of India could be understood in the context of it being the only country to have suffered from a nuclear weapon attack. But its being specially critical of India was contradictory to its overall attitude towards nuclear weapons powers that have closer relations with it and are also geographically closer to it. The reaction of the US and European democracies was as anticipated.

India refused a suggestion from the US in 1963 that it produce a nuclear bomb to counter China's anticipated nuclear weapons programme. An additional point of importance needs to be mentioned: in 1967, three years after China's nuclear weaponisation and two years after the Indo-Pakistani war of 1965, India approached all the nuclear powers except China to enquire whether they would provide security guarantees to India against a nuclear threat. The response of the nuclear powers was ambiguous, bordering on the negative. This confirmed the conviction there is no substitute for self-reliance in safeguarding national security.

The nuclear tests carried out by India in 1998 perhaps reflected the most momentous decision taken by its leaders after the initial policy decisions at Independence. Sections of public opinion were fairly well informed about our nuclear policies. These sections were also quite articulate. It was certain aspects of public reactions were a matter of concern in coping with the fallout of Pokhran II. Reactions varied from unnecessary and avoidable boastfulness on TV shows, by some strategic analysts who claimed the tests indicated that India had outdistanced China in several nuclear capacities (a patently irrational claim), to intense advocates of nuclear non-proliferation describing the nuclear tests as a "cheap and partisan political trick". There are elements in political circles and in the media who have genuine doubts as to whether undertaking nuclear tests was necessary. While respecting the diversity of opinions is imperative in a democracy, the point to note is that between 87 and 89 per cent of Indian citizens endorsed the decision, according to opinion polls. There was a general feeling of self-confidence and national pride generated by the tests.

What has India achieved by taking this radical and internationally unpopular decision of becoming a nuclear weapons state? The first point to be made is that it is the capacity of a country and its people to go down a lonely path, in its own interests, which is the ultimate test of its will to safeguard its territorial integrity. The tests perhaps affirm this capacity. Second, the people of India, leaving aside the experts and the pillars of the power structure, were quite uncertain about their scientific and technological capacities. The tests confirmed to the people India's capacities and potentialities in a definite manner. Third, the tests have infused a sense of confidence and decisiveness in India's foreign and defence policies. A positive psychological and emotional repercussion has been felt in India through the phenomenon. It cannot be quantified. Fourth, India sent clear and unambiguous messages to the international community that it is a nuclear weapons power and that it has indigenously developed its capabilities to a satisfactory level. This is a ground reality which the world has to come to terms with, whatever be the legal quibbling about India's status as a nuclear weapons state because its did not acquire this capacity before 1 January 1968. Fifth, the achievement has sent out a signal to the world as well as to the public that the restraint and discipline, despite provocation and restrictions, were not a result of technological incapacities. It was voluntary. Sixth, India laid the foundation for a credible response to the strategic and security environment around us. Seventh, it profoundly changed the strategic balance between nuclear weapons powers in the political sense. It also changed the strategic equations in Asian power relations. Eighth, the technological spin-off should serve peaceful purposes and contribute to economic development. And lastly, in any new global arrangement, India will be a force to be reckoned with. India cannot be ignored.

Pakistan's Nuclear Weapons Status

Let us now turn our attention to the overt nuclear weaponisation of Pakistan between 28 and 30 May 1998. Neither the speed with which Pakistan redressed the balance of India's formal acquisition of nuclear weapons status nor the accompanying political and technological rhetoric about Pakistan's superior missile and nuclear weapons capabilities from prominent people like Gohar Ayub Khan (then Pakistan foreign minister) and presiding scientist Dr. Abdul Qadir Khan came as a surprise to India. This prospect was taken into account when the Vajpayee Government took the radical decision to conduct nuclear tests. The debate about whether Pakistan really conducted seven nuclear tests or whether only three or four were successful or whether Pakistan's other claims are valid is not relevant. The basic fact is that Pakistan claims to have achieved macro-level strategic military and political parity with India.

The impact of these developments on India's foreign policy and future prospects is pertinent. Some background information on the process by which Pakistan has emerged as a nuclear weapons state is also relevant.

It is well-known that Pakistan entertained nuclear ambitions from the mid-1960s onwards. It decided to acquire nuclear weapons by January 1972 within three weeks of its defeat in the 1971 war. Bhutto, who succeeded Yahya, was clear in his mind that the acquisition of nuclear weapons and the related delivery systems by Pakistan was imperative if it was to match India's superior conventional technology and military capacities. This was the force multiplier Pakistan sought, and achieved. Bhutto had called a meeting of eminent Pakistani scientists in Multan in January 1972, announced his desire to make Pakistan a nuclear weapons state, and urged his scientists to help him achieve his aim, if possible, within three years. There is a wealth of published information available about the evolution of Pakistan as a nuclear weapons power through clandestine means. It was helped in terms of material, technology, maps and designs and sophisticated equipment by France, the UK, the US, Holland, Germany, Italy and the Scandinavian countries indirectly and, above all, China. China has also been actively assisting Pakistan in developing its military missile capacities. Aircraft of US and French manufacture belonging to the Pakistani Air Force were given suitable weapons configuration structures to carry and deliver nuclear warheads. Records assiduously maintained and collated by the Center for Non-Proliferation Studies in the Monterey Institute of International Studies, California, indicate that Pakistan went into high gear to become a nuclear weapons state from 1977 onwards, after having collected the basic material necessary to launch its tests of 28 and 30 May 1998. Between 1972 and 1974, Pakistan had persuaded Libya, Saudi Arabia, and, to some extent, Iraq, to fund its nuclear weapons programme. By 1986, Pakistan had acquired the capacity to manufacture raw material for nuclear weapons and to assemble them.

Ultimately, it was China that emerged as the main supplier. It has been discerned from technological documents and reports covering the 1980s and 1990s that China assisted Pakistan in developing nuclear technological capacities. China sold special industrial furnaces and high-technology diagnostic equipment to unsafeguarded nuclear facilities in Pakistan. China's Nuclear Energy Industrial Corporation was the source of this equipment.

China also supplied Pakistan with ring magnets, drawings and designs for the manufacture of nuclear bombs. Chinese high-temperature furnaces facilitated Pakistan's manufacture of tritium moulds for the nose cones of the missiles that would carry warheads. The US has been the source of material such as zirconium and Kryton electric triggers for nuclear bombs. Germany and some Scandinavian countries have been the source of electronic components, tritium purification and production facilities. China supplied Pakistan both highly enriched uranium and complete drawings and designs for a 25 kiloton nuclear bomb in 1983.

A Pakistani nuclear device was reportedly tested at the Chinese testing site at Lop Nor in Xiniiang in 1987. By 1992, both Abdul Qadir Khan and Foreign Secretary Shahryar Khan had confirmed that Pakistan was a nuclear weapons capable state. By 1995-96, Pakistani political leaders had started threatening India with a nuclear response if India took decisive military action against Pakistani intrusion into Jammu and Kashmir. Certain aspects of Pakistan's nuclear programme are quite clear. First, the primary motivation of Pakistan was to harness nuclear energy only for military and weapon purposes. Second, the programme was generally under the control of the Pakistani military establishment. Third, Pakistan's nuclear weapons programme was mostly a clandestine operation, connived at by the US during the Soviet intervention in Afghanistan.

Pakistan will woo the nuclear weapons powers by giving them assurances that it will unconditionally adhere to all discriminatory non-proliferation regimes if India were to do the same, which India evidently cannot. Yet, in some respects, India should be relieved Pakistan has gone ahead and tested its nuclear devices and declared itself a nuclear weapons state. Such a move has ensured greater transparency about Pakistan's capacities and intentions. It also removes the complexes, suspicions and uncertainties about each other's nuclear capacities. A certain parity in nuclear weapons and missile capacities will put in place structured and mutual deterrents. These could persuade the Governments of India and Pakistan to discuss bilateral disputes in a more rational manner.

While being alert about threats inherent in Pakistan's nuclear weapons capacities, India should engage in a purposive and continuous dialogue with Pakistan in order to forge a stable security environment in South Asia. We should attempt to put in place credible mutual and equal security guarantees. I think India and Pakistan should seriously discuss and finalise agreements on the "no first use" of nuclear capacities. The manner in which India and Pakistan will cope with this challenge depends on the motivations that led to their decision to acquire nuclear weapons. Ultimately, it will depend on the extent to which the acquisition of such enormous military capacities will make them mature and self-disciplined in resolving antagonisms.

A reference to public opinion in India and Pakistan to the holding of tests would be pertinent at this juncture. While the majority of people in both countries supported the decision to become nuclear weapons states, there was one difference in public reactions to these developments between the two countries. Compared to Pakistan, there was more dissent and criticism in India. A fair segment of intellectuals and academics in India questioned the wisdom of the Vajpayee Government's decision to make India a nuclear weapons state. The criticism ranged from questioning the decision on moral grounds to objections based on economic, strategic, security and political considerations. While there was mass support, it has to be acknowledged that there is still no national consensus amongst the political elite. In contrast, there was greater unanimity in Pakistani public reaction. Their reaction was that Pakistan's acquiring this capacity was not just desirable but imperative to counter possible threats from India. There was also the undercurrent of feeling that Pakistan's achievement went beyond national dimensions, that Pakistan had done the Islamic countries proud and that Pakistan had emerged as a major Islamic power.

Reports over the past two years, since the beginning of 2000, estimate that though Pakistan may have fewer nuclear warheads, it has a more effective and deployable delivery system both in terms of aircraft and missiles. The speculative assessment is that Pakistan has converted its F-16 and Mirage aircraft to carry nuclear warheads. It is believed that while India is still developing and perfecting various categories of its missiles, Pakistan has tested the M-11 missiles supplied by China and the Nodong missiles supplied by North Korea. There have also been reports that Pakistan has finalised its command and control systems to manage its nuclear weapons systems and related arrangements. Most of these reports emanate from Western academic and specialised sources. While India may have more nuclear warheads and the capacity to produce a larger number, it is believed that India's delivery systems are still in the experimental stage and that India has not as yet finalised its command and control systems to manage its nuclear weapons and missile capacities. Neither the Government of India nor the Government of Pakistan has given out any definitive information on these speculative assessments.

The rationale for Pakistan's nuclear weapons programme continuously harped on is that Pakistan has always been quantitatively and technologically weaker than India in military terms. India's counter-argument is that in terms of the ratio between defence responsibilities and the size of the armed forces, specially in terms of territorial defence from external aggression, this argument is not valid. It would be relevant, therefore, to mention the factual position in terms of conventional military balance between the two countries, which would include not just the regular armed forces, but also the paramilitary forces and the equipment which they have. The most fundamental factor while undertaking this comparative assessment is the territorial factor. India has a roughly 2000-kilometre border with Pakistan (including the Line of Control). It has another 3500–3800-kilometre boundary stretching from Ladakh in the northwest to Arunachal Pradesh in the east. In addition, it has a 1600-kilometre border with Myanmar and southwestern China. This is apart from India's borders with Bangladesh, and the coastline stretching from West Bengal to the Gulf of Cambay. India has a regular land army of 1,303,000 and an additional reserve of 535,000. India has 3414 battle tanks (out of which about 1100 are not readily deployable). It has about 4500 artillery pieces, about 2400 air defence guns and about 1800 surface-to-air missiles of various categories. The size of the Indian Navy is about 53,000 including 5000 naval aviation personnel and 1000 marines. It has 16 submarines, most of them obtained from the former Soviet Union. It has 26 surface combat ships which include 8 destroyers, 12 frigates and 5 corvettes. India has 38 corvettes in its Coastguard services. The navy is equipped with a variety of conventional weapons and missiles. The naval aviation wing is primarily equipped with Sea Harrier and Chetak helicopters and has 37 combat aircraft. The Indian Air Force has a strength of 150,000 personnel. It has 774 combat aircraft and 34 armed helicopters of the larger size. India's paramilitary forces consist of the National Security Guard, the Special Frontier Force, the Rashtriya Rifles, the Defence Security Corps, the Indo-Tibetan Border Police, the Assam Rifles, the Railway Protection Force, the Central Industrial Security Force, the Central Reserve Police Force, the Border Security Force, the Home Guard, the State Armed Police, the Civil Defence Corps and the Coastguard. The total strength of these 14 paramilitary cadres is roughly 1,066,000.

Compared to this, the strength of the Pakistani armed forces is 1,225,000. The army has 550,000 personnel, 2885 battle tanks, 1467 artillery pieces, more than 2000 air defence guns and nearly 400 surface-to-air missiles which include Stingers, M-11 and M-9 missiles. The Pakistani Navy has 22,000 personnel, 10 submarines and 8 surface combat ships, mostly frigates. It has 9 coastal patrol seacraft and an air wing with 40 aircraft. The Pakistani marine force has a strength of 12,000 men. The Pakistani Air Force has 40,000 personnel, 353 main combat aircraft and bombers. The Pakistani Navy is equipped with Exocet missiles and surface-to-air missiles. The Air Force is equipped with Exocet, Harpoon, Sparrow, Sidewinder and Magic missiles. Pakistan has 6 paramilitary cadres with a strength of 288,000. The para-military cadres are the National Guard, the Frontier Corps, the Pakistan Rangers, the Northern Light Infantry, the Maritime Security Agency and the Coastguard.

Though Pakistan is less than one-third the size of Indian territory and it has to guard frontiers roughly one-sixth of the frontiers India has to, Pakistan's armed forces, paramilitary forces and equipment measure more than 60 per cent of the strength of the armed forces of India. Given India's defence responsibilities, apart from the frontier with Pakistan, the most optimistic interpretation would be of India and Pakistan being evenly matched in terms of their conventional military strengths, in the sectors in which they are likely to confront each other. Pakistan's nuclear weapons programme and its substantive defence cooperation with China in the spheres of nuclear and missile weapons, therefore, constitute an additional tangible and perceptible threat. One cannot also avoid coming to the conclusion that China's continuing help to Pakistan to build up its military strength is a calculated step aimed at keeping India under pressure. India's nuclear and missile weapons programme, therefore, has been and is unavoidable and can be reasonably termed as a pre-emptive measure in defence preparedness.

What are the nuclear weapons capabilities of India and Pakistan? Since the nuclear tests, by the International Institute of Strategic Studies and the US Natural Resources Defence Council have estimated that India's stockpile of separated-weapons grade plutonium would be between 330 and 400 kilograms plus or minus 30 per cent, enough to manufacture between 65 and 100 nuclear warheads by the year 2005. The US agencies have also acknowledged that India has a capacity to manufacture, deploy and deliver two such thermonuclear weapons. The Congressional Research Service of the US projects a higher estimate of India's nuclear capacities, putting it at between 390 and 470 warheads. As far as delivery systems go, India has the more sophisticated categories of fighter bomber aircraft from Russia and the French Mirage. India has also tested the medium-range Prithvi and the intermediate-range Agni missiles. India has also some initial capacities to launch nuclear weapons from sea-based platforms, such as the "Delhi" class destroyers or submarines of Russian origin. The same sources mentioned above estimate that as Pakistan's nuclear weapons and missiles are based on tested weapons systems supplied by China and North Korea, its nuclear weapons capacities therefore would be more proven and reliable than ours.

Dr. Abdul Qadir Khan, assessing the ramifications of the six nuclear tests carried out by Pakistan at the Chagai Hills at the end of May 1998, confirmed that Pakistan's nuclear weapons tests were based on boosted fission devices using Uranium 235. He asserted that Pakistan has a sufficient stockpile of fissile material for the production of nuclear weapons, namely, highly enriched uranium produced at the centrifuge plant at Katuha near Islamabad. Pakistan's stockpiles in 1999 were estimated at between 450 and 600 kilograms, sufficient to produce 20 to 30 nuclear warheads. Making long-term projections, US experts have suggested that Pakistan is capable of possessing about 100 nuclear warheads by the year 2020. Apart from being able to deliver the warheads by F-16 aircraft, Pakistan also has sufficient stocks of fully tested Ghauri and M-11 missiles, apart from Hatf-I and Hatf-II missiles for delivering tactical nuclear weapons.

The general rationale behind India's nuclear weapons programme was articulated by Prime Minister Vajpayee in his statement in the Indian Parliament a fortnight after India's nuclear tests on 27 May 1998. It is worthwhile quoting relevant extracts of this statement in extenso because there is no clearer articulation of India's policies:

"The decades of the 1980s and 1990s had witnessed the gradual deterioration of our security environment as a result of nuclear and missile proliferation. In our neighbourhood, nuclear weapons had increased and more sophisticated delivery systems inducted. In addition, India has also been the victim of externally aided and abetted terrorism, militancy and clandestine war.

"At a global level, we see no evidence on the part of the nuclear weapons states to take decisive and irreversible steps in moving towards a nuclear weapon-free world. Instead, we have seen that the NPT has been extended indefinitely and unconditionally, perpetuating the existence of nuclear weapons in the hands of the five countries.

"Under such circumstances, the government was faced with a difficult decision. The touchstone that has guided us in making the correct choice clear was national security. These tests are a continuation of the policies set into motion that put this country on the path of self-reliance and independence of thought and action.

"India is now a nuclear weapons state. This is a reality that cannot be denied. It is not a conferment that we seek, nor is it a status for others to grant. It is an endowment to the nation by our scientists and engineers. It is India's due, right of one-sixth of humankind. Our strengthened capability adds to our sense of responsibility. We do not intend to use these weapons for aggression, or for mounting threats against any country; these are weapons of self-defence, to ensure that India is not subjected to nuclear threats or coercion. We do not intend to engage in an arms race.

"We had taken a number of initiatives in the past, we regret that these proposals did not receive a positive response from other nuclear weapons states. In fact, had their response been positive, we need not have gone in for our current testing programme. We have been and will continue to be in the forefront of the calls for open negotiations for a Nuclear Weapons Convention, so that this challenge can be dealt with in the same manner that we have dealt with the scourge of two other weapons of mass destruction — through the Biological Weapons Convention and the Chemical Weapons Convention.

"Traditionally, India has been an outward-looking country. Our strong commitment to multilateralism is reflected in our active participation in organisations like the United Nations. This engagement will continue. The policies of economic liberalisation introduced in recent years have increased our regional and global linkages and my government intends to deepen and strengthen these ties.

"Our nuclear policy has been marked by restraint and openness. We have not violated any international agreements either in 1974 or now, in 1998. The restraint exercised for 24 years, after having demonstrated our capability in 1974, is in itself a unique example. Restraint, however, has to arise from strength. It cannot be based upon indecision or doubt. The series of tests recently undertaken by India have led to the removal of doubts. The action involved was balanced in that it was the minimum necessary to maintain what is an irreducible component of our national security calculus.

"Subsequently, the government had already announced that India will now observe a voluntary moratorium and refrain from conducting underground nuclear test explosions. We have also indicated willingness to move towards de jure formalisation of this declaration.

"The House is no doubt aware of the different reactions that have emanated from the people of India and from different parts of the world.

"The overwhelming support of our citizens is our source of strength. It tells us not only that this decision was right but also that our country wants a focused leadership, which attends to their security needs. This, I pledge to do as a sacred duty. We have also been greatly heartened by the outpouring of support from Indians abroad. They have, with one voice, spoken in favour of our action. To the people of India, and to Indians abroad I convey my profound gratitude. We look to the people of India and Indians abroad for support in the difficult period ahead.

"In this, the fiftieth year of our Independence, we stand at a definite moment in our history. The rationale for the government's decision is based on the same policy tenets that have guided us for five decades. These policies have been sustained successfully because of an underlying national consensus. It is vital to maintain the consensus as we approach the next millennium. In my statement today, and in the paper placed before the House, I have elaborated on the rationale behind the government's decision and outlined our approach for the future. The present decision and future actions will continue to reflect a commitment to the sensibilities and obligations of an ancient civilisation, a sense of responsibility and restraint, but a restraint born of the assurance of action, not of doubts and apprehension. Avoiding triumphalism, let us work together towards our shared objective in ensuring that as we move towards a new millennium, India will take its rightful place in the international community."

Like space, India's nuclear weapons programme therefore was a response to four factors. First, the general deterioration of the security environment in the West Asian, Central Asian and South Asian region, characterised by the presence of nuclear weapons in the area. Second, the incremental nuclear and missile weapons programme of Pakistan and China posed a threat to India in security and strategic terms. Third, there were clear indications that the existing nuclear weapons states had no intention of giving up their nuclear weapons. And fourth, there was clearly a discernible attempt by these nuclear states to try to forge and impose restrictive regimes aimed not only at non-proliferation but also at preventing the transfer and evolution of sophisticated technologies by and for developing countries. The Missile Control Technology Regime, the stipulations about transfer of nuclear material and related technologies, the London and Australian Clubs, the manner in which the Comprehensive Test Ban Treaty was finalised, and the indefinite extension of the Non-Proliferation Treaty characterised this last factor. Another consideration which impelled India towards its nuclear weapons programme was the governing awareness of Pakistan's nuclear capability.

India's nuclear doctrine is rooted in the prime minister's parliamentary statement quoted above and the factors just mentioned. The doctrine was drafted by a subcommittee of the National Security Advisory Board comprising strategic analyst K. Subrahmanyam, former foreign secretary, M.K. Rasgotra, former chairman of the Atomic Energy Commission Raja Ramana, then professor at the Centre for Policy Research defence expert and professor at the Centre for Policy Research, Bharat Karnard, and former chief of army staff, General S.F. Rodrigues. This draft was discussed by the full National Security Advisory Board and submitted to the Government of India in August-September 1999. The cardinal elements in the doctrine are: first, that India would not use nuclear weapons for aggression or as a threat to any country. Second, that the purpose of India's nuclear weapons is not to engage in an arms race with Pakistan or China or any other country. Third, that India's acquisition of nuclear weapons and missile capacity is essentially for purposes of self-defence and to ensure that India does not become subject to nuclear threats or politico-strategic coercion based on any other country's nuclear weapons capacity. Fourth, that consistent with India's commitment to the ultimate objective of elimination of all weapons of mass destruction, India will unilaterally observe a moratorium on conducting further nuclear tests of all categories. Fifth, that India will adhere to the principle of no-first-use of nuclear weapons against Pakistan or any other nuclear weapons state, nor would India use nuclear weapons against any state that has no nuclear weapons and is not under the nuclear weapons security umbrella of any other country. Sixth, the objective of India's nuclear programme is to create, maintain and sustain a minimum credible and effective deterrent capacity against external nuclear threats. Seventh, that the authority to exercise the nuclear weapons option in self-defence will rest entirely with the civilian segment of the Government of India, with the elected prime minister of India who is accountable to the Indian Parliament. And eighth, that the operational command and control systems would be entrusted to the armed forces, who would implement the option in consultation with relevant scientific and technical personnel once the overall strategic and tactical decision is taken by the civilian authority.

While the nuclear doctrine document has been submitted to the government by the National Security Advisory Board, it is still described as a recommendatory document. The doctrine has yet to be discussed by the Cabinet and is in Parliament for finalisation, at the time of writing this chapter. One anticipates nevertheless that the constituent elements of the doctrine document as summarised above will not be changed, and that it is likely to be accepted with some minor modifications. The doctrine also states that if subjected to nuclear attack by any country, India's endeavour and approach would be to retaliate by a second strike, which would be punitive, and aim at imposing acceptable damage on the concerned nuclear adversary.

There has been curiosity about the quality and quantity of nuclear weapons systems and missiles that would constitute the minimum credible effective deterrent — not only from Pakistan but from a number of important powers. India's response has been that effective minimum deterrence cannot be a static phenomenon. The quality and quantity of deterrent capacities will change according to the perceived threat, the nuclear weapons posture of potential enemies and the required extent of the second strike response. This is logical in keeping with the nuclear doctrines of the older nuclear powers.

I must also mention the populist emotionalism that followed the nuclear tests in Pokhran in 1998. It was equally jingoistic and irrational. I was witness to this particular phenomenon because I was participating in a seminar in Jodhpur (near Pokhran) on the day the second Indian Shakti test was held, namely, 13 May 1998. Cadres of the Bharatiya Janata Party and its organisations like the Rashtriya Swayamsevak Sangh (RSS) and Vishwa Hindu Parishad (VHP), announced plans to proceed to Pokhran and collect sand and debris from around the site of the nuclear tests and carry it in sanctified urns to different parts of India to install as centres for political and social celebrations. It was only the sobriety and rationality of Prime Minister Vajpayee that prevented this foolishly emotional exercise. The prime minister personally intervened, refusing public access to the sites of the nuclear tests for some time.

I have already mentioned that there was general public support for India's nuclear weapons programme. But this did not translate into an untrammelled national consensus. Fairly influential Indian intellectuals, academics and journalists were critical of India's decision to conduct nuclear tests. Their argument was that the exercise was an expensive one which India could not afford. Second, by conducting tests India provoked Pakistan to conduct tests, thereby commencing a disastrous arms race in the South Asian region. They averred that India lost the high moral ground on disarmament and the non-proliferation issues. Also that India had moved away from the Nehruvian idealism of commitment to disarmament and peace, and that acquisition of these weapons have only augmented threats to India instead of reducing them. Further, there was no specific event or development that required India to conduct these nuclear tests and declare itself a nuclear weapons state. The answers to these criticisms are available in the earlier portions of this chapter dealing with the evolution and history of India's nuclear weapons programme and therefore need no repetition.

Pakistan's response to the Indian nuclear tests in terms of attitudes and policies has been ambiguous and less formally documented. First came Nawaz Sharif's statement that Pakistan was obliged to exercise the nuclear option due to the weaponisation of India's nuclear programme. Pakistan had to respond to the radically altered strategic balance in the South Asian region because of this. Pakistan then decided to acquire nuclear weapons and to equip itself with delivery systems in the interest of national self-defence, to deter aggression whether nuclear or conventional. It is the last portion of his statement which spells out the most significant element of Pakistan's nuclear doctrine. The point made is that Pakistan will use its nuclear weapons capacity to deter even a conventional military threat. Though Pakistan has not announced any formal nuclear doctrine like India, the main elements of Pakistan's nuclear doctrine can be discerned as follows:

First, Pakistan will use its nuclear weapons to counter even a primarily conventional conflict situation if it feels threatened with military defeat. Pakistan will resort to "first use" of nuclear weapons without limiting them to deterring only a nuclear threat from India. Pakistan's ambassador to the UN Conference on Disarmament in Geneva elaborated the concept in July 1998 stating that with Pakistan's aquisition of nuclear weapons, a situation of overall mutual deterrence now exists between India and Pakistan. Pakistan will seek to maintain this situation of deterrence in future. The level at which this deterrence is maintained and will be maintained will be determined, in accordance with any escalatory steps taken by India. Though its interest is maintaining nuclear deterrence at the lowest possible level, the governing consideration would be to safeguard Pakistan's strategic vulnerability in certain areas such as fissile materials, and ballistic missiles. The Government of Pakistan in official statements advocated that permanent members of the Security Council and the industrially advanced "Group of 8" countries should persuade India not to deploy its nuclear weapons delivery systems. Pakistan, however, did not give any similar undertaking not to deploy its own weapons systems. The next element in Pakistan's nuclear doctrine is that given the asymmetry of conventional weapons capabilities between India and Pakistan, in which India has superiority, Pakistan reserves the right of "first use" of nuclear weapons against India. Pakistan has announced that it has put in place its command and control systems to manage its nuclear weapons capacities. This command and control system and the final authority for exercising the nuclear weapons options rests with the Pakistani military high command which will exercise this authority in consultation with the prime minister. For the present this provision for consulting civilian authorities is redundant because Pakistan is under the military rule of General Pervez Musharraf.

Pakistan has so far not given any commitment about not holding further nuclear tests. Its stand is that it will adhere to the provisions of these regimes only if India first abides by such provisions whenever they come into force. The Pakistani nuclear doctrine found expression at the highest political levels during the Kargil conflict between May and July 1999. Prime Minister Nawaz Sharif stated in the initial stages that Pakistan was fully equipped to meet any nuclear threat from India. Foreign Minister Sartaj Aziz and Foreign Secretary Shamshad Ahmed Khan went one step further to say that Pakistan will not hesitate to use any weapon in its arsenal to defend its territorial integrity. India interpreted these as veiled nuclear threats during the Kargil conflict. The speculative assessment in India at that time was that Pakistan's lack of geo-strategic depth and the reach of India's conventional forces, especially Indian aircraft, would mean that Pakistani leaders would be inclined to use their nuclear weapons capacities early, to pre-empt any defeat by Indian conventional forces. Given this juxtaposition of India's and Pakistan's doctrines and postures, foreign experts have suggested that there is a risk of a dangerous misunderstanding between India's and Pakistani's perceptions of what they would do in terms of their respective nuclear weapons utilisation when a conflict situation between them reaches levels of criticality. As Pakistan claims to be at a military disadvantage, it would be interested in maintaining deterrence power and be ready to use nuclear weapons in the early stages of a conflict if it felt seriously threatened. Indian authorities, on the other hand, may believe that Pakistan would be restrained from early use of nuclear weapons due to massive Indian nuclear retaliation. The result is and would be a highly uncertain situation with dangerous implications. Pakistan's inclination to be trigger-happy in nuclear terms seems plausible, given the fact that the final authority of command and control over nuclear weapons would rest with the joint staff headquarters aided by a military secretariat. Neither is responsible to any elected institutions.

India and Pakistan therefore face a volatile predicament in managing the ramifications of their nuclear and missile weapons programmes. It was the profound awareness of this situation that animated Atal Behari Vajpayee's visit to Lahore on 22 February 1999. The most important item on the agenda of Vajpayee's discussions with Nawaz Sharif was to come to some agreement with Pakistan on avoiding nuclear confrontation, and preparations for discussing this item on the agenda were undertaken nearly three months before the visit took place. The result, a separate memorandum of understanding signed between India and Pakistan at this Lahore meeting to create a joint working group of technical experts and officials from the concerned departments of the two governments to negotiate and finalise an agreement maintaining strategic restraints between the two countries in the context of their nuclear weaponisation. The stated objective of this memorandum was to prevent nuclear confrontation and, more important, accidental nuclear conflict between the two countries. The memorandum was also based on the confidence-building measures agreed upon between the two countries between 1989 and 1994. These were that neither country would attack the other's nuclear installations. A suggestion from India in 1994 that this non-attack provision should be expanded to cover population centres and major economic facilities was rejected by Pakistan.

Second, neither country would intrude into the other's airspace. Both countries agreed to give advance notice to each other about military movements and exercises. It was also agreed that military exercises would be conducted by both countries at stipulated distances from the international frontier. India and Pakistan had also signed a bilateral agreement on the complete prohibition of chemical weapons, even before the UN Convention on Chemical Weapons came into force in 1997. Apart from these, provisions were made for telephone hotlines to be established between armed forces headquarters, offices of foreign secretaries and between the two prime ministers. Experience has shown that while confidence-building measures served their purpose to a limited extent, the telephone hotlines were not used much after 1994, except for a weekly routine conversation every Thursday between the director-generals of military operations of the two countries. None of the hotlines were used during the Kargil conflict, except towards the end of June as the Indian military campaign succeeded and Pakistan came under US pressure to pull back.

The memorandum of understanding on strategic restraint remained an exercise on paper because of the Kargil conflict. Matters were made worse when General Pervez Musharraf after he took over power described the Lahore process and resulting agreements as a farce. The result has been a stalemate on the nuclear confrontation issue. Though this is the position at the governmental level, people with reason and common sense from both countries have commenced discussions using non-governmental channels to remedy the dangerous ramifications. Non-governmental think-tanks from Pakistan and from India have been engaged in serious discussions since the beginning of 2000 to suggest procedures to prevent a nuclear conflict and to create confidence-building measures and an atmosphere of strategic stability between the two countries. Organisations like the Delhi Policy Group, the Centre for Policy Research, the Centre for Peace and Conflict Resolution, all from India, and entities like the Institute of Strategic Studies and the Centre for Defence and Strategic Studies of Pakistan have been engaged in discussions.

It is an irony of history that within one year of both countries completing the 50th anniversary of their independence, they have completed the process of becoming overt nuclear weapons powers. They have entered the

21st century bringing upon themselves the challenge of tackling the implications of being endowed with enormous destructive power. Future generations of Indians and Pakistanis will judge the current leaders on the basis of the options they choose. One hopes that reason and common sense will prevail.

Ten

Retrospect and Prospects

There is a theory among certain schools of Indian historians that but for three events stretching from the 16th to the 20th centuries, subcontinental India would not have been partitioned on the basis of Islam and Hinduism. The first event was Aurangzeb defeating his older brother, Crown Prince Dara Shikoh, at the battle of Samugarh in the summer of 1658. The second event was Ahmed Shah Abdali defeating combined Maratha and Mughal forces in the third battle of Panipat in June 1761. The third event was Motilal Nehru suggesting and Mahatma Gandhi agreeing to Jawaharlal Nehru becoming president of the Congress Party at the young age of 40, marginalising Mohammad Ali Jinnah in national politics.

Despite his princely arrogance and bad public relations, Dara Shikoh would have been an emperor in the mould of Akbar the Great governing the Indian empire on the basis of tolerance, mutual accommodation and non-discrimination between Muslims and Hindus. Aurangzeb's victory and his deep adherence to orthodox Islam divided his subjects on the basis of religion, despite his having many Hindus in his administrative and military setup. Abdali destroyed the political and military power of the Marathas. Jinnah, before moving to convictions about a two-nation theory, was acknowledged as an "ambassador to Hindu-Muslim unity" and was an active member of the Indian National Congress. His being denied its leadership, combined with Mahatma Gandhi's personal charisma rooted in Hindu philosophical thought, led him to become an advocate of a separate Muslim

351

state in subcontinental India. The point being made is that the adversarial relationship between India and Pakistan pre-dates the Partition of India by a long span of time. The British Imperium found it both useful and necessary to nurture and accentuate the socio-cultural divide between the Hindus and Muslims of India, giving it political expression. Curzon dividing the province of Bengal on the basis of communal demography, and the British Government making reserved seats, communal awards and separate electorates for Hindus and Muslims respectively and incrementally in their constitutional reforms between 1909 and 1935 germinated the seeds not only of Partition, but of political antagonism between the two communities. It is an interesting footnote to history that the All India Muslim League was founded soon after Curzon's dividing Bengal into two provinces consisting of Muslim and Hindu majorities. The Muslim League was founded by Aga Khan Sultan Mohammad Shah, the religious and socio-political leader of the Khoja Muslim Ismaili community. He along with Nawab Viqarul Mulk, founded the League on 31 December 1906 with active encouragement from the British Government. The main objectives of the League, as declared in its initial charter, were to promote loyalty to the British Government, to protect and advance the socio-political and economic interests of Indian Muslims, and lastly and ironically, to prevent feelings of hostility towards other communities. By the late 1920s, the Muslim League was expressing the aspirations of Muslims advocating the continuation of British rule in India, the separate representation of Muslims in the legislatures and the executive branches of the British Government (both at the centre and in the provinces) and an insistence that Muslims should find separate reserved representation in the entire administrative structure of the Government of India and Indian armed services. In 1932-33, a young Indian Muslim student at Cambridge, Chaudhuri Rahmat Ali, had written his now-famous paper on the need for a separate homeland for Muslims. By the mid-1930s, prominent Muslim scholar, poet and litterateur Allama Iqbal, endorsed the idea of the creation of "a Muslim India within the body politic of India".

The years 1929 and 1930 were also the period when Mohammad Ali Jinnah became disillusioned with the Congress because of Mahatma Gandhi and the two Nehrus (Motilal and Jawaharlal) dominating the Congress and in consequence, national politics, diminishing his chances of personifying a composite national leadership. Allama Iqbal encouraged him to assume the leadership of the Muslim community, as Iqbal was also disillusioned with the Congress by then. British authorities both in India and from London encouraged his inclination towards the communal division of civil society in the subcontinent. Muslim League representatives were invited as a separate entity to participate in the Round Table Conferences for Indian constitutional review in 1929 and 1931.

Jinnah added new ingredients to the political platform of the Muslim League.

First and foremost, he claimed that he and the Muslim League should be acknowledged as the sole representatives of the Muslim community in India. Second, he proceeded to assert that the Muslim homeland in India should consist of the Muslim-majority provinces (even though the majority was only marginal) and that the whole of Assam and Bengal should be part of it. Third, he took the deliberate decision to project the Indian National Congress as "a Hindu party". He went to the extent of labelling Muslim public figures like Khan Abdul Ghaffar Khan, Dr M.A. Ansari, Hakim Ajmal Khan and Maulana Abul Kalam Azad as Hindu stooges. However, the advocacies of the Muslim League, as summed up above, failed to evoke enthusiasm and response from the Muslims of Punjab, the North West Frontier Province, Sindh and even in Uttar Pradesh and Assam. Nevertheless, Jinnah managed to convert the Muslim League into a mass party of Muslims between 1937 and 1940. His unequivocal and unconditional support for Britain against Germany at the beginning of the Second World War contrasted with the conditional support the Indian National Congress offered. The conditions stipulated by the Indian National Congress were that decisions regarding Indian participation in the Second World War should be taken in consultation with Indian political representatives, and second, that Britain should commit in advance the grant of dominion status and then freedom to India as a quid pro quo.

Winston Churchill's government naturally felt good about the Muslim League as compared to the negotiating tactics of the Congress. Britain also felt that sustaining its hold over India would depend on having two separate territorial entities in its empire, one a Muslim homeland and another for the Hindus, with the Muslims of India guaranteeing their continuation in power in India. There was active support from the British Government to what is known as the Pakistan Resolution, passed by the Lahore Session of the Muslim League in March 1940. The resolution propounded the two-nation theory, asserting that Muslims constituted a separate nation and that areas in which Muslims were numerically in the majority should be autonomous and sovereign. The resolution did not demand full independence, but envisaged the continuation of general British control over the subcontinent, with the Muslim League and its desired territorial identity being treated on a par with the political aspirations of the Indian National Congress. After the defeat of Churchill's Conservative Government in

Britain, the Labour Government led by Clement Attlee declared its intention of relinquishing control over India. In fact, the British Government had initiated the process of giving more self-government to India in 1942 itself, as envisaged in the proposals put forward by the Cripps Mission. Sir Stafford Cripps had suggested extensive delegation of powers to a federal government of India with dominion status and providing for separate power-sharing arrangements for the Muslims. Mahatma Gandhi had described the Cripps proposals as "a post-dated cheque on a crashing bank". Jinnah and the Muslim League, however, took full advantage to consolidate their campaign and make their demands acceptable to the British.

By 1945, the British Government had realised that it could not hold on to the Indian empire. There was a groundswell of assertive demands for independence among the Indian people. Indian military personnel in the British Indian armed forces were becoming progressively alienated from the British Government. Their loyalty could not be relied on. Indians in the civil administration of India were also deeply influenced by the Indian Freedom Movement, particularly the Quit India Movement of 1942. International public opinion and the declared policies of the allied powers during the Second World War, particularly those of the US, had expressed support for the self-determination and independence of the colonial peoples. Britain could hold on to the Indian empire only at unaffordable economic cost. So by late 1945, the Labour Government in England decided to disengage from India and give it full dominion status by the summer of 1948.

Once the Cripps Mission and the UK Cabinet Mission led by Lord Pethick Lawrence failed in persuading Indian political parties to accept the creation of an Indian dominion under loose confederational arrangements, Britain took the decision to partition India on the basis of the religious identities of Hindus and Muslims, accepting the two-nation theory put forward by Ali Jinnah. The discussions and negotiations that led to Partition need no repetition here. However, one aspect of the British geo-strategic objectives is not too well known and merits recall.

The British authorities' aim was ensuring the emergence of the newly-created Pakistan as the most homogeneous, cohesive and strong state in the South Asian region. Their predication was that Islam would be the cementing factor in the creation of the Muslim nation-state of Pakistan. It was also the anticipation that Britain, by granting a separate state to the Muslims of India, would have the assurance of Pakistan becoming a trusted political and strategic ally of the United Kingdom. The new dominion of India, in contrast, was planned as a geopolitical entity with centrifugal prospects. It was to consist of the former British Indian provinces, including those partitioned, like Bengal and Punjab. The 560-odd princely states were to be reverted back to completely independent status they had had in the 18th and 19th centuries. Their treaty obligations with the British Government were to be abolished. These princely states were given complete freedom of option to remain independent or to join India or Pakistan. British expectations were that the princes, nawabs and maharajas, particularly of the larger princely states like Jammu and Kashmir, Hyderabad, Gwalior, Baroda, Bhopal, Travancore, as well as of the princely states of what is today Rajasthan, would opt for independence. The result would be the emergence of a territorially fragmented Indian dominion interspersed with large chunks of territories of the bigger princely states of India. The further hope was that these princely states would also desire a special relationship with the British Government. So the major portion of the subcontinent would still remain subject to British political and strategic influence even after the termination of British imperial rule. It is significant that the India Independence Act left the decision about determining the future status of the princely states to the ruling princes alone and not to the people's movements, which had strong linkages with the freedom movement led by the Congress.

The Foreign and Political Departments of the British Government of India, which functioned under the direct charge of the viceroy, were active in encouraging Indian princes to opt for independence. They even advocated that the Muslim princes accede their territories to the Dominion of Pakistan. Discussions for this purpose were held by the British Political Resident in different native states under the directions of the former foreign secretary, Sir Olaf Caroe, and his British successors, till 1948, when K.P.S. Menon (Sr) took over charge as foreign secretary of India. The proof that the British Government and its officials instigated these fissiparous trends was manifest in the initial policy orientations of the maharajas of Kashmir and Travancore, the nizam of Hyderabad, the nawab of Junagadh and even by the nawab of Bhopal. What the British planners of this scenario did not anticipate was the political acumen and firmness in terms of objectives of Sardar Vallabhbhai Patel, the first deputy prime minister of India, who became the architect of Indian unity by ensuring the accession of the majority of Indian princely states to the newly created Dominion of India. Except in the cases of Hyderabad and Junagadh, Sardar Patel did not have to use coercive force to ensure these accessions. The Muslim League was privy to these machinations because of the close and continuous interaction between the concerned British officials of the Government of India and the leaders of the Muslim League — people like Liaqat Ali Khan, Ghaznafar Ali Khan,

Mumtaz Daulatana and Sardar Abdur Rab Nishtar. Despite all these plans, aimed at making Pakistan emerge as a strong and cohesive power in the subcontinent as compared to India, Pakistan, as it emerged, was subject to frustrations and disappointments. The Muslim League leadership did not get the whole of Punjab, the whole of Bengal and the whole of Assam to be part of Pakistan.

Despite being created as a homeland for Muslims of the subcontinent, the Muslim-majority provinces of Punjab and the North West Frontier Province were not in favour of the creation of Pakistan. The then prime ministers of the two provinces, Dr Khan Sahib of the North West Frontier Province (NWFP) and Sardar Sikandar Hayat and Khizr Hayat Khan of Tiwana in Punjab, opposed the creation of Pakistan. Even more significantly, the majority of Muslims in the British Indian provinces in north, central and south India did not migrate to Pakistan. Jinnah was, therefore, right when he talked about receiving a "moth-eaten and truncated Pakistan".

The consequence was that by the end of the 20th century India had a larger number of Muslim citizens than the whole of Pakistan. There was profound bitterness among the Pakistani leadership and decision-making elite about Jammu and Kashmir and Hyderabad not becoming part of Pakistan at Partition and its immediate aftermath. Pakistani leaders were also not happy about the division of financial and physical assets and the assets of the British Indian armed forces between India and Pakistan, which was based on the territorial size and population of the new entities. Pakistani leaders desired parity, which was neither practical nor logical. Another disappointment was India being declared the successor state to British India, while Pakistan was given the status of a newly created independent country. There were some Pakistani scholars and academics who indulged in the somewhat extraordinary argument that Pakistan should be declared the successor state and not India, because India was under Muslim rule at the point of time when the East India Company and then the British Crown took over the governance of India.

The Pakistani leadership was also unhappy about the geophysical arrangements of Partition. Not getting Assam deprived Pakistan of the oil and potential natural gas resources of Assam. The partition of Bengal resulted in India getting the port of Calcutta and much of the industrial sector of Bengal's economy involving the production of jute, iron, steel and coal. This is apart from Pakistan losing the tea gardens of Assam and north Bengal. Pakistan faced similar disappointments in the western wing also. The Radcliffe Award, which resulted in the district of Gurdaspur and adjacent areas being awarded to India, cut off Pakistan's access to Jammu and

Kashmir from the south. Maharaja Hari Singh acceding the state of Jammu and Kashmir to India resulted in the headwaters of the river systems of Punjab falling under the control of the Government of India. The broad consequences were Pakistan suffering from a sense of territorial inadequacy, and its civil society and leadership suffering from an identity crisis and economic and military insecurity because of the asymmetry between India and Pakistan. Another dimension of this insecurity was the Pakistani view that the machinations of Lord Mountbatten and the Indian National Congress prevented the emergence of a Pakistan encompassing the entire Muslim population of India. This bitterness remains part of the psyche of the power structure of Pakistan.

India's strong action in integrating Jammu and Kashmir, Hyderabad and Junagadh heightened this bitterness and, more important, generated a genuine apprehension that India would try to nullify Partition by subverting the state of Pakistan, by breaking it up or reabsorbing it into what Pakistanis called the Hindu plan of "Akhand Bharat". India's role in the liberation of Bangladesh only reinforced this Pakistani fear psychosis. If this is so, why did Pakistan indulge in military adventures against India in 1948 and 1965? The answer lies in the artificially nurtured memories of Muslim superiority and a subconscious desire to rectify the unfair arrangements of the Partition. The conflict of 1971 tempered Pakistan's inclination towards military adventurism for getting even with India, but short of that, its power structure continues to have the same mindset. The proof of this mindset was Field Marshal Ayub Khan's assessment before he launched the military offensive in Jammu and Kashmir in September 1965 that Hindu India did not have the stamina or determination to face some hard knocks from the Pakistani armed forces.

Another element in the Pakistani mindset is of a certain envy Pakistanis would not acknowledge, but certainly exists. Both countries achieved independence at the same time but while India, despite all its diversities, tensions and problems, has gradually consolidated its democratic and administrative institutions, Pakistan has gone through a roller-coaster ride of constantly changing political arrangements and political institutions which have no coherence and stability. The armed forces remain the ultimate centre of authority. This bothers Pakistanis when they compare themselves with Indians. Instead of taking a practical view of their predicament and being rational about it, they tend to justify the aberrations. They even assert that being different from India in respect of practising democracy is necessary for safeguarding Pakistani identity. This was unwittingly but profoundly reflected in a speech given by Pakistan's then high commissioner in New

Delhi, Riaz Khokhar, on 17 June 1994. He was one of the principal speakers at a function organised to release Mani Shankar Aiyer's book *Pakistan Papers*. Khokar's opening remark was, "Pakistan does not consider India or the Indian political experiment as a relevant model for Pakistan." In this one sentence, he said it all.

The net result of all these trends is of a consistent and continuing policy on the part of Pakistan not to allow normal and easy people-to-people contacts between Indians and Pakistanis. If this were allowed, many of the dogmas, myths and misinterpretations of Indian intentions would be exploded. But this would not suit the vested interests of the existing power structure in Pakistan. The closure of the Indian consulate general in Karachi in January 1995 is but one more manifestation of this phenomenon.

India's Complexes

The Indian mindset also has its complexes. While there is a general cohesiveness in the attitudes and reactions of the Pakistani decision-making groups towards India, this is not so this side of the border. That the people of India have not accepted Partition and that there are undercurrents to re-absorb Pakistan back into India are, however, totally incorrect. They hope that those Muslims who had decided to break away from the Indian (not Hindu) political identity and are now in Pakistan do not add to India's problems. In fact, Hindu extremists are of the view that the remaining Muslims in India should also go away to Pakistan, a prospect Pakistan would not welcome. It is not allowing even its own Mohajir citizens in Bangladesh to come home. That a fair number of Muslims stayed back in India, that they have increased in number and are now an integral part of the Indian polity also generates forces of reason and moderation in the Indian mindset. This approach, however, is eroded each time Pakistan resorts to provocative pronouncements and acts.

The large Muslim citizenry of India is an element within and of the Indian psyche. Muslim citizens who did not opt to go to Pakistan or who could not because of economic and socio-cultural constraints were certainly not happy about Partition. However, when it became a fact, their attitude and mindset confirmed Maulana Azad's prophetic insight that the partition of the subcontinent on communal lines would subject the Muslim community of India to socio-political schizophrenia. Pakistan has taken advantage of the existence of a large Muslim community in India to sow dissension within the polity by arrogating to itself the role of protector. That Indian Muslims remain subject to greater economic pressures and resulting socio-political limitations cannot be denied despite India's genuine and deep commitment to secularism. Consequently, some segments of India's Muslim leadership are not averse to using the leverage of Pakistan's intrusive policies.

Some of my friends, both Indian Muslims and foreign Muslims, have told me that there is also an unarticulated but subconscious feeling among this country's Muslims that the Islamic state of Pakistan generally guarantees a sense of security for them. This is provocative, but could be true nevertheless. This is reflected in the fact that whenever it was, in 1948, 1965 or 1971, the general reaction of India's Muslim community was one of apprehension rather than an acceptance of the reality of Pakistani military adventurism resulting in the firm reactions of India. There is no questioning its patriotism, just its mindset, which has a particular view about Pakistan's role in the subcontinent. I should also mention that there was not much enthusiasm when Bangladesh was liberated. When I state this, I am referring to Muslim reactions and attitudes in generic terms. Muslim leaders active in our national politics, across the spectrum, have been part of the mainstream of political orientations in India. The problem has always been their inability to reach out to the Muslim masses and educate them about their profound relevance to the ideology underpinning the Indian state.

Since claims based on the religious argument on Kashmir do not find international acceptability, depending on the fora in which Pakistan wishes to articulate them, its arguments vary from "Muslims and Islam being in danger" to emphasising the doctrine of self-determination and the ultimately flexible and selective advocacy of human rights. It has gone even further, by crossing the threshold of political and socio-moral arguments to threatening the world at large with possibilities of nuclear holocaust if India is not compelled to accept Pakistani claims. Whatever the later denials by official sources, Pakistan's foreign minister Aseef Ali speculating on this possibility at Tashkent in January 1994 and Nawaz Sharif threatening India with nuclear war on Kashmir at Neela Butt on 24 August 1994, are only a culmination of the calculated whisperings to this effect in the chancellories of the world since 1990. There is also an abiding intellectual and ideological conviction that a successful, plural, multi-religious, democratic and united India is a permanent question mark against the logic by which Pakistan was created. The passing of two generations of Pakistanis into adulthood since Partition has not changed this, notwithstanding the fact that Pakistani people in general are objective and rational.

It is the assessment and orientation of the decision-making and public opinion-making sections of Pakistani society that Pakistan's leadership of the Islamic community can become unchallenged only by the failure of the

Indian socio-political experiment. Pakistani cogitations on the state of minorities in India, its concern about Muslim religious places being harmed in India despite a number of such structures having been affected similarly in Pakistan itself over the past 40 years, and the selective demand for the application of human rights norms through the prism of the Muslim religious identity are only facets of this basic predilection.

Since 1965, and more so since 1971, defence strategists and the military establishment of Pakistan have cultivated an almost self-inflicted masochistic aspiration that its martial traditions and military credibility can only be retrieved by another conflict with India (though for a limited duration), which should result in a decisive victory over India, and that Kashmir provides the catalyst and the opportunity for this purpose. One has only to look through the military doctrines articulated by General Mirza Aslam Beg during his tenure to confirm this. He advocated "offensive defence", etc. This thought-process forms the undercurrent of thinking among the intellectuals and decision-makers in Pakistan. That general bilateral and international political pressure and, where possible, military pressure, should be generated on India to weaken its cohesion and territorial unity comes through clearly in the official memoranda and policy papers of the decades of the 1960s and the 1970s. One has only to read through the relevant portions of Stanley Wolpert's biography of Zulfiqar Ali Bhutto, and the revelations regarding policies towards Indian Punjab and Jammu and Kashmir during Zia's time to confirm these Pakistani motivations.

East Pakistan separating from West Pakistan and emerging as independent Bangladesh has had a traumatic impact on both the ideology of Pakistan and its national identity. Bangladesh claiming separation on the basis of ethnicity and language was a decisive rejection of the two-nation theory. This has been further compounded by centrifugal pressures on the Pakistani polity. The objective reality is that Pakistan is as much a multi-lingual, multi-ethnic, even multi-religious state as is India. The people of Pakistan are divided into the distinct ethnic groups of Sindh, Punjab, the North West Frontier Province and Baluchistan. Even Punjab itself is characterised by a subregional division. The people of southern Punjab claim an identity separate from northern Punjab, with their own language (Saraiki) which they claim to be different from Punjabi. One has to note that Sindhi, Punjabi, Baluchi and Pushto, and Hindustani or Urdu, spoken by the Muslim migrants from Uttar Pradesh and Bihar, are distinct and separate languages, with which the peoples of these Pakistani provinces are linked. The Shia-Sunni divide in Pakistani civil society has remained a constant factor of tension. This is apart from the persecution of smaller Islamic sects like the

Ahmediyas and the Ismailis by the Pakistani authorities since the time of Bhutto. The Pakistani power structure faces the challenge of reconciling the contradiction between the normative terms of reference of Islamic nationhood as a determinant of monolithic homogeneity and the realities of its plural society with multiple linguistic, ethnic and religious identities. The point is, it refuses to acknowledge these contradictions and resolve them by rational political means. It continues to harp on the ideology of Pakistan rooted in Islam. The consequence of this refusal to acknowledge the widening political realities has been the decision-making elite nurturing the conviction that Pakistan's Islamic national identity can only be sustained by having an adversarial relationship with Bharat, that is "Hindu India". One dimension of this reaction, as already mentioned is the aspiration to fragment India territorially and politically. The second dimension has been the feeling that East Pakistan's breaking away and the emergence of Bangladesh should be avenged by ensuring the elimination of Jammu and Kashmir, Punjab and the eastern provinces of India from the Indian republic.

It would be pertinent to mention that officer-cadets of the Pakistani National Military Academy at Kakul, while taking the oath of loyalty when completing training, have to commit themselves to two objectives: first, of upholding the ideology of Pakistan, and second, to avenge the military defeat of 1971. These characteristics of Pakistani politics are not a matter of wide public knowledge, but they exist nevertheless. During my tenure as India's ambassador and high commissioner in Pakistan, I heard senior political administrative and military figures telling me that if Pakistan does not exist on its Islamic identity, the justification for the partition of India, the logic of it, will stand negated. The very *raison d'être* of Pakistan will stand nullified. I was also told by them that there is a deep-seated desire among the Pakistani armed forces and political circles to redress the humiliation of the military defeat of 1971, of India having taken 93,000 prisoners of war, the release of whom had to be pleaded for by Z.A. Bhutto.

Mutual Hyperbole

Having referred to the factors affecting the Pakistani mindset, it is necessary to refer to the other side of the coin, namely, the complexes and prejudices characterising the Indian attitude towards Pakistan. Various governments and civil society in India have reconciled themselves to Partition and have no desire to reverse the division of the subcontinent. Yet, at emotional and intellectual levels, the people of India remain opposed to the two-nation theory rooted in Islam. Pakistan's agitations about states belonging to

Muslim nawabs and princes acceding to India and Pakistan continuing territorial claims on Jammu and Kashmir result in a threat perception in India that the long-term political and strategic objective of Pakistan is the territorial fragmentation of the Indian republic by the generation of external tensions and the support of domestic fissiparous trends in Indian civil society. Pakistan's oft-articulated claim of being the protector of the rights and safety of the Muslim minority in India is a major irritant to the people of India. What bothers Indian public opinion more in this regard is the fact of certain Muslim political circles in India accepting this role of Pakistan. The decimation and expulsion of the Hindu minority, particularly from West Pakistan, exacerbates this irritation. Then there are extremist Hindu groups who talk about "Akhand Bharat", advocating the undoing of Partition and unification of the subcontinent. Somewhat paradoxically, some groups also advocate that since Pakistan was created as a homeland for the Muslims of the subcontinent, all the Muslims living in India should migrate to Pakistan. It is fortunate that this approach is not shared by the majority of the people of India.

Pakistan's questioning the credibility of India's commitment to secularism and its derisively critical evaluation of Indian democracy does not help matters. Examples of how such irritants are created are plentiful. The former foreign minister and speaker of the Pakistani National Assembly, Gauhar Ayub Khan — son of Field Marshal Ayub Khan — asserted in a press conference in New Delhi in 1993 that peace and stability could come to the subcontinent only if India broke up into smaller states. He went on to state that Indian unity was an artificial phenomenon and that India would inevitably break up under the pressure of centrifugal, ethnic, linguistic and casteist forces. I recall a conversation in late 1990 or early 1991 when I went to call on him as Indian high commissioner in Islamabad. During the course of the conversation, he proceeded to give a holistic analysis of subcontinental history. He told me that the partition of India was inevitable as the minimal solution to Hindu-Muslim relations in the subcontinent. He stated that Muslims had ruled India for nearly a thousand years and that they could not stay in a unified India as a minority where they did not have supreme power. Muslims were natural rulers. He went on to say that the partition not only geographically conformed to the religious affiliations of Muslims and Hindus, but that it affirmed the basic difference in the nature of the Hindu and Muslim populations. The Muslims, according to him, were religiously committed, they were warlike and aggressive, and they were not given to softness and compromises, whereas Hindus were exactly the opposite: submissive, manoeuvring and clever. He moved on to hyperbole, informing me that even the flora and fauna had a linkage with Partition. While East and West Pakistan had tigers, wild boar, leopards, bulls, etc., India had bison, nilgai, gazelle and deer, most of the latter vegetarian and natural prey to animals on the other side. He came to the high point in this argument while referring to Kashmir. He said that Kashmir will ultimately become part of Pakistan, that this was inevitable. He told me that Indians should all realize the profound capacity for commitment to struggle (*jehad*) amongst the *momin* (Muslim faithful). This commitment, according to him, was underpinned by a win-win situation. If the *jehadi* lost his life in the struggle, he became a *shahid* and went to heaven. If he won the struggle and the war, he became a *gazi* (effulgent, religious victor). He then asked, "What is your response to this analysis of mine?" I gave him a two-part answer. I said that the first point I noticed was that even the animals chose to live in Pakistan or India according to their temperament. While Pakistan became the home of violent and aggressive carnivores, India became the home of the gentler species, though some of them were not lacking in strength. I went on to say that his theories about Muslim politico-military superiority involved a reciting of history as well as of the socio-cultural ingredients of civil societies in the subcontinent. I added that if the *jehadis* are in a win-win situation on the lines mentioned by him, it would be my continuing prayer that they all became *shahids*, so that the violence would come to an end. He told me that this was not how a diplomat should respond. He suggested that I was being impolite. I told him that at times even diplomats are carried away due to the reality of a situation or the extraordinary nature of analyses which are given to them. (I must mention in parentheses that Gauhar Ayub's press conference was given while he was leading a parliamentary delegation to a meeting of the Inter-Parliamentary Union in Delhi. One does not have to speculate too much about the nature of the Indian response to such views.)

There are also some India political and strategic thinkers who feel that India should resort to military means to expel Pakistani forces from those areas of Jammu and Kashmir which they occupy. This school of thought is convinced that the only durable solution to the Kashmir problem is to reunite "Azad Kashmir" with Jammu and Kashmir as part of the Indian republic. The same school of thought also expresses the speculative aspiration that peace in the subcontinent can only be achieved if Pakistan is divided into three or four states — the exact opposite of Ayub's fragmentation dream!

This mutually adversarial canvas does not complete the picture. As if to balance these trends, there has been positive interaction between the people of India and Pakistan. Those Muslims who migrated from Uttar

Pradesh, Bihar, Rajasthan, Hyderabad and Tamil Nadu to Pakistan left behind a large number of their relatives in India. Barring the short periods when actual conflicts take place, on an average, 600,000 to a 1,000,000 people regularly travel from India to Pakistan and from Pakistan to India to meet their relatives. Familial relations and marriages between Mohajir citizens of Pakistan and Indian Muslims continue. In culture and entertainment, there is mutual appreciation and attraction. Despite bans and restrictions imposed occasionally, Indian films have great popularity in Pakistan, as does Indian film music. Conversely, Pakistani artistes are held in high esteem in India. Mehdi Hassan, Iqbal Bano, Ghulam Ali and Nusrat Fateh Ali are cult figures for Indian audiences. Randhir Kapoor and Rishi Kapoor produced a film in the early 1990s in which the heroine was Pakistani Zeba Bakhtiar. In Islamabad, they had to do some shooting in the outer courtyard of the Faisal mosque. There were initial objections from religious authorities. Once the authorities met the Kapoor brothers, permission came through. The Kapoors were treated with equal warmth and affection when they went to Lahore. I also received film actors Shatrughan Sinha and Dilip Kumar and his wife Saira Bano during my stay in Islamabad. They were received by all sections of Pakistani society with courtesy and open-hearted hospitality. The same harmonious and warm interaction characterises the exchanges of poets, authors, senior journalists and intellectuals from both countries. One remembers in this connection, Haroon of the *Dawn* newspaper coming to India, Dr Asma Jehangir participating in conferences in Delhi, and Shekhar Gupta of the *Indian Express* and Bharat Bhushan, then of the *Hindustan Times* going to Pakistan. Kaifi Azmi, Ali Sardar Jafri and Amrita Pritam still fascinate Pakistanis while poets like Faiz captivate Indians. One of the largest and most colourful literary functions I was asked to organise — by then foreign minister, Atal Behari Vajpayee, in 1978-79 — was in honour of Faiz when I was director-general of the Indian Council for Cultural Relations.

I still recall the manner in which the fifth round of official-level talks between the foreign secretaries of Pakistan and India concluded in Islamabad in October 1991. After the official-level discussions, characterised by the usual differences of opinion, Pakistani foreign secretary Shahryar Khan, asked his counterpart Muchkund Dubey what he would like to do in the evening after the concluding session. Dubey said that he would like, if possible, a dinner with a limited number of guests, followed by a musical soiree of Urdu ghazals, possibly sung by Iqbal Bano. The acrimonies of the official discussions were swept away in the enchantment of the evening which Shahryar Khan organised. Iqbal Bano swept all of us off our feet at a concert that lasted for three hours after the dinner, almost till midnight. Unavoidable political realities over Indo-Pak relations were transcended by the cultural and linguistic symbiosis personified in Iqbal Bano and her singing.

Safety Matters

Though there is a general restriction on free distribution of Indian books and literature in Pakistan, a large number of books published in India, particularly on technical, scientific and technological subjects, find their way to the Pakistani market and are lapped up by scholars and students. This proves the point that ideas and intellectual impulses cannot be restricted by decree or national boundaries. Nor can human interest and curiosity be subject to such restrictions. A significant example was the Islamabad Women's International Club seeking my assistance to go on a tour of Delhi, Rajasthan and Jammu and Kashmir immediately after Rajiv Gandhi concluded his visit to Islamabad in July 1989. The chairperson of the club was the wife of the Iraqi ambassador, and the club had a large number of Pakistani ladies as members. The club delegation was to consist mostly of Pakistani women. I referred the matter to Delhi and received an immediate positive response. A week before proceeding on their tour, one of the vice-presidents of the club, a Pakistani lady, called on me and made inquiries on the following lines: Would Pakistani women be safe while travelling in India? Would they have to observe purdah to safeguard themselves? Would they really be allowed to go to Jammu and Kashmir? I told her that I had a clearance for them to go wherever they wanted according to their proposed itinerary. The delegation consisting of 12 to 15 ladies came to India. They visited Delhi and Jaipur, but their culminating positive experience was their visit to Jammu and Kashmir. The then governor of Jammu and Kashmir, General K.V. Krishna Rao, personally received them, ensured that they visited all the interesting tourist spots in the state and, to top it all, personally hosted a reception for them at Gulmarg. The delegation called on me when it returned and expressed satisfaction, not only about the arrangements made for the visit but specially mentioned the fact that their apprehensions about the attitude of the Indian people towards Pakistanis were totally wrong. They marvelled at the freedom with which Indian women carried on their lives and were surprised at the complete lack of any antagonism towards them among the common people.

The purpose of detailing these non-political trends in Indo-Pakistani relations is that perhaps at the fundamental human level, the peoples of

India and Pakistan have no antagonism towards each other. Whatever antagonism there is, is essentially a political phenomenon which does not touch the lives and attitudes of common people in either country. It is only when people-to-people contacts have political ingredients or motivation that antagonism surfaces. An illustrative example is that of Rajya Sabha member and senior journalist Kuldip Nayar proceeding to the Wagah-Attari border on Pakistan's and India's Independence Days, 14 and 15 August in 1997 and 1998. He led a group of 500 Indians to hold a candlelight vigil at the border inviting his friends from Pakistan to come with lighted candles from the other side. This proved to be an unrequited exercise, because nobody came from the Pakistani side. The reason given was that the Government of Pakistan had not approved of such an exercise on the other side of the Wagah-Attari boundary post. It is obvious that the Pakistani authorities perceived Nayar's move to be a thinly disguised political exercise in discrediting the Pakistani Government, in proving that the people of Pakistan do not share the Pakistani government's adversarial attitude towards India.

I have mentioned the background of Prime Minister Vajpayee's significant and unorthodox initiative for normalising relations, his journey by land to the Wagah-Attari border and then on to Lahore in February 1999, in the earlier portions of this book. The visit actually originated in an interview given by then prime minister Nawaz Sharif to Shekhar Gupta, editor-in-chief of the *Indian Express*. Nawaz Sharif expressed willingness to meet Vajpayee at a place and time of mutual convenience. Vajpayee's response was prompt. He decided to use the inauguration of the bus service between Delhi and Lahore to respond to Nawaz Sharif's invitation. The factors that led to his decision were, first and foremost, the promises Nawaz Sharif had made about desiring the restoration of friendly relations during the election campaign that had brought him to power in Pakistan. Second, Nawaz Sharif had given the impression of being constructive and rational in his discussions with Indian leaders preceding Vajpayee. He was also the prime minister of Pakistan, after the restoration of democracy there, who had maximum contact with his Indian counterparts. He had dealt with Chandra Shekhar, Narasimha Rao and Gujral on more or less a continuous basis. Though his public pronouncements were positive about normalising relations with India, the ground realities did not manifest any significant change, particularly in Jammu and Kashmir. Vajpayee, however, felt that responding to Nawaz Sharif's invitation and having a meeting in Lahore would be an imaginative and constructive step in creating the right political atmosphere, as he was also of the view that the nuclear weapons programme of India and Pakistan had created a more critical strategic and security environment in the subcontinent. The hope was that given the ramifications of this programme, Pakistan would be willing to engage India in a substantive dialogue with greater self-confidence and an equally greater awareness of the dangers of a nuclear confrontation. To sum up the objectives of Vajpayee's Lahore initiative, he had first desired India and Pakistan to focus specifically on the critical implications of their nuclear programme and he sought to revive the composite dialogue on all the issues negatively affecting Indo-Pakistani relations. Also, he wanted India and Pakistan to focus specifically on the critical implications of their nuclear programme and missile capacities and to come to some understanding about nuclear risk reduction and to put in place procedures to avoid any accidental nuclear confrontation. At the psychological level, Vajpayee had memories of his being considered one of the most constructive and positive political figures by the government and the people of Pakistan during his two-year tenure as the foreign minister of India in the Morarji Desai Government (1977 and 1979). His anticipation was that both governmental and public response to his visit would be rooted in the trust and positive feelings of the people in Pakistan about him, despite his linkages with what Pakistanis felt was a Hindu party. The visit resulted in a declaration stipulating the restoration of a bilateral dialogue on all the subjects affecting bilateral relations and a separate memorandum of understanding to create a joint working group of experts to discuss and evolve mutual confidence-building measures for nuclear risk reduction and the avoidance of accidental nuclear confrontation.

I have already described the atmospherics and the public mood in both countries that the visit generated. The effort proved to be abortive, with Pakistan's incursions into the Kargil area and the resulting conflict occurring within three months of this imaginative move on the part of India. The denouement of the conflict in political terms, was the coup d'etat organised by the Pakistani chief of army staff, General Pervez Musharraf, and his assuming charge as head of Government, dismissing Nawaz Sharif. India's reaction to Musharraf assuming power by force was negative, because it brought an end to democracy in Pakistan. Even more important, General Musharraf was perceived as the architect of what Indians considered the betrayal of the Lahore process at Kargil. The Musharraf Government gave additional reasons for strengthening India's critical and negative perceptions of the new dispensation in Pakistan. Pervez Musharraf, in a lengthy interview to the *The Hindu*, described the discussions held between Nawaz Sharif and Vajpayee as a farce. He went on to state that he would have to re-examine the contents of the Lahore Declaration and the Lahore Memorandum of

Understanding to see if they would serve any meaningful purpose. He also stated more than once in public pronouncements that he would continue his support to the militant separatist movement in Jammu and Kashmir and added that even if the Kashmir problem were solved, the Indo-Pakistan adversarial relationship would continue because of the profound suspicion and mistrust which Pakistanis had of India.

The Indian response to these attitudes was equally trenchant, with a refusal to deal with Musharraf for having scuttled democracy in Pakistan. Policy pronouncements were made that India would not have any dialogue with Pakistan unless the Musharraf Government stopped supporting cross-border terrorism and undertook to create an atmosphere of normality in Jammu and Kashmir. India refused to participate in SAARC meetings from the second half of 1999 onwards and indicated that it did not wish to interact with General Musharraf. India also initiated a campaign to isolate the Musharraf Government in the Non-Aligned Movement, in Commonwealth conferences, and at the UN. This was accompanied by a sustained Indian diplomatic campaign in the capitals of the important powers questioning the legitimacy of the Musharraf Government. Mutual antagonisms stood highly exacerbated till mid-2000.

Though General Musharraf was to be on the defensive because of these moves by India in the initial months after his assuming power, he and his government broke through this isolation, first because the Musharraf regime had undoubted and widespread support from the people of Pakistan, who were highly dissatisfied with the inefficiency and corruption of the elected governments that had been in power from 1988 onwards. Second, Musharraf undertook an extensive diplomatic and political campaign to the important countries of Western Europe and the Islamic states. His domestic acceptability and the pronouncements which he made about restoring democracy resulted in a general consensus in the international community to deal with him. Added to this was the general indication he gave to the US in particular and the international community in general that Pakistan would fall in line with non-proliferation stipulations if India also accepted them. While there was incremental acceptability for his regime, his expelling a democratic government and Pakistan's involvement with cross-border terrorism, particularly its links with the Taliban in Afghanistan, generated undercurrents of reservation about his policies, resulting in consequent pressures on him on issues related to narco-terrorism, religious extremism (*jehad*) and cross-border terrorism activities originating in Pakistan.

The manner in which the then president of the US, Bill Clinton, structured his visit to the subcontinent characterised this pressure, which had a significant impact on Pakistani policies. Clinton visited India, Bangladesh and Pakistan in March 2000. He spent five days in India, approximately five hours in Bangladesh and about four hours in Pakistan. Clinton's demeanour and public pronouncements in Islamabad were deliberately dour and admonitory. He suggested a four-point formula for subcontinental peace and normalisation, namely, respect for the Line of Control in Jammu and Kashmir, restraint and giving up violence on this Line, the restoration of dialogue, and restraint on military posturing rooted in nuclear and missile weaponisation. He conveyed a clear message on Jammu and Kashmir, stating that the US would not endorse attempts to change frontiers and territorial arrangements by violence. It is also to be recalled that Clinton's visit to Pakistan was preceded by the visits of the Commander-in-Chief of the Central Command of the US and the Deputy National Security Adviser of the Russian Federation, both of whom conveyed insistent cautionary messages to Pervez Musharraf. US concerns about Pakistan's involvement with Osama bin Laden and his terrorist operations against the US and Western democracies was an important factor influencing American attitudes and policies. The pressures generated by these events seemed to have a salutary impact on the Pakistani power structure. Pakistan's lenient treatment of the hijackers of the Indian aircraft in December 1999-January 2000 and its insistence on supporting terrorist violence in Kashmir were also part of the critical advocacies of the important powers. The consequence was the emergence of a certain practicality in Pakistan's India policies without it having diluted its basic positions on critical issues affecting Indo-Pakistan relations. Pakistan's foreign minister, Abdul Sattar, and General Musharraf himself started talking about the desire to restore political dialogue with India by the summer of 2000. Musharraf expressed a willingness to have discussions with Indian leaders at any time and at any place.

Indications were also given that Pakistan was willing to restore what is called the Lahore process. The previous stand, that the decisions taken at Lahore by Nawaz Sharif, had no relevance, was changed. Parallel to this, Pakistani authorities endorsed a series of non-governmental contacts between India and Pakistan, to which India responded positively. Organisations and entities like the Islamabad Policy Research Institute, the Qaid-e-Azam University and the Institute of Strategic Studies of Pakistan were allowed to interact with their Indian counterparts like the Delhi Policy Group, the Centre for Policy Research and the Democratic Movement for Indo-Pakistan Relations. Dialogue was restored under the aegis of bilateral NGO contacts like BALUSA and the Neemrana process.

Former diplomats and military figures from both countries exchanged visits and held discussions to explore the possibility of restoring a dialogue and resolving the inter-governmental impasse. It was with this background that the largest Kashmir-based militant group, Hizbul Mujahideen, announced a unilateral ceasefire in July 2000, expressing a willingness to commence a dialogue with representatives of the Government of India. The Indian response to this move was prompt and positive. There is still no clarity and a number of unanswered questions as to why the Hizbul made this move remain. Speculative analyses at that time contained the following points: that the Hizbul Mujahideen had developed resentment and strong disagreement with Pakistan-based foreign terrorist groups who were operating in Jammu and Kashmir; that the population, particularly in the Valley, was tired of the violence and was becoming progressively less supportive of terrorist activities; that Pakistan gave a limited endorsement to this move to convey a signal to the international community that it was willing to initiate a graduated dialogue with India, beginning with the Hizbul and then moving on to intergovernmental talks between India and Pakistan. This initiative proved to be stillborn, because the controlling headquarters of the Hizbul Mujahideen in Pakistan, headed by Salauddin, refused to endorse the unilateral ceasefire declared by the Hizbul leader in Jammu and Kashmir. Pakistan insisted that its representatives should be included in the dialogue between the Hizbul Mujahideen and representatives of the Government of India. The ultimatum was given that if India did not accept this demand within three days, that is, by the evening of 8 July 2000, the unilateral ceasefire would be withdrawn. Though India sent a delegation to Srinagar led by Home Secretary Kamal Pande to initiate the discussions, the talks did not take place.

The background and dynamics of this aborted initiative merit detailed recall. As mentioned, there was a flurry of activity on the part of the Government of India and various militant groups in Jammu and Kashmir over resuming a dialogue despite the escalation of terrorist violence during June and July. One agreed, of course, that this attempt at peace was a much-desired objective but it would be inaccurate to call the steps taken at that time a peace initiative. They were only initiatives to start a discussion to bring about arrangements that could have eventually brought about peace. Events and measures that led to the declaration of a ceasefire by the Hizbul Mujahideen merit recounting. The government decided to resume a meaningful dialogue with all parties and segments of public opinion in Jammu and Kashmir early in 2000. By late summer, many senior leaders of the Hurriyat Conference were released from jail. Meanwhile, the prospects of New Delhi making an offer to the Hurriyat generated concern in the minds of Chief Minister Farooq Abdullah and his party, which led to the State Assembly endorsing autonomy for Jammu and Kashmir.

Conduits for Contacts

Simultaneously, the government had orchestrated back-channel contacts with the leaders of the All Parties Hurriyat Conference. R.K. Mishra of the *Observer* group, former foreign secretary M.K. Rasgotra, and even the RAW chief, were deployed for this purpose. Track II contacts with Pakistan were also activated. There was also participation by Kashmiri activists based in the US individuals, like Farooq Kathwari, Ghulam Nabi Fai of the Kashmiri American Council, Mohammad Ayub Thakur of the World Kashmir Freedom Movement, Mushtaq Jeelani of the Kashmiri Canadian Council, and Mansoor Ejaz, a New York banker, have all been conduits for contacts with Kashmiri militants. Their efforts had the backing of the State Department. Former diplomat Rasgotra was also authorised to initiate contacts with the Pakistani establishment unofficially.

All these initiatives resulted in the Hizbul Mujahideen declaring a three-month ceasefire and indicating a willingness to talk to the Indian Government without any preconditions. While the local leader of the organisation, Abdul Majid Dar, made this offer, its Supreme Council reluctantly agreed to exploratory discussions. Other Pakistan-based militant groups like the Lashkar-e-Toiba, Jaishe-e-Mohammad and Harkat-ul-Mujahideen labelled Hizbul's initiatives as a betrayal. The head of the Lashkar-e-Toiba, Mohammed Saeed, stated on 31 July 2000 that the *jehad* against India would continue until Kashmir became part of Pakistan.

Before assessing the prospects, one should take note of the motivations and impulses underpinning these recent initiatives. There was definitely behind-the-scenes American pressure on both Pakistan and India to resume discussions with the militants as well as between themselves. The US wanted some tangible progress to occur by the time Vajpayee visited the US in mid-September for bilateral talks with President Clinton. Pakistan agreed to support the dialogue without giving any commitment about withdrawing support to terrorist groups. Pakistan's support to the dialogue would have enabled it to claim to the US that it had persuaded the militants to declare a ceasefire. It would also be able to make the same claim before the UN General Assembly and the UN Security Council in September, when Vajpayee was also in New York. If India refused to resume the dialogue, it could be projected as being unreasonable. If the dialogue ended in a stalemate, India could continue to be accused of obduracy. Other major world powers desired a dialogue leading to normality primarily to avoid a nuclear confrontation between India and Pakistan. None of the five permanent members of the Security Council see Jammu and Kashmir as being wholly an integral part of India. The inclination of the international community would, therefore, be towards a territorial adjustment in Jammu and Kashmir to avoid a subcontinental nuclear confrontation. It is significant that the offer had come from the Hizbul, the most indigenous of the various militant groups. The other groups with large components of foreign mercenaries, had not made any ceasefire offer. Thus Pakistan and these groups, including the Hizbul, retained the option of reverting to violence if they found the dialogue not going their way. A matter of equal significance was the fact that the militants' delegation for talks had individuals based in the US. The Hizbul was also insisting that Pakistan must be present at the dialogue, making it a tripartite exercise.

It is against this background that one had to assess the prospects of the dialogue. First, there seemed to be a lack of clarity in India's basic approach to the dialogue. One only hoped that it was a calculated stance. While the government had indicated that it would not stipulate any unalterable preconditions, National Security Adviser Brajesh Mishra had stated that any solution emerging from the discussions had to be within the parameters of the Constitution. The Left parties had suggested unconditional talks. The Congress had not made any clear policy pronouncement on the subject. Meanwhile, the Hizbul as well as the Hurriyat leaders had categorically rejected any solution within the Indian Constitution. If one were to speculate on the possible negotiating stances of the militants' delegation on the substance of the Kashmir issue, an approach would have been to suggest the options of a plebiscite, interim status under UN supervision, or a trifurcation of Jammu and Kashmir, which now falls within the jurisdiction of India. It would be suggested that the LoC be radically readjusted until the new arrangements were in place.

India faced a complex and serious predicament while entering into this dialogue. Its participation in discussions with a Pakistani delegation present in a tripartite framework would have meant that it formally recognised Pakistan's *locus standi* in dealing with the problem. If practical proposals for autonomy for the region were rejected by the militants and they insisted on territorial arrangements, they would erode India's formal jurisdiction over the state and this would be the first step towards the separation of the Valley from India and its joining Pakistan, while India's capacity to maintain its jurisdiction and strategic control over Ladakh and Jammu would be dangerously affected. Any alienation of the Valley or Jammu and Kashmir from India would affect the economy and water resource management of portions of Jammu and the Indian Punjab. Such a separation, apart from giving a fillip to Pakistan's two-nation theory, would encourage separatist tendencies in other parts of India.

Important powers like the US and the international community in general welcomed the tentative attempts at restoration of dialogue. The failure of this attempt by mid-July resulted not only in general disappointment but in criticism of Pakistan and Pakistan-based militant and terrorist groups. The permanent members of the Security Council led by the US, conveyed messages to Pakistan regretting the failure of this attempt and suggesting that Pakistan should not stand in the way of the dialogue, nor should it insist on immediate tripartite talks with its participation. This pressure was to have some fallout from December 2000–January 2001 onwards, tenuously reviving the processes for peace in Jammu and Kashmir.

A major domestic political development in Pakistan needs to be noted, as it signalled the possibility of a continuation of the Musharraf regime for a period longer than constitutionally envisaged by the Supreme Court of Pakistan. Musharraf's tenure as chief executive was to end by the year 2001 according to the Pakistani Supreme Court stipulation. By December 2000, Musharraf, both in public pronouncements and by political decisions, indicated his intention of staying on in power for a longer period. Musharraf had put former prime minister Nawaz Sharif on trial on serious charges of treason, conspiracy to murder, high corruption, generating disaffection in the armed forces, and so on. Nawaz Sharif was in the process of being convicted of one crime after another and being sentenced to life imprisonment, with even a threat of being condemned to death. There was pressure on Musharraf from the US and important Islamic countries to desist from taking drastic measures against Nawaz Sharif. His domestic difficulties and external constraints made him amenable to such pressure. He decided to send Nawaz Sharif into long-term exile in Saudi Arabia, and negotiations for the former prime minister's departure were conducted by Musharraf himself, with Saudi Arabian Crown Prince Abdullah. Sharif left towards the end of December.

It was not the first time that the leader of a military coup had exiled political leaders from Pakistan. Ayub Khan exiled the front man of the military coup he conducted in 1958-59, Major General Iskander Mirza, to England. He also generated sufficient pressure on political leaders like Mohammad Ali and Nazimuddin to go out of Pakistan. It is the inevitable logic followed by military rulers, that to establish their credibility they neutralise credible political rivals by ensuring their departure from the scene, either through exile or through elimination, as was the case with Zulfiqar Ali Bhutto. Nawaz Sharif being exiled, however, is unique. A prime minister in office, who was in power on the basis of a general election, was ousted from power and then exiled.

The background of Nawaz Sharif's expulsion from Pakistan is relevant in analysing the ramifications of his departure from the scene in Pakistan's domestic politics. It cannot be denied that Nawaz Sharif had come to power with general popular support. His forcible removal was the result of two factors. His betrayal of the trust vested in him by the people of Pakistan, manifested in his increasing authoritarianism and unbridled corruption, There was also ineptitude and lack of political judgement, that characterised his attempt to dismiss his chief of army staff, General Musharraf. It was an extraordinary example of his refusal to perceive the profoundest reality facing Pakistani politics, the reality of the clout of the Pakistani armed forces as an institutional entity in the power structure. It is worthwhile analysing the reason why General Musharraf sent him into exile. Sharif and his family members, along with a number of officials who coalesced with him in defying the armed forces were put on trial on charges of corruption, high treason, attempt to murder, disrupting the discipline of the Pakistani armed forces, and so on. He would have been subject to a long period of imprisonment and a death sentence. General Musharraf perhaps judged that the Pakistan of the years 1999 and 2000 was different from the Pakistan of 1977 to 1979, when General Zia-ul-Haq could get away with the execution of a prime minister. There was also international pressure from the US and from the influential countries of the Gulf, on whom Pakistan is dependent. Whatever his shortcomings, Nawaz Sharif had an extensive rapport and influence with the leaders of the US and the countries of the Gulf and West Asia. General Musharraf did not wish to be seen as a harsh military figure. His aim was to project himself as a catalytic figure who would bring back genuine democracy to Pakistan after the inefficiency and corruption that characterised the democratic governments of Pakistan from 1988 to October 1999.

Historical patterns were repeated in Pakistan between October 1999 and the end of 2000. Just as it happened after Zia's taking over power in 1977, Pakistani political parties were again in disarray after Musharraf's coup. But by the autumn of 2000, all the political parties had moved towards creating a united front against General Musharraf's military regime. The culminating point of this process was the Pakistan Muslim League of Nawaz Sharif and the People's Party of Pakistan agreeing to join each other to launch a campaign against the military government. The expectation of Musharraf and his colleagues that with Benazir Bhutto being exiled and the Pakistan Muslim League being divided after Nawaz Sharif's arrest and incarceration, political parties in Pakistan would not be able to be an active factor in Pakistani politics was proved wrong. Earlier, the Pakistan Supreme Court had given a verdict that the present military regime should finish its tenure by the middle of 2002, which was accepted by General Musharraf. He, therefore, had two options: either to voluntarily relinquish power and let the political parties of Pakistan fight an election in the coming year or two, or to initiate arrangements for his continuation in power within the framework of democratic institutional arrangements accepted by the judiciary as well as the people of Pakistan. He chose the second option. Regardless of public disappointment about political leaders, both Benazir Bhutto and Nawaz Sharif still have a certain stature and charisma in Pakistani public opinion, which Musharraf could not eliminate. Nor could he allow them to remain active in Pakistani politics. Benazir has remained outside Pakistan, under threat of corruption trials by the Musharraf government. The practical solution chosen by General Musharraf was to exile Nawaz Sharif too, after significantly eroding his economic assets and related capacities to influence Pakistani politics. His keeping the leaders of major political parties of Pakistan exiled is in preparation for his continuing in power under new and more domestically and internationally acceptable institutional arrangements. Pervez Musharraf himself gave indications regarding this in a radio and television broadcast to the nation in the second half of December 2000. There were interesting points in his speech: first, that he could not have succeeded in overthrowing Nawaz Sharif's corrupt regime and in assuming power without divine support, which, according to him, entailed his being entrusted with certain profound responsibilities to ensure the well-being of Pakistan "as a wish of Allah Talah". General Musharraf went on to assert that he was not an escapist and that he would relinquish power only after he fulfilled these responsibilities. Second, he said that he wanted to restore democracy in Pakistan. He exhorted the people of Pakistan not to perceive democracy in terms of an exercise in conventional party politics. He urged the people of Pakistan to put up qualified, sincere, honest candidates, dedicated to genuine public service, instead of relying on the corrupt party system in Pakistan. Third, he announced that he would be holding elections for local self-governing bodies and panchayats in Pakistan, as a first step in moving forward to democracy.

Incremental Change

Benazir's residential base is between London and Dubai. At the formal level, the likelihood of Benazir Bhutto returning to Pakistan in the foreseeable future is remote. Nawaz Sharif has been exiled for 10 years and has been banned from politics and public office for 21 years, though some Pakistani analysts hold the view that both Benazir Bhutto and Nawaz Sharif will continue to influence Pakistani political processes and that they cannot be kept outside the country beyond a decade or so. There are unconfirmed reports that the Musharraf Government has persuaded the governments of the Gulf not to allow these political leaders to get back into the country, so that General Musharraf can prolong his tenure in power.

The speculation is that General Musharraf will incrementally make his government a civilian government after the panchayat elections are over; moving up from the district to provincial levels. One is reminded of Field Marshal Ayub Khan's experiment with what he called "Basic Democracies" in the 1960s. There are also reports from Pakistan that General Musharraf will appoint some civilian prime minister before he organises general elections in the coming year. The names of the Speaker of suspended National Assembly Elahi Bux Soomro, and Pakistan People's Party vice-president, Amin Fahim are being mentioned. In the meantime, none of the political parties of Pakistan wants the national and provincial assemblies suspended by General Pervez Musharraf to be revived or restored. Indications are that General Musharraf will complete the process of giving his government an incremental but partial civilian identity by mid-2002, by which time he may create a political platform, assuming the leadership of this platform himself. There is no likelihood of General Musharraf and the Pakistani armed forces relinquishing power in the near future.

It soon became obvious that it would be impractical for India to refuse to deal with General Musharraf on the basis of our arguments regarding the means by which he came to power. Practicality demands that India move on to deal with him at least during the coming three to five years. This is the only way that India could hope to manage the current difficult and complicated phase in Indo-Pakistani relations.

There were purposive initiatives by India from November 2000 to bring relations back on track, though the prospects remained tentative and uncertain. Prime Minister Vajpayee unilaterally announced a ceasefire in operations against militant groups during the period of the holy month of Ramzan (in November 2000). This initiative was based on an assessment that the citizens of Jammu and Kashmir were weary of the violence.

Second, since July 2000, there have been clear signals that the indigenous secessionist groups and opposition parties are also coming round to the view that violent agitation will not bring about the desired results, and that having a political dialogue would be a more practical approach. The unilateral stoppage of military and security operations during the whole month of Ramzan has perhaps struck a responsive chord in the Muslim population of Jammu and Kashmir at the emotional and psychological level, as these assessments of the Prime Minister have proved to be correct — the Kashmir-based units of the Hizbul Mujahideen welcomed the decision. The general reaction of the people was that of relief and satisfaction. The international community welcomed the decision, as it was accompanied by statements from the Government of India that if the ceasefire held, the government would be willing to resume the dialogue with all Kashmiri groups. It has also indicated that it would not stand in the way of the All Party Hurriyat Conference of Jammu and Kashmir and other militant groups sending their representatives to Pakistan, so that they could contact their controlling headquarters, persuading them to abide by the ceasefire and to agree to a dialogue. The Government of Pakistan did not welcome the ceasefire, but accepted the declaration as an interim step that could lead to a dialogue. In a specific response to the cease-fire, Pakistan announced on 2 December that apart from having withdrawn some of its forces from the Line of Control, it would observe maximum restraint on the LoC. It must be remembered that Vajpayee's initiative in November, mentioned here, was taken in spite of the failure of similar effort in July 2000 because of the insistence of Pakistan that it should be participant in the dialogue proposed to be held with the Hizbul Mujahideen and others, an insistence stridently supported by the headquarters of the Hizbul Mujahideen located in Pakistan and by the leaders of other foreign mercenary militant groups like the Lashkar-e-Toiba and Jaish-e-Mohammad. These Islamabad-based militant groups, while endorsing the Pakistani stand on talks, rejected the ceasefire declared at that point of time. In many ways, therefore, Vajpayee was taking an unorthodox initiative, primarily to emphasise two ingredients of his Kashmir and Pakistan policies: first, that the well-being and desire for peace amongst the people of Jammu and Kashmir is a primary factor in Indian policies; and second, that India was willing to normalise relations with Pakistan in spite of the negative signals from Pakistan and from the militant groups based in that country.

Heightened violence against civilians and military installations characterised the period between July and November 2000, so there was no compulsion on India to declare the November ceasefire. The ceasefire declaration in November was to last only for the month of Ramzan. Separatist and terrorist elements interested in scuttling this initiative continued to perpetrate violence during the month of Ramzan. Military camps and installations in Jammu and Kashmir were subjected to attacks. The civilian population of Jammu and Kashmir, where the ceasefire was welcomed, was targeted for similar violence. Pakistan-based militant cadres extended their operations into the Red Fort in Delhi, killing military personnel within the fort, and the Lashkar publicly declared its intention to kill the prime minister of India and to attack the Prime Minister's Office and other offices of the Central Government in New Delhi. Parallel to these events in November and December, the All Party Hurriyat Conference declared its willingness to engage in a dialogue with the Government of India. So did the leaders of the Hizbul Mujahideen in Jammu and Kashmir. The Hurriyat leader, however, stipulated that they would like to visit Pakistan for discussions with their associates, and the Government of Pakistan, keeping in mind the reaction of the international community and the mood of the people of Jammu and Kashmir, agreed that Pakistan need not be a part of the dialogue between India and Kashmir groups "in the initial stages" and that Pakistan would allow the ground to be prepared through these discussions for its eventual participation in the dialogue. Pakistan underlined that it was being flexible in the matter, but that no durable solution to the Kashmir problem could be forged without tripartite talks between India, the Kashmiri groups and Pakistan. Continued violence by the Pakistan-based militant groups in Jammu and Kashmir and in other parts of India led to a fair amount of pressure on Prime Minister Vajpayee not to extend the ceasefire beyond the month of Ramzan. This pressure mounted even from Vajpayee's own party. However, he held his ground and extended the ceasefire twice, once in December and then again towards the end of January. The ceasefire stood extended till the end of May 2001.

Meanwhile the Islamabad-based secessionist groups continued to reject the ceasefire insisting they would continue what they called "*jehad*", holy war, going to the extent of stating that the problems of Kashmir could be solved only by the jehad and not by dialogue. The months of December 2000 and January 2001 witnessed considerable confusion and contradictions within the Hurriyat and other Kashmiri militant groups. The state Government of Jammu and Kashmir, led by Farooq Abdullah, was legitimately concerned about getting marginalised. This concern was compounded by the Hurriyat objecting to the state government organising panchayat elections. These were held with a fair amount of success, increasing its credibility among the people even if the exercise remained under doubt. I undertook an analysis of these trends up to the middle of January 2001 commenting on various factors impinging on this emerging political process. Soon after, I visited Pakistan from 12 to 16 January. The impressions I gathered are summarised at the end of this analysis.

The Analysis

Since Prime Minister Vajpayee's announcement of a unilateral ceasefire for the month of Ramzan on 20 November 2000 there has been a spurt of discussions, statements and initiatives to move towards a negotiated settlement of all issues related to Jammu and Kashmir. There is cautious expectation and hope that these initiatives will lead to purposive and substantive discussions and futher to a solution acceptable to all concerned. Whether these expectations and hopes will be met would primarily depend on realities on the ground as they occur. The prospects of the initiatives have to be assessed in three dimensions: first, the manner in which the dialogue between the Hurriyat, the Hizbul and other Kashmiri groups would progress; second, the orientation that discussions between the Hurriyat and other dissident groups with the Government of Pakistan and jehadist organisations there will take; and third, the direction talks between India and Pakistan will follow, once the two countries agree to engage in direct discussions again, on Kashmir.

As one analyses the prospects of the current initiatives on Kashmir in these dimensions, it is axiomatic that all parties concerned realise that a durable solution can be achieved only through dialogue underpinned by a realistic and practical approach rather than on maximalist stances rooted in the collective psychological and political complexes or prejudices of India and Pakistan. What then are the ground realities as they evolve since the announcement of a ceasefire by Vajpayee?

Indian security forces are maintaining the ceasefire despite provocative violence. Pakistan responded by declaring its intention of practising strategic restraint on the Line of Control. Consequently, firing and direct skirmishes on the Line of Control have diminished. It must be noted that Pakistan's strategic restraint is also a result of the setting in of winter in Jammu and Kashmir. The Government of India has extended the ceasefire beyond the month of Ramzan to facilitate and encourage the negotiations. A.S. Dullat, who was recently in charge of India's external intelligence organisation RAW, has been appointed officer on special duty in the Prime Minister's Office to deal with the processes of the dialogue with Kashmiri dissident groups now under way. Dullat is an officer who has been dealing with Kashmiri affairs for a long time and has both the necessary experience and contacts. The Government of India did not stand in the way of Hurriyat leaders going to Pakistan for discussions. It has been indicated to dissident groups in Kashmir that the Government of India would be willing to recommence negotiations with them on or around 15 January. Hashim Qureshi, one of the founding members of the JKLF, who was also involved in the hijacking of an aircraft in 1971, has been brought back to India as an additional contact with dissident elements both in Jammu and Kashmir and Kashmiris in Pakistan-occupied Kashmir. While the Hizbul Mujahideen in Jammu and Kashmir seems willing to participate in discussions, the other militant organisations based in Pakistan like Lashkar-e-Toiba, have not respected the ceasefire and have continued their violence not only inside Jammu and Kashmir, but as far afield as Delhi's Red Fort, where they succeeded, and Hyderabad and Karnataka, where their violent plans were thwarted. As far as political parties and groups in Jammu and Kashmir are concerned, differences have emerged within the Hurriyat between pro-Pakistani elements and others who visualise a solution to the Kashmir problem outside Pakistani plans. Leaders like Syed Ali Shah Gilani, who are pro-Pakistan, have fallen out with Abdul Ghani Lone. Their differences of opinion became public in the first week of January 2001. Some Hurriyat leaders would be visiting Pakistan for discussions. The National Conference, led by Dr Farooq Abdullah, is in the process of organising panchayat elections in Jammu and Kashmir, to prove political influence and its credibility as the dominant democratic force in Jammu and Kashmir.

Pakistan has tactically, though not fundamentally, resiled from its negotiating position of July 2000 that it should participate in any negotiations being held between India and the dissidents in Jammu and Kashmir from the initial stages. Pakistani Foreign Minister Abdul Sattar has declared that Pakistan would not insist on participation *ab initio*, but would come into a tripartite negotiations process at a later stage. Public opinion in India is divided about these initiatives, one segment being against negotiations, because of the continuing violence, and the other supporting the initiatives, hoping that these would eventually result in a peaceful solution being evolved.

In terms of ground realities, therefore, the initiative taken by the Government of India is still subject to confusion and political uncertainty. As far as the first dimension impacting on prospects of dialogue, namely, discussions between the Government of India and Kashmiri groups is concerned, India faces two problems: first, to determine which group genuinely represents the aspirations of the people of Kashmir. Given Pakistani influence on the leaders of some of these groups, this is a difficult dilemma to resolve. The government cannot allow the isolation or marginalisation of the National Conference by the other groups in these discussions. Second, though India agrees that the dialogue should not have any preconditions except that all Kashmiri groups give up violence during the talks, there is no clarity or unity in the objectives of the dissident groups about objectives that would constitute a solution. India's dialogue with the Kashmiri groups would continue to be subject to attempts at disrupting and scuttling them by Pakistan-based militants and mercenaries. India, on the other hand, is clear about one objective, that there should be no territorial alienation of Jammu and Kashmir from the republic. India is willing to discuss other political compromises.

As far as the second dimension about the orientations of discussions between Hurriyat and Pakistani authorities is concerned, it is logical to anticipate that Pakistan will encourage the Hurriyat to negotiate for the separation of Jammu and Kashmir from India while suggesting that the Hurriyat should not advocate Jammu and Kashmir becoming part of Pakistan in the initial period. This latter suggestion is and would be patently a stratagem to change the status quo, the ultimate objective being to seek Jammu and Kashmir's linkages with Pakistan, while initially assuaging elements among the dissident groups who do not wish Jammu and Kashmir to be part of Pakistan. Pakistan is also likely to suggest to the Hurriyat that they revive suggestions for a referendum under the aegis of international entities to determine the future status of Kashmir in their talks with India. Pakistani authorities would primarily endorse the Inter-Services Intelligence to keep the pressure on India through violence and terrorist acts by organisations like Lashkar-e-Toiba and others. The third dimension about Indo-Pakistan discussions on Kashmir is subject to fundamental differences in the objectives of India and Pakistan. India aims at a solution of the issues related to Kashmir on the basis of ground realities without diluting India's territorial unity and integrity in any way. Pakistan's objective is the exact opposite. It desires a solution that would finish what it calls "the unfinished task of the partition of India". The Indian view is that discussions with Kashmiri dissident groups would be a separate set of problems related to the aspirations of the people of Jammu and Kashmir and that discussions with Pakistan would be on another category of problems rooted in Pakistan's Kashmir policies over the past 50 years, particularly during the last 10. India's approach is to discuss these problems in separate compartments, but Pakistan wants to be an integral part of the discussions for a solution in any tripartite framework, though for tactical purposes, Pakistan has agreed to join the talks only at a later stage.

Given the predicaments and situations described above, it is obvious that one should not expect any early breakthrough. These negotiations are on the anvil, due to Vajpayee's initiatives, but it is going to be a long haul. The question is how India should manage these negotiations in the face of the political uncertainties and contradictions affecting the internal situation in Jammu and Kashmir and the ultimate objectives of Pakistan. A possible approach on the part of India would be to sustain the dialogue, anticipating violent disruptions against it which would continue. Second, to respond decisively in terms of security operations in a focused manner against those elements which try to disrupt the dialogue. This has to be a highly calibrated exercise so that the dialogue does not get disrupted. Third, India should convey a clear message to important powers and to the international community bilaterally and through multilateral fora that a durable solution to the Kashmir issue can only be one which is rooted generally in ground realities in Jammu and Kashmir. To be specific, a solution has to be on the basis of the Line of Control with some adjustments (as far as Pakistan is concerned) and qualitatively responsive to political arrangements for the governance of Jammu and Kashmir and responsive to the aspirations of the people of that state. Further, India should recommence the direct dialogue in graduated stages with Pakistan. This could ultimately lead to a high-level political meeting in about a year. Such a measured approach would be practical though there is no guarantee that it will succeed. It should also be acknowledged that the process would be gradual and slow. India should not succumb to external pressures or be in a hurry. If the current efforts fail, we should have the stamina and grit to remain firm in protecting our vital interests in Jammu and Kashmir.

Impressions of My Visit to Pakistan

I visited Pakistan from 12 to 16 January 2001 to participate in a conference between the Islamabad Policy Research Institute and the Delhi Policy Group on nuclear risk reduction. This was a non-governmental effort though the participants in the conference on both sides were former diplomats, and government and military officials. We were also invited to speak at the Department of Defence Studies of the Qaid-e-Azam University in Islamabad and the Institute of Strategic Studies of Pakistan and the Foreign Service Academy of Pakistan. Our group was led by India's former ambassador to China, the US and Pakistan, K.S. Bajpai. Other members of the delegation were Lt. General Raghavan, Rear Admiral (Retd.) K. Raja Menon, Air Chief Marshal S.K. Mehra, Matin Zuberi, professor on disarmament, Jawaharlal Nehru University (JNU), and myself.

The primary focus of our discussions in Pakistan was to exchange views with members of the Islamabad Policy Research Institute — which is the think-tank backed by the Pakistan Government and its armed forces — on methods by which India and Pakistan could reduce the risk of a nuclear confrontation. The lectures and discussions organised at the other institutions were also focused on specific issues of concern. Our delegation was to discuss developments in Afghanistan at the Qaid-e-Azam University, the phenomenon of cross-border and international terrorism at the Institute of Strategic Studies of Pakistan and exchange views on the comparative experiences of Pakistan and India in their respective nation-building activities at the Foreign Service Academy of Pakistan.

This trip was of particular interest to me because I was returning to Islamabad after seven years. My last visit was in the first week of January 1994, as India's foreign secretary, during Benazir Bhutto's last tenure as prime minister. I was curious whether there had been any transformation in the Pakistani world-view and mindset about India. There were changes and transformations, but I came back chastened and worried. I must preface this description and analysis of my visit with a rider that my value judgements may not be entirely accurate in terms of their applicability to all segments of Pakistani public opinion, or civil society. The value judgements are based on views conveyed (and resulting impressions) by those segments of the Pakistani government, academia and think-tanks, with whom one interfaced.

I must also mention that apart from the conferences and seminars in which we participated, our delegation from the Delhi Policy Group was received by the foreign minister of Pakistan, Abdul Sattar, and foreign secretary of Pakistan, Inamul Haq, with whom we spent nearly three hours on 13 January. This meeting was preceded by an hour-long briefing by the additional secretary in charge of multilateral affairs at the Pakistan Foreign Office, Riaz Hussain. The logic of Hussain's briefing was that he was in charge of non-proliferation matters in the Pakistani Foreign Office.

While welcoming the Delhi Policy Group having a technical discussion with the Islamabad Policy Research Institute on nuclear risk reduction, Hussain emphasised that the efforts of mutual nuclear restraint are rooted in the removal of the basic cause of tension between India and Pakistan, namely, the Kashmir issue. He stressed that nuclear risk reduction cannot be considered in isolation, as a separate issue affecting regional security. He went on to say that unless the Kashmir problem was solved, based on the right of self-determination of the people of Jammu and Kashmir, the necessary atmosphere of mutual trust would not be created for Pakistan to agree to nuclear confidence-building measures. When the Indian side pointed out that the risk of nuclear confrontation and war is a more dangerous phenomenon than Pakistan viewing the Kashmir issue as a territorial dispute, Hussain indulged in a colourful simile in Hindi. He said both India and Pakistan know that the water in the well of mutual peace is dirty and poisoned. Just drawing out the dirty water will not result in the well being cleaned because the reason for the water being poisoned and dirty is that there is a dead dog in the well — and the dead dog is the Kashmir dispute. Unless we take out the dog and dispose of it, we cannot hope for fresh water.

The Indian side could have responded to this bizarre simile by pointing out that it was Pakistan that killed the dog and put it in the well when it invaded Kashmir in 1948 but we did not because the argument could not have led anywhere. A substantive political point made in this Foreign Office briefing was that Pakistan considers nuclear risk reduction intrinsically linked with its views on Kashmir and thus an affirmation that Pakistan's nuclear weapons programme in one dimension is an instrumentality to further its Kashmir policies. The full-day technical discussions with the Islamabad Policy Research Institute on nuclear matters were characterised by a contrast between the approach of the Indian and Pakistani delegations. The Indian side presented structured and written papers on three aspects of nuclear risk reduction. The first paper was on the political and strategic context in which Indo-Pakistan confidence-building measures had evolved since 1989. The second paper was on possible technical proposals and measures both sides could adopt to reduce the prospects of nuclear confrontation or accidental nuclear conflict. The third paper was on whether the contradictions between the Indian nuclear doctrine and the Pakistani nuclear doctrine could be reconciled, given the Pakistani doctrine of retaining the option of first strike and the Indian doctrine of "no-first-use" of its nuclear weapons. The Indian papers and Indian presentations focused on this specific issue for which the conference was organised. The Pakistani delegation in contrast did not present any written papers. It would be pertinent to mention that like the Indian delegation, the Pakistani delegation also consisted of former foreign secretaries, retired military officers and academics. While the Indian approach was technical and focused on the issue, the Pakistani presentations consisted of broader political perspectives. It was interesting to note that in these intellectual exchanges the Pakistani side reflected the approach outlined to us in the Foreign Office briefing. They emphasised with greater vigour that nuclear risk reduction is dependent on, and intrinsically linked with, the solution of the Kashmir issue within the framework of the Pakistani terms of reference.

Even when touching upon technical aspects, the Pakistani delegation emphasised that India's "no-first-use" doctrine and its abjuring the option of first strike has no meaning, because a Pakistani first strike may obliterate India's capacity for a second nuclear strike. Alternatively, India's "no-first-use" approach is a public relations exercise and in a conflict situation, what is there to prevent India resorting to a first strike? The Pakistanis put forward the familiar argument that their nuclear weapons programme was a response to India's nuclear weapons and missile capacities and that it was a necessary measure to safeguard Pakistan's security in relation to the Kashmir dispute. The Pakistani side was not willing to examine the technical feasibility of the confidence-building measures on nuclear risk reduction that India had presented.

The meetings at the other academic institutions mentioned were even more revealing. In discussions on developments in Afghanistan and their fall-out on the Indian subcontinent and Central Asia, Pakistani academics assertively justified the Taliban's policies and objectives. The Indian apprehension about the Taliban exporting or conniving at cross-border terrorism in Jammu and Kashmir and in the Central Asian republics, was rejected with the assertion that the Taliban were not involved in such activities. It was a flat denial. As far as the Taliban's extremist domestic policies — violating human rights, particularly of women within Afghanistan — are concerned, the Pakistani view was that external criticism was misinformed and was based on deliberate misrepresentations. That such views were expressed by Pakistani academics who have had exposure to foreign universities and media, left one wondering about the vigour of orthodoxy that influenced their thought processes.

The theme for discussion at the Institute of Strategic Studies was the implications of religious extremism and cross-border terrorism on regional peace. Instead of a dispassionate and objective discussion on the phenomenon, the Pakistani academics proceeded to argue at great length that the world at large and India in particular was deliberately labelling the intensively spiritual and religious phenomenon of jehad to malign Pakistan. This argument was further expanded with the assertion that the international community led by the US and the West is deliberate in its opposition to the rise of pan-Islamic movements and Islamic religious resurgence in the world, which finds expression in the success of the Taliban in the jehadist campaigns in different countries and the continuation of the struggle in Jammu and Kashmir. Indian advocacies that jehad in the religious sense is different from militant separatist terrorism and violence was polemically rejected. When these discussions meandered into the ups and downs of Indo-Pakistan relations, the director of the Institute justified the Pakistani intrusion into Kargil in 1999, stating that India should evaluate the intrusion in contextual terms, because Pakistani moves in Kargil were justified as a retaliation to India's violating the Line of Control at Siachen in 1984. An additional point was made that Pakistan would not have withdrawn from Kargil but for the US pressure.

The comparative analysis of the experience in nation-building and building of institutions of state at the Foreign Service Academy was remarkable because the Pakistani participants questioned the credibility of India's democracy and India's secularism citing the contradictions of Indian civil society in terms of the treatment of minorities, the caste system, the fragmentation of political parties, the rise of Hindu religious extremism in India, etc. In contrast, discussions with Foreign Minister Abdul Sattar and his colleagues were a comparative relief to the Indian delegation. Sattar affirmed Pakistan's desire to restore a dialogue with India. In response to specific queries, he said that Pakistan was willing to revive the Lahore process and that Pakistan remained committed to the decisions taken at Lahore. But then he neutralised the potential impact of his remarks by saying the same of all the previous agreements between India and Pakistan, including the UN resolutions and the Simla Agreement. It is important to note that one found government representatives more rational and practical than the non-governmental Pakistani interlocutors.

The overall impression one came away with could be summed up as follows. There was no intense anxiety among the Pakistani elite to restore democracy. There was an acceptance of General Musharraf's regime. There seems to be widespread belief in these circles that India was getting exhausted in Kashmir and would not be able to hold on to Jammu and Kashmir for long, and therefore political and militant pressure should be continued. While there was an awareness about the dangers of nuclear confrontation, there was a parallel feeling that the threat of such confrontation would become an incremental pressure on India on the Kashmir issue. While Pakistan had to be responsive to concerns about cross-border terrorism in the Western democracies led by the US, there was no need for such responsiveness towards India. The ceasefire and peace initiatives of the Vajpayee Government were an interim phase through which Pakistan could work towards its objectives in Jammu and Kashmir.

One acknowledges that these impressions may not reflect the views of all of Pakistani society but they certainly reflect the views of an influential section of the decision-making elite. This cannot be ignored.

Meanwhile, ceasefire or no ceasefire, sporadic violence organised by Pakistan-based terrorist groups continued in Jammu and Kashmir. General Musharraf engaged himself in carefully calculated pronouncements about his policies towards India. He promptly offered relief assistance in the aftermath of the Gujarat earthquake on 26 January 2001. India accepted his offer. Pakistan Airways flights brought tents, medicines and blankets directly to Ahmedabad. Musharraf spoke to Prime Minister Vajpayee on 2 February conveying his sympathy and concern for the earthquake victims. Vajpayee thanked him. The conversation was brief and did not touch upon the broader political issue about the resumption of dialogue. The media on both sides of the border, however, interpreted this conversation as "breaking the ice" and the "beginning of a thaw" between India and Pakistan, which could lead to the resumption of intergovernmental dialogue. This simplistic optimism was dampened by General Musharraf's statement at Muzaffarabad on 4 February, the eve of Pakistan's "Kashmir Solidarity Day" that the Government and people of Pakistan would continue to support the cause of the Kashmiri people and of the separation of Jammu and Kashmir from India. The euphemism used was "support to the right of self-determination of the Kashmiri people". The Government of India, however, took this statement in its stride. The internal and knowledgeable assessment in the Indian Government was that Musharraf could not avoid making such a statement on 4 and 5 February given the long tradition of Pakistan agitating on this issue on 5 February every year for the past four decades. What was more significant was Musharraf trying to sow dissension within the Indian Government in his public pronouncements. He said on 6 February 2001 that Vajpayee was inclined to resume the dialogue at high political levels, but he was surrounded by hawkish political colleagues who would not allow him the freedom to exercise this option. He urged Vajpayee to break free from these elements and come for a high-level discussion to Islamabad. On all counts, India considered this a naïve exercise in psychological and propaganda warfare.

Back-channel and track II contacts continued, despite these ups and downs occurring practically every alternate day. The Neemrana group met in Islamabad in the second week of February. The BALUSA group of diplomats, academics and retired military officers also met in February, with American academic and national security expert, Sheerin Tahir Khel playing an active role in discussions in Delhi. The chief minister of Jammu and Kashmir, Farooq Abdullah, claimed the consolidation of democratic processes in Jammu and Kashmir, having held panchayat elections for local self-governing bodies. He also emphasised that in the anxiety to resume a dialogue with the militant groups and the All Party Hurriyat Conference, the Government of India should not marginalise his leadership and his party, the National Conference, which is committed to India and to a solution to the Kashmir issue within the framework of the Indian Constitution. This was a legitimate and logical argument in terms of India's overall interests. The Indian ceasefire initiative was making slow progress. There were no indicators of a change in the basic negotiating stances of India and Pakistan on the Kashmir issue.

The possible interaction with the Hurriyat was the focus of political and media attention. The question to be asked was whether it would be right to deal with the Hurriyat as the sole or major group representing the people of Jammu and Kashmir. The objective answer to this question would have been in the negative. The Hurriyat did not and does not have any representatives from Ladakh or Jammu. It does not even have any representatives from some militant groups which are not part of it. The Hizbul and Pakistan-based militant groups insist on retaining their separate identity. Equally important, India cannot ignore or marginalise Chief Minister Farooq Abdullah. The Hizbul or other violent groups arrogating to themselves the role of being the sole representatives of the citizens of Jammu and Kashmir was not actually correct and is not and should not be politically acceptable. The second question to be asked was whether there was any clarity amongst Kashmiri and other groups about what the solution to the Kashmir problem should be. Here again, the reply was negative.

There are some Kashmiri groups and foreign mercenaries linked with them who want Jammu and Kashmir to be an integral part of Pakistan. There are others who want Jammu and Kashmir to be an independent state. The people of Ladakh and Jammu are clearly in favour of the state remaining an integral part of India. The National Conference led by Farooq Abdullah remains committed to the state being a part of India, but with qualitatively enhanced political, administrative and financial autonomy. Farooq Abdullah also wants the territorial dimensions of the Jammu and Kashmir issue to be resolved on the basis of the Line of Control. Then there are others who visualise Ladakh and Jammu remaining part of India, with the Kashmir valley being ceded to Pakistan or given the status of some kind of an autonomous region under international guarantees and supervision.

Another dimension of the Kashmir issue is the predicament of nearly 250,000 Kashmiri Hindus who were forced to flee Jammu and Kashmir owing to terrorist violence. Their returning to their homes and the restoration of their properties has to be an essential ingredient of any solution that may be discussed. A certain elaboration of this issue is important. What the Pakistan-trained terrorist groups have been doing over the past decade is undertaking a systematic campaign of ethnic and religious cleansing, the objective being to expel as many Hindus as possible. The violence against the Sikhs has the same objective: expelling the Sikh community also from Jammu and Kashmir. The past violence against Buddhists in Ladakh and Kargil district is a part of this exercise. The latest information about the changing demography of Jammu is also a matter of concern. The population of Jammu has trebled during the past five years and the largest segment of people who have come and settled there are Muslims. It is obvious, therefore, that while advocating a dialogue for a peaceful solution, Pakistan and the militant groups supported by it are systematically working at changing the communal and religious demography of Jammu and Kashmir to ensure a larger Muslim majority in the state. This should constitute a critical issue in India's negotiations with Kashmir groups and eventually with Pakistan. The process of pushing out non-Muslims has to be stopped and reversed.

Let us for a moment speculate on what would happen to Jammu and Kashmir if it is separated from India and becomes an independent entity even under interim international guarantees, and guarantees of non-interference by India and Pakistan. The population would be disadvantaged under the new dispensation dominated by Islamic militant groups. Kashmir is a landlocked entity depending entirely for its access to the sea on Pakistan or on India. There would be bitterness in India about this new entity. India may not be inclined to be of assistance. Such a Jammu and Kashmir's dependence on Pakistan would be unavoidable. This dependence would first be translated into economic and political influence and through the instrumentality of the militant groups, integration into Pakistan after a short period of time. The ramifications of its alienation from the Indian republic on Indian civil society and communal harmony would be negative, eroding both the ideological and political unity of India, leaving aside the violation of India's territorial integrity. If Kashmir becomes a separate entity or state, Pakistan would have achieved two objectives: first, the process of absorbing Jammu and Kashmir would have started; and second, the Pakistani power structure would have fulfilled its oft-declared desire of avenging Bangladesh's breakaway.

A further question can be asked: would Jammu and Kashmir's separation from India lead to a normal relationship between India and Pakistan? Here again, one goes by the intellectual and ideological orientations of Pakistani strategic thinkers of various hues. A fair section of them, with whom one has personally interacted, have expressed the view that as long as India remains the largest polity in south Asia, tensions are inevitable and will continue. They hold that the Indian republic is territorially too vast and consists of completely different ethnicities and languages and, therefore, India should break itself into smaller states which would create a geo-strategic equilibrium in south Asia from the point of view of India's smaller neighbours. That is considered by segments of the power structure of Pakistan as the first step to generate the desired centrifugal impulses within the Indian republic.

The factors and trends analysed here go beyond the declared negotiating stances of Pakistan and the separatist groups. They have long-term and critical implications for the unity, stability and territorial integrity of India. India's negotiating stance on Kashmir should be rooted in a deep consideration of these factors. It is not a question of a new ceasefire, or restoring the dialogue. India must be clear about the objectives of the interim and ultimate objectives of the dialogue before it engages in the exercise.

Having ruminated on the profound complexities affecting a resolution of the Kashmir problem, which remains a distant prospect, one factor which has contributed to this complexity is the interpretation of Islam and *jehad* the power structure and Pakistan has adopted as an instrumentality both for national consolidation and for the implementation of certain foreign and strategic policy objectives. The founding father of Pakistan, Jinnah, did not envision Pakistan as a theocratic Islamic state. He recognised the pluralities of the civil society that would constitute the new state of Pakistan. His objective was to create a modern democracy in which Muslims would constitute the majority. He did not anticipate the inner contradictions which would affect the new state of Pakistan rooted in ethnic and linguistic diversities. East Pakistan could not totally identify with the socio-ethnic ethos of West Pakistan. West Pakistani political and economic discrimination only accentuated this alienation, ultimately leading to East Pakistan breaking away into the independent state of Bangladesh, thereby posing a terminal challenge to the two-nation theory, on the basis of which Pakistan was created.

The emergence of independent Bangladesh confirmed that religion alone cannot be the basis for the creation of a national identity. Actually, the establishment of Bangladesh not only constituted a rejection of the two-nation theory, but also created a conundrum in terms of retrospective history. East Pakistanis or Bangladeshis, if they were overwhelmingly committed to an exclusively Bengali ethnic or linguistic identity, should have been inclined to be reunited with Indian West Bengal. This was definitely not the case. They wanted to emerge not only as an independent Bengali country, but as an independent Bengali Muslim country. In this they proved the British Viceroy Lord George Curzon (1899-1905) correct. His partition of Bengal in 1905 creating two provinces, one with a Muslim majority and the other with a Hindu majority, seems to have been confirmed by Bangladesh's emergence as a Muslim state. So one should not be carried away by the claim of the two-nation theory having been disproved.

The separation of Bangladesh, however, generated impulses leading to the incremental Islamisation of Pakistan. It is worth remembering that it was Bhutto who declared Pakistan an Islamic republic. He claimed that Bangladesh's breaking away was a result of a Hindu-inspired anti-Islamic conspiracy. He proceeded to argue that given the pluralities affecting the remnant of Pakistan, that is, West Pakistan, there should be a greater emphasis on Islam as the cementing factor in nation-building in the face of the trauma which Pakistan had gone through with its break-up in 1971-72. Like India, Pakistan is also a multi-lingual, multi-ethnic state, though it may not be multi-religious in terms of a broad definition. The majority of Pakistanis are adherents of Islam, though there are differences between Shias and Sunnis and other subsects. The nurturing and cultivating of Islam as a political instrumentality to consolidate the nation became state policy from the early 1970s onwards. This approach transmuted itself into processes of governance, the incremental application of the Shariat and the introduction of religious courses on Islam from the school level up to the university level, including in the syllabus of the National military and administrative institutes.

The presence of a large Muslim population in India living under a constitutional and political arrangement that is secular and non-discriminatory, became a greater challenge to Pakistan's sense of national identity. It became not only necessary to affirm and enhance the orthodox Islamic ethos for consolidating the Pakistani nation; it also became equally necessary to question India's secular democracy, particularly in terms of the predicament of the Muslim citizens of India. The Pakistani power structure came to the view that one method to challenge India's credibility in these respects was to constantly project the Hindu majority and the Government of India as being discriminatory and oppressive against the Muslims in the Indian republic. Having an adversarial relationship with India was considered necessary if Pakistan were to survive, overcoming its own internal disunity. This paranoia also manifested itself in the ostracisation of the Ahmediya (Qadiani) Muslims and certain subsects of the Ismaili community. The alienation of the Muslims living in Kashmir became the tool for implementing the adversarial policies towards India. Another facet of this approach is the oft-repeated assessment by the Pakistani leaders that the Indian republic is an artificial entity, too large geographically, and too varied socially, ethnically, linguistically and from the religious point of view.

In other words, the unarticulated ambition and hope is that in such a situation, Pakistan will emerge as the strongest and most powerful political entity in South Asia. Strengthening and nurturing Islamic cohesion, therefore, is, according to them, the most effective means to achieve the objectives of internal unity and regional predominance. The majority of ordinary people in Pakistan are sincerely and emotionally committed to the faith of Islam. Left to themselves, this is a spiritual force, a social corrective and a unifying phenomenon. The vested interests of the power structure in Pakistani society have, however, vitiated the process. The more extremist, aggressive and intolerant interpretation of Islam being put forward is the foundation on which the Pakistani state should be strengthened and on which only can the advocacy of this power structure survive. Pakistan not having much of an urban middle class and a large number of Pakistanis being rural and illiterate, the local religious leaders who are subject to the influence of the power structure, make a distinct impact on public opinion. The absence of democracy, the domination of the feudal gentry and the civil and military officers combine to take Pakistan down the path of religious extremism, intolerance and adversarial approach towards India. As mentioned earlier in this chapter, this approach was visible during my recent visit to Pakistan.

Pakistan refuses to accept international perceptions regarding religious extremism and cross-border terrorism. It considers the activities of various terrorist groups as 'jehad', which, according to their interpretation of Islamic scriptures, is a continuing struggle for religious self-reliance both internally and externally. Jehad is a spiritual and religious phenomenon, according to them, and its purpose is to go to the defence of the *Ummah*, Muslims anywhere in the world. To the Pakistani, jehad is a struggle and a fight for freedom and resistance against all oppression and injustice against Muslims. Jehad should not be confused with terrorism. Pakistan goes further in this argument. Pakistani policy-makers assert that India and the Western democracies are raising the bogey of religious extremism and international terrorism, because they resent the vibrant resurgence of a pan-Islamic movement, from North Africa in the west to the Philippines in the east. Pakistanis frequently quote Samuel Huntington's thesis about a conflict of civilisations as an example of the phenomenon of non-Muslim states uniting against Islam. Though there are smaller segments of Pakistani intellectuals and analysts who comprehend the dangers that such an extremism can pose to Pakistan's unity and stability, they do not make any impact on the broad scheme.

It would be pertinent to describe the wellsprings of this phenomenon and how it is being sustained and nourished in that country. It must be noted that nearly 60 per cent of Pakistanis are illiterate. Most of rural Pakistan lacks modern educational facilities at the school level. In contrast, Islamic religious schools *(madrasas)* are located all over the country, down to the village level. These religious schools not only provide free education but also free food, clothing and shelter. General Zia encouraged the establishment and spread of such *madrasas* through his 11-year rule as a means of getting the support of Muslim religious parties, like the Jamaat-e-Islam and its sub-groups. Another objective of his encouraging the spread of such institutions was to recruit cadre to fight the Soviet troops in Afghanistan. The finances for these institutions came from *zakat*, the Islamic tax collected by the state. But since the mid-1980s, more and more of these *madrasas* are financed by the governments of Gulf states like Saudi Arabia, to some extent by Iran and by Islamic private and government-funded NGOs. Practically all these *madrasas* do not teach any modern subjects. They offer religious, theological education and many of them preach violent jehad. The priests and teachers of these madrasas in Pakistan equate jehad with violent warfare against non-believers, totally ignoring the real meaning of the concept of Islam — is "to strive and struggle to purify oneself".

American scholar Jessica Stern of Harvard University's Kennedy School of Government, in an article published in the November-December 2000 issue of *Foreign Affairs* writes that there are 40,000 to 50,000 *madrasas* in Pakistan, of which only 4000 have registered themselves with the government. Pakistan's minister for the interior, Moinuddin Haider, has acknowledged "that the Islamic teaching is not good for Pakistan — some in the garb of religious training are fanning sectarian violence". Haider's reaction was a response to the growing pressure from Western democracies that Pakistan should control the activities of these religious institutions. In contrast, leading figures presiding over the *madrasas* like the Chancellor of the Darul-Uloom, Haqqani, state that any move against the *madrasas* is aimed at destroying the spirit of these religious schools. Another leading figure in the movement, Mujibur Rahman Inqalabi, asserted that closing down or controlling them is against Islam. The students now constitute the cadre of the most militant terrorist groups operating against India, namely, the Lashkar-e-Toiba, Ahle Hadith and the Karkaz-e-dawa and the Wal-Irshad. The funding comes, as mentioned before, from the ISI and from countries like Saudi Arabia and Libya. It must also be noted that the jehadis in Pakistan are not only Pakistanis but mercenaries from as far away as Saudi Arabia, Egypt, Libya, Sudan and Algeria. Equally significant is the policy orientation and belief of these cadres that the jehad should continue "even if India gives up Kashmir to Pakistan". Reports from Pakistan indicate that Pakistani *madrasas* are now imparting jehad training to Muslim youths from Myanmar, Bangladesh, Afghanistan, Mongolia, Kuwait, Yemen, Chechnya, and even Nepal. There are also jehadis recruited from the Central Asian republics of Uzbekistan, Tajikistan and Turkey.

India's concern, of course, is the continuing infiltration of these violent terrorist cadres into Jammu and Kashmir, most of whom are volunteers, who now have a vital interest in not allowing any Indo-Pakistan peace initiative to succeed — who have vested interests not only in terms of extreme religious factions, but because most of these mercenaries were unemployed and are unemployable, given their violent background. Terrorism labelled as jehad is good business. The general assessment is that an average *jehadi* earns between Rs 10,000 and Rs 15,000 a month (which is three or four times what a college- or school-educated Pakistani can earn).

In the ultimate analysis, India can withstand the pressure of these jehadi groups, though Pakistan may continue to support them, because the Pakistanis' tactical and strategic theory is that fomenting a low-cost war against India in Jammu and Kashmir would serve the Pakistani objective of absorbing Jammu and Kashmir even if this takes time, whereas for India such a situation would be an incrementally costly proposition both financially and in terms of human resources. To some extent the Government of Pakistan may not be in a position to control the activities of these terrorist groups fully. However, the basic fact is that if Pakistan withdraws its territorial sanctuaries and logistical support, these groups may not be able to function very long.

The more problematic predicament the Government of Pakistan faces is that if it clamps down effectively on these terrorist groups, their violence would be turned inwards against the government. This is apart from the government having to cope with the agitational reaction of these groups and religious parties, who have support in the rural population. Decisive action against them could be a prescription for an internal crisis, the origins of which unfortunately lie in the policies of the Government of Pakistan since the late 1970s. India has to keep in mind the fact that the jehadis' policies of Pakistan are not territory specific to Kashmir. At the most fundamental level, they are a threat to India's territorial integrity and unity, a threat that will continue in the foreseeable future.

The assessment given above is not entirely speculative. General Musharraf in a manner confirmed it in an address to the Pakistan Institute of International Affairs on 23 June 2000. He said that in the foreseeable future Pakistan faces threats on two fronts — the first from India in terms of Pakistan's political stability and territorial integrity, and the second, from the fallout of the Afghanistan crisis and due to Iranian policies in Afghanistan. He went on to make the following points:

1. Pakistan has developed and should further develop good relations with Iran and ensure the stabilisation of Afghanistan in order to have a friendly neighbour, and not a region where Russia may yet intervene; any friendly government of Pushtoons is welcome because the NWFP and Baluchistan has large Pushtoon populations amongst whom irredentist feelings have to be countered. The defeat of the Taliban has, of course, destroyed the calculation.

2. Mutual nuclear deterrence rules out any war with India. But there is no question of letting down the guard or of any reduction of defence strength as some (evidently sizeable) sections, including some in the military, are advocating. Musharraf sees the real threat from India as its desire to "dominate" Pakistan and its stand on Kashmir as a means of doing so. Hence Pakistan should "engage" India by "diplomacy". Low-intensity conflicts cannot be ruled out. Support for the "freedom fighters" in Kashmir will be extended. The idea of the integration of Kashmir with Pakistan may be given up if it is expedient to do so. Independence for it will be supported but even that may be postponed if local support cannot be mobilised. Other means will be adopted in order to enhance Pakistan's security and foil India's plan to be a regional power and an international player with US support. China too would resist such a plan because China wants to emerge as the "second pole".

3. Pakistan wishes to emerge as the leader of an Islamic bloc comprising Afghanistan, the Central Asian States (CAS) and Iran, with peripheral support from the Gulf States and Turkey. It claims this status by virtue of the fact that in this "the century of gas", no longer one of oil, all gas supplies to India, southeast Asia and the further east have to pass through Pakistan. So does the trade of all the landlocked states of the bloc. As the geographic-economic centre of this region, it has to become its leader.

4. Inasmuch as it is aware of Russian opposition to this ambition, Pakistan is including Turkey as an ally. Turkey is a member of NATO and possibly is eyeing some adjoining areas in the CAS for economic exploitation.

5. Musharraf condemned terrorism and narcotics trafficking, but in ambiguous terms, obviously to please the US and Russia as is his declaration of the desirability of eliminating terrorism from Pakistan. There is an implicit conceding of US interests in the CAS so long as its own leadership of this Islamic bloc is not undercut.

6. China's support is an essential element of Pakistan's foreign policy. Its defence production and upgrading are dependent on it (not to say defence itself).

7. Next in order of importance to the strategic defence of Pakistan is the second component of national strategy on economic development. They go together. No one in Pakistan doubts that its economy is in a bad way. The message is that it cannot be assertive vis-à-vis India till the gas and other trading gets going in this Islamic bloc.

8. Pakistan has to preserve its Islamic identity with deep relationships with all Islamic states, and has, rather surprisingly, expressed its concern over Chechnya, Azerbaijan and even distant Bosnia, but none specifically for Palestine or Iraq.

9. Surprisingly, Musharraf placed Kashmir as the "last" (not even as "the last but not the least") item of foreign policy. He takes it up as a matter of "principle", one continuing to hurt Pakistan since its formation. He neither elucidates nor gives priority to that point. Nor is he willing to take Pakistan to war to get Kashmir. Instead of taking it up as a direct responsibility, he wants the Kashmiris to wage a "freedom struggle". He concedes that some mujahideen groups are terrorists and presumably therefore not worthy of receiving Pakistani support.

10. He elaborates that for Pakistan to pursue its Islamic bloc leadership agenda, it needs "internal strength". This he defines as the sum total of economic (first) and military strength. Thus, it is not for the generals of Pakistan alone to safeguard and promote the national interest nor for the mullahs to do so.

Commenting on these points, the former head of RAW, Anand Varma, gave this assessment of General Musharraf's foreign policy and strategic objectives. Its prime objectives would appear to be:

1. The leadership of its own Islamic bloc with the endorsement of China and despite the opposition of Russia, while avoiding any direct resistance from the US. This is Musharraf's slogan to reorient the country's political obsession with Kashmir without saying so.

2. The weakening of the Indian state and subverting its relations with the SAARC countries and helping China to do the same so that India cannot emerge as the leader of south Asia.

3. To not offend the US on terrorism and narcotics traffic while maintaining close relations with China and supporting it as the second pole.

4. Giving the fundamentalists a higher objective than the total Islamisation of Pakistan and its people and the acquisition of Kashmir, thus undercutting the Islamic generals and the mullahs and even putting the mujahideen on notice not to defy the state. Neither the generals nor the mullahs should take unanimity for granted among Pakistanis in taking on India frontally.

5. That the export and transmission of gas and trade with India is essential to Pakistan's economy and, therefore, to its foreign policy, that is, its military strength and Islamic bloc leadership.

We must conclude this chapter ruminating on the reasons for the adversarial attitudes of India and Pakistan going beyond the territorial and political controversies between the two countries, because these controversies are only manifestations and symptoms of deeper factors. These factors merit description and analysis to understand the complexities that are due to afflict Indo-Pakistan relations for time to come. That there are such factors going beyond the disputes and controversies in bilateral relations, was acknowledged with frankness about four years ago, by the former foreign minister of Pakistan, Sahibzada Yaqub Khan. The Rajiv Gandhi Foundation had organised a seminar on Indo-Pakistan relations in New Delhi in January 1997. The participants were senior political figures, bureaucrats, journalists and academics from both countries. As is the practice during such seminars, the concluding session was for discussing an agreed summary of the discussions or conclusions arrived at. This draft document was couched in the positive terms of courtesy and optimism. After listening to various people emphasising the normative requirements of peace and cooperation between India and Pakistan, Sahibzada Yaqub Khan intervened to bring the discussion back to reality. He said that he had no objection to optimism and a rationale being embodied in the concluding statement of the seminar, but he wanted to remind the audience at the seminar that Indo-Pakistan normalcy and cooperation was not going to come about by seminars and general expressions of goodwill. He stated that "there is a fundamental line of hatred between India and Pakistan which generates suspicion, mistrust and antagonism". He concluded by saying that unless the reasons for this hatred and suspicion are removed, seminars and positive conclusions have only limited and cosmetic relevance.

What Sahibzada Yaqub Khan said was unpalatable and was definitely a jarring note in the contrived atmosphere of rationality and goodwill sought to be created at the seminar. But what he said was perhaps factually correct. There are segments of Indian public opinion that are profoundly antagonistic towards Pakistan. Equally, there are similar attitudes permeating the collective psyche of Pakistanis.

There are sections of public opinion in both countries that acknowledge the need to move away from these attitudes and influences and to forge a cooperative relationship. But they are not sufficiently influential in terms of policy-making. The governments of both countries themselves have become the prisoners of policy stances and attitudes they have created in public opinion and, therefore, cannot be bold and innovative beyond a certain threshold. There are two glimmers of hope about India and Pakistan getting over their Catch-22 predicament. First, both acknowledge the need to restore a dialogue, a need which is actively supported by the important powers, given the nuclear potential of both countries. Second, the economic phenomenon of globalisation and the technological phenomenon of the information revolution will eventually break the barriers of entrenched policies and attitudes which will become progressively irrelevant. Patience is required. One should take note of Aristotle's sage advice in his *Poetics*. He said more than two thousand years ago, "It is not a sign of wisdom to be desperate about things." India and Pakistan would do well to heed this advice.

One would add a caveat. While it is not a sign of wisdom to be desperate about things, one must not and cannot wish away attitudes and acts of desperation. There is a segment of conventional wisdom that suggests that Pakistan is likely to be a failed state. This is not a valid assessment on any account. Pakistan has territorial cohesion, the people of Pakistan, despite their ethnic and linguistic diversities and contradictions, have a general sense of unity rooted in the faith of Islam, whatever the country's economic difficulties. It is generally self-sufficient in food, and so far the land-to-people ratio in Pakistan seems to be manageable. Despite these sustaining factors of national identity and survival, a pervading anxiety about this identity characterises the Pakistani power structure and intellectual elite. This anxiety is rooted in misperceptions about potential Indian hegemonism.

I would conclude by recalling a remark made by India's first Prime Minister Jawaharlal Nehru, to Foreign Service officers of my batch (1958) speculating on the future security of India in response to questions we asked about Pakistani and Chinese attitudes. He said there may be external threats to India, off and on, but the most serious threat that India will face in the initial decades of its existence would be from the extremist communal and religious forces in the subcontinent that caused the partition of the country and which may lead to Pakistan encouraging such forces. He was prescient, given emerging realities. India has to cope with this challenge, both in times of peace and in times of conflict with Pakistan.

Eleven

The Agra Summit and After

$\mathcal{T}$ he Vajpayee-Musharraf summit at Agra held on the 15 and 16 July, was anticipated with high hopes and expectations. But it barely managed to ensure the continuity of the dialogue that had reopened after a gap of more than two and a half years.

The background, motivations and the approach which India and Pakistan had towards the summit was worth narrating before going on to analyse the proceedings, results and implications.

I had the occasion to speak with persons at the highest political levels in the Government of India about the reasons why Vajpayee extended the invitation to General Musharraf to come to India. My insistent curiosity was impelled by the fact that the invitation was a complete about turn from the policy pronouncements of the Government of India since October 1999 that India would not deal with a military government of Pakistan which had come to power by unconstitutional means, overthrowing an elected prime minister. India had continued to refuse the offer by Musharraf to have bilateral discussions "at any level, at any time and at any place." Why then a sudden change of policy resulting in an invitation on 24 May 2001 to Pervez Musharraf to come to India for a summit?

The information I have is that Prime Minister Vajpayee was not keen on a bilateral summit meeting with Musharraf in India. His preference was to re-commence such contacts on the margins of the SAARC summit and the UN General Assembly session, then scheduled for December and September respectively. It was L.K. Advani and other senior cabinet colleagues who advised Vajpayee to do something bold and dramatic in a bilateral framework so that India and Pakistan could break out of the logjam since the Kargil war in 1999. Vajpayee accepted this advice, particularly from Advani. Some senior BJP Party figures indicated that the decision to invite Musharraf to the Agra summit was finalised at a one-to-one lunch at Advani's residence to which Vajpayee had gone in April 2001. The other reasons for this invitation were inherent in political developments in Jammu and Kashmir. The ceasefire offers and extensions that commenced from July 2000 and were continued till the end of May 2001 had not improved the law and order situation. Pakistani intrusions and terrorist violence continued, though the situation on the Line of Control was less tense upto the middle of July 2001.

The ceasefire did not result in any meaningful discussions between Indian Government representatives and secessionist groups and other Kashmir opposition political parties. The Hurriyat's insistence that it should first have discussions with the Government of Pakistan before entering into negotiations with India was unacceptable to the Government of India, based on the assessment that India formally endorsing such discussions with Pakistan would legitimise Pakistan's claim to be a participant in discussions on the political future and territorial status of Kashmir. Personally I have a different view. The Government of India need not have developed high blood pressure about the Hurriyat's desire to go and have discussions with Pakistan. India should have allowed the Hurriyat team to go as it would have enabled India to finally prove to the world that the secessionist parties, including the Hurriyat are not genuine representatives of the people of Kashmir but are mere instrumentalities of Pakistani policies aimed at challenging the territorial integrity of India.

Therefore no serious discussions occurred. The Government of India's initiative nominating K.C. Pant, deputy chairman of the Planning Commission and former defence minister as the special representative for discussions with separatist groups and other political parties of Jammu and Kashmir was also unsuccessful. So the Government decided to give the Hurriyat and its associates time to decide what they wished to do and simultaneously taking steps to reach out to the Musharraf Government, the expectation being that resumption of the dialogue with Pakistan through the instrumentality of Musharraf-Vajpayee summit would generate parallel pressures on the secessionists in Jammu and Kashmir to talk to the Government of India. India also wished to respond to advocacies and pressures from the major powers of the world to resume contacts with Pakistan to discuss issues related to Kashmir and nuclear risk reduction.

Vajpayee's invitation of May the 24th was accepted by Musharraf on May the 27th. Dates for the summit were tentatively scheduled for mid-July, the summit ultimately took place between the 14th and 16th of July. A contextual analysis of Pakistani policies and attitudes immediately preceding the summit is equally relevant.

First and foremost, certain presumptions and predications were articulated in the Indian media about Pakistan responding to the Indian invitation, that were not entirely valid. These predications were, Musharraf is coming to India because Pakistan is economically on the verge of bankruptcy and serious political instability. Second, that after two years in power, he is genuinely interested in finding a practical compromise on the Kashmir issue and in normalising relations with India. This second predication is based on the view that Musharraf thinks that his credibility will increase if he comes to agreement with India on Kashmir in a manner acceptable to Pakistan.

While it is true that Pakistan was in some economic difficulties, that did not seem to be a major impelling factor pushing Musharraf to the proposed summit. Granted that Pakistan's GDP had come down from $62.2 billion in 1996 to a little over $50 billion in the year 2000, granted that 74 per cent of Pakistan's budget is frittered away in debt servicing and defence expenditure, true that Pakistan's industrial production and exports have declined and that the foreign exchange reserves stood at an all-time low of only $1.5 billion or so, but the fact remained that Pakistan was sustaining an annual growth at the rate of 4 per cent per annum till the year 2000. It was generally self-sufficient in food, it could presume on continuing energy supplies from the Gulf countries, particularly Saudi Arabia due to the Islamic connection. The most fundamental fact was that the United States and Western democracies would do their utmost to prevent Pakistan from economic disintegration when the chips are down. Musharraf's assuming the presidency just before coming to the summit underlined he was confident enough about support from all important agencies of the Pakistani establishment and public opinion. Otherwise, he would not have taken the decision to elevate himself to the presidency. Public opinion and Islam-pasand parties had endorsed his coming to Delhi, as shown in his consultations with these entities on 24 June. He told them his objective was to persuade India to compromise on Kashmir within the framework of Pakistani objectives. He had conveyed a message to India that this was his expectation.

Before coming to the governmental and public responses from Pakistan that preceded the summit, it is relevant to mention the initiatives taken by

India signalled its genuine desire to bring Indo-Pakistan relations back on track towards normalisation and cooperation. Between the 1 and 12 July, India announced a series of unilateral initiatives. It offered 20 scholarships to Pakistani students to come and study in India in subjects of their choice including science and technology. It also offered to implement the provisions of the cultural agreement signed in July 1989 to enhance people-to-people contacts. India announced that it would not capture Pakistani fishermen who strayed into its territorial waters. India also announced a decision to release such Pakistani fishermen in Indian custody. India made public its plan to expand bilateral trade with Pakistan within the frame-work of the MFN status which India has granted to Pakistan several years ago, subject to Pakistan reciprocating the gesture. India announced it was liberalising the visa regime for Pakistani nationals to extend them greater facilities to visit India not only across the international border but also across the Line of Control in Jammu and Kashmir. The Government of India announced that visa issuing offices would be opened at designated points on the Line of Control in Jammu and Kashmir and on the international frontier in Rajasthan and Punjab so that Pakistanis who wanted to visit India or Kashmiris from Pakistan-held Kashmir desiring to visit Jammu and Kashmir did not have to go to Islamabad to get a visa. It was clarified that India had taken this initiative despite possible adverse security considerations.

The prime minister instructed the director general, military operations of India to proceed to Islamabad to have discussions with his Pakistani counterparts on expanding mutual military confidence-building measures, including CBMs related to the nuclear weaponisation of India and Pakistan. India also indicated its willingness to move forward in implementing agreements that had been reached on issues like Siachen, completion of the Wullar Barrage (Tulbul navigation project), delineating the boundary at Sir Creek, etc. India's motivation in announcing these unilateral gestures was to convey two signals. First, that India was serious about finding a negotiated settlement of the Kashmir issue in its internal dimensions. That is why India announced unilateral ceasefire, a willingness to have discussions with all Kashmiri groups and appointed K.C. Pant as special representative of the government to conduct these discussions. Second, unilateral initiatives announced in relation to Pakistan were a continuation of this process conveying that India aimed at doing whatever was necessary to create an environment conducive to a rational discussion on Kashmir and other issues.

Pakistani responses to these moves were deliberately negative. First and foremost, there was no positive reciprocal response to the specific unilateral initiative detailed above. In fact, the Pakistani Foreign Office reacted to the initiatives by saying these gestures were a calculated attempt by India to shift the focus of the Agra summit from the Kashmir issue. Musharraf himself repeatedly harped on the point in his interviews that he was coming to the summit to discuss only the Kashmir issue and to find a solution within the framework of the aims of Pakistan. He further announced that changing the status of Jammu and Kashmir is "the unfinished part of the partition". He went on to say that all other issues affecting Indo-Pakistan relations can be addressed only after a solution is found to the Kashmir issue from Pakistan's point of view, though he had no objection in discussing those issues with Prime Minister Vajpayee. The most important point he made was that his objective was to persuade India to find a solution to the Kashmir problem within a definite time-frame. This in fact sounded like an ultimatum to India. When queried by senior Indian journalists about what solution to the Kashmir issue he had in mind, he said that the only acceptable solution would be to hold a plebiscite in Jammu and Kashmir on the basis of the UN resolutions of 1947/48. He also conveyed to the Hurriyat in a formal communication that Pakistan would continue to give diplomatic, moral and political support to their struggle for self-determination of the people of Jammu and Kashmir. In other words, Pakistan would continue to support the secessionist movement by employing mercenaries, sponsoring cross-border terrorism and de-stabilising Jammu and Kashmir.

Pakistan's commerce minister, Razak Daud, told a business delegation from India in June 2001 that he would like Indo-Pakistani economic cooperation to expand but stated in the second week of July that no expansion of economic relations or giving India MFN status would be possible unless the Kashmir issue is resolved. In between government-backed trial balloons were floated by the Pakistani media — that Prime Minister Vajpayee may agree to withdrawal of Indian troops from Siachen; he may reduce the strength of the India security forces in Jammu and Kashmir; India might agree at the end of the summit to relinquish control over the Kashmir valley giving it some kind of an autonomous status while retaining Ladakh and Jammu. The most extraordinary proposition was that India in a bold move would allow Jammu and Kashmir a semi-independent status under some kind of a UN observers' group for a period of 15 years, after which India and Pakistan would jointly agree to a referendum in the state on its future.

This was both a pressure tactic and a ploy to tell the world that Pakistan had several suggestions to resolve the Kashmir issue to which India was not responding. India was absolutely justified in refusing any of these hare-brained proposals. There was no signal from Musharraf acknowledging the serious implications of the nuclear weaponisation of India and Pakistan and the need to have discussions on nuclear risk reduction. To compound all this he (Musharraf) changed the composition of the original Pakistani delegation which was coming to the summit. He was planning to bring Foreign Minister Abdul Sattar, Finance Minister Shaukat Aziz and Commerce Minister Daud. But the evented delegation consisted only of Sattar; known for his negative attitude towards India. The finance minister and commerce minister did not come, a clear indication that Musharraf approached the summit with a tunnel vision, to discuss only Kashmir, and was not even prepared to have exploratory discussion on possibilities of broader cooperation between the two countries, which could create a positive environment and general mutual trust.

It is also worthwhile examining the pronouncements and orientations of President Musharraf and the Pakistani Government, particularly after he received Prime Minister Vajpayee's invitation on 24 May 2001. In fact, it would be pertinent to go back to further Musharraf's repeated announcements that he was willing to meet Vajpayee at any time, on any date, any place. His lengthy interview to M.J. Akbar published in April 2001 in *Asian Age*, was the first detailed articulation by him of his India policies. The second instance was an equally lengthy interview given to Dileep Padgaonkar for *The Times of India* just a week before he came to Delhi and Agra. In both these interviews he clearly underlined the following points. His primary and overarching objective was to discuss the Kashmir issue from his point of view. He clarified that while he was willing to discuss other issues, affecting Indo-Pakistan relations, he will be willing to discuss those other issues in a substantive and meaningful manner only after the solution satisfactory to him was achieved on Kashmir. When queried about his views on terrorist violence and secessionism, his response was that he was opposed to violence and terrorism but did not consider the secessionist violence in Jammu and Kashmir was terrorism. In his view it was a violent struggle for self-determination. That the jehad in Kashmir was justified. That it was a freedom struggle Pakistan supported politically, morally and diplomatically. At the same time he resorted to obfuscation stating that Pakistan was not playing any role in the violence in Jammu and Kashmir and that this was an entirely indigenous phenomenon. He flatly denied Pakistan's sponsorship and support to various violent groups in terms of sanctuaries, supplies and training. When pressurised in these interviews to be specific about a solution he may have in mind, he said that an acceptable solution could be found only by going back to holding a plebiscite envisaged in the UN Resolutions of 1947 and 1948. But he wanted these resolutions to be applied only selectively without implementing the provisions in these resolutions for vacation of the territory of Jammu and Kashmir by Pakistani raiders and regular Pakistani armed forces. In an interview to *Gulf News* just 48 hours before his arrival in Delhi, Musharraf stated that neither the Simla Agreement nor the Lahore Declaration and accompanying documents, had any relevance to the summit at Agra. These agreements had not served any purpose according to him. His foreign minister and he himself of course claimed later that he was quoted out of context by the Indian media. That he was willing to take cognisance of the Simla and Lahore agreements as benchmarks for future of Indo-Pakistan relations.

Addressing a women's delegation in Islamabad in the first week of July, he said he desired a new status for the entire state of Jammu and Kashmir unlinked from India. When the ladies' delegation asked him what he thought of Kashmir valley being given to Pakistan and Jammu and Ladakh remaining with India, his reported response was that there must not be any ill-informed suggestions on these lines. He told the delegation that there were Muslims in Ladakh, Kargil and Jammu, and they could not be abandoned. So the whole state of Jammu and Kashmir had to be de-linked from India to move towards a solution. Responding to speculation that the Line of Control could be the basis for a solution, he said a week before arriving in Delhi that "The Line of Control is the problem". He implied that he did not accept the relevance or sanctity of the Line of Control. He kept harping on the point that he was the first head of government and state of Pakistan who had persuaded India to invite him to come and discuss only the Kashmir question. Under instructions from him Finance Minister Shaukat Aziz made public pronouncements in the second week of July that Indo-Pakistani cooperation can be structured only after the Kashmir problem was solved. As mentioned earlier Musharraf did not show any response to suggestions regarding nuclear risk reducation. In fact, he re-affirmed the legitimacy of Pakistani nuclear weapons and missiles as a deterrence against India and linked these to the Kashmir issue. He also remained adamant about tripartite talks, with Pakistan the Hurriyat and India being participants, to find a solution to the Kashmir issue. Though he agreed to suggestions that the contacts with Hurriyat could be separately undertaken by India and Pakistan, he insisted that Hurriyat should be acknowledged by India as the sole representative of the people of Jammu and Kashmir, which is politically and factually unjustified.

These signals should have been sufficient for India to realise that he was coming for the summit with a narrow agenda and a single aim. The Agra summit was accompanied by emotional euphoria and hyperbole. This was despite Musharraf desiring to concentrate on his one point agenda on Kashmir and his collateral objective of projecting himself as some kind of a protector of Muslims not only in Kashmir but also in India. The latter motivation manifested itself in a number of requests his government made about his itinerary. India originally wanted the summit to be held in Goa as a working visit without Musharraf visiting Delhi. Musharraf, however, wanted his visit to be treated as a "state visit". This was one of the reasons for his assuming the presidency of Pakistan. He wanted to offer namaz at the Jama Masjid in Delhi. He also desired to address a meeting of Muslims in Delhi. He wanted to go to offer prayers at the shrines of both at Nizamuddin Auliya and at Ajmer Sharif. All this apart from his successful insistence about meeting representatives of the All Parties Hurriyat Conference.

It is also relevant to note that at the Pakistan high commission reception he kept senior Indian leaders, including former prime minister V.P. Singh, waiting while he carried on his discussions with Hurriyat members. Details of the proceedings of the summit need no repetition. In overall terms it was an anti-climax, both in ambience and in substance.

Musharraf departed for Islamabad grimfaced at midnight on 16 July. He was deprived even of the spiritual succour by not being able to visit the shrines of the Chisti saints in Delhi and Ajmer. India's official spokesperson Nirupama Rao expressed disappointment at the joint declaration not being made. Two things became clear at midnight of 16 July. The first, that high expectations built up between 14 and 16 July afternoon among the people of both India and Pakistan were abruptly shattered. Second, that the fundamental differences between India and Pakistan on the core issues of cross-border terrorism and Kashmir, instead of being resolved at the high level Vajpayee-Musharraf interaction, were only re-affirmed by the two leaders. Foreign Ministers Jaswant Singh and Abdul Sattar at their press conferences on 17 July, asserted that the summit though not leading to any forward looking conclusions, was not a failure. It, according to them, marked the beginning of a process of re-engagement and dialogue between the two countries. Public perceptions, however, remain that the summit failed. So, did the summit break down or did it mark the beginning of a continuous dialogue between India and Pakistan? Discerning an answer from the complex negotiations between the Indian and Pakistan delegations at the summit requires a retrospective analysis before one comes to any conclusions.

First of all, one considers the question whether Pervez Musharraf should have been invited to come for separate bilateral official talks with India. On balance perhaps it would have been better if the first contacts between Vajpayee and Musharraf were made on the margins of the SAARC summit meeting or of the UN General Assembly session. The decision to house a bilateral meeting was implemented nevertheless on the collective advice of the Indian cabinet. This fact is confirmed by Foreign Minister Jaswant Singh's assertion in the press conference on 17 July that there was no division in the Vajpayee cabinet on the proceedings of the summit. Similarly, Musharraf's positive response to Vajpayee's invitation was based on detailed consultations between him and the Pakistani military high command and other important segments of the Pakistani establishment. The logic behind his coming to New Delhi was that his credibility as an effective ruler of Pakistan and as a reasonable statesman would increase by his engaging India in high level discussions.

There were, however, deep contradictions between the impulses and motivations of the two leaders and the two governments in coming to these summit negotiations. India's motivations were the following, first to explore an alternative track of political discussions to resolve the Kashmir issue as the unilateral ceasefire and other initiatives taken by India since November 2000, had not succeeded till the middle of May. Second, India felt that by engaging Pakistan in direct high-level negotiations, it would reduce the insistence and stringency of Hurriyat's demands to be recognised as the sole representative of the people of Jammu and Kashmir and to move towards tripartite talks by going to Pakistan. That there was a sincere and genuine desire by Vajpayee to start a process of normalising relations with Pakistan in response to the desire for a negotiated settlement broadly shared by public opinion and political parties in India. Fourth, India wanted to focus attention on linkages between cross-border Pakistan sponsored terrorism and the requirements of a rational solution to the Kashmir problem. Fifth, India was particularly interested in initiating mechanisms and procedures to manage the serious ramifications of the nuclear weaponisation of India and Pakistan on regional security. Sixth, India also aimed at responding to international concerns and anxieties about the conflict in Kashmir accidentally resulting in a nuclear confrontation between India and Pakistan.

In overall terms, Vajpayee wanted to project India as a country, committed to peaceful means, even when, its unity and territorial integrity stood threatened by the continuing adversarial attitude of Pakistan. Pervez Musharraf and his government's aims were in sharp contrast to the above Indian objectives. First, being recognised by India and participating in negotiations with India would confirm his political and institutional legitimacy as the head of Government of Pakistan. Second, he wished to prove that he was the first Pakistani head of state and government who persuaded India to discuss the Kashmir problem as a separate and high priority issue. Third, the series of statements which he and his governmental colleagues made prior to the summit clearly stated that Pakistan considers a solution to the Kashmir problem according to Pakistani terms of reference an unalterable precondition for the general normalisation of relations. Fourth, Musharraf's objective was to ensure that India agrees to discuss a change in the political and jurisdictional status of Jammu and Kashmir at this summit discussion. Inherent in this objective was also the purpose of obliterating the sanctity of the Line of Control from his point of view. Fifth, he clearly indicated that the Simla Agreement was no longer relevant and the Lahore Process could be selectively revised only if the issue of Kashmir became the only item on the agenda at the Agra summit. Sixth, he of course calculated that his image as a reasonable statesman would get a boost by engaging Vajpayee in discussions. It was this dichotomy in objectives that was the first reason for the Agra discussions ending "inconclusively" as Foreign Minister Abdul Sattar put it in his press conference on 17 July.

The second category of reasons contributing to the break in talks (if not a break down) were, Pakistani perceptions about India's attitudes and predicaments. Pakistan felt that India's stamina and political will to hold on to Kashmir had qualitatively diminished. That the Indian army and security forces were exhausted and losing the will to fight terrorism and proxy war sponsored by Pakistan. Third, that in the context of its nuclear weaponisation India was under direct pressure from the US to compromise with Pakistan on Kashmir. Fourth, that the coalition Government led by Vajpayee was not only subject to internal factional pressure but also his government would not get the support of political parties in opposition to take a strong stand. Fifth, since Vajpayee took the unilateral initiative to invite Musharraf, he would find it difficult, if not impossible, not to show some concrete results at the end of the Agra summit. Sixth, that Vajpayee would be apprehensive about higher levels of jehad terrorism activities in Jammu and Kashmir and in other parts of India and would therefore be willing to respond to Pakistani demands to a great extent. It was this assumption perhaps which made Pervez Musharraf announce before coming to Delhi and Agra, that he wanted a solution to the Kashmir problem within a definite time-frame. Each one of these presumptions proved to be wrong.

The mutually contradictory approach to the summit was also reflected in the composition of the Indian and Pakistani delegations. India's objective was to restore the processes of multifaceted normalisation, Vajpayee being accompanied by the Home Minister Advani, Foreign Minister Jaswant Singh,

Commerce Minister Murosoli Maran and Finance Minister Yashwant Sinha. Musharraf in conformity with his one-point agenda of "Kashmir only" brought Foreign Minister Abdul Sattar, his personal staff and Foreign Office officials. The third reason was the meddlesome role played by audio-visual and print media during the summit. Both India, and Pakistan particularly, instead of controlling and tempering the media's intrusive enthusiasm consciously utilised the media as an instrument of high policy instead of focusing on the negotiations. Information Minister Sushma Swaraj, whatever her latter rationalisation, briefed the press about the item discussed at the summit in a manner that seemed an exercise to stress the Indian side was successful in structuring an agenda for the meeting. She omitted mentioning the Pakistani side's insistence on discussing Kashmir. Musharraf, in response, addressed senior editors on the morning of 16 July, without giving them advance warning that his interaction was going to be televised by Pakistan TV. His main statement and his interaction with senior media representatives detail his negotiating stance on all issues. His articulation, was direct but, more significantly, uncompromisingly assertive. Senior ministers and heads of government do not hold press conferences while engaged in important and sensitive negotiations, on the very subjects on which negotiations are taking place. His breakfast press conference completely destroyed the elbow-room and adjustment spaces in the negotiating process. The failure to make a joint declaration was therefore inevitable.

There was confirmed information that Prime Minister Vajpayee was absolutely firm on issues of vital territorial, security and political interests of India with Musharraf who was clearly informed that his political and media ploys are not going to pressurise India, regardless of criticism which India might have to face if the summit does not result in joint decisions or declarations.

The basic compulsions of both leaders remained operative in that the summit should not mark a breakdown in negotiations. The press conferences of Jaswant Singh and Abdul Sattar on 17 July announcing that Vajpayee would meet Musharraf in New York and at the SAARC summit and would eventually go to Islamabad and their confirming that discussions at various levels would continue, was a positive development. These press conferences led to the following conclusions. First, they were essentially damage control exercises. Second, whatever the gloss put on the differences of opinion and whatever the hopes expressed by the foreign ministers to overcome them, the fact is that profound divergence exist between India and Pakistan on all important issues. One of the signal shortcoming of the summit was its not addressing the nuclear issue which in the long term is more important than the Kashmir issue. Though both sides have affirmed that negotiations would continue, there is ambiguity about the timings of further discussions and the manner in which the subjects would be discussed which created the deadlock at Agra.

At the formal governmental and political level, the assessment is that the summit marked an important beginning. But one has to take note, the beginnings are tentative and the prospects uncertain.

Months have passed since the Agra summit. Media and political analysts have indulged in an orgy of recall, and post facto descriptive analyses which seem to have missed the main points for rumination, that is, what are the realistic rather than speculative prospects of Indo-Pakistan relations. The focus has been on what was done and said at Agra and analyses of pronouncements thereafter. The need is to examine as to where India and Pakistan go from the impasse which occurred at Agra. First, one should look at the official pronouncements of government representatives of India and Pakistan after the summit about what is planned for the future of bilateral dialogue. Secondly, there has to be an assessment of what will actually happen in terms of bilateral discussions. And, thirdly one has to test the validity of these public pronouncements and the possible prospects in the context of ground realities as they have occurred after the Agra summit.

The policy pronouncements by the representatives of both the governments are characterised by a certain amount of contradiction and ambiguity. In their press conferences held on 17 July, both Sattar and Jaswant Singh described the summit discussions as useful. They attempted to rationalise the failure to agree on a joint declaration in terms of certain last-minute complexities and lack of sufficient time and affirmed that high-level political contacts will continue and the dialogue will proceed without break, the objective being to carry forward the positive processes of normalisation of Indo-Pakistan relations. This damage control exercise has however, proved to be tentative and stillborn. General Pervez Musharraf in his widely publicised press conference of 20 July unhesitatingly laid the responsibility of the Agra summit on the Government of India, nuancing this approach with personal praise for Prime Minister Vajpayee. More significant was his categorical re-assertion that all other facets of Indo-Pakistan relations can be attended to only after India agrees to discuss the status of Kashmir within the frame-work of Pakistani objectives. (This is not a quote from Press conference but this is the clear implication of all that he said on Kashmir.) He again indulged in brazen mendacity asserting that Pakistan is not giving any support to terrorist mercenaries and secessionists claiming that they were indigenous freedom fighters. He compared their activities with the struggle of the Palestinians and secessionist elements in Chechnya, Kosovo, etc. He compared Pakistan's attitude on the Kashmir issue with India's role in the creation of Bangladesh. He went on to rationalise Pakistani aggression in Kargil in the context of India's pre-emptive action against Pakistani intrusions in Siachen. His claim that he had taken a compromising position on Kashmir by agreeing to Kashmir being described as an "issue" and not a "dispute", was an exercise in semantic irrelevance in the context of the policy outlined by him in the summit press conferences.

Indians were also strangely adulatory. In policy pronouncements on Pakistan, post-summit, after giving initial indications of the prime minister adhering to his acceptance of Musharraf's invitation to go to Pakistan and about continuing political and other official-level contacts, India stressed that the summit failed because Pakistan was not willing to accept the reality of cross-border terrorism and its role in nurturing this terrorism. While initially agreeing to consider Kashmir as an important issue, we proceeded to re-assert that the whole of Jammu and Kashmir was an integral part of India, that India did not accept it as a territorial dispute and that any change in the status of Jammu and Kashmir is a challenge to India's national identity.

Much was made in the Indian media about the lofty views expressed by General Musharraf in the visitor's book at Rajghat about non-violence and of the irrelevance of military solutions at his banquet speech at Rashtrapati Bhavan, on 14 July. Words did not match deeds as Pakistan-sponsored violence occurred in Jammu and Kashmir even as the summit was taking place. The litmus test on the basis of which the prospects of a positive and purposive dialogue can be assessed is the situation on the ground as it has evolved and is evolving after the summit. Pakistan has rejected all the unilateral efforts for confidence-building measures which India made during the summit. The suggestions for doing some ground level work at the officials level before the summit, of sending the director general, military operations, to Islamabad, of liberalising the travel facilities and visa regimes, including in Jammu and Kashmir, were rejected out of hand. Hindu pilgrims going to Amarnath were being attacked by Pakistan-backed terrorists. Levels of violence perpetrated by them against civilians, especially Hindu civilians, increased in ferocity and frequency as after Musharraf's return to Islamabad. Heavy exchange of fire was resumed along the Line of Control. Islam-pasand parties of Pakistan began questioning the ethno-religious affiliations and identities of the people of

Ladakh and Jammu, asserting that they are subject to the over-arching Islamic identity of Jammu and Kashmir.

Prime Minister Vajpayee aptly assessed Pakistan's India policies in his address to the National Executive of the BJP on 28 July when he stated, General Musharraf came to Agra as a military man with a specific self-serving goal and was not serious about restoring peace. An inescapable conclusion to be drawn is that there is not even a tentative meeting ground on the substance of political issues at discussion between India and Pakistan. Secondly, Pakistan is not willing to accept the objective realities of its supporting the secessionist forces against India. More importantly Pakistan is not willing to pull back from giving this support. Third, Pakistan has decided to continue its undeclared war against India not only in Jammu and Kashmir but in other parts of our country, which leads one to a more critical conclusion that the macro-level agenda of Pakistan is to generate centrifugal impulses in India on communal lines and to disrupt the Indian economy and stability, aimed at the fragmentation of India. This is not a speculation. Gauhar Ayub, former Speaker of the Pakistan National Assembly and son of Field Marshal Ayub Khan publicly stated in 1993 in a press conference in Delhi that peace in the South Asian subcontinent can only be achieved with the break up of India into smaller units. In a way he echoed the strategic designs of the British Imperium at the time of partition which India neutralised due to the genius of Sardar Patel and syncretic and secular political vision of Jawaharlal Nehru.

The Agra summit had only very marginal achievements. The Indian leadership made the personal acquaintance of General Musharraf in terms of his vision and objectives. It conveyed its firmness in safeguarding national interests but indicated a willingness to continue the dialogue with Pakistan in the larger interests of peace and stability. Indo-Pakistan discussions should certainly be continued but Vajpayee and Jaswant Singh should make haste slowly.

Twelve

Uncertainties or Opportunities

$\mathcal{T}$he entire matrix of Indo-Pakistani relations and the regional security environment unravelled with the terrorist attacks on the Pentagon in Washington and the World Trade Center in New York on September 11. The organisation led by Osama bin Laden was found to be the perpetrator. The concept and presumption of "Fortress America" on which US security policies were based for nearly 200 years stood shattered. The last time the continental US, particularly Washington, came under direct physical attack from a foreign source was during the Anglo-US war of 1812.

Osama's headquarters being in Afghanistan and the active nexus between him, the Taliban government of Afghanistan and pan-Islamic terrorist militancy, focused intensive punitive altert against Afghanistan, and political interest on the Central and South Asian region by the US and the international community. The Musharraf Government of Pakistan, isolated and ostracised because of its origins in a military coup regained acceptance and international credibility, particularly with the US. This was because of General Musharraf's reluctant but prompt support to the US-led international campaign against terrorism. India was equally prompt in supporting the international coalition. While both India and Pakistan developed a closer equation with the US in the process, operational interaction between the US and Pakistan on the one hand, and the US and India on the other, have had long-term ramifications. The involvement of the US, NATO powers, Russia and China in the anti-terrorist campaign against the Taliban have made them more active influences on Indo-Pakistani relations.

A number of issues form the ingredients of this assessment. Will General Pervez Musharraf's legitimisation and credibility make him more confident in continuing his adversarial policies towards India, due to the US and other powers being grateful to him for the support extended by him to the international anti-terrorist campaign? Will the US and the Russian Federation in particular, and other powers in general, move to persuade him to stop supporting terrorist militancy against India after the Afghan phase of the anti-terrorist campaign is completed? Can India and Pakistan possibly seize the opportunity for negotiations for finding a practical solution to the Kashmir issue?

While there have been initial doubts in India about the last prospect, the violence of September 11 has the potentialities of an opportunity for both India and Pakistan to come to terms with each other, if India and Pakistan collectively evolve the political will to seize this opportunity.

One facet of the US-led anti-terrorist military campaign in Afghanistan and Pakistan's involvement in this campaign that did not immediately attract the attention it should have, was its impact on the domestic political situation in Pakistan and the complex predicament in which Pakistan had got enmeshed.

When one talks of Pakistan, one is referring primarily to the policies of the Government of General Musharraf. The main point to remember is that the terrorist attacks on the US and the US's response to it have complex implications for Pakistan in terms of stability of its government and the cohesion of civil society of Pakistan. One must go beyond the manifest policy orientations of Pakistan and public pronouncements in Pakistan relating to these orientations to comprehend as to what is happening and what is likely to happen inside Pakistan. It must be noted that Pervez Musharraf extended support to the US reluctantly and under pressure. Reluctantly because public opinion in Pakistan was not supportive of any US military campaign against a neighbouring Muslim country or against the religious movement led by the charismatic Osama.

Nearly three-and-a-half decades of incremental Islamisation of Pakistani civil society and Pakistan's power structure resulted in this mindset. Musharraf was conscious that his decision to support the US and cooperation with it would attract widespread opposition from the people of Pakistan regardless of the claim of government spokesman that it was only some minority segments that were opposing Musharraf's decision. The pressures that led to Musharraf's joining the US campaign were twofold: first, if he had not joined the US-led coalition, there was the possibility of the US dealing with Pakistan as a state supporting and sponsoring terrorism specially in the context of the close linkages between Pakistani military establishment and the Taliban as well as with Al Qaeda. Then there was the possibility Musharraf himself mentioned publicly, that the US might have destroyed what he called "the strategic assets of Pakistan", its nuclear and missile capacities and related technological wherewithal. Third, the Musharraf Government was facing a critical economic situation as well as considerable shortfall in military supplies and equipment, due to sanctions after the nuclear tests of 1998. Musharraf calculated that if he did not cooperate with the United States, these sanctions would continue, debilitating Pakistan, while if he joined the US, it would lift the sanctions and resume various categories of assistance to Pakistan across the board, a calculation that has been proved correct. It must also be remembered that Musharraf did not have the unqualified support of the higher command of the Pakistani armed forces in the decision he took to cooperate with the US. There were reports that in the meeting of the corps commanders of Pakistan held in the second week of September 2001, after the terrorist attacks on the US, 7 out of 11 corps commanders had reser-vations about Pakistan extending political support. There was even greater opposition to Pakistan providing logistical support and launching facilities to US forces in Pakistan and Pakistani territorial waters. It was only after Musharraf assured his senior colleagues about the revival of flows of defence supplies and defence cooperation that they reluctantly agreed.

The conclusion that Musharraf's decision has been against profound undercurrents of opposition and doubts amongst the people and the power structure of Pakistan was inescapable. Internal developments in Pakistan confirm the validity of this conclusion. There were massive demonstrations against President Musharraf's policy in Quetta, Karachi, Rawalpindi and Lahore led by all the Islam-pasand parties of Pakistan. The two major political parties of Pakistan, the Muslim League and the PPP did not give full support to President Musharraf. That Musharraf Government reached levels of serious concerns about these demonstrations was proved by the fact that he had had to put the leaders of Jamat-e-Islami and other religious parties under house arrest. He had to fall in line with the US in freezing the assets and resources of militant Islamic groups in Pakistan that had been listed by the US as entities involved with international terrorism. This generated widespread resentment against Musharraf and his government. By mid-October Musharraf was concerned about possible serious opposition from the high command of his armed forces. He had to take the drastic step of transferring or retiring seven of his eleven seniormost military colleagues including Lt. General Aziz, who actually brought Musharraf to power in 1999, and the chief of the ISI, General Mehmood Ahmed, who had very close connections with the Taliban. Musharraf was engaged in walking the tightrope of being in the good books of the US on the one hand, and at the same time not losing his credibility as a Pakistani ruler and leader committed to the ideology and interests of Islam. This was the motivation that made him demand from the US that Israel and India be kept out of the anti-terrorist coalition. His second demand was that the struggle for self-determination in Jammu and Kashmir should not be brought within the ambit of the campaign against international terrorism. Further demands from him reflecting his difficult predicament were that the US military operation, particularly aerial strikes should be short, swift and targeted. He also suggested that US military operations should be either completed before the beginning of Ramzan or be suspended during this holy Islamic month.

President George W. Bush did not accept many of the demands of Musharraf which embarrassed him further. The positioning of US warships in Pakistan's western coastal territorial waters, Musharraf's allowing US forces to use the air force bases at Dalbandin, Jacobabad, Pesni and Penjgur, had attracted not only public criticism but criticism from Pakistan's strategic and security analysts. The most trenchant elements in this criticism were that Musharraf's decisions were contrary to general public feelings and that he has taken these policy decisions without taking the people and political parties of Pakistan into confidence. There had been reports in the third week of October that protests and agitations against Musharraf's policies have spread to rural areas. There had also been enough speculation that apart from 50 per cent of the commanders of the Pakistan army being opposed to Musharraf's pro-US policies, the middle-level officers of the Pakistan Army were generally upset too by the policies. This was valid speculation given the fact that since the tenure of General Zia-ul-Haq, the officer cadre of the Pakistan Army has been incrementally Islamised and permeated by orthodox religious ideology.

Pakistan trounced India diplomatically and politically by joining the anti-terrorist campaign. Musharraf's first public reaction to the terrorist attacks in Washington and New York came about 24 hours after the incident, in which he condemned the violence, condoled with the US, declared that Pakistan was opposed to all categories of terrorism and offered to cooperate in countering international terrorism. In messages conveyed through Pakistani Ambassador Maleeha Lodhi, Musharraf stated that Pakistan's cooperating with the US in the anti-terrorist campaign being planned by the latter was subject to the following conditions:

First, that the US lift the economic and technological sanctions imposed on Pakistan, particularly after the Chagai nuclear tests. Second, the US restore the flow of financial assistance of various categories bilaterally as well as from multilateral financial institutions. Third, the US extend debt relief concessions on external debts to be paid by Pakistan. Fourth, that Pakistan would only join the US-led international coalition against terrorism if the US kept Israel and India out of the coalition despite these two countries having offered full support and cooperation Fifth, the US restore bilateral financial and defence assistance to Pakistan. Sixth, the US clearly commit that the campaign was not anti-Islamic but only against specific acts of terrorism. Seventh, the involvement of Osama and the Taliban. The US has accepted almost all the conditions stipulated by Musharraf de facto, though the US Government did not give any formal or public response to these pre-conditions.

Some significant nuances in shifts in Musharraf's policies should be noted. Musharraf had clearly stated that the violence in Jammu and Kashmir is not terrorism, implying that the US-led campaign should not cover the violence originating from Pakistan in Jammu and Kashmir. He also underlined that while Pakistan will offer operational and logistical facilities to the US and members of the anti-terrorist coalition in the campaign against Osama bin Laden and Taliban, Pakistani armed forces will not participate in any operations in Afghanistan. When Bush announced that one of the objectives of the international campaign would be to remove the Taliban from power in Afghanistan and replace it with a more acceptable government through the instrumentality of the Northern Alliance, Musharraf objected asserting that Pakistan could not condone the removal of the Taliban from power. Musharraf also opposed the negotiations between the US representatives and Zahir Shah in Rome aimed at bringing the former Afghan back as titular head of the proposed new government. It was only after the failure of negotiations between Pakistani government delegation and the delegation of religious leaders of Pakistan with the Taliban that Musharraf changed this approach. Another reason for this was perhaps the Taliban showing no enthusiasm about Musharraf's proposal that he himself would go to Kabul for further round of negotiations with Taliban. Musharraf invited King Zahir Shah to send a special envoy to Islamabad for discussions with the Government of Pakistan. This, however, did not mean that Musharraf had decided to abandon the Taliban.

The ground realities which provided the contact for these policy orientations were: first, high political and diplomatic pressure from the US on Pakistan to compromise. Pakistan had agreed to US and allied forces using

Pakistani air space, Pakistani territory and Pakistani territorial waters for the planned operations. A US naval force led by aircraft carrier Kitty Hawk was deployed in Pakistani territorial waters between the ports of Karachi and Gwadar. The air and military bases in Gwadar have been made available to the US forces. Pakistani armed forces personnel from these places have been withdrawn. Pakistan security forces were deployed on the Pakistan-Afghanistan border to prevent the flow of large number of Afghan refugees moving out of central and eastern Afghanistan.

There were two reasons for this. First, Pakistan did not want the Taliban to move into North West Frontier Province and Baluchistan as refugees thereby increasing potential of disruptive violence in these sensitive provinces of Pakistan. Second, Pakistan found it extremely difficult to take on additional burden of refugees economically and in terms of social implications of such an influx. The Musharraf government also closed down training camps of organisations named in the prohibitory list of the US as terrorist groups. Even otherwise closing down of camps and dispersing of cadres temporarily was logical and politic. The most significant ground reality is that certain segments of Pakistani public opinion and most of the Islamic parties are opposed to Musharraf cooperating with the US.

Having said this, one acknowledges that the major political parties of Pakistan as well as the power structure in the armed forces establishment are generally supportive of Musharraf's policies at present. The rationale and motivations of Musharraf's interactions with the US are clear. Pakistan has been in an extremely difficult economic predicament since 1998-99, Musharraf needed US assistance to overcome this situation. Had Musharraf refused to cooperate with the US, Pakistan could have been labelled as a state supporting terrorist extremism given Pakistan's close connections with the Taliban and the known contacts between various terrorist organisations based in Pakistan and Al Qaeda led by Osama bin Laden. Musharraf with the background of his memories of American reactions to his Kargil adventure also apprehended US endorsing Indian punitive actions against Pakistan, if he did not fall in line with the US.

Leaving aside the general economic difficulties, Pakistani armed forces have been in need of a wide range of defence supplies from the US. Musharraf's calculations were that if he cooperated with the US, the defence relationship, specially defence supplies relationship, between the US and Pakistan would be restored. This has already happened with the announcement by Bush that countries cooperating with the US in its anti-terrorist campaign would be provided with military assistance. Another motivation of Musharraf was that if military supplies were restored from the US and defence cooperation revived, the power structure of the armed forces headquarters would be supportive of him. This was an important consideration for him because in the initial stages at least four or five of the 11 corps commanders of Pakistan were not terribly enthusiastic about his cooperating with the US. Former chief Lt. General Hamid Gul is on public record as saying that Musharraf's policies are wrong and that they do not serve the long-term interests of Pakistan.

A very important expectation on which Musharraf has predicated his policy of cooperation with the United States is that the US will be more understanding if not supportive of Musharraf's Kashmir policies and Musharraf's foreign policy objectives relating to India. The positive chemistry of Indo-US relations beginning with Clinton's visit was neutralised by Pakistan's cooperating actively with the United States. This expectation stands partially fulfilled with the US not naming Pakistan specially as one of the states from where terrorism originates. The US has also formally advised the Government of India not to take any punitive action against Pakistan-based terrorists. There is no doubt that Musharraf is walking on a high-tension political tightrope in terms of domestic pressures. One has to accept that he is doing it adroitly so far. India need not get high blood pressure because of the importance being given to Pakistan by the US in terms of the US's short-term interests and priorities. If the current Pakistan-US cooperation evolves into any policy orientation detrimental to Indian interests, India should be prepared with remedial political and diplomatic options, even operational options against Pakistan. There is no logic in India competing with Pakistan to attract the US's strategic and foreign policy attention. The approach should be tempered by a continuing awareness. Both the US and Pakistan will basically function within the framework of their respective national interests.

Prime Minister Vajpayee in a lengthy interview towards the end of September had expressed the view that there was some disappointment in India that the US perhaps was not as sensitive to Indian concerns regarding terrorism as India had expected. Parallely, I was told by senior members of the US establishment in October 2001 that the US was also disappointed about Indians not appreciating the extent to which the US campaign against terrorism was safeguarding Indian interests and security concerns. Leaving aside the background of events and military developments in which Secretary of State Colin Powell visited Pakistan and India between 15 and 17 October, it is in this psychological and political context of mutual disappointments that Powell held discussions in New Delhi on 16 and 17 October. The details of his discussions with Jaswant Singh, Advani and

Prime Minister Vajpayee to the extent they could be made public had been reported upon by the media; so had the press conference addressed by Powell been reported upon. The objective should go beyond the descriptive dimensions and related analysis of the visit to draw up a balance sheet, so to say, on Indo–US relations post–September 11.

The negative perceptions or reactions in India that disappointed the US government were the following:

- The US chose Pakistan over India as an active partner in its campaign against international terrorism rooted in Afghanistan, despite India offering unreserved and complete support to the United States.

- As a consequence, the US tilted towards Pakistan and perhaps supported it on issues like Jammu and Kashmir against Indian interests.

- US was not interested in acting against terrorism sponsored by Pakistan against India. US was only concerned with terrorism directed against the US and its allies in Western Europe and against countries like Japan.

- The US would complete its anti-terrorist campaign against Afghanistan and against perhaps some countries in West Asia and leave India to tackle problems of terrorism affecting India, on its own.

- The restoration of economic and military assistance to Pakistan in return for its support would strengthen Pakistan's position in its hostile stances against India.

- A possible expansion of US-Pakistan defence cooperation arrangements resulting from Pakistan support to US, will adversely affect Indian security interests resulting in an arms race in the subcontinent.

- Powell's statement that Jammu and Kashmir is a central issue in Indo-Pakistan relations has been objected to by India. India asserts that it is cross-border terrorism and not Jammu and Kashmir which is the central issue.

- India is disappointed that the US has not designated Government of Pakistan as a terrorism-sponsoring entity.

- There is no public or media appreciation in India about the positive consequences accruing for India from the anti-terrorist campaign launched by the US.

Some of these points were conveyed to Powell during his discussions on 17 October. It is to be noted that Secretary of State Powell's responses were not assertive, polemical or insensitive towards Indian concerns. His responses were based on the following factual developments in trends of direct interest to India.

There is a genuine appreciation of the sympathy and support extended by India to the US, since the violent events of September 11 in US public opinion as well as in the executive and legislative branches of the US Government.

- Pakistan has been made a partner in the coalition due to substantive geo-strategic and operational reasons as Pakistan is and could be most effective instrumentality in operations against the Taliban and Al Qaeda in terms of its capacities to give logistical and operational facilities and most authentic human intelligence inputs for this operation.

- This cooperation between Pakistan and the US is not going to erode or diminish Indo-US relations in any manner.

- Though not publicly stated, the US co-opted Pakistan into the anti-terrorist coalition (especially in operational terms) under some pre-conditions.

- These have resulted in Musharraf dissociating his government from the extremist Taliban and the Al Qaeda movements.

- Musharraf has also been persuaded to take restrictive actions against extremist Islamic parties and political groups in Pakistan.

- Musharraf transferred or removed 7 seniormost out of the 11 army commanders who were opposed to his support to the USA and cooperating with it. These generals particularly General Aziz and ISI chief, General Mehmood Ahmed, were active in fomenting terrorism in Jammu and Kashmir.

- While stating that Kashmir is central to normalising Indo-Pakistan relations, Powell also pointedly mentioned that the terrorist bombing of the Jammu and Kashmir State Assembly on 1 October was wrong and unacceptable. He also emphasised that a solution to the Kashmir issue had to be achieved through bilateral negotiations between India and Pakistan.

- In earlier official statements, the US Government had stressed that while these negotiations take place, the existing Lines of Control and boundaries should be respected by all concerned.

- The US froze the assets of not just the Al Qaeda movement but other foreign organisations linked with it in Europe and elsewhere. The US has also frozen the assets of some of the extremist Islamic groups located in Pakistan.

- The US repeatedly emphasised that the campaign against terrorism will be a long campaign and will target all categories of international terrorism in all parts of the world.

- It should also be noted that the US military campaign in Afghanistan leading to the elimination of terrorist training camps and arms stockpiles, will significantly reduce the capacities and potentialities of terrorists originating in Afghanistan and Pakistan to operate against India and in Jammu and Kashmir and elsewhere.

- The US is also going to destroy opium and other narcotic-producing capacities in Afghanistan in addition to its anti-narcotics campaign in Pakistan and other parts of the world. This will drastically reduce the financial resources of terrorist groups operating in the South Asian region.

- India remained an integral part of bilateral and multilateral consultations being held by leading members of the current international coalition against terrorism.

- The United States and India have signed an agreement during Powell's visit to New Delhi to counter international terrorism activities, with legal and juridical provisions. This consolidates the existing institutional consultative arrangements between India and United States to counter terrorism.

- The US Government is not intending to tilt towards Pakistan to the detriment of the evolving substantive positive trends in Indo-US relations.

- The Musharraf Government could be persuaded to adopt a more rational and practical approach towards India in the momentum of Pakistani policies supporting the US against terrorism, even if this phenomenon emerges under pressure and with reservations. This may be conducive to the beginning of a cordial exercise of resuming a substantive Indo-Pakistan dialogue.

As far as one gathers, the US government felt the Indian media and public opinion were not taking sufficient cognisance of positive trends, the best that the US can do for India at this stage within the framework of its own national interests. To expect the US to designate Pakistan as a terrorism sponsoring state when Pakistan is an active participant in the US campaign against terrorism is impractical.

The central message for India in these developments is twofold: first, that it should not predicate its policies taking the US or Pakistan policies for granted. These would be focused on their respective national interests. Second, that India would have to primarily be self-reliant in resolving its problems related to terrorism and in managing its security environment.

India's attention was so focused on the anti-terrorist campaign led by the US against Afghanistan that we seemed to be unaware of the consequences of this campaign in terms of the struggle against terrorism sponsored by Pakistan, terrorism of which India has been the victim specially since 1989. The Indian Government in its initial reactions to the terrorist attacks on the US conveyed full and unreserved support to the US in its anti-terrorist campaign. In retrospect, India seemed to have predicated its policies on the assumption that the campaign of the US against international terrorism would automatically cover within its ambit terrorism perpetrated by Pakistan-sponsored extremist Islamic mercenaries. This was an optimistic and unrealistic predication. There were speedy signals within a week after the catastrophic violence in New York and Washington that Pakistan was going to be the main operational and logistical instrumentality in the USA's anti-terrorism campaign.

The US gave specific advice to India not to take any action against the Government of Pakistan in response to violence in Jammu and Kashmir within the first ten days after the terrorist attacks in US in September. While the US condemned the Jaish-e-Mohammed attack on the State Assembly building in Jammu and Kashmir early in October in which nearly 40 people died, it did not acknowledge Jaish-e-Mohammed being an organisation sponsored by Pakistan and based in Pakistan.

Despite Musharraf's January 12 spends, India should expect a continuation of terrorist violence in Jammu and Kashmir. Another dilemma the Government of India faces and will continue to face is the groundswell of public opinion within the country in support of India taking decisive, punitive action against Pakistani terrorism. This view is shared by segments of the Indian political and security establishment. Defence Minister Fernandes and Home Minister Advani's pronouncements should be perceived in this context. It must also be clearly acknowledged by the Government and people of India that there is little likelihood of the US politically or operationally supporting any anti-terrorist campaign undertaken by India against Pakistan. This is a campaign which India will have to undertake on its own wherever and whenever it becomes necessary.

India has been fighting terrorism of far within its own territorial limits. The question is can we or should we take the battle across the Line of Control to strike at the roots of Pakistan-sponsored terrorism. If we undertake such a fight again it will be an exercise which we would have to undertake alone. The best scenario one can visualise is of the international community not taking action against us as long as these operations do not deteriorate into a nuclear confrontation with Pakistan.

Four considerations that should influence India's decision in this regard are: first, India must be prepared for Pakistani threatening nuclear and missile retaliation against punitive action in its territory. Second, any effective action by India in response to a manifestly serious terrorist incident could justify action in the eyes of the international community. Third, it must carefully examine whether it has the operational capacity to undertake such action at least for proportionate retaliation, there is no guarantee that Pakistan will reconcile itself to the concept of proportionate retaliation, or it will want to expand the conflict. Fourth, does India have the political will to undertake such punitive action and more importantly the mindset to cope with the military consequences.

Two visual clippings on CNN television on 11 November 2001 brought out the confusing and critical predicament in which Pakistan finds itself, after the US-led military campaign commenced against the Taliban and Al Qaeda—one television clipping showed an Afghan Pushtun near Kandahar lamenting the destruction caused by the US bombing. He stated that it is the common people who are greater sufferers than the Taliban forces. He then proceeded to say that "real Talibs are our people, they are Afghans who brought stability in recent years. It is the foreigners who joined them who have brought this tragedy and violence upon us — the Arabs, the Pakistanis, the Chechens and Egyptians. These foreigners should not have come to my country which has ultimately led to Americans killing us."

The second visual was an interview with a Pakistani anti-Musharraf demonstrator in Islamabad. He said that Pakistan has not even gained what Musharraf told the people that he was going to gain by supporting the United States. The Taliban Government which Pakistan had established in Afghanistan now stands totally destroyed. Acknowledging his Pathan identity, the demonstrator said that the Pushtuns who always had an important role in Afghan Government may no longer have it. The non-Muslim soldiers who started being permanently located in Muslim countries from the time of the Gulf War are now located in Pakistan and in Afghanistan. Pakistan is becoming a slave country because of Musharraf."

These perceptions by common people may not be analytical, nuanced or knowledgeable about the intricacies of the politics of the anti-terrorist campaign and Musharraf's role in it, but they do reflect the general assessment close to the disappointing realities which General Musharraf is facing and is likely to face in coming weeks and months.

The most accomplished foreign minister/diplomat in contemporary history was Charles Maurice Talleyrand (1754-1838). He stipulated that three phenomena should be avoided in the conduct of any country's foreign relations, namely, there should be no overzealousness (or enthusiasm); there should be no excessive anxiety; and third, once a policy is decided upon, there should be consistency in implementing it. If one were to judge characteristics of Indo-US relations since September this year, and the results of Prime Minister Vajpayee's visit to Washington and New York between 7 and 10 November, the conclusion is inescapable that the three stipulations of Tallyrand have been completely ignored by the Government of India.

First, the issue of being overzealous. Vajpayee's visit took place in the context of India being the first country to announce complete, unreserved support and full cooperation to the US in the aftermath of 11 September. It took this decision even before the nearest allies of the US in NATO announced their support and spelt out the operational elements. In contrast, the Russians and Chinese while condoling the tragedy in the US and announcing general support for the campaign against international terrorism stated that the campaign would be more effective and credible if it were undertaken under the auspices of the United Nations. China went a step further including its particular national concerns in its policy reactions, expressing the view that terrorism and separatism in Tibet, Taiwan and Xinjiang should be included in the proposed international anti-terrorist campaign.

India did not mention anything specific about Pakistan-sponsored terrorism in its initial policy statements. The argument given by the government's representatives was that it would have looked like an exercise in cheap and opportunistic bargaining. No other country suffered from this inhibition in its policy reactions. India's motivations were also rooted in over-optimistic and unilateral expectations from the US which were not logical.

What were the results of Prime Minister Vajpayee's discussions with Bush in Washington and his interaction with other world leaders in New

York? The visit led to Vajpayee and his senior advisers making personal acquaintances of the highest leadership in the US. This was followed by wide-ranging discussions on all aspects of Indo-US relations going beyond the issue of the campaign against international terrorism.

There are prospects now of expanded defence cooperation between India and the US as confirmed by Defence Secretary Donald Rumsfeld when he declared his conviction of the need for "strategic cooperation with India" to structure the long-term stability and security in the Asian region. Vajpayee and Bush agreed to take specific initiatives to stimulate and expand bilateral economic relations, particularly, hitech commerce. The US ambassador to India, Robert Blackwill, stated that after Vajpayee's discussions, the expectation is that Indo-US bilateral hitech commerce could increase by 70 to 80 per cent in the coming decade. Brajesh Mishra and President Bush's chief economic adviser Larry Lindsay, have been designated to oversee implementation.

The important agreement reached between Bush and Vajpayee was the instructions issued by them to their respective officers and experts to find ways to work around the Wassenaar and Nuclear Suppliers Group technology regimes so that Indo-US cooperation in nuclear and space technologies could be revived by procedural compromises dealing with hitech export controls inhibiting such cooperation at present. This means a qualitative moderation in the USA's approach towards India's nuclear and missile weaponisation, though the US will remain committed to its non-proliferation agenda.

The attack on the Jammu and Kashmir Assembly building in October confirmed the anticipation that the Government of Pakistan would continue its support to separatist terrorism in Jammu and Kashmir, taking advantage of the new equations Pakistan had achieved with the United States. Further, the cadre of the Pakistan-based Lashkar-e-Toiba attacked the Indian Parliament on 13 December 2001. This attack qualitatively changed the subcontinental security environment and hardened the Indian position against Pakistan's focused subversive violence against India. The attack also introduced a new and critical chemistry in the triangular relationship between India, the US and Pakistan.

Events and trends between December 2001 and end-January 2002 will have a profound impact on India's relations with Pakistan in the coming months and years. US policies towards India and Pakistan will have incremental influence on subcontinental affairs. By coincidence I was in the United States from 14 December 2001 to 16 January 2002. So I had the opportunity to gain direct impressions about US policies and attitudes on the basis of personal discussions and interactions. The months of December and January also saw Musharraf announcing radical changes in his policies towards terrorism and religious extremism. His address to the people of Pakistan on 12 January and another speech he gave to Islamic religious leaders of Pakistan a week later contained announcements regarding this transformation. It is pertinent to broadly review developments since 13 December in these concluding pages.

My primary curiosity as I reached the US on 15 December was to assess how the government and people of that country are reacting to the terrorist attack on Parliament on 13 December. American reaction to the trauma was varied. There were formal statements from the State Department and the Defence Department condemning the terrorist attack on the Indian Parliament. The US Government froze the assets of the Jaish-e-Mohammed and Lashkar-e-Toiba, including them in the list of terrorist organisations. There were telephone calls from President Bush and Powell to Vajpayee and Jaswant Singh, conveying sympathy and general support. Nuances in US policy statements, however, must not go unnoticed. There was no acknowledgement of links between these terrorist organisations and the Government of Pakistan. India was also insistently advised to react with caution and restraint.

The quid pro quo from the US was the offer to generate pressure on Musharraf to act against these terrorist groups and their leaders. Such pressure from the US has apparently resulted in Musharraf putting restraint on the leaders of the Jaish and the Lashkar and initiating some action to freeze their financial assets in Pakistan. It is worthwhile noting that the US Government, while welcoming the steps, has generally supported the Pakistani demand that India should provide hard evidence about these terrorist organisations having been involved in the attack. One wonders whether the same detached meticulousness for hard evidence would have underpinned US reactions had the US Capitol been attacked as the Indian Parliament was. As these governmental interactions were taking place, Indo-Pakistani tensions increased with the deployment of Indian and Pakistani troops along the international border and the Line of Control in Jammu and Kashmir. The situation was compounded by Pakistan's ambiguous and dilatory responses to the legitimate demands made by the Government of India for action against the Lashkar and the Jaish and for the extradition of their leaders.

The media coverage in the US of Indo-Pakistani relations post–13 December left one bemused in contrast to the manner in which US media reacted to the attack on the World Trade Center and the Pentagon. The attack on the Indian Parliament was consistently described as attack by "militants from Kashmir who India claims operated with the support of Pakistan". Pakistan's denial of links with this attack and Musharraf's messages of sympathy to India were given high prominence. Then there was the projection that India had yet to come up with hard evidence about Pakistani involvement. Following the analysis came the prognosis on rising Indo-Pakistani tensions. Armchair American experts in the audio-visual media, instead of taking note of the violence against the Parliament as an act of terrorism needing an appropriate punitive response, proceeded to theorise on Kashmir being a disputed territory and this unresolved dispute being the cause of the violence in New Delhi in December. These pundits were critical of India for having deployed troops on the Pakistan border and announcing intention of decisive action. The American public was reminded that India and Pakistan were nuclear weapon powers and that any military confrontation between them could lead to a nuclear war. Everybody was also informed that Pakistan was a close ally operationally important to the United States in its anti-terrorist war in Afghanistan.

Then came the articulation of the primary American concern: India's generating military and diplomatic pressure on Pakistan would compel Pakistan to focus political attention on India and divert troops from the Pakistan-Afghanistan border, thereby slowing down or creating difficulties in the ongoing anti-terrorist campaign by the United States. The expression of this concern was followed by the advocacy that India has a particular responsibility to act with restraint and not put a spanner in the works of the campaign against the Taliban and Al-Qaeda.

While the US government has been more forthcoming and concrete in its support to India, the substantive concerns of the US were reflected in the media reports and analyses. There is general sympathy regarding terrorism India faces but the primary concern is to complete America's own terrorist campaign. That Osama bin Laden and Mullah Omar have not still been captured or killed; that Taliban and Al-Qaeda cadre still remain in Afghanistan with potentialities of destabilising the new Afghan government and uncertainties about US being supported by the Arab allies in expanding its counter-terrorist operations to other countries like Iraq, are more significant concerns in US policies.

Nevertheless, there is a general awareness about Pakistan's two-decade long involvement and links with pan-Islamic militancy and cross-border terrorism. Nor is there any amnesia about the US government's involvement in supporting Islamic militancy during the final two decades of the previous century for serving its broader strategic interests. There is a greater acknowledgement of India being not only a committed democracy but a strategic entity supportive of the forces of democracy, human rights and plurality in the international order. These perceptions of the American people, one hopes, will balance off somewhat self-centred orientation articulated by the US media.

It is with this background that India should anticipate US policies towards our region. The first priority would remain the destruction of the inter-national Islamic terrorist networks threatening the US's own security and then the security of western democracies. Its second priority would be to eradicate the resources of these networks in terms of narcotic smuggling and illegal acquisition of arms. This campaign will not be limited to Afghanistan but will expand to other countries in the coming months. India can expect general political support in its anti-terrorist campaign as far as its campaign remains confined within Indian territory, responding to specific incidents of terrorism. The United States will not countenance any punitive action against Pakistan across the border or across the Line of Control. In fact there are clear enough indications that the United States would be inclined to intervene more actively in the subcontinent. Secretary of Defence Donald Rumsfeld stated in the last week of December that apart from being in constant touch with the leaders of India and Pakistan, the United States is considering contingency options to prevent an India-Pakistan conflict.

It is obvious, therefore, that if India refuses to abide by the advice for restraint given by the United States, the new beginnings made in Indo-US relations will be negatively affected. It is equally obvious that India would have to fight its own battles against terrorism in the foreseeable future in the context of US perceptions of its own interests and Pervez Musharraf's adroitly cosmetic gestures to remain on the right side of the United States. India has to conduct this struggle not only in terms of carefully structured anti-terrorist operations but more importantly by engaging in an intense publicity and diplomatic campaign to make the US and world public opinion aware of our concerns and the linkage of these concerns with issues of global security which interest the United States and the major powers of the world.

As most of my travels were in southcentral and western United States, away from the eastern states of the country, I presume to claim that my perceptions are based on the views and attitudes of the Americans living away from the direct impact of governmental thinking and the influence of the traditional establishment of that country. First, the impact on the domestic front within the United States. The foremost element in this impact is the feeling of vulnerability in terms of domestic security. The collective self-confidence in the American people about "Fortress America" stands eroded. Continental United States, surrounded by oceans on the east and west and by friendly neighbours in the north and south, coming under direct attack was not just unexpected but an unthinkable prospect. The 9/11 terrorist strikes in New York and Washington were the first attacks to occur within the continental territory of the United States after 1812, when British forces briefly captured Washington. "Homeland security" has emerged as a major political concept and policy objective of high priority. President Bush has created a new Department of Homeland Security. Executive orders and organisational arrangements are being evolved to reactivate the role of the US armed forces and paramilitary forces in safeguarding domestic security in all its dimensions.

The second noticeable phenomenon is the appearance of emotional patriotism. This attitude finds expression in the fact that practically every decision taken, every policy suggested by President Bush to counter the terrorist threat, has not encountered any opposition from the US Congress or at the level of the governments of constituent states of the US. The groundswell of patriotism has been nurtured and strengthened by political functions and religious ceremonies in remembrance of the September attacks. Though there is an absence of aggressive jingoism, one can discern a certain amount of paranoia about foreigners, particularly from Asia and the Arab countries.

There is fear about Islam, though President Bush and the US leadership have tried to educate public opinion about the distinction between Islam as a religion and terrorists who pervert its teachings. While the US Government stresses that its anti-terrorist campaign is not animated by motives of revenge, public opinion feels that the massive violence perpetrated against innocent US citizens should be avenged clearly and decisively. A corollary of this approach is the general view that countries and people, who do not fully support the anti-terrorist campaign of the United States and suggest reticence or moderation in this campaign are not friends of the US and should be treated accordingly.

There is also the feeling that the other major powers of the world should take on a more active role in dealing with international terrorism without leaving the burden on the United States. That the US government is responsive to this broad undercurrent in domestic public opinion is indicated by the fact that Defence Secretary Donald Rumsfeld has been comparatively ambiguous about expanding the US campaign beyond Afghanistan in his public statement since the beginning of January. He has also indicated that in the short term the US military campaign will be focused on eastern and southern Afghanistan and the border areas with Pakistan. He has taken note of the emerging frustration within his government and in public opinion about Osama bin Laden and Mullah Omar not having been captured or eliminated as yet. He has stressed that the operations against them remain an objective. The State Department echoed his views when a US spokesman, for the first time, publicly stated that General Musharraf's credibility and Pakistan's future will depend on how the Government of Pakistan deals with Al Qaeda and other terrorists.

India shifted its Pakistan policies into a high proactive gear in the aftermath of the terrorist attack on Parliament on 13 December. The macro-level political consequences have been higher and palpable levels of tension in Indo-Pakistani relations. Three broad patterns of reactions have emerged about India's diplomatic, political and military moves to generate pressure on Pakistan, and to signal India's determination to be more decisive in responding to the proxy war. There is a collective international consensus and concern that India and Pakistan should not get enmeshed in a military conflict with possibilities of a nuclear confrontation. Second, there are advocacies in Indian public opinion that India should not resile from the policy of generating pressure on Pakistan, particularly, military pressure based on the large-scale deployment of Indian armed forces on the India-Pakistan border and on the Line of Control. Third, there is the view that the pressure generated by India has achieved India's objectives to the extent feasible at this stage, both in terms of the impact on President Musharraf and in terms of the international community responding to the Indian concern, and therefore India should consider shifting from high gear to a stance of reasonableness.

In early 2002, representatives of four out of five Permanent Members of the UN Security Council — the US, the UK, Russia and China — met India's prime minister, home minister and foreign minister in New Delhi to give unanimous advice to India to be moderate, restrained and cautious. They also conveyed a general consensual assessment that India's politico-diplomatic and military moves have had the desired effect on Musharraf resulting in restraining actions against extremist religious groups and terrorist organisations within Pakistan. Shorn of courtesy and diplomatic tact, the substantive assessment of the US and other important powers is that President Musharraf has started a genuine move to curb and eradicate religious extremism and terrorism in his country and, therefore, India should not maintain high pressure on him which might result in his having to move back from policy initiatives in this regard. Linked with these is the longer-term objective that India and Pakistan should take some substantive steps to resolve the Kashmir problem, because if not attended to it is a hair-trigger for a conflict. While there is an acknowledgement of India's trauma and concerns by these powers, their view is that India should be temperate in larger interests of regional stability. India's Pakistan policies have to be responsive to these trends because of unanimity of approach of all the important powers in the world on these issues.

One, therefore, proceeds to assess the most recent ingredients of Pakistan's policies towards India. Much has been made of Musharraf's speech of 12 January, his banning Jaish-e-Mohammed and Lashkar-e-Toiba, freezing their assets and Pakistani authorities detaining nearly 2000 Islamic activists. General Musharraf's speech is being interpreted as the beginnings of qualitative change in Pakistan's India policies. The question is whether these positive interpretations of Musharraf's policies are an emerging reality or are they cosmetic and tactical moves by him which have resulted in positive anticipatory speculations (as far as India is concerned, the latter seems to be the case). Musharraf in his speech has reiterated that there will be no change in Pakistan's support to the secessionist movements in Jammu and Kashmir. "Kashmir remains a part of bloodstream of Pakistanis," according to him. He has ruled out any compromise with India on Kashmir. There is no declaration from his government that they will stop supporting separatists in Kashmir. He has specially emphasised that his actions against various extremist groups within Pakistan are a part of his policy of general support to the international campaign against terrorism led by the US and is aimed at stabilising the internal situation in Pakistan.

Given this overall context, India faces a complex predicament in dealing with Pakistan. First, there is no clear shift in Pakistan's India policies. Second, Musharraf's credibility as a reasonable moderate leader committed to the international anti-terrorism campaign and as a person desirous of defusing tension with India has increased in international perceptions. Whatever the facts, whatever India's reservations, this international perception is a compelling phenomenon. Third, the politico-military stance having achieved the initial desired objective to some extent is now subjected to law of diminishing returns. It is necessary for India to appear practical and reasonable without lowering its guard or pulling back from the principled approach on the question of Pakistani involvement in terrorism. It is equally important that New Delhi not lose the general support of the international community, gained since last September.

India must examine options to de-escalate the military tension in a gradual and measured manner. It should agree to bilateral discussions with

Pakistan at the sufficiently high official level with a defined time-frame of the coming two to three months. It should continue the diplomatic campaign with the important powers of the world to sustain international pressure on Pakistan to transmute the general policy pronouncements of Musharraf into operational realities. Parallely, it should initiate substantive negotiations with leaders of all groups in Jammu and Kashmir to resolve the domestic dimensions of the Kashmir problem.

Since the terrorist attacks against the United States and against Parliament on 13 December 2001, international concerns are focused on South Asia, particularly on Afghanistan, Pakistan and India. A consequence has been an incrementally activist role adopted by the United States and other major powers in the subcontinent within the framework of the international anti-terrorist campaign. Visits of high-level leaders of foreign governments to Delhi since mid-December to defuse Indo-Pakistan tension have not been advisery exercises. In objective terms, these exercises are a third party intervention in Indo-Pakistani relations. This is just a statement of fact and not a value judgement.

The likelihood of international involvement/intervention, particularly by the US, is on the cards due to the following reasons. First, whatever India's convictions, the international community considers the problems of Jammu and Kashmir as a territorial dispute in which Pakistan has a status and stake. Neither the accession of the state to India nor the issue of Pakistani aggression is part of their perceptions. Second, despite the passage of more than 50 years, the dispute remains unresolved and it has sparked off major conflicts between India and Pakistan. Third, the anxiety about such conflicts has qualitatively increased in the international community because of the acquisition of nuclear weapons and missiles capacities by India and Pakistan over the last decade. The Kashmir issue is perceived as a nuclear flashpoint. Fourth, the phenomenon or cross-border terrorism and pan-Islamic militancy has become a matter of international concern and the assessment is that this pernicious phenomenon finds fertile ground in disputes like those of Jammu and Kashmir. There is also a speculative assessment that the stabilisation of Afghanistan is indirectly dependent on the resolution of Kashmir and the normalisation of India-Pakistan relations.

Therefore, India must clearly understand that there is every possibility of the US intervening in the subcontinent, not just politically but operationally if there is an impending nuclear confrontation between the two countries in Washington's assessment. It will have the support of the international community in such an exercise. India has to be responsive to the realities described above. If it wants to avoid third party involvement, it must give the highest priority to resolving the internal dilemmas of Jammu and Kashmir.

There have been reports that the United States wanted expanded defence cooperation with India in the following specific areas: (a) Indian Naval Protection for the US ships in the Indian Ocean, (b) training facilities to be provided for American troops inside Indian territory, (c) berthing and repair facilities for American ships in Indian ports and (d) logistical support for the US Navy in the Bay of Bengal and in the Arabian Sea. These proposals were publicised in the media with the comment that India had refused some of these suggestions. Jaswant Singh dismissed these reports as fiction. While he was saying this in Washington, Defence Minister George Fernandes said in Delhi that some of these proposals were discussed between him and Rumsfeld and that India was not averse to cooperating with the US on these proposals after careful consideration.

India's policy at present on all counts seems to be to fully support the US and establish close relationship with that country. If that is so, one finds the views expressed by Jaswant Singh as a contradiction of this policy of which he has been the principal architect over the past three years. Fernandes contradicting Jaswant Singh's assertions projects India as an ambivalent country that has not made up its mind on very vital aspects of Indo-US cooperation. One is conscious that this contradiction reflects the division in Indian public opinion about the United States. But being perceptive about long-term interests, being clear about priorities, and being cohesive and definite about decisions, is important in structuring relations with major power centres of the world, particularly the US. Depsite the positive results of Vajpayee-Bush meeting, Indian policies towards the US remain subject to contradictions, doubts and lack of clarity.

While Musharraf's capability and inclination to support violent terrorist organisations may be eroded because of international pressure, he will not be able to completely distance himself from such organisations as far as India is concerned because his survival in power depends on not antagonising them beyond a point.

While the international campaign against terrorism provides India and Pakistan with an opportunity to move towards a reasonable dialogue, this opportunity can be effectively used only if there is a fundamental transformation of the power structure in Pakistan, not only in terms of its military components but also in terms of the social background and political inclinations of the plutocratic and feudal leadership of the major political parties of Pakistan. The hope for rationality in Indo-Pakistani relations, therefore, has to be tempered with abundant political caution.

Annexures

Annexure 1

Pakistan—Birth and Objectives

*P*akistan grew out of the two-nation theory of the Muslim, which for the last twenty years or more has been synonymous with its permanent president, the late Mohammed Ali Jinnah, called by the Muslims Qaid-i-Azam or the Supreme. Leader. The career of Qaid-i-Azam Jinnah indicates a curious and ironic development from being 'the apostle of Hindu-Muslim Unity', as he was called by admiring Congressmen, to being the chief exponent, advocate and creator of Pakistan — a state based upon the thesis that the Muslims of India are a separate nation, and as such need a homeland and state for themselves, separate from Hindu-land. Pakistan is now a predominantly Muslim state, so predominantly Muslim in its population that its western and more important portion has in the course of a few months of its establishment, been almost completely rid of its Hindu, Sikh and to a great extent of its Christian and untouchable populations. By what processes this development has been brought about is what this booklet is designed to relate. The present overlords of Pakistan have declared frequently that Pakistan is *in character* a Muslim State — the largest Muslim State in the world. This description of its character, when placed side by side with the declared character of India as a secular state, has unnerved the Hindu population of faraway East Bengal, let alone in Pakistan where Hindus in appreciable numbers are found. Since last October a deliberate policy on the part of the Muslim majority in East Bengal, with the connivance of the East Bengal Muslim League Government, forced the Hindus out of that province. This exodus of Hindus became such a vast movement of emigration, that in October 1948 official estimates put the number of Hindu immigrants from Eastern Pakistan into India at 15 lakhs. More and more were following over the border into Assam and West Bengal everyday, and the refugee problem for the Indian Government already preoccupied with the rehabilitation of about a crore of people from Western Pakistan and Kashmir, began to assume a desperate look. That is what made Sardar Patel declare that if the Pakistan Government did not take effective steps to stop the exodus of Hindus from East Bengal the India Government would claim proportionate territory from East Bengal for the resettlement of the Hindu immigrants. This exodus is only an illustration of the fact that the driving out of minorities and non-Muslim population is something inherent in the very nature, conception and scope of the kind of state which the Muslims have achieved through the good offices of the British in the shape of Pakistan. No amount of reasonableness and accommodation, no attempts at friendship and understanding on the part of India could avert what occurred in West Punjab, in the North Western Frontier Province, in Sindh, in Bahawalpur, in raider-occupied Kashmir and is at present occurring in East Bengal. The thing is inevitable and inherent in the nature of the State of Pakistan and the entire attitude and mentality of which this State is the result. It is a significant fact that while in India, the Government discourages *communal* groups and parties, in Pakistan no group or parties other than communal are encouraged. A Pakistan Peoples' Congress is inconceivable. When the Hindu leaders of Sindh planned the establishment of a political party which might draw its membership from people belonging to various communities the reply of the Pakistan Government was characteristic. The Hindus of Sindh, (such of them as are still there) might have a Hindu Party, but not one which Muslims also might join. In the *Muslim* State of Pakistan, no Muslim may join any organisation other than a purely Muslim one. It is such an attitude which bred the riots of 1946 and 1947-Calcutta, Noakhali, NWFP, the Punjab, Sindh and Bahawalpur.

The very name of the State which the Muslim League envisaged — and achieved — is, in the context in which it was adopted, a standing insult to other non-Muslims living in India. This name, *Pakistan*, means literally "the Land of the Pure" or of Purity. This implies clearly that Hindus and all that belongs to them credally and materially is impure, defiled and unholy. In a communally-charged atmosphere to have broadcast such an offensive name and concept among the Muslims was to extend an open invitation to racial and communal arrogance, contempt of others, challenges and counter-challenges.

The origin of the Pakistan idea is briefly this:

Dr Mohammad Iqbal in his presidential address at the Annual Muslim League Session held at Allhabad in 1930, advocated the establishment of a separate Muslim State or Federation in India on the basis of the Muslim's separate political identity, in these words: "The Muslim demand for the creation of Muslim India within India is, therefore, perfectly justified.... I would like to see the Punjab, North West Frontier Province, Sindh and Baluchistan amalgamated into a single state. Self-Government within the British Empire, or without the British Empire, the formation of a consolidated North-West Indian Muslim State appears to me to be the final destiny of the Muslims at least of North-West India.

This was the first hint thrown into the atmosphere of Indian politics of a separate Muslim State or Federation. But the thing at this stage was a vague aspiration, the desire towards a separate state was formed in anybody's mind as a concrete programme — symptomatic nevertheless of a dangerous way of thinking and an explosive kind of mentality.

Dr Mohammad Iqbal's thesis did not immediately find much support with the Indian Muslims. At the Round Table Conference which was held in London soon after, the Muslim delegates talked in terms only of safeguards and the proportions of seats the Muslims might get in the various legislatures of India in addition to pleas for the creation of a new Muslim-majority province, namely Sindh. The official policy of the Muslim League in these years continued to be very much the same — any thought of setting up a separate state being regarded as the vision of an idealist, a poet, but in no way practical politics.

But Dr Mohammad Iqbal was by no means the only Muslim who thought in terms of a separate Muslim State in India. In January 1933 there appeared, on behalf of certain Indian Muslim students at Cambridge, headed by Chaudhari Rehmat Ali, a pamphlet entitled *Now or Never*. This pamphlet advocated a complete breakaway of the Muslims of North-Western zones of India from the rest of the Indian nation. "India," it said, "is not the name of single country, nor the home of one single nation. It is in fact, the, the designation of a state created for the first time in history by the British." The Muslims are shown in this pamphlet to be altogether separate in their way of life from the other people of India, and hence the unmistakable conclusion is suggested that they must have a separate state of their own. Says the pamphlet, "We do not inter-dine, we do not intermarry. Our national customs and calendars, even our diet and dress, are different. Hence the Muslims demand the recognition of a separate national status."

It is necessary here to point out that the essence of this last argument given above has been repeated ever since 1940 by all Muslim Leaguers, down from Mr Jinnah. Differences and cleavages have been emphasised and the doctrine of hate and animosity has been preached. Muslim separatism has been bolstered up; all attempts made in the past — both remote and recent — by far-sighted Hindus and Muslims, kings, poets, founders of faiths and others, have been sought to be written off. This exaggerated account of the cleavage between the Muslims and the Hindu (and Sikh) way of life led, when factors favourable to such a consummation had developed fully, to the orgy of rioting in Bengal, the NWFP, the Punjab and Sindh. As a matter of fact, it would have been a surprising thing if after the gospel of hate which the Muslim League had been preaching to the Indian Muslims for so many years, these riots and their accompanying horrors and devastation had not occurred.

The word "Pakistan", which so powerfully caught the imagination of the Muslims of India, and which pinned the vague, floating idealism of savants like Dr Mohammad Iqbal to a concrete objective and programme, is a coinage of Chaudhari Rehmat Ali, who has been mentioned above. He has been hailed among the Muslims as the founder of the Pakistan National Movement. The coinage is said to have been formed from the initial letters of the names of the Provinces designed to compose the original Pakistan. These provinces were: Punjab, Afghania (NW Frontier Province), Kashmir and Baluchistan (which contributed the end letters to the name). Apart from this genesis of the name, which perhaps was an afterthought, the name is a Persian compound formation, and an offensive challenge to the non-Muslims. Pakistan means the Land of the Pure, in this case the Muslims.

Pakistan, as has been told above, was originally conceived to comprise only the northwestern areas of the Punjab, Sindh, Kashmir, the N.W. Frontier Province and Baluchistan. But in a later concept of the thing, issued in the form of a revised version of the original scheme, it was devised to comprise, besides the areas originally earmarked for it, also Assam and Bengal in the east, and Hyderabad and Malabar in the south. In addition to these extensive strongholds of Muslim power in the north west, east and south beleaguering non-Muslim India from all strategic points, there were also to be several smaller though by no means small, Muslim pockets, studded all over the country — one in the United Provinces, one in the heart of Rajputana and another still in Bihar. Thus, the Muslims of all India, and not only those of the Muslim majority areas, were to have independent countries of their own, parcelling out India into so many new Muslim-dominated States.

This process in its conception carried with itself certain very far-reaching, and in the light of the communal developments of 1946 and 1947, very significant and pregnant corollaries. Rehmat Ali, whatever else he might be, has been quite fertile in the devising of catching, though somewhat megalomaniac, names. Besides Pakistan, he has been responsible for the concept of India as *Dinia*, a cleverly suggestive anagram. Dinia would be the continent which, if not at the moment the home of an Islamic State, was such, in immediate conception, waiting to be converted and subordinated to Islam through the proselytising zeal of its sons. Bengal and Assam, conceived as a joint Muslim-majority area by a logic partial to Muslim reasoning was rechristened by Rehmat Ali, Bang-i-Islam or Bangistan, redolent of the Feudal Mughal name of Bengal, *Bangush*, which has been offensive to the Hindu, suffering for centuries under the hell of the Muslim. The Muslim homelands parcelled out of Bihar, the UP and Rajputana (the Ajmer area, where the shrine of the great Muslim Saint, Khawaja Muinuddin Chisti is located) were to be called respectively Faruquistan, Haideristan and Muinistan. Hyderabad, ruled over by a Muslim prince, with its 86% Hindu population, was to be called Osmanistan, after the name of the present nizam; and the Moplah tracts of Malabar were named Moplistan. There would, besides, be areas known as Safistan and Nasaristan. On the map of India (or Dinia) as drawn by Rehmat Ali, non-Muslim areas make unimpressive, miserable patches, interspersed on all sides with Muslim states, born out of conflict with Hindu India, and pursuing a set policy of converting, conquering and amalgamating this Hindu India into themselves. Such was the conception of Pakistan, at any rate the first push, made popular among the Indian Muslims by the tremendous force of propaganda which communal and fanatical zeal could lend to the Muslim League of which we have been witnessing the grimly tragic consequences since August 1946.

All this mentioned above was elaborated by Rehmat Ali in 1940, the year in which his concept had been so successful that the Lahore Session of the Muslim League passed the famous Pakistan Resolution, adopting the achievement of an independent "Muslim State" out of the United India of British formation, as the immediate goal of the Muslim League policy. Rehmat Ali's pamphlet of 1940 was entitled *Millat of Islam and the Menace of Indianism*. By the Menace of Indianism was implied the conception of the Indian Muslims as a separate nation, who must refuse to be of India, and must demand a separate state or several "states" to be in alliance with one another, for themselves. The elucidation of this conception by Rehmat Ali is very revealing for a student of the trends forming the Indian Muslim mentality of the last decade or so.

In 1942 Rehmat Ali came out with still another pamphlet, called *The Millat and its Mission*. In this pamphlet, apart from the concept of India as Dinia or the land which was destined to be converted in its entirety to Islam and to Muslim hegemony, there was a very revealing attitude about minorities. As has been pointed out by all, those who have been critical of the programme of Pakistan, the problem of minorities to be left in Pakistan and Hindustan would be the chief stumbling block of any future policy in these states. Vast Hindu-Sikh and Muslim minorities would be left in Pakistan and Hindustan respectively, and to settle with them would require imagination, tact and a high degree of fairness. The Muslim League advocates of Pakistan have been prolific with assurances of fair treatment towards minorities — assurances never seriously meant to be kept, and broken in the most unworthy manner in all the territories which became part of the Pakistan State. What the Muslim League had been planning all these years was really to drive out minorities from Pakistan, and in this way to solve the minority problem. Listen to the illuminating remarks of Rehmat Ali on minorities.

"What is the fundamental truth about minorities ... remember that, in the past 'Minorityism' has ever proved itself a major enemy of the Millat; that at present it is sabotaging us religiously, culturally, and politically even in our national lands; and that in the future, it would destroy us throughout the Continent of Dinia and its dependencies, Hence the Commandment (one of the seven commandments laid down in the pamphlet "The Millat and its Mission"), Avoid 'Minorityism', which means *that we must not leave our minorities in Hindu lands, even if the British and the Hindus offer them the so-called constitutional safeguards.* For no safeguards can be substituted for the nationhood which is their birthright. *Nor must we keep Hindu and/ or Sikh minorities in our lands, even if they themselves were willing to remain with or without any special safeguards.* For they will never be of us. Indeed, while in ordinary times they will retard our national reconstruction, in times of crisis they will betray us and bring about our redestruction.

"This is the gist of the Commandment. It may be expanded into the factual statement that

"(a) To leave our minorities in Hindu lands is:-

(1)   To leave under Hindu hegemony 35 million Muslims who form no less than 1/3 of the whole Millat, which in her struggle for freedom has no allies in the continent.

(2)   To deny their resources to the cause of the Millat at a time when

she needs the maximum contribution of every one of her sons and daughters.

(3) To devote their lives and labour to the cause of the Hindu *Jati*. I hope people who argue that an equal number of (35 millions) Hindu and Sikh minorities in Pakistan, Bangistan and Osmanistan will be working for the Millat overlook the fact that the work of one can never compensate for that of the other...."

To reinforce still further the lesson and the determination for the total elimination of minorities, Rehmat Ali argues further on, more uncompromisingly,

"(b) To keep Hindu and/or Sikh minorities in our lands is:

"(1) To keep in Muslim lands 35 million Hindus and Sikhs who form no more than 1/8 of the total strength of the force opposing the Millat in the Continent of Dinia.

(2) To condemn to permanent servitude our 35 million brethren living in Hindu Dinia, i.e., outside Pakistan, Bangistan and Osmanistan. The reason is that unless and until we accept this commandment we cannot liberate them from the domination of 'Indianism'.

(3) To forget even the unforgettable lesson taught to us by the disappearance of our own Pak Empire[1] and of the Turkish Empire, namely that one of the major causes of their decline, defeat and downfall was the treachery and treason of their religious, racial and political minorities."

Thus, in a thorough and relentless way Rehmat Ali has pleaded for the total elimination of minorities from Pakistan. How deeply the lesson sank into the minds of the Muslim League and the average Muslim, will be seen from the pronouncements given below of the leaders of Muslim Opinion in India from Qaid-i-Azam Jinnah downwards, on the question of minorities and the exchange of population. It was this lesson, thoroughly learnt, which led to the hounding out of the non-Muslim populations from Eastern Bengal (1946), NW Frontier Province (1946 and 1947), Western Punjab, Sindh and its adjoining areas, and now from the East Bengal Province of Pakistan.

Mr Jinnah replying to a question seeking suggestions for the restoration of peace in India, said: In view of the horrible slaughter in various part of

India, I am of the opinion that the authorities, both Central and Provincial, should take up immediately the question of exchange of population to avoid brutal recurrence of that which had taken place where small minorities have been butchered by the overwhelming majorities.

> The Viceroy — because he alone can do it — as the representative of the Crown and as the Governor-General with powers that are vested in him, should adopt every means and measures to restore, first, peace and order. In the present conditions there is no room for reason, intelligence and fair-play. Negotiations in these conditions can hardly yield fruitful results and produce a settlement satisfactory to both parties.

It may be pointed out here that exchange of population has been in the mind of all Muslim exponents of Pakistan, or whatever the Muslim State designed to be carved out of India has been called. Dr Latif of Hyderabad (Deccan) in his book, *The Muslim Problem in India*, in spite of the temperate language used by him and the reasoned way in which he has made out the case for creating Hindu and Muslim zones, has advocated the exchange of population. On this problem he says, "One of the objects of the transitional consitution[2] is to *facilitate and prepare the ground for migration of Muslims and the Hindus* into the zones specified for them so as to develop them into culturally homogeneous States.

"During the transitional period migration should be on a voluntary[3] basis. For this the necessary legislation will have to be passed for each region, and a machinery set up to organise and regulate this voluntary migration."

There is unconscious humour and irony in the use of the epithet "voluntary" for this migration, for which Dr Latif's scheme postulates the provision of legislation and a suitable machinery by the Government or the Government concerned. Of course, when the Muslim League did actually come to establish a government of their own on 15 August, 1947, they drove the non-Muslim population out of their country with scant ceremony — by a campaign of pillage, murder, rape and arson. This method effected the exchange desired much quicker and in a more thorough way than could be done by any human legislation. As a matter of fact, the driving out of minorities had begun as early as November 1946 with Noakhali, when the whole of northern India was flooded with destitutes begging for a morsel or a piece of cloth to cover their shivering bodies. Later this was effected in December 1946 and January 1947 in the Hazara District of the N-W Frontier Province, when Sikhs and Hindus had to flee for dear life into the Punjab. And then came March 1947 with its horrors. August 1947 let loose a vast flood of persecution of millions. So, the Muslim scheme was being translated into historic fact to the letter.

To return now for a while to Rehmat Ali, whose pamphlets provided the germ of the Pakistan idea, and the Muslim League Plans and such bodies as the Muslim National Guards, which were subsidiary to it. Rehmat Ali had the dream of reviving the old Muslim glory. His ultimate vision was of a Muslim India or Dinia, over which Islam must rule in its traditional manner. The areas carved out for Muslims in the midst of Hindu India mentioned above, were called by Rehmat Ali, "footholds". Footholds from which presumably the Muslims were to plan expansion into the heart of the neighbouring non-Muslim areas, and to link up with one another, for tightening up their stranglehold in these non-Muslim areas. Jinnah's own abortive proposals for a "corridor" to link up Eastern and Western Pakistan was somewhat of this nature — have an area running all over northern India, cutting India into two-and plan for the rest from this advantageous position.

Presumably, had Hyderabad been in a position to accede to Pakistan, a corridor would have been demanded for linking it up with Pakistan in the shape of an outlet to the sea. This has been the tempo, the character and the insatiably ambitious nature of the Pakistan Plan, conspiring for the conquest of Hindu India. Rioting and pillaging would be accounted only as minor rehearsary exercises in such a mighty and vast programme of action!

On the exchange of population, Mr Jinnah expressed himself quite clearly on a number of occasions, as already quoted. His views were not those of a mere idealist like Rahmat Ali, or of an intellectual like Dr Latif, but of the leader of the most powerful Muslim Party in India, whose words would carry tremendous influence with the Muslim masses and would be effective in forming their reactions. Speaking in Kingsway Hall in London on 13 December 1946, when he had gone there to have consultations with the British Government regarding the future functioning or killing of the Constituent Assembly, to which talks the Congress leaders too had been invited, Mr Jinnah made a passionate plea for the Muslim State of Pakistan, which would be inhabited by "one hundred million people, *all Muslims*." The implication of this is very clear. The Muslim population of India was, according to the Muslim League plan, to be concentrated in Pakistan, and as a necessary corollary, the non-Muslims were to be packed off. 'The important implications of such remarks were not lost upon the Muslims of the Muslim majority areas of India, and they formulated their plans for effecting a clean sweep of the non-Muslim minorities from their lands.

A few excerpts from the text of this speech of Mr Jinnah, made at a time when the situation in the country was very explosive, and any provocation provided to the Muslims would lead to widespread rioting, should serve to reveal the real nature of the campaign started by the Muslim League. The terrible Calcutta riots had already occurred; Noakhali was hardly a month-old affair and stirrings of the Muslim population of Hazara District in the NWFP against the Sikhs were becoming visible. At such a time to have propounded the twin theories of complete cultural and credal separation and the exchange of population was only to inflame rioting on the part of the Muslims still further. Said Mr Jinnah at Kingsway Hall:

In the North-West and North-East zones of India which are our homeland and where we are in a majority of 70% we say we want a separate State of our own. There we can live according to our own notions of life. *The differences between Hindus and Muslims are so fundamental there is nothing that matter in life upon which we agree.*

It is well known to any student of History that our heroes, our culture, our language, our music, our architecture, our jurisprudence, our social life are absolutely different and distinct. We are told that the so-called one India is British-made. It was by the sword. It can only be held as it has been held. Do not be misled by anyone saying that India is one and why, therefore, should it not continue to be one. What do we want? I tell you, Pakistan. Pakistan presupposes that Hindustan should also be a free State.

What would Hindus lose? Look at the map. They would have three-quarters of India. They would have the best parts. They have a population of nearly 200,000,000. Pakistan "is certainly not the best of India". We should have a population of 100,000,000, *all Muslims*.

On July the 27th, we decided to change our policy and to resort to "Direct Action" — a big change of policy — and we decided to tell our people this on August the 16th.

Reviewing the whole position, there is no other way but to divide India. Give Muslims their homeland and give Hindus Hindustan.

The Muslim League's famous "Pakistan Resolution" was passed in its Annual session at Lahore in April 1940. It declared for the first time the objective of Muslim league policy in India thus:

Resolved that it is the considered view of this session of the All-India Muslim League that no constitutional plan would be acceptable in this country or acceptable to the Muslims, unless it is designed on the following basic principles, namely that geographically contiguous units are demarcated into regions which should be so constituted with such territorial readjustments as may be necessary, that the areas in which Muslims are numerically in a majority, as in the northwestern and northeastern zones of India should be grouped to constitute eight independent states in which the constituent units shall be autonomous and sovereign....

Non-Muslim India did not readily give acceptance to this proposal which on the very face of it was outrageous and the consequences of which appeared to be nothing less than a relentless and destructive civil war in the country. Large sections of the Muslims too did not find this solution of the country's constitutional problem, acceptable, as it would mean endless rioting in which Muslims as surely as non-Muslims would suffer. But the British Government found in this resolve of the Muslim League a fresh sign of the perpetuation of the communal rift in India and they were not slow to lend it countenance in a way, and as Congress leaders repeatedly declared, to put a premium on Muslim League intransigence which made any reasonable settlement well-nigh impossible. The viceroy, Lord Linlithgow, whose regime in India was marked for the campaign of repression launched by the British Government against the Freedom Movement in India, said in the well-known August 1940 "offer" to India, "It goes without saying that they (the British Government) could not contemplate transfer of their present responsibilities for the peace and welfare of India to any system of Government whose authority is directly denied by large and powerful elements in India's national life. Nor could they be parties to the coercion of such elements into submission to such a Government."

Here was a clear hint to all such groups as would decide to dissociate themselves from the Congress, that any such dissociation on their part would be duly noted and respected. The princes, the Muslim League and all others that might come along. But as this declaration came not long after the passing of the "Pakistan Resolution" it is clear that it was meant as an acceptance by the British Government of the right of Muslim separation. Such was the joint Anglo-Muslim conspiracy out of which Pakistan was born. And the two forces — the British Government and the Muslim League — worked hand in hand right up till the 15 August 1945 to make Pakistan a fact, and to create such a temper of hate and lack of confidence between the communities as would make any thought of their living together an utter impossibility.

But the British Government did not stop short at this above declaration. In the Prime Minister's Statement in the House of Commons on 11 March, 1942 on the eve of the departure of Sir Stafford Cripps on his historic mission to India it was said: "He (Sir Stafford) carries with him the full confidence of His Majesty's Government, and he will strive in their name to procure the necessary measure of assent, not only from the Hindu majority, but also from those great minorities among whom the Muslims are the most numerous and on many ground pre-eminent."

With these and other declarations of the British Government's policy in their pocket, with the full support of the British bureaucracy in India with whom in Pandit Nehru's famous words the Muslim League had "a mental alliance" and with the confidence that any and every act of intransigence on its part would be respected by the British Government, the Muslim League devised plans for creating sanctions behind its extreme demands. The sanctions were to be riots against Hindus, and when these came into the Punjab, against the Sikhs as well. Very evidently the Muslim League was not at war with the British Government. Its war was with Hindu India, and so against Hindu India it would start a fierce campaign. While the war lasted, it did not suit the British Government to have any large-scale rioting or conflict inside India, as that would have meant hindering the war effort. But all this while the propaganda campaign for Pakistan was kept on at full blast. When the Congress started its 1942 Movement, Mr Jinnah made vituperative speeches against the Congress and called upon Muslims to oppose this movement. The Muslim League press all through this struggle used words like "goondas" in describing the Congress fighters against British rule. Even the British press did not say harder things against the Congress leaders and workers than did the Muslim.

A good deal has been written regarding the psychological, political and historical factors which led to the formulation of the Muslim demand for Pakistan. Leaving aside the issues which may be controversial and may reflect only individual reactions, two or three things appeared to be quite clear as to the factors which made this demand possible. One was the clear need of the British Government in the event of parting with power in India which they well knew, could not be long delayed, of leaving behind them a warring and divided India. The other was the peculiarly arrogant and narcissistic temperament of Mr Jinnah which kept him perpetually in conflict with the great personalities inside the Congress, a number of whom were his equals, and so he would have to work with them in a team and not dictate to them, as he could unquestionably do inside the Muslim League, made up of mediocrities for the most part. Added to these was the general temper and behaviour of the Muslims, especially in the important Muslim-majority provinces of Bengal and the Punjab in which the Muslim-dominated ministries, which to begin with were not Muslim League but became so in 1940, were ruling over the Hindus and in the latter province over the Hindus and Sikhs, in a most discriminatory manner.

In these two provinces, of which the Punjab had been called by Mr Jinnah the "corner stone" of Pakistan, and which was, between them to constitute the bulk of the territory and about 80 per cent of the population of Pakistan, a policy of thoroughly beating down the non-Muslims had been in operation for some time. In Bengal, and to a still greater extent in the Punjab, the administration was placed in its most important aspects in Muslim hands. Hindus and Sikhs were removed from key positions, and Hindu or Sikh officers who were occupying such positions, were transferred to routine office work, and those whose promotions were due were kept down under one pretext or the other. Wherever any District Magistrate or other senior administrative officer showed impartiality and dared to put down the aggressive Muslim elements within his area, the wrath of the Muslim ministers inevitably descended upon him, and he soon found himself cast into the wilderness of the secretariat or such work as would keep him in a position of utter impotence, under the check of some Muslim favourite of the ministry. In administration there were glaring instances of discrimination against non-Muslims, while they made the average Muslim very arrogant and aggressive, put the non-Muslims in a mood of desperation against the injustice of the administrative machinery. It was the opinion openly held in these times among the Hindus and Sikhs of the Punjab and the Hindus of Bengal, that in these two provinces, the Muslims already had Pakistan *in action* though not in name. As a matter of fact, that astute politician, the late Sir Sikandar Hyat Khan, premier of the Punjab from 1937 to the end of 1942, suggested in vain to his Muslim League colleagues not to press for a formal division of India into independent states, but to ask only for the creation of Hindu and Muslim zones within an Indian Federation with a weak centre, as that would give the Muslims all the advantages of Pakistan without the liabilities, financial and political, of having an independent State, which would be deprived of the rich economic backing of the more productive parts of India. He and his Unionist Party succeeded to a great extent in making the Punjab very much a Muslim province. Protests of Hindu and Sikh politicians and legislators were of no avail. Sir Sikandar died in the December of 1942, and his death removed from the field of Muslim politics, perhaps the only figure who could have successfully helped to modify at least some of the extreme theories of Mr Jinnah. His successor,

Sir Khizar Hyat Khan, although a capable man and one who got ample support from Hindus and Sikhs as against the rabid Punjab Muslim League, became as time passed, altogether helpless to resist the onslaught of the League on his party and the Hindu and Sikh minorities of the Punjab.

After the passing of the Pakistan Resolution by the League and the declaration by the British Viceroy and the British Prime Minister that the Muslim point of view would be given a place of importance in all constitutional negotiations, the next Annual Session of the Muslim League (1941) held at Madras showed still greater vehemence in the expression of the Pakistan demand by the Muslim League. While repeating the substance of the Pakistan demand in its resolutions, this session drew forth an exposition of this demand from its President, Mr Jinnah. He said, "The goal of the All-India Muslim League is that we want to establish a completely independent State in the northwest and eastern zones of India with full control on defence, foreign affairs, communications, customs, currency, exchange, etc. We do not want under any circumstances a constitution of all-India character with one Government at the centre. We will never agree to that. If you once agree to it, let me tell you that the Muslims would be absolutely wiped out of existence. We shall never be a feudatory of any power or of any Government at the Centre so far as our free national homelands are concerned. Muslim India will never submit to an All-Indian constitution and one Central Government. The ideology of the League is based on the fundamental principle *that the Muslims of India are an independent nationality and that any attempt to get them to merge their national and political identity and ideology will be resisted....*"

The last portion, italicized by the present writer, is worthy of note. Resistance, direct action, struggle — these words have been the keynote of the Muslim League in defining its relations with Hindu India. As early as 1938, at its Patna Session, the Muslim League had passed a resolution declaring: "The time has come to authorise the Working Committee of the All-India Muslim League to decide and resort to direct action if and when necessary". This was to launch a struggle against the Congress ministries on whose resignation in November 1939 in protest against the drafting by the British Government of India into the war without prior consent of the people, the Muslim League celebrated its "Thanksgiving Day".

Mahatma Gandhi was released from prison in 1944, and while in prison he had addressed a letter to Mr Jinnah asking him to come and see him for a talk regarding the political settlement in the country. This letter the British Government withheld, but Mr Jinnah and the country knew of it from a Government *communique*. The Muslim press was moved at this gesture on the part of the incarcerated Mahatma, but not Mr Jinnah. He found occasion, even in the Mahatma's writing an invitation to him, to abuse and vilify the latter, and so he never applied to the Government for permission to see the Mahatma. On coming out of prison, with the Congress still in jail, the Mahatma went to meet Mr Jinnah at his Bombay residence, day after day. But Mr Jinnah really did not want a settlement. So the Mahatma's approach proved unavailing. Then, in 1945, after the surrender of Germany when the Congress leaders were released, Lord Wavell, the Viceroy called the famous conference at Simla, of the Congress, League, Sikh and other leaders. Nothing short of complete severance of relations with the rest of India would satisfy Mr Jinnah. Parity was offered with the Congress to the Muslim League on a basis of 5:5 in a cabinet of 14.

This was to be an interim measure, with the permanent settlement to come a little later. But Mr Jinnah would have none of it. The Muslim temper of hostility to the Hindus was kept up by the resolutions of the Muslim League, the speeches of Mr Jinnah and the Muslim League leaders and the comments of the Muslim League–controlled press.

During the period the Muslim League was preparing, as is now evident from what happened in 1946 and 1947, for a large struggle against Hindu India, and in the Punjab inevitably against the Sikhs and Hindus, the Muslim League had been gathering a private army of its own, to which training was being imparted in fighting, stabbing and assaults. Arms were being collected, and demobilized Muslim personnel of the Indian Army were freely enlisted in the League army. This army, begun about the year 1938, continued to expand and grow better equipped. It had two famous organizations; one was the Muslim League Volunteer Corps, which was parallel to the Congress Seva Dal. But there was a great difference between the Congress body and this League body. The Congress adopted and followed its creed of non-violence. The Congress volunteers were forbidden even under the gravest provocation to retaliate with physical force. They were to regulate crowds, to organise picketing, anti-Government processions to arrange protest strikes, but no way to fight. But the Muslim League creed was not non-violent. Every town with any Muslim population had a large proportion of its Muslim inhabitants who could be counted only as riff-raff, and who very often with the connivance of the black sheep among the police force, lived on crime. Such unprincipled elements were the favourite recruiting ground for the Muslim League volunteer corps. Any hooligan with the badge and uniform of a political organisation, which was day in and day out preaching the gospel of hatred against other communities, would be formidable in a well-organised group, which could back him up, and direct him in secret and violent action.

Still more important and more dangerous was the Muslim National Guards, which by the bye, is now converted into the Pakistan National Guards.

The Muslim National Guards did not owe any formal allegiance to the Muslim League, though it had the same flag as the Muslim League had. It is well-known that the National Guards was the secret arm of the Muslim League. Its membership was secret and it had its own centres and headquarters, where its members received military training and such instruction as would make them affective in times of rioting, such as using the lathi, the spear and the knife. The Unit Commander of the Muslim National Guards was known as *Salar*, over whom were higher officers, but all functioning secretly and with clearly such instructions as would make them formidable in rioting against unarmed non-Muslims populations. When in January 1947 the Lahore office of the Muslim National Guards was raided by the Punjab police, a good deal of military equipment including steel helmets and badges were recovered. The National Guards had their own jeeps and lorries, which helped them in swift mobility for attack on Hindu and Sikh localities, in sniping and stabbing lonely passers-by and in carrying away loot. One of the articles the Muslim National Guards prized and stored was petrol, which would be used not only as fuel in transport, but as an excellent means of incendiarism on a large and devastating scale. Hundreds of burnt town and villages in the two provinces of Punjab and Bengal are tragic evidence of how thorough the preparations of the Muslim League had been for its war on Hindus and Sikhs.

Regular tests were held of the Muslim National Guards in feats of fighting and attack. Marks were given and certificates granted. So the Muslims had a widespread and well-trained semi-military organisation to back up its programme and policy.

So alarming was the rise of the Muslim National Guards that the Punjab Government took serious notice of this development, which proved to be so dangerous for the peace of the Province. But the entire machinery to the Government being pro-Muslim, nothing serious was done about the Muslim National Guards.

In April 1947 Mr Akhtar Hussain, Chief Secretary to the Punjab Government reported to the Governor of the Punjab:

The necessity for recruitment and re-organisation of the Muslim League National Guards is occupying the attention of the Provincial Salar. An increase of 5,630 Guards has been reported and accelerated activity has been noticeable in the western and northwestern Punjab.

In the eastern Punjab, active training has been confined mainly in Simla, Ambala Cantt. and Panipat where Guards have been exercising secretly in lathi fighting and in the Central Punjab and in Jullundar District, where Khaksars have undertaken their training. Open activity has been confined to the collection of Relief Funds, and in the Rawalpindi area to warning Muslims to destroy looted property and refrain from giving evidence in connection with the recent disturbances.

The Chief Secretary's report dated a fortnight later says:

There are already indications that the Guards are being used as secret messengers, and their general activities are becoming less open, and in some places, they are active in arming the Community[5]. It has been reported that financial aid from the Centre has been promised, particularly for the Western Districts which are to act as recruiting grounds for the entire Province. Enlistment in the Rawalpindi and Campbellpore Districts has been particularly brisk and efforts have been made to enlist the services of ex-soldiers. The increase membership is noticeable in all districts however and it is estimated that the number of Muslim League National Guards in the Province now is in the neighbourhood of 39,000.

The Muslim League, therefore, had this two-pronged thrust to make in its assault on the non-Muslims of the Muslim majority areas. In the first place it was preaching its two-nation theory and its uncompromising opposition to the Hindus, and in the Punjab, to the Sikhs as well. It tried to write off all such things as a common Indian Culture and an Indian Nationhood. In the name of self-determination for the Muslims of India, it inculcated in them the creed of intolerance, arrogance and hate. All this made any compromise with Hindu India an impossibility for the Muslims; they must fight against the Hindus to enforce their extreme demands. And this fight came in 1946, when the Muslim League gave its Direct Action call on the 27 July of that year, which part of the story is to be narrated in the next chapter.

Second, the Muslim League had been preparing Muslims physically and militarily for such a fight, which when it came, the Hindus and Sikhs were caught unawares, and suffered heavily in the dead and in the injured, in women abducted and dishonoured, in property looted and houses and religious and educational places burnt. Such retaliation as came from the Hindus and Sikhs was only belated, and after the Muslim onslaught was becoming continuous and a threat to their very existence. Before August

1947 such retaliation wherever it came, even served the purpose of the Muslim League, for it created that atmosphere of a civil war in India, which the Muslim League found necessary for the furtherance of its programme and policy. It could trot out atrocity stories and incite Muslims elsewhere to fall upon Hindus and Sikhs, as they actually did in the NW Frontier Province in December 1946, and January 1947. Such was the aim and method of the Muslim League.

---

[1] Meaning the Muslim Empire in India (Present writer's note).
[2] As advocated in Dr Latif's scheme adumberated in "The Muslim Problem in India".
[3] One, however, fails to see how it would be voluntary, if effected by law.
[4] The original is in the possession of a Hindu gentleman.
[5] Muslims.

Annexure 2

Chronology of Significant Bilateral Meetings Between 1994–2000

January (1-3) 1994	7th round of FS levels talk took place in Islamabad between J. N. Dixit and Shahryar Khan. Kashmir main issue. J. N. Dixit meets Prime Minister Bhutto at Karachi on 2 January 1994 – Talks fail.
July (31) 1994	MOS R. L. Bhatia and Pak Foreign Minister Assef Ahmed Ali met briefly at Dhaka on the margins of the SAARC Council of Ministers Meeting.
September (15-16) 1994	Secretary level meeting held between India and Pakistan in New Delhi for combating Drugs Trafficking and Smuggling.
November (21-25) 1994	FS Kris Srinivasan led Indian delegation to Commonwealth Senior Official meeting held at Islamabad. The Pak side declined to engage in any bilateral talks.
November (26-29) 1994	Shri Arjun Singh, minister for HRD, visits Islamabad in connection with the 12th Commonwealth Education Ministers' Conference.

January (15-16) 1995	India and Pakistan hold a Task Force level meeting in Islamabad on technical cooperation for control of drug trafficking.
April (5-6) 1995	The second round of Indo – Pak Secretary level talks on Narcotics Control were held in Islamabad.
April (27-29) 1995	Foreign Secretary Najmuddin Sheikh led Pak delegation to the SAARC Standing Committee meeting in Delhi.
May (2-4) 1995	President Leghari visits India for the SAARC summit. He held a 46 minute meeting with PM Narsimha Rao on 2 May.
August (24-26) 1995	Pak Foreign Secretary Najmuddin Sheikh attends special session of SAARC Foreign Society Secretary in New Delhi.
December (18-19) 1995	Foreign Minister Assef Ali participated in a two-day meeting of the SAARC Council of Ministers on 18-19 December at New Delhi.
January (3-4) 1996	V.A Jaffrey, Advisor to PM on finance and Qazi Ali, deputy chairman planning Commission attended two-day SAARC Finance and Planning Ministers meeting in New Delhi.
May (8-9) 1996	80th Indo – Pakistan Indus Commission meeting at Islamabad.
September (17-20) 1996	N. K. Singh, secretary revenue visits Pakistan for talks on Narcotics Control and Drugs trafficking.
November (21) 1996	Three member delegation led by Indian commissioner, Indus Water Commission visits Pakistan.
December (18) 1996	Caretaker Foreign Minister Sahibzada Yakub Khan visits India for the SAARC Council of Ministers meeting. He calls on EAM.
March (1) 1997	First round of revised Indo-Pak Foreign Secretary level talks held at Delhi.

April (9) 1997	Foreign Minister Gohar Ayub Khan visiting New Delhi for the NAM Ministerial meeting. Has breakfast meeting with EAM I. K. Gujral.
April (26) 1997	Meeting between revenue secretary and Pak secretary at New Delhi on drug trafficking agreed to exchange information to combat drug trafficking.
May (12) 1997	PM I. K. Gujral and PM Nawaz Sharif have 50 minutes meeting at Male while attending the SAARC summit.
June (19-23) 1997	Second round of revived Indo-Pakistan foreign secretary level talks held at Islamabad.
June (19) 1997	PM I. K. Gujral calls PM Nawaz Sharif on the newly installed hot lines between the two PMs.
September (16-18) 1997	Third round of revived Indo-Pak foreign secretary level talks held in New Delhi.
September (15-18) 1997	S. R. Bomai, minister for HRD visits Pakistan to participate in E–9 Ministerial meeting. Calls on Pakistan president.
September (23) 1997	PM I. K. Gujral and PM Nawaz Sharif have an hour-long meeting in New York.
October (24-29) 1997	Speaker of Lok Sabha P.A. Sangma accompanied by MPs, participate in conference of SAARC Speakers and Parliamentarians at Islamabad.
October (25) 1997	PM I. K. Gujral and PM Nawaz Sharif have 80 minutes meeting at Edinburgh on the margins of the Commonwealth summit.
January (15) 1998	India Pakistan FS level meeting at Dhaka on the margins of the trilateral business summit. Discuss modalities to resume bilateral dialogue at FS level. PM I. K. Gujral and PM Nawaz Sharif also meet on the margins.

March (6) 1998	Meeting of the Parliament Indus Waters Commission at Islamabad.
April (28) 1998	Commerce Minister R. K. Hegde visits Islamabad in connection with SAARC Commerce Ministers conference in Islamabad.
July (29) 1998	PMs of India and Pakistan meet at Colombo on the sidelines of the 10th SAARC summit.
September (1) 1998	Indian MOS Vasundhara Raje calls on Pak FM on the sidelines of Durban NAM summit.
September (23) 1998	PM A. B. Vajpayee meets PM Nawaz Sharif at New York. Decision taken to begin the composite dialogue.
October (16-18) 1998	Composite dialogue between India and Pakistan on the issue for Peace and Security including CBMs and Jammu and Kashmir held in Islamabad.
November (5-13) 1998	Composite dialogue held at New Delhi on Sir Creek, Tulbul Navigation Project Siachen, Terrorism and Narcotics, Economic and Commercial Cooperation. Friendly exchanges in various fields.
December (1) 1998	Five-member Indian delegation led by R. S. Bhatti, JS, Water and Surface Transport Ministry, visits Islamabad to work out technical details of the Delhi-Lahore Bus Service.
January (28) 1999	Five-member delegation visits New Delhi to finalise export of electricity to India. Pak delegation included Chairman WAPDA Lt. General Zulfiqar Ali Khan. Indian delegation led by Pradip Baijal.
February (2) 1999	PM Atal Behari Vajpayee visits Lahore on the occasion of the inaugural Delhi-Lahore Bus Service.
March (18) 1999	Foreign Secretary K. Raghunath meets his Pakistani counterpart on the sidelines of the

	21st session of the SAARC Council of Ministers in Sri Lanka.
May 6 – July 15, 1999	The Kargil war.
June (12) 1999	Foreign Minister Sartaj Aziz visits New Delhi during Kargil crisis.
October (12) 1999	Military Coup — General Pervez Musharraf takes over.
May (24) 2001	PM Vajpayee invites Musharraf to India for a summit meeting.
May (29) 2001	Musharraf accepts invitation to come to India.
July (14-16) 2001	Indo-Pak summit at Agra.
September (11) 2001	Terrorist attack on the World Trade Center, New York, and Pentagon in Washington.
October (7) 2001	United States launches military operations against the Taliban and Al Qaeda in Afghanistan.
October (30) 2001	Jaishe-e-Mohammad terrorists attack the J&K Assembly in Srinagar
December (13) 2001	Indian Parliament is attacked by Jaishe-e-Mohammad cadres.
December (30) 2001	India hands over list of 20 terrorists to Pakistan demanding their extradition.
January (12) 2002	General Musharraf addresses the people of Pakistan, announcing decisions to curb religious extremism and terrorism; but at the same time declares that Pakistan will not compromise its traditional stand on Jammu & Kashmir. India responds announcing that India will not resume the dialogue with Pakistan unless Pakistan stops cross-border terrorism and hands over the terrorists mentioned in the list given on the 30 December 2001.

Joint Statement

1. In respose to an invitation by the Prime Minister of Pakistan, Mr Muhammad Nawaz Sharif, the Prime Minister of India, Shri Atal Behari Vajpayee visited Pakistan from 20-21 February, 1999, on the inaugural run of the Delhi-Lahore bus service.

2. The Prime Minister of Pakistan received the India Prime Minister at the Wagah border on 20 February 1999. A banquet in honour of the Indian Prime Minister and his delegation was hosted by the Prime Minister of Pakistan at Lahore Fort, on the same evening. Prime Minister Atal Behari Vajpayee visited Minar-e-Pakistan, Mausoleum of Allama Iqbal, Gurudwara Dera Sahib and Samadhi of Maharaja Ranjeet Singh. On 21st February, a civic reception was held in honour of the visiting Prime Minister at the Governor's House.

3. The two leaders held discussions on the entire range of bilateral relations, regional cooperation within SAARC, and issues of international concern. They decided that:

    a. The two Foreign Ministers will meet periodically to discuss all issues of mutual concern, including nuclear related issues.

    b. The two sides shall undertake consultations on WTO related issues with a view to coordinating their respective positions.

    c. The two sides shall determine areas of cooperation in Information Technology, in particular for tackling the problems of Y2K.

d. The two sides will hold consultations with a view to further liberalizing the visa and travel regime.

e. The two sides shall appoint a 2-member committee at ministerial level to examine humanitarian issues relating to Civilian detainees and missing POWs.

4. They expressed satisfaction on the commencement of a Bus Service between Lahore and New Delhi, the release of fishermen and civilian detainees and the renewal of contacts in the field of sports.

5. Pursuant to the directive given by the two Prime Ministers, the Foreign Secretaries of Pakistan and India signed a Memorandum of Understanding on 21 February 1999, identifying measures aimed at promoting an environment of peace and security between the two countries.

6. The two Prime Ministers signed the Lahore Declaration embodying their shared vision of peace and stability between their countries and of progress and prosperity for their peoples.

7. Prime Minsiter Atal Behari Vajpayee extended an invitation to Prime Minister Muhammed Nawaz Sharif to visit India on mutually convenient dates.

8. Prime Minister Atal Behari Vajpayee thanked Prime Minister Muhammed Nawaz Sharif for the warm welcome and gracious hospitality extended to him and members of his delegation and for the excellent arrangements made for his visit.

Lahore
February 21, 1999

Memorandum of Understanding

The Foreign Secretaries of India and Pakistan:

Reaffirming the continued commitment of their respective governments to the principles and purposes of the UN Charter:

Reiterating the determination of both the countries to implementing the Simla Agreement in letter and spirit;

Guided by the agreement between their Prime Ministers of 23 Septemeber 1998 that an environment of peace and security is in the supreme national interest of both sides and that resolution of all outstanding issues, including Jammu and Kahsmir, is essential for this purpose;

Pursuant to the directive given by their respective Prime Ministers in Lahore, to adopt measures for promoting a stable environment of peace, and security between the two countries;

Have on this day, agreed to the following:-

1. The two sides shall engage in bilateral consultations on security concepts, and nuclear doctrines, with a view to developing measures for confidence building in the nuclear and conventional fields, aimed at avoidance of conflict.

2. The two sides undertake to provide each other with advance notification in respect of ballistic missile flight tests, and shall conclude a bilateral agreement in this regard.

3. The two sides are fully committed to undertaking national measures to reducing the risks of accidental or unauthorized use of nuclear weapons

under their respective control. The two sides further undertake to notify each other immediately in the event of any accidental, unauthorized or unexplained incident that could create the risk of a fallout with adverse consequences for both sides, or an outbreak of a nuclear war between the two countries, as well as to adopt measures aimed at diminishing the possibility of such actions, or such incidents being misinterpreted by the other. The two sides shall identify/establish the appropriate communication mechanism for this purpose.

4.   The two sides shall continue to abide by their respective unilateral moratorium on conducting further nuclear test explosions unless either side, in exercise of its national sovereignty decides that extraordinary events have jeopardized its supreme interests.

5.   The two sides shall conclude an agreement on prevention of incidents at sea in order to ensure safety of navigation by naval vessels, and aircraft belonging to the two sides.

6.   The two sides shall periodically review the implementation of existing Confidence Building Measures (CBMs) and where necessary, set up appropriate consultative mechanisms to monitor and ensure effective implementation of these CBMs.

7.   The two sides shall undertake a review of the existing cmmunication links (e.g. between the respective Directors-General, Military operations) with a view to upgrading and improving these links, and to provide for fail-safe and secure communications.

8.   The two sides shall engage in bilateral consultations on security, disarmament and non-proliferation issues within the context of negotiations on these issues in multilateral fora.

Where required, the technical details of the above measures will be worked out by experts of the two sides in meetings to be held on mutually agreed dates, before mid 1999, with a view to reaching bilateral agreements.

Done at Lahore on 21 February 1999 in the presence of Prime Minister of India Mr Atal Behari Vajpayee and Prime Minister of Pakistan Mr Muhammad Nawaz Sharif.

(K. Raghunath)   (Shamshad Ahmad)
Foreign Secretary of the   Foreign Secretary of the
Republic of India   Islamic Republic of Pakistan

Annexure 5

Lahore Declaration

The Prime Ministers of the Republic of India and the Islamic Republic of Pakistan:-

Sharing a vision of peace and stability between their countries, and of progress and prosperity for their peoples;

Convinced that durable peace and development of harmonious relations and friendly cooperation will serve the vital interests of the peoples of the two countries, enabling them to devote their energies for a better future;

Recognizing that the nuclear dimension of the security environment of the two countries adds to their responsibility for avoidance of conflict between the two countries;

Committed to the principles and purposes of the Charter of the United Nations, and the universally accepted principles of peaceful co-existence;

Reiterating the determination of both countries to implementing the Simla Agreement in letter and spirit;

Committed to the objectives of universal nuclear disarmament and non-proliferation;

Convinced of the importance of mutually agreed confidence building measures for improving the security environment;

Recalling their agreement of 23 September, 1998, that an environment of peace and security is in the supreme national interest of both sides and that the resolution of all outstanding issues, including Jammu and Kashmir, is essential for this purpose;

Have agreed that their respective Governments:-

- Shall intensify their efforts to resolve all issues, including the issue of Jammu and Kashmir.

- Shall refrain from intervention and interference in each other's internal affairs.

- Shall intensify their composite and integrated dialogue process for an early and positive outcome of the agreed bilateral agenda.

- Shall take immediate steps for reducing the risk of accidental or unauthorized use of nuclear weapons and discuss concepts and doctrines with a view to elaborating measures for confidence building in the nuclear and conventional fields, aimed at prevention of conflict.

- Reaffirm their commitment to the goals and objectives of SAARC and to concert their efforts towards the realization of the SAARC vision for the year 2000 and beyond with a view to promoting the welfare of the peoples of South Asia and to improve their quality of life through accelerated economic growth, social progress and cultural development.

- Reaffirming their condemnation of terrorism in all its forms and manifestations and their determination to combat this menace.

- Shall promote and protect all human rights and fundamental freedoms.

Signed at Lahore on the 21st day of February 1999.

Atal Bihari Vajpayee
Prime Minister of the
Republic of India

Muhammad Nawaz Sharif
Prime Minister of the Islamic
Republic of Pakistan

Annexure 6

Simla Agreement 1972

Agreement on Bilateral Relations between the Government of India and the Government of Pakistan

1. The Government of India and the Government of Pakistan are resolved that the two countries put an end to the conflict and confrontation that have hitherto marred their relations and work for the promotion of a friendly and harmonious relationship and the establishment of durable peace in the sub-continent, so that both countries may henceforth devote their resources and energies in the pressing task of advancing the welfare of their peoples.

   In order to achieve this objective, the Government of India and the Government of Pakistan have agreed as follows:

   (i)   That the principles and purposes of the Charter of the United Nations shall govern the relations between the two countries.

   (ii) That the two countries are resolved to settle their differences by peaceful means through bilateral negotiations or by any other peaceful means mutually agreed upon between them. Pending the final settlement of any of the problems between the two countries, neither side shall unilaterally alter the situation and both shall prevent the organisation, assistance or encouragement of any acts detrimental to the maintenance of peaceful and harmonious relations.

(iii) That the pre-requisite for reconciliation, good neighbourliness and durable peace between them is a commitment by both the countries to peaceful co-existence, respect for each other's territorial integrity and sovereignty and non-interference in each other's internal affairs on the basis of equality and mutual benefit.

(iv) That the basic issues and causes of conflict which have bedeviled the relations between the two countries for the last 25 years shall be resolved by peaceful means.

(v) That they will always respect each other's national unity, territorial integrity, political independence and sovereign equality.

(vi) That in accordance with the Charter of the United Nations they will refrain from the threat or use of force against the territorial integrity or political independence of each other.

2. Both government will take all steps within their power to prevent hostile propaganda directed against each other. Both countries will encourage the dissemination of such information as would promote the development of friendly relations between them.

3. In order progressively to restore and normalise relations between the two countries step by step, it was agreed that

(i) Steps shall be taken to resume communications, postal, telegraphic, sea, land including border posts, and air links including overflights.

(ii) Appropriate steps shall be taken to promote travel facilities for the nationals of the other country.

(iii) Trade and cooperation in economic and other agreed fields will be resumed as far as possible.

(iv) Exchanges in the fields of science and culture will be promoted. In this connection delegations from the two countries will meet from time to time to work out the necessary details.

4. In order to initiate the process of the establishment of durable peace both the government agree that:

(i) Indian and Pakistani forces shall be withdrawn to their side of the international border.

(ii)   In Jammu and Kashmir, the Line of Control resulting from the ceasefire of December, 1971 shall be respected by both sides without prejudice to the recognised position of either side. Neither side shall seek to alter it unilaterally, irrespective of mutual differences and legal interpretations. Both sides further undertake to refrain from the threat or the use of force in violation of this Line.

(iii)   The withdrawals shall commence upon entry into force of the Agreement and shall be completed within a period of 30 days thereof.

5. This agreement will be subject to ratification by both countries in accordance with their respective constitutional procedures and will come into force with effect from date on which the Instruments of Ratification are exchanged.

6. Both Governments agree that their respective Heads will meet again at a mutually convenient time in the future and that in the meanwhile, the representatives of the two sides will meet to discuss further the modalities and arrangements for the establishment of durable peace and normalisation of relations including the question of repatriation of prisoners-of-war and civilian internees, a final settlement of Jammu and Kashmir and the resumption of diplomatic relations.

Indira Gandhi   Zulfikar Ali Bhutto
Prime Minister   President
Republic of India   Islamic Republic of Pakistan

Tashkent Declaration, 10 January 1966

Text of the Tashkent Declaration on 10 January 1966 by the Prime Minister of India and President of Pakistan. The initiative for a meeting of the Prime Minister of India and President of Pakistan at Tashkent was taken by Kosygin, Chairman of the Council of Ministers of the USRR, Swaran Singh, Minister for External Affairs had said that Kosygin, not only sponsored the idea of the conference, but also at all stages and particularly when difficulties arose, acted as a messenger of peace and helped to resolve all obstacles. He did not propose, much less impose, any particular solutions. Yet without his good offices, the Tashkent declaration could not have taken shape.'

The Prime Minister of India and the President of Pakistan having met at Tashkent and having discussed the existing relations between India and Pakistan, hereby declare their firm resolve to restore normal and peaceful relations between their countries and to promote understanding and friendly relations between their peoples. They consider the attainment of these objectives of vital importance for the welfare of the 600 million people of India and Pakistan.

I

The Prime Minister of India and the President of Pakistan agree that both sides will exert all efforts to create good neighbourly relations between India and Pakistan in accordance with the United Nations Charter. They re-affirm their obligation under the Charter not to have recourse to force and to settle their disputes through peaceful means. They considered that the interests of peace in their region and particularly in the Indo-Pakistan subcontinent and, indeed, the interests of the peoples of India and Pakistan were not served by the continuance of tension between the two countries. It was against this background that Jammu and Kashmir was discussed and each of the sides set forth its respective positions.

II

The Prime Minister of India and President of Pakistan have agreed that all armed personnel of the two countries shall be withdrawn not later than 25th February 1966 to the positions they held prior to 5 August, 1965, and both sides shall observe the cease-fire terms on the cease-fire line.

III

The Prime Minister of India and President of Pakistan have agreed that relations between India and Pakistan shall be based on the principles of non-interference in the internal affairs of each other.

IV

The Prime Minister of India and the President of Pakistan have agreed that both sides will discourage any propaganda directed against the other country, and will encourage propaganda which promotes the development of friendly relations between the two countries.

V

The Prime Minister of India and the President of Pakistan have agreed that the High Commissioner of India in Pakistan and the High Commissioner of Pakistan in India will return to their posts and that the normal functioning of diplomatic missions of both countries will be restored. Both Governments have observed the Vienna Convention of 1961 on Diplomatic Intercourse.

VI

The Prime Minister of India and the President of Pakistan have agreed to consider measures towards the restoration of economic and trade relations, communications, as well cultural exchanges between India and Pakistan, and to take measures to implement the existing agreement between India and Pakistan.

VII

The Prime Minister of India and President of Pakistan, have agreed that they give instructions to their respective authorities to carry out the repatriation of the prisoners of War.

VIII

The Prime Minister of India and President of Pakistan have agreed that both the sides will continue the discussion of questions relating to the problems of refugees evictions/illegal immigration. They also agreed that both sides will create conditions which will prevent the exodus of people. They further agreed to discuss the return of the property and assets taken over by either side in connection with the conflict.

IX

The Prime Minister of India and President of Pakistan have agreed that the two sides will continue meetings both at the highest and at other levels on matters of direct concern to both countries. Both sides have recognised the need to set up joint Indian-Pakistani bodies which will report to their Governments in order to decide what further steps should be taken.

*****

The Prime Minister of India and the President of Pakistan record their feelings of deep appreciation and gratitude to the leaders of the Soviet Union, the Soviet Government and personally to the Chairman of the Council of Ministers of the USSR for their constructive friendly and noble part in bringing about the present meeting which has resulted in mutually satisfactory results. They also express to the Government and friendly people of Uzbekistan their sincere thankfulness for their overwhelming reception and generous hospitality.

They invite the Chairman of the Council of Ministers of the U.S.S.R. to witness this Declaration.

India and Pakistan: Military Balance
(Year 2000/2001)

India

		1998	1999	2000	2001
GDP	Rs	17.0tr	18.9tr.		
	US$	412bn	440bn		
per capita	US$	1,700	1,800		
Growth	%	6.7	5.9		
Inflation	%	13.2	4.7		
Debt	US$	94bn	99bn		
Def exp[a]	Rs	580bn	610bn		
	US$	14.1bn	14.2bn		
Def bdgt	Rs	412bn	533bn	709bn	
	US$	10.0bn	12.4bn	15.9bn	
FMA[b] (US)	US$	0.2m	0.5m	0.5m	0.5m
FMA (Aus)	US$	0.2m	0.2m		
US$1=Rs	4.13	43.0	44.4		

[a] Incl exp on para-mil org
[b] UNMOGIP 1997 US$7m 1998

Population			**1,016,242,000**
(Hindu 80%, Muslim 14%, Christian 2%, Sikh 2%)			
Age	*13-17*	*18-22*	*23-32*
Men	53,812,000	49,257,000	87,033,000
Women	50,432,000	45,713,000	79,562,000

Total Armed Forces

ACTIVE 1,303,000

Reserves 535,000

Army 300,000 (first line reserves within 5 years' full time service, a further 500,000 have commitment until age 50) **Territorial Army** (volunteers) 40,000 **Air Force** 140,000 Navy 55,000

Army 1,100,000

HQ: 5 Regional Comd, 4 Fd Army, 12 Corps (3 armd div (each 2-3 armed, 1 SP arty (2 SP fd, 1 med regt) bde) • 4 RAPID div (each 2 inf, 1 mech bde) • 18 inf div (each 2-5 inf, 1 arty bde; some have armd regt) • 9 mtn div (each 3-4 bde, 1 or more arty regt) • 1 arty div (3 bde) • 15 indep bde: 7 armd, 5 inf, 2 mtn, 1 AB/cdo • 1 SSM regt (*Prithvi*) • 4 AD bde (plus 14 cadre) • 3 engr bde

These formations comprise

59 tk regt (bn) • 355 inf bn (incl 25 mech, 8 AB, 3 cdo) • 190 arty regt (bn) reported: incl 1 SSM, 2 MRL, 50 med (11 SP), 39 mtn, 29 AD arty regt; perhaps 2 SAM gp (3-5 bty each) plus 15 SAM regt • 22 hel sqn: incl 5 ATK

Reserves

Territorial Army 25 inf bn, plus 29 'department' units

Equipment

MBT £3,414 (£1,100 in store): some 700 T-55 (450 op), £1,500 T-72/M1, 1,200 *Vijayanta*, £14 *Arjun* LT TK £90 I'I-76

RECCE £100 BRDM-2

AIFV 250+BMP-1, 1,000 BMP-2 (*Sarath*)

APC 157 OT-62/-64 (in store), some *Casspir*

TOWED ARTY 4,175 (perhaps 600 in store) incl: **75mm**: 900 75/24 mtn, 215 FRY M-48; **105mm**: some 1,300 IFG Mk I/II, 50 M-56; **122mm**: some 550 D-30; **130mm**: 750 M-46; **155mm**: 410 FH-77B

SP ARTY **105mm**: 80 *Abbot* (£30 in store); **130mm**: 100 mod M-46 (£70 in store); **152mm**: some 2S19

MRL 122mm: **£100 incl BM-21, LRAR;** 214mm: *Pina ha* **(being deployed)**

MOR **81mm**: 116A1, E1; **120mm**: 500 Brandt AM-50, E1; **160mm**: 500 M-1943

SSM *Prithvi* (3-5 launchers)

ATGW *Milan*, AT-3 *Sager*, AT-4 *Spigot* (some SP), AT-5 *Spandrel* (some SP)

RCL **84mm**: *Carl Gustav;* **106mm**: 1,000+M-40A1

AD GUNS some 2,400 **20mm**: Oerlikon (reported); **23mm**: 300 ZU 23-2, 100 ZSU-23-4SP; **30mm**: 24 2S6 SP; **40mm**: 1,200 L40/60, 800 L40/70

SAM 180 SA-6, 620 SA-7, 50 SA-8B, 400 SA-9, 45 SA-3, SA-13, 500 SA-16

SURV MUFAR, *Green Archer* (mor)

UAV *Searcher, Nishant*

HEL 120 *Chetak*, 40 *Cheetah*

LC 2 LCVP

DEPLOYMENT

North 3 Corps with 8 inf, 2 mtn div **West 3** Corps with 1 armd, 5 inf div, 3 RAPID Central 1 Corps with 1 armd, 1 inf, 1 RAPID **East 3** Corps with 1 inf, 7 mtn div South 2 Corps with 1 armd, 3 inf div

Navy 53,000

(incl, 5,000 Naval Aviation and 1,000 Marines, £2,000 women)

Principal Command Western, Southern, Eastern (incl Far Eastern sub command)

Sub-Command Submarine, Naval Air

Bases Mumbai (Bombay) HQ Western Comd), Goa (HQ Naval Air), Karwar (under construction), Kochi (Cochin) (HQ Southern Comd),

Vishakhapatnam (HQ Eastern), Calcutta, Madras, Port Blair (Andaman Is (HQ Far Eastern Comd), Arakonam (Vaval Air)

Fleets Western base Bombay Eastern base Visakhapatnam

Submarines 16

SSK 16

10 *Sindhughosh* (Sov *Kilo*) with 533mm TT 4 *Shishumar* (Ge T-209/1500) with 533mm TT 2 *Kursura* (Sov *Foxtrol*) + with 533mm TT (plus 3 in reserve)

Principal Surface Combatants 26

Carries 1 *Viraat* (UK *Hermes*) 29,00t) CVV

Air group typically ac 6 *Sea Harrier* ftr/attack hel 6 *Sea* King ASW/ASUW (*Sea Eagle* ASM) in refit until April 2001

DESTROYERS 8

DDG 8

5 *Rajput* (Sov *Kashin*) with 4 SS-N-2C Styx SSM, 2x2 SA-N-1 *Goa* SAM, 2 x 76mm gun, 5 x 533mm ASTT, 2 ASW RL, 1 Ka-25 or 28 hel (1 in refit)

3 *Delhi* with 16 SS-N-25 *Switchblade* SSM, 2xSA-N-7 *Gadfly* SAM, 1 x 100mm ASTT, 2 hel

FRIGATES 12

FFG 4

1 *Brahmaputra* with 8 x SS-N-25 *Switchblade* SSM, 20 SA-N-4 *Gecko* SAM, 1 x 76mm gun, 2 x 3 324mm ASTT, 1 hel

3 *Godavari* with SS-N-2D *Styx* SSM, 1 x 2 SA-N-4 *Gecko* SAM, 2 x 3 324mm ASTT, 1 *Sea King* hel

FF 8

4 *Nilgiri* (UK *Leander*) with 2 x 114mm guns; 2 x 3 ASTT, 1 x 3 *Limbo* ASW mor, 1 *Chetak* hel (2 with 1 *Sea King*)

1 *Krishna* (UK *Leander*) trg role)

3 *Arnala* (Sov *Petya*) with 4 x 76mm gun, 3 x 533mm ASTT, 4 ASW RL

CORVETES 5

4 *Khukri* FSG with 2 or 4 SS-N-2C *Styx* SSM, 1 x 76mm gun, hel deck

1 mod *Khukri* FSG with 8 x SS-N-25 *Switchblade* SSM, SA-N-5 *Grail* SAM, 1 x 76mm gun

Patrol and Coastal Combatants 38

CORVETTES 14

1 *Vijay Durg* (Sov *Nanuchka* II) FSG with 4 SS-N-2C *Styx* SSM, SA-N-4 *Gecko* SAM (Plus 1 non-op)

3 *Veer* (Sov *Tarantul*) FSG, with 4 *Styx* SSM, SA-N-5 *Grail* SAM, 1 x 76mm gun (plus 2 non-op)

6 *Vibhuti* (similar to *Tarantual*), armament as *Veer* 4 *Abhay* (Sov *Pauk* II) FS with SA-N-5 *Grail* SAM, 1 x 76mm gun, 4 x 533mm ASTT, 2 ASW mor

Missile Craft 6 *Vidyut* (Sov Osa II) with 4 *Styx* SSM†

Patrol, Offshore 7 *Sukanya* PCO

Patrol, Inshore 11

7 SDB Mk 3

4 *Super Dvora* PCI<

MINE WARFARE 17

Minelayers 0

None, but *Kamorta* FF and *Pondicherry* MSO have minelaying capability

Mine Countermeasures 17

11 *Pondicherry* (Sov *Natya*) MSO, 6 *Mahé* (Sov *Yevgenya*) MSI<

AMPHIBIOUS 9

2 *Magar* LST, capacity 500 tps, 18 tk, 1 hel

7 *Ghorpad* (Sov *Polnocny* C) ISM, capacity 140 tps, 6 tk Plus craft: 10 *Vasco da Gama* LCU

1 *Adiyta* (mod *Deepak*) AO, 1 *Deepak* AO, 1 *Jyoti* AO, 4 small AOT; 1 YDT, 1 Tir trg, 2 AT/F, 3 TRV, 1 AH; 6 *Sandhayak* AGHS, 4 *Makar* AGHS, 1 *Sagardhwani* AGOR

Naval Aviation (5,000)

37 cbt ac, 72 armed hel Flying hours some 180

Attack 2 sqn with 23 *Sea Harrier* FRS Mk-51, 1 T-60 trg* plus 2 T-4 (on order)

ASW 6 hel sqn with 24 *Chetak*, 7 Ka-25, 14 Ka-28, 25 *Sea King* Mk 42A/B

MR 3 sqn with 5 II-38, 8 Tu-142M *Bear* F, 19 Do-228, 18 BN-2 *Defender*

Comms 1 sqn with ac 10 Do-228 hel 3 *Chetak*

Sar 1 hel sqn with 6 *Sea King* Mk 42C

TRG 2 sqn with ac 6 HJT-16, 8 HPT-32 hel 2 *Chetak**, 4 Hughes 300

MISSILES

AAM R-550 *Magic* I and II

ASM *Sea Eagle*, *Sea Skua*

Marines (1,200)

1 regt (3 gp)

Air Force 150,000

774 cbt ac, 34 armed hel Flying hours 150

Five regional air commands: Central (Allabhada),

Western (New Delhi), Eastern (Shillong), **Southern** (Tiruvettipuram), **South-Western** (Gandhinagar); 2 spt cmds: trg and maint

FGA 18 sqn

1 with 10 Su-30k, 3 with 53 MiG-23 BN/UM,4 with 88 *Jaguar* S(I), 6 with 147 MiG-27, 4 with 69 MiG-21 MF/PEMA

FTR 20 sqn

4 with 66 MiG-21 FL/U, 10 with 169 MiG-21 bis/U,1 with 26 MiG-23 MF/UM, 3 with 64 MiG-29, 2 with 35 *Mirage* 2000H/TH (believed to have secondary GA capability), 8 Su-30MK

ECM 4 *Canberra* B(I) 58 (ECM/target towing, plus 2 *Canberra* TT-18 target towing)

Elint 2 Boeing 707, 2 Boeing 737

AEW 4 HS-748

Tanker IL-78

Maritime Attack 6 *Jaguar* S(I) with *Seq Eagle*

Attack Hel 3 sqn with 32 Mi-25

Recce 2 sqn

1 with 8 *Canberra* (6 PR-57, 2 PR-67)

1 with 6* MiG-25R, 2* MiG-25U

Mr/Survey 2 *Gulfstream* IV SRA, 2 *Learjet* 29

TRANSPORT

ac 12 sqn

6 with 105 An-32 *Sutlej*, 2 with 45 Do-228, 2 with 28 Bae-748, 2 with 25 II-76 *Gajraj*

hel 11 sqn with 73 Mi-8, 50 Mi-17, 10 Mi-26 (hy tpt)

VIP 1 HQ sqn with 2 Boeing 737-200, 7 Bae-748, 6 Mi-8

TRG ac 28 Bae-748 (trg/tpt), 120 *Kiran* I, 56 *Kiran* II, 88 HPT-32, 38 *Hunter* (20 F-56, 18 T-66), 14* *Jaguar* B(1), 9* MiG-29UB, 44 TS-11 *Iskara* hel 20 *Chetak*, 2 Mi-24, 2* Mi-35

MISSILES

ASM AS-7 *Kerry*, AS-11B (ATGW), AS-12, AS-30, *Sea Eagle*, AM 39 *Exocet*, AS-17 *Krypton*

AAM AA-7 *Apex*, AA-8 *Aphid*, AA-10 *Alamo*, AA-11 *Archer*, R-550 *Magic*, *Super* 530D

SAM 38 sqn with 280 *Divina* V75SM/VK (SA-2), *Pechora* (SA-3), SA-5, SA-10

Forces Abroad

UN and Peacekeeping

Droc (Monuc): 12 obs Ira/Kuwait

(Unikom): 6 obs Lebanon (Unifil): 618 Sierra

Lone (Unamsil): 3,161 incl 14 obs

Paramilitary 1,069,000 active

NATIONAL SECURITY GUARDS 7,400
(Cabinet Secretariat)

Anti-terrorism contingency deployment force, comprising elements of the armed forces, CRPF and Border Security Force

SPECIAL PROTECTION GROUP 3,000

Protection of VVIP

SPECIAL FRONTIER FORCE 9,000
(Cabinet Secretariat)

mainly ethnic Tibetans.

Rashtriya Rifles 36,000 (Ministry of Defence) 36 bn in 12 Sector HQ

Defence Security Corps 31,000 provides security at Defence Ministry sites

Indo-Tibetan Border Policy 30,000 (Ministry of Home Affairs) 28 bn, Tibetan border security

Assam Rifles 52,000 (Ministry of Home Affairs) 7 HQ, 31 bn, security within north-eastern states, mainly Army-officered; better trained than BSF

Railway Protection Foces 70,000

Central Industrial Security Force 88,600 (Ministry of Home Affairs)[a] guards public-sector locations

Central Reserve Polices Force (CRPF) 160,000 Ministry of Home Affairs) 130-135 bn incl 10 rapid action, 2 *Mahila* (women); internal security duties, only lightly armed, deployable throughout the country

Border Security Force (BSF) 174,000 (Ministry of Home Affairs) some 150 bn, small arms, some it arty, tpt/liaison air spt

Home Guard (R) 472,000 authorised, actual str 416,000 in all states except Arunachal Pradesh and Kerala; men on lists, no trg

State Armed Police 400,000 For duty primarily in home state only, but can be moved to other states, incl 24 bn India Reserve Police (commando-trained)

Civil Defence 394,000 (R) in 135 towns in 32 states

Coast Guard over 8,000

Patrol Craft 36

3 *Samar* PCO, 9 *Vikram* PCO, 21 *Jija Bai*, 3 SDB-2 plus 16 boats

Aviation

3 sqn with ac 14 Do-228, hel 15 *Chetak*

[a]Lightly armed security guards only

Opposition £2,000+

Hizbul Mujahideen: str n.k. Operates in Indian Kashmir

Harkat-Ul-Mujahideen: str n.k. Operates from Pakistan Kashmir

Lashkar-E-Jihad: str n.k. Operates from Pakistan Kashmir

Al-Badr: str n.k. Operates in Indian Kashmir

Pakistan

		1998	*1999*	*2000*	*2001*
GDP	Rs	2.8tr	3.0tr		
	US$	60.8bn	61.6bn		
per capita	US$	2,400	2,500		
Growth	%	4	3.1		
Inflation	%	6.2	4.1		
Debt	US$	32bn	34.5bn		
Def exp	Rs	180bn	173bn		
	US$	4.0bn	3.5bn		
Def bdgt	Rs	145bn	142bn	170bn	
	US$	3.2bn	2.9bn	3.3bn	
FMA[a] (US)	US$	1.5m	2.9m	04m	–
FMA (Aus)	US$	0.02m	0.02m		
US$1=Rs		45.0	49.1	52.0	

[a] UNMOGIP 1997 US$7m 1998 US$8m

Population		**148,012,000** (less than 3% Hindu)	
Age	13-17	18-22	23-32
Men	8,755,000	7,501,000	12,112,000
Women	8,337,000	6,815,000	10,735,000

Total Armed Forces

Active 612,000

Reserves 513,000

Army £500,000; obligation to age 45 (men) or 50 (officers); active liability for 8 years after service Navy 5,000 Air Force 8,000

Army 550,000

9 Corps HQ * armd div * 9 Corps arty bde * 19 inf div * engr bde * 1 area comd (div) * 3 armd recce 7 indep armd bde * 1 SF gp (3 bn) * 9

indep inf 1 AD comd (3 AD gp: 8 bde) 17 sqn 8 hel, 1 VIP, 1 obs flt

MENT

I 2,285+: 15 M-47, 250 M-48A5, 50 T-54/55, 200 PRC Type-59, 250 PRC Type-69, 200+PRC pe-85, 320 T-80UD 1,000+ M-113

Ved Arty 1,467: **85mm**: 200 PRC Type-56; **6mm**: 300 M-101, 50 M-56 pack; **122mm**: 200 C Type-60,250 PRC Type-54; **130mm**: 227 PRC be-59-1; **155mm**: 30 M-59, 60 M-114, 124 M-198; mm: 26 M-115

RTY 105mm: 50 M-7; **155mm**: 150 M-109A2; mm: 40 M-110A2 **122mm**: 45 *Azar* (PRC Type-83) **81mm**: 500; **120mm**: 225 AM-50, M-61 30 *Hatf 1*, *Hatf 3* (PRC M-11), *Shaheen* 1, 12 *Ghauri*

ATGW 800 incl: *Cobra*, 200 TOW (incl 24 on M-901 SP), *Green Arrow* PRC *Red Arrow*)

RL 89mm: M-20 3,5in

RCL 75mm: Type-52; **106mm**: M-40A1

AD GUNS 2,000+ incl: **14.5mm**; **35mm**: 200 GDF-002; **37mm**: PRC Type-55/-65; **40mm**: M1, 100L/60; **57mm**: PRC Type-59

SAM 350 *Stinger, Redeye*, RBS-70, 500 *Anza* Mk-1-2

SURV RASIT (veh, arty), AN/TPQ-36 (arty, mor)

Aircraft

Survey 1 *Commander* 840

Liaison 1 Cessna 421, 2 *Commander* 690, 80 *Mashshaq*, 1 F-27, 2 Y-12 (II)

OSB 40 O-1E, 50 *Mashshaq*

Helicopters

Attack 20 AH-1F (TOW)

TPT 12 Bell 47G, 7 -205, 10 -206B, 16 Mi-8, 61AR/SA-315B, 23 IAR/SA-316, 35 SA-330, 5 UH-1H

Navy 22,000

(incl Naval Air, £1,200 Marines and £2,000 Maritime Security Agency (see *Paramilitary*)

Base Karachi (Fleet HQ) (2 bases being built at Gwadar and Ormara)

SUBMARINES 10

SSK 7

1 *Khalid* (Fr Agosta 90B) with 533mm TT, *Exocet* SM39 USGW

2 *Hashmat* (Fr Agosta) with 533mm TT (F-17 HWT), *Harpoon* USGW

4 *Hangor* (Fr *Daphné*) with 533mm TT (L-5HWT), *Harpoon* USGW

SSI 3 MG110 (SF delivery)

PRINCIPAL SURFACE COMBATANTS 8

FRIGATES 8

FFG 6 *Tariq* (UK *Amazon* with 4 x *Harpoon* SSM (in 3 of class), 1 x LY-60N SAM (in 3 of class), 1 x 114mm gun, 6 x 32mm ASTT, 1 *Lynx* HAS-3

FF 2 *Shamsher* (UK *Leander*) with 2 x 114mm guns, 1 x 3 ASW mor, 1 SA-319B hel

PATROL AND COASTAL COMBATANTS 9

MISSILE CRAFT 5

4 *Sabqat* (PRC *Huangfeng*) PFM with 4 HY 2 SSM 1x *Jalalat* II with 4 C-802 SSM

Patrol, Coastal 1 *Larkana* PCC

Patrol, Inshore 3

2 *Quetta* (PRC *Shanghai*) PFI

1 *Rajshahi* PCI

Mine Countermeasures 3

3 *Munsif* (Fr *Eridan*) MHC

Support and Miscellaneous 9

1 *Fuqing* AO, 1 *Moawin* AOT, 1 *Attack* AOT; 3 AT; 1 *Behr Paima* AGHS

NAVAL AIR

5 cbt ac (all operated by Air Force), 9 armed hel

ASW/MR 1 sqn with 3 *Atlantic* plus 2 in store, 2 P-3C (operated by Air Force)

ASW/SAR 2 hel sqn with 6 *Sea King* Mk 45 (ASW), 3 *Lynx* Has Mk-3 (ASW)

Comms 5 Fokker F-27 ac (Air Force) hel 4 SA-319B

ASM *Exocet* AM-39

MARINES (£1,200)

1 cdo/SF gp

Air Force 40,000

353 cbt ac, no armed hel **Flying hours** some 210 3 regional cmds: **Northern** (Peshawar) **Central** (Sargodha) **Southern** (Faisal). The Composite Air Tpt Wg, Combat Cdrs School and PAF Academy are Direct Reporting Units.

FGA 6 sqn

1 with 16 *Mirage* (13 IIIEP (some with AM-39 ASM), 3 IIIDP (trg)

3 (1 OCU) with 52 *Mirage* 5 (40-5PA/PA2, 105PA3 (AsuW), 2 5DPA/DPA2

2 with 42 Q-5 (A-5III *Fantan*), some FT-6

FTR 12 sqn

3 (1 OCU) with 40 F-6/FT-6 (J-6/JJ-6), 2 (1 OCU) with 32 F-16 (22 –A, 10 –B), (1 OCU) with 77 F-7P/FT-7), 1 with 43 *Mirage* IIIO/7-OD

Recce 1 sqn with 11* *Mirage* IIIRP

ELINT/ECM 2 *Falcon* DA-20

SAR 1 hel sqn with 15 SA-319

TPT at 12 C-130 (11 B/E, 1 L-100), 2 Boeing 707, 1 Boeing 737, 1 *Falcon* 20, 2 F-27-200 (1 with Navy), 1 Beech *Super King Air* 200, 2 Y-12 (II), hel 15 SA 316/319, 4 Cessna 172, 1 Cessna 560 *Citation,*1 *Piper* PA-3 *Seneca*, 4 MFI-17B *Mashshaq*

TRG 30 FT-5, 15 FT-6, 13 FT-7, 40* MFI-17I-17B *Mashshaq*, 30 T-37B/C, 12 K-8

AD 7 SAM bty

6 each with 24 *Crotale*, 1 with 6 CSA-1(SA-2)

Missiles

ASM AM-39 *Exocet*, AIM-9L/P *Sidewinder*, R-530 *Magic*

ARM AGM-88 *Harm*

Forces Abroad

UN AND PEACEKEEPING

Croatia (UNMOP): 1 obs DROC (MONUC): 29 obs

East Timor (UNTAET): (804 incl 30 obs GEORGIA (UNOMIG): 7 obs Iraq/Kuwait (UNIKOM): 6 obs

Sierra Leone (UNAMSIL): 10 obs Western Sahara (MINURSO): 6 obs

Paramilitary £288,000 active

NATIONAL GUARD 185,000

incl *Janbaz* Force, *Mujahid* Force, National Cadet Corps, Women Guards

Frontier Corps up to 65,000 reported (Ministry of Interior)

11 regt (40 bn), 1 indep armd car sqn; 45 UR-416 APC

Pakistan Rangers £25,000-30,000 (Ministry of Interior)

Northern Light Infantry £12,000; bn

Maritime Security Agency£1,000

1 *Alamgir* (US *Gearing* DD) (no ASROC or TT), 4 *Barkat* POC, 2 (PRC *Shanghai*) PFI<

COAST GUARD

some 23 craft

Foreign Forces

UN (UNMOGIP): 46 mil obs from 8 countries.

Index